The
HUMAN RECORD

SOURCES OF GLOBAL HISTORY

SIXTH EDITION / Volume I: To 1700

Alfred J. Andrea

Emeritus Professor of History, University of Vermont

James H. Overfield

Professor of History, University of Vermont

HOUGHTON MIFFLIN COMPANY   BOSTON   NEW YORK

Executive Publisher: Patricia A. Coryell
Publisher: Suzanne Jeans
Senior Sponsoring Editor: Nancy Blaine
Senior Marketing Manager: Katherine Bates
Discipline Product Manager: Lynn Baldridge
Senior Development Editor: Tonya Lobato
Senior Project Editor: Margaret Park Bridges
Senior Media Producer: Lisa Ciccolo
Senior Content Manager: Janet Edmonds
Art and Design Manager: Jill Haber
Cover Design Director: Tony Saizon
Senior Photo Editor: Jennifer Meyer Dare
Senior Composition Buyer: Chuck Dutton
New Title Project Manager: Susan Peltier
Associate Editor: Adrienne Zicht
Marketing Associate: Lauren Bussard

Cover image: India Office Library / The British Library, MS Ras Loan 5 fol. 128r

Source credits appear on pages 465–469, which constitute an extension of the copyright page.

Printed in the U.S.A.

Library of Congress Control Number: 2006939645

Instructor's examination copy
  ISBN-10: 0-618-83424-9
  ISBN-13: 978-0-618-83424-2

For orders, use student text ISBNs
  ISBN-10: 0-618-75110-6
  ISBN-13: 978-0-618-75110-5

123456789-CRS-12 11 10 09 08

The
HUMAN
RECORD

Volume I

Contents

Geographic Contents

Topical
Contents

Preface

The sixth edition of *The Human Record: Sources of Global History* follows the principles that have guided the book since its inception in 1990. Foremost is our commitment to the proposition that all students of history must meet the challenge of analyzing primary sources, thereby becoming active inquirers into the past. Working with primary source evidence enables students to see that historical scholarship is an intellectual process of drawing inferences and discovering patterns from clues yielded by the past, not of memorizing someone else's judgments. Furthermore, such analysis motivates students to learn by stimulating their curiosity and imagination, and it helps them develop into critical thinkers who are equipped to deal with the complex intellectual challenges of life.

Themes and Structure

We have compiled a source collection that traces the course of human history from the rise of the earliest civilizations to the present. Volume I follows the evolution of cultures that most significantly influenced the history of the world from around 3500 B.C.E. to 1700 C.E., with emphasis on the development of the major social, religious, intellectual, and political traditions of the societies that flourished in Eurasia and Africa. Although our focus in Volume I is on the Eastern Hemisphere, we do not neglect the Americas. Volume I concurrently develops the theme of the growing links and increasingly important exchanges among the world's cultures down to the early modern era. Volume II, which begins just before 1500 C.E. and covers the two centuries of overlap in far greater detail than Volume I, picks up this theme of growing human interconnectedness by tracing the gradual establishment of Western global hegemony; the simultaneous historical developments in other civilizations and societies around the world; the anti-Western, anticolonial movements of the twentieth century; and the emergence of the twenty-first century's integrated but still often bitterly divided world.

To address these themes in the depth and breadth they deserve, we have chosen primary sources that present an overview of global history in mosaic form. Each source serves two functions: It presents an intimate glimpse into some meaningful aspect of the human past and simultaneously contributes to the creation of a single large picture — an integrated history of the world. With this dual purpose in mind, we have tried to avoid isolated sources that provide a taste of some culture or age but, by their dissociation, shed no light on patterns of cultural creation, continuity, change, and interchange — the essential components of world history.

In selecting and arranging the various pieces of our mosaic, we have sought to create a balanced picture of human history that reflects many different perspectives and experiences. Believing that the study of history properly concerns every aspect of past human activity and thought, we have chosen sources that mirror the practices and concerns of as wide a variety of representative persons and groups as availability and space allow.

Our pursuit of historical balance has also led us into the arena of artifactual evidence. Although most historians center their research on documents, the discipline of history requires us to consider all of the clues surrendered by the past, and these include its artifacts. Moreover, we have discovered that students enjoy analyzing artifacts and remember vividly the insights they draw from them. For these reasons, we have included works of art and other artifacts that users of this book can and should analyze as historical sources.

New to This Edition

We have been gratified with the positive response by colleagues and especially students to the first five editions of *The Human Record*. Many have taken the trouble to write or otherwise contact us to express their satisfaction. No textbook is perfect, however, and these correspondents have been equally generous in sharing their perceptions of how we might improve our book and meet more fully the needs of its readers. Such suggestions, when combined with continuing advances in historical scholarship and our own deeper reflections on a variety of issues, have mandated periodic revisions. In the current revision, as was true in the previous four, our intent has been to make the book as interesting and useful as possible to students and instructors alike.

In this continuing (and never-ending) pursuit of trying to find the best and most useful documents and artifacts, we have added eighty-three new sources to these volumes, thirty-one in Volume I and fifty-two in Volume II. Needless to say, in order to keep these volumes within manageable boundaries, we have had to excise almost a like number of sources, many of which undoubtedly have their advocates, who will be disappointed at their excision from the present edition. Persons who disagree with our judgments as to what to cut and what to add should feel free to contact us (see "Feedback" below) and to argue their case. There will be a seventh edition.

Instructors who have used earlier editions of *The Human Record* will recognize immediately that we have added a new feature that we call "Multiple Voices." Two of the most important skills that every student of history must acquire and sharpen are an ability to identify, evaluate, and use evidence that reflects different perspectives and an ability to trace historical development over time. Earlier editions of *The Human Record* have contained occasional clusters of sources that have challenged students to grapple with problems that require these skills, but now we have endeavored to increase substantially the number of such exercises, to give each a certain uniformity and coherence, and to highlight each as a distinctive entity. Together, the two volumes contain fifteen Multiple Voices units, with each containing three to five sources and clearly set apart from other elements in the chapter. We believe that this will enable instructors to use them easily as in-class lessons and as focal points for out-of-class essays. Beyond that, we believe that each Multiple Voices unit will help students acquire and deepen habits of the mind that are necessary for not only their successful mastery of history but also, more important, their functioning in the world as educated individuals and citizens. These include, but are not limited to, a high degree of comfort with nuance and ambiguity; a sensitivity to the ways in which personality, time, place, culture, and other circumstances influence perspectives; an understanding that change and continuity are equally important elements in the dynamics of human history; a willingness to offer provisional answers to complex phenomena in which some or much of the desired evidence is not available; and an intellectual humility that allows one to modify and even radically change previous judgments once new evidence or insights become available.

Beyond helping to stimulate these skills and habits of the mind, we also have an obligation to reflect in our work the most up-to-date scholarly discoveries and controversies. With that in mind, we have revised many of our introductions and commentaries. More than one-third of the pages dedicated to editorial commentary and notes have been rewritten.

Learning Aids

Source analysis can be a daunting challenge for any student. With this in mind, we have labored to make these sources as accessible as possible by providing the student-user with a variety of aids. First there is the *Prologue*, in which we explain, initially in a theoretical manner and then through concrete examples, how a historian interprets written and artifactual sources. Instructors who have used previous editions of our book will note that the new Prologue offers a sample Multiple Voices exercise as a means of introducing student-readers to the art of source analysis. Next we offer *part, chapter, sub-chapter*, and *individual source introductions* — all to help the reader place each selection into a meaningful context and understand each source's significance. Because we consider *The Human Record* to be an interpretive overview of global history and therefore a survey of the major patterns of global history that stands on its own as a text, our introductions are significantly fuller than what one normally encounters in a book of sources.

Suggested *Questions for Analysis* precede each source; their purpose is to help the student make sense of each piece of evidence and wrest from it as much insight as possible. The questions are presented in a three-tiered format designed to resemble the historian's approach to source analysis and to help students make historical comparisons on a global scale. The first several questions are usually quite specific and ask the reader to pick out important pieces of information. These initial questions require the student to address two issues: What does this document or artifact say, and what meaningful facts can I garner from it? Addressing concrete questions of this sort prepares the student researcher for the next, more significant, level of critical thinking and analysis: drawing inferences. Questions that demand inferential conclusions follow the fact-oriented questions. Finally, whenever possible, we offer a third tier of questions that challenge the student to compare the individual or society that produced a particular source with an individual, group, or culture encountered earlier in the volume. We believe such comparisons help students fix more firmly in their minds the distinguishing cultural characteristics of the various societies they encounter in their survey of world history. Beyond that, it underscores the fact that global history is, at least on one level, comparative history.

Another form of help we offer is to *gloss the sources*, explaining words and allusions that students cannot reasonably be expected to know. To facilitate reading and to encourage reference, the notes appear at the bottom of the page on which they are cited. A few documents also contain *interlinear notes* that serve as transitions or provide needed information.

Some instructors might use *The Human Record* as their sole textbook. Most, however, will use it as a supplement to a standard narrative textbook, and most of these will probably decide not to require their students to analyze every source. To assist instructors (and students) in selecting sources that best suit their interests and needs, we have prepared *two analytical tables of contents* for each volume. The first lists readings and artifacts by geographic and cultural area, the second by topic. The two tables suggest to professor and student alike the rich variety of material available within these pages, particularly for essays in comparative history.

In summary, our goal in crafting *The Human Record* has been to do our best to prepare the student-reader for success — *success* being defined as comfort with historical analysis, proficiency in critical thinking, learning to view history on a global scale, and a deepened awareness of the rich cultural varieties, as well as shared characteristics, of the human family.

Using The Human Record: *Suggestions from the Editors*

Specific suggestions for assignments and classroom activities appear in the online manual *Using* The Human Record: *Suggestions from the Editors*, which may be accessed through the textbook website at www.college.hmco.com/history/instructors. It is also available in print format. In it we explain why we have chosen the sources that appear in this book and what insights we believe students should be capable of drawing from them. We also describe classroom exercises for encouraging student thought and discussion on the various sources. The advice we present is the fruit of our own use of these sources in the classroom.

Feedback

As already suggested, we want to receive comments and suggestions from instructors and students who use this book. Comments on the Prologue and Volume I should be addressed to A. J. Andrea, whose e-mail address is <Alfred.Andrea@uvm.edu>; comments on Volume II should be addressed to J. H. Overfield at <James.Overfield@uvm.edu>.

Acknowledgments

We are in debt to the many professionals who offered their expert advice and assistance during the various incarnations of *The Human Record*. Scholars and friends at The University of Vermont who generously shared their expertise with us over the years as we crafted these six editions include Abbas Alnasrawi, Doris Bergen, Holly-Lynn Busier, Ernesto Capello, Robert V. Daniels, Carolyn Elliott, Bogac Ergene, Erik Esselstrom, Shirley Gedeon, Erik Gilbert, William Haviland, Walter Hawthorn, Richard Horowitz, William Mierse, George Moyser, Kristin M. Peterson-Ishaq, Abubaker Saad, Wolfe W. Schmokel, Peter Seybolt, John W. Seyller, Sean Stilwell, Mark Stoler, Marshall True, Diane Villemaire, Janet Whatley, and Denise Youngblood. Additionally, Ms. Tara Coram of the Arthur M. Sackler Gallery and Freer Gallery of Art of the Smithsonian Institution deserves special thanks for the assistance she rendered A. J. Andrea in his exploration of the Asian art holdings of the two museums.

We wish also to acknowledge the following instructors whose comments on the fifth edition helped guide our revision: Janet Bednarek, University of Dayton; Sharon Cohen, Springbrook High School; Michael Davidson, Southern Illinois University; Jay Harmon, Catholic High School; Brian Hodson, Fort Hays State University; Patrick Patterson, Honolulu Community College; Daniel Sarefield, The Ohio State University; and John Wilson, Rowen University.

Finally, our debt to our spouses is beyond payment, but the dedication to them of each edition of this book reflects in some small way how deeply we appreciate their constant support and good-humored tolerance.

A. J. A.
J. H. O.

The
HUMAN
RECORD
Volume I

Prologue

Primary Sources and How to Read Them

Imagine a course in chemistry in which you never set foot in a laboratory or a course on the history of jazz in which you never listen to a note of music. You would consider such courses deficient and would complain to your academic advisor or college dean about flawed teaching methods and wasted tuition. And you would be right. No one can understand chemistry without doing experiments; no one can understand music without listening to performances.

In much the same way, no one can understand history without reading and analyzing *primary sources*. Simply defined, *in most instances, primary sources are historical records produced at the same time the event or period that is being studied took place or soon thereafter.* They are distinct from *secondary sources* — books, articles, television documentaries, and even historical films — produced well after the events they describe and analyze. Secondary sources — *histories* in the conventional sense of the term — organize the jumble of past events into understandable narratives. They provide interpretations, sometimes make comparisons, and almost always discuss motive and causation. When done well, they provide pleasure and insight. But such works, no matter how well done, are still *secondary*, in that they are written well after the fact and derive their evidence and information from primary sources.

History is an ambitious discipline that deals with all aspects of past human activity and belief. This means that the primary sources historians use to recreate the past are equally wide-ranging and diverse. Most primary sources are written — government records, law codes, private correspondence, literary works, religious texts, merchants' account books, memoirs, and the list goes on almost endlessly. So important are written records to the study of history that many historians refer to societies and cultures with no system of writing as prehistoric. This does not mean they lack a history; it means there is no way to construct a detailed narrative of their histories due to the lack of written records. Of course, even so-called prehistoric societies leave behind evidence of their experiences, creativity, and belief systems in their *oral traditions* and their *artifacts*.

Let us look first at oral traditions, which can include legends, religious rituals, proverbs, genealogies, and a variety of other forms of wisdom and knowledge. Simply put, they constitute a society's remembered past as passed down by word of mouth. The difficulty of working with such evidence is significant. You are aware of how stories change as they are transmitted from person to person. Imagine how difficult it is to use such stories as historical evidence. Yet, despite the challenge they offer us, these sources cannot be overlooked.

Although the oral traditions of ancient societies were often written down long after they were first articulated, they are often the only recorded evidence that we have of a far-distant society or event. So, the farther back in history we go, the more we see the inadequacy of the definition of primary sources that we offered above ("historical records produced at the same time the event or period that is being studied took place or soon thereafter"). The early chapters of Volume I contain quite a few primary sources based on oral traditions; in some cases, they were recorded many centuries after the events and people they deal with. We will inform you when this is the case and offer you sufficient information and suggestions as to which questions you can validly ask of them to enable you to use them effectively.

Artifacts — essentially anything, other than a document, that was crafted by hand or machine — can help us place oral traditions into a clearer context by producing tangible evidence that supports or calls into question this form of testimony. Artifacts can also tell us something about prehistoric societies whose oral traditions are lost to us. They also serve as primary sources for historians who study literate cultures. Written records, no matter how extensive and diverse, never allow us to draw a complete picture of the past, and we can fill at least some of those gaps by studying what human hands have fashioned. Everyday objects — such as fabrics, tools, kitchen implements, weapons, farm equipment, jewelry, pieces of furniture, and family photographs — provide windows into the ways that people lived. Grander cultural products — paintings, sculpture, buildings, musical compositions, and, more recently, film — are equally important because they also reflect the values, attitudes, and styles of living of their creators and those for whom they were created.

To be a historian is to work with primary sources in all their diverse forms. But to do so effectively is not easy. Each source provides only one glimpse of reality, and no single source by itself gives us the whole picture of past events and developments. Many sources are difficult to understand and can be interpreted only after the precise meaning of their words has been deciphered and their backgrounds thoroughly investigated. Many sources contain distortions and errors that can be discovered only by rigorous internal analysis and comparison with evidence from other sources. Only after all these source-related difficulties have been overcome can a historian hope to achieve a coherent and reasonably accurate understanding of the past.

To illustrate some of the challenges of working with primary sources, let us imagine a time in the future when a historian decides to write a history of your college class in connection with its fiftieth reunion. Since no one has written a book or article about your class, our historian has no secondary sources to consult and must rely entirely on primary sources. What primary sources might he or she use? The list is a long one: the school catalogue, class lists, academic transcripts, yearbooks, college rules and regulations, and similar official documents; lecture notes, syllabi, examinations, term papers, and textbooks; diaries and private letters; articles from the campus newspaper and programs for sporting events, concerts, and plays; posters and handbills; recollections written down or otherwise recorded by some of your classmates long after they graduated. With a bit of thought you could add other items to the list, among them some artifacts, such as souvenirs sold in the campus store, and other unwritten sources, such as recordings of music popular at the time and photographs and videotapes of student life and activity.

Even with this imposing list of sources, our future historian will have only an incomplete record of the events that made up your class's experiences. Many of those moments — telephone conversations, meetings with professors, and gossip exchanged at the student union — never made it into any written record. Also consider the fact that all the sources available to our future historian will be fortunate survivors. They will represent only a small percentage of the material generated by you, your classmates, professors, and administrators over a two- or four-year period. Wastebaskets and recycling bins will have claimed much written material; the "delete" key, inevitable changes in computer technology, and old websites dumped as "obsolete" will make it impossible to retrieve some basic sources, such as your college's website, e-mail, and a vast amount of other online materials. It is also probable that it will be difficult to find information about certain groups within your class, such as part-time students, nontraditional students, and commuters. The past always has its so-called silent or near-silent groups of people. Of course, they were never truly silent, but often nobody was listening to them. It is the historian's task to find whatever evidence exists that gives them a voice, but often that evidence is tantalizingly slim.

For these reasons, the evidence available to our future historian will be fragmentary at best. This is always the case when doing historical research. The records of the past cannot be retained in their totality, not even records that pertain to the recent past.

How will our future historian use the many individual pieces of surviving documentary evidence about your class? As he or she reviews the list, it will quickly become apparent that no single primary source provides a complete or unbiased picture. Each source has its own perspective, value, and limitations. Imagine that the personal essays submitted by applicants for admission were a historian's only sources of information about the student body. On reading them, our researcher might draw the false conclusion that the school attracted only the most gifted, talented, interesting, and intellectually committed students imaginable.

Despite their flaws, however, essays composed by applicants for admission are still important pieces of historical evidence. They reflect the would-be students' perceptions of the school's cultural values and the types of people it hopes to attract, and usually the applicants are right on the mark because they have studied the college's or university's website and read the brochures prepared by its admissions office. Admissions materials and, to a degree, even the school's official catalogue (assuming it still has a printed catalogue and has not gone totally online) are forms of creative advertising, and both present an idealized picture of campus life. But such publications have value for the careful researcher because they reflect the values of the faculty and administrators who composed them. The catalogue also provides useful information regarding rules and regulations, courses, instructors, school organizations, and similar items. Such factual information, however, is the raw material of history, not history itself, and certainly it does not reflect anything close to the full historical reality of your class's collective experience.

What is true of the catalogue is equally true of the student newspaper and every other piece of evidence pertinent to your class. Each primary source is a part of a larger whole, but as we have already seen, we do not have all the pieces. Think of historical evidence in terms of a jigsaw puzzle. Many of the pieces are missing, but it is possible to put the remaining pieces together to form a fairly accurate and coherent picture. The picture that emerges will not be complete, but it is valid and useful, and from it one can often make educated guesses as to what the missing pieces look like. The keys to putting together this historical puzzle are hard work and imagination. Each is absolutely necessary.

Examining Primary Sources

Hard work speaks for itself, but students are often unaware that historians also need imagination to reconstruct the past. After all, many students ask, doesn't history consist of irrefutable dates, names, and facts? Where does imagination enter into the process of learning these facts? Again, let us consider your class's history and its documentary sources. Many of those documents provide factual data — dates, names, grades, statistics. While these data are important, individually and collectively they have no historical meaning until they have been *interpreted*. Your college class is more than a collection of statistics and facts. It is a group of individuals who, despite their differences, shared and molded a collective experience. It was and is a community evolving within a particular time and place. Any valid or useful history must reach beyond dates, names, and facts and interpret the historical characteristics and role of your class. What were its values? How did it change and why? What impact did it have? These are some of the important questions a historian asks of the evidence.

To arrive at answers, the historian must examine every piece of relevant evidence in its full context and wring from that evidence as many *inferences* as possible. *An inference is a logical conclusion drawn from evidence*, and it is the heart and soul of historical inquiry. Facts are the raw materials of history, but inferences are its finished products.

Every American schoolchild learns at an early age that "in fourteen hundred and ninety-two, Columbus sailed the ocean blue." In subsequent history classes, he or she might learn other facts about the famous explorer: that he was born in Genoa in 1451; that he made three other transatlantic voyages in 1493, 1497, and 1503; that he died in Spain in 1506. Knowing these facts is of little value, however, unless it contributes to our understanding of the motives, causes, and significance of Columbus's voyages. Why did Columbus sail west? Why did Spain support such enterprises? Why were Europeans willing and able to exploit, as they did, the so-called New World? What were the short- and long-term consequences of the European presence in the Americas? Finding answers to questions such as these are the historian's ultimate goal, and these answers can be reached only by studying primary sources.

One noted historian, Robin Winks, has written a book entitled *The Historian as Detective*, and the image is appropriate although inexact. Like a detective, the historian examines evidence to reconstruct events. Like a detective, the historian is interested in discovering "what happened, who did it, and why." Like a detective interrogating witnesses, *the historian also must carefully examine the testimony of sources.*

First and foremost, the historian must evaluate the *validity* of the source. Is it what it purports to be? Artful forgeries have misled many historians. Even authentic sources still can be misleading if the author lied or deliberately misrepresented reality. In addition, the historian can easily be led astray by not fully understanding the *perspective* reflected in the document. As is soon learned by any detective who has examined eyewitnesses to an event, even honest witnesses' accounts can differ widely. The detective has the opportunity to re-examine witnesses and offer them the opportunity to change their testimony in the light of new evidence and deeper reflection. The historian is not so fortunate. Even when the historian compares a piece of documentary evidence with other evidence in order to uncover its flaws, there is no way to cross-examine its author. Given this fact, it is absolutely necessary for the historian to understand as fully as possible the source's perspective. Thus, the historian must ask several key questions — all of which share the letter *W*.

- *What* kind of document is it?
- *Who* wrote it?
- For *whom* and *why*?
- *Where* was it composed and *when*?

What is important because understanding the nature of a source gives the historian an idea of what kind of information he or she can expect to find in it. Many sources simply do not address the questions a historian would like to ask of them, and knowing this can prevent a great deal of frustration. Your class's historian would be foolish to try to learn much about the academic quality of your school's courses from a study of the registrar's class lists and grade sheets. Student and faculty class notes, copies of syllabi, examinations, student papers, and textbooks would be far more useful.

Who, for whom, and *why* are equally important questions. The official catalogue (if, as noted above, the school still prints one) and publicity materials prepared by the admissions office undoubtedly address some issues pertaining to student social life. But should documents like these — designed to attract potential students and to place the school in the best possible light — be read and accepted uncritically? Obviously not. They must be tested against student testimony discovered in such sources as private letters, memoirs, posters, the student newspaper, and the yearbook.

Where and *when* are also important questions to ask of any primary source. As a rule, distance from an event in space and time colors perceptions and can diminish the reliability of a source. Recollections of a person celebrating a twenty-fifth class reunion could be an insightful and valuable source of information for your class's historian. Conceivably this graduate would have a perspective and information that he or she lacked a quarter of a century earlier. Just as conceivably, that person's memory of what college was like might have faded to the point where his recollections have little value.

You and the Sources

This book will actively involve you in the work of historical inquiry by asking you to draw inferences based on your analysis of primary source evidence. This might prove difficult at first, but it is well within your capability.

You will analyze two types of evidence: documents and artifacts. Each source will be authentic, so you do not have to worry about validating it. Editorial material in this book also supplies you with the information necessary to place each piece of evidence into its proper context and will suggest questions you legitimately can and should ask of each source.

It is important to keep in mind that historians approach each source with questions, even though they might be vaguely formulated. Like detectives, historians want to discover some particular truth or shed light on an issue. This requires asking specific questions of the witnesses or, in the historian's case, of the evidence. These questions should not be prejudgments. *One of the worst errors a historian can make is setting out to prove a point or to defend an ideological position.* Questions are essential, but they are starting points, nothing else. Therefore, as you approach a source, have your question or questions fixed in your mind, and constantly remind yourself as you work your way through a source what issue or issues you are investigating, but at the same time, keep an open mind. You are not an advocate or a debater. Your mission is to discover the truth, insofar as you can, by following the evidence and asking the right questions of it. Each source in this anthology is preceded by a number of suggested *Questions for Analysis.* You or your professor might want to ask other questions. Whatever the case, keep focused on your questions and issues, and take notes as you read a source. Never rely on unaided memory; it will almost inevitably lead you astray.

Above all else, you must be honest and thorough as you study a source. Read each explanatory footnote carefully to avoid misunderstanding a word or an allusion. Try to understand exactly what the source is saying and what its author's perspective is. Be careful not to wrench items, words, or ideas out of context, thereby distorting them. Be sure to read the entire source so that you understand as fully as possible what it says and does not say.

This is not as difficult as it sounds. But it does take concentration and work. And do not let the word "work" mislead you. True, primary source analysis demands attention to detail and some hard thought, but it is also rewarding. There is great satisfaction in developing a deeper and truer understanding of the past based on a careful exploration of the evidence. What is more, an ability to analyze and interpret evidence is a skill that will serve you well in whatever career you follow.

Analyzing Sample Sources

To illustrate how you should go about this task and what is expected of you, we will now take you through an exercise. One of the new features of the sixth edition of this source book is a feature we call "Multiple Voices." Each volume is divided into four Parts, and each Part contains one or more Multiple Voices sections. Each Multiple Voices feature is a set of short source excerpts that illustrates one of three phenomena: (1) multiple, more-or-less contemporary perspectives on a common event or phenomenon; (2) multiple sources that illustrate how something changes over time; (3) multiple perspectives from different cultures regarding a common concern or issue. The sample exercise we have constructed for this Prologue is a Multiple Voices feature. We have chosen three documents and an artifact that shed light on the importance and economic policies of the Indian port city of Calicut in the years preceding the entry on a large scale of Europeans into the Indian Ocean. We present this grouping of sources as it would appear in the book: first a bit of background; next a discussion of the individual sources; then suggested Questions for Analysis; and finally the sources themselves, with explanatory notes.

Everyone Meets in Calicut

BACKGROUND

On May 20, 1498, after almost eleven months of sailing, the Portuguese captain-major Vasco da Gama anchored his three ships a few miles from Calicut on India's Malabar, or southwestern, Coast, thereby inaugurating Europe's entry into the markets of the Indian Ocean. At the time of da Gama's arrival, Calicut (or Kozhikode), which had been established in the thirteenth century, was the capital of the most important state in a region dotted with small powers. Despite lacking a good natural harbor, Calicut prospered as a center of trade for reasons suggested in the following sources. However, with the establishment of competitive Portuguese trading stations along the Malabar Coast and elsewhere in the Indian Ocean following da Gama's initial contact with India, Calicut's fortunes rapidly declined, and its prominence ended.

THE SOURCES

We begin with an account of Calicut contained in the anonymous *Logbook (Roteiro) of the First Voyage of Vasco da Gama*, often referred to simply as the *Roteiro*. The journal, which is incomplete, was kept by one of da Gama's crew members aboard the *San Rafael*. Several persons, namely the notary João de Sã and the soldier Álvaro Velho, have been offered as candidates, but neither has a definitive claim on its authorship. What is certain, however, is that the *Roteiro* is authentic.

The second source, Ibn Battuta's *Rihla*, or *A Gift to Those Who Contemplate the Wonders of Cities and the Marvels Encountered in Travel*, predates the *Roteiro* by a century and a half. Abu Abdallah Muhammad Ibn Battuta (1304–1368?) left his home in Tangier on the coast of Morocco in 1325 at the age of twenty-one to begin a twenty-six-year journey throughout the Islamic World and beyond. When he returned to Morocco in 1349, he had logged about 73,000 miles of travel, including more than seven years spent as a *qadi*, or religious judge, in the Islamic sultanate of Delhi in north India. In 1341 Sultan Muhammad Tughluq (r. 1325–1351) invited Ibn Battuta to travel to China as his ambassador. On his way to China, Ibn Battuta stopped at Calicut. In 1354 the traveler began to collaborate with a professional scribe, Ibn Juzayy, to fashion his many adventures into a *rihla*, or book of travels, one of the most popular forms of literature in the Islamic World. It took almost two years to complete his long and complex story. Some of that story was fabricated, as even contemporaries noticed, but most of the *rihla* has the ring of authenticity. The excerpt describes Calicut as seen in 1341 and remembered about fifteen years later, and there is no good reason to doubt that this is an eyewitness account.

The third source, *The Overall Survey of the Ocean's Shores*, is Chinese. Its author, Ma Huan (ca. 1380–after 1451), accompanied the fourth (1413–1415), sixth (1421–1423), and seventh (1431–1433) expeditions of the great Ming fleets that the Yongle Emperor (r. 1402–1424) and his successor sent into the Indian Ocean under the command of Admiral Zheng He (1371–1433). The main purpose of the seven expeditions, which began in 1405 and ended in 1433, was to reassert Chinese hegemony in coastal lands touched by the Indian Ocean. Ma Huan, who was a Chinese Muslim, served as an Arabic translator on his first voyage and upon his return home transcribed his notes into book form. After sailing on two other expeditions, he amended his account accordingly and published a book in 1451 that encapsulated all three expeditions and described in detail the lands visited and actions taken by the fleets during those voyages. In this excerpt he describes Calicut, known to the Chinese as Guli.

The fourth source, an artifact, is a detail of the western portions of India and the adjoining Arabian Sea from the *Catalan World Atlas*, which was drawn in 1375 on the island of Majorca, probably by Abraham Cresques (1325–1387), a Jewish "master of maps of the world" who served the king of Aragon in northeast Spain (Catalonia), which had seized Majorca from the Moors in 1229. Cresques's map, which wound up in the possession of the king of France in 1380 (and today is one of the treasures of Paris's Bibliothèque Nationale), was based on the best available literary and cartographic sources and reflected the facts and fictions regarding the Afro-Eurasian World that circulated in educated circles in late-fourteenth-century Western Europe. In the segment shown here, we see at the top the Three Magi on their way to visit the Christ Child. Below them is the sultan of Delhi, whose Muslim state dominated north India; below him is the raja of Vijayanagara, who presided over the most powerful Hindu state in south India. Between them are an elephant and its handler. In the Arabian Sea at the bottom of the map are pearl divers, as described by Marco Polo. Above the pearl divers is a vessel with two men in conical hats.

QUESTIONS FOR ANALYSIS

1. According to the *Roteiro*, why was Calicut so important, and, by implication, why was it necessary for Portugal to gain direct access to it?
2. What does Ibn Battuta tell us about the roles of foreigners in Calicut, and specifically which foreigners?
3. From what all three documentary sources tell us, what factors contributed to Calicut's prosperity?
4. What does the *Catalan World Atlas* tell us about Western Europe's knowledge of the Malabar Coast and India in general by the late fourteenth century?
5. Overall, what can we say with certainty about Calicut prior to its rapid decline in the sixteenth century?

---

1 ▾ ROTEIRO

From this country of Calicut . . . come the spices that are consumed in the East and the West, in Portugal, as in all other countries of the world, as also [are] precious stones of every description. The following spices are to be found in this city of Calicut, being its own produce: much ginger and pepper and cinnamon, although the last is not of so fine a quality as that brought from an island called Çillon [Ceylon],[1] which is eight days journey from Calicut. Calicut is the staple for all this cinnamon. Cloves are brought to this city from an island called Melqua [Malacca].[2] The Mecca vessels carry these spices from there to a city in Mecca[3] called Judeâ [Jeddah],[4] and from the said island to Judeâ is a voyage of 50 days sailing before the wind. . . . At Judeâ they discharge their cargoes, paying customs duties to the Grand Sultan.[5] The merchandise is then transshipped to smaller vessels, which carry it through the Red Sea to a place close to Santa Catarina of Mount Sinai,[6] called Tuuz [El Tûr][7] where customs dues are paid once more. From

[1]The modern island nation of Sri Lanka. At this time, Ceylon alone produced true cinnamon. The other cinnamon-like spice is cassia, which is made from the bark of a related tree that originated in China.

[2]The straits and city of Malacca were not the source. Cloves came from the Southeast Asian islands known as the Moluccas (or Spice Islands), which today constitute the province of Maluku in the Republic of Indonesia.

[3]Actually Arabia, Mecca [or Makkah] being the inland holy city of Islam in the Arabian Peninsula. Today Mecca is located in Saudi Arabia.

[4]Jeddah (or Jidda) is the Arabian Peninsula's main port city on the Red Sea.

[5]The Mamluk dynasty of sultans that ruled Egypt from 1250 to 1517.

[6]Saint Catherine's Monastery — an ancient Christian monastery in Egypt that still exists.

[7]A port on Egypt's Sinai Peninsula.

that place the merchants carry the spices on the backs of camels . . . to Quayro [Cairo], a journey occupying ten days. At Quayro duties are paid again. On this road to Cairo they are frequently robbed by thieves. . . .

At Cairo the spices are embarked on the river Nile . . . and descending[8] that river for two days they reach a place called Roxette [Rosetta],

where duties have to be paid once more. There they are placed on camels, and are conveyed in one day to a city called Alexandria, which is a sea-port.[9] This city is visited by the galleys of Venice and Genoa, in search of these spices, which yield the Grand Sultan [an annual] revenue of 600,000 cruzados.[10]

---

[8]Sailing north.
[9]On the Mediterranean.

[10]A Portuguese gold coin that received its name from the crusader's cross emblazoned on it.

---

2 ▼ Ibn Battuta, A GIFT TO THOSE WHO CONTEMPLATE THE WONDERS OF CITIES AND THE MARVELS ENCOUNTERED IN TRAVEL

The sultan of Calicut is an infidel,[1] known as "the Sámarí."[2] . . . In this town too lives the famous ship-owner Mithqál,[3] who possesses vast wealth and many ships for his trade with India, China, Yemen, and Fars.[4] When we reached the city, the principal inhabitants and merchants and the sultan's representative came out to welcome us, with drums, trumpets, bugles and standards on their ships. We entered the harbor in great pomp. . . . We stopped in the port of Calicut, in which there were at the time thirteen Chinese vessels, and disembarked. Every one of us was lodged in a house, and we stayed three months as the guests of the infidel, awaiting the season of the voyage to China.[5] On the Sea of China traveling is done in Chinese ships only. . . .

The Chinese vessels are of three kinds: large ships called *chunks* [junks], middle-sized ones called *zaws* [dhows], and small ones called *kakams*. The large ships have from twelve down to three sails, which are made of bamboo rods plaited like mats. They are never lowered, but turned according to the direction of the wind. . . . A ship carries a complement of a thousand men, six hundred of whom are sailors and four hundred men-at-arms, including archers . . . and arbalists, who throw naptha.[6] . . . The vessel has four decks and contains rooms, cabins, and salons for merchants; a cabin has chambers and a lavatory, and can be locked by its occupant, who takes along with him slave girls and wives. Often a man will live in his cabin unknown to

---

[1]A Hindu.
[2]In the local language, the title was *Samudri raja*, which means "Lord of the Sea." The Portuguese would corrupt this to "Zamorin."
[3]A strange name, very much like being called "Goldie" in English. A measure of weight throughout the Islamic world, a *mithqal* was 4.72 grams of gold. This might mean the man was a Muslim from across the Arabian Sea.
[4]Yemen is the southwestern tip of the Arabian Peninsula; Fars is the southern region of Iran along the Gulf of Oman.

[5]They awaited the lessening of the northeast monsoon winds, which blow from late November to April. The period around 11 April was considered the best time to begin a voyage from the Malabar Coast to the Bay of Bengal, which lay east of India.
[6]Crossbowmen who shoot missiles containing a mixture of fiery materials.

any of the others on board until they meet on reaching some town. The sailors have their children on board ship, and they cultivate green stuffs, vegetables, and ginger in wooden tanks. The owner's factor [agent-in-charge] on board ship is like a great amir.[7] When he goes on shore he is preceded by archers and Abyssinians[8] with javelins, swords, drums, trumpets, and bugles. On reaching the house where he stays, they stand their lances on both sides of the door, and continue thus during his stay. Some of the Chinese own large numbers of ships on which their factors are sent to foreign countries. There is no people in the world wealthier than the Chinese.

When the time came for the voyage to China, the sultan Sámarí made provision for us on one of the thirteen junks in the port of Calicut. The factor on the junk was called Sulayman of Safad,[9] in Syria. . . .

> ▷ Disaster strikes. Ibn Battuta's ship sinks in a storm in the harbor before he boards it, but it carries with it to the bottom all of his baggage, servants, and slaves.

Next morning we found the bodies of Sumbal and Zahir ad-Din,[10] and having prayed over them buried them. I saw the infidel, the sultan of Calicut . . . a fire lit before him on the beach; his police officers were beating the people to prevent them from plundering what the sea had cast up. In all the lands of Malabar, except in this one land alone, it is the custom that whenever a ship is wrecked all that is taken from it belongs to the treasury. At Calicut, however, it is retained by its owners, and for that reason Calicut has become a flourishing city and attracts large numbers of merchants.

---

[7]Lord or commander.
[8]Persons from the Horn of Africa — modern Ethiopia, Eritrea, and Somalia — and maybe even farther south along the Swahili Coast.

[9]Zefat in present-day Israel.
[10]Envoys whom the sultan of Delhi had dispatched to accompany him.

---

3 ▼ Ma Huan, THE OVERALL SURVEY OF THE OCEAN'S SHORES

THE COUNTRY OF GULI

The king of the country is a Nankun[1] man; he is a firm believer in the Buddhist religion[2] and he venerates the elephant and the ox. . . .

The king of the country and the people of the country all refrain from eating the flesh of the ox. The great chiefs are Muslim people; they all refrain from eating the flesh of the pig. Formerly there was a king who made a sworn compact with the Muslim people [who said to him], "You do not eat the ox; I do not eat the pig; we will reciprocally respect the taboo"; [and this compact] has been honored right down to the present day. . . .

The king has two great chiefs who administer the affairs of the country; both are Muslims.

The majority of the people in the country all profess the Muslim religion. There are twenty or thirty temples of worship,[3] and once in seven days they go to worship. . . .

---

[1]High caste — probably a member of the Kshatriya, or warrior-ruler, caste.
[2]Actually, he was a Hindu. His veneration of an ox (probably a bull) suggests he was a devotee of Shiva.
[3]The preceding sentence and the following reference to the weekly day of worship make it appear that these temples

were mosques. It seems unlikely, however, that the majority of the population was Muslim and that Calicut had twenty or thirty mosques. More likely, it had several mosques and many Hindu temples. As a Muslim, Ma Huan might have thought, incorrectly, that Hindus, like Muslims, have a once-a-week day of communal prayer.

If a [Chinese] treasure-ship goes there,[4] it is left entirely to the two men to superintend the buying and selling; the king sends a chief and a Zhedi Weinoji[5] to examine the account books in the official bureau; a broker comes and joins them; [and] a high officer who commands the ships discusses the choice of a certain date for fixing prices. When the day arrives, they first of all take the silk embroideries . . . and other such goods that have been brought there [by the ship], and discuss the price of them one by one; when [the price] has been fixed, they write out an agreement stating the amount of the price, [which] is retained by these persons.

The chief and the Zhedi, with his excellency the eunuch,[6] all join hands together, and the broker then says, "In such and such a moon, on such and such a day, we have all joined hands and sealed our agreement with a hand-clasp; whether [the price] be dear or cheap, we will never repudiate or change it."

After that, the Zhedi and the men of wealth then come bringing precious stones, pearls, corals, and other such things, so that they may be examined and the price discussed; [this] cannot be settled in a day; [if done] quickly, [it takes] one moon; [if done] slowly, two or three moons.

Once the money-price has been fixed after examination and discussion, if a pearl or other such article is purchased, the price that must be paid for it is calculated by the chief and the Weinoji who carried out the original transaction. As to the quantity of the hemp-silk or other such article that must be given in exchange for it, goods are exchanged according to [the price fixed by] the original hand-clasp — there is not the slightest deviation. . . .

The king uses gold of 60 percent to cast a coin for current use. . . . He also makes a coin of silver . . . for petty transactions. . . .

The people of the country also take the silk of the silk-worm, soften it by boiling, dye it all colors, and weave it into kerchiefs with decorative stripes at intervals . . . ; each length is sold for 100 gold coins.

As to pepper; the inhabitants of the mountainous countryside have established gardens, and it is extensively cultivated. When the period of the tenth moon arrives, the pepper ripens. It is collected, dried in the sun, and sold. Of course, big pepper-collectors come and collect it, and take it to the official storehouse to be stored; if there is a buyer, an official gives permission for the sale. The duty is collected according to the amount [of the purchase price] and is paid to the authorities. . . .

Foreign ships from every place come there; and the king of the country also sends a chief and a writer and others to watch the sales; thereupon they collect the duty and pay it to the authorities.

---

[4]The fleets commanded by Zheng He contained a significant number of treasure ships — large ships along the lines described by Ibn Battuta that carried Chinese trade goods and gifts, but which also were meant to carry back tribute, foreign trade goods, exotic items, and persons of importance invited (or compelled) to visit the imperial court at Nanjing. By extension, Ma Huan means any Chinese trading vessel.

[5]Probably his attempt to transliterate *Waligi Chitty*, or accountant.

[6]The reference is to Zheng He, a eunuch, who commanded the treasure ships that visited Calicut during these voyages, but more broadly it probably also refers to the commander of any Chinese ship.

4 ▾ THE CATALAN WORLD ATLAS

Interpreting the Sources

These four pieces of evidence allow us to say quite a bit about Calicut before Europeans established a strong presence in the Indian Ocean. Let us begin with the two Western sources.

The *Catalan World Atlas* depicts what is unmistakably a Chinese vessel off the west coast of India. The plaited bamboo sails, which Ibn Battuta described, as well as the distinctive hats worn by the two men, make that identification easy. Clearly, Westerners realized as early as the fourteenth century that the Chinese were major players in the commerce of the Indian subcontinent. The West's knowledge of the great wealth of India, as well as its high degree of urbanization and its political fragmentation, is obvious from the portraits of the sultan of Delhi and the raja of Vijayanagara, as well as the symbols for the many cities dotting the coastline and interior. The pearl divers, elephant, and Three Magi only add to the overall picture of India's riches and wonders. The fact is that between roughly 1250 and 1350 a significant number of Europeans, especially missionaries and merchants, had traveled, largely by land, to China and India, and some of them, such as Marco Polo, had written widely circulated accounts of their experiences. Even if you did not know that, you can infer from this map segment alone that the fourteenth-century West was not totally ignorant of India's geography and dynamics, including the importance of Chinese merchants in the commerce of the Malabar Coast.

The *Roteiro* illustrates why the Portuguese desired direct overseas access to the rich markets of India and beyond. Given the numerous duties and profit margins placed on spices that made their way to Egypt and from there to Europe, the Portuguese realized that access to the markets of the Malabar Coast and beyond would enable them cut out many of the middle agents who profited greatly from this lucrative trade. At this point there is no good reason for you to know that the overland trade routes between Europe and the "Indies" (India, China, and other distant lands in Asia and East Africa) had largely broken down after about 1350 (see Vol. I, Chapter 12) and that the closing down of those routes spurred Portugal and Spain to find alternate ways by sea. What you can easily infer from this source is that the Portuguese expected to make much more per year than the 600,000 *cruzados* that the sultan of Egypt enjoyed, once they had direct access to Calicut. As we learn from this anonymous author, not only was Calicut a major commercial emporium, it was also a center of spice and gemstone production.

The *Roteiro* makes clear how important Calicut was to the commerce of Arabia and Egypt, Venice, Genoa, and the Spice Islands; Ibn Battuta and Ma Huan show us how central Calicut was to the overseas trade of China and other segments of the Islamic world. Our Moroccan and Chinese eyewitnesses further depict Calicut as an international city, where Muslims served both Chinese shipowners and the Hindu ruler of Calicut as trusted, high-ranking officials in charge of commercial activities. Both authors also shed light on policies adopted by the rulers of Calicut to encourage commerce and friendly relations with neighboring and far-distant powers.

Ibn Battuta tells us how his diplomatic party was received with great ceremony and how the *Samudri raja* arranged for his transportation aboard a Chinese vessel. Even more revealing are his descriptions of the sizes and types of the Chinese ships that did business at Calicut; the high status and honor accorded the factors, or agents-in-charge, of these Chinese ships; and the manner in which the ruler of Calicut protected the goods of shipwrecked merchants. The size of their ships alone suggests that the Chinese invested heavily in their trade with Calicut, but they did so because they knew that they would be welcomed and treated fairly at the port city. And why not? The rulers of Calicut understood that the prosperity of their city depended on the satisfaction of visiting merchants.

Ma Huan provides additional detail in this regard. The rajas of Calicut maintained a policy of religious toleration, which, given how much they depended on Muslim officials and merchants, was the only logical policy to follow. And this was in an age when bitter wars were fought between the sultanate of Delhi and Vijayanagara. The rajas also provided for a well-run and honest marketplace by commissioning officials who were responsible for facilitating all commercial transactions and guaranteeing all contracts. Inasmuch as a tax on all sales was paid into the ruler's treasury, it was in his best interest to grease the wheels of trade and to guarantee that once a deal was struck, it was inviolate. The fact that the raja minted gold and silver coins suggests that these policies worked well.

Finally, Ma Huan supports and supplements evidence from the *Roteiro* regarding Calicut's industries. Pepper production, which was carefully regulated by the state in regard to collection, storage, and sale (although the trees were apparently cultivated in small family garden plots), was a major staple of Calicut's economy. Likewise, Calicut's silk industry produced expensive bolts of silk, and the region was also a major source for coral and gemstones, especially pearls. Despite its native silk production, however, Calicut was a center for trade in Chinese embroidered silk. Apparently the high quality of this product allowed it to compete favorably with Indian silk.

Well, as you can see, interpreting historical sources is not an arcane science or esoteric art. Yes, it is challenging, but it is a skill that you can master. Look at it this way: It is an exercise that mainly requires close attention and common sense. You must first read and study each source carefully and thoroughly. Then, using the evidence you have picked up from the documents and artifacts, answer the Questions for Analysis. It is that straightforward. If you work with us, trusting us to provide you with all of the necessary background information and clues that you need to make sense out of these sources, you will succeed.

One last word: Have fun doing it because you should find it enjoyable to meet the challenge of reconstructing the past through its human records.

Part One

The Ancient World

THE TERM *ANCIENT WORLD* presents a problem to the student of world history because it is a creation of Western historical thought. Historians in the West originally used the term to refer only to the early history of one small region of the world — the area that stretches from the northwest corner of the Indian subcontinent to the Atlantic Coast of Europe. Understood within this narrow context, ancient history was seen as encompassing the period from the rise of *civilizations*, or *complex urban societies*, in Mesopotamia in Southwest Asia and Egypt in eastern North Africa to the collapse of Roman civilization: from approximately 3500 *Before the Common Era* (B.C.E.) to about 500 in the *Common Era* (C.E.). Within this scheme of history, antiquity passed away about 1,500 years ago, but not before it had laid the roots of Western civilization. Having spent itself, the Ancient World was followed by the so-called *Middle Ages* (500–1500), and this era, in turn, was followed by the early modern (1500–1789), modern (1789–1914), and contemporary eras.

Such neat divisions of the past, which once were thought to reflect the Western historical experience (and today there is serious doubt as to their accuracy in regard to the history of the West), make little sense when history is studied globally. Nevertheless, the category *Ancient World* is useful for the world historian if we redefine it in two ways: (1) by expanding the term to include all of the world's earliest complex societies, which are also known as *primary civilizations*, and (2) by distinguishing between the *Afro-Eurasian* and *American* worlds of antiquity.

The first primary civilizations arose independently and somewhat contemporaneously on two grand *world islands*: the Afro-Eurasian landmass and the Americas. Apparently the first to witness this phenomenon was the Afro-Eurasian supercontinent, where urban societies appeared in rough chronological sequence in the river valleys of Mesopotamia (essentially present-day Iraq), Egypt, northwest India, and China, between approximately 3750 and 2200 B.C.E. Although distinct and largely indigenous, these four early centers of civilization influenced one another in varying degrees.

Across the Atlantic and Pacific oceans, unknown to and uninfluenced by the civilizations of Eurasia and Africa, an urban, complex society had already emerged by 2600 B.C.E. (and possibly as early as 3100 B.C.E.) along Peru's Pacific coastal zone, as shown by recent radiocarbon dating of artifacts found at Caral in the Supe Valley. Later, by at least 1500 B.C.E., civilization had emerged along the Gulf Coast of Mexico. Significantly, the earliest cities of Peru and Mexico were constructed around monumental stone mounds that served as temple complexes, but hard evidence of cross-cultural linkage at this early date is lacking. What is clear is that these original centers of civilization in the Americas served as the Western Hemisphere's dominant matrices of civilized culture for thousands of years and well beyond the period of Afro-Eurasian antiquity. Due to extensive trade networks, Mexico's first civilization eventually influenced cultures throughout ancient *Mesoamerica* (Mexico and Central America) and far into North America, whereas Peru's first civilization influenced the development of complex societies throughout the Pacific coastal and Andes regions and into the Amazon rainforest.

The four original centers of civilization within the Afro-Eurasian World — Mesopotamia, Egypt, the Indus Valley, and China — were fairly self-contained, compact, and separate, but never isolated. Plenty of evidence (such as source 7) indicates that the river-valley civilizations of Mesopotamia, Egypt, and the Indus enjoyed a measure of commercial and cultural exchange from early days. The vast steppes, deserts, and mountain ranges of Central Asia also meant that China, at the eastern end of the Eurasian landmass, was more isolated than the three other primary centers of civilization, but its isolation was never absolute. By the middle of the second millennium (the 1000s) B.C.E., wheat and barley had made their way from *Southwest Asia* (today often called the *Middle East*) to China. The techniques of painted pottery and bronze casting might also have made the same journey, but the process of transmission is obscure and disputed. Less controversial is the horse chariot, an invention of northern Iran, which appeared in China before the twelfth century B.C.E. On the other end of the scale of exchange, scraps of Chinese silk have been found in Egyptian tombs dating from around 1000 B.C.E.

As these separate but connected civilizations evolved over the course of several thousand years, each spread outward, encompassing a large region on which it imprinted a distinctive culture. By 300 B.C.E. the four major Afro-Eurasian cultural regions were Southwest Asia, India, China, and the Mediterranean. Of these, China's relative isolation dictated that its culture would be the most singular and least stimulated by foreign influences. Conversely, the culture of Southwest Asia was the most variegated and eclectic because geography made it the crossroads of the Afro-Eurasian World. A close second in the realm of diversity was the Mediterranean, which drew deeply from the cultural traditions of Mesopotamia, Egypt, and all of the various peoples of the Mediterranean Basin, especially the Greeks and the diverse inhabitants of *Syria-Palestine* and *Anatolia* (the Asian peninsula of present-day Turkey).

During the last few centuries B.C.E. and the first several centuries C.E., the cultures at both ends of the great Eurasian expanse of land, China and the Mediterranean, achieved political unity and consequently expanded at the expense of their less organized neighbors, such as Koreans and Southeast Asians in the East and various Celtic peoples in the West. The result was two massive empires — Han China and the Roman Empire — linked by Central Asian, Indian, Southwest Asian, and East African intermediaries. Consequently, goods, ideas, and diseases were exchanged throughout Eurasia and portions of Africa more freely and quickly than ever before, especially along the so-called *Silk Road*, a complex network of caravan routes that opened up around 100 B.C.E. and connected China with Central Asia, India, and the Mediterranean Sea.

Between approximately 200 and 550 C.E., internal and external pressures, including diseases that traveled along the trade routes and incursions by various nomadic and semi-nomadic peoples, precipitated the collapse of empires in China, India, Southwest Asia, and the Roman Mediterranean. With those disasters, which were neither totally contemporaneous nor equally severe, the first grand epoch of Afro-Eurasian history — the Ancient World — was at an end. The era that followed rested on the foundations of antiquity but also differed substantially from the Ancient World, in part because of three *world religions* — Mahayana Buddhism, Christianity, and Islam — that played transforming roles throughout Eurasia and Africa between roughly 600 and 1500 C.E.

Across the oceans, the civilizations of Mesoamerica and South America continued their development in isolation from the cares and trends of the Eastern Hemisphere. Cities and empires rose and fell, and societies continued to develop along cultural lines set down by the Americas' first civilizations. To be sure, changes took place. One important new trend between roughly 600 and 1200 C.E. was the rise of North American complex societies in what are today the deserts of the southwestern United States and the lands washed by the Mississippi and Ohio rivers. Despite these new centers of civilization, the American Indian World was only wrenched out of its ancient patterns when European invaders and colonists began arriving in significant numbers in the early sixteenth century.

Because of a relative lack of documentary evidence relating to preconquest American Indian cultures and civilizations, the sources in Part One deal almost exclusively with ancient Afro-Eurasian history. We will consider the story of antiquity in the Western Hemisphere more fully in Part Three, Chapter 11.

The First Civilizations

THE TERM *CIVILIZATION* arouses heated discussion among world historians. First, they do not agree as to what constitutes a civilization. Moreover, many deplore the value judgment that the term seems to imply: Civilizations are better or "more advanced" (more "civilized") than non-civilizations. Rather than use this value-laden word, many have opted for the apparently more neutral "complex society." Leaving aside the obvious objection that this alternative term contains its own apparent value judgment, we have opted for the often-misused and misunderstood term *civilization*, but we do so only to delineate a society that has created a *state*.

The word derives from the Latin adjective *civilis*, which means "political" or "civic." No matter how else we define civilization, an organized civic entity, a state, serves as its core. A state is a sovereign public power that binds large numbers of people together at a level that transcends the ties of family, clan, tribe, and local community and organizes them for projects far beyond the capabilities of single families or even villages and towns.

Modern states tend to be *secular*, or oriented toward this world, and most rulers today claim no particular spiritual or religious authority. In fact, many modern states are based on the principle that legitimate power derives solely from the people. In contrast, the world's first states were *sacred states*, in which rulers claimed to govern by divine mandate. Such rulers either governed in the name of some divine or heavenly authority or were themselves perceived as gods. Religious beliefs, as well as political and social institutions, varied greatly among the world's ancient civilizations, but ancient civilized peoples shared a common perception that authority is indivisible because it is divine. In other words, they saw no distinction between the state's sacred and secular functions.

Rulers and those who carried out their wills — priests, bureaucrats, and soldiers — were a small minority and maintained power by exploiting the many. This was a fact of early civilized life largely because, until recent times, states could produce only severely limited surpluses of resources, due to the narrow agrarian base of their economies. That surplus of goods, which is so necessary for the creation of a state, could be channeled into state-building activities only if rulers kept the majority of their subjects at a fairly low level of subsistence by exacting from them a major portion of the surplus through taxes, labor services, and military conscription. Consequently, the more agreeable benefits of civilization, such as literature and the other arts, were largely the exclusive property and tools of the few.

Many of the world's first civilizations evolved systems of writing, and in each case the art of writing served, at least initially, to strengthen the authority of rulers. Whether writing was used to record temple possessions or tax obligations, to give permanence to laws, or to provide priests with a coherent body of sacred texts, writing set apart the powerful from the powerless. At the same time, however, writing was only one means of communicating the will of the gods and of rulers and of preserving cultural traditions, and it was a far less effective and popular vehicle than word of mouth, images, and architecture. The point is that written records from the long-distant past can give us only a partial glimpse of reality, and that glimpse is given to us by antiquity's elites. Rarely, if ever, do we hear the voice of the common person, and almost never do we hear the folk stories and myths of an ancient society in their original, raw condition. When myths, folk tales, and popular songs were finally set down in writing, they were probably almost always overlaid with "more literary" elements.

Added to this is the problem that not all of the records left behind by the first civilizations are open to us. Some ancient systems of writing still defy decipherment, such as those of early Crete and India. Happily, this is not the case with the written languages of Mesopotamia, Egypt, and China. The documentary sources left behind by these three civilizations, for all of their limitations, reveal societies that were strikingly different in perspective and structure, even as they shared characteristics common to all early civilizations. We do not know all that we want to know about these civilizations, but their records do give us privileged insights into their values and makeup.

Mesopotamia: The Land of Two Rivers

It is in *Sumer*, which lay just to the north of the Persian Gulf in an area encompassed by the southern regions of present-day Iraq, that we discover the first evidence of human civilization, although archaeological evidence from sites in other areas of the world might someday force us to revise that statement.

Around 3750 B.C.E. Uruk (or Erech) emerged as a city — apparently Sumer's first city — and other Sumerian city-states followed in succeeding centuries. The origin of the Sumerians is a mystery. Their language is unique, with no connection to any other known language or language family. Evidence of a number of non-Sumerian words in their language, especially for terms associated with such basic skills as farming and metalworking, suggests that the Sumerians were immigrants who learned the techniques essential for a settled life from an indigenous population that they absorbed, or at least controlled.

Generally we call the Sumerians, and the other peoples who inhabited this region of Southwest Asia, *Mesopotamians*. The term is Greek, and it means "those who dwell between the rivers." The rivers are the Tigris in the east and the Euphrates to its west. The former is about 1,180 miles long, and the latter flows for about 1,740 miles. Rising in the mountains, they descend southeast, providing water to the inhabitants of the steppe, desert, and marshes through which they pass. Without the fertile soil produced by these two rivers and the challenge of harnessing this life-giving water through irrigation systems, Sumerian civilization is inconceivable.

By approximately 1800 B.C.E., the Sumerians had been absorbed by waves of infiltrators and invaders and ceased to exist as an identifiable people. Moreover, the cultural center of gravity within Mesopotamia had shifted northward to the region of middle Mesopotamia, centering on the city of *Babylon* on the Euphrates.

Despite their disappearance as a people, the Sumerians had set the framework for a dynamic Mesopotamian civilization that exercised profound cultural influence throughout West Asia and beyond for about 3,000 years. Between roughly 3750 and 500 B.C.E., Mesopotamia was the cultural and political center of West Asia.

Ancient Mesopotamians are credited with having created the world's first system of writing (although some scholars credit Egypt with this "first"), as well as its first governments, schools, codes of law, and epic literature. Just as prominent in Mesopotamian life were disasters, both natural and human generated.

As noted, the geography of Mesopotamia provided its people with the challenge of harnessing the waters of its two great rivers, and from that cooperative effort civilization arose. Yet those rivers also threatened to destroy the fragile fabric of civilized society because they were unpredictable and could easily turn into uncontrollable torrents, especially in the south. Moreover, most of southern Mesopotamia was covered by either arid plains or marsh. Consequently, Sumerian civilization was built upon heroic labor in the midst of a hostile environment.

Another significant geographic aspect of Mesopotamian life, which also proved to be an important factor throughout its history, is the land's openness to incursions. To the north and east lie the hills and mountains of Iran and Armenia, from which wave after wave of invaders descended into the inviting valley of cities. To the south and west lies the desert of Arabia, out of which came countless nomads century after century. In many instances these invaders toppled a preexisting state and then settled down to become, in turn, Mesopotamians.

Some came from the desert fringes, such as the *Amorites*, speakers of a *Semitic* language who established the first Babylonian Empire in the eighteenth century (1700s) B.C.E. Others were mountain folk, such as the chariot-driving *Kassites*, speakers of an Indo-Iranian language who toppled Babylon late in the seventeenth century B.C.E. Regardless of their origin, language, or native culture, all eventually became part of a Mesopotamian cultural complex, with modes of life and thought the Sumerians had set in place at the dawn of human civilization.

Life and Death in Mesopotamia
▼▼▼
1 ▼ *THE EPIC OF GILGAMESH*

Humans share many basic concerns, and among them two are of primary importance: finding meaning in life and confronting the reality of death. In Mesopotamia, where life and human fortune were so precarious, people deeply probed these issues and made them the subjects of numerous myths. The word *myth* derives from the ancient Greek word for "a poetic story." As understood by modern scholars, a myth is not just any poetic story, and it certainly is not a deliberate piece of fiction or a story told primarily to entertain, although myths have entertainment value. Primarily, a myth is a vehicle through which prescientific societies explain the workings of the universe and humanity's place within it. Whereas the scientist objectifies nature, seeing the world as an *it*, the myth-maker lives in a world where everything has a soul, a personality, and its own story. A raging river is not a body of water responding to physical laws but an angry or capricious god. In the same manner, the fortunes of human society are not the consequences of chance, history, or any patterns discoverable by social scientists. Rather, the gods and other supernatural spirits intervene directly into human affairs, punishing and rewarding as they wish, and divine interventions become the subjects of mythic stories. The stories, in turn, provide insight into the ways of the gods, thereby largely satisfying the emotional and intellectual needs of the myth-maker's audience.

So far as the issues of the meaning of life and death were concerned, ancient Mesopotamia created its classic mythic answer in the form of its greatest work of literature, *The Epic of Gilgamesh*. An *epic* is a long narrative poem that celebrates the feats of a legendary hero who is involved in a journey or similar severe test. In the process of his trials, the hero gains wisdom and, because of that wisdom, greater heroic stature.

The most complete extant version of *The Epic of Gilgamesh* exists in Akkadian, a Semitic language that gradually supplanted Sumerian as the dominant language of Mesopotamia after about 2300 B.C.E. and became *the* language of diplomacy and commerce throughout Southwest Asia after about 1450 B.C.E. The text was discovered on fragments of about seventy clay tablets in the ruins of an Assyrian library that dated to the late seventh century B.C.E. Other, earlier versions of the epic show, however, that the story, at least in its basic outline, is Sumerian in origin and goes back to the third millennium B.C.E. (2000s). The Akkadian version of the epic that survives is about 80 percent complete. About 575 lines are missing out of an original 3,000 or so. Despite these holes, some of which might have been filled from yet-to-be-translated cuneiform tablets looted or destroyed in 2003 in the wake of the Second Gulf War, the story that survives is coherent, and its characters emerge as multidimensional.

The hero, Gilgamesh, was a historical figure. Originally known by his Sumerian name, Bilgames, he ruled the city-state of Uruk sometime around 2800–2700 B.C.E. and was remembered as a great warrior, as well as the builder of Uruk's massive walls. His exploits were so impressive that he became the focal point of a series of sagas that recounted his heroic deeds. Around 1700 B.C.E. an unknown Babylonian poet reworked some of these Sumerian tales, along with other stories — such as the adventure of Utnapishtim that appears in our selection — into an epic masterpiece that became widely popular and influential throughout Southwest Asia and beyond.

The epic contains a profound theme, the conflict between humanity's talents and aspirations and its mortal limitations. Gilgamesh, "two-thirds a god and one-third human," as the poem describes him, is a man of heroic proportions and appetites who still must face the inevitability of death.

As the epic opens, an arrogant Gilgamesh, not yet aware of his human limitations and his duties as king, is exhausting the people of Uruk with his manic energy. The people cry to Heaven for relief from his abuse of power, and the gods respond by creating Enkidu, a wild man who lives among the animals. Enkidu enters Uruk, where he challenges Gilgamesh to a contest of strength and fighting skill. When Gilgamesh triumphs, Enkidu embraces him as a brother, and the two heroes set out on a series of spectacular exploits.

In the course of their heroic adventures, they insult Ishtar (Inanna in Sumerian), goddess of sexual love and fertility, and for this a life is owed. The one chosen by the gods to die is Enkidu. As the selection opens, Enkidu, after having cursed his heroic past, which has brought him to this fate, tells Gilgamesh of a vision he has had of the place Mesopotamians knew as "the land of no return."

QUESTIONS FOR ANALYSIS

1. What was the Mesopotamian view of the afterlife?
2. What is the message of Siduri's advice to Gilgamesh?
3. Consider Utnapishtim's initial response to Gilgamesh's request for the secret of eternal life. How does his message complement what Siduri has said?

4. Consider the story of Utnapishtim. What do the various actions of the gods and goddesses allow us to infer about how the Mesopotamians viewed their deities?
5. According to the epic, what are the respective roles of the gods and humans? What do the Mesopotamian deities require of humanity? What do humans expect of their gods?
6. What has Gilgamesh gained from his epic quest? Has it changed him?
7. In the epilogue the poet lays out the moral of the story. What does it tell us about the Mesopotamian view of the meaning of life?

As Enkidu slept alone in his sickness, in bitterness of spirit he poured out his heart to his friend. . . . "Listen, my friend, this is the dream I dreamed last night. The heavens roared, and earth rumbled back an answer; between them stood I before an awful being, the somber-faced manbird; he had directed on me his purpose. His was a vampire face, his foot was a lion's foot, his hand was an eagle's talon. He fell on me and his claws were in my hair, he held me fast and I smothered; then he transformed me so that my arms became wings covered with feathers. He turned his stare towards me, and he led me away to the palace of Irkalla, the Queen of Darkness,[1] to the house from which none who enters ever returns, down the road from which there is no coming back.

"There is the house whose people sit in darkness; dust is their food and clay their meat. They are clothed like birds with wings for covering, they see no light, they sit in darkness. I entered the house of dust and I saw the kings of the earth, their crowns put away forever; rulers and princes, all those who once wore kingly crowns and ruled the world in the days of old. They who had stood in the place of the gods like Anu and Enlil,[2] stood now like servants to fetch baked meats in the house of dust, to carry cooked meat

and cold water from the waterskin. In the house of dust which I entered were high priests and acolytes, priests of the incantation and of ecstasy; there were servers of the temple, and there was Etana, that king of Kish whom the eagle carried to Heaven in the days of old.[3] There was Ereshkigal[4] the Queen of the Underworld; and Belit-Sheri squatted in front of her, she who is recorder of the gods and keeps the book of death. She held a tablet from which she read. She raised her head, she saw me and spoke: 'Who has brought this one here?' Then I awoke like a man drained of blood who wanders alone in a waste of rushes; like one whom the bailiff has seized and his heart pounds with terror."

⊳   Enkidu dies. Gilgamesh, now aware of the reality of his own death, begins a search for immortality. He travels to the end of the Earth, where he encounters Siduri, a female tavern keeper/goddess, who advises him:

"Gilgamesh, where are you hurrying to? You will never find that life for which you are looking. When the gods created man they allotted to him death, but life they retained in their own keeping. As for you, Gilgamesh, fill your belly with good things; day and night, night and day,

---

[1]Goddess of the Underworld and sister of Ishtar/Inanna.
[2]Dead earthly kings. Anu, whose name meant "heaven," was the supreme but remote king of the gods and the ultimate source of all order and government. Enlil, second only to Anu in power and importance, directed the forces of nature and bestowed royal authority on earthly leaders.

[3]A legendary king of the Sumerian city of Kish who flew to Heaven on the back of an eagle in order to obtain a magical plant that would give him the potency to father an heir.
[4]The more common name of the goddess of the Underworld (see note 1).

dance and be merry, feast and rejoice. Let your clothes be fresh, bathe yourself in water, cherish the little child that holds your hand, and make your wife happy in your embrace; for this too is the lot of man."

▷ Gilgamesh refuses to be deflected from his quest. After a series of harrowing experiences, he finally reaches Utnapishtim, a former mortal whom the gods had placed in an eternal paradise, and addresses him.

"Oh, father Utnapishtim, you who have entered the assembly of the gods, I wish to question you concerning the living and the dead, how shall I find the life for which I am searching?"

Utnapishtim said, "There is no permanence. Do we build a house to stand forever, do we seal a contract to hold for all time? Do brothers divide an inheritance to keep forever, does the flood-time of rivers endure?. . . From the days of old there is no permanence. . . . What is there between the master and the servant when both have fulfilled their doom? When the Anunnaki,[5] the judges, come together, and Mammetun[6] the mother of destinies, together they decree the fates of men. Life and death they allot but the day of death they do not disclose."

Then Gilgamesh said to Utnapishtim the Faraway, "I look at you now, Utnapishtim, and your appearance is no different from mine; there is nothing strange in your features. I thought I should find you like a hero prepared for battle, but you lie here taking your ease on your back.

Tell me truly, how was it that you came to enter the company of the gods and to possess everlasting life?" Utnapishtim said to Gilgamesh, "I will reveal to you a mystery, I will tell you a secret of the gods."

"You know the city Shuruppak,[7] it stands on the banks of Euphrates? That city grew old and the gods that were in it were old. There was Anu, lord of the firmament, their father, and warrior Enlil their counselor, Ninurta[8] the helper, and Ennugi[9] watcher over canals; and with them also was Ea.[10] In those days the world teemed, the people multiplied, the world bellowed like a wild bull, and the great god was aroused by the clamor. Enlil heard the clamor and he said to the gods in council, 'The uproar of mankind is intolerable and sleep is no longer possible by reason of the babel.' So the gods agreed to exterminate mankind. Enlil did this, but Ea because of his oath[11] warned me in a dream. He whispered their words to my house of reeds, 'Reed-house,[12] reed-house! Wall, O wall, hearken reed-house, wall reflect; O man of Shuruppak, son of Ubara-Tutu; tear down your house and build a boat, abandon possessions and look for life, despise worldly goods and save your soul alive. Tear down your house, I say, and build a boat. . . . Then take up into the boat the seed of all living creatures.'

"When I had understood I said to my lord, 'Behold, what you have commanded I will honor and perform, but how shall I answer the people, the city, the elders?' Then Ea opened his mouth and said to me, his servant, 'Tell them this: I

---

[5]An assemblage of lesser deities (numbering either 60 or 600) who had multiple functions.
[6]A mother goddess of fate.
[7]Located at present-day Fara, about equidistant between Baghdad in the north and Basra in the south, the ruins of Shuruppak contain a two-foot-thick layer of mud, evidence of a local flood that took place around 2750 B.C.E. The flood did not cover all of Sumer, much less all of Mesopotamia, but it might have served as the basis for a flood epic. Evidence also shows that the city survived the flood and life went on.
[8]Originally a god of irrigation and agriculture, Ninurta became a god of war with the rise of Mesopotamian imperialism.
[9]God of irrigation and of the dead.

[10]Also known as Enki, Ea was the god of water and the secret wisdom of sorcery and crafts. He was also the god of providence who protected those in crisis.
[11]An oath to protect humanity, because he was the god of life-giving water and good fortune.
[12]Reed houses probably go back to Neolithic times. Because of their fragility, they served Mesopotamians as a metaphor for impermanence. The so-called Marsh Arabs of southern Iraq built reed houses well into the late twentieth century, until Saddam Hussein destroyed the marshes following the 1991 Gulf War in order to root out their opposition to his rule. Almost the entire marshland was turned into desert, and most of its inhabitants were displaced.

have learnt that Enlil is wrathful against me, I dare no longer walk in his land nor live in his city; I will go down to the Gulf to dwell with Ea my lord. But on you he will rain down abundance, rare fish and shy wildfowl, a rich harvest-tide. In the evening the rider of the storm will bring you wheat in torrents.' . . .

"On the seventh day the boat was complete. . . .

"I loaded into her all that I had of gold and of living things, my family, my kin, the beast of the field both wild and tame, and all the craftsmen. I sent them on board. . . . The time was fulfilled, the evening came, the rider of the storm sent down the rain. I looked out at the weather and it was terrible, so I too boarded the boat and battened her down. . . .

"For six days and six nights the winds blew, torrent and tempest and flood overwhelmed the world, tempest and flood raged together like warring hosts. When the seventh day dawned the storm from the south subsided, the sea grew calm, the flood was stilled; I looked at the face of the world and there was silence, all mankind was turned to clay. The surface of the sea stretched as flat as a roof-top; I opened a hatch and the light fell on my face. Then I bowed low, I sat down and I wept, the tears streamed down my face, for on every side was the waste of water. I looked for land in vain, but fourteen leagues distant there appeared a mountain, and there the boat grounded; on the mountain of Nisir the boat held fast, she held fast and did not budge. . . . When the seventh day dawned I loosed a dove and let her go. She flew away, but finding no resting-place she returned. Then I loosed a swallow, and she flew away but finding no resting-place she returned. I loosed a raven, she saw that the waters had retreated, she ate, she flew around, she cawed, and she did not come back. Then I threw everything open to the four winds, I made a sacrifice and poured out a libation[13] on

the mountain top. Seven and again seven cauldrons I set up on their stands, I heaped up wood and cane and cedar and myrtle. When the gods smelled the sweet savor, they gathered like flies over the sacrifice.[14] Then, at last, Ishtar also came, she lifted her necklace with the jewels of Heaven that once Anu had made to please her. 'O you gods here present, by the lapis lazuli round my neck I shall remember these days as I remember the jewels of my throat; these last days I shall not forget.[15] Let all the gods gather round the sacrifice, except Enlil. He shall not approach this offering, for without reflection he brought the flood; he consigned my people to destruction.'

"When Enlil had come, when he saw the boat, he was wroth and swelled with anger at the gods, the host of Heaven, 'Has any of these mortals escaped? Not one was to have survived the destruction.' Then the god of the wells and canals Ninurta opened his mouth and said to the warrior Enlil, 'Who is there of the gods that can devise without Ea? It is Ea alone who knows all things.' Then Ea opened his mouth and spoke to warrior Enlil, 'Wisest of gods, hero Enlil, how could you so senselessly bring down the flood?' . . . It was not that I revealed the secret of the gods; the wise man learned it in a dream. Now take your counsel what shall be done with him.

"Then Enlil went up into the boat, he took me by the hand and my wife and made us enter the boat and kneel down on either side, he standing between us. He touched our foreheads to bless us saying, 'In time past Utnapishtim was a mortal man; henceforth he and his wife shall live in the distance at the mouth of the rivers.' Thus it was that the gods took me and placed me here to live in the distance, at the mouth of the rivers."

Utnapishtim said, "As for you, Gilgamesh, who will assemble the gods for your sake, so that you may find that life for which you are searching?"

---

[13]Poured out wine or some other beverage as an offering to the gods.
[14]Many myth-making people believe that the gods gain nourishment from the greasy smoke of burnt sacrifices.

[15]The necklace is a rainbow. Lapis lazuli is not indigenous to Mesopotamia and was imported from Afghanistan.

> After telling his story, Utnapishtim challenges Gilgamesh to resist sleep for six days and seven nights. When Gilgamesh fails the test, Utnapishtim points out how preposterous it is to search for immortality when one cannot even resist sleep. Out of kindness, Utnapishtim tells Gilgamesh where he can find a submarine plant that will at least rejuvenate him. Consequently, the hero dives to the bottom of the sea and plucks it. However, humanity is denied even the blessing of forestalling old age and decrepitude when the plant is stolen from Gilgamesh by a serpent (which annually rejuvenates itself by shedding its skin). His mission a failure, Gilgamesh returns to Uruk.

The destiny was fulfilled which the father of the gods, Enlil of the mountain, had decreed for Gilgamesh: "In nether-earth the darkness will show him a light: of mankind, all that are known, none will leave a monument for generations to come to compare with his. The heroes, the wise men, like the new moon have their waxing and waning. Men will say, 'Who has ever ruled with might and with power like him?' As in the dark month, the month of shadows, so without him there is no light. O Gilgamesh, this was the meaning of your dream. You were given the kingship, such was your destiny, everlasting life was not your destiny. Because of this do not be sad at heart, do not be grieved or oppressed; he has given you power to bind and to loose, to be the darkness and the light of mankind. He has given unexampled supremacy over the people, victory in battle from which no fugitive returns, in forays and assaults from which there is no going back. But do not abuse this power, deal justly with your servants in the palace, deal justly before the face of the Sun.". . .

Gilgamesh, the son of Ninsun, lies in the tomb. At the place of offerings he weighed the bread-offering, at the place of libation he poured out the wine. In those days the lord Gilgamesh departed, the son of Ninsun, the king, peerless, without an equal among men, who did not neglect Enlil his master. O Gilgamesh, lord of Kullab,[16] great is thy praise.

---

[16]Part of Uruk.

The Search for Justice in Mesopotamia

▼▼▼

2 ▼ *THE JUDGMENTS OF HAMMURABI*

Mesopotamia's sense of insecurity resulted in its producing not only great philosophical literature but also detailed legal codes. The so-called *Code of Hammurabi* is the most famous but certainly not the earliest of the many collections of law produced throughout the first 3,000 years of Mesopotamian civilization. Discovered in 1901, this Babylonian text from the eighteenth century B.C.E. is inscribed on a stone pillar (technically known as a *stele*) that measures over seven feet in height and more than six feet in circumference. Apparently Hammurabi (r. ca. 1792–1750 B.C.E.), who briefly united Mesopotamia through conquest and transformed Babylon into the capital of an empire, wanted it to last forever.

Whether Mesopotamia's numerous compilations of law were Sumerian, Babylonian, Assyrian, or Chaldean, they shared common elements. Chief among them was the expressed purpose, as the prologue to Hammurabi's collection declares, "to promote the welfare of the people . . . to cause justice to prevail in the land, to destroy the wicked and the evil, that the strong might not oppress the weak."

Hammurabi's code is actually not a coherent and systematic code of laws but rather a compilation of decisions, or *misharum* (equity rulings), that the king made in response to specific cases and perceived injustices. Nevertheless, this collection of judgments covers a wide variety of crimes and circumstances, thereby allowing extensive insight into the structure and values of eighteenth-century Babylonian society.

QUESTIONS FOR ANALYSIS

1. What specific actions did Hammurabi take in his attempt to provide for the good order of society and the basic welfare of his subjects?
2. What evidence is there of class distinctions in Babylon?
3. What was the status of women and children in this society? Did they enjoy any protection or liberties?
4. Mesopotamian society has been characterized as a *patriarchal* (dominated by male heads of households) society. Does the evidence in this collection of decisions tend to support or refute that judgment?
5. What principles and assumptions underlay these judgments? In other words, what does this collection reveal about the worldview, basic values, and ideals of Hammurabi's Babylon?

PROLOGUE

When Marduk[1] had instituted me governor of men, to conduct and to direct, Right and Justice I established in the land, for the good of the people.

THE ADMINISTRATION OF JUSTICE

3. If in a lawsuit a man gives damning evidence, and his word that he has spoken is not justified, then, if the suit be a capital one,[2] that man shall be slain. . . .

5. If a judge has heard a case, and given a decision, and delivered a written verdict, and if afterward his case is disproved, and that judge is convicted as the cause of the misjudgment, then he shall pay twelve times the penalty awarded in that case. In public assembly he shall be thrown from the seat of judgment; he shall not return; and he shall not sit with the judges upon a case. . . .

FELONS AND VICTIMS

22. If a man has perpetrated brigandage, and has been caught, that man shall be slain.

23. If the brigand has not been taken, the man plundered shall claim before god[3] what he has lost; and the city and governor in whose land and boundary the theft has taken place shall restore to him all that he has lost.

24. If a life, the city and governor shall pay one mina[4] of silver to his people.[5] . . .

PROPERTY

29. If his son is under age, and unable to administer his [deceased] father's affairs, then a third part of the field and garden shall be given to his mother, and his mother shall bring him up. . . .

---

[1]The chief god of Babylon.
[2]A case in which death is the penalty.
[3]The god or goddess of the city. Each city had its special protector deity.

[4]A unit of measure that equaled eighteen ounces of silver. Coins were invented around 700 B.C.E. in the Anatolian kingdom of Lydia.
[5]The family of the slain person.

38. A captain, soldier, or official may not give his field, or garden, or house to his wife or his daughter; neither can they be given as payment for debt.[6]

39. He may bequeath in writing to his wife or daughter a field, a garden, or a house that he may have bought, and may give it as payment for debt. . . .

WINESELLERS AND TAVERNS

109. If rebels meet in the house of a wineseller and she[7] does not seize them and take them to the palace, that wineseller shall be slain.

110. If a priestess who has not remained in the temple,[8] shall open a wine-shop, or enter a wine-shop for drink, that woman shall be burned. . . .

DEBT SLAVERY

117. If a man has contracted a debt, and has given his wife, his son, his daughter for silver or for labor, three years they shall serve in the house of their purchaser or bondsmaster; in the fourth year they shall regain their original condition. . . .

MARRIAGE AND THE FAMILY

129. If the wife of a man is found lying with another male, they shall be bound and thrown into the water. If the husband lets his wife live, then the king shall let his servant[9] live. . . .

134. If a man has been taken prisoner, and there is no food in his house, and his wife enters the house of another, then that woman bears no blame.

135. If a man has been taken prisoner, and there is no food before her, and his wife has entered the house of another, and bears children,

and afterward her husband returns and regains his city, then that woman shall return to her spouse. The children shall follow their father. . . .

137. If a man has decided to divorce . . . a wife who has presented him with children, then he shall give back to that woman her dowry,[10] and he shall give her the use of field, garden, and property, and she shall bring up her children. After she has brought up her children, she shall take a son's portion of all that is given to her children, and she may marry the husband of her heart.

138. If a man divorces his spouse who has not borne him children, he shall give to her all the silver of the bride-price,[11] and restore to her the dowry which she brought from the house of her father; and so he shall divorce her.

139. If there was no bride-price, he shall give her one mina of silver for the divorce.

140. If he is a peasant, he shall give her one-third of a mina of silver.

141. If a man's wife, dwelling in his house, has decided to leave, has been guilty of dissipation, has wasted her house, and has neglected her husband, then she shall be prosecuted. If her husband says she is divorced, he shall let her go her way; he shall give her nothing for divorce. If her husband says she is not divorced, her husband may marry another woman, and that [first] woman shall remain a slave in the house of her husband.

142. If a woman hates her husband, and says "You shall not possess me," the reason for her dislike shall be inquired into. If she is careful, and has no fault, but her husband takes himself away and neglects her, then that woman is not to blame. She shall take her dowry and go back to her father's house. . . .

148. If a man has married a wife, and sickness has seized her, and he has decided to marry

---

[6]The monarch retained ultimate ownership of the property handed out to soldiers and bureaucrats who received land as payment for their services.
[7]Women traditionally filled this role in ancient Mesopotamia. See Siduri in source 1.

[8]Thereby breaking her vow to devote her life to serving the temple deity.
[9]The wife's lover.
[10]The required money or goods she brought to the marriage.
[11]The price he paid her family in order to marry her.

another, he may marry; but his wife whom the sickness has seized he shall not divorce. She shall dwell in the house he has built, and he shall support her while she lives. . . .

168. If a man has decided to disinherit his son, and has said to the judge, "I disown my son," then the judge shall look into his reasons. If the son has not been guilty of a serious offense which would justify his being disinherited, then the father shall not disown him.

169. If the son has committed a serious offense against his father which justifies his being disinherited, still the judge shall overlook this first offense. If the son commits a grave offense a second time, his father may disown him. . . .

PERSONAL INJURY

195. If a son has struck his father, his hands shall be cut off.

196. If a man has destroyed the eye of another free man, his own eye shall be destroyed. . . .

198. If he has destroyed the eye of a peasant, . . . he shall pay one mina of silver.

199. If he has destroyed the eye of a man's slave, . . . he shall pay half his value. . . .

202. If a man strikes the body of a man who is superior in status, he shall publicly receive sixty lashes with a cowhide whip. . . .

206. If a man has struck another man in a dispute and wounded him, that man shall swear, "I did not strike him knowingly"; and he shall pay for the physician.

207. If he dies of his blows, he shall swear like-wise; and if it is the son of a free man, he shall pay half a mina of silver.

208. If he is the son of a peasant, he shall pay a third of a mina of silver.

209. If a man strikes the daughter of a free man, and causes her fetus to abort, he shall pay ten shekels[12] of silver for her fetus.

210. If that woman dies, his daughter shall be slain.

211. If he has caused the daughter of a peasant to let her fetus abort through blows, he shall pay five shekels of silver.

212. If that woman dies, he shall pay half a mina of silver. . . .

CONSUMER PROTECTION

215. If a physician has treated a man with a metal knife for a severe wound, and has cured the man, or has opened a man's tumor with a metal knife, and cured a man's eye, then he shall receive ten shekels of silver.

216. If the son of a peasant, he shall receive five shekels of silver. . . .

218. If a physician has treated a man with a metal knife for a severe wound, and has caused the man to die, or has opened a man's tumor with a metal knife, and destroyed the man's eye, his hands shall be cut off. . . .

229. If a builder has built a house for a man, and his work is not strong, and if the house he has built falls in and kills the householder, that builder shall be slain.

230. If the child of the householder is killed, the child of that builder shall be slain.

231. If the slave of the householder is killed, he shall give slave for slave to the householder.

232. If goods have been destroyed, he shall replace all that has been destroyed; and because the house that he built was not made strong, and it has fallen in, he shall restore the fallen house out of his own personal property.

233. If a builder has built a house for a man, and his work is not done properly, and a wall shifts, then that builder shall make that wall good with his own silver. . . .

EPILOGUE

The oppressed, who has a lawsuit, shall come before my image as king of justice. He shall read the writing on my pillar, he shall perceive my

---

[12]Three ounces of silver. A mina (note 4) was divided into sixty shekels, each of which was three-tenths of an ounce of silver.

precious words. The word of my pillar shall explain to him his cause, and he shall find his right. His heart shall be glad [and he shall say,] "The Lord Hammurabi has risen up as a true father to his people; the will of Marduk, his god, he has made to be feared; he has achieved victory for Marduk above and below. He has rejoiced the heart of Marduk, his lord, and gladdened the flesh of his people for ever. And the land he has placed in order.". . .

In after days and for all time, the king who is in the land shall observe the words of justice which are written upon my pillar. He shall not alter the law of the land which I have formulated, or the statutes of the country that I have enacted. . . . If that man has wisdom, and desires

to keep his land in order, he will heed the words which are written upon my pillar. . . . The . . . people he shall govern; their laws he shall pronounce, their statutes he shall decide. He shall root out of the land the perverse and the wicked; and the flesh of his people he shall delight.

Hammurabi, the king of justice, am I, to whom Shamash[13] has granted rectitude. My words are well weighed: my deeds have no equal, leveling the exalted, humbling the proud, expelling the haughty. If that man heeds my words that I have engraved upon my pillar, departs not from the laws, alters not my words, changes not my sculptures, then may Shamash make the scepter of that man to endure as long as I, the king of justice, and to lead his people with justice.

---

[13]The sun-god: god of justice and vindicator of the oppressed. During the eighteenth century B.C.E., he rose in prominence among the deities of Babylon. The sculpture that is carved at the top of the stele on which Hammurabi's

judgments are inscribed shows the king humbly receiving from Shamash a measuring-line and a rod, the symbols of equity and justice.

Egypt: The River of Two Lands

Civilization seems to have arisen in Egypt shortly after it first appeared in Sumer. Although there is evidence of early Sumerian contact with the Egyptians, Egypt's civilization was largely self-generated, and its history and cultural patterns differed substantially from those of Mesopotamia. Egyptians, however, shared the same myth-making way of perceiving reality.

An integral element of Egyptian myth was the belief that Egypt was the land of divine harmony ruled by a living god-king, or *pharaoh*, who balanced all conflicting cosmic forces. Around 3100 B.C.E. the land of the Nile was unified into a single state, although culturally it remained two distinctive lands: the rich delta region of the north, known as *Lower Egypt* (because the Nile flows north), and the long but narrow strip of green land that borders the Nile to the south, known as *Upper Egypt*. Before their unification, Lower and Upper Egypt had been separate kingdoms. As far as Egyptians were concerned, they forever remained two antithetical yet complementary lands brought into harmony by a unifying king who was a god on Earth. As the embodiment of the union of Upper and Lower Egypt, the king was likewise the personification on Earth of the goddess *Ma'at*, whose name meant "what is right." In other words, the god-king of Egypt *was* truth, law, and justice.

The state that resulted from the union of Egypt's two lands enjoyed about 3,000 years of prosperity and stability. Between approximately 3100 and 343 B.C.E.,

Egypt experienced only a handful of relatively short-lived periods of either internal turmoil and the breakdown of central authority or domination by foreign powers. This long history of centralized monarchy and native rule was largely due to the blessings of geography. Unlike Mesopotamia, Egypt was fairly secure behind its barriers of sea and desert, and the Nile's annual flooding was normally predictable and usually beneficial.

The sense of security that resulted from these geographic and historical circumstances was reflected in much of ancient Egypt's religion, philosophy, and arts. At the same time, codes of law, which figure so prominently in the historical records of Mesopotamia, are not to be found in the literature of ancient Egypt. Although the Egyptians were equally concerned with maintaining a well-ordered and equitable society, their avenue to this goal differed greatly from that of the Mesopotamians.

Life and Death in Egypt
▼▼▼
3 ▼ *THE PERSON WHO WAS TIRED OF LIFE*

Historians divide the first 2,000 years of Egyptian civilization into six ages: the Early Dynastic Period (ca. 3100–2600 B.C.E.); the Old Kingdom (ca. 2600–2125); the First Intermediate Period (ca. 2125–2025); the Middle Kingdom (ca. 2060–1700); the Second Intermediate Period, or the Age of the Hyksos (ca. 1700–1550); and the New Kingdom, or Empire (ca. 1550–1069).

Multiple Voices I describes these six ages. For the moment, it is sufficient to know that the First Intermediate Period was a time of turmoil that witnessed the breakdown of central authority and the rise of regional petty lords. The following document probably reflects the anxieties of that troubled age, even though its sole surviving manuscript dates to the Middle Kingdom's Twelfth Dynasty (ca. 1976–1793), a time of relative stability, peace, and prosperity. Here we read an unusual dialogue between a despondent individual and his soul (*ba*). Alone and friendless, he contemplates suicide but wonders if death will be any better.

In this excerpt, which concludes the dialogue, the soul refers to the West, the ancient Egyptian term for the region of the dead. For further insight into how the Egyptians viewed the West and the ways one attained it, see the three mortuary texts in "Multiple Voices I: Shifts in the Search for Eternal Life in Egypt."

QUESTIONS FOR ANALYSIS

1. Compare this anonymous individual with Gilgamesh. In what ways do their crises differ?
2. Consider the soul's advice: "Love me here (and now), and forget about the West." How does it compare with the advice that Siduri and Utnapishtim give Gilgamesh?
3. Compare the soul's resolution of the troubled man's crisis with the *Epic of Gilgamesh*'s epilogue, or resolution. Which strike you as more significant, the similarities or the differences?

4. **What do your answers to questions 1–3 allow you to infer about the world-views of these two civilizations?**

"Behold, my very being is loathsome,
Behold, more than the dung of vultures
On summer days when the sky is hot. . . .

Whom can I trust today?
One's brothers have become evil,
And friends of today have no compassion.

Whom can I trust today?
Hearts are greedy,
And every man steals his neighbor's goods. . . .

Whom can I trust today?
I am laden down with sorrow,
And there is none to comfort me.

Whom can I trust today?
Evil runs rampant throughout the land,
Endless, endless evil.

Death is before me today
(Like) the healing of a sick man,
Like going outside after illness.

Death is before me today
Like the fragrance of myrrh,
Like sitting under the sails on a windy day.

Death is before me today
Like the fragrance of the lotus,
Like tottering at the verge of drunkenness.

Death is before me today
Like the course of the Nile,
As when men return home from a campaign.

Death is before me today
Like the clearing of the sky,
As when a man understands what had been
    unknown to him.

Death is before me today
Like a man's yearning to see his home
After passing many years in exile.

But surely, he who is yonder[1] will be a living god,
Having purged away the evil which had
    afflicted him.

Surely, he who is yonder will be one who stands
    in the sun barque,[2]
Having made the necessary offerings to the
    temples.

Surely, he who is yonder will be one who knows
    all things,
Who will not be prevented from standing in the
    presence of Re when he speaks."

What my *ba* said to me:

"Lay your complaining aside, my companion
    and my brother.
Make offerings on the altar and struggle for
    your life,
Just as you have declared.
Love me here (and now),[3] and forget about the
    West.
Continue indeed in your desire to reach the
    West,
But only when your body is buried in the earth.
I shall alight after you have become weary,[4]
And we shall make our dwelling place together."

---

[1]In the West, the land of the dead.
[2]The bark, or boat, of Re, the sun and creator god, who daily sails across the sky from east to west.

[3]Appreciate life here and now.
[4]After you fall asleep in death.

The Search for Justice in Egypt

▼▼▼

4 ▼ *TALE OF THE ELOQUENT PEASANT*

In this story that comes down from the Middle Kingdom, a peasant is robbed of his meager possessions, a donkey and food for his family, by a subordinate of the royal chief steward. The peasant appeals for justice to the chief steward, who is so impressed with the peasant's eloquence that he informs King Nebkaure the Just of the man's rhetorical skill. Nebkaure decides that he wishes to hear more, and he instructs his chief steward to keep the peasant coming back and to record his eloquent appeals for the royal pleasure. At the same time, the chief steward is to anonymously provide daily food for the peasant and his family. The peasant is forced to make eight additional appeals. Following the ninth appeal, the peasant is convinced that he will now be punished for his impudence. Instead, the chief steward sends the peasant's appeals to the king. Pleased by what he reads, Nebkaure instructs the chief steward to render a verdict. The chief steward orders the arrest of the malefactor and the confiscation of all his goods, animals, and servants and bestows them all on the eloquent peasant.

The following excerpt is the peasant's eighth appeal.

QUESTIONS FOR ANALYSIS

1. Compare the eloquent peasant's description of the proper role of magistrates with the epilogue of *The Judgments of Hammurabi*. Which strike you more, the similarities or the differences? What do you conclude from your answer?
2. Consider Ma'at, to which the peasant appeals. Is it the same as the "Right and Justice" that Hammurabi claimed to have established in the land, or was it different? Explain your answer.
3. Compose Hammurabi's commentary on this story.

Then the peasant came to petition him an eighth time, saying, "O Chief Steward, my lord:

Men flounder because of selfishness;
The greedy man lacks success,
For his (only) success is failure.
You are greedy, but it (gains) you nothing;
You steal, but it is no profit to you.
Now, permit a man to stand up for his cause
  which is truly good.
You have your provisions in your house, and
  your belly is full.
Your grain is excessive and even overflows,

And what issues forth perishes on the earth.
(You are) a rogue, a thief, an extortioner!
Yet magistrates are commissioned to suppress
  evil,
As safeguards against the aggressor;
Magistrates are empowered to fight falsehood.

It is not fear of you which causes me to petition
  you.
You do not know my heart:
A lowly man who turns again and again to
  make complaint to you,
One who does not fear him to whom he makes
  his petition,

One whose equal will not be brought to you
  from any quarter (of town).

You have a plantation in the country,
You have a salary in the administration,
You have provisions in the storehouse,
The officials pay you, and still you steal.
Are you an extortioner?
Do men bring (bribes) to you
And to the henchmen with you at the allotment
  of the farmlands?

Perform Ma'at for the sake of the Lord of Ma'at,[1]
For the constancy of his Ma'at is absolute.
(You are) the pen, papyrus and palette of
  Thoth,[2]
So keep far from the doing of wrong.
That goodness should be potent is excellent
  indeed,
For Ma'at will endure unto eternity
And go down to the grave with him who
  performs it.
He will be buried, and the earth will enfold
  him,
But his name will never vanish upon the earth,
For he will be remembered because of his
  goodness.
Such is the integrity of the decree of God:

It is a balance, and it does not tilt;
It is a scale, and it does not lean to the side.

Whether it is I or another who comes (before
  you),
You must acknowledge (him).
Do not give back (to him) the reply of a silent
  man.
Do not abuse one who himself has done no
  abuse.

But you show no compassion!
You are neither concerned nor perturbed!
You do not give me due recompense for this fine
  speech
Which comes from the mouth of Re[3] himself.
Speak Ma'at! Perform Ma'at!
For it is great, it is exalted, it is enduring,
Its integrity is evident,
And it will cause (you) to attain the state of
  veneration.

Can a balance tilt?
It is its scale-pans which bear things,
And there must be no exceeding the measure.
A criminal action does not reach safe harbor,
But he who is humble will reach land."

---

[1]The king.
[2]The god of wisdom, who invented language, writing, and
mathematics, he served as the scribe and messenger of the

gods. At the judgment of the dead (see Multiple Voices I),
he recorded the deceased's guilt or innocence.
[3]See source 3, note 2.

▼▼▼

China: The Land of the Yellow and Yangzi Rivers

The study of history has been one of China's most revered and continuous traditions for more than 2,000 years. By the second century B.C.E., the Chinese claimed
a detailed history that reached back into the early third millennium. According to
their vision of the past, Chinese civilization was sparked by extraordinary men,
beginning with the *Three Sovereigns*, who laid the basis of Chinese culture by bestowing such gifts as agriculture and fire. The last of the three was the *Yellow Em-*
peror, who established an organized state around 2700 B.C.E. Four other emperors

succeeded in turn, each ascending the throne through merit and genius rather than by birth. Known as the *Five Sage Emperors*, they crafted all of the basic elements of Chinese civilization, such as hydro engineering (harnessing the waters of the violent Yellow River) and silk production. The last of the five was succeeded onto the throne by his son, thereby establishing China's first royal dynasty — the Xia (pronounced "shah") family, which ruled from 2205 to 1766 B.C.E. After Xia's collapse, the *Shang* Dynasty succeeded and held power, until it gave way to the *Zhou* (pronounced "joe") Dynasty.

Until the late 1920s, scholars lacked hard evidence that either the Xia or Shang dynasties ever existed, and Western historians generally dismissed them as romantic legends. The work of archaeologists over the past sixty years, however, proved that the Shang Era was a historical reality, and recent evidence suggests that its period of efflorescence stretched from about 1600 to around 1050 B.C.E. Xia remains an enigma due to a lack of conclusive evidence. Recent excavations, however, show that China enjoyed a period of civilization long before Shang. The discovery in Henan province of a tiny spinning wheel with what appears to be a Daoist inscription (see Chapter 4) suggests that the art of writing in China might stretch back to at least 2500 B.C.E. Whether there was a full-fledged Xia Dynasty of kings during those pre-Shang centuries is an open question.

One theory that has some evidentiary support holds that Xia, Shang, and Zhou were three coexisting centers of civilization in northern China in the area of the Yellow River and that the Xia, Shang, and Zhou eras were largely the shifting of dominance through warfare from one state and family of royal warlords to another. It appears that from as early as the late third millennium B.C.E., northern China was home to many competing small states, each centered on a clan and its walled town. Warfare and alliances allowed some states to grow at their neighbors' expense and others to lose their independence. Apparently none of the families or their states ever totally dominated northern China until the victory of the Qin (pronounced cheen) state in 221 B.C.E. (see Chapter 4), but certain families, certainly Shang and Zhou and possibly Xia, successively and successfully claimed wide-sweeping royal hegemony.

Although the details of early Chinese history still largely elude us, archaeology is providing tantalizing clues that cause us to question and even abandon once-dominant notions regarding early Chinese civilization. In the 1980s discoveries south of the Yangzi River and also in the southwestern province of Sichuan led scholars to reevaluate the prevailing diffusionist theory of the origins of Chinese civilization. According to that model, civilization began in the north, around the Yellow River, in the late third millennium B.C.E. and slowly spread out from there, not fully penetrating the southern region of the Yangzi River Valley until the early centuries C.E. The first four editions of *The Human Record* reflected that picture. However, the discovery of bronzes and other artifacts far to the south and the southwest of the Yellow River has forced a rethinking of that model. Many of the artifacts in the Yangzi River area, which date to the late Shang Era, show clear Shang characteristics, indicating that Shang cultural influences had spread far beyond its political borders. More significant, the artifacts discovered in the southwestern region of Sichuan, as well as some items from the Yangzi River area, exhibit styles and forms that differ greatly from those of Shang. This has led many scholars to posit the theory that Chinese civilization emerged out of the confluence of several independent cultures, all of which were flourishing around 1200 B.C.E. It certainly seems as though the Yangzi River Valley, which previous generations of historians thought was a latecomer to Chinese culture, played a role in the evolution of early Chinese civilization. It might not have been as dominating as that of the Yellow River, but it was significant.

The history of early southern Chinese civilization has yet to be written, so we must turn to the north, to the states of the Yellow River, for the story of early Chinese political development.

Our knowledge of the Xia state, if there was one, and its presumed age of predominance is less than just sketchy. We know much more about the Shang, thanks to the work of archaeologists, who have unearthed two huge capital cities, royal tombs, magnificent bronze ceremonial vessels, and an early form of Chinese ideographic writing on what are known as *oracle bones*. Because they served the purpose of magical divination of the future, the inscriptions on oracle bones are brief and often cryptic. Nevertheless, in the hands of experts, they provide useful insights into Shang society and culture.

The Shang kings reigned over a loose confederation of family-centered states that collectively encompassed most but not all of northern China. Their world was precarious because military alliances and loyalties were constantly shifting. Despite limitations on the Shang kings' political powers, they enjoyed substantial authority as chief priests in the worship of Di, the high god of the Shang. It was believed that the ancestral spirits of the Shang family gave the king a privileged avenue of communication to Di. Moreover, excavated royal tombs indicate that the Shang kings were able to mobilize large numbers of workers and extensive resources in a world in which slavery and ritual sacrifice of human victims were accepted practices.

If, however, we desire a fuller story based narrative documents, we must wait until the Zhou Dynasty (ca. 1050–256). Because China's earliest extant literary and political documents date from the age of Zhou rule, we know much more about the Zhou Dynasty than about the Xia and Shang combined. The era of Zhou rule began around 1050, when the Zhou conquered the Shang and established a royal dynasty that lasted eight centuries. The Zhou Era is divided into two periods: Western and Eastern. The age of Western Zhou witnessed a fairly strong but decentralized monarchy that presided over fifty or more subordinate states. Zhou kings delegated authority to the rulers of these states in elaborate ceremonies that emphasized the king's primacy. As time went on, however, power tended to slip away from the Western Zhou kings into the hands of local lords. In 771 B.C.E. a group of rebellious northern nobles killed King Yu and overran the capital city, Chang'an (present-day Xi'an), and the royal heir fled east to Luoyang, where the Zhou continued to reside as kings until 256 B.C.E. But the kings of Eastern Zhou never enjoyed the power of their western forebears. For 500 years they reigned over but did not rule a kingdom where military and political power resided in the smaller regional states and the families that controlled them. As the *Son of Heaven*, however, the king continued to enjoy the exclusive right to offer sacrifices to Heaven and to preside over ceremonies dedicated to the royal ancestors.

The Mandate of Heaven
▼▼▼
5 ▼ *THE BOOK OF DOCUMENTS*

The *Shujing*, or *Book of Documents*, is the oldest of the *Five Confucian Classics*. These five works, which also include the *Book of Songs* (source 6), the *Book of Changes*, the *Book of Rites*, and the *Spring and Autumn Annals*, are incorrectly ascribed to the editorship of *Confucius* (Chapter 4, source 20). Known collectively as the *Wujing* (*The Five Scriptures*), the books became the basic elements of the Confucian educational system during the second century B.C.E., when they were reconstructed by order of several emperors of the Han Dynasty (202 B.C.E.– 220 C.E.), who reversed the policy of the earlier *Qin Dynasty* to destroy all traces of Confucian ideology. Regardless of this reconstruction and later editing, the *Shujing* that has come down to us is probably pretty much the same already-ancient text that Confucius admired, studied, and accepted as an authentic record of Chinese civilization.

Also known in English translation as the *Classic of History*, the *Shujing* is not a work of historical narration. Rather, it is a collection of documents spanning about 1,700 years of Chinese history and legend, from 2357 to 631 B.C.E. Despite their ascriptions, many of the documents are the spurious creations of much later periods and therefore reflect the attitudes of those subsequent eras.

The document that appears here was composed in the age of Zhou but purports to be the advice given by the faithful Yi Yin to King Tai Jia, the second Shang king. According to the story behind the document, when the first Shang king, Zheng Tang, died around 1753, his chief minister, Yi Yin, took it upon himself to instruct the new, young king in the ways and duties of kingship and the workings of the Mandate of Heaven.

The *Mandate of Heaven* (*Tianming*) was a political-social-cosmological philosophy that served as the basic Chinese explanation for the success and failure of monarchs and states down to the end of the empire in 1911 C.E. Whenever a dynasty fell, the reason invariably offered by China's sages was that it had lost the mandate, or authorized right, to rule, which is given by Heaven alone. In this context, Heaven did not mean a personal god but a cosmic, all-pervading power. The theory of the Mandate of Heaven and the very concept of Heaven were probably joint creations of the Zhou, who used them to justify their overthrow of the Shang around 1050 B.C.E. The king, after all, was the father of his people, and paternal authority was the basic cement of Chinese society from earliest times. Rebellion against a father needed extraordinary justification.

QUESTIONS FOR ANALYSIS

1. How does a ruler earn the Mandate of Heaven? How and why is it lost?
2. What are the consequences of losing the Mandate of Heaven?
3. Modern politicians often promise "innovative answers to the challenges of tomorrow." What would Yi Yin think about such an approach to statecraft?

What would Yi Yin think about modern politicians who attempt to appear youthful? What would he think of popular opinion polls?

4. What does the theory of the Mandate of Heaven suggest about the nature of Chinese society and the Chinese worldview?

5. Compare the Chinese vision of its ideal monarch with Egyptian and Mesopotamian views of kingship. Despite their obvious cultural differences, did each society expect its king to perform essentially the same task? If so, what was that task?

In the twelfth month of the first year . . . Yi Yin sacrificed to the former king, and presented the heir-king reverently before the shrine of his grandfather. All the princes from the domain of the nobles and the royal domain were present; all the officers also, each continuing to discharge his particular duties, were there to receive the orders of the chief minister. Yi Yin then clearly described the complete virtue of the Meritorious Ancestor[1] for the instruction of the young king.

He said, "Oh! of old the former kings of Xia cultivated earnestly their virtue, and then there were no calamities from Heaven. The spirits of the hills and rivers likewise were all in tranquility; and the birds and beasts, the fishes and tortoises, all enjoyed their existence according to their nature. But their descendant did not follow their example, and great Heaven sent down calamities, employing the agency of our ruler[2] who was in possession of its favoring appointment. The attack on Xia may be traced to the orgies in Ming Tiao.[3] . . . Our king of Shang brilliantly displayed his sagely prowess; for oppression he substituted his generous gentleness; and the millions of the people gave him their hearts. Now your Majesty is entering on the inheritance of his virtue; — all depends on how you commence your reign. To set up love, it is for you to love your relations; to set up respect, it is for you to respect your elders. The commencement is in the family and the state. . . .

"Oh! the former king began with careful attention to the bonds that hold men together. He listened to expostulation, and did not seek to resist it; he conformed to the wisdom of the ancients; occupying the highest position, he displayed intelligence; occupying an inferior position, he displayed his loyalty; he allowed the good qualities of the men whom he employed and did not seek that they should have every talent. . . .

"He extensively sought out wise men, who should be helpful to you, his descendant and heir. He laid down the punishments for officers, and warned those who were in authority, saying, 'If you dare to have constant dancing in your palaces, and drunken singing in your chambers, — that is called the fashion of sorcerers; if you dare to set your hearts on wealth and women, and abandon yourselves to wandering about or to the chase, — that is called the fashion of extravagance; if you dare to despise sage words, to resist the loyal and upright, to put far from you the aged and virtuous, and to seek the company of . . . youths, — that is called the fashion of disorder. Now if a high noble or officer be addicted to one of these three fashions with their ten evil ways, his family will surely come to ruin; if the prince of a country be so addicted, his state will surely come to ruin. The minister who does not try to correct such vices in the sovereign shall be punished with branding.' . . .

---

[1]Zheng Tang, founder of the Shang Dynasty, who was supposedly enthroned in 1766 B.C.E.
[2]Zheng Tang (see note 1).

[3]According to legend, Jie, the last Xia king, held notorious orgies at Ming Tiao.

"Oh! do you, who now succeed to the throne, revere these warnings in your person. Think of them! — sacred counsels of vast importance, admirable words forcibly set forth! The ways of Heaven are not invariable: — on the good-doer it sends down all blessings, and on the evil-doer it sends down all miseries. Do you but be virtuous, be it in small things or in large, and the myriad regions will have cause for rejoicing. If you not be virtuous, be it in large things or in small, it will bring the ruin of your ancestral temple."

Zhou Viewed from Above and Below
▼▼▼
6 ▼ THE BOOK OF SONGS

The *Shihjing*, or *Book of Songs*, another of the Five Confucian Classics that served as basic texts of an educational system that molded China's leaders for more than 2,000 years, consists of 305 poetic songs, composed largely between about 900 and 600 B.C.E. Some of them were sung at the Zhou court on ceremonial occasions, but others, such as ballads that complain about Zhou rule, celebrate love, or depict ordinary people at work, probably began as folk songs. We know nothing about the process by which songs were selected for inclusion, especially certain love songs that scandalized some later commentators. Regardless of the high percentage of lighthearted, homey, and even frankly sexual songs in the collection, the *Book of Songs* ultimately became Confucian because Confucius and his many generations of disciples interpreted these troublesome songs as metaphors and allegories, transforming them into texts of moral instruction.

The following songs illustrate several important aspects of early Chinese civilization and thought: marriage customs, relations between men and women, the perceived role of Heaven (and women) in human affairs, and the cult of ancestor veneration. The first song is that of a young woman who loves someone her family does not favor. The second tells of a moment shared between a woman and a man. The third reflects on troubles and the reasons for them. The fourth is a hymn meant to be sung in a ceremony in which the spirits of the ancestors are offered wine and food.

QUESTIONS FOR ANALYSIS

1. Consider the first two songs. What do they suggest about marriage customs and the status and role of women in Zhou China? Is the picture that emerges simple or complex?
2. What are the author's specific complaints in the third song? Whom does he blame for China's woes?
3. Compare the philosophy that undergirds the third song with that of the selection from the *Book of Documents* (source 5). What conclusions do you reach?
4. Compose a reply by the author of either of the first two songs to the third song. A prose answer is sufficient.
5. According to the third and fourth songs, how and why were the ancestors honored?

I BEG YOU, ZHONG ZI

I beg of you, Zhong Zi,
Do not climb into our homestead,
Do not break the willows we have planted.
Not that I mind about the willows,
But I am afraid of my father and mother.
Zhong Zi I dearly love;
But of what my father and mother say
Indeed I am afraid.
I beg of you, Zhong Zi,
Do not climb over our wall,
Do not break the mulberry-trees we have
    planted.
Not that I mind about the mulberry-trees,
But I am afraid of my brothers.
Zhong Zi I dearly love;
But of what my brothers say
Indeed I am afraid.

I beg of you, Zhong Zi,
Do not climb into our garden,
Do not break the hard-wood we have planted.
Not that I mind about the hard-wood,
But I am afraid of what people will say.
Zhong Zi I dearly love;
But of all that people will say
Indeed I am afraid.

SPLENDID

How splendid he was!
Yes, he met me between the hills of Nao.[1]
Our chariots side by side we chased two boars.
He bowed to me and said I was very nimble.

How strong he was!
Yes, he met me on the road at Nao.
Side by side we chased two stags.
He bowed to me and said "well done."

How magnificent he was!
Yes, he met me on the south slopes of Nao.
Side by side we chased two wolves.
He bowed to me and said "that was good."

HIGH REGARD

In high regard we hold mighty Heaven,
But even it is unkind to us.
We are forever without peace;
It brings down this scourge upon us.
All the states are filled with unrest,
Low and noble both suffer this disease.
As with parasites and pests,
There is no controlling it.
The guilty are not apprehended,
There is no respite, no cure.
The people have farm and field,
But these you seize without warning.
The people have working folk,
But these you commandeer.
There are some people quite innocent,
But still you have them jailed.
Then there are those with offenses
Whom you let go free.

A clever man builds a city;
A clever woman tears it down.
Oh, that clever woman,
She is an owl, she is a shrike.
The wagging tongues of women
Are the instruments of our decline.
No, disorder does not come down from Heaven,
Rather it is the spawn of these women.
You can neither teach, nor instruct
Women and their eunuchs.[2]

They attack others in anger and spite,
Slander arises, backs are turned.
You ask if they are not right,

---

[1]In northeastern China.
[2]Castrated court officials. They were castrated so that they would have no family ties. Often they and the women of the court were accused of intrigues aimed at grabbing power.

You ask what harm can they do.
They are like merchants with a three-fold
    profit;[3]
Noble lords understand this well.
Thus no woman serves the public,
They stay with their weaving and their loom.

Why does Heaven so reprove you?
Why do spirits not give their blessings?
Because you pay the enemy no attention,
And yet view us with resentment.
This is neither good nor auspicious;
Your demeanor is not fitting.
People flee for their lives,
The state is injured and exhausted.

Heaven casts down its net,
Indeed it is very wide.
People flee for their lives,
Their hearts filled with grief.
Heaven casts down its net,
It is very close-knit indeed.
People flee for their lives.
Their hearts filled with melancholy.

The geyser spews high in the sky;
It must be very deep indeed.
Our hearts are filled with grief
Why has this come to us now?
And not before?
Or not after?
Expansive is mighty Heaven;

There is nothing it cannot assure.
Insult not the august ancestors,
And your descendants will be secure.

GLORIOUS ANCESTORS

Ah, the glorious ancestors —
Endless their blessings,
Boundless their gifts are extended;
To you, too, they needs must reach.
We have brought them clear wine;
They will give victory.
Here, too, is soup well seasoned,
Well prepared, well mixed.
Because we come in silence,
Setting all quarrels aside,
They make safe for us a ripe old age,
We shall reach the withered cheek, we shall go
    on and on.
With our leather-bound naves,[4] our bronze-clad
    yokes,
With eight bells a-jangle
We come to make offering.
The charge put upon us is vast and mighty,
From Heaven dropped our prosperity,
Good harvests, great abundance.
They come,[5] they accept,
They send down blessings numberless.
They regard the paddy-offerings,[6] the offerings
    of first-fruits
That Tang's descendant brings.[7]

---

[3]Exorbitant profit.
[4]The hubs of wheels. The image is of their driving a chariot.
[5]The spirits of the ancestors.
[6]An offering of rice.

[7]Zheng Tang, founder of the Shang Dynasty (see source 5).
This hymn comes from the state of Song (pronounced
"suung"), whose people claimed descent from the Shang.

▼▼▼

Mute Testimony

Some of the world's earliest civilizations have left written records that we cannot yet decipher and might never be able to read. These include India's *Harappan* civilization, which was centered in the Indus Valley from around 2600 to about 1700 B.C.E.; the *Minoan* civilization of the Aegean island of Crete, which flourished from roughly 2500 to about 1400 B.C.E.; and the African civilization of *Kush*, located directly south of Egypt, which reached its age of greatness after 800 B.C.E. but with much earlier origins as a state. For many other early civilizations and cultures, we have as yet uncovered no written records.

The following pieces of artifactual evidence provide glimpses into several of these so-called mute cultures. As is always the case when dealing with unwritten sources, the historian discovers that such clues from the past raise more questions than they answer.

Cultural Impressions
▼▼▼

7 ▼ *INDUS, MESOPOTAMIAN, AND CRETAN SEALS*

The stamps and seals that grace the many documents certifying who we are and what we have attained have their origins in the carved magic amulets of prehistory. As official signatures and tokens of authority, seals and stamps have been used by individuals and states since the dawn of civilization. In Mesopotamia carved stone cylinder seals that were rolled into soft clay were used at Uruk and other Sumerian cities as early as 3500 B.C.E. and continued to be produced throughout Southwest Asia for the next 3,000 years. When papyrus and parchment replaced clay as preferred writing surfaces, stamps and stamp seals replaced cylinder seals in popularity.

Ancient Southwest Asians did not have a monopoly on such marks of ownership, authenticity, and official approval. More than 2,000 stamp seals and seal impressions have been discovered at Harappan sites in the Indus Valley of what is today the nation of Pakistan. Collectively, the seals contain about 400 different characters of what appears to be a pictographic form of writing. However, scholars have been unable to crack the code represented by these signs. Happily, the seals also contain carved images that allow us to infer something about this largely mysterious civilization.

The first grouping contains six modern drawings (done in negative for clarity) of Indus seal impressions from the period 2100–1750 B.C.E., the age of Harappan cultural maturity. Seal 1 depicts a hairy person holding two tigers by the throat. Seal 2 portrays a horned, tailed, and cloven-footed individual grappling with a horned tiger under a tree. Seal 3 depicts two unicorn (single-horned) heads twisted around what appears to be a stylized *pipal*, or fig, tree, the sacred tree of India. Seal 4 shows four human figures somersaulting forward and backward over the raised horns of a bull. Seal 5 shows a humped bull, often called a Brahman bull. Seal 6 presents a male individual with a deeply furrowed or painted face who is wearing a water-buffalo-horn headdress, numerous bangles, bracelets, and a V-shaped collar or necklace. The individual is sitting with his knees angled to either side and the soles of his feet pressed together in front of him. His arms extend away from his body, and his hands rest on his knees, with fingers pointed downward. Surrounding him are wild animals: a rhinoceros and water buffalo to his left; an elephant and tiger to his right; underneath him are two antelope-like creatures (one is largely broken off; only its horns remain). A stick-figure human also stands or walks to his right. Some viewers see two side faces in this seated figure.

1

4

2

5

3

6

Indus Seals

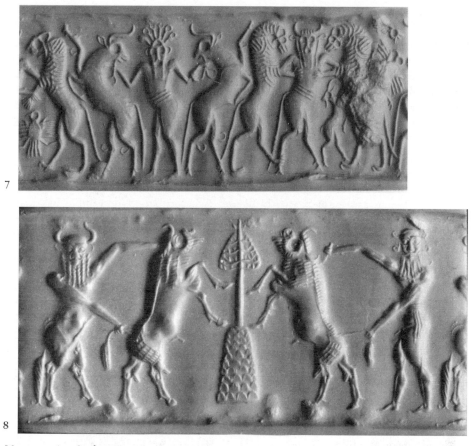

7

8

Mesopotamian Seals

9

Cretan Seal

By way of comparison, consider the second group of three seal impressions. Items 7 and 8 are rolled-out impressions from Mesopotamian cylinder seals. Number 7, which is from Sumer and dates to somewhere between 2600 and 2350 B.C.E., depicts two heroes struggling with animals. On our left is a nude, muscular, hairy man fighting two bulls. This is probably Gilgamesh (source 1). On the right is a creature who is half bull and half human grasping two lions. This is probably Gilgamesh's companion Enkidu. Number 8 was crafted in Akkad in central Mesopotamia in the period 2340–2180 B.C.E. and shows a bull-man on the left and a hairy hero on the right (probably Enkidu and Gilgamesh). Each holds a rampant bull by the mane and tail. The forelegs of each bull touch the top of a stylized mountain and what seems to be a sacred tree on the mountain. The final impression (9) is of a seal from the island civilization of Crete. The seal dates to ca. 1550–1500 B.C.E. and depicts two bulls and two acrobats. One athlete has just vaulted over a bull, while the second bull-leaper stands ready to vault.

QUESTIONS FOR ANALYSIS

1. Seals 2–9 contain horned figures. What do you suppose the horn symbolized to these societies? Why, of all horned creatures, do you think the bull figures so prominently in these seals? Based on your answers, what can you infer about the religious and social values of these societies?
2. Consider the hairy males in seals 1, 7, and 8. What does hairiness seem to symbolize in each instance? Again, what do you infer about their societies' religious and social values from this evidence?
3. Consider the central figure in seal 6. How do you interpret his posture, and what does your answer suggest about the individual and his function? Consider his dress and the figures that surround him. Do these suggest humanity or divinity? If a human, what is his class? If a god, what sort of god?
4. What can you infer from these seals about possible lines of cultural contact and influence? Who *seems* to have influenced whom, and how? On a map, trace the possible routes of cultural exchange.

Sacred Kingship Along the Nile
▼▼▼
8 ▾ *TWO TEMPLE RELIEFS*

It is unclear whether several of the Indus seals that we have studied portray humans or deities, but the two temple *reliefs* (raised carvings on flat backgrounds) that follow clearly depict gods and kings. The piece on the top is Egyptian and dates from the thirteenth century B.C.E. Located at the temple of King Seti I at Abydos in Upper Egypt, it portrays, from right to left, Horus the falcon-god, King Seti, and the goddess Isis (see Multiple Voices I, source 3, note 1). We will use it solely for comparison with the relief below it. This piece of art is Kushitic and dates from after 300 B.C.E. It is a small fragment of a temple tablet from Meroë, a

Nubian city considerably distant from Abydos. It portrays a Nubian king of *Kush* and Apedemak, the lion-god of war.

The Nubians, who inhabited the region directly south of Egypt, were drawn into the orbit of their powerful neighbor to the north at an early date. Yet while they borrowed quite a bit from the Egyptians, the Nubians managed to retain their indigenous culture. Around 800 B.C.E. the Nubians created the independent kingdom of Kush and around 730 B.C.E. were strong enough to conquer Egypt, which Kushite pharaohs ruled for close to a century. After being driven out of Egypt by the Assyrians, the Kushites eventually established a new capital for their kingdom at Meroë on the Middle Nile. Between about 350 B.C.E. and the early fourth century C.E., Kush was a major economic power in northeast Africa, largely because of Meroë's rich iron deposits.

In the bottom relief, one of those mighty monarchs of Kush stands face-to-face with the Nubians' most powerful deity. Unfortunately, we cannot decipher the writing above each figure, so we can only guess at the meaning of this scene. Perhaps the relief of Seti I provides a vital clue. There Horus, the divine son of Isis, is handing the scepter of power to Seti, who, as long as he lives on Earth, will be identified with Horus, upon whose throne he sits. Note that the Meroitic tablet also portrays both god and king with what appear to be scepters.

QUESTIONS FOR ANALYSIS

1. What do these two sculptures allow us to infer about the nature of royal power in Kush?
2. What do these reliefs tell us about the balance that the Kushites struck between accepting Egyptian influences and retaining traditional Nubian ways?

Temple Relief: Isis, Seti I, and Horus

Temple Relief: Kushite King and Apedemak

Multiple Voices I ▾▾▾
Shifts in the Search for Eternal Life in Egypt

BACKGROUND

As already noted in the introduction to source 3, historians divide the first 2,000 years of Egyptian civilization into six ages. The *Early Dynastic Period* (ca. 3100–2600 B.C.E.) was Egypt's era of unification and state-building. The *Old Kingdom* (ca. 2600–2125) centered on Egypt's god-kings, whose mummified remains were reverently entombed in pyramids in preparation for the journey to eternal life in the *Land of the West*. During this age Egyptians believed (or at least the priests taught) that immortality was the exclusive preserve of the divine king, members of the royal family, the priests, and a handful of favored royal servants. They further believed that the necessary element that ensured the king's safe journey to the afterlife was proper attention to the rituals of the royal funeral ceremony.

Toward the end of the third millennium B.C.E., royal power collapsed, plunging Egypt into an era of civil turmoil known as the *First Intermediate Period* (ca. 2125–2025). A century later this age of local rule and social upheaval gave way to the *Middle Kingdom* (ca. 2060–1700), an era of revived central authority and of a deepening awareness of social justice and moral responsibility. Befitting the new spirit, many Egyptians came to view the means to eternal life in a new way.

The Middle Kingdom collapsed in the face of invasion. During the *Second Intermediate Period* (ca. 1700–1550), Lower Egypt (the delta area of the north) was held in bondage by invaders from the east known as the Hyksos (best translated as "foreign kings"), and Upper Egypt (the south) was divided into petty states that became vassals of the Hyksos. Following the reassertion of native pharaonic authority around 1550 B.C.E. by the princes of Thebes, who established the powerful Eighteenth Dynasty, Egyptian imperial power spread beyond its traditional borders. The *New Kingdom*, or *Empire* (ca. 1550–1069), was also characterized by a continued concern on the part of all classes who shared in the benefits of Egypt's imperial prosperity to continue to enjoy in the afterlife the good life that they had on Earth. It is an exaggeration to say that the path to eternal life was now open to all, but the path was wider and easier than ever before.

THE SOURCES

Beginning around 2345 B.C.E., Egyptians carved magical incantations on the walls of royal burial chambers as a means of assuring the king's safe journey into eternal life. Scholars have discovered more than 750 distinct incantations, which they term collectively the *Pyramid Texts*. We do not know what the Egyptians called them; regardless, they provide a privileged view of funeral practices and beliefs regarding immortality during the Old Kingdom. The first selection comes from the tomb of King Teti, the founder of the Sixth Dynasty, who died around 2333 B.C.E.

A new body of funerary inscriptions appeared during the Middle Kingdom. Known today as the *Coffin Texts*, these texts, usually inscribed within the wooden coffins of people who could afford elaborate funerals, were ritual resurrection spells. Some were modeled on the earlier *Pyramid Texts*, but most were new and displayed an obsession with the dangers of Earth and the terrors of death that was lacking in the pyramid inscriptions. Despite their hope in a blissful afterlife, Egyptians were not immune to the miseries and fears, especially fear of disaster and death, that beset all humans.

The second selection is a much-used coffin spell that takes the form of a two-part speech. In the first part, the sun-god Re speaks, reminding humanity of his four good deeds at the time of creation. In the second part, the deceased speaks, laying his claim on eternal life.

The third stage in this search for access to the afterlife is evident in the so-called *Book of the Dead*. This is the modern name for a collection of papyrus texts that the Egyptians knew as *The Chapters for Coming Forth by Day*. Although it did not reach its final form until around the sixth century B.C.E., this collection of chapters was largely a creation of the New Kingdom. Like the pyramid and coffin inscriptions from which it evolved, it was a body of magical incantations for use in burial ceremonies, but unlike the pyramid and coffin inscriptions, it had a fairly standardized text. It was also available to a larger but still necessarily prosperous clientele. Divided into more than 150 chapters, which were gathered together into papyrus scrolls, the book had a certain mass-produced quality. One could purchase a scroll, fill in the name of the deceased, and bury it with the person's body.

Of all the chapters, the most famous is Chapter 125, the lengthy "Judgment of the Dead," from which we have extracted *The Negative Confession*. The scene is the Hall of the Two Truths, or the Double Ma'at, where *Osiris*, king of the Underworld, presides over an assembly of forty-two minor deities. It is these forty-two who judge the deceased's suitability to become an eternally blessed spirit. Upon entering the hall, the deceased (N, or fill in the name) proclaims her or his purity.

QUESTIONS FOR ANALYSIS

1. What are the underlying assumptions of King Teti's pyramid text?
2. According to the coffin text, how does a person guarantee eternal life?
3. Consider the speech of Re. Does it contain a moral element? If so, how is that message connected, if at all, with the dead person's spell?
4. What does *The Negative Confession* allow us to infer about Egyptian values in the New Kingdom?
5. Each of the three texts provides a path to eternal life. What do their similarities and differences suggest about continuities and changes within Egyptian society over this millennium?
6. Ma'at figures prominently in both *The Negative Confession* and the roughly contemporaneous *Tale of the Eloquent Peasant* (source 4). Is it the same Ma'at? What inferences follow from your answer?

I ▾ A PYRAMID TEXT

Oho! Oho! Rise up, O Teti!
Take your head,
Collect your bones,
Gather your limbs,
Shake the earth from your flesh!
Take your bread that rots not,
Your beer that sours not,
Stand at the gates that bar the common people!
The gatekeeper comes out to you,
He grasps your hand,
Takes you into heaven, to your father Geb.[1]
He rejoices at your coming,
Gives you his hands,

Kisses you, caresses you,
Sets you before the spirits, the imperishable
    stars.
The hidden ones worship you,
The great ones surround you,
The watchers wait on you.
Barley is threshed for you,
Emmer is reaped for you,
Your monthly feasts are made with it,
Your half-month feasts are made with it,
As ordered done for you by Geb, your father,
Rise up, O Teti, you shall not die!

---

[1]The god of Earth and father of Osiris, the god of resurrection and king of the dead.

---

2 ▾ A COFFIN TEXT

Words spoken by Him-whose-names-are-hidden, the All-Lord, as he speaks before those who silence the storm, in the sailing of the court:[1]

Hail in peace! I repeat to you the good deeds which my own heart did for me from within the serpent-coil,[2] in order to silence strife. I did four good deeds within the portal of lightland:

I made the four winds, that every man might breathe in his time. This is one of the deeds.

I made the great inundation,[3] that the humble might benefit by it like the great. This is one of the deeds.

I made every man like his fellow; and I did not command that they do wrong. It is their hearts that disobey what I have said. This is one of the deeds.

I made that their hearts are not disposed to forget the West,[4] in order that sacred offerings be made to the gods of the nomes.[5] This is one of the deeds.

I have created the gods from my sweat, and the people from the tears of my eye.

THE DEAD SPEAKS

I[6] shall shine and be seen every day as a dignitary of the All-Lord, having given satisfaction to the Weary-hearted.[7]

---

[1]The deities who accompany Re as he sails daily across the sky (note 8).
[2]The serpent-dragon Apophis, a mythic symbol of the lurking dangers in the world.
[3]The annual flooding of the Nile.
[4]The Land of the Resurrected Dead.

[5]The forty-two religious and administrative districts into which Egypt was divided. Note that the dead person is being judged by forty-two deities.
[6]The dead person now becomes the speaker, assuming the identity of Re.
[7]One of Osiris's titles. One must first satisfy Osiris before joining Re.

I shall sail rightly in my bark,[8] I am lord of eternity in the crossing of the sky.

I am not afraid in my limbs, for Hu and Hike[9] overthrow for me that evil being.

I shall see lightland, I shall dwell in it. I shall judge the poor and the wealthy.

I shall do the same for the evil-doers; for mine is life, I am its lord, and the scepter will not be taken from me.

I have spent a million years with the Weary-hearted, the son of Geb, dwelling with him in one place; while hills became towns and towns hills, for dwelling destroys dwelling.

I am lord of the flame who lives on truth; lord of eternity, maker of joy, against whom that worm shall not rebel.

I am he who is in his shrine, master of action who destroys the storm; who drives off the ser-pents of many names when he goes from his shrine.

Lord of the winds who announces the north-wind, rich in names in the mouth of the Ennead.[10]

Lord of lightland, maker of light, who lights the sky with his beauty.

I am he in his name! Make way for me, that I may see Nun[11] and Amun![12] For I am that equipped spirit who passes by the guards.[13] They do not speak for fear of Him-whose-name-is-hidden, who is in my body. I know him, I do not ignore him! I am equipped and effective in opening his portal!

As for any person who knows this spell, he will be like Re in the eastern sky, like Osiris in the netherworld. He will go down to the circle of fire, without the flame touching him ever!

---

[8]Re sails across the sky in a bark, or boat.
[9]Personifications of effective speech and magic, they are probably a reference to this magical spell, which has been uttered at entombment and carved in the coffin.
[10]The company of Egypt's nine chief deities.
[11]The watery void outside of the temporal and spatial boundaries of creation from which the creator emerged, Nun was personified as the god of the Abyss.

[12]A primeval god who existed as a force before creation, he became the chief god of Thebes. He rose to preeminence in Egypt when the princes of Thebes reunited Egypt after the Second Intermediate Period.
[13]The guards to the Land of the West.

---

3 ▾ THE NEGATIVE CONFESSION

(1) To be said on reaching the Hall of the Two Truths[1] so as to purge N of any sins committed and to see the face of every god:
Hail to you, Great God, Lord of the Two Truths!
I have come to you, my Lord,
I was brought to see your beauty.
I know you, I know the names of the forty-two gods,
Who are with you in the Hall of the Two Truths.

Who live by warding off evildoers,
Who drink of their blood,
On that day of judging characters before Wennofer.[2]
Lo, your name is "He-of-Two-Daughters,"
(And) "He-of-Ma'at's-Two-Eyes."
Lo, I come before you,
Bringing Ma'at to you,
Having repelled evil for you.

---

[1]Ma'at takes a dual form here in Isis, goddess of Right, and Nephthys, goddess of Truth. Isis was the sister and wife of Osiris. It was she who brought the dead and dismembered Osiris back to life, thereby assuring his status as god of res-urrection and king of the Underworld. Nephthys, also Osiris's sister, had assisted in his resurrection.
[2]One of Osiris's names.

I have not done crimes against people,
I have not mistreated cattle,
I have not sinned in the Place of Truth.[3]
I have not known what should not be known,[4]
I have not done any harm.
I did not begin a day by exacting more than my due,
My name did not reach the bark of the mighty ruler.[5]
I have not blasphemed a god,
I have not robbed the poor.
I have not done what the god abhors,
I have not maligned a servant to his master.
I have not caused pain,
I have not caused tears.
I have not killed,
I have not ordered to kill,
I have not made anyone suffer.
I have not damaged the offerings in the temples,
I have not depleted the loaves of the gods,
I have not stolen the cakes of the dead.[6]
I have not copulated nor defiled myself.[7]
I have not increased nor reduced the measure. . . .

I have not cheated in the fields.
I have not added to the weight of the balance,
I have not falsified the plummet of the scales.
I have not taken milk from the mouth of children,
I have not deprived cattle of their pasture.
I have not snared birds in the reeds of the gods,
I have not caught fish in their ponds.
I have not held back water in its season,
I have not dammed a flowing stream,
I have not quenched a needed fire.
I have not neglected the days of meat offerings,
I have not detained cattle belonging to the god,
I have not stopped a god in his procession.

I am pure, I am pure,
I am pure, I am pure! . . .
No evil shall befall me in this land,
In this Hall of the Two Truths;
For I know the names of the gods in it,
The followers of the great God!

---

[3]He has not sinned in any holy place.
[4]Secrets of the gods.
[5]As he sails across the sky in his bark, Re has not heard of any misdeeds by the deceased.

[6]Food to accompany the dead on the their journey
[7]Presumably, in a holy place.

▲▲▲

❖ Chapter 2 ❖

Newcomers
From Nomads to Settlers

*T*HE OLDEST TOWN excavated to date by archaeologists is Jericho, which has been inhabited fairly continuously, but with some significant breaks, for the past 10,000 years. Around 8000 B.C.E. this site, which lies west of the Jordan River, covered more than eight acres and supported a population of 2,000 to 3,000 people. Most impressive are the town's massive watchtower, walls, and encircling ditch — silent witnesses of the residents' fear of outsiders.

Archaeological evidence shows that Jericho was destroyed on several occasions, and some of those catastrophes were probably the handiwork of invaders, attracted by the town's wealth. Not all of Jericho's assailants were *nomads*, or groups of related individuals who migrated along well-established seasonal routes, tending herds of domesticated animals as they moved. But some were.

The tension between nomadic peoples and settled farmers is as old as agriculture itself, and it was a major factor in world history well into modern times. At the same time, settled communities and the peoples who wandered their borders enjoyed many mutually beneficial relationships. Nomads served as mercenary soldiers, traders, consumers of a settled community's manufactured wares and foods, and carriers of new ideas. But they could also be formidable foes, threatening the very existence of some civilizations. Threats and incursions cut both ways, and often nomads found their ways of life disrupted and imperiled by the outward expansion of neighboring civilizations.

In this chapter we consider the impact, settlements, and evolving cultures of three newcomers: the *Aryans*, the *Greeks*, and the *Israelites*, all of whom appeared on the historical scene during the second millennium B.C.E. The state of current scholarship suggests that all three engaged in some limited agriculture prior to their moving into their new homelands. Many of the Israelites, however, seem to have been more purely pastoralists when they marched into the light of history, very much like modern Bedouins who still wander the arid regions of Southwest Asia with their flocks.

▼▼▼

The Indo-Europeans

By the late first millennium B.C.E., many of Eurasia's settled peoples, from the *Celts* of the British Isles to the *Tocharians* of Central Asia, spoke a variety of related languages that linguists classify as *Indo-European*. As far as we can tell, a core group of people who spoke a language known as *Proto-Indo-European* lived in western Asia about 6,500 years ago. Some scholars push that date back as far as 6500 B.C.E.; a majority is more comfortable with the vague date ca. 4500–4000 B.C.E. Some linguists place the ancestral homeland of this language family in *Anatolia* (the Asian peninsula of present-day Turkey); a majority finds the steppe region of southern Ukraine and Russia, just north of the Black and Caspian seas, a more likely location. Whatever the time and place of Proto-Indo-European's origins, beginning possibly as early as 4500 B.C.E. and continuing for several thousand years, groups who spoke various forms of this language moved out of their ancestral homeland in waves and migrated east, west, north, and southeast. Once under way, the migration waves seem to have moved at a slow pace, but their historical impact was profound. The fact that *Aryan, Eire* (the Gaelic name for the Republic of Ireland), and *Iran* derive from the common archaic root-word *aryo*, which means "nobleman," eloquently attests to the extent of the ancient Indo-European wanderings and settlements. Today almost all of the languages of Europe (Basque, Finnish, Georgian, and Hungarian are the exceptions) belong to subgroups of the Indo-European family, as also do such disparate tongues as Armenian, Farsi (Persian), Tajik, Hindi, Kurdish, and Romany (the language of the Gypsies).

In the course of these Indo-European migrations, the Aryans (the self-named "noble people") moved across the Hindu Kush mountain range and into the fertile Indus Valley, where they encountered the vestiges of Harappan civilization (source 7), and the Greeks moved into the Balkans, where they absorbed or displaced the native people they encountered. The dates of their respective arrivals are uncertain, but both were securely settled in their new homelands by the mid second millennium B.C.E.

Life, Death, and the Gods in Aryan India
▼▼▼

9 ▼ *THE RIG VEDA*

Until fairly recently, historians generally credited the Aryans with conquering and destroying a vigorous Harappan civilization. The evidence now suggests that these Indo-European immigrants moved into a region where organized society was already in shambles, due probably to a series of natural disasters around 1700 B.C.E. What is clear is that by 1500 B.C.E. the Aryans were ruling northwestern India as an illiterate warrior aristocracy and that the arts of writing and statecraft had disappeared. India would not reemerge into the light of recorded history until around 600 B.C.E.

Because the early Aryans were a preliterate people, what little we know about them we derive from their *oral tradition*, which survives in four great collections of priestly hymns, chants, incantations, and ritual formulas known as the *Vedas*, all of which were composed in the Aryans' sacred language, *Sanskrit*, and written down many centuries after their initial formulation. *Veda* means "wisdom" or "knowledge," and the Aryans accepted these collections of sacred poetry as the eternal word of the gods. For modern historians, however, the Vedas provide tantalizing glimpses into the historical dynamics of the era from roughly 1500 to about 600 B.C.E., a near millennium that is often referred to as India's *Vedic Age*.

As is common in preliterate societies, Aryan priests, known as *Brahmins*, were trained to perform prodigious feats of memory. Generation after generation they sang these songs and passed them on. As a result, although the Vedas would not be written down until around 600 B.C.E. (or later), many of the songs reflect the religious, social, and political realities of Aryan life around 1500 (or earlier). Conversely, other Vedic hymns were the products of later centuries and mirror the more sophisticated culture of an emerging Indo-Aryan civilization. It is the historian's task to identify and make sense out of these different elements.

The most celebrated and earliest of the four Vedic collections is the *Rig Veda* (*Verses of Knowledge*), a compilation of 1,017 songs, which probably was largely put together in the form that we know it between 1200 and 900 B.C.E., although it contains many elements that stretch back to long before the Aryans arrived in India. This Sanskrit masterpiece remains, even today, one of the sacred books of *Hinduism* (see Chapter 3). It is also, as far as we can determine, the earliest extant major work of literature in an Indo-European tongue, predating by several centuries the Homeric Greek epics.

The following three poems from the *Rig Veda* illustrate the evolution of Indo-Aryan religious thought. The first celebrates the victory over *Vritra*, the dragon of drought, by *Indra*, the early Aryans' chief deity. In this particular hymn, Indra conquers Vritra, known as the *Encompasser*, and liberates the universe, which Vritra has swallowed. The victory releases life-giving monsoon rains, irrigating waters that were vital to the Aryans, who were now settling down and farming the land. As the Aryans were absorbed into the rich cultural fabric of India, their manner of religious expression also changed. Indra, whose worship was the central reality of early Vedic religious life, largely fell out of favor as a major deity in post-Vedic India, becoming simply the god of weather. The second hymn hints at the change in religious perception that was taking place in later Indo-Aryan society. The third hymn, which is clearly one of the last Vedic songs to be crafted, presents another, quite different religious vision. In this poem the gods create the universe (and themselves) by sacrificing *Purusha*, the Cosmic Man, to himself. The paradoxical view of reality presented in this hymn would become a hallmark of classic Hindu thought, as we shall see in Chapter 3 and elsewhere.

QUESTIONS FOR ANALYSIS

1. The hymn regarding the victory over Vritra is the earliest of the three poems. What does its vision of Indra suggest about the society that worshiped him as its chief deity?
2. Consider the overall message of the second hymn. How does it portray Indra? Now focus on the fifth stanza. What is its message? What do your answers suggest to you about what was happening in Indo-Aryan society?
3. What clues in the "Hymn to Purusha" point to its late composition?
4. What are the core messages of the "Hymn to Purusha"?
5. Compare Indra and Purusha. In what ways do they represent significant historical changes that were taking place in Indo-Aryan society?

VICTORY OVER VRITRA

I will declare the manly deeds of Indra, the first that he achieved, the thunder-wielder.

He slew the dragon, then disclosed the waters, and cleft the channels of the mountain torrents.

He slew the dragon lying on the mountain: his heavenly bolt of thunder Twashtar[1] fashioned.

Like lowing cows in rapid flow descending, the waters glided downward to the ocean.

Impetuous as a bull, he chose the Soma,[2] and quaffed in threefold sacrifice the juices.

Maghavan[3] grasped the thunder for his weapon, and smote to death this firstborn of the dragons.

When, Indra, you had slain the dragon's first-born, and overcome the charms of the enchanters,

Then, giving life to sun and dawn and heaven,[4] you found not one foe to stand against you.

Indra with his own great and deadly thunder smote into pieces Vritra worst of Vritras.[5]

As trunks of trees, what time the axe has felled them, low on the earth so lies the prostrate dragon.

He, like a mad weak warrior, challenged Indra, the great impetuous many-slaying hero.

He, brooking not the clashing of the weapons, crushed — Indra's foe — the shattered forts in falling.[6]

---

[1]The divine artisan.
[2]A sacred hallucinogenic drink reserved for the gods and their priests.
[3]Lord Bountiful — another of Indra's names.

[4]See the next hymn.
[5]"Dragon, worst of dragons."
[6]The clouds are pictured as forts imprisoning moisture.

Footless and handless still[7] he challenged Indra, who smote him with his bolt between the shoulders.

Emasculated yet claiming manly vigor, thus Vritra lay with scattered limbs dissevered. . . .

Nothing availed him. Lightning, nothing, nor thunder, hailstorm or mist which he had spread around him.[8]

When Indra and the dragon strove in battle, Maghavan gained the victory for ever. . . .

Indra is king of all that moves and moves not, of creatures tame and horned, the thunder-wielder.

Over all living men he rules as sovereign, containing all as spokes within a rim.

WHO IS INDRA?

The god who had insight the moment he was born, the first who protected the gods with his power of thought, before whose hot breath the two world-halves[9] tremble at the greatness of his manly powers — he, my people, is Indra.

He who made fast the tottering earth, who made still the quaking mountains, who measured out and extended the expanse of the air, who propped up the sky — he, my people, is Indra.

He who killed the serpent[10] and loosed the seven rivers, . . . who gave birth to fire between two stones,[11] the winner of booty in combats — he, my people, is Indra.

He by whom all these changes were rung, who drove the race of Dasas[12] down into obscurity, who took away the flourishing wealth of the enemy as a winning gambler takes the stake — he, my people, is Indra.

He about whom they ask, 'Where is he?,' or they say of him, the terrible one, 'He does not exist,' he who diminishes the flourishing wealth of the enemy as a gambler does — believe in him! He, my people, is Indra.

He who encourages the weary and the sick, and the poor priest who is in need, who helps the man who harnesses the stones to press Soma, he who has lips fine for drinking — he, my people, is Indra.

He under whose command are horses and cows and villages and all chariots, who gave birth to the sun and the dawn and led out the waters, he, my people, is Indra. . . .

He without whom people do not conquer, he whom they call on for help when they are fighting, who became the image of everything,[13] who shakes the unshakeable — he, my people, is Indra.

He who killed with his weapon all those who had committed a great sin, even when they did not know it, he who does not pardon the arrogant man for his arrogance, who is the slayer of the Dasyus,[14] he, my people, is Indra. . . .

He who helps with his favor the one who presses and the one who cooks,[15] the praiser and the preparer, he for whom prayer is nourishment, for whom Soma is the special gift, he, my people, is Indra.

You[16] who furiously grasp the prize for the one who presses and the one who cooks, you are truly real. Let us be dear to you, Indra, all our days, and let us speak as men of power in the sacrificial gathering.

---

[7] Vritra is serpent-like, lacking feet and hands.
[8] Vritra used magic to surround himself with storms and mist, but they failed him. Thunderstorms and heavy lightning presage and accompany India's seasonal monsoon rains.
[9] Heaven and Earth.
[10] Vritra.
[11] Indra is the bringer of fire, which is kindled by striking two flints. He is also the creator of lightning (the fire between [the stones of] Heaven and Earth) and Soma, which

is crushed between stones. He also created the sun, another fire between Heaven and Earth.
[12] The indigenous, dark-skinned people whom Indra and the Aryans, a fairer "wheat-colored" people, conquered and subjugated. The word *dasa* came to mean "slave" in Sanskrit.
[13] Compare the next hymn.
[14] The Dasas.
[15] Those who press and those who cook Soma.
[16] Indra.

TO PURUSHA

A thousand heads had Purusha,[17] a thousand eyes, a thousand feet.

He covered earth on every side, and spread ten fingers' breadth beyond.

This Purusha is all that yet has been and all that is to be;

The lord of immortality which waxes greater still by food.

So mighty is his greatness; yea, greater than this is Purusha.

All creatures are one-fourth of him, three-fourths eternal life in heaven.[18]

With three-fourths Purusha went up: one-fourth of him again was here.

Thence he strode out to every side over what eats not and what eats.

From him Viraj[19] was born; again Purusha from Viraj was born.

As soon as he was born he spread eastward and westward o'er the earth.

When gods prepared the sacrifice with Purusha as their offering,

Its oil was spring, the holy gift was autumn; summer was the wood.

They balmed as victim on the grass[20] Purusha born in earliest time.

With him the deities and all Sadhyas[21] and Rishis[22] sacrificed.

From that great general sacrifice the dripping fat was gathered up.[23]

He formed the creatures of the air, and animals both wild and tame.

From that great general sacrifice Richas and Samahymns[24] were born:

Therefrom the meters were produced,[25] the Yajus[26] had its birth from it.

From it were horses born, from it all creatures with two rows of teeth:

From it were generated cows, from it the goats and sheep were born.

When they divided Purusha how many portions did they make?

What do they call his mouth, his arms? What do they call his thighs and feet?

The Brahmin[27] was his mouth, of both his arms was the Rajanya[28] made.

His thighs became the Vaisya,[29] from his feet the Sudra[30] was produced.

The Moon was gendered from his mind, and from his eye the Sun had birth;

Indra and Agni[31] from his mouth were born, and Vayu[32] from his breath.

---

[17]Purusha, the all-pervading universal spirit and source of all life, is conceived as a god with countless eyes, hands, and feet. Purusha is both limitless and able to be enclosed in the smallest of spaces. In an act celebrated by this poem, Purusha is simultaneously the sacrifice and the sacrificer.

[18]One-quarter of Purusha is found in all mortal creation; three-fourths of Purusha is divine and eternal.

[19]The female creative germ.

[20]Special grasses laid out during Vedic sacrifices for the gods to sit upon.

[21]A class of demigods.

[22]Sages.

[23]Compare the sacrifice offered by Utnapishtim (source 1).

[24]The constituent elements of the *Rig Veda*.

[25]The verses of the *Sama Veda*. It is largely a collection of parts of the *Rig Veda* arranged for religious ceremonial use.

[26]The ritual formulas of the *Yajur Veda*. It was compiled a century or two after the *Rig Veda* and served as a collection of sacrificial chants.

[27]An Aryan priest.

[28]The *Rajanyas*, or *Kshatriyas*, comprised the ruling or warrior class, which later became a caste.

[29]This class initially encompassed free herders and farmers; later, when it was a caste, it included traders and artisans.

[30]The slave and servant class, which later became the fourth and lowest caste. The term was originally applied to the Dasas (note 12).

[31]The god of fire and sacrifice. This Sanskrit word is cognate with *ignis*, the Latin word for "fire" (hence, *ignite* in English).

[32]The wind.

Forth from his navel came mid-air; the sky was fashioned from his head;

Earth from his feet, and from his ear the regions. Thus they formed the worlds.

Seven fencing-logs had he, thrice seven layers of fuel were prepared,[33]

When the gods, offering sacrifice, bound, as their victim, Purusha,

Gods, sacrificing, sacrificed the victim: these were the earliest holy ordinances.

The mighty ones attained the height of heaven, there where the Sadhyas, gods of old, are dwelling.

---

[33]For a sacrificial fire.

A Journey to the Underworld
▼▼▼
10 ▼ *Homer, THE ODYSSEY*

By 1600 B.C.E. history's first identifiable Greeks, a people who called themselves the *Achaeans*, had created a decentralized warrior civilization in the Balkan Peninsula. We term that culture *Mycenaean*, which derives from *Mycenae*, a city that exercised a loose leadership over the petty principalities of southern and central Greece. Around 1450 B.C.E. the Achaeans were masters of the island civilization of Crete (source 7) and, as accomplished pirates and maritime merchants, were a major force in the eastern Mediterranean. It is against this background that historians place the Achaean expedition against *Troy*, a city in western Anatolia, which took place around 1200.

The sack of rival Troy was the high-water mark for the Achaeans. Within a century Mycenaean civilization was collapsing, in part because of internecine wars among the Achaean principalities. What other factors were involved remains a mystery. By 1100 B.C.E., the highly specialized arts and crafts, including literacy, that had characterized Bronze Age Greece at its height had disappeared or were severely reduced in quality and quantity. Greece entered a period we call the *Greek Dark Age* (ca. 1100–ca. 800), a term that, more than anything else, implies our overall ignorance of the details of what was happening in the Greek World during these centuries. About all we can say with any degree of certainty is that the Greeks lost the art of writing, their political and economic structures were drastically reduced in size, and a relatively weak and impoverished Greek World ceased to be a major power in the eastern Mediterranean. At the same time, however, recent archaeological finds have underscored the continuities between late Mycenaean society and the classical *Hellenic World* that arose after 800 B.C.E., despite the losses and retrenchments. What is more, during this so-called Dark Age the Greek *polis*, or city-state, emerged as a major (many would say *the* major) component of Greek civilization. By 800 B.C.E., *poleis* (the plural of *polis*) were scattered all over the Greek World.

When Greek civilization (with its accompanying literacy) reemerged around the middle of the eighth century B.C.E., it was centered along the western shores of Anatolia, where Greek colonists had begun settling around the mid eleventh century B.C.E. Because so many of these Greek refugees spoke a Greek dialect known as *Ionian*, the region became known as *Ionia*. Here Greek settlers, benefiting from contact with the far-older civilizations of Southwest Asia (and, to a lesser extent, Egypt), produced the first Greek literature known to us (as opposed to the bureaucratic lists left behind by Mycenaean civilization). Of all of this early literature, the most significant are two epic poems, the *Iliad* and the *Odyssey*, both ascribed to a bard called *Homer*.

The ancients believed there was a historical Homer. Modern scholars are less certain, and most agree that we will never know the truth about Homer's identity or the exact process by which these epics were fashioned. Yet there are some points on which scholars are generally agreed. Internal evidence (the words, phrases, and allusions within each poem) has led most researchers to conclude that, regardless of whether Homer was one, two, or many poets, these two poems largely reached their final form in Anatolia during the late eighth century B.C.E. Whether they were written down that early or still continued to be transmitted orally is impossible to say. What is clear is that both epics exhibit all of the hallmarks of oral poetry, suggesting strongly that in the act of creation the poet or poets whom we call Homer drew heavily from a long tradition of oral poetic stories, which had been preserved for centuries in the memories of wandering professional bards.

Very much like the *Rig Veda*, therefore, the Homeric epics preserve vestiges of a much earlier age — in this case the Late Mycenaean Age — but are also overlaid with the values, social practices, and modes of perception of later Greek society. When used judiciously, the two epics tell us a good deal about life in the thirteenth century B.C.E. — the age of the Trojan War. At the same time, they often reflect the culture of Late Dark Age society, especially that of the ninth and eighth centuries. The problem is to separate one from the other.

On one level both Homeric poems celebrate warrior virtues, such as personal honor, bravery, and loyalty to one's comrades, and on a deeper level they probe the hidden recesses of human motivation and emotion. On a third level the poems address the issue of the meaning of human suffering. Why do humans experience pain and sorrow? Are they captive to the whims of the gods? Are they and the gods subject to an overarching destiny that neither can avoid?

More to human scale than the *Iliad*, the *Odyssey* tells two intertwined stories. One traces the ten-year-long homeward voyage of the Achaean hero *Odysseus*. This clever adventurer battles, with cunning and skill, the enmity of Poseidon, god of the sea, and a variety of superhuman opponents before arriving home to his island kingdom of Ithaca. The second story details the efforts of Odysseus's wife and son, Penelope and Telemachus, who, with equal cunning and skill, attempt to stall indefinitely the advances of a group of suitors who seek to marry the presumed widow. As the suitors impatiently wait to see whom she will marry, they despoil Odysseus and Penelope's home and waste Telemachus's patrimony. The two story lines merge when Odysseus returns and, with the aid of his son and several loyal servants, wreaks vengeance on the suitors by killing them all. Unlike most epics, the story ends happily with Penelope and Odysseus reunited and Telemachus assured of his inheritance.

The following selection describes one of Odysseus's most daring adventures on his troubled homeward journey — a visit to the House of Hades, or the Land of the Dead. Here he consults Teiresias, the blind Theban seer, who even in death retains his prophetic powers. Odysseus also meets the shades of many famous women and men, including Achilles, the Achaeans' greatest warrior and the central character of the *Iliad*, who was killed prior to the fall of Troy.

QUESTIONS FOR ANALYSIS

1. What values did Odysseus's society hold in highest esteem?
2. How does Homer address the issue of human responsibility for ill fortune? Is there a destiny that humans cannot escape? If so, what role do the gods play in this destiny?
3. It is often stated that the Greeks focused on human beings and human concerns. Indeed, it is said that for the Greeks the human was the standard of measurement for all things. Does this selection support or contradict that judgment?
4. Compare Achilles' sentiment toward the Land of the Dead with Enkidu's vision in *The Epic of Gilgamesh* (source 1). What do you conclude from your analysis?

Now the spirit of Teiresias of Thebes came forward, bearing a golden staff in his hand. Knowing who I am, he addressed me: "Son of Laertes, sprung from Zeus,[1] Odysseus, known for your many wiles, why, unhappy man, have you left the sunlight to behold the dead in this cheerless region? Step back from the trench and put aside your sharp sword so that I might drink the blood[2] and thereby prophesy the truth to you." Thus he spoke. I, stepping backward, drove my silver-studded sword into its scabbard. When he had drunk the black blood, this noble prophet addressed me with these words.

"Lord Odysseus, you seek a honey-sweet homeward journey, but a god will make your travels difficult. I do not think you can escape the notice of the Earth-shaker,[3] who has set his mind in enmity against you, enraged because

you blinded his beloved son.[4] Even so, you still might be able to reach home, although in sorry circumstances, if you are willing to restrain your desires, and those of your comrades, beginning when your seaworthy ship leaves the deep blue waters and approaches the island of Thrinacie,[5] where you will see the grazing cattle and fat sheep of Helios,[6] who sees and hears everything. If you leave the animals untouched and concentrate solely on getting home, it is possible that all of you might reach Ithaca, although in sorry circumstances. If you injure these animals, however, I foresee destruction for your ship and its crew, and even if you yourself manage to escape, you will return home late, in a sorry state, in an alien ship, having lost all your companions.[7] And even there at home you will find troubles. Overbearing men will be consuming your

[1]The greatest of the Greek gods. The title implies Odysseus's godlike heroic qualities.
[2]The spirits of the dead can communicate with Odysseus only after they drink blood from animals he has sacrificed.
[3]Poseidon, god of the sea and of earthquakes.
[4]The Cyclops, a son of Poseidon, was a one-eyed, cannibal giant whom Odysseus had blinded in self-defense.
[5]The mythical island of the sun-god Helios, where he pastured his sacred cattle; ancient Greek commentators on Homer identified it as the island of Sicily.
[6]The sun-god.
[7]The crew will kill and eat the sun-god's flocks, and all, except Odysseus, will die as a result.

wealth, wooing your goddess-like wife, and offering her bridal gifts. Certainly, following your arrival, you will gain revenge on these suitors for their evil deeds. When you have slain the suitors in your halls, whether by stratagem or in an open fight with sharp bronze weapons, you must again set out on a journey. You must take a well-fashioned oar and travel until you reach a people who are ignorant of the sea and never eat food mixed with salt, and who know nothing about our purple-ribbed ships and the well-fashioned oars that serve as ships wings. And I say you will receive a sign, a very clear one that you cannot miss. When another traveler upon meeting you remarks that you are carrying a winnowing-fan across your broad back,[8] plant your well-fashioned oar in the earth and offer Lord Poseidon the sacrifice of a ram, a bull,[9] and a boar, the mate of the wild she-swine. Then return home and there make sacred offerings to all the immortal gods who inhabit wide Heaven, and do so to each in order of rank. As for death, it will come to you at last gently out of the sea in a comfortable old age when you are surrounded by a prosperous people. This I tell you truly.". . .

Next came the spirit of Achilles, son of Peleus . . . [who] recognized me, and mournfully spoke in winged words: "Son of Laertes, sprung from Zeus, Odysseus, known for your many wiles! Rash man, what greater deed than this remains for you to devise in your heart? How did you dare to descend to Hades'[10] realm, where the dead dwell as witless images of worn-out mortals?"

Thus he spoke, and I answered in return. "Achilles, son of Peleus, by far the mightiest of the Achaeans, I came to consult with Teiresias in the hope of his giving me a plan whereby I might reach rocky Ithaca. For I have not yet come near the land of Achaea,[11] nor yet set foot on my own island, but have been constantly beset by misfortunes. How different from your situation, Achilles, you who are more fortunate than any man whoever was or will be. For in the old days, when you were alive, we Argives[12] honored you as though you were a god, and now that you are here, you rule nobly among the dead. Therefore, grieve not, Achilles, that you are dead."

So I spoke, and he immediately answered, saying: "Do not endeavor to speak soothingly to me of death, Lord Odysseus. I would rather live on Earth as the hired help of some landless man whose own livelihood was meager, than be lord over all the dead who have perished. Enough of that. Tell me about my son, that lordly young man. Did he follow me to war and play a leading role in it? And tell me about noble Peleus. . . . I am not there in the sunlight to aid Peleus with that great strength that was once mine on the broad plains of Troy, where I slew the best of the enemy's army in defense of the Argives. If, but for an hour, I could return to my father's house with such strength as I once had, I would give those who do him violence and dishonor him cause to rue my might and my invincible hands."

So he spoke, and I answered: "I have heard nothing about noble Peleus, but I will give you all the news you desire of your dear son, Neoptolemus. It was I who brought him . . . in my well-fashioned, hollow ship to join the ranks of the well-armed Achaeans. Whenever we held a council meeting during the siege of Troy, he was always the first to speak, and his words never missed the mark. . . . As often as we fought with bronze weapons on the Trojan plain, he never lagged behind in the ranks or crowd, but would always run far out in front, yielding first place to no one, and he slew many men in mortal combat. I could not name all whom he killed in defense of the Argives. . . . Again, when we, the best of the Argives, were about to enter into the horse that

---

[8]Odysseus will be in a region where no one knows what an oar's function is. Rather, they will mistake it for the long-handled shallow basket in which grain is tossed to separate cereal from the chaff.

[9]The bull was sacred to Poseidon. (See source 7 for examples of the popularity of the bull as a sacred animal.)

[10]The god of the dead.

[11]The land of the Achaeans.

[12]Another name for the Achaeans.

Epeus made,[13] and responsibility lay solely with me to either open or keep closed the door of our stout-built ambush, the other Danaan[14] leaders and chieftains were wiping away tears from their eyes and each man's limbs shook beneath him. But never did my eyes see his fair face grow pale, nor did I see him wiping away tears from his cheeks. Rather, he earnestly begged me to allow him to sally forth from the horse, and he kept handling his sword-hilt and his heavy bronze spear in his eagerness to inflict harm on the Tro-jans. Following our sack of the lofty city of Priam,[15] he boarded his ship with a full share of the spoils and his special prize.[16] And he was un-scathed, never cut by a sharp sword or wounded in close combat, as often happens in war, since Ares[17] rages in a confused fashion."

So I spoke, and the spirit of the son of Aeacus departed with long strides across the field of as-phodel,[18] rejoicing that his son was preeminent among men.

---

[13]The so-called Trojan Horse, by which the Achaeans cap-tured Troy.
[14]Another name for the Achaeans.
[15]The last king of Troy.
[16]At the division of the Trojan survivors, Neoptolemus was awarded Andromache, widow of Hector, Troy's greatest hero, whom Achiles had killed in single combat.

[17]The god of war.
[18]A flower that carpeted the Elysian Fields, where the spirits of dead heroes, such as Achilles, resided.

▼▼▼

The Israelites and Their Neighbors

Excavations at the city of Ebla in northern Syria reveal that the land of Palestine-Syria (the region covered by the present-day nations of Israel, Jordan, Lebanon, Syria, and the emerging Palestinian state) has known urban civilization since about 3000 B.C.E., although its cities did not begin to reach significant size until around 2500. A landbridge between Egypt and Mesopotamia, it has suffered the fate of all crossroads regions, being prey to numerous invaders. Its first known conqueror was Sargon the Great of Akkad in Mesopotamia, who sacked Ebla in the twenty-fourth century. Proximity to Egypt and Mesopotamia, especially the latter, also enriched the land of Palestine-Syria and its people with trade and cul-tural imprints. The Eblaites wrote mainly in Sumerian on clay tablets, in imitation of their Mesopotamian neighbors, but they also adopted Sumerian *cuneiform* (wedge-shaped) script and words to write their own language — Eblaite. Ebla dis-appeared from history by 1600 B.C.E., but the region continued to be a focal point of exchange and invasion.

During the thirteenth century B.C.E., in the midst of a number of invasions and upheavals that tested all civilizations in Southwest Asia and the eastern Mediter-ranean, several groups of invaders penetrated the region of *Canaan* (roughly present-day Israel, Palestine, and southern Lebanon) and established themselves there at the expense of an indigenous, ethnically diverse population. One of the in-vaders was a mixed group from the Aegean that settled in cities along the coast of what is today the state of Israel. These people, who included a large percentage of uprooted Mycenaean Greeks and Cretans, became known as the *Philistines*. A sec-ond wave was composed of another hybrid mass of people, the *Israelites*, who spoke a Semitic language — *Hebrew*.

As is the case with the Indo-European language family, Semitic origins are lost in the mists of time. We know, however, that the Akkadians, who spoke a Semitic language, inhabited the middle Tigris-Euphrates Valley as early as 2900 B.C.E., and the Eblaites also spoke a Semitic tongue. Evidence suggests that the early Semites migrated into Mesopotamia and northern Syria from the western and southern deserts, and consequently historians believe that the original homeland of the Semitic language family was Arabia.

Whatever the distant origins of their language, the people whom history identifies as the Israelites seem to have been originally an ethnically mixed mass of Semitic peoples who infiltrated into Canaan out of the southern and eastern deserts and settled the inland high ground overlooking the Philistine cities. Egyptian sources suggest that the forerunners of the Israelites were viewed by their more settled neighbors as outlaws and raiders.

Prior to the arrival of waves of invaders, the Hittite and Egyptian empires had fought for mastery over Syria-Palestine. With the destruction of Hittite civilization and the concurrent severe weakening of the Egyptian empire around 1200, a momentary power vacuum occurred along the eastern rim of the Mediterranean. In the absence of any outside imperial power, the various cultural groups of Syria-Palestine, including the Israelites, had several centuries of relative freedom in which to struggle with one another and to amalgamate.

For the Israelites, amalgamation was seductively easy and potentially disastrous. The vast majority of the peoples who already inhabited Canaan also spoke Semitic languages and shared other cultural characteristics with these ruder newcomers. Something, however, set the Israelites apart and enabled them to mold a distinctive culture. As they coalesced as an identifiable people, the Israelites evolved the idea that they enjoyed the special protection of a god whom they called *YHWH* (probably pronounced "Yahveh"). In return for protection, this deity demanded their sole devotion. Moreover, if the Israelites were to prosper in Canaan, a land that YHWH had promised them, they had to maintain religious purity and cultural distance from all other peoples.

Establishing a Covenant with Humanity
▼▼▼
11 ▼ THE BOOK OF GENESIS

Other than a late-thirteenth-century B.C.E. Egyptian note that there was an entity called Israel inhabiting the land of Canaan, contemporary foreign records were silent regarding the settlement and even the very existence of the Israelites. Likewise, archaeological evidence of their activities during the first several centuries of their residence in Canaan is scanty and ambiguous. The major documentary source for both the process of cultural fusion and the fierce struggles that took place among the various groups of settlers in Syria-Palestine is a collection of sacred Hebrew writings known as the Bible (from the Greek *biblos*, which means "book").

The exclusively Hebrew portion of the Bible, known to Jews as the *Tanakh* but called by Christians the Old Testament, consists of a wide variety of different types of literature. These scriptures were mainly composed, edited, and reedited between roughly 1000 B.C.E. to possibly as late as the second century B.C.E., although Jewish religious authorities did not fix the Tanakh's final *canon*, or official body of accepted texts, until after 100 C.E. This means that biblical accounts of early Israelite history are, in many cases, centuries removed from the events they narrate, although these later authors apparently used early oral and written sources that are now lost to us. At the same time, we must keep in mind that these authors wrote history primarily from a theological perspective and consequently clothed their stories in myth. That is, history for them was not a narrative of verifiable human events. It was, rather, the story of Israel's special relationship with its god, and in telling that story, the Bible's authors employed a variety of literary devices, many of which they adapted to their needs from the literary traditions of their neighbors.

The first book of the Bible, known as *Genesis* (the beginning), recounts the story of humanity's relationship with YHWH from Creation through the settlement of the Children of Israel in Egypt. Tradition ascribes its authorship to *Moses*, one of the most enigmatic and elusive figures in the Bible. Modern scholars divide on the question of whether there was a historical Moses who led the Israelites out of Egypt and passed on to them a set of laws that made them uniquely YHWH's people (source 12). Later Israelites did not doubt Moses' historicity, but this did not necessarily mean they believed Moses wrote or dictated Genesis. Rather, calling this book "Mosaic" meant they understood Moses to be the one who provided the initial and pervading spirit behind the work. In all likelihood, a number of different authors composed and reworked Genesis over the period from before 900 to after 721 B.C.E., but they might have drawn on traditions that stretched back to the time of the Israelites' infiltration into Canaan or soon thereafter.

The following selection recounts a popular Southwest Asian theme that we saw in Chapter 1: the Flood. As you read it, be aware of the striking parallels between it and the story told by Utnapishtim (source 1) and their significant differences. Remember that this author or group of authors is making a religious statement. The primary question that you must continually ask yourself as you compare the two stories is: What do the Mesopotamian gods demand of humans, and what does Noah's god demand?

QUESTIONS FOR ANALYSIS

1. Why does YHWH destroy all humanity except Noah and his family? How does YHWH's reasoning compare with the Mesopotamian gods' reason for wanting to destroy humans and Ea's decision to warn Utnapishtim?
2. Compare YHWH's covenant (binding agreement) with Noah and his descendants following the Flood with the Mesopotamian gods' treatment of Utnapishtim after the waters had receded. From your analysis, what picture emerges of the god of the Israelites? In what ways is their god similar to the gods of Mesopotamia? In what ways does their god differ?

3. Note YHWH's different instructions regarding the number of animals to be brought into the ark. What might that suggest about the way this story was crafted?
4. Consider the story of Noah's curse on Canaan. What has Ham done to deserve such anger, and why is it that his son suffers as a consequence? Do your answers tell us anything about Israelite social values and practices at this time? (Hint: Review *The Judgments of Hammurabi*, source 2).
5. How does the story of the curse on Ham have relevance to the Israelites' settlement in the land of Canaan? What does this suggest about the story's date of composition? How does this illustrate the Israelites' use of myth to explain and justify historical events?

The Lord saw that the wickedness of man was great in the Earth, and that every imagination of the thoughts of his heart was only evil continually. And the Lord was sorry that he had made man on the Earth, and it grieved him to his heart. So the Lord said, "I will blot out man whom I have created from the face of the ground, man and beast and creeping things and birds of the air, for I am sorry that I have made them." But Noah found favor in the eyes of the Lord. . . .

Noah was a righteous man, blameless in his generation; Noah walked with God. And Noah had three sons, Shem,[1] Ham, and Japheth.

Now the Earth was corrupt in God's sight, and the Earth was filled with violence. And God saw the Earth, and behold, it was corrupt; for all flesh had corrupted their way upon the Earth. And God said to Noah, "I have determined to make an end of all flesh; for the Earth is filled with violence through them; behold, I will destroy them with the Earth. Make yourself an ark of gopher wood; make rooms in the ark, and cover it inside and out with pitch. . . . For behold, I will bring a flood of waters upon the Earth, to destroy all flesh in which is the breath of life from under Heaven; everything that is on the Earth shall die. But I will establish my covenant with you; and you shall come into the ark, you, your sons, your wife, and your sons' wives with you. And of every living thing of all flesh, you shall bring two of every sort into the ark, to keep them alive with you; they shall be male and female. Of the birds according to their kinds, and of the animals according to their kinds, of every creeping thing of the ground according to its kind, two of every sort shall come in to you, to keep them alive. Also take with you every sort of food that is eaten, and store it up; and it shall serve as food for you and for them." Noah did this; he did all that God commanded him.

Then the Lord said to Noah, "Go into the ark, you and all your household, for I have seen that you are righteous before me in this generation. Take with you seven pairs of all clean animals,[2] the male and his mate; and a pair of the animals that are not clean, the male and his mate; and seven pairs of the birds of the air also, male and female, to keep their kind alive upon the face of all the Earth. For in seven days I will send rain upon the Earth forty days and forty nights; and every living thing that I have made will blot out from the face of the ground." And Noah did all that the Lord had commanded him.

---

[1]Shem was the eldest of Noah's sons and the one from whom the Israelites claimed direct descent. The term *Semite* is derived from the name.

[2]According to the Mosaic Law, a ritually clean animal, such as a sheep, was one worthy of sacrifice to YHWH. An unclean animal, such as a predator or a scavenger, would never be offered in sacrifice.

Noah was six hundred years old when the flood of waters came upon the Earth. And Noah and his sons and his wife and his sons' wives with him went into the ark, to escape the waters of the flood. Of clean animals, and of animals that are not clean, and of birds, and of everything that creeps on the ground, two and two, male and female, went into the ark with Noah, as God had commanded Noah. And after seven days the waters of the flood came upon the Earth.

In the six hundredth year of Noah's life, in the second month, on the seventeenth day of the month, on that day all the fountains of the great deep burst forth, and the windows of the heavens were opened.[3] And rain fell upon the Earth forty days and forty nights. . . .

And the waters prevailed so mightily upon the Earth that all the high mountains under the whole Heaven were covered. . . . He blotted out every living thing that was upon the face of the ground, man and animals and creeping things and birds of the air; they were blotted out from the Earth. Only Noah was left, and those that were with him in the ark. And the waters prevailed upon the Earth a hundred and fifty days.

But God remembered Noah and all the beasts and all the cattle that were with him in the ark. And God made a wind blow over the Earth, and the waters subsided; the fountains of the deep and the windows of the heavens were closed, the rain from the heavens was restrained, and the waters receded from the Earth continually. At the end of a hundred and fifty days the waters had abated; and in the seventh month, on the seventeenth day of the month, the ark came to rest upon the mountains of Ararat. . . .

At the end of forty days Noah opened the window of the ark which he had made, and sent forth a raven; and it went to and fro until the waters were dried up from the Earth. Then he sent forth a dove from him, to see if the waters had subsided from the face of the ground; but the dove found no place to set her foot, and she returned to him to the ark, for the waters were still on the face of the whole Earth. So he put forth his hand and took her and brought her into the ark with him. He waited another seven days, and again he sent forth the dove out of the ark; and the dove came back to him in the evening, and lo, in her mouth a freshly plucked olive leaf; so Noah knew that the waters had subsided from the Earth. Then he waited another seven days, and sent forth the dove; and she did not return to him any more.

In the six hundred and first year,[4] . . . the waters were dried from off the Earth; and Noah removed the covering of the ark, and looked, and behold, the face of the ground was dry. . . . Then God said to Noah, "Go forth from the ark, you and your wife, and your sons and your sons' wives with you. Bring forth with you every living thing that is with you of all flesh — birds and animals and every creeping thing that creeps on the earth — that they may breed abundantly on the Earth, and be fruitful and multiply upon the Earth." So Noah went forth, and his sons and his wife and his sons' wives with him. And every beast, every creeping thing, and every bird, everything that moves upon the Earth, went forth by families out of the ark.

Then Noah built an altar to the Lord, and took of every clean animal and of every clean bird, and offered burnt offerings on the altar. And when the Lord smelled the pleasing odor, the Lord said in his heart, "I will never again curse the ground because of man, for the imagination of man's heart is evil from his youth; neither will I ever again destroy every living creature as I have done. While the Earth remains, seedtime and harvest, cold and heat, summer and winter, day and night, shall not cease."

---

[3]The view of the world shared by the peoples of Southwest Asia at this time was that the world's firmament, or land, was totally surrounded, above and below, by water. The water above was normally kept in place by a translucent crystalline sphere. Rain was the seepage of water through that sphere.
[4]Of Noah's life.

And God blessed Noah and his sons, and said to them, "Be fruitful and multiply, and fill the Earth. The fear of you and the dread of you shall be upon every beast of the Earth, and upon every bird of the air, upon everything that creeps on the ground and all the fish of the sea; into your hand they are delivered. Every moving thing that lives shall be food for you; and as I gave you the green plants, I give you everything. Only you shall not eat flesh with its life, that is, its blood.[5] For your lifeblood I will surely require a reckoning; of every beast I will require it and of man; of every man's brother I will require the life of man. Whoever sheds the blood of man, by man shall his blood be shed; for God made man in his own image. And you, be fruitful and multiply, bring forth abundantly on the Earth and multiply in it."

Then God said to Noah and to his sons with him, "Behold, I establish my covenant with you and your descendants after you, and with every living creature that is with you, the birds, the cattle, and every beast of the earth with you, as many as came out of the ark. I establish my covenant with you, that never again shall all flesh be cut off by the waters of a flood, and never again shall there be a flood to destroy the Earth." And God said, "This is the sign of the covenant which I make between me and you and every living creature that is with you, for all future generations: I set my bow[6] in the cloud, and it shall be a sign of the covenant between me and the Earth. When I brink clouds over the Earth and the bow is seen in the clouds, I will remember my covenant which is between me and you and every living creature of all flesh; and the waters shall never again become a flood to destroy all flesh. When the bow is in the clouds, I will

look upon it and remember the everlasting covenant between God and every living creature of all flesh that is upon the Earth." God said to Noah, "This is the sign of the covenant which I have established between me and all flesh that is upon the Earth."

The sons of Noah who went forth from the ark were Shem, Ham, and Japheth. Ham was the father of Canaan. These three were the sons of Noah; and from these the whole Earth was peopled.

Noah was the first tiller of the soil. He planted a vineyard; and he drank of the wine, and became drunk, and lay uncovered in his tent. And Ham, the father of Canaan, saw the nakedness of his father, and told his two brothers outside. Then Shem and Japheth took a garment, laid it upon both their shoulders, and walked backward and covered the nakedness of their father; their faces were turned away, and they did not see their father's nakedness. When Noah awoke from his wine and knew what his youngest son had done to him, he said

"Cursed be Canaan;
a slave of slaves shall he be to
his brothers."[7]

He also said,

"Blessed by the Lord my God be Shem;
and let Canaan be his slave.
God enlarge Japheth,
and let him dwell in the tents of Shem;[8]
and let Canaan be his slave."

After the flood Noah lived three hundred and fifty years. All the days of Noah were nine hundred and fifty years; and he died.

---

[5] Raw meat or meat dripping with blood could not be consumed.
[6] A rainbow. Compare this with Ishtar's rainbow (source 1).
[7] According to Hebrew legend, Ham and his son Canaan were the direct ancestors of the Canaanites, a Semitic people whom the Israelites were dispossessing of their lands.

[8] Japheth, according to Israelite tradition, was the ancestor of the Indo-European peoples of northern Syria and beyond, such as the Hittites and Hurrians. From the Israelite perspective, the Israelites and the northern Indo-Europeans were dividing up the land of Syria-Palestine between them.

Establishing a Covenant with a Chosen People
▼▼▼
12 ▼ *THE BOOK OF DEUTERONOMY*

The story of Noah tells of YHWH's post-Deluge covenant with all living creatures; the story of the Israelites' *Exodus* (going out) from Egypt tells of their special *Covenant*, or pact, with this god and their becoming a *Chosen People* with a new identity.

Forerunners of the Israelites had probably entered Egypt in the time of the conquest of Lower Egypt, or the delta region, by the Hyksos (rulers from foreign lands), who came in from the deserts of western Asia around 1700 B.C.E. With the overthrow of the Hyksos and the re-establishment of native Egyptian rule around 1570, significant numbers of these people were probably enslaved, as happened to many Asian prisoners of war in Egypt at that time. That at least seems to be a likely scenario if we seek to fit the story told in the Bible's Book of Exodus with the sketchy picture we have of Egyptian history during the Second Intermediate Period and the New Kingdom that followed.

At this point reconstruction of the next stage of Israelite history becomes even more problematic, due to the many, sometimes contradictory, layers of legend and folktale motifs that we find in the biblical story of their flight from Egypt. Yet several aspects of the story have the ring of validity and lead many (but certainly not all) historians to accept the basic historicity of the Exodus, even though most question many of the details of the story as narrated in the Bible. The fact that the Israelites trace their origins as a people to an age of bondage and oppression, rather than claiming kings and heroes as their progenitors, suggests that this less-than-glorious beginning was rooted in historical reality. Equally telling is the origin of Moses' name, which most likely derives from the Egyptian verb *msy* (born). This hint of Egyptian heritage lends a certain credence to his presumed historicity, even though there is no known record of Moses outside of the Bible. Assuming that the Israelites' oral traditions retained a valid core memory of their flight from Egypt and subsequent wanderings, we can say with hesitant confidence that a charismatic leader, whom history remembers as Moses, arose to lead a heterogeneous band of Semitic wanderers out of Egypt and to the borders of Canaan, probably sometime around the reign of Ramses the Great (r. 1279–1213 B.C.E.). Further, and most important of all, in the process of their migration, Moses molded these disparate wanderers into a single people and wedded them to his god YHWH. No longer a loose band of nomads, they were now the Israelites — descendants of the patriarchs Abraham, Isaac, and Jacob (see note 1).

The story of this transformation is told in several books of the Bible. This selection comes from *Deuteronomy*, which was initially shaped during the reign of King Josiah of Jerusalem (r. 640–609 B.C.E.) and subsequently revised in the following century. Deuteronomy was composed at a time of religious reformation, when Josiah and several successors were attempting to abolish all other forms of worship in the kingdom, especially the practices of the Assyrians, who had conquered the northern kingdom of the Israelites. Although Deuteronomy, as we know it, is essentially a creation of the seventh and sixth centuries B.C.E., there is good reason to conclude that it is based on sources dating from an earlier era.

The setting of the excerpt is the frontier of Canaan, which the Israelites have reached after forty years of wandering in the desert. Moses, realizing he will die before his people cross the Jordan River into the *Promised Land*, delivers a final message.

QUESTIONS FOR ANALYSIS

1. What is the covenant between YHWH and the people of Israel? What does God promise and demand in return? What does YHWH threaten for those who break the covenant?
2. Consider YHWH's promises again. What does YHWH have to say about rewards after death? What do you infer from your answer?
3. Which elements of Moses' message would the religious reformers of Jerusalem wish to emphasize?
4. Compare the Ten Commandments with *The Judgments of Hammurabi* (source 2). Which strike you as more significant, the similarities or the differences? What do you conclude from your answer?

And Moses summoned all Israel,[1] and said to them, "Hear, O Israel, the statutes and the ordinances which I speak in your hearing this day, and you shall learn them and be careful to do them. The Lord our God made a covenant with us in Horeb.[2] Not with our fathers did the Lord make this covenant, but with us, who are all of us here alive this day. The Lord spoke with you face to face at the mountain, out of the midst of the fire, while I stood between the Lord and you at that time, to declare to you the word of the Lord; for you were afraid because of the fire, and you did not go up into the mountain. He said:

"'I am the Lord your God, who brought you out of the land of Egypt, out of the house of bondage.

"'You shall have no other gods before me.

"'You shall not make for yourself a graven image, or any likeness of anything that is in Heaven above, or that is on the Earth beneath, or that is in the water under the Earth; you shall not bow down to them or serve them; for I the Lord your God am a jealous God, visiting the iniquity of the fathers upon the children to the third and fourth generation of those who hate me, but showing steadfast love to thousands of those who love me and keep my commandments.

"'You shall not take the name of the Lord your God in vain: for the Lord will not hold him guiltless who takes his name in vain.

"'Observe the sabbath day, to keep it holy, as the Lord your God commanded you. Six days you shall labor, and do all your work; but the

---

[1]They referred to themselves as *Israel* and also as the *Children of Israel* and the *Israelites* because they traced their lineage to Jacob, whose name God had changed to Israel (God rules). Jacob, the grandson of Abraham and the son of Isaac, had twelve sons, each of whom became the patriarch of one of the twelve tribes of the Children of Israel. Whether Abra-

ham and the other patriarchs were historic figures or just figments of mythic imagination is another issue that defies definitive resolution.

[2]Also known as *Mount Sinai*. Here Moses had received the Law from YHWH during the period of desert wandering.

seventh day is a sabbath to the Lord your God; in it you shall not do any work, you, or your son, or your daughter, or your manservant, or your maidservant, or your ox, or your ass, or any of your cattle, or the sojourner who is within your gates, that your manservant and your maidservant may rest as well as you. You shall remember that you were a servant in the land of Egypt, and the Lord your God brought you out thence with a mighty hand and an outstretched arm; therefore the Lord your God commanded you to keep the sabbath day.

"'Honor your father and your mother, as the Lord your God commanded you; that your days may be prolonged, and that it may go well with you, in the land which the Lord your God gives you.

"'You shall not kill.

"'Neither shall you commit adultery.

"'Neither shall you steal.

"'Neither shall you bear false witness against your neighbor.

"'Neither shall you covet your neighbor's wife; and you shall not desire your neighbor's house, his field, or his manservant, or his maidservant, his ox, or his ass, or anything that is your neighbor's.'

"These words the Lord spoke to all your assembly at the mountain out of the midst of the fire, the cloud, and the thick darkness, with a loud voice; and he added no more. And he wrote them upon two tables of stone, and gave them to me. . . .

"Now this is the commandment, the statutes and the ordinances which the Lord your God commanded me to teach you, that you may do them in the land to which you are going over, to possess it; that you may fear the Lord your God, you and your son and your son's son, by keeping all his statutes and his commandments, which I command you, all the days of your life; and that your days may be prolonged. Hear therefore, O Israel, and be careful to do them; that it may go well with you, and that you may multiply greatly, as the Lord, the God of your fathers, has promised you, in a land flowing with milk and honey.

"Hear, O Israel: The Lord our God is one Lord; and you shall love the Lord your God with all your heart, and with all your soul, and with all your might. And these words which I command you this day shall be upon your heart; and you shall teach them diligently to your children, and shall talk of them when you sit in your house, and when you walk by the way, and when you lie down, and when you rise. And you shall bind them as a sign upon your hand, and they shall be as frontlets between your eyes. And you shall write them on the doorposts of your house and on your gates.

"And when the Lord your God brings you into the land which he swore to your fathers, to Abraham, to Isaac, and to Jacob, to give you, with great and goodly cities, which you did not build, and houses full of all good things, which you did not fill, and cisterns hewn out, which you did not hew, and vineyards and olive trees, which you did not plant, and when you eat and are full, then take heed lest you forget the Lord, who brought you out of the land of Egypt, out of the house of bondage. You shall fear the Lord your God; you shall serve him, and swear by his name. You shall not go after other gods, of the gods of the peoples who are round about you; for the Lord your God in the midst of you is a jealous God; lest the anger of the Lord your God be kindled against you, and he destroy you from off the face of the Earth. . . .

"When the Lord your God brings you into the land which you are entering to take possession of it, and clears away many nations before you . . . seven nations greater and mightier than yourselves, and when the Lord your God gives them over to you, and you defeat them; then you must utterly destroy them; you shall make no covenant with them, and show no mercy to them. You shall not make marriages with them, giving your daughters to their sons or taking their daughters for your sons. For they would turn away your sons from following me, to serve other gods; then the anger of the Lord would be kindled against you, and he would destroy you quickly. But thus shall you deal with them: you shall break down their altars, and dash in pieces their pillars, and hew down their Asherim,[3] and burn their graven images with fire.

"For you are a people holy to the Lord your God; the Lord your God has chosen you to be a people for his own possession, out of all the peoples that are on the face of the Earth. It was not because you were more in number than any other people that the Lord set his love upon you and chose you, for you were the fewest of all peoples; but it is because the Lord loves you, and is keeping the oath which he swore to your fathers, that the Lord has brought you out with a mighty hand, and redeemed you from the house of bondage, from the hand of Pharaoh king of Egypt. Know therefore that the Lord your God is God, the faithful God who keeps covenant and steadfast love with those who love him and keep his commandments, to a thousand generations, and repays those who hate him, by destroying them; he will not be slack with him who hates him. . . . You shall therefore be careful to do the commandments, and the statutes, and the ordinances, which I command you this day.

"And because you hearken to these ordinances, and keep and do them, the Lord your God will keep with you the covenant and the steadfast love which he swore to your fathers to keep; he will love you, bless you, and multiply you; he will also bless the fruit of your body and the fruit of your ground, your grain and your wine and your oil, the increase of your cattle and the young of your flock, in the land which he swore to your fathers to give you. You shall be blessed above all peoples; there shall not be male or female barren among you, or among your cattle. And the Lord will take away from you all sickness; and none of the evil diseases of Egypt, which you knew, will he inflict upon you, but he will lay them upon all who hate you. And you shall destroy all the peoples that the Lord your God will give over to you, your eye shall not pity them; neither shall you serve their gods, for that would be a snare to you."

[3]Sacred poles raised to Astarte (or Asherah), the Canaanite counterpart of Ishtar, the Mesopotamian goddess of fertility and love (source 1).

❖ Chapter 3 ❖

Transcendental Reality
Developing the Spiritual Traditions of India and Southwest Asia: 800–200 B.C.E.

*B*ETWEEN ABOUT 800 AND 200 B.C.E., profound changes in thought, belief, social organization, and government took place in China, India, Southwest Asia, and *Hellas* (the land of the Greeks). So pivotal were the changes, some historians favor calling this era the *Axial Age*. During these six centuries, the Chinese, Indians, Southwest Asians, and *Hellenes* (the name by which the Greeks of classical antiquity identified themselves) formulated traditions and institutions that became core elements of their civilizations. In essence, their classical cultures took shape.

These developments became especially pronounced around the sixth and fifth centuries B.C.E. Perhaps it was no coincidence that Confucius, the Buddha, several authors of the Upanishads, Second Isaiah, and the earliest Greek scientists and philosophers all lived around this time. What accounts for these parallel phenomena? The *Age of Iron*, which began roughly after 1000 B.C.E., witnessed the emergence of considerably larger, more complex, and more competitive political and economic entities that challenged older social systems and values. This disruption of life was unsettling and led to the search for new answers to some fundamental questions: What is the meaning of life? How does one relate to the spiritual world? To the natural world? To other humans? What is the ideal government?

The frameworks of the various civilizations posing such questions often differed radically. Hence, their respective answers varied significantly. In one way, however, they displayed a striking similarity. Each emerging tradition challenged the myth-making notion that humankind is held hostage by a capricious, god-infested nature.

Indian thinkers did this by denying that the tangible world of observable nature is real in any meaningful sense and seeking, instead, reality in the transcendental world of the spirit. China witnessed several other approaches. One school of thought — *Daoism* — sought mystical union with nature; two other schools — *Confucianism* and *Legalism* — sought to control nature by imposing human discipline upon it. Whereas Confucians saw the solution in a moral order of virtuous behavior, Legalists found it in the order of strict and dispassionately applied human law. In Southwest Asia freedom from myth-laden nature was partially achieved through worship of and obedience to a totally spiritual yet personal God of the universe, who stood completely outside nature yet imposed moral order upon it. In Hellas the attempt to master nature took the form of philosophy and science. Here certain thinkers sought to control nature by studying it objectively, thereby discovering laws that would enable humans to define more surely their place in the universe. In this manner, four major world traditions emerged: Indian transcendental spirituality; China's distinctive blend of practical worldliness with a mystical appreciation of nature; Southwest Asia's preoccupation with ethical monotheism; and Greek rationalism, with its special focus on the human condition.

In this chapter we explore the spiritual and religious traditions that took shape in India and Southwest Asia. Religion has played a central role in human history, especially in the region of southern Asia that stretches from the eastern coast of the Mediterranean Sea to the Bay of Bengal. This vast area, which encompasses all of Southwest Asia and the whole Indian subcontinent, has been the birthplace of most of the world's major religions. Time and again we will return to this region of the world to marvel at its spiritual fertility. For the present, we focus on the emergence of two major spiritual traditions. The first is a world- and self-denying transcendentalism that took shape in India. Its most classic expressions were *Brahminical Hinduism* and *Buddhism*. Both sprang out of a common Indian notion that true peace and bliss do not lie in the momentary pleasures that come from satisfying the illusory desires of this world. Rather, lasting tranquillity comes only with the discovery of Immutable Reality through a radical transformation of one's self. The second major religious tradition of southern Asia was the concept of a single, sole God of the universe. This God is transcendental, existing totally outside of time, space, and matter, all of which are this deity's creations. But this Universal God is also a personal, caring deity who directs human history and uses humans as historical agents. Moreover, this God demands a high degree of moral behavior from those called to divine service because by directing human history, God has sanctified it. This notion, which we term *ethical monotheism*, found its origins in Persia's *Zoroastrianism* and Israel's *Judaism*.

▼▼▼

The Emergence of Brahminical Hinduism

Religion for the early Aryans of India, as was also true for the early Greeks and Persians, centered on the sacrifice by fire of animals, especially horses and cattle. Chanting ritual hymns, which were later preserved in the four great Vedic collections, Aryan priests, known as *Brahmins*, offered sacrifices in the hope of winning the favor of the gods, especially Indra (source 9). As important as the Brahmins were, however, early Aryan society appears to have been led by its warriors. Yet by the time of the composition of the *Rig Veda*'s "Hymn to Purusha," the Brahmins, who composed and recited the hymn, claimed a position of primacy over the other three classes: *Rajanya*s or *Kshatriyas* (rulers and warriors); *Vaisyas* (workers); and *Sudras* (slaves and servants). This claim did not go uncontested by the Kshatriyas, and for many centuries both classes jockeyed for leadership. In the end, the Brahmins won out, at least on a religious plane, and their victory was manifested in a uniquely Indian religious-social system known as *caste*.

The Sanskrit term for caste is *varna*, which means "color," and might derive from the Aryans' early attempt to distinguish themselves from the darker-skinned natives of the subcontinent. It seems likely that initially the Aryans relegated these much-despised *Dasas* (slaves) to the fourth and lowest class — the Sudras — although over time many members of the native upper classes were incorporated into the higher strata of the Indo-Aryan World. Whatever its origins, sometime in the course of the so-called Axial Age, varna came to mean, at least insofar as the Brahmin priests were concerned, the four groups of humanity that inhabited the *Hindu* (Indian) World, and at the top of this hierarchy stood the Brahmins. According to brahminical teachings, the four traditional Indo-Aryan classes were now castes, and strict rules codified each one. The four castes became theoretically hereditary and permanent, with few exceptions, and they defined the most intimate aspects of each member's life. What was more important, caste defined one's place in the painful cycle of rebirth (*samsara*) as each soul journeyed from incarnation to incarnation in search of release (*moksha*) and return to the World Soul (*Brahman*). Needless to say, male Brahmins stood at the doorstep of release because of the merits of their previous lives that had brought them this far. With the evolution of caste, which in itself is based on the belief that the tangible world is a shadow of the true world of the spirit, *Brahminical Hinduism* had arrived, at least in its early stages of evolution.

On one level Hinduism can be defined as the entire body of Indian religious beliefs and ways of life that are centered on a caste system in which Brahmins hold the most exalted position. Yet on a more profound level, Hinduism defies all attempts at simple definition. In fact, it is wrong to think of it, either today or several thousand years ago, as a single set of beliefs and practices. To the contrary, it is and always has been a fluid mass of religious and social expressions. It encompasses archaic folk rituals and the most abstract and speculative thought on the nature of Divine Reality. Although Brahmins constitute its priestly caste, historically its great *gurus*, or religious teachers, have come from all castes and walks of life. It is both polytheistic and monotheistic. It has thousands of gods and goddesses, but it also focuses on Brahman, the True One — limitless Divine Reality. One deity can have countless manifestations, but all the deities are manifestations of the One. Because Divine Reality is without bounds, Hindu religious expression is simultaneously earthy and metaphysical, and both erotic sexuality and extreme asceticism are equally valid religious traditions. More than a single religion, it is a family of connected religions that encompasses the living faiths of all the diverse peoples of India who call themselves Hindu, or Indian. Indeed, Hindus embrace an apparently endless variety of beliefs and modes of worship because one of the key religious insights of Hinduism is that *there are an infinite number of paths to and manifestations of the limitless One.* Consequently, Hindus do not believe that the fullness of religious truth can be summed up in a neat package of doctrinal statements, nor do they believe that religion consists of a clear-cut struggle of truth versus error, good versus evil. The notion that a thing either is or is not, but cannot be both, has no place in a Hindu world where countless apparent contradictions exist comfortably alongside one another.

The Hindu Search for Divine Reality
▼▼▼
13 ▼ *THE UPANISHADS*

Despite the growing importance of the Brahmins, between roughly 700 and 500 B.C.E., a number of religious revolutionaries in the region of northeast India's Ganges Plain, the new demographic and cultural center of the subcontinent, created a form of spiritual literature known as the *Upanishads.*

Upanishad means "sitting down in front [of a teacher]," and these texts take the form of dialogues between teachers and pupils who seek to go beyond the Vedas in their search for ultimate wisdom. Many of the authors were probably Brahmins, but it seems clear that just as many, if not more, were Kshatriyas. This fact reflects not only a continuing struggle for supremacy between the two castes but also a discontentment by many Brahmins, as well as Kshatriyas, with what they perceived to be the empty formalism of brahminical rituals.

Without necessarily rejecting the ancient Vedas and brahminical sacrifices or even the far-more-recent, still-evolving, and far-from-universally accepted caste system, the Upanishadic teachers took certain concepts that were implied in the later Vedic hymns, such as the "Hymn to Purusha" (source 9), and articulated a vision of an all-inclusive Being, or Ultimate Reality, called *Brahman.* More than that, they articulated a way by which anyone, regardless of caste, could immediately attain Brahman.

As we might expect, there is a good deal of contradiction among the 108 extant Upanishadic texts (108 being a sacred number in India), yet a fundamental message binds them: Not only is there a Universal Soul, or Brahman, but the innermost essence of a person, the *atman*, or spiritual self, is one with Brahman, the True Self. Humans, therefore, are not outside Divine Reality; they are part of it. Those who wish to throw off the painful bonds of rebirth and earthly nonreality must reach that divinity within themselves.

The first selection, which comes from the early and especially revered *Chandogya Upanishad*, presents two analogies to explain this theological message. Here we meet Svetaketu, a youth who thinks that he has mastered all he needs to know in order to win release from the shackles of life's cycle of suffering by virtue of his twelve-year apprenticeship with Brahmin priests, who have taught him all the sacred rituals. His father, however, teaches him an additional lesson: Reality transcends the world of tangible phenomena and yet is attainable. The second excerpt, taken from the later but equally important *Brihadaranyaka Upanishad*, deals with the issue of how that spark of Brahman, the Self, which is contained within each mortal body, migrates from one body to another until it finally achieves release and rejoins the One. Here we see an early enunciation of what are becoming two essential elements of Hindu religious thought: reincarnation and the law of *karma*, or the fruits of one's actions (see also source 14). The third selection, also from the *Brihadaranyaka*, describes the state of consciousness of a person who is on the verge of attaining release from the cycle of rebirth and union with Brahman.

QUESTIONS FOR ANALYSIS

1. What does the father mean when he states, "You, Svetaketu, are it"?
2. What is the law of karma?
3. Why are souls reincarnated, and how does one end the cycle of rebirth?
4. Why do even good and evil cease to have meaning to the soul that has found Brahman?
5. Consider the closing lines of the *Brihadaranyaka Upanishad*. What hope does this text hold out to persons of the lowest castes and even to casteless *Untouchables*?
6. Is the Upanishadic vision of Brahman a logical development from the message of the "Hymn to Purusha"? If so, how?

THE CHANDOGYA UPANISHAD

There lived once Svetaketu. . . . To him his father Uddalaka . . . said: "Svetaketu, go to school; for no one belonging to our race, dear son, who, not having studied, is, as it were, a Brahmin[1] by birth only."

Having begun his apprenticeship when he was twelve years of age, Svetaketu returned to his father, when he was twenty-four, having then studied all the Vedas, — conceited, considering himself well-read, and stern.

His father said to him: "Svetaketu, as you are so conceited, considering yourself so well-read, and so stern, my dear, have you ever asked for that instruction by which we hear what cannot be heard, by which we perceive what cannot be perceived, by which we know what cannot be known?"

"What is that instruction, Sir?" he asked. . . .

"Fetch me . . . a fruit of the Nyagrodha tree."

"Here is one, Sir."

"Break it."

"It is broken, Sir."

"What do you see there?"

"These seeds, almost infinitesimal."

"Break one of them."

"It is broken, Sir."

"What do you see there?"

"Not anything, Sir."

The father said: "My son, that subtle essence which you do not perceive there, of that very essence this great Nyagrodha tree exists.

"Believe it, my son. That which is the subtle essence, in it all that exists has its self. It is the True. It is the Self, and you, . . . Svetaketu, are it."

"Please, Sir, inform me still more," said the son.

"Be it so, my child," the father replied.

"Place this salt in water, and then wait on me in the morning."

The son did as he was commanded.

The father said to him: "Bring me the salt, which you placed in the water last night."

The son having looked for it, found it not, for, of course, it was melted.

The father said: "Taste it from the surface of the water. How is it?"

The son replied: "It is salt."

"Taste it from the middle. How is it?"

The son replied: "It is salt."

"Taste it from the bottom. How is it?"

The son replied: "It is salt."

The father said: "Throw it away and then wait on me."

He did so; but the salt exists forever.[2]

Then the father said: "Here also, in this body,[3] . . . you do not perceive the True, my son; but there indeed it is.

"That which is the subtle essence,[4] in it all that exists has its self. It is the True. It is the Self, and you, Svetaketu, are it."

THE BRIHADARANYAKA UPANISHAD

"And when the body grows weak through old age, or becomes weak through illness, at that time that person, after separating himself from his members, as a mango, or fig, or pippala-fruit is separated from the stalk,[5] hastens back again as he came, to the place from which he started, to new life. . . .

"Then both his knowledge and his work take hold of him[6] and his acquaintance with former things.[7]

"And as a caterpillar, after having reached the end of a blade of grass, and after having made another approach to another blade, draws itself together towards it, thus does this Self, after having thrown off this body and dispelled all

---

[1]Note that *Brahmin* is the male gender variation of the neuter noun *Brahman*.
[2]The salt, although invisible, remains forever in the water.
[3]The human body.
[4]The soul, or atman.
[5]The image is of a fruit that carries the seed of new life, even as it decays.

[6]The law of karma, which is defined more fully later in this source.
[7]Acquaintance with things in a former life explains the peculiar talents and deficiencies evident in a child.

ignorance, and after making another approach to another body, draw himself together towards it.

"And as a goldsmith, taking a piece of gold, turns it into another, newer and more beautiful shape, so does this Self, after having thrown off this body and dispelled all ignorance, make unto himself another, newer and more beautiful shape. . . .

"Now as a man is like this or like that, according as he acts and according as he behaves, so will he be: — a man of good acts will become good, a man of bad acts, bad. He becomes pure by pure deeds, bad by bad deeds.

"And here they say that a person consists of desires. And as is his desire, so is his will; and as is his will, so is his deed; and whatever deed he does, that he will reap.

"And here there is this verse: 'To whatever object a man's own mind is attached, to that he goes strenuously together with his deed; and having obtained the consequences of whatever deed he does here on Earth, he returns again from that world . . . to this world of action.'[8]

"So much for the man who desires. But as to the man who does not desire, who, not desiring, freed from desires, is satisfied in his desires, or desires the Self only, his vital spirits do not depart elsewhere, — being Brahman, he goes to Brahman.[9]

"On this there is this verse: 'When all desires which once entered his heart are undone, then does the mortal become immortal, then he obtains Brahman.'"

▼▼▼

"Now as a man, when embraced by a beloved wife, knows nothing that is without, nothing that is within, thus this person, when embraced by the intelligent Self, knows nothing that is without, nothing that is within. This indeed is his true form, in which his wishes are fulfilled, in which the Self only is his wish, in which no wish is left, — free from any sorrow.

"Then a father is not a father, a mother not a mother, the worlds not worlds, the gods not gods, the Vedas not Vedas. Then a thief is not a thief, a murderer not a murderer, a Kandala not a Kandala,[10] a Sramana not a Sramana,[11] a Tapasa not a Tapasa.[12] He is not followed by good, not followed by evil, for he has then overcome all the sorrows of the heart."

---

[8]The law of karma, which means "action."
[9]By discovering and becoming one with the spark of Brahman within, the person ends the painful cycle of samsara.
[10]*Kandalas* were the lowest of all casteless persons. Beneath the lowly Sudra stood certain casteless persons whose inherited occupations, or subcastes (*jatis*), rendered them "unclean." Hence, they were Untouchables.
[11]A holy beggar.
[12]A person performing penance.

Dharma: The Imperative of Caste Law
▼▼▼
14 ▼ *THE BHAGAVAD GITA*

The Upanishadic texts offer one *yoga* (pathway of discipline) to total detachment from this world and, therefore, release: the *Yoga of Knowledge*, by which the atman acquires the sure knowledge of its own divinity. The *Bhagavad Gita* (*Song of the Blessed Lord*), Brahminical Hinduism's most beloved sacred text, offers several others, of which we shall, at this time, consider only one: the *Yoga of Action*, by which one detaches oneself from this world through selfless devotion to caste duties (see Chapter 6, sources 34 and 35, for the *Yoga of Devotion*).

The *Gita* appears as an interjected episode in the *Mahabharata* (*The Great Deeds of the Bharata Clan*), the world's longest epic poem. Like the Homeric

Greek epics, the *Mahabharata* is ascribed to a single legendary poet, Vyasa. In fact, however, it was the work of many authors over an extensive period of time, from perhaps 500 B.C.E. to possibly 400 C.E. Also like the Homeric epics, the *Mahabharata* deals on one level with the clash of armies and the combat of individual heroes, and simultaneously on a higher plane it expounds theological and philosophical insights. Among all of its spiritual passages, the *Bhagavad Gita* is the most profound.

Younger than most of the epic into which it was placed, the *Gita*'s date of final composition is uncertain; scholars fix it anywhere between 300 B.C.E. and 300 C.E. Whatever its date, Hindu commentators have consistently considered the song to be the last and greatest of the Upanishadic texts, for they see it as the crystallization of all that was expressed and implied in the Upanishadic tradition.

The core question addressed in the *Bhagavad Gita* is how a person can become one with Brahman while still functioning in this world. Answers to that primary quest of Hindu theology come from Lord *Krishna*, the incarnation of the god *Vishnu*, the Divine Preserver. Vishnu had been a minor deity in the Vedas, but by the fourth century C.E., he had become a major god in the Hindu pantheon, who was believed to assume corporeal form periodically in order to re-establish cosmic harmony. In this particular incarnation, or *avatara* (descent), Krishna/Vishnu serves as charioteer to the warrior-hero *Arjuna*. Arjuna, son of a mortal mother and the god Indra, is a fearless warrior, but he shrinks from entering battle because his foes are kinsmen. Overcome by a sense of the futility of this fratricidal war and overwhelmed by compassion, he wants no part in creating more suffering. The hero-god Krishna then proceeds to resolve Arjuna's quandary by explaining to him the moral imperative of caste-duty, or *dharma*.

QUESTIONS FOR ANALYSIS

1. "There is no existence for that which is unreal; there is no non-existence for that which is real." What does Krishna mean by these words, and what relevance does it have to Arjunta's unwillingness to fight his kinsmen?
2. Why should one perform one's caste-duty in a totally disinterested fashion?
3. According to Krishna, what constitutes sin? What is evil?
4. Is Krishna's message the same as that of the Upanishads? If so, how?

The deity said, you have grieved for those who deserve no grief. . . . Learned men grieve not for the living nor the dead. Never did I not exist, nor you, nor these rulers of men; nor will any one of us ever hereafter cease to be. As in this body, infancy and youth and old age come to the embodied self, so does the acquisition of another body; a sensible man is not deceived about that. The contacts of the senses, O son of Kunti![1] which produce cold and heat, pleasure and pain, are not permanent, they are ever coming and going. Bear them, O descendant of Bharata![2] For, O chief of men! that sensible man whom they (pain and pleasure being alike to him) afflict not, he merits

---

[1]The secondary name of Arjuna's mother (see note 4).

[2]King Bharata was the ancestor from whom Arjuna and his foes were descended.

immortality. There is no existence for that which is unreal; there is no non-existence for that which is real. And the correct conclusion about both is perceived by those who perceive the truth. Know that to be indestructible which pervades all this. . . . He who thinks it[3] to be the killer and he who thinks it to be killed, both know nothing. It kills not, is not killed. It is not born, nor does it ever die, nor, having existed, does it exist no more. Unborn, everlasting, unchangeable, and primeval, it is not killed when the body is killed. O son of Pritha![4] how can that man who knows it thus to be indestructible, everlasting, unborn, and inexhaustible, how and whom can he kill, whom can he cause to be killed? As a man, casting off old clothes, puts on others and new ones, so the embodied self casting off old bodies, goes to others and new ones. . . . It is everlasting, all-pervading, stable, firm, and eternal. It is said to be unperceived, to be unthinkable, to be unchangeable. Therefore knowing it to be such, you ought not to grieve. But even if you think that it is constantly born, and constantly dies, still, O you of mighty arms! you ought not to grieve thus. For to one that is born, death is certain; and to one that dies, birth is certain. . . . This embodied self, O descendant of Bharata! within every one's body is ever indestructible. Therefore you ought not to grieve for any being. Having regard to your own duty also, you ought not to falter, for there is nothing better for a Kshatriya than a righteous battle. Happy those Kshatriyas, O son of Pritha! who can find such a battle . . . an open door to Heaven! But if you will not fight this righteous battle, then you will have abandoned your own duty . . . and you will incur sin. . . . Your business is with action alone; not by any means with fruit. Let not the fruit of action be your motive to action. Let not your attachment be fixed on inaction. Having recourse to devotion . . . perform actions, casting off all attachment, and being equable in success or ill-success; such equability is called devotion. . . . The wise who have obtained devotion cast off the fruit of action,[5] and released from the shackles of repeated births, repair to that seat where there is no unhappiness. . . . The man who, casting off all desires, lives free from attachments, who is free from egoism, and from the feeling that this or that is mine, obtains tranquility. This, O son of Pritha! is the Brahmic state; attaining to this, one is never deluded; and remaining in it in one's last moments, one attains the Brahmic bliss.[6] . . .

I have passed through many births, O Arjuna! and you also. I know them all, but you, O terror of your foes! do not know them. . . . Whensoever, O descendant of Bharata! piety languishes, and impiety is in the ascendant, I create myself. I am born age after age, for the protection of the good, for the destruction of evil-doers, and the establishment of piety. . . . The fourfold division of castes was created by me according to the appointment of qualities and duties. . . . The duties of Brahmins, Kshatriyas, and Vaisyas, and of Sudras, too, O terror of your foes! are distinguished according to the qualities born of nature.[7] Tranquility, restraint of the senses, penance, purity, forgiveness, straightforwardness, also knowledge, experience, and belief in a future world, this is the natural duty of Brahmins. Valor, glory, courage, dexterity, not slinking away from battle, gifts, exercise of lordly power, this is the natural duty of Kshatriyas. Agriculture, tending cattle, trade, this is the natural duty of Vaisyas. And the natural duty of Sudras, too, consists in service. Every man intent on his own respective duties obtains perfection. Listen, now, how one intent on one's own duty

---

[3]The atman, or individual soul, and Brahman, which are one and the same (see source 13).

[4]The primary name of Arjuna's mother (see note 1).

[5]They do not concern themselves with the earthly consequences of their actions and develop no attachments to the rewards of this world (fame, wealth, family) that might result from those actions.

[6]*Brahma-nirvana*, or merging with Brahman and release (*moksha*) from the cycle of rebirth. It is a state of simultaneous being and nonbeing.

[7]Each caste consists of persons born to that station by virtue of their nature. Each person's karma has made that person's nature suitable for a particular caste and only that caste. Brahmins teach and offer sacrifices; Kshatriyas rule and fight; Vaisyas work; and Sudras serve (see source 9).

obtains perfection. Worshiping, by the performance of his own duty, him from whom all things proceed, and by whom all this is permeated, a man obtains perfection. One's duty, though defective, is better than another's duty well performed. Performing the duty prescribed by nature, one does not incur sin. O son of Kunti! one should not abandon a natural duty though tainted with evil; for all actions are enveloped by evil, as fire by smoke.

▼▼▼

A Challenge to Caste: The Teachings of the Buddha

By 600 B.C.E. the central spiritual question in Indian society was how to find liberation from karma and the painful cycle of rebirth. The Upanishadic teachers and the *Bhagavad Gita* offered different but complementary answers, and both sources of wisdom held out the possibility that anyone, regardless of caste, could find release in the present life by achieving a state of absolute selflessness. Regardless, Brahmin teachers continued to emphasize the fourfold division of society, and by about 300 B.C.E., the idea and even reality of caste divisions and duties were pretty well established throughout most of northern and central India (but not yet in the south). Moreover, there was a widespread consensus — at least among the Brahminical teachers — that conformity to one's dharma, no matter how lacking in perfect selflessness it might be, and slow karmic progress up the chain of caste through a series of reincarnations were the dual keys to release from the bonds of matter. In opposition to this notion, however, some spiritual teachers offered their followers avenues to liberation that challenged the entire caste system.

Even as the Brahmin class was in the process of defining itself as the dominant Hindu caste, several teachers emerged from the Kshatriya class to offer alternatives to caste. The most significant of these was *Siddhartha Gautama*, better known as the *Buddha* (the Enlightened One).

The Buddha and his doctrine are understandable only within the context of Hindu cosmology. Although he formulated a spiritual philosophy that denied certain concepts basic to what was emerging as classical Brahminical Hinduism, the questions he asked and the answers he offered were predicated on the world-denying assumptions that underlie all Indian spiritual thought.

Although grounded in Indian spirituality, *Buddhism* eventually expanded well beyond the cultural and geographic boundaries of India. By the first century C.E., the Buddha's teachings had been transformed into a family of related religious sects, many of which worshiped the Buddha himself as a divine being. For well over 2,000 years, Buddhism in its various forms has profoundly shaped the lives of countless devotees throughout South, Central, and East Asia and remains a vital religious force today.

The Path to Enlightenment

▼▼▼

15 ▼ *The Buddha,* *SETTING IN MOTION THE* *WHEEL OF THE LAW*

Most details of the Buddha's life are uncertain. Unanimous tradition places Siddhartha Gautama's birth into a princely family residing in the Himalayan foothills of Nepal, but the written sources for his life and teachings, all composed long after his time, differ as to his birth and death dates; the three strongest traditions are 624–544, 563–483, and 448–368 B.C.E. Significantly, all three agree that he lived to the age of eighty. Recent scholarship, based on archaeological evidence, has led to a growing consensus that the approximate dates 480–400 make the most sense.

Tradition holds that the prince led a sheltered court life up to age twenty-nine, when he viewed evidence of human aging, suffering, and death for the first time. Shrinking in horror at these manifestations of misery, he fled his comfortable life, his wife, and his newborn son and became an *ascetic* (someone who denies the pleasures of the body in order to liberate the soul), determined to find a remedy for suffering. *Mendicant* (begging) ascetics, known as *Shramanas*, who rejected the religious traditions of the Vedas and the primacy of the Brahmins, were already a major religious force in India. Siddhartha Gautama, however, found that the ascetic life offered him no insight as to how one might escape the sorrows of mortal existence. In an act of desperation, he sat under a sacred *pipal tree* (see source 7, seal 3), vowing to meditate until he achieved his goal. Despite the attempts of the armies of *Mara,* "the Evil One," the divine Lord of the Realm of Desire, to deflect Siddhartha from his course, he persisted. Shortly after his victory over Mara's temptations, he achieved his goal. He was now the Buddha, the Enlightened One.

Legend tells us that seven weeks later he proceeded to share the path to Enlightenment, which he termed the *Middle Path,* by preaching a sermon in a deer park at Sarnath in northeastern India to five ascetics, former companions and students who had abandoned him as a false teacher when he had renounced asceticism as the path to Enlightenment. Through the aura of compassion that he now radiated, as well as by the words of his first sermon, the Buddha converted these five into his first disciples. Buddhists refer to that initial sermon as "Setting in Motion the Wheel of the Law," which means that the Buddha had embarked on a journey (turning the wheel) on behalf of the Law of Righteousness (Dharma). Now at age thirty-five, he had forty-five years ahead of him to preach his doctrine.

Our text is a reconstruction of that sermon as preserved in a body of Buddhist literature known as the *Pali Canon,* which contains the most authentic texts relating to the Buddha and his doctrine known to exist today. Assembled as an authoritative collection, or canon, of orally transmitted remembrances during the period between the Buddha's death and the late third century B.C.E., the texts were probably not written down in the form in which we have them until the late first century B.C.E. Composed in Pali, a language that is close to classical Sanskrit, they first appeared on the island of Ceylon (present-day Sri Lanka) and traveled from there to Burma and Thailand, where they became the core canonical books of the branch of Buddhism known as *Theravada* (see Chapter 6). Each text is located in one of three groupings, or "baskets," a designation whose origin traces back to a time when the palm-leaf manuscripts of the texts were kept in three separate baskets. For this reason the entire collection is known as the *Tipitaka* (also spelled *Tripitaka*), or *Three Baskets*. The following source comes from *The Discipline Basket*, which consists of a number of books that concern the discipline, or regimented life, of Buddhist monks and nuns.

QUESTIONS FOR ANALYSIS

1. What is the Middle Path? According to the Buddha, why is it the proper path to Enlightenment?
2. What are the *Four Noble Truths*, and how does one's total comprehension and acceptance of them lead to *Nirvana*, or escape from the cycle of suffering?
3. Buddhists call the Law taught by the Buddha *Dharma*. How does Buddhist Dharma differ from that of Brahminical Hinduism?

And the Blessed One thus addressed the five Bhikkhus.[1] "There are two extremes, O Bhikkhus, which he who has given up the world ought to avoid. What are these two extremes? A life given to pleasures, devoted to pleasures and lusts: this is degrading, sensual, vulgar, ignoble, and profitless; and a life given to mortifications: this is painful, ignoble, and profitless. By avoiding these two extremes, O Bhikkhus, the Tathagata[2] has gained the knowledge of the Middle Path which leads to insight, which leads to wisdom, which conduces to calm, to knowledge, to the Sambodhi,[3] to Nirvana.[4]

"Which, O Bhikkhus, is this Middle Path the knowledge of which the Tathagata has gained . . . ?

It is the Holy Eightfold Path, namely, Right Belief,[5] Right Aspiration,[6] Right Speech,[7] Right Conduct,[8] Right Means of Livelihood,[9] Right Endeavor,[10] Right Memory,[11] Right Meditation.[12] . . .

"This, O Bhikkhus, is the Noble Truth of Suffering: Birth is suffering; decay is suffering; illness is suffering; death is suffering. Presence of objects we hate, is suffering; Separation from objects we love, is suffering; not to obtain what we desire, is suffering. Briefly, . . . clinging to existence is suffering.

"This, O Bhikkhus, is the Noble Truth of the Cause of suffering: Thirst,[13] that leads to rebirth, accompanied by pleasure and lust, finding its delight here and there. This thirst is threefold,

---

[1] Ascetics. The term later was used to refer to Buddhism's mendicant monks.

[2] One of the Buddha's titles. Literally it means "one who has gone thus," which is a way of saying "He who has arrived at the Truth."

[3] Total Enlightenment.

[4] The state of release from the limitations of existence and rebirth. The word means literally "extinction," in the sense that one has extinguished all worldly desires. In essence, it is Buddhahood. Like the Hindu Brahma-nirvana, Buddhist Nirvana is a state of absolute being and nonbeing.

[5] Understanding the truth about the universality of suffering, knowing the path leading to its extinction, and realizing it is attainable.

[6] Preparing for the journey to Enlightenment by freeing one's mind of ill will, sensuous desire, and cruelty.

[7] Abstaining from lying, harsh language, and gossip.

[8] Acting honestly by avoiding killing, stealing, and unlawful sexual intercourse.

[9] Avoiding any occupation that harms directly or indirectly any living being.

[10] Going beyond simply acting morally, a person now avoids all distractions and temptations of the flesh.

[11] Now that one has put aside distractions, one focuses the entire mind fully on important issues, such as life, suffering, and death.

[12] Total discipline of the mind, body, and spirit leading to a state of absolute awareness that transcends consciousness.

[13] Desire.

namely, thirst for pleasure, thirst for existence, thirst for prosperity.

"This, O Bhikkhus, is the Noble Truth of the Cessation of suffering: it ceases with the complete cessation of this thirst, — a cessation which consists in the absence of every passion — with the abandoning of this thirst, with the doing away with it, with the deliverance from it, with the destruction of desire.

"This, O Bhikkhus, is the Noble Truth of the Path which leads to the cessation of suffering: that Holy Eightfold Path, that is to say, Right Belief, Right Aspiration, Right Speech, Right Conduct, Right Means of Livelihood, Right Endeavor, Right Memory, Right Meditation. . . .

"As long, O Bhikkhus, as I did not possess with perfect purity this true knowledge and insight into these four Noble Truths . . . so long, O Bhikkhus, I knew that I had not yet obtained the highest, absolute Sambodhi in the world of men and gods. . . .

"But since I possessed, O Bhikkhus, with perfect purity this true knowledge and insight into these four Noble Truths . . . then I knew, O Bhikkhus, that I had obtained the highest, universal Sambodhi. . . .

"And this knowledge and insight arose in my mind: The emancipation of my mind cannot be lost; this is my last birth; hence I shall not be born again!"

The Poison Arrow of Needless Speculation

▼▼▼

16 ▼ *The Buddha,* *QUESTIONS THAT TEND NOT TO EDIFICATION*

The *Pali Canon* contains thousands of sermons ascribed to the Buddha. Other than "Setting in Motion the Wheel of the Law," none is more famous or central to the Buddha's teaching than "Questions That Tend Not to Edification," also known as the "Poison Arrow." The sermon displays two characteristics common to most of the lessons ascribed to the Buddha in the *Tipitaka*: his use of earthy parables and analogies to convey his profound spiritual insights; and teaching by means of a dialogue between Enlightened Master and pupil.

QUESTIONS FOR ANALYSIS

1. Which issues or questions did the Buddha refuse to consider?
2. Did the Buddha consider such speculation simply a waste of time, or was there a more profound reason for his antipathy to the search for answers to such questions?
3. What does his refusal to speculate on these issues suggest about his core doctrine?
4. Now that you have studied these four Indian sources, you are ready for the Big Questions: What assumptions and values do Brahminical Hinduism and Buddhism share? Where do they differ? Which are more significant, the similarities or the differences? What conclusions follow from your answers?

On certain occasion the Blessed One[1] was dwelling at Savatthi in Jetavana monastery. . . . Now it happened to the venerable Malunkyaputta,[2] being in seclusion and plunged in meditation, that a consideration presented itself to his mind as follows:

"These theories that the Blessed One has left unexplained, has set aside and rejected — that the world is eternal, that the world is not eternal, that the world is finite, that the world is infinite, that the soul and the body are identical, that the soul is one thing and the body another, that the saint[3] exists after death, that the saint does not exist after death, that the saint both exists and does not exist after death, that the saint neither exists nor does not exist after death — these the Blessed One does not explain to me. And the fact that the Blessed One does not explain them to me does not please me nor suit me. Therefore I will draw near to the Blessed One and inquire of him concerning this matter. If the Blessed One will explain them to me, . . . I will lead the religious life under the Blessed One. If the Blessed One will not explain them to me, . . . I will abandon religious training and return to the lower life of a layman."

Then the venerable Malunkyaputta arose in the evening from his seclusion, and drew near to where the Blessed One was; and having drawn near and greeted the Blessed One, he sat down respectfully at one side. And . . . the venerable Malunkyaputta spoke to the Blessed One as follows:

"Reverend Sir, it happened to me, as I was just now in seclusion and plunged in meditation, that a consideration presented itself to my mind, as follows: . . .

▷   He repeats verbatim the questions that vex him.

"If the Blessed One knows that the world is eternal, let the Blessed One explain to me that the world is eternal; if the Blessed One knows that the world is not eternal, let the Blessed One explain to me that the world is not eternal. If the Blessed One does not know either that the world is eternal or that the world is not eternal, the only upright thing for one who does not know, or who has not that insight, is to say, 'I do not know; I have not that insight.'"

"Pray Malunkyaputta, did I ever say to you, 'Come, Malunkyaputta, lead the religious life under me, and I will explain to you either that the world is eternal, or that the world is not eternal . . . or that the saint neither exists nor does not exist after death'?"

"No, indeed, Reverend Sir."

"Or did you ever say to me, 'Reverend Sir, I will lead the religious life under the Blessed One, on condition that the Blessed One explain to me either that the world is eternal, or that the world is not eternal . . . or that the saint neither exists nor does not exist after death'?"

"No, indeed, Reverend Sir." . . .

"That being the case, vain man, whom are you so angrily denouncing?

"Malunkyaputta, any one who should say, 'I will not lead the religious life under the Blessed One until the Blessed One shall explain to me either that the world is eternal. Or that the world is not eternal . . . or that the saint neither exists nor does not exist after death'; — that person would die, Malunkyaputta, before the Tathagata had ever explained this to him.

"It is as if, Malunkyaputta, a man had been wounded by an arrow thickly smeared with poison, and his friends and companions, his relatives and kinsfolk, were to procure for him a physician or surgeon; and the sick man were to say, 'I will not have this arrow taken out until I have learned whether the man who wounded me belonged to the warrior caste, or to the Brahmin caste, or to the agricultural caste, or to the menial caste.'

---

[1]The Buddha.
[2]One of the Buddha's disciples.

[3]An *arahat*, or "one worthy of reverence," who has achieved the fourth and highest stage leading to Nirvana. The title is also spelled *arahant* and *arhat*.

"Or again he were to say, 'I will not have this arrow taken out until I have learned the name of the man who wounded me, and to what clan he belongs.'

"Or again he were to say, 'I will not have this arrow taken out until I have learned whether the man who wounded me was tall, or short, or of the middle height.'

"Or again he were to say, 'I will not have this arrow taken out until I have learned whether the man who wounded me was black, or dusky, or of a yellow skin.'

"Or again he were to say, 'I will not have this arrow taken out until I have learned whether the man who wounded me was from this or that village, or town, or city.' . . .

▷   Many similar possibilities are mentioned.

"That man would die, Malunkyaputta, without ever having learned this.

"In exactly the same way, Malunkyaputta, any one who should say, 'I will not lead the religious life under the Blessed One until the Blessed One shall explain to me either that the world is eternal, or that the world is not eternal . . . or that the saint neither exists nor does not exist after death'; — that person would die, Malunkyaputta, before the Tathagata had ever explained this to him.

"The religious life, Malunkyaputta, does not depend on the dogma that the world is eternal; nor does the religious life, Malunkyaputta, depend on the dogma that the world is not eternal. Whether the dogma obtain, Malunkyaputta, that the world is eternal, or that the world is not eternal, there still remain birth, old age, death, sorrow, lamentation, misery, grief, and despair, for the extinction of which in the present life I am prescribing. . . .

"Accordingly, Malunkyaputta, bear always in mind what it is that I have not explained, and what it is that I have explained. And what, Malunkyaputta, have I not explained? I have not explained, Malunkyaputta, that the world is eternal; I have not explained that the world is not eternal; I have not explained that the world is finite; I have not explained that the world is infinite; I have not explained that the soul and the body are identical; I have not explained that the soul is one thing and the body another; I have not explained that the saint exists after death; I have not explained that the saint does not exist after death; I have not explained that the saint both exists and does not exist after death; I have not explained that the saint neither exists nor does not exist after death. And why, Malunkyaputta, have I not explained this? Because, Malunkyaputta, this profits not, nor has to do with the fundamentals of religion, nor tends to aversion, absence of passion, cessation, quiescence, the supernatural faculties, supreme wisdom, and Nirvana; therefore I have not explained it.

"And what, Malunkyaputta, have I explained? Misery, Malunkyaputta, have I explained; the origin of misery have I explained; the cessation of misery have I explained; and the path leading to the cessation of misery have I explained.[1] And why, Malunkyaputta, have I explained this? Because, Malunkyaputta, this does profit, has to do with the fundamentals of religion, and tends to aversion, absence of passion, cessation, quiescence, knowledge, supreme wisdom, and Nirvana; therefore have I explained it. Accordingly, Malunkyaputta, bear always in mind what it is that I have not explained, and what it is that I have explained."

Thus the Blessed One spoke and, delighted, the venerable Malunkyaputta applauded the speech of the Blessed One.

---

[1]The Four Noble Truths. See source 15.

Persians, Israelites, and Their Gods

Two peoples of Southwest Asia, the Persians and the Israelites, evolved visions of a single, uncreated God of the universe. The Creator of all goodness, He demanded wholehearted devotion and imposed an uncompromising code of moral behavior upon all believers. Both the Persian *Ahura Mazda* (Lord Wisdom) and the Israelite YHWH (I am Who am) were originally perceived as male sky-gods, existing among a multiplicity of other gods of nature; by the sixth century B.C.E., however, their respective devotees worshiped each as the sole source of all holiness. What is more, each of these two divinities was perceived as *the* sole God of history. That is, each God alone used humans as agents to serve the Divine Will and, thereby, to assist in the realization of the Divine Plan for humanity. For both the Persians and the Israelites, human history had a purpose and a goal. By serving as agents in the working out of God's holy plan for creation, humans assumed a spiritual dignity and importance that they could otherwise never have hoped to attain.

The Persian faith, known as *Zoroastrianism*, admitted the existence of a number of lesser divinities and, therefore, was not strictly monotheistic. Moreover, evidence strongly suggests that the religion of the early Israelites (Chapter 2) was *monolatric* (worshiping a single god while acknowledging the existence of others) rather than monotheistic (believing there is only one God). Nevertheless, both religions laid the basis for Southwest Asia's distinctive vision of ethical monotheism.

The Struggle Between Good and Evil

▼▼▼
17 ▼ *Zarathustra, GATHAS*

During the second millennium B.C.E., about the same time that one branch of the Aryans wandered into the Indian subcontinent, another branch settled the highlands of *Iran* (the land of the Aryans). Initially, the religion and general culture of the people who settled Iran were almost identical to that of the Vedic Aryans of India. For example, the Iranians celebrated the slaying of Verethra, the drought, by their war-god Indara. The parallel with Indra's striking down Vritra, the dragon of drought, is obvious (see source 9). In time, however, the Iranians developed a civilization that differed radically from that of the Indo-Aryans. We call that ancient civilization *Persian*.

By the late sixth century B.C.E., the Persians possessed the largest empire the world had yet seen. For nearly two centuries, they united Southwest Asia and portions of Central Asia, Northeast Africa, and the Balkan region of Europe into a politically centralized yet culturally diverse entity. During the reign of Darius the

Great (r. 522–486 B.C.E.), who styled himself King of Kings, the royal house of Persia adopted as its religion the teachings of a native son, *Zarathustra* (or *Zoroaster*, as he was called by the Greeks). The highly ethical message of this Persian religious visionary appears to have been one of the major factors contributing to the empire's general policy of good government.

We know very little about the life of Zarathustra. According to a late Persian tradition, he lived 258 years before Alexander the Great, or around the first quarter of the sixth century B.C.E. As appealing as this putative date is for those who would place this religious revolutionary squarely into the so-called Axial Age, it seems likely that Zarathustra flourished many centuries earlier. The archaic language of his few extant hymns strongly suggests that he lived no later than 1000 B.C.E., probably closer to 1200, and possibly as early as the 1300s, although some scholars state that his use of archaic language indicates only that he drew from much earlier rituals. Whatever his dates, he apparently belonged to the priestly class that performed fire sacrifices, very much like the Indo-Aryan Brahmins. The religious world into which he had been born was filled with a multiplicity of lesser gods known as *daevas* (called *devas* by the Indo-Aryans) and three greater gods, each of whom bore the title *Ahura* (Lord), and all of these deities commanded worship. Zarathustra's great religious breakthrough seems to have been that he preached that one of these divine beings, *Ahura Mazda* (Lord Wisdom), was the sole God of creation and the supreme deity of the universe. This uncreated God and source of all goodness alone was worthy of the highest worship. To be sure, Ahura Mazda had created lesser benign spirits, known as *yazatas,* to aid him, and they merited devotion, but all of the traditional Iranian daevas were evil demons, who deserved no worship. Indeed, these daevas were the creation of another uncreated entity, *Angra Mainyu* (Hostile Spirit), whose evil existence was the source of all sin and misery in the universe.

It is clear that Zarathustra claimed to be the *prophet* (a person speaking by divine inspiration and, thereby, revealing the will of God) of Ahura Mazda. Equally clear, Zarathustra taught his disciples that Ahura Mazda required all humans to join in the cosmic struggle against Angra Mainyu. Although coeternal with Lord Wisdom, Hostile Spirit was nowhere his equal. Angra Mainyu (also known as the *Liar*) and his minions afflicted human souls with evil and led them away from the path of righteousness, but in the end Angra Mainyu and his daevas would be defeated. Strictly speaking, such a vision, which sees the universe engaged in a contest between two divine principles, one good and the other evil, is not monotheistic but rather *dualistic*. Nevertheless, Zarathustra's dualistic theology focused on a single God of goodness and should be seen as one of the major roots of Southwest Asian ethical monotheism.

Zarathustra's teachings took hold in Persia, especially with the rise of the first Persian Empire in the sixth century B.C.E. From 224 to 651 C.E., Zoroastrianism was the official state religion of a revived Persian Empire under the Sassanian house, and it was only in the Sassanian Era, possibly as late as the sixth century C.E., that the *Avesta*, the Zoroastrian collection of holy scripture, was written down in its final form. Although the *Avesta* encompasses many texts that date from well after Zarathustra's time, it contains a few short devotional hymns, known as *Gathas*, that seem to date to the age of Zarathustra and probably owe their composition to him or an early disciple. Their archaic language and often unclear references make them hard, even impossible to interpret with full confidence. Yet, they are our only reliable sources for the original teachings of the Persian prophet. As such, they illustrate, but ambiguously so, his vision and message.

QUESTIONS FOR ANALYSIS

1. What evidence indicates that Zarathustra saw Ahura Mazda as the sole creator of the universe?
2. How does each person's life become a microcosm of the battle between Ahura Mazda and the Liar?
3. How do we know that Zarathustra believed Ahura Mazda would ultimately triumph over evil?
4. Does Zarathustra see his faith as only one of many paths to the truth, or is it the Truth?
5. What is promised to those who serve Ahura Mazda faithfully? What about those who do not accept and serve this God?

This I ask you, tell me truly, Ahura. Who is by generation the Father of Right, at the first? Who determined the path of sun and stars? Who is it by whom the moon waxes and wanes again? This, O Mazda, and yet more, I want to know.

This I ask you, tell me truly, Ahura. Who upheld the Earth beneath and the firmament from falling? Who the waters and the plants? Who yoked swiftness to winds and clouds? Who is, O Mazda, creator of Good Thought?[1]

This I ask you, tell me truly, Ahura. What artist made light and darkness? What artist made sleep and waking? Who made morning, noon, and night, that call the understanding man to his duty? . . .

This I ask you, tell me truly, Ahura. Who created together with Dominion the precious Piety? Who made by wisdom the son obedient to his father? I strive to recognize by these things you, O Mazda, creator of all things through the holy spirit. . . .

This I ask you, tell me truly, Ahura. The Religion which is the best for all that are, which in union with Right should make prosperous all that is mine, will they duly observe it, the religion of my creed, with the words and action of Piety, in desire for your future good things, O Mazda?

This I ask you, tell me truly, Ahura — whether Piety will extend to those to whom your Religion shall be proclaimed? I was ordained at the first by you: all others I look upon with hatred of spirit.

This I ask you, tell me truly, Ahura. Who among those with whom I would speak is a righteous man, and who a liar? On which side is the enemy? . . .

This I ask you, tell me truly, Ahura — whether we shall drive the Lie away from us to those who being full of disobedience will not strive after fellowship with Right, nor trouble themselves with counsel of Good Thought. . . .

---

[1]Zarathustra conceived of Good Thought, Piety, and other such moral entities as spiritual beings whom Ahura Mazda had created to help in the battle against the forces of evil.

This I ask you, tell me truly, Ahura — whether through you I shall attain my goal . . . and that my voice may be effectual, that Welfare and Immortality may be ready to unite according to that promise with him who joins himself with Right.

This I ask you, tell me truly, Ahura — whether I shall indeed, O Right, earn that reward, even ten mares with a stallion and a camel,[2] which was promised to me, O Mazda, as well as through you the future gift of Welfare and Immortality.

▼▼▼

I will speak of that which Mazda Ahura, the all-knowing, revealed to me first in this earthly life. Those of you that put not in practice this word as I think and utter it, to them shall be woe at the end of life. . . .

I will speak of that which the Holiest declared to me as the word that is best for mortals to obey: he, Mazda Ahura said, "They who at my bidding render him[3] obedience, shall all attain Welfare and Immortality by the actions of the Good Spirit." . . .

In immortality shall the soul of the righteous be joyful, in perpetuity shall be the torments of the Liars. All this does Mazda Ahura appoint by his Dominion.

---

[2]Symbols of good fortune and earthly prosperity.

[3]Zarathustra.

A New Covenant for All Peoples
▼▼▼
18 ▼ THE BOOK OF ISAIAH

Once settled in the land of Canaan (Chapter 2), the Israelites waged a continuing battle to retain their independence, cultural identity, and exclusive devotion to YHWH. According to the biblical account, in the late eleventh century B.C.E., largely in response to Philistine pressure, the Israelites created a kingdom. Around 1020 B.C.E. their second king, David, captured Jerusalem and converted it into the Israelites' religious and political capital.

The political stability of this kingdom was precarious. In 922 it was split into two independent entities: the larger kingdom of Israel in the north and the kingdom of Judah, centering on Jerusalem, in the south. In 722 the Assyrians obliterated Israel. The more compact and remote kingdom of Judah survived until 586 B.C.E., when a Semitic people from Mesopotamia known as the *Chaldeans* captured and destroyed Jerusalem and carried off most of Judah's upper classes into exile in Babylon, an episode known forever after as the *Babylonian Captivity*.

Cultural and religious stability was equally precarious. The cult of YHWH was in many ways more suitable to the life of the desert herder than to that of the settled farmer. As the Israelites settled down, they adopted many of the religious practices of their neighbors (and there is good reason to conclude that many Israelites were themselves of Canaanite stock). This embracing of so-called alien deities occasioned angry protests from a group of religious reformers known as the *prophets*. The prophets, who claimed inspiration from YHWH, now increasingly referred to as the *Lord*, protested vehemently against debasement of the Mosaic religion, but in the process of their protest, they broadened considerably the moral and theological scope of the worship of the Lord.

One of the greatest and last of these prophets was a person we know only as *Second Isaiah*. He served as the voice of a new faith that was born out of the anguish of the Babylonian Captivity. We call that faith *Judaism*.

The original Prophet Isaiah had towered over the religious scene of Jerusalem from the middle to the late eighth century B.C.E. and left behind a rich legacy of teaching on the Lord's role as the God who controls the destinies of all people. Second Isaiah, who lived in the mid and late sixth century B.C.E., carried on this tradition. Consequently, the prophecies of this otherwise unknown person were appended to the writings of the earlier Isaiah and appear as chapters 40 through 55 in the Bible's Book of Isaiah (and Third Isaiah was the author or authors of chapters 56–66).

The following passages were composed around 538 B.C.E., when Cyrus the Great, king of Persia and conqueror of the Chaldean (Neo-Babylonian) Empire, released Israelite leaders from captivity in Mesopotamia and allowed them to rebuild Jerusalem and its Temple. Here Second Isaiah metaphorically describes the people of Israel as the Lord's *Suffering Servant* and delineates the historical role that the Lord has decreed for this servant.

This notion of a God of goodness who uses human agents to drive history forward certainly reminds us of Zarathustra's message, and clearly elements of Zoroastrian belief — such as angels, the Devil, Heaven, Hell, Limbo, the Resurrection of the dead, a Savior-to-Come, and a Day of Judgment — would later surface in some forms of Judaism, as well as in Christianity and Islam. Nevertheless, it is impossible to say with any certainty what influence, if any, Zoroastrian teachings might have had on Second Isaiah's prophetic vision. We can only speculate.

QUESTIONS FOR ANALYSIS

1. What does Second Isaiah mean by the prophecy that the Lord will present Israel "as a light to the nations"? How will the Children of Israel's redemption from exile in Babylon serve a universal purpose?
2. Compare this text with Zarathustra's *Gathas* with an eye toward the ways in which Ahura Mazda and the Lord are portrayed. Are there any parallels or common elements? Are there any major differences? Which are more significant — the similarities or the differences. Why?
3. Consider YHWH's covenants with Noah (source 11) and with the wandering Israelites (source 12). To which of those covenants is this one closer? What do you conclude from your answer?
4. How do Ahura Mazda and the Lord differ from Brahman?

Thus says the Lord, the King of Israel[1]
and his Redeemer, the Lord of hosts:
"I am the first and I am the last;
besides me there is no God. . . .
Remember these things, O Jacob,[2]
and Israel, for you are my servant;
I formed you, you are my servant;
O Israel, you will not be forgotten by me.
I have swept away your transgressions like a
    cloud,
and your sins like mist;
return to me, for I have redeemed you. . . .
I am the Lord, who made all things,
who stretched out the heavens alone,
who spread out the Earth — Who was with
    me? —
who frustrates the omens of liars,
and makes fools of diviners;
who turns wise men back,
and makes their knowledge foolish;
who confirms the word of his servant,
and performs the counsel of his messengers;
who says of Jerusalem, 'She shall be inhabited,'
and of the cities of Judah, 'They shall be built,
and I will raise up their ruins,' . . .
who says of Cyrus, 'He is my shepherd.
and he shall fulfill all my purpose';
saying of Jerusalem, 'She shall be built,'
and of the temple, 'Your foundation shall be
    laid.'"
Thus says the Lord to his anointed, to Cyrus,
whose right hand I have grasped,
to subdue nations before him
and ungird the loins of kings,
to open doors before him
that gates may not be closed:
"I will go before you
and level the mountains,
I will break in pieces the doors of bronze
and cut asunder the bars of iron,[3]
I will give you the treasures of darkness

and the hoards in secret places,
that you may know that it is I, the Lord,
the God of Israel, who call you by your name.
For the sake of my servant Jacob,
and Israel my chosen,
I call you by your name,
I surname you,[4] though you do not know me.
I am the Lord, and there is no other,
besides me there is no God;
I gird you, though you do not know me,
that men may know, from the rising of the sun
and from the west, that there is none besides
    me;
I am the Lord, and there is no other. . . .
I made the Earth,
and created man upon it;
it was my hands that stretched out the heavens,
and I commanded all their host.
I have aroused him[5] in righteousness,
and I will make straight all his ways;
he shall build my city[6]
and set my exiles free,
not for price or reward,"
says the Lord of hosts. . . .
"I the Lord speak the truth,
I declare what is right.
"Assemble yourselves and come,
draw near together,
you survivors of the nations![7]
They have no knowledge
who carry about their wooden idols,
and keep on praying to a god
that cannot save.
Declare and present your case;
let them take counsel together!
Who told this long ago?
Who declared it of old?
Was it not I, the Lord?
And there is no other god besides me, a right-
    eous God and a Savior;
there is none besides me.

---

[1]All Israelites and not just the inhabitants of the former
kingdom of Israel.
[2]Here *Jacob* means all of Jacob's descendants — the Children
of Israel.
[3]A reference to the great walls of Babylon.

[4]The Lord bestows on Cyrus the title *the Great*.
[5]Cyrus.
[6]Jerusalem.
[7]All peoples who survive the collapse of the Chaldean, or
Neo-Babylonian, Empire.

"Turn to me and be saved,[8]
all the ends of the Earth!
For I am God, and there is no other.
By myself I have sworn,
from my mouth has gone forth in righteousness
a word that shall not return:
'To me every knee shall bow,
every tongue shall swear.'
"Only in the Lord, it shall be said of me,
are righteousness and strength;
to him shall come and be ashamed,
all who were incensed against him.
In the Lord all the offspring of Israel
shall triumph and glory." . . .
Listen to me, O coastlands,
and hearken, you peoples from afar.
The Lord called me[9] from the womb,
from the body of my mother he named my
    name.
He made my mouth like a sharp sword,
in the shadow of his hand he hid me;
he made me a polished arrow,
in his quiver he hid me away.

And he said to me, "You are my servant,
Israel, in whom I will be glorified."
But I said, "I have labored in vain,
I have spent my strength for nothing and
    vanity;
yet surely my right is with the Lord,
and my recompense with my God."
And now the Lord says, . . .
"It is too light a thing that you should be my
    servant
to raise up the tribes of Jacob
and to restore the preserved of Israel;
I will give you as a light to the nations,
that my salvation may reach to the end of the
    Earth."
Thus says the Lord,
the Redeemer of Israel and his Holy One,
to one deeply despised, abhorred by the nations,
the servant of rulers:
"Kings shall see and arise;
princes, and they shall prostrate themselves;
because of the Lord, who is faithful,
the Holy One of Israel, who has chosen you."

---

[8]Most scholars conclude that the terms *save* and *salvation* used by Second Isaiah do not imply a promise of Paradise after death but only earthly peace and prosperity.

[9]The Children of Israel.

❖ Chapter 4 ❖

The Secular Made Sacred

Developing the Humanistic Traditions of China and Hellas: 600–200 B.C.E.

THE CHINESE AND THE GREEKS had deities and spirits for every imaginable function and a wide range of religious taboos and rituals. But while contemporaries in India and Southwest Asia were raising religious speculation to high levels of abstract thought, religion for the Chinese and the Greeks remained, for the most part, a practical affair. One sacrificed to the gods and spirits in order to assure their benevolence. Religion was largely a form of magical insurance and not a relationship with Ultimate Reality.

At the same time, the social and psychic crises of the Age of Iron were as real in China and Greece as elsewhere. In fashioning responses to the questions occasioned by the dislocation of traditional ways of life, both the Chinese and the Greeks looked more toward this world than the Beyond and created cultures that were essentially *humanistic* (human centered) and *secular* (of this world) in the sense that they focused on humanity's position within an observable universe of finite space and time. Social and political philosophy rather than theology engaged the intellectual energies of the Chinese and the Greeks as they faced the challenges of the Iron Age.

In China various philosophers offered insights into how humans should behave in regard to their families, the state, and nature. These philosophers also struggled with the issue of personal excellence. They first inquired whether such a goal was achievable or even desirable, and many ultimately concluded that the cult of individuality that was inherent in such a quest for personal perfection threatened the harmony of the family, the state, and even the natural order. Therefore, it was to be avoided. For those who accepted, however tentatively and reluctantly, even a modified search for personal excellence, several questions remained: How is it achieved, and what purposes does it serve? Does cultivation of virtue have only personal value, or is it subordinate to a higher social purpose?

Many of the same concerns preoccupied Greek thinkers. Two issues particularly dominated Greek social thought: (1) How does the individual achieve excellence (*arete*), a quality they assumed to be the natural goal of all human striving? (2) How does the individual function as an effective citizen within the city-state (*polis*)? Most Greek social philosophers assumed that cultivation of personal talents and good citizenship were complementary pursuits. Accomplished individuals were the best citizens.

Additionally, a small but highly influential group of Greeks turned their attention to an objective study of the physical environment, thereby becoming the West's first natural scientists. Like its social philosophers, Greece's scientists attempted to explain the workings of the physical universe in response to human needs, the most basic of which was to provide knowledge that would allow people to control their lives and environment.

The Chinese and the Greeks fashioned cultures in which humanity and the natural world were the measure of what was most important to them, and in this sense they made the secular sacred.

▼▼▼

China: Thought in Search of Harmony

The collapse of the Western Zhou monarchy (ca. 1050–771 B.C.E.) and its replacement by the weaker Eastern Zhou (770–256 B.C.E.) signaled the end of all effective royal power in China (limited though it had been) and ushered in a 500-year period when regional states held center stage. Zhou kings continued to perform their traditional religious roles and received tokens of nominal obedience from the great lords. True power, however, lay in the hands of the regional lords, who developed bureaucratic governments and strong standing armies. With each local prince essentially a sovereign, military and diplomatic maneuvering among their states became a constant fact of life.

As disruptive as all of this was at times, it also proved to be a stimulus to intellectual activity. The demands of statecraft at the regional level and the occasional social dislocation that resulted from the conflicts among these states stimulated the development of political theory and social philosophy.

This was especially true from the fifth century B.C.E. onward, as wars became more frequent and bitter. Chinese historians traditionally catalogue the period from 403 to 221 B.C.E. as the *Age of Warring States*. Innovations such as cavalry, cheap, mass-produced iron weapons, and the crossbow broke the battlefield superiority of the chariot-driving aristocracy. Armies of conscripted foot and horse soldiers became larger and more deadly. Concomitantly, intellectuals sought to keep pace with this changing world.

Between 260 and 221 B.C.E., *Qin*, the most aggressive and best organized of the warring states, conquered all rival powers in China and established a new ruling family, the short-lived but pivotal Qin Dynasty (221–206 B.C.E.). The triumph of the lord of Qin, the self-styled *Qin Shi Huangdi* (the First Emperor of Qin), not only inaugurated China's first age of empire but also brought with it the momentary victory of a political philosophy known as *Legalism*. In conforming to the principles of Legalism, the Qin regime was ruthless and brutal in its drive for complete centralization of authority. Undone by the harshness of its laws and policies, the Qin Dynasty collapsed in early 206. Within four years, however, a commoner general, Liu Bang, reformulated the empire by establishing the successful and long-lived *Han Dynasty* (202 B.C.E.–220 C.E.).

Although the extreme measures of the Qin regime discredited Legalism as a philosophy, Legalist-inspired organizational structures and administrative procedures served as the framework of the highly centralized Han Empire. By the late second century B.C.E., however, the Han Dynasty adopted as its official ideology the gentler and more humane philosophy of *Confucianism*, which had also taken shape in the disturbing period of Eastern Zhou.

Han imperial policies and institutions were, therefore, the products of a Confucian-Legalist synthesis, but these were not the only modes of thought to play a prominent role then and ever after in China. *Daoism*, an antirational, quite antipolitical, and somewhat antisocial philosophy, had also emerged from the confusion of Eastern Zhou and survived the hostility of Qin censors to become an integral part of Chinese thought and aesthetics.

Although they offered different answers to the ills of their day and presented some striking differences of perspective, all three schools of thought claimed to offer the correct *Way*, or path, to harmony. Daoism emphasized harmony with nature; Confucianism emphasized the harmony of human relationships; and Legalism emphasized the harmony of a well-regulated state. A fourth school of thought that emerged during this era of profound intellectual fertility also emphasized harmony, but harmony on a grander scale. Philosophers who developed the dualistic theory of *Yin* and *Yang* encapsulated the entire universe in their explanation of the intrinsic harmony that infuses everything that exists. Integral to their philosophy was the belief that by understanding the natural harmony of the universe that results from the balance of Yin and Yang, one could set aright anything that had fallen into a state of disharmony — be it some element of nature, human relations, the social-political order, or even the human body (see Multiple Voices II).

Daoism: The Way That Is and Is Not
▼▼▼

19 ▼ Laozi,
THE CLASSIC OF THE WAY AND VIRTUE

Few if any philosophies are as enigmatic as *Daoism* — the teachings of the Way (*Dao*). The opening lines of this school's greatest masterpiece, *The Classic of the Way and Virtue* (*Dao Dejing*), which is ascribed to the legendary *Laozi*, immediately confront the reader with Daoism's essential paradox: "The Dao that can be trodden is not the enduring and unchanging Dao. The name that can be named is not the enduring and unchanging name." Here is a philosophy that purports to teach *the* Way of truth but simultaneously claims that the True Way transcends human understanding. Encapsulated within a little book of some 5,000 words is a philosophy that defies definition, spurns reason, and rejects words as inadequate.

The Dao is limitless, and its origins are infinite. Somewhat like the Way that it purports to teach and not teach, Daoism has many manifestations and numerous origins. No one knows when or where it originated, but its roots probably lie in the animistic religions of prehistoric China. Daoism's earliest sages are equally shadowy. According to tradition, Laozi supposedly was born around 604 B.C.E. and died about 517, making him an older contemporary of Confucius (source 20). According to one popular story, when Confucius visited him, Laozi instructed the younger man to rid himself of his arrogant airs and then bade him farewell. As another story has it, the aged Laozi decided to leave the state in which he lived because he foresaw its imminent decay. At the frontier he was delayed by a border official, who implored him not to depart without first leaving behind his wisdom. In response, Laozi dashed off the *Dao Dejing* and left, never to be heard from again (although according to one story that sprang up in Daoist circles in the fourth century C.E., Laozi went to India, where he became the Buddha). The fact that Laozi means "Old Master" suggests to many that this sage was more a composite figure of legend and imagination than a historic individual of flesh and blood. Indeed, many scholars conclude that the bulk of the language, ideas, and allusions contained within this classic indicate an intellectual environment closer to 300 than to 500 B.C.E.

Whatever its date and circumstances of composition, the *Dao Dejing* is one of the most profound and beautiful works ever written in Chinese and one of the most popular. Daoism, especially as articulated in this little book, has exercised an incalculable influence on Chinese life, thought, and art over the centuries.

As you study the following selections, pay particular attention to the Daoist notion of *Actionless Activity*. Known in Chinese as *wuwei* and also translated as "Effortlessness," "Nonaction," and "Nonstriving," this idea pervades all Daoist thought and comes closest to being Daoism's universal principle and driving force, if such is possible.

QUESTIONS FOR ANALYSIS

1. How does Laozi define the Way? How permanent is it? What are its limitations?
2. Does the Way acknowledge right and wrong?
3. How does the sage ruler who is in harmony with the Way govern?
4. What are the *Dao Dejing*'s major criticisms of Confucianism and Legalism? Before addressing this issue, study sources 20 and 21.
5. When Buddhism initially entered China, many Chinese thought it to be a variation of Daoism. How and why was this perception possible? In what ways was this a misperception?

THE WAY

The Dao that can be trodden is not the enduring and unchanging Dao. The name that can be named is not the enduring and unchanging name.

▾ ▾ ▾

The Dao produces all things and nourishes them; it produces them and does not claim them as its own; it does all, and yet does not boast of it; it presides over all, and yet does not control them. This is what is called "The mysterious quality" of the Dao.

▾ ▾ ▾

When the Great Dao ceased to be observed, benevolence and righteousness came into vogue. Then appeared wisdom and shrewdness, and there ensued great hypocrisy.[1]

▾ ▾ ▾

Man takes his law from the Earth; the Earth takes its law from Heaven; Heaven takes its law from the Dao. The law of the Dao is its being what it is.

▾ ▾ ▾

All-pervading is the Great Dao! It may be found on the left hand and on the right.

All things depend on it for their production, which it gives to them, not one refusing obedience to it. When its work is accomplished, it does not claim the name of having done it. It clothes all things as with a garment, and makes no assumption of being their lord; — it may be named in the smallest things; . . . it may be named in the greatest things.

▾ ▾ ▾

He who has in himself abundantly the attributes of the Dao is like an infant.

▾ ▾ ▾

The Dao in its regular course does nothing, for the sake of doing it, and so there is nothing which it does not do.[2]

THE WISE PERSON

When we renounce learning we have no troubles.[3]

▾ ▾ ▾

If we could renounce our sageness and discard our wisdom, it would be better for the people a hundredfold. If we could renounce our benevo-

---

[1] This is a criticism of the supposed hypocrisy of Confucians who claim to know and practice virtue (see source 20).

[2] The principle of *wuwei*, or "achieving through non-effort."
[3] According to the Confucians, careful study and emulation of the virtues of the past is the primary avenue to harmony.

lence and discard our righteousness, the people would again become filial and kindly.[4] If we could renounce our artful contrivances and discard our scheming for gain, there would be no thieves nor robbers.

▼ ▼ ▼

The sage manages affairs without doing anything, and conveys his instructions without the use of speech.

▼ ▼ ▼

Therefore the sage holds in his embrace the one thing of humility, and manifests it to all the world. He is free from self-display, and therefore he shines; from self-assertion, and therefore he is distinguished; from self-boasting, and therefore his merit is acknowledged; from self-complacency, and therefore he acquires superiority. It is because he is thus free from striving that therefore no one in the world is able to strive with him.

▼ ▼ ▼

When gold and jade fill the hall, their possessor cannot keep them safe. When wealth and honors lead to arrogance, this brings its evil on itself. When the work is done, and one's name is becoming distinguished, to withdraw into obscurity is the way of Heaven.

IDEAL GOVERNMENT

A state may be ruled by measures of correction;[5] weapons of war may be used with crafty dexterity; but the kingdom is made one's own only by freedom from action and purpose.

How do I know that it is so? By these facts: — In the kingdom the multiplication of prohibitive enactments increases the poverty of the people; the more implements to add to their profit that the people have, the greater disorder is there in the state and clan; the more acts of crafty dexterity that men possess, the more do strange contrivances appear; the more display there is of legislation, the more thieves and robbers there are.

Therefore a sage has said, "I will do nothing, and the people will be transformed of themselves; I will be fond of keeping still, and the people will of themselves become correct. I will take no trouble about it, and the people will of themselves become rich; I will manifest no ambition, and the people will of themselves attain to the primitive simplicity."

▼ ▼ ▼

Not to value and employ men of superior ability is the way to keep the people from rivalry among themselves;[6] not to prize articles which are difficult to procure[7] is the way to keep them from becoming thieves; not to show them what is likely to excite their desires is the way to keep their minds from disorder.

Therefore the sage, in the exercise of his government, empties their minds, fills their bellies, weakens their wills, and strengthens their bones.

He constantly tries to keep them without knowledge and without desire, and where there are those who have knowledge, to keep them from presuming to act on it. When there is this abstinence from action, good order is universal.

---

[4]These first two sentences reject the Confucian values of wisdom (saintliness), knowledge, human-heartedness, and righteousness, all of which, according to the Confucians, will result in *filial piety* (proper devotion and service to parents, ancestors, and superiors). See the introduction to source 20 for further discussion of the history of this Confucian principle.

[5]See source 21.
[6]Confucian political philosophy centered on the wise and learned superior man, also known as the gentleman (see source 20).
[7]Legalist policy favored trade.

Confucianism: The Moral Way of the Past
▼▼▼
20 ▼ *Confucius, THE ANALECTS*

The Chinese refer to the period of Eastern Zhou as the *Age of a Hundred Schools.* Of the many schools of thought that flourished then, none has had a more substantial impact on Chinese culture than *Confucianism*, a philosophy ascribed to a teacher whom history identifies as *Confucius*.

Tradition records that this sage was born in 552 or 551 B.C.E. into the aristocratic but impoverished Kong family, which traced its lineage to the Shang Dynasty. Young Kong Qiu, as he was named, became an authority on court rituals and statecraft and rose to high office in his native state of Lu in northeastern China. In 497 he resigned his position when proper rituals were not performed during a state sacrifice to Heaven. Already an established teacher, he embarked on a fourteen-year period of wandering with his students. Traveling to the courts of various small states, he attempted without success to convince their princes to employ his philosophy of life and government — his *Moral Way* — which he believed would return Chinese society to a state of harmony and justice. Finally in 484, at age sixty-seven, Master Kong was recalled to Lu but not offered an office. He spent his remaining years teaching and died at age seventy-two in 479, convinced that he had failed to halt what he believed to be the moral corruption and political chaos of his day.

If Confucius died thinking himself a failure, he was wrong. His students achieved high positions of responsibility and became teachers themselves of the Moral Way. Through their students and the generations of students that followed, Confucius's ideas were widely disseminated. In the Age of Tang (618–907 C.E.), Confucianism became virtually synonymous with Chinese culture and played an almost equally important role in shaping Korean and Japanese thought. Because of Master Kong's profound impact on Chinese civilization, posterity accorded him the elegant title *Kongfuzi* (Reverend Master Kong), which seventeenth-century Western scholars Latinized into Confucius.

Recently some historians have challenged this story. Several claim that the historical Confucius was not a scholar-official but a conservative warrior-noble who held very few of the values that tradition later ascribed to him. Several others even question the historicity of Confucius, concluding that the man was a fictional construct of a much later age. Notwithstanding these challenges, most historians accept the overall outlines of the traditional story, even though they generally agree that later generations ascribed to Confucius some ideas and emphases that were never his.

Although later disciples of Confucian thought, such as *Mengzi*, or *Mencius* (ca. 370–300 B.C.E.), carried the ideas of the Master to points that he never imagined, it seems possible to identify the principles that served as bedrocks of Confucius's thinking. First, we must realize that Master Kong was a conservative. He sought to transform Chinese society and government by returning it to the values and practices of the era of the duke of Zhou, a twelfth-century B.C.E. legislator and consolidator of the early Zhou Dynasty who, Kong was convinced, presided over a Golden Age of harmony and prosperity. In order to achieve this end, Kong Qiu emphasized several virtues. Chief among them were *xiao, li*, and *ren*. *Xiao* is best translated as "filial piety" (devotion and service to parents, ancestors, and superiors). *Li* is best understood as both "proper behavior" and "performance of the rituals." *Ren* is the richest of the terms and is variously translated as "human-heartedness," "benevolence toward humanity," "nobility of heart," and "humaneness."

As noted, Confucius revered the ways of the past. Consequently, he urged his students to master ancient traditions and texts, such as the *Book of Documents* and the *Book of Songs* (sources 5 and 6). But his philosophy went well beyond simple admiration and emulation. He took age-old Chinese values, such as filial piety and proper performance of ancient rituals, and turned them into moral principles. His genius was that he insisted human beings are moral creatures with social obligations and are, by that fact, obliged to comport themselves humanely and with integrity. He also taught that humans, or at least males, are capable of perfecting themselves as upright individuals. His ideal moral agent, so far as we can infer from the evidence, was the superior man (or gentleman), who cultivated virtue through study and imitation of the Moral Way of the past. This person by knowing the good would choose the good. What is more, he would act as an example to others, who would irresistibly follow the path he set along the Way of Goodness.

Although a traditionalist, Confucius was an innovator in that he was one of the first Chinese educators to offer instruction to any intelligent young man who sought the Moral Way, regardless of his social or economic status. Even so, Confucius's pupils were few. Tradition records that they numbered seventy-two, but we know the names of only about thirty-five.

As is true of so many great teachers whose words and example have placed a permanent stamp on a civilization, Confucius was not a productive writer. As far as we know, nothing he wrote or edited survives. Early Confucian disciples, however, managed to transmit to posterity a number of sayings ascribed to Master Kong and his immediate pupils. In time they were gathered into a book known as the *Lunyu* (*Ethical Dialogues*), which the modern West knows as the *Analects*, a term that means "Literary Gleanings." We do not know which of these maxims Confucius actually uttered, but collectively they provide us with the best available view of Master Kong's teachings as remembered by those who knew and followed him.

To assist your study, we have grouped our selections by general topic but have retained the traditional numbering of the maxims. Ancient editors arranged these Confucian aphorisms into twenty chapters of unequal length. Thus 16.8 is saying 8 in Chapter 16. At the same time, be aware that there is a fair amount of thematic overlap. Several of the selections under the heading "The Well-Lived Life," for example, also deal with *ren*.

QUESTIONS FOR ANALYSIS

1. How and why does filial piety serve as a bedrock of Confucius's philosophical system?
2. Describe the superior man, or gentleman, as envisioned by Confucius. What are his qualities, and how does he employ them?
3. What is Confucius's concept of good government and the ideal state?
4. Define what *ren* meant to Confucius. Was it absolute? Was it all-encompassing? In other words, did it have limitations? In what ways did it animate other virtues?
5. "For Confucius, propriety (*li*) meant proper performance of all rituals, which in turn meant much more than good manners, proper etiquette, or correct procedures. Like *ren* and filial piety, it was an interior quality that set the superior man apart from all other humans." Comment on this anonymous statement. Is this a correct analysis of Confucius's philosophy? Be specific in your answer.

FILIAL PIETY

1.2 Master You[1] said: "Those who are filial to their parents and obedient to their elder brothers but are apt to defy their superiors are rare indeed; those who are not apt to defy their superiors, but are apt to stir up a rebellion simply do not exist. The gentleman applies himself to the roots. Only when the roots are well planted will the Way grow. Filial piety and brotherly obedience[2] are perhaps the roots of humanity,[3] are they not?"

1.9 Master Zeng[4] said: "Show genuine grief at a parent's death,[5] keep offering sacrifices to them as time goes by, and the people's moral character shall be reinforced."

2.5 When Meng Yi-zi[6] asked about filial piety, the Master said: "Do not act contrary."[7]

When Fan Chi[8] was driving, the Master said to him: "When Meng-sun[9] asked

me about filial piety, I replied: 'Do not act contrary.'"

Fan Chi said: "What do you mean?"

The Master said: "When your parents are alive, serve them in accordance with the rituals; when they die, bury them in accordance with the rituals; offer sacrifices to them in accordance with the rituals."

4.18 The Master said: "In serving your parents, be gentle in remonstration. Seeing that they are not inclined to comply, remain reverent, and do not disobey them. Though weary, do not feel resentful."

THE GENTLEMAN

1.8 The Master said: "If a gentleman is not grave, he will not be awe-inspiring. If he learns, he will not be benighted.[10] He keeps whole-hearted sincerity and truthfulness as his major principles and does

---

[1]You Ruo, one of Confucius's chief disciples.
[2]The virtue of *ti*, whereby a younger brother obeys an older brother.
[3]*Ren.*
[4]Zeng Shen, one of Confucius's most important pupils. Mengzi (Mencius), the greatest Confucian after Kongfuzi himself, studied in the school begun by Zeng Shen.

[5]Here he addresses a ruler.
[6]A minister of Lu.
[7]Contrary to the ancient rituals.
[8]Also known as Fan Xu, he was a major disciple of the Master.
[9]Meng Yi-zi, who came from the aristocratic family of Meng-sun.
[10]He will not be ignorant of the rituals.

not befriend those beneath him. When he makes a mistake, he is not afraid to correct it."

4.10 The Master said: "The gentleman, in his attitude toward all under Heaven,[11] neither favors anyone nor disfavors anyone. He keeps close to whoever is righteous."

4.16 The Master said: "The gentleman is conversant with righteousness; the small man is conversant with profit."

12.16 The Master said: "The gentleman helps others achieve their good ends; he does not help them achieve their evil ends. The small man does the opposite."

15.18 The Master said: "A gentleman considers righteousness his major principle: he practices it in accordance with the rituals, utters it in modest terms, and fulfils it with truthfulness. A gentleman indeed!"

15.34 The Master said: "The gentleman may not be recognized for small skills but can undertake great responsibilities; the small man cannot undertake great responsibilities but may be recognized in small skills."

16.8 Master Kong said: "The gentleman has three fears: he fears the decree of Heaven; he fears great men;[12] he fears the sage men's words. The small man, not knowing the decree of Heaven, does not fear it; he scorns great men and mocks the sage men's words."

GOOD GOVERNMENT

1.5 The Master said: "In governing a thousand-chariot state,[13] be reverent to your duties and truthful; economize expenditure and love men; employ the people at proper times."[14]

2.1 The Master said: "He who conducts government with virtue may be likened to the North Star, which, seated in its place, is surrounded by multitudes of other stars."

2.3 The Master said: "If you govern them with decrees and regulate them with punishments, the people will evade them but will have no sense of shame. If you govern them with virtue and regulate them with the rituals, they will have a sense of shame and flock to you."

2.19 Duke Ai[15] asked: "What must we do to make the people obedient?"

Master Kong replied: "Promote the upright, place them above the crooked, and the people shall be obedient. Promote the crooked, place them above the upright, and the people shall be disobedient."

2.20 Ji Kang-zi[16] asked: "How do you make the people reverent, loyal, and mutually encouraging?"

The Master said: "If you preside over them with dignity, they will be reverent; if you are filial and loving,[17] they will be loyal; if you promote the good and instruct the incapable, they will be mutually encouraging."

REN

3.3 The Master said: "If a man is not humane, what can he do with the rituals? If a man is not humane, what can he do with music?"[18]

---

[11]"All under Heaven" are all the Chinese.
[12]He is in awe of rulers.
[13]The military power of a state was computed by the number of chariots it could muster. A thousand-chariot state was fairly small.
[14]Employ their conscripted labor on public works during the slack times of the agricultural year.
[15]The prince of Lu (r. 494–466 B.C.E.), whom several of Confucius's disciples served.
[16]Prime minister to Duke Ai of Lu.
[17]Filial toward one's parents and loving to one's children.

[18]The rituals were an elaborate, detailed code of proper etiquette governing all aspects of life, including sacrificial rites, state affairs, social relations, and day-to-day family matters. Specific rituals performed by an individual differed according to sex, age, social status, and context. Their purpose was to create harmony within a society where everyone knew his or her place and role and acted accordingly. Music, which represents the principle of harmony, accompanied court and family rituals. According to tradition, Confucius had a particular love of music and recommended that his followers become adept at it.

4.1 The Master said: "To live among humane men is beautiful. Not to reside among humane men — how can one be considered wise?"

4.4 The Master said: "If you bend your mind on humanity, you are free from evil."

13.19 When Fan Chi asked about humanity, the Master said: "Conduct yourself with respect; perform your duties with reverence; treat others with wholehearted sincerity. Even if you should journey to the Yis and Dis,[19] you cannot abandon these."

15.24 Zi-gong[20] asked: "Is there one single word that one can practice throughout one's life?"

The Master said: "It is perhaps 'like-hearted considerateness.' 'What you do not wish for yourself, do not impose on others.'"

17.23 Zi-gong said: "Does the gentleman also have people he loathes?"

The Master said: "Yes, I do. I loathe those who babble about other people's vices; I loathe those who, being in the lower stream, slander their superiors; I loathe those who are courageous but have no regard for the rituals; I loathe those who are resolute and daring but stubborn."

Then he said: "Ci,[21] are there also people you loathe?"

"I loathe those who plagiarize and consider themselves wise; I loathe those who are impertinent and consider themselves courageous; I loathe those who divulge other people's unseemly secrets and consider themselves straightforward."

THE RITUALS[22]

6.27 The Master said: "A gentleman who is extensively learned in culture and restrains himself with the rituals is not likely to betray."

12.1 When Yan Yuan[23] asked about humanity, the Master said: "'To restrain oneself and return to the rituals constitutes humanity.' One day one can restrain oneself and return to the rituals, all under Heaven will turn to humanity. The practice of humanity rests with oneself. Does it rest with anyone else?"

Yan Yuan said: "May I ask the details?"

The Master said: "That which does not conform to the rituals — do not look at it; that which does not conform to the rituals — do not listen to it; that which does not conform to the rituals — do not say it; that which does not conform to the rituals — do not do it."

Yan Yuan said: "Slow-witted as I am, I beg to practice these remarks."

17.10 The Master said: "'The rituals, the rituals,' they say. Do they merely refer to jade and silk? 'Music, music,' they say. Do they merely refer to bells and drums?"[24]

THE WELL-LIVED LIFE

6.22 When Fan Chi asked about wisdom, the Master said: "To apply oneself to the duties of man and, while revering the spirits and gods, to keep away from them[25] — this may be called wisdom."

---

[19]*Yi* is an ancient Chinese term for the non-Chinese, or barbarian, tribes to the east, especially Korea; *Di* is a similar term for the tribes to the north. "The Yis and Dis" meant, therefore, all the barbarian tribes on the borders of China.
[20]Also known as Duan-mu Ci (see note 21), he was one of Master Kong's most faithful disciples. He later became prime minister of Lu and a famous diplomat.
[21]Zi-gong. See note 20.
[22]See note 18.

[23]Better known as Yan Hui (521?–481 B.C.E.), he had the reputation of being the most humane of Master Kong's students.
[24]The external signs of the rituals and the instruments used to perform music are differentiated from the moral purposes behind them. See note 18.
[25]The spirits of the ancestors can influence a family's (or state's) fortunes for good or evil. The wise person employs rituals to keep the spirits happy and at a distance. In this aphorism Confucius also shows his all-consuming concern with human relations in the here and now.

When he asked about humanity, the Master said: "A man of humanity places hard work before reward. This may be called humanity."

7.3 The Master said: "Virtue uncultivated, learning undiscussed, the inability to move toward righteousness after hearing it, and the inability to correct my imperfections — these are my anxieties."

7.6 The Master said: "Aspire after the Way; adhere to virtue; rely on humanity; ramble among the arts."[26]

7.33 The Master said: "As for sageness and humanity, how dare I claim them? But to learn it[27] insatiably and instruct others indefatigably — that much may be said of me, that is all."

Gong-xi Hua[28] said: "This is exactly what we disciples are unable to learn."

9.25 The Master said: "Keep wholehearted sincerity and truthfulness as your major principles. Do not befriend those beneath you. When you make a mistake, do not be afraid to correct it."

---

[26]The Six Arts in the Era of Western Zhou were mastery of rituals, music, archery, charioteering, language, and arithmetic.

[27]The Way.
[28]This student of the Master became a respected diplomat.

Legalism: The Way of the State
▼▼▼
21 ▼ *Qin Shi Huangdi, QIN PENAL LAWS*

Daoism offered no active political program, whereas Confucius and his disciples preached a doctrine of benevolent reform based on virtuous imitation of the past. A third school of thought that emerged in the chaos of the late Zhou Era (and the several decades that followed) was *Legalism*, which rejected Daoism's Way of Nature and Confucianism's Moral Way. On their part, Legalist writers emphasized *law* as government's formulative force and advocated a radical restructuring of society in ways that were totally rational and up-to-date.

Legalism reached its apogee in the late third century B.C.E. in the policies of the First Emperor of China, *Qin Shi Huangdi* (r. 221–210 B.C.E.). As King Zheng of Qin (r. 247–221 B.C.E.), he completed the conquest of "All under Heaven" in 221 B.C.E. and forged the First Chinese Empire — a unified entity upon which he imposed an empire-wide uniformity of law administered by a bureaucracy that was answerable to a central authority. Envisioning an empire that would last for centuries, he grandly styled himself Qin Shi Huangdi — the First Emperor of Qin (from which the term *China* is derived). The Qin Dynasty collapsed in 206 B.C.E., four years after Qin Shi Huangdi's death, in large part because of rebellions against Qin's imperial structure and policies. In 202 B.C.E. China was united by a new imperial dynasty, the Han, which adopted many of the policies of Legalist Qin but softened them by employing Confucian ideology. Thus, a Legalist-Confucian synthesis began to take shape — a synthesis that served Chinese emperors and their officials very well for more than 2,000 years.

In 1975, 625 bamboo strips were uncovered in central China. The pages of a book, they contain a variety of Qin laws. Those excerpted here deal with offenses that merited penal punishment and regulations regarding the treatment of convicts. Combined, they illustrate Legalism in practice.

Five degrees of penal servitude and punishment are listed here. The least oner-
ous was the status of "debt worker," a person who was incarcerated in order to
pay off a debt, including debts to the state. In rising order of severity, there followed "convict servant," "convict worker," "intact convict laborer," and "mutilated convict laborer." An intact convict laborer received no physical marks or
wounds on his or her body. Mutilation varied from tattooing to cutting off one or
more parts of the body.

QUESTIONS FOR ANALYSIS

1. The great theorist of Legalism, Han Feizi (d. 233 B.C.E.), wrote, "To warn the
   officials and overawe the people, to rebuke obscenity and danger, and to
   forbid falsehood and deceit, nothing can match penalty." How, if at all, do
   these regulations conform to that principle? Please be specific.
2. Going beyond your answer to question 1, describe the other values and
   principles of the Qin regime as reflected in these regulations.
3. Compose a Confucian or Daoist critique of these regulations.

SOME OFFENSES LEADING
TO PENAL SERVITUDE

Criminals who owe fines . . . and others who
have debts to the government are told to pay immediately. Those unable to pay must work off
their debt from the day the order is given. Each
day they work off eight cash,[1] or six cash if they
are fed by the government.

When five men jointly rob something worth
one cash or more, they should have their left foot
amputated, be tattooed, and made convict laborers. If fewer than five men were involved but what
they robbed was worth more than 660 cash, they
should be tattooed, their noses cut off, and made
convict laborers. When the value falls between
220 and 660 cash, they should be tattooed and
made convict laborers. Under 220 cash, they are
banished.

Suppose a slave gets his master's female slave
to steal the master's ox, then they sell it, take the
money, and flee the country, only to be caught at

the border. How should they each be sentenced?
They should be made convict laborers and tattooed. [At the end of their term] they should be
returned to their master.

Suppose A stole an ox when he was only 1.4
meters tall, but after being in detention for a
year, he was measured at 1.57 meters [i.e. adult
height]. How is A to be sentenced? He should
be left intact and made a convict laborer. . . .

Anyone who kills a child without authoriza-
tion is to be made a convict laborer. This does
not apply to killing a deformed or abnormal
newborn. Suppose a child is born whole and normal, and a person kills it merely because he or
she already has too many children. What is the
sentence? It counts as killing a child.

Suppose someone arresting a person charged
with a crime punishable with a fine stabs him on
purpose with a sword or sharp weapon. What is
the sentence? If he killed him, he is left intact
and made a convict laborer. If he wounded him,

---

[1]Known to the Chinese as *wen*, they were small coins of low
value. Made of copper, iron, or brass, they had square holes
in the center so that they could be strung together, often in
hundreds, to create higher denominations.

he has his beard shaved off and is made a convict servant. . . .

When commoners need to pay fines, commutation fees,[2] or debts, they may have their male or female slave, horse, or ox work it off for them.

Prisoners of war are made convict servants.

TREATMENT OF CONVICTS

Male convict servants and convict laborers who are not 1.5 meters and female convict servants and convict laborers who are not 1.43 meters are classed as undersized. When convicts reach 1.2 meters they are all put to work.

Convict laborers are to wear red clothes and red head cloths. They are to be manacled and fettered. They are not to be supervised by capable convict laborers, but only by those assigned the task. Convict laborers sent out to work are not to enter the market and must stay outside the outer gate of buildings. If they have to go past a market, they should make a detour, not pass through it.

When working for the government, male convict servants are given two bushels of grain a month, female convict servants one and a half. Those not engaged in work are not given anything. When working, undersized convict laborers and convict servants are given one and a half bushels of grain a month; those still too young to work get one bushel. Working undersized female convict servants and convict laborers get one bushel and two and a half pecks a month; those still too young to work get one bushel. Infants, whether in the care of their mother or not, get a half bushel a month. Male convict servants doing agricultural work get two and a half bushels from the second to the ninth month, when rations stop.

Overseers who increase the rations for convict laborers performing easy tasks will be judged according to the rules on infringing the ordinances.

Male convict servants without wives and all male convict laborers get money to cover their clothing: 110 cash in winter and 55 in summer; undersized ones get 77 in winter and 44 in summer. Women convict laborers get 55 cash in winter and 44 in summer; undersized ones get 44 in winter and 33 in summer. Women convict servants, if old or undersized and thus unable to provide their own clothes, are clothed like the women convict laborers.

Officials need not petition to use convict laborers to enlarge or repair government buildings and storehouses.[3]

When convict laborers break pottery vessels or iron or wooden tools or break the rims of cart wheels, they should be beaten ten strokes for each cash of value, up to twenty cash, and the object is to be written off. An official who does not immediately beat them is to be charged half the value.

A commoner not guilty of any crime who has a mother or sister serving as a convict servant may if he wishes be assigned to the frontier[4] for five years without pay to free her.

In exchange for two degrees of aristocratic rank a person may free a father or mother who has been made a convict servant.

If a convict servant lets a convict laborer escape, he will be made an intact convict laborer himself and his wife and children outside will be confiscated.

Debt workers may return home for ten days when it is time to plow or weed.

---

[2]The penalties for some offenses could be commuted to a cash payment in place of penal servitude.

[3]Male convict laborers were generally put to work on public construction projects. Therefore, no special permission was needed to engage them in this work.

[4]Serve there as a soldier.

▼▼▼

Hellenic Civilization: An Inquiry into Life

Early in the sixth century B.C.E., a small group of Greek intellectuals in Ionia began to challenge age-old mythic ways of explaining the workings of the universe by looking at the world as an objective phenomenon that could be studied in a systematic manner. These thinkers, who sought to discover the physical underpinnings of the universe, are acknowledged as ancient Hellas's first philosophers and scientists and the people who established the Greek intellectual tradition of rational inquiry into all aspects of the physical and moral world.

As important as reason was in the formation of Greek thought, it never threatened to displace myth, mysticism, and religion. We would very much misunderstand ancient Greek civilization by concluding that rational inquiry dominated every element of Greek life from the sixth century onward. Indeed, the nonrational, or suprarational, permeated Greek society. This should not be surprising, nor should it cause us to undervalue the achievements of Greek rationalists, whose modes of analysis became a hallmark of Greek civilization.

The period from about 750 B.C.E. down to the death of Alexander the Great in 323 B.C.E. is known as the *Hellenic Age* because, as we have seen, the people we call *Greeks* referred to themselves as *Hellenes* and their land as *Hellas*. (It was the Romans who began the tradition of calling all Hellenes *Greeks*.)

During the Hellenic Age, the Greek World was very much a frontier society along the western periphery of the ancient civilized world. As a result, the Greeks were able to draw from the experiences of their more deeply rooted neighbors while simultaneously enjoying a certain amount of freedom to experiment culturally, especially in the areas of politics, thought, and art. This age was characterized by general Greek independence from foreign domination, political decentralization, intense rivalry among Hellas's many city-states, and a deep-seated ethnocentrism and even contempt for the non-Hellenic World. The two dominating events of the Hellenic Age were the Persian Wars (499–450 B.C.E.) and the Peloponnesian War (431–404 B.C.E.). In the first, Greeks, under the leadership of Athens and Sparta, successfully withstood the threat of Persian domination. In the latter, again under Athenian and Spartan leadership, the whole Greek World was embroiled in a bitter family bloodletting. Despite the wars that dominated so much of the fifth century B.C.E., this hundred-year period is rightly regarded as the classical era of Hellenic civilization — an age when Hellas's intellectuals and artists soared to new heights as they explored the place of humans in a world that they confidently assumed was understandable and human-sized.

Analyzing a Failed War

▼▼▼

22 ▼ *Thucydides,*
HISTORY OF THE PELOPONNESIAN WAR

During the eighth century B.C.E., Homer, the putative author of the *Iliad* and the *Odyssey*, interpreted the past through the medium of poetic myth. By the mid fifth century, a few Hellenic researchers were recapturing and interpreting the past through the more prosaic but accurate medium of history. The word *historia* is Greek and means "knowledge achieved through inquiry." As we have seen, the Israelites and the Persians had already evolved a sense of divinely directed history. However, it was the Greeks who became western Eurasia's first students of worldly events that were divorced from any consideration of divine intervention or control. The particular genius of Greek *historiography* (the writing of history) was that certain thinkers, beginning with *Herodotus* (ca. 484–424 B.C.E.), believed that human events could be reconstructed and made comprehensible through careful research into the human record.

One such student of the human past was *Thucydides* (ca. 460–ca. 400 B.C.E.), widely considered classical Hellas's greatest historian and often also recognized as its premier political scientist. Thucydides was a citizen of Athens in an age when Hellenic civilization was dominated by rivalry among its many different city-states, or *poleis* (the plural of *polis*). During Thucydides' youth and young manhood, Athens was led by *Pericles*, who from 461/460 to his death in 429 B.C.E. was a major force in shaping Athenian democracy.

In 431 B.C.E. Pericles led Athens into the *Peloponnesian War* against the oligarchic polis of *Sparta* and its allies in the Peloponnesian League. The war dragged on for a generation, ending in 404 with a total Spartan victory. In the early stages of the conflict, it had seemed as though there was no way Athens could lose the war, given its command of the sea-lanes and its maritime empire. Events as they unfolded proved the contrary.

In 424/423, when the war was still far from lost, Thucydides commanded a naval squadron that failed to relieve a besieged Athenian infantry force, and for that failure he was forced into exile. An avid student of human affairs, especially politics, Thucydides used his enforced retirement to study the war and write its history. As he noted in the opening lines of his *History*, he had begun writing about the war from its outbreak because he believed it would prove to be the most memorable conflict in all of Hellenic history. In the course of witnessing Athens's errors, declining fortunes, and eventual defeat, he fixed upon a higher purpose: to provide all Hellenes with "an everlasting possession," a careful study of which would enable them to avoid similar errors in the future. Although he lived to see Athens's defeat, death apparently interrupted his work, and he managed to complete his history of the war only down to the year 411. Despite this abrupt ending, the history from beginning to end foreshadows Athens's humiliating defeat — a defeat precipitated by human overreaching and miscalculations.

Throughout his history Thucydides constantly paused to probe the deeper meaning of the events he narrated and to analyze the motives and personalities of the actors in this human drama. One of his most telling moments of reflection is his commentary on Pericles, following this Athenian leader's speech in the summer of 430, when he defended his war policy and strategy before a populace that already was questioning the war and seeking to make peace with the Spartans. Pericles' plan for winning the war, which he thought necessary to protect Athens's way of life and its maritime empire (see note 5 in the source), was for the city's citizens to abandon their country estates and seek the security of the city's walls, trusting in their naval supremacy to wear down the enemy. The immediate result was two summers of Spartan invasion, destruction of the countryside, and a plague in the overcrowded city that killed off large numbers of its inhabitants.

QUESTIONS FOR ANALYSIS

1. According to Thucydides, what qualities made Pericles an exceptional leader?
2. According to Thucydides, what were the failings of those who followed him, and how did those flaws lead to Athens's defeat?
3. Thucydides cannot avoid exhibiting his own political philosophy in this passage. What is it?
4. How does Thucydides address the issues of human agency and responsibility? Does his view of the human's role in shaping events differ from that of Homer's *Odyssey* (source 10)? What conclusions follow from your answers?
5. Compose an essay on this passage by either a Confucian or a Legalist.

By this speech,[1] Pericles attempted to divert the Athenians' anger away from himself and to take their minds off of their current hardships. . . . In fact, their public displeasure toward him did not abate until they had fined him a sum of money. . . . But not long afterward, in the way that the masses tend to act, they again elected him general[2] and committed everything to him, having become less concerned about their private affairs and thinking him the best man for all of the state's needs. As long as he was at the head of the state in time of peace, he governed moderately and kept it safe, and in his time Athens was at the height of its greatness. When the war broke out, he also seems to have correctly gauged the city's power. He survived the war's outbreak by two years and six months, and after he died, his foresight regarding the war's course became better appreciated. For he said that if they waited patiently, paid attention to their navy, made no attempt to extend their empire during the war, and did not expose the city to dangerous enterprises, they would have the upper hand in the struggle. But they did the very opposite. They allowed private ambition and personal interests, in matters that seemed to have nothing whatsoever

---

[1]Thucydides inserted 141 speeches into his *History*. He admitted that they were not verbatim accounts, but he claimed that when they were speeches he had heard, he adhered as closely as possible to the general sense of what was said. Undoubtedly he attended this important public speech.

[2]Most offices in Pericles' Athens were filled by lot, but the city's ten generals (one from each tribe) were elected annu-

ally, the position being too important to trust to luck (or the gods). A general was more than a military commander; he had the authority to call and preside over extraordinary meetings of the general assembly of all citizens, and he could thereby influence public policy. Pericles held the office continuously from 461/460 to his death in 429, except when he was fined and briefly voted out of office in 430.

to do with the war, to lead them to adopt projects that proved injurious to themselves and their allies. These projects, if successful, would only lead to the honor and benefit of private individuals, but when they failed, they proved disastrous for the state so far as the war was concerned. The reason [for Pericles' superior leadership] was that he, by virtue of his high rank, integrity, and incorruptability so far as bribes were concerned, controlled the masses with an independence of spirit, and was not led by them but, rather, led them. He never felt the need to flatter them; he never sought power by improper means. On the contrary, given the strength of his position, he was free to risk their displeasure by contradicting them. . . . And so, what was called a "democracy" was, in fact, government administered by the First Citizen. Whereas, those who came after him, being more on one another's level, and each grasping to gain supremacy, ended up committing even the policies of the state to the whims of the people. As might have been expected in a great and sovereign state, many

blunders were committed, especially the expedition to Sicily.[3] Yet, this was not so much a miscalculation in regard to the people against whom they sent this expedition, as it was the fault of those who did the sending in not afterward voting the necessary supplies for the expeditionary force. Rather, they engaged in private squabbles in their quest to gain leadership of The People. Consequently, they not only paralyzed military operations but also for the first time were embroiled in civil discord at home. Yet, even after they had endured the loss of the greater part of their fleet in Sicily, as well as the loss of other forces, and were simultaneously involved in sedition at home, they still held out for three years against their original enemies,[4] who were now joined by the Sicilians and, moreover, the majority of their [the Athenians'] allies, who were in rebellion,[5] and Cyrus, the king's son, who later joined them, and who supplied the Peloponnesians with money for their fleet.[6] Indeed, they did not succumb until they overthrew and ruined themselves through their private quarrels.

---

[3]In the winter of 416/415, the Athenian assembly voted to send a fleet to conquer Sicily. The expedition, which was resisted primarily by the Sicilian-Greek city of Syracuse (with the assistance of the Peloponnesian League and the Spartan general Gylippus), ended in disaster in the summer of 413 after the Athenians had suffered terrible losses in two years of fighting, and the surviving remnants of the expeditionary force were taken captive and enslaved as quarry workers.
[4]The Spartans and their allies in the Peloponnesian League.
[5]Originally set up as a confederation of Greek maritime cities and islands to counter the Persian menace in the Aegean Sea, the Delian League, which originally kept its common treasury in a sanctuary on the island of Delos, had

metamorphosed into the Athenian Empire by the 450s, with its member states paying tribute to an increasingly oppressive and tyrannical Athens. In the latter years of the war, especially after the disaster in Sicily, a substantial number of these tributary "allied" states revolted.
[6]Following the Athenian disaster in Sicily, various Persian governors in Anatolia began lending open support to the Peloponnesian League, especially by supplying ships. In 407 Prince Cyrus the Younger, son of King Darius II, began giving increasingly generous support to help the Peloponnesian League construct a navy that could rival that of Athens. The result was a decisive victory at Aegospotomi in 405 that led directly to Athens's humiliating surrender.

Bacchic Maenads: Feminine Religious Ecstasy
▼▼▼
23 ▼ *Euripides, THE BACCHAE*

Athens created one of the Hellenic World's most enduring art forms — tragic drama. In the sixth century B.C.E., improvised songs and dance performed at festivals honoring *Dionysus* (also known as *Bacchus*), the god of wine, evolved into formal lyric narratives and dances, and from there became full-fledged dramas. The first known dramatic contest at which a prize was offered took place in Athens around the year 534. By the fifth century, tragic dramas were annually offered in competition during Athens's six-day spring festival dedicated to Dionysus. The competition and production of the plays were supported by public funds, and money was put aside to allow the poorest of Athens's citizens leisure time to attend the festivities and plays.

As Athenian tragic drama evolved, three playwrights emerged as the city's preeminent dramatists and dramatic innovators: *Aeschylus* (ca. 525–456), *Sophocles* (ca. 496–406), and *Euripides* (ca. 480–406). Of the three, Euripides won the fewest first prizes, despite having composed about ninety plays, but more of his tragedies have survived (nineteen, but one is of doubtful authenticity) than those of Aeschylus and Sophocles combined. The reason for his later popularity, which assured the survival of so many of his plays, is that, more than any other Hellenic playwright, Euripides explored the dark side of the human psyche and the underside of Athenian life. Put simply, he was a master psychologist and an outspoken critic of the indignities suffered by those whom Athenian society exploited or overlooked: war victims, slaves, foreigners, and especially women.

Late in life he left Athens, probably because his outspoken opposition to Athenian atrocities in the Peloponnesian War made his native city an unwelcome place for him, and he took up residence in Macedon. Following Euripides' death in 406, his son returned to Athens, bearing with him three plays that his father had written in exile. One of them, the *Bacchae*, was produced for the City Dionysia in 405, where it won first prize — only the fifth first prize that the Athenians accorded the great playwright.

The *Bacchae* is a troubling play. Some interpret it as the aged Euripides' recantation of the rationalism that pervaded his earlier work. Others see it as a final indictment of religion by an unregenerate skeptic. It is neither. The play unfolds as a rationalist's argument for a balanced acceptance of all religious expressions. Its underlying theme is that rejection of one religion in favor of another, no matter how irrational the rejected cult might appear to be, is intellectual arrogance that leads to dangerous imbalance and inevitable disaster. Composed of mind and body, humans need both lofty spirituality and earthy emotionalism.

The story revolves around the return of Dionysus to Thebes, where he was born from a union of Zeus, king of the gods, and a mortal, Semele, the daughter of Cadmus, who was then king of the city. The god has come out of western Asia (where his cult originated), followed by a group of ecstatic female devotees. His purpose is to redeem the reputation of his deceased mother, whose sisters said she lied when claiming Dionysus was the son of Zeus. Because they refused to recognize his divinity, Dionysus drove the sisters and every other woman in Thebes mad with frenzy, whereupon they took to the mountains to perform bacchanal rites in devotion to him. The young king of Thebes, Pentheus, grandson of Cadmus, refuses to accept this new religion. Determined to root out a pernicious rite that has led women to abandon their traditional roles, Pentheus disguises himself as a woman and goes to the mountains to spy on the bacchants. Dionysus blinds the women to Pentheus's identity and convinces them he is a mountain lion. Led by Pentheus's mother, Agave, and her two sisters (the three sisters who had rejected Semele's story of her divine pregnancy), the women tear Pentheus apart and carry his head back to Thebes in triumph. The still-living former king, Cadmus, informs Agave of her murderous error, which has extinguished the male line of his royal house. Dionysus then appears and justifies Pentheus's death. He also announces that the three sisters will be banished from the city because of their blood guilt and that Cadmus and his wife will undergo great trials before eventual redemption. Full price has been paid for the blasphemy of not recognizing Dionysus's godhood.

Our selection comes from the play's midpoint, where a herdsman describes to Pentheus the activities of the bacchants, known as *Maenads* (literally, "mad women"), whom he observed on Mount Cithaeron.

QUESTIONS FOR ANALYSIS

1. Maenads were often accused of indulging in orgiastic rites of sexual license. Where does Euripides stand on the issue?
2. Maenads were accused of uninhibited drunkenness. Where does Euripides stand on the issue?
3. Maenads were accused of violence. Where does Euripides stand on the issue?
4. Why do you think Euripides has the herdsman report miracles performed by the Maenads?
5. It has been argued that bacchanal worship included "rituals of inversion," whereby women participated in acts that inverted, or turned on their head, normal female activities or modes of behavior. Can you find any in this passage?
6. Some scholars argue that the bacchanal rites were a safety valve that allowed women to break out momentarily from the confines of the roles assigned them by their society. Do you see any evidence to support that thesis in this source?
7. Some scholars argue that whatever other purposes the bacchanal rites served, rumors regarding what transpired during them reinforced men's stereotypes of women as out-of-control creatures when restraints were lifted, and helped justify male domination of them. Comment.

MESSENGER: Pentheus, king of Thebes, I come from Cithaeron[1] where the gleaming flakes of snow fall on and on forever —

PENTHEUS: Get to the point. What is your message, man?

MESSENGER: Sir, I have seen the holy Maenads, the women who ran barefoot and crazy from the city, and I wanted to report to you and Thebes what weird fantastic things, what miracles and more than miracles, these women do. But may I speak freely in my own way and words, or make it short? I fear the harsh impatience of your nature, sire, too kingly and too quick to anger.

PENTHEUS: Speak freely. You have my promise: I shall not punish you. Displeasure with a man who speaks the truth is wrong. However, the more terrible this tale of yours, that much more terrible will be the punishment I impose upon that man who taught our womenfolk this strange new magic.

MESSENGER: About that hour when the sun lets loose its light to warm the Earth, our grazing herds of cows had just begun to climb the path along the mountain ridge. Suddenly I saw three companies of dancing women, one led by Autonoë, the second captained by your mother Agave, while Ino led the third.[2] There they lay in

---

[1]The mountain was sacred to Dionysus and the Muses.

[2]The three were sisters.

the deep sleep of exhaustion, some resting on boughs of fir, others sleeping where they fell, here and there among the oak leaves — but all modestly and soberly, not, as you think, drunk with wine, nor wandering, led astray by the music of the flute, to hunt their Aphrodite[3] through the woods.

But your mother heard the lowing of our hornèd herds, and springing to her feet, gave a great cry to waken them from sleep. And they too, rubbing the bloom of soft sleep from their eyes, rose up lightly and straight — a lovely sight to see: all as one, the old women and the young and the unmarried girls. First they let their hair fall loose, down over their shoulders, and those whose straps had slipped fastened their skins of fawn[4] with writhing snakes[5] that licked their cheeks. Breasts swollen with milk, new mothers who had left their babies behind at home nestled gazelles and young wolves in their arms, suckling them. Then they crowned their hair with leaves, ivy and oak and flowering bryony. One woman struck her thyrsus[6] against a rock and a fountain of cool water came bubbling up. Another drove her fennel in the ground, and where it struck the Earth, at the touch of god, a spring of wine poured out. Those who wanted milk scratched at the soil with bare fingers and the white milk came welling up. Pure honey spurted, streaming, from their wands. If you had been there and seen these wonders for yourself, you would have gone down on your knees and prayed to the god you now deny.

We cowherds and shepherds gathered in small groups, wondering and arguing among ourselves at these fantastic things, the awful miracles those women did. But then a city fellow with the knack of words rose to his feet and said: "All you who live upon the pastures of the mountain, what do you say? Shall we earn a little favor with King Pentheus by hunting his mother Agave out of the revels?" Falling in with his suggestion, we withdrew and set ourselves in ambush, hidden by the leaves among the undergrowth. Then at a signal all the Bacchae whirled their wands for the revels to begin. With one voice they cried aloud: *"O Iacchus![7] Son of Zeus!" "O Bromius!"[8]* they cried until the beasts and all the mountain seemed wild with divinity. And when they ran, everything ran with them.

It happened, however, that Agave ran near the ambush where I lay concealed. Leaping up, I tried to seize her, but she gave a cry: "Hounds who run with me, men are hunting us down! Follow, follow me! Use your wands for weapons."

At this we fled and barely missed being torn to pieces by the women. Unarmed, they swooped down upon the herds of cattle grazing there on the green of the meadow. And then you could have seen a single woman with bare hands tear a fat calf, still bellowing with fright, in two, while others clawed the heifers to pieces. There were ribs and cloven hooves scattered everywhere, and scraps smeared with blood hung from the fir trees. And bulls, their raging fury gathered in their horns, lowered their heads to charge, then fell, stumbling to the earth, pulled down by hordes of women and stripped of flesh and skin more quickly, sire, than you could blink your royal eyes.[9] Then, carried up by their own speed, they flew like birds across the spreading fields along Asopus' stream[10] where most of all the ground is good for harvesting. Like invaders they swooped on Hysiae and on Erythrae[11] in the foothills of Cithaeron. Everything in sight they pillaged and destroyed. They snatched the children from their homes. And when they piled their plunder on their backs, it stayed in place, untied. Nothing, neither bronze

[3]Goddess of erotic love.
[4]Maenads wore cloaks of animal skin, usually a fawn's skin because it was considered holy. See source 25.
[5]Some apparently also adorned their heads with snakes. See source 25.
[6]A shaft of fennel topped with ivy. It was carried in the right hand, with the ivy to the rear. See source 25.
[7]One of Dionysus's titles, it probably derives from a cry of joy in his honor.
[8]Another of his titles, it means "roarer" and refers to his manifestations as a bull-god and a lion-god.
[9]Maenads were accused of tearing living animals apart and eating their raw flesh during their ecstasies. We do not know what rites they performed, but it is imaginable that they ritually slaughtered and consumed animals, possibly raw, as a communion feast.
[10]The god of the river that also bore his name.
[11]Two nearby villages.

nor iron, fell to the dark earth. Flames flickered in their curls and did not burn them. Then the villagers, furious at what the women did, took to arms. And *there*, sire, was something terrible to see. For the men's spears were pointed and sharp, and yet drew no blood, whereas the wands the women threw inflicted wounds. And then the men *ran*, routed by women! Some god, I say, was with them. The Bacchae then returned where they had started, by the springs the god had made, and washed their hands while the snakes licked away the drops of blood that dabbled their cheeks.

Whoever this god may be, sire, welcome him to Thebes. For he is great in many other ways as well. It was he, or so they say, who gave to mortal men the gift of lovely wine by which our suffering is stopped. And if there is no god of wine, there is no love, no Aphrodite either, nor other pleasure left to men.

(Exit messenger.)

Body and Soul

▼▼▼

24 ▼ *Plato, PHAEDO*

Terms such as "rational," "secular," and "humanistic" have great validity when applied to classical Greek thought, especially of the fifth and early fourth centuries B.C.E. Yet it is very much of an oversimplification to say that Hellas's thinkers focused exclusively on the human in the here and now. A case in point is the philosopher Plato (427–348), the most profound and influential of the students of *Socrates* of Athens (ca. 469–399), Hellas's first great social philosopher.

Almost all that we know, or think that we know, about Socrates derives from Plato's *Dialogues*, which purport to be conversations between Socrates and others in which the philosopher probed the true meaning of such abstractions as "the Good," "piety," and "knowledge." Here we see the Socratic method of analysis — dialectical reasoning in which assumptions, opinions, and received wisdom are tested through a process of intellectual volleying. Propositions are tendered, their inherent contradictions or flaws are pointed out, a new proposition is offered, only to be greeted by more objections, and so it goes in this "investigation through discussion," which is what the Greek verb *dialego* means. And there is no good reason to doubt that this was the method by which Socrates turned himself into the "gadfly of Athens," and through which he enraged a number of people by questioning and demonstrating the logical flaws within some of their most cherished opinions.

The problem for Socrates was that he incurred such animosity that he was condemned to death in 399 B.C.E. on charges of atheism and corrupting the youth. The problem for modern scholars is that it is almost impossible on most points to separate clearly Plato's ideas from those of Socrates. One dialogue, however, that most historians think is much more Platonic than Socratic is the *Phaedo*. The scene is Socrates' prison cell, where he is consoling some of his friends and students minutes before drinking the condemned prisoner's cup of hemlock that will kill him. Pointedly, Plato puts into the mouth of Phaedo, Socrates' disciple who recounts his master's last moments, the fact that Plato was not present because he was ill.

Here Socrates discusses the soul, and the views put into his mouth illustrate the spiritual bent of Plato's philosophy. His vision had a profound impact on later Hellenistic and Greco-Roman philosophy and religion, much of which emphasized a mystical otherworldliness (see Chapter 5, source 27). Beyond that, Platonic and Neo-Platonic thought profoundly influenced Christian theology.

QUESTIONS FOR ANALYSIS

1. Did Plato believe that the attainment of true wisdom is possible in this world? Why or why not?
2. Plato's philosophy has been characterized as "mystical rationalism." Whatever is meant by this, and is that a proper term to apply to it?
3. In what ways might Platonic thought have influenced Christianity?
4. Can you think of any traditions exemplified by a source or sources in Chapter 3 that might have influenced Plato's thought? Be specific.

And when real philosophers consider all these things, will they not be led to make a reflection which they will express in words something like the following? "Have we not found," they will say, "a path of thought which seems to bring us and our argument to the conclusion, that while we are in the body, and while the soul is infected with the evils of the body, our desire will not be satisfied? and our desire is of the truth. For the body is a source of endless trouble to us by reason of the mere requirement of food; and is liable also to diseases which overtake and impede us in the search after true being: it fills us full of loves, and lusts, and fears, and fancies of all kinds, and endless foolery, and in fact, as men say, takes away from us the power of thinking at all. Whence come wars, and fightings, and factions? whence but from the body and the lusts of the body? Wars are occasioned by the love of money, and money has to be acquired for the sake and in the service of the body; and by reason of all these impediments we have no time to give to philosophy; and, last and worst of all, even if we are at leisure and betake ourselves to some speculation, the body is always breaking in upon us, causing turmoil and confusion in our inquiries, and so amazing us that we are prevented from seeing the truth. It has been proved to us by experience that if we would have pure knowledge of any-

thing we must be quit of the body — the soul in herself must behold things in themselves: and then we shall attain the wisdom which we desire, and of which we say that we are lovers; not while we live, but after death; for if while in company with the body, the soul cannot have pure knowledge, one of two things follows — either knowledge is not to be attained at all, or, if at all, after death. For then, and not till then, the soul will be parted from the body and exist in herself alone. In this present life, I reckon that we make the nearest approach to knowledge when we have the least possible intercourse or communion with the body, and are not surfeited with the bodily nature, but keep ourselves pure. . . . And thus having got rid of the foolishness of the body we shall be pure and converse with the pure, and know of ourselves the clear light everywhere, which is none other than the light of truth." For the impure are not permitted to approach the pure. These are the sort of words . . . which the true lovers of knowledge cannot help saying to one another, and thinking. . . .

If this be true, there is great reason to hope that, going whither I go, when I have come to the end of my journey, I shall attain that which has been the pursuit of my life. And therefore I go on my way rejoicing, and not I only, but every other man who believes that his mind has been made ready and that he is in a manner purified. . . .

And what is purification but the separation of the soul from the body, as I was saying before; the habit of the soul gathering and collecting herself into herself from all sides out of the body; the dwelling in her own place alone, as in another life, so also in this, as far as she can; — the release of the soul from the chains of the body? . . .

Clearly.

And the true philosophers . . . are always occupied in the practice of dying, wherefore also to them least of all men is death terrible. Look at the matter thus: — if they have been in every way the enemies of the body, and are wanting to be alone with the soul, when this desire of theirs is granted, how inconsistent would they be if they trembled and repined, instead of rejoicing at their departure to that place where, when they arrive, they hope to gain that which in life they desired — and this was wisdom — and at the same time to be rid of the company of their enemy. Many a man has been willing to go to the world below animated by the hope of seeing there an earthly love, or wife, or son, and conversing with them. And will he who is a true lover of wisdom, and is strongly persuaded in like manner that only in the world below he can worthily enjoy her, still repine at death? Will he not depart with joy? Surely he will, O my friend, if he be a true philosopher. For he will have a firm conviction that there, and there only, he can find wisdom in her purity.[1] And if this be true, he would be very absurd, as I was saying, if he were afraid of death.

---

[1] *Sophia* (wisdom) is a feminine Greek noun. Socrates personifies wisdom as a beloved woman.

Art and the Human Form

▼▼▼

25 ▼ *THREE HELLENIC WORKS OF ART*

It is often said that the ancient Hellenes used the human as the measure of all things (although Plato probably would have disagreed). Their gods were humanlike in appearance and in their passions, and human concerns, especially morality and politics, consumed most Greek thinkers and writers. Humanity, particularly the human form, was also the consuming interest of fifth-century B.C.E. Hellenic sculptural and graphic artists, as the following three pieces of art illustrate.

The first example is a black-on-white painting found on the interior of a wine cup. The work, crafted around 490 B.C.E. by an artist known simply as the Brygos Painter, depicts a Maenad. Note the animal pelt around her neck, the panther she holds in her left hand, and the other accouterments of bacchic worship that Euripides described in the *Bacchae*.

The second work is the *Bronze Charioteer of Delphi*, which dates from around 470 B.C.E. This life-size (5'11") charioteer was originally part of a four-horse chariot ensemble that stood near the Temple of Apollo at Delphi. An inscription records that it was dedicated to celebrate a chariot victory at the Pythian Games, which were held every four years near Delphi in honor of Apollo.

The early dates of the first two pieces place them on the cusp of the classical period of Hellenic art, but the third piece is unmistakably classical. Known as the *Girl with Doves*, it is a grave monument from the island of Paros. Its style places it squarely in midcentury, around 450 B.C.E. Carved from Parian marble, this raised relief depicts a young girl who died unmarried (the doves symbolize virginity).

The artist has created an especially poignant work of art by contrasting the subject's head with her body. The body is that of a child (note the arms and hands), but her stylishly coiffured head is that of the young woman she would never become. Note also how the sculptor has used the maiden's draped robe to give form to her figure.

QUESTIONS FOR ANALYSIS

1. "The art of fifth-century classical Hellas expressed the importance of the human person." Based on these three examples, do you agree or disagree? Be specific in articulating your reasons.
2. It has also been said that Hellenic artists created idealized human forms that conveyed a sense of serene balance without losing reality. Based on these three examples, do you agree or disagree? Be specific in articulating your reasons.
3. "Simplicity, dignity, and restraint were the hallmarks of classical Hellenic art, and all three qualities reflected the Greek vision of a world that was understandable and controllable." Based on these three examples, do you agree or disagree? Be specific in articulating your reasons.

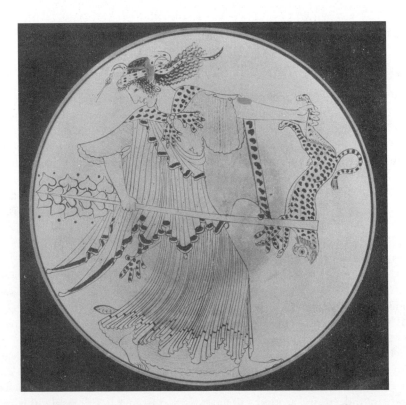

A Maenad

The Bronze Charioteer of Delphi

Girl with Doves

Multiple Voices II   ▼▼▼
The Healing Arts in China and Greece

BACKGROUND

The search for effective cures of humanity's manifold ailments and injuries is almost as old as the species itself. The following three documents illustrate how two of Eurasia's most distantly separated cultures, China and Hellas, approached that challenge.

Each culture developed a medical science that reflected its distinctive way of explaining the natural world and the manner in which it functions. For the Chinese, this was the cosmology of Yin and Yang. Yin and Yang theory assumes that the universe is composed of two principles: Yang is the male principle of light and life, the day and the sun, strength and activity; Yin is the female principle of darkness and death, the night and the moon, weakness and passivity. Heaven is the creation of Yang; Earth is the creation of Yin. But precisely because Yin and Yang are polar opposites, they complement and complete each other. Every part of nature, including humans, contains its unique blend of Yin and Yang, and each element's mixture of Yin and Yang defines its essence and characteristics. It follows, therefore, that maintaining the harmonious balance of Yin and Yang that is special to each element of nature is essential for preserving its well-being and proper function.

For the Greeks, there were two defining principles: the direct intervention into human affairs of anthropomorphic deities, as articulated in such revered texts as Homer's *Iliad* and *Odyssey*, and the theory of bodily *humors*, a notion that the body contains four basic fluids, or humors, namely, blood, phlegm, black bile, and yellow bile. Greek physicians further concluded that an excess of any humor — by reason of hereditary factors, environment, or accident — causes psychic and physical imbalance. Depending on the humor that has thrown the body out of balance, the patient becomes sanguine, phlegmatic, melancholy, or bilious. Moreover, given human variability, no person's humors are ever in perfect balance; some humor always is dominant, and this explains why people have different personalities and physical qualities. When, however, the imbalance becomes so acute as to cause clinical illness, the physician must intervene. The physician's art and science consisted of helping the body re-establish its natural harmony by administering or withholding foods and medicines that either reduced or increased one or more of the humors.

THE SOURCES

The first source is an excerpt from *The Yellow Emperor's Classic of Internal Medicine*. The first of the mythic Five Sage Emperors, the *Yellow Emperor (Huangdi)*, who supposedly reigned in the twenty-seventh century B.C.E., was credited with fashioning China's first state. Daoists claimed the Yellow Emperor had articulated the basic principles of their philosophy, and Chinese physicians believed he had laid down the foundations of their healing art.

The earliest known Chinese medical text, *The Yellow Emperor's Classic of Internal Medicine* was composed probably between 1000 and 300 B.C.E. All we can say for certain is that it was known and used during the Han Era (202 B.C.E.– 220 C.E.), and scholars are certain that it could not have been composed anywhere near the supposed time of the Yellow Emperor. One indicator is the classic's focus on the theory of *Yin* and *Yang*, which was developed during the Zhou Era.

As this source shows, the Chinese translated this cosmological theory into a philosophy of holistic, preventative medicine. Here we encounter an explanation of how the wise person must act in conformity with the four seasons, each a manifestation of the cyclic interplay of Yin and Yang: Spring is when Yang is on the rise and Yin on the wane; summer is the season of Yang when Yin is dormant; fall is when Yin is on the rise and Yang on the wane; winter is the season of Yin when Yang is dormant.

The second source contains testimonials inscribed on a *stele* (an upright stone slab) erected around the mid fourth century B.C.E. at the Temple of Asklepios (Aesculapius in Latin and English; also Asclepius) at Epidauros in Greece's Peloponnesian Peninsula, the largest, most revered, and most visited sanctuary of the god of healing in the Hellenic World. Suppliants in search of a cure or other favor touching on the body would ritually bathe, offer sacrifices to the god, and spend the night in the sanctuary, where they expected to be visited by the god in a vision in which their petitions would be answered. Alternatively, the suppliant might be approached and aided by a sacred serpent or dog.

This cult, which rose to prominence in fifth-century B.C.E. Hellas, became pan-Mediterranean in the age of the Roman Empire and died out only after the triumph of Christianity (Chapter 7) and the emergence of saints as the new wonder-workers. As late as the fifth century C.E., the great Christian writer Augustine of Hippo (354–430) felt compelled to attack the cult as theologically false and incapable of effecting cures. Asklepios/Aesculapius had his minor revenge, however. His symbol, the staff entwined with a snake, is the insignia of the modern medical profession.

The island of Cos (or Kos) housed an *Asklepieion*, or temple of Asklepios, but Cos was also the birthplace of Greek medical science, which might or might not have had its origins in that temple. Whatever its origins, Hellenic medical science turned away from the religious practices of the priesthood of Asklepios. It came to dominate the healing arts on the island by the 430s B.C.E., and for the time in which this science was predominant, the temple gave way to a public hospital, where patients received free treatment. Later, the cult of the god of healing made a comeback on the island, and medical science and Aesculapian remedies continued to provide the Greco-Roman World with alternate and often complementary avenues of healing until the end of the Ancient World.

The most famous physician of Cos was *Hippocrates* (Hippokrates), yet we know very little about his life. Born around 460 B.C.E., his abilities as a practitioner and teacher of medicine eventually earned him a pan-Hellenic reputation, and he found himself traveling from city to city teaching an art and science that stressed careful clinical observation of the nature and course of diseases. A late tradition holds that he died in Thessaly in northern Greece around 377 B.C.E.

Hippocrates' legend grew as the years passed. By 300 B.C.E., some seventy-two books were ascribed to him, but this Hippocratic body of medical knowledge clearly shows the hands of many different authors. It is impossible to say precisely which, if any, of these books Hippocrates composed, but it is reasonable to assume that they represent the medical tradition that he and generations of his students practiced and taught.

An integral part of that tradition was the theory of bodily humors, which apparently grew out of the practice of the physicians of Cos to record carefully the courses of various diseases. This theory underlies the document that appears here, an excerpt from *On the Sacred Disease*, one of the earliest treatises within the body of medical texts ascribed to Hippocrates, in which the author deals with epilepsy.

QUESTIONS FOR ANALYSIS

1. How, if at all, does *The Yellow Emperor's Classic of Internal Medicine* offer a program for psychological and physical harmony? Please be specific in your answer.
2. Belief in supernatural intervention pervades the *Testimonials at Epidauros*, yet there is a hint of how this cult and some of its priests might have given an impetus to more naturalistic forms of healing. What is that hint?
3. *On the Sacred Disease* clearly ridicules Aesculapian approaches to healing, and it appears to be antithetical to that cult's belief system. Why then was it possible for both systems of healing to have coexisted and even served as complements to each other for so many centuries? Indeed, by the fourth century B.C.E., Asklepieia (the plural of Asklepieion) tended to have sanctuaries along with attached hospitals and sanitariums. Even surgical instruments have been unearthed at these sites.
4. Compare the Chinese and Hellenic approaches to healing as illustrated in these three sources. Which strike you as more significant, the differences or the similarities? What conclusions follow from your answer?

I ▾ THE YELLOW EMPEROR'S CLASSIC OF INTERNAL MEDICINE

GREAT TREATISE ON THE HARMONY OF THE ATMOSPHERE OF THE FOUR SEASONS WITH THE HUMAN SPIRIT

The three months of *Spring* are called the period of the beginning and development of life. The breaths of Heaven and Earth are prepared to give birth; thus everything is developing and flourishing.

After a night of sleep people should get up early in the morning; they should walk briskly around the yard; they should loosen their hair and slow down their movements; by these means they can fulfill their wish to live healthfully.

During this period one's body should be encouraged to live and not be killed; one should give to it freely and not take away from it; one should reward it and not punish it.

All this is in harmony with the breath of Spring and all this is the method for the protection of one's life.

Those who disobey the laws of Spring will be punished with an injury of the liver. For them the following Summer will bring chills and bad changes; thus they will have little to support their development in Summer.

The three months of *Summer* are called the period of luxurious growth. The breaths of Heaven and Earth intermingle and are beneficial. Everything is in bloom and begins to bear fruit.

After a night of sleep people should get up early in the morning. They should not weary during daytime and they should not allow their minds to become angry.

They should enable the best parts of their body and spirit to develop; they should enable their breath to communicate with the outside world; and they should act as though they loved everything outside.

All this is in harmony with the atmosphere of Summer and all this is the method for the protection of one's development.

Those who disobey the laws of Summer will be punished with an injury of the heart. For them Fall will bring intermittent fevers; thus they will have little to support them for harvest in Fall; and hence, at Winter solstice they will suffer from grave disease.

The three months of *Fall* are called the period of tranquility of one's conduct. The atmosphere of Heaven is quick and the atmosphere of the Earth is clear.

People should retire early at night and rise early in the morning with the rooster. They should have their minds at peace in order to lessen the punishment of Fall. Soul and spirit should be gathered together in order to make the breath of Fall tranquil; and to keep their lungs pure they should not give vent to their desires.

All this is in harmony with the atmosphere of Fall and all this is the method for the protection of one's harvest.

Those who disobey the laws of Fall will be punished with an injury of the lungs. For them Winter will bring indigestion and diarrhea; thus they will have little to support their storing of Winter.

The three months of *Winter* are called the period of closing and storing. Water freezes and the Earth cracks open. One should not disturb one's Yang.[1]

People should retire early at night and rise late in the morning and they should wait for the rising of the sun. They should suppress and conceal their wishes, as though they had no internal purpose, as though they had been fulfilled. People should try to escape the cold and they should seek warmth, they should not perspire upon the skin, they should let themselves be deprived of breath of the cold.

All this is in harmony with the atmosphere of Winter and all this is the method for the protection of one's storing.

Those who disobey the laws of Winter will suffer an injury of the kidneys; for them Spring will bring impotence,[2] and they will produce little. . . .

The sages followed the laws of nature and therefore their bodies were free from strange diseases; they did not lose anything which they had received by nature and their spirit of life was never exhausted. . . .

Thus the interaction of the four seasons and the interaction of Yin and Yang is the foundation of everything in creation. Hence the sages conceived and developed their Yang in Spring

---

[1]Yang is dormant and should be allowed to rest.
[2]The kidneys were believed to be the organ from which the sexual life force emanated.

and Summer, and conceived and developed their Yin in Fall and Winter in order to follow the rule of rules; and thus, together with everything in creation, maintained themselves at the gate of life and development.

Those who rebel against the basic rules of the universe sever their own roots and ruin their true selves. Yin and Yang, the two principles in nature, and the four seasons are the beginning and the end of everything and they are also the cause of life and death. Those who disobey the laws of the universe will give rise to calamities and visitations, while those who follow the laws of the universe remain free from dangerous illness, for they are the ones who have obtained Dao, the Right Way.

Dao was practiced by the sages and admired by the ignorant people. Obedience to the laws of Yin and Yang means life; disobedience means death. The obedient ones will rule while the rebels will be in disorder and confusion. Anything contrary to harmony with nature is disobedience and means rebellion to nature.

Hence the sages did not treat those who were already ill; they instructed those who were not yet ill. They did not want to rule those who were already rebellious; they guided those who were not yet rebellious. This is the meaning of the entire preceding discussion. To administer medicines to diseases which have already developed and to suppress revolts which have already developed is comparable to the behavior of those persons who begin to dig a well after they have become thirsty, and of those who begin to cast weapons after they have already engaged in battle. Would these actions not be too late?

---

2 ▾ *TESTIMONIALS AT EPIDAUROS*

Ambrosia of Athens, blind of one eye. She came as a suppliant to the god. As she walked about in the Temple she laughed at some of the cures as incredible and impossible, that the lame and the blind should be healed by merely seeing a dream. In her sleep she had a vision. It seemed to her that the god stood by her and said that he would cure her, but that in payment he would ask her to dedicate to the Temple a silver pig as a memorial of her ignorance.[1] After saying this, he cut the diseased eyeball and poured in some drug. When day came she walked out sound.

▾▾▾

A voiceless boy. He came as a suppliant to the Temple for his voice. When he had performed the preliminary sacrifices and fulfilled the usual rites, thereupon the temple servant who brings in the fire[2] for the god, looking at the boy's father, demanded he should promise to bring within a year the thank-offering for the cure if he obtained that for which he had come. But the boy suddenly said, "I promise." His father was startled at this and asked him to repeat it. The boy repeated the words and after that became well.

▾▾▾

A man had his toe healed by a serpent.[3] He, suffering dreadfully from a malignant sore in his toe, during the daytime was taken outside by the servants of the Temple and set upon a seat. When sleep came upon him, then a snake issued

---

[1] As the required thanksgiving offering for her cure. See the next testimonial.
[2] Fire for the animal sacrifice that was part of the required rituals.

[3] The serpent was sacred to Aesculapius because of its presumed regenerative powers, and a number were kept at each temple dedicated to the god.

from the Abaton[4] and healed the toe with its tongue, and thereafter went back again to the Abaton. When the patient woke up and was healed he said that he had seen a vision: it seemed to him that a youth with a beautiful appearance had put a drug upon his toe.

▼▼▼

Heraieus of Mytilene. He had no hair on his head, but an abundant growth on his chin. He was ashamed because he was laughed at by others. He slept in the Temple. The god, by anointing his head with some drug, made his hair grow thereon.

Hermon of Thasus. His blindness was cured by Asclepius. But, since afterwards he did not bring the thank-offerings, the god made him blind again. When he came back and slept again in the Temple, he [the god] made him well.

▼▼▼

Agameda of Ceos. She slept in the Temple for offspring and saw a dream. It seemed to her in her sleep that a serpent lay on her belly. And thereupon five children were born to her.

---

[4]The "Unapproachable," the innermost sanctuary of the temple in which suppliants slept, but only after they had ritually purified themselves.

---

3 ▼ Hippocrates, ON THE SACRED DISEASE

In regard to the disease called "sacred," it seems to me to be no more divine or sacred than other diseases but has a natural cause from which it originates, like other afflictions. People regard its nature and cause as divine out of ignorance and credulity, because it is unlike other diseases. This notion of its divinity persists by virtue of people's inability to comprehend it and the simplicity of the means by which it is cured, for those afflicted are supposedly freed from it by purifications and incantations. If people reckon it divine because it incites awe, then instead of one sacred disease there would be many. As I will show, other diseases are no less awe-inspiring and strange, yet no one considers them sacred. . . . For example, one can see people grow mad and demented for no apparent reason and doing many strange things. I have known many persons to groan and cry out in their sleep . . . some jumping up and rushing out of doors, all deprived of their reason until they wake up. Afterward they are as healthy and rational as before,

although pale and weak. And this will occur not once but frequently. There are many similar phenomena that it would be tedious to enumerate.

In my view, they who first associated this disease with the gods were people just like our present-day magicians, purifiers, charlatans, and quacks, who claim great piety and superior knowledge. Such persons, using superstition as camouflage for their own inability to offer any help, proclaimed the disease sacred . . . and instituted a method of treatment that protected them, namely purifications, incantations, and enforced abstinence from bathing and from many types of food. . . . Their course of treatment forbids the patient to have a black robe, because black is symbolic of death, or to sleep on a goatskin, or to wear one, or to put one foot on another, or one hand on another. All these things are reputed to be impediments to healing. . . . If the patient recovers they reap the honor and credit; if the patient dies, they have a perfect defense: The gods, not they, are to blame, seeing as they had administered nothing to eat or drink in the way of medicine, and they had not over-heated the patient with baths. . . .

If such things, when administered as food, aggravate the disease, and if it is cured by abstinence from them, then the disease cannot be divine in origin, and the rites of purification provide no benefit. It is the food which is either beneficial or harmful. . . . Therefore, they who attempt to cure this disease in such a manner appear to me to be incapable of believing the disease is sacred or divine. . . .

Consequently, this disease seems to me to be no more divine than others. It has the same nature and cause as other diseases. It is also no less curable than other diseases. . . . The key to its origin, as is the case with other diseases, lies in heredity. . . . Where one or the other parent suffers from this malady, some of their children likewise suffer from it. . . . Another strong proof that this disease is no more divine in origin than any other is that it afflicts those who are by nature phlegmatic,[1] but it does not attack the bilious.[2] If this disease were more divine than other diseases, it should afflict all groups equally, making no distinction between the bilious and the phlegmatic. . . .

Since the brain, as the primary center of sensation and of the spirits, perceives whatever occurs in the body, if any unusual change takes place in the air, due to the seasons, the brain is changed by the state of the air. . . . And the disease called "sacred" arises from . . . those things that enter and leave the body, such as cold, the sun, and winds, which are constantly changing and never at rest. . . . Therefore the physician should understand and distinguish each individual situation, so that at one time he might add nourishment, at another time withhold it. In this disease, as in all others, he must endeavor not to feed the disease, but he must attempt to wear it out by administering whatever is most contrary to each disease and not that which favors and is allied to it. For it grows vigorous and increases through that which is allied to it, but it wears out and disappears under the administration of whatever is opposed to it.[3] Whoever is knowledgeable enough to render a person humid or dry, hot or cold by regimen can also cure this disease, if the physician recognizes the proper season for administering remedies. The physician can do so without attention to purifications, spells, and all other forms of hocus-pocus.

---

[1] A calm temperament that can reach sluggishness due to excessive phlegm.
[2] Those who, by reason of the dominance of bile in their systems, have peevish, sour-tempered dispositions.

[3] Specific foods and ministrations stimulate the production of specific humors; others reduce them.

▲▲▲

Chapter 5

Regional Empires and Afro-Eurasian Interchange

300 B.C.E.–500 C.E.

*B*Y 300 B.C.E. THE CULTURAL TRADITIONS of China, India, Southwest Asia, and Hellas were solidly in place and ready to expand beyond their original boundaries. Expand they did, but expansion followed no single pattern. Imperial aggrandizement, largely by means of military conquest, played a major role in spreading Chinese, Southwest Asian, and Hellenic cultural influences, but it was not a factor in the creation in Southeast Asia of a *Greater India* (as many historians term it).

As early as the first century C.E., people of the coastal areas of Southeast Asia accepted elements of Indian culture, including Hindu and Buddhist religious traditions, from merchants traveling across the Bay of Bengal. Colonists, including Indian priests and scholars, soon followed the merchants. Traffic, however, was not all one-way, as youths from various emerging Hindu and Buddhist kingdoms throughout Southeast Asia traveled to India for advanced religious instruction. Although the Hindu caste system failed to take root in Southeast Asia, other Indian traditions flourished there, including the cults of Shiva and Vishnu (Chapter 6, sources 34 and 35) and the notion of the *devaraja* (sacred king) — an idea embraced by native ruling elites.

Chinese cultural influences traveled south, northeast, and west as a consequence of military adventure and more peaceful exchanges, especially the travels of merchants and the slow, steady southward migration of China's expanding peasant population. The armies of Han conquered Manchuria and northern Korea and established hegemony over non-Chinese peoples to the south in northern Vietnam and along the Himalayan foothills. To the west, the armies of Han China penetrated deeply into Central Asia. Wherever its soldiers went, its merchants were not too far behind. The roads that China opened to the West also served as conduits for the influx of new ideas into the Middle Kingdom, particularly *Mahayana Buddhism* (see Chapter 6, sources 32–33, and Chapter 9, Multiple Voices VI), which flowed into China along its overland trade routes.

From the late sixth to the late fourth century B.C.E., the *Persian Empire*, centered in Southwest Asia, encompassed an area from the Nile to the Indus, from the Mediterranean to the Persian Gulf, from the Black Sea to the Red Sea. Although the Persians were respectful of local traditions, their massive empire was a fertile medium for the blending and transmission of many cultures. Then, in the late fourth century, Persia and Greece were merged into a single empire for one brief but significant moment. The conquest of the Persian Empire by *Alexander the Great* (r. 336–323 B.C.E.) and his penetration as far east as Central Asia and the Indus Valley ushered in a new era for western Eurasia — the *Hellenistic Age*. Whereas the Hellenic World had been parochial, the Hellenistic World was cosmopolitan and culturally eclectic. The armies of Alexander and the state-builders who followed helped create a cultural amalgamation of Southwest Asian, Egyptian, and even some Indian elements, over which was laid a layer of Greek language, thought, and artistic expression. What emerged was, to use a Greek word, a cultural *ecumene* (a unity of diverse civilized peoples). This world culture stretched from western Central Asia and northwest India to the central Mediterranean, and much of it was Greek in form and inspiration.

Alexander's empire did not survive him, but the amalgamation of peoples and cultures that he forged laid the basis for Hellenistic successor states in Egypt, Southwest Asia, and the Mediterranean. Of these, the most impressive was the *Roman Empire*. To be sure, Romans spoke Latin and not Greek, and their civilization was as deeply influenced by the Etruscans of north-central Italy as it was by Greeks and other Hellenistic cultures. Moreover, their empire was centered on the central Mediterranean— far away from the heartland of the original Hellenistic Ecumene. Notwithstanding, it is reasonable to see the Roman Empire as the last and greatest of the Hellenistic states and as the carrier of Hellenistic culture into such faraway western regions as Gaul, Germany, and Britain.

Rome and Han China were certainly not Eurasia's only great empires. By the end of the first century B.C.E., four great regional empires linked China, India, Southwest Asia, and the Greco-Roman Mediterranean in a chain of civilization from the Pacific to the Atlantic: Han China, the *Kushan Empire* of Central Asia, the *Parthian Empire* of Southwest Asia, and Rome.

The Kushans, who spoke an Indo-European language, were a confederation of nomadic peoples, many of whom had been pushed west from the borders of China in the second century B.C.E. Settling down in a region that was centered on what are today the nations of Afghanistan and Pakistan, they established a Central Asian empire that included the northern plains of India. Kushan history remains to be reconstructed, but our fragmentary sources indicate that their empire flourished from the early first century C.E. to the late third century and served as an important conduit for Indian goods on their way to China and the West. It is also clear that the Kushans adopted and transmitted some forms of Indian culture. Many of the Kushan aristocracy and their subjects became Buddhists, especially Mahayana Buddhists, and under Kushan rule a region of Pakistan known as *Gandhara* became the center of an exciting new form of Buddhist art (see Multiple Voices III, source 3).

Sometime in the first half of the third century B.C.E., the *Parni,* a tribe that inhabited lands just to the east of the Caspian Sea (present-day Turkmenistan), expanded southwest into *Parthia*, an ancient Persian province in northern Iran, which they consolidated into a state around 200 B.C.E. The Parni were soon absorbed by the settled peoples of Parthia and disappeared as a separate, identifiable people, but before their disappearance the Parni set Parthia on the road to empire. After 190 B.C.E. the Parni-Parthian state expanded westward at the expense of the *Seleucid Empire*, the most eastern of the Hellenistic states. Around 147 B.C.E. the Parthians conquered Babylon in Mesopotamia and were well on their way to carving out an empire that at its height stretched from the Caspian Sea to northern Syria and aggressively butted up against the Roman Empire. Not only did the Parthians fight the Romans, they also traded with them. Until its collapse around 224 C.E., when the empire was taken over by the *Sassanians*, the Parthian Empire served as an important intermediary along the network of caravan routes that linked the Mediterranean, India, Central Asia, and China and to which historians have given the romantic name the *Silk Road*.

Indeed, not only land routes but sea-lanes as well, were now joined in complex patterns to create the first age of Afro-Eurasian linkage.

Although most of the major trade routes traversed the lands and waters of Eurasia, Africa also shared in this unification to the extent that its northern regions were an integral part of the Roman Empire, and northern portions of its eastern coast were linked by regular trade with Arabia, India, and Southeast Asia.

This age of grand-scale linkage began to suffer retrenchment and shrinkage around 200 C.E., when both China and the Roman Empire entered periods of severe crisis. Despite political and economic disasters, however, trade across the Silk Road and along the sea-lanes never totally ceased in the centuries that followed, even though it experienced periods of severe recession.

▼▼▼

The Greco-Roman World

Alexander the Great died in Babylon in 323 B.C.E., and several of his generals divided the Hellenistic World into a number of rival successor states. The two mightiest and most brilliant were the kingdom of the *Seleucids*, centered on Anatolia, Mesopotamia, and Syria, and the kingdom of Egypt, which fell to the family of *Ptolemy*, a Macedonian Greek.

Ptolemy and his successors lavished money on their capital, *Alexandria*, transforming this new city, located in Egypt's northern delta region, into the most impressive cosmopolitan setting in the Hellenistic World. Two of the city's glories were the Museum, which functioned as a center of advanced research, and the Library. In an attempt to gather under one roof the entire Hellenistic World's store of written knowledge, it contained perhaps as many as half a million separate scrolls.

Both institutions enjoyed the continuous generous patronage of the Macedonian god-kings of Egypt and served as focal points for scientific and literary studies that were Greek in form and substance but cosmopolitan in scope and clientele. Educated Persians, Jews, Mesopotamians, Syrians, Italians, and members of many other ethnic groups flocked to Alexandria, where they formed an ecumenical community of scholars and artists whose common tongue and intellectual perspective were as Greek as that of their Ptolemaic hosts.

In 30 B.C.E. Cleopatra VII, the last Ptolemaic ruler of Egypt, died in Alexandria, and Egypt passed under the direct control of the rising imperial power of Rome. By this time Rome had already seized control of Italy, Greece, major portions of Anatolia (which it termed *Asia Minor*), Syria, most of North Africa, all of the major Mediterranean islands, Spain, and the area north of the Alps and Pyrenees known as *Gaul*. The Mediterranean had truly become Rome's *Mare Nostrum* (Our Sea), and the Roman Empire now controlled a large portion of the Hellenistic World. As inheritor by conquest of eastern Mediterranean lands and culture, Rome would disseminate a Greco-Roman form of Hellenistic culture throughout the western Mediterranean, as well as among various barbarian peoples living in European lands well beyond the Mediterranean coastline. Well before the end of the first century C.E., Roman legions would be erecting Greek-style temples to the Persian god Mithras along the Rhine and in Britain, and Greek literature would be studied in schools throughout lands recently wrested from Gallic tribes.

Images of the Hellenistic World
▼▼▼
26 ▼ *FOUR HELLENISTIC SCULPTURES*

The Hellenistic Ecumene was exceedingly cosmopolitan, but cosmopolitanism often carries a price. Parochial societies — such as fifth-century B.C.E. Hellas, which centered on small, fairly homogeneous poleis — offer their inhabitants the security that comes from living in a friendly and understandable environment. Conversely, societies open to the world and filled with a bewildering array of different and often contradictory cultural stimuli can be frightening and alienating. Such alienation and confusion can have profound effects on artistic expression. But even when people are comfortable with cultural differences and at home in a *universal city* (the literal meaning of *cosmopolitan*), they tend to view the world and themselves differently from people whose horizons are more limited. This comfort with a wider world also finds expression in the arts.

As we saw in source 25, Hellenic artists of the fifth century B.C.E. idealized the human body and placed the human being securely in the center of an ordered world — a world that they saw reflected in the poleis in which they were citizens. As the following four sculptures suggest, later Hellenistic sculptors had different visions.

The first item is a marble bust of King Euthydemos I of *Bactria* (r. ca. 235–200 B.C.E.), which dates from around 200 B.C.E. The Greek-speaking kings of Bactria had carved out a realm on the far horizon of the Hellenistic World, a wild mountainous region in western Central Asia shared by the present-day nations of Turkmenistan, Tajikistan, Uzbekistan, and Afghanistan. A native of Anatolia, Euthydemos had risen to power by overthrowing his predecessor. The second piece is a Roman marble copy of a bronze original that had been created around 230–220 B.C.E. Known as *The Gaul and Wife*, the original had served as one of a number of statues gracing a victory monument of King Attalos I of *Pergamon* (r. 241–197 B.C.E.) that celebrated his victories over invading Gallic, or Celtic, tribes. The kings of Pergamon, a city located near the northwestern coast of Anatolia, lavished money on their city's beautification, using art to trumpet their policies and achievements. The third sculpture is *The Old Woman*, also known as *The*

The Gaul and Wife

King Euthydemos I of Bactria

The Boxer

The Old Woman

Old Market Woman, an original work in marble that dates from the late second or early first century B.C.E. One interpretation of the sculpture is that the woman is depicted in the act of calling out to potential customers, hoping that they purchase the chicken and basket of vegetables and fruits that she holds in her left hand. Another interpretation, which we favor, is that the laurel wreath on her head suggests she is offering the goods as part of a religious festival, possibly one in honor of Dionysus (see source 23). The fourth sculpture is a bronze boxer by the Athenian sculptor Apollonius. Created around 60 B.C.E. in Italy, possibly for some rich fan of the Greek sport of pugilism, the work shows us a veteran boxer, whose broken nose, battered face and ears, muscular body, and leather gloves with bands of lead at the knuckles clearly indicate his profession.

In your study of the three full-body sculptures, pay particular attention to three artistic elements: facial expression, drapery, and *contrapposto* (the turning of the hip and leg away from the shoulders and the head). Hellenistic sculptors employed all three to add psychological insight, dramatic effect, and movement to their art.

QUESTIONS FOR ANALYSIS

1. Consider the bust of King Euthydemos. How does the sculptor present the king? What reaction do you think the sculptor desired to evoke from the viewer?
2. Compare the bust of Euthydemos with the face of the *Bronze Charioteer* in source 25. What conclusions follow from your study?
3. Compare the *Girl with Doves* (source 25) with *The Gaul and Wife*. Does it appear that the artists expected to elicit similar emotional responses from viewers? If so, what techniques did each employ? What conclusions follow from your answers?
4. Consider *The Old Woman* and *The Boxer*. How have their sculptors dealt with them? Compare them with the three Hellenic works of art in source 25. Which strike you as more significant, the similarities or the dissimilarities? What conclusions follow from your analysis?
5. Some commentators have characterized Hellenistic art as an attempt to create psychological portraits. Do any or all of these four works seem to fall into that category? If so, what was there about the Hellenistic World that might have led some artists to emphasize the individual human psyche?
6. If art is a window on the society that produces it, what do these four sculptures allow you to infer about the Hellenistic World?

Rome Viewed from the Underworld

▼▼▼

27 ▾ Virgil, THE AENEID

By 200 B.C.E. the Roman Republic was the major power in the Mediterranean and an empire in fact, if not in name. Rome's acquisition of an empire had major repercussions at home, and the resultant strains triggered more than a century of class discord and civil war. The civil wars ended in 30 B.C.E., when Octavian, the great-nephew and adopted son of Julius Caesar (ca. 100–44 B.C.E.), defeated Mark Antony and became sole master of the Roman World. In 27 B.C.E. the Senate accorded him the title *Augustus* (Revered One), implying he possessed divine authority. Posterity remembers Octavian as *Caesar Augustus* (63 B.C.E.–14 C.E.), Rome's first emperor and the man who created and presided over the first generation of the *Pax Romana*, or Roman Peace.

Augustus used his age's leading artists and intellectuals to trumpet his accomplishments, and of these publicists of the Roman Peace, none was more important than Publius Vergilius Maro (70–19 B.C.E.), better known as *Virgil*. Virgil was classical Rome's greatest poet, and his most important creation, the *Aeneid*, was an epic that centered on nothing less than the divinely ordained destiny of Rome. The poem tells the story of the warrior-hero Aeneas, a refugee from Troy, whose settlement in Italy, following a long series of trials and troubled travels, would lead ultimately to the foundation of Rome. As the title and topic might suggest, Virgil borrowed liberally from Homer's *Iliad* and *Odyssey*, but he never slavishly imitated his Greek models. Rather, Virgil crafted a unique Latin masterpiece that deserves recognition on its own merits as one of the Ancient World's greatest epics.

The following excerpt comes from the pivotal point of the epic. Aeneas has just reached Italy. There, accompanied by the Sibyl of Cumae, a prophetess of the god Apollo, he enters the Underworld to consult the spirit of his father, Anchises. We begin at the point when Aeneas and the Sibyl, having passed by Tartarus, the place of torment for the wicked, arrive at Elysium. The view of the Underworld that Virgil presents here was deeply influenced by Plato's *Phaedo* (source 24).

QUESTIONS FOR ANALYSIS

1. How does Virgil's Underworld differ from that of Gilgamesh (source 1)? From that of Homer (source 10)?
2. What do the last two excerpts from this source suggest about the Roman self-image in the Age of Augustus?

They arrived at a land of joy, the green gardens and blessed abodes of the Blissful Groves. Here a fuller air clothes the meadows with a violet luminescence, and they have their own sun and starlight. Some exercise their limbs on the grassy playing fields, contend in sports, and wrestle on the yellow sand. Others beat out dances with their feet and sing songs. . . . Here is a band of men who incurred wounds fighting for their fatherland. Here are they who remained pure in their priesthood as long as they lived. Here are they who were true poets and who spoke in ways worthy of Phoebus.[1] And here are they who improved life by the arts of their inventions. Here are they who merited by their service remembrance before all others. The brows of all are encircled with snowy-white garlands. . . .

But Father Anchises, deep in the verdant valley, was surveying with intent mind the imprisoned souls that were to ascend to the light above, and by chance was counting numbers of men — his beloved descendants, their fates and their fortunes, their ways and their works.

And when he saw Aeneas coming toward him across the flowery meadow, he eagerly stretched out both hands, while tears flowed down his cheeks and a cry slipped from his mouth. "Have you come at last, and has the devotion that your father has expected of you conquered the path of adversity? My son, is it given to me to gaze on your face and to hear and respond in familiar speech? . . ." Aeneas replied: "Your shade, Father, your sad shade, appearing to me so often drove me to steer toward these portals. . . . Grant that I might clasp your hand, grant it, Father, and do not withdraw from our embrace." While thus speaking, his face was drenched with copious tears. Three times there he tried to put his arms about his neck; three times the shade, embraced

in vain, escaped out of his hands like weightless winds and even more so like a winged dream.

And now Aeneas sees within a hidden valley a secluded grove, rustling forest thickets, and the River Lethe flowing past peaceful dwellings. Around it hovered peoples and individuals beyond count. . . . Startled by this sudden vision, the uncomprehending Aeneas asks for an account: What is that river over there? Who are those people who throng on its banks in such great numbers? Father Anchises then answers: "Spirits to whom Fate owes another body drink the soothing waters of deep amnesia at the River Lethe's stream. Indeed, for quite a while I have wanted to tell you about these and show them to you face to face and to count the offspring of my descendants, so that you might rejoice with me the more for having reached Italy." "Father, must we think that some souls, soaring upwards, travel from here to the upper world and once again return to bodily fetters?"[2] "Why do these sad souls have such a dreadful longing for the light of day?" "Surely, I will tell you, my son, and I will not hold you in suspense," replies Anchises, and he lays everything out in order, one by one.

"First of all, one intrinsic Spirit sustains the heavens and the Earth and the watery expanses, the shining globe of the moon and the Titanian stars,[3] and one Mind flows through all its parts, drives the entire entity, and mingles with the mighty structure. From them[4] are generated humanity and beasts, the lives of flying creatures, and those monsters that the sea contains beneath its marbled surface. Fire is their life force and their seeds originate in Heaven,[5] inasmuch as sinful bodies do not hamper them, and earthly frames and mortal limbs do not render them sluggish. Bodies are the cause of fear and desire, of sorrow and joy, and souls cannot discern the light of Heaven when shut up in the gloom of a dark

---

[1]Phoebus Apollo, the god of prophecy and of poetry.
[2]These are the words of a world-weary Aeneas, who has been exhausted by the trials he has undergone due to his devotion to duty.
[3]The sun and the stars.

[4]Spirit and Mind.
[5]Spirit and Mind spring from the primal element of fire (see note 8), and their seeds are particles of divine fire born out of heavenly air.

dungeon.[6] Indeed, on the very last day when life has fled, all evil and all the ills of the body do not totally pass from these sad souls,[7] for it must be the case that many evils, long set hard, are deeply ingrained within them in ways beyond understanding. As a consequence, they are disciplined with punishments and pay the penalty for old evil ways. Some are hung, helplessly suspended before the winds; from others the stain of guilt is washed away under a swirling flood or burned off by fire.[8] Each of us endures his own ghost.[9] Then we are released to wander through wide Elysium. A few of us possess the Fields of Happiness until, once the cycle of time is completed, the passing days have removed the hardened stain and have left unsoiled the ethereal sentient spirit and the fire of pure air.[10] The god summons all these in a vast procession to the River Lethe once the wheel of time has revolved a full thousand years, so that they might revisit the vaulted world above[11] without memories and might begin to wish to return to bodily forms."[12]

Anchises finished speaking and drew his son, and the Sibyl along with him, into the midst of the crowded and murmuring throng. . . .

"Come now, I will teach you about your destiny. I will make clear by my words what glory will eventually befall the progeny of Dardanus[13] and what sort of descendants will spring from Italian stock[14] — souls of renown who shall inherit our name. . . .

▷ Anchises begins to point out the souls of the great men, still awaiting rebirth, who will create Rome and bring it to glory. After describing Romulus, the son of Mars (the god of war) and founder of Rome, Anchises abandons a strict chronological sequence and jumps to Caesar Augustus, the second founder of Rome.

"This man, this is he whom so often you heard promised to you. This is Caesar Augustus, son of a god,[15] who shall again establish a Golden Age in Latium[16] amid the fields where Saturn once ruled.[17] He shall extend his rule beyond the Garamantians[18] and the Indians. His dominion will extend beyond the paths of the zodiac and of the sun.[19] . . . Even now, in anticipation of his coming as prophesied by the oracles, the kingdoms of the Caspian Sea[20] and the region around Lake Moeotis[21] shudder in horror, and the seven mouths of the Nile[22] tremble in terror.[23] Yes, not even Alcides[24] strode over such a space of earth. . . . Do we

---

[6]The dungeon of the sinful, mortal body.
[7]Here Anchises picks up Aeneas's reference to "sad souls" and gives the term new meaning.
[8]In other words, sinful souls are cleansed in this purgatory by air, water, or fire, three of the four primal elements of the universe (the other being earth). Irredeemably evil souls are condemned to eternal torment in Tartarus, the place that Aeneas just passed on his way to Elysium.
[9]Each soul suffers in accord with its unique imperfections. By using the term "us," Anchises implies that he also has undergone this purgation.
[10]The soul (the sentient spirit) has been returned to its primal purity — the fire and air from which it was generated. See what Anchises says about the origins of Spirit and Mind (note 5).
[11]Earth, which is vaulted by the heavens.
[12]Were they to remember the miseries of life and the process of purgation they underwent after death, they would not want to return.
[13]The mythical founder of Troy.
[14]Aeneas's future descendants, who will bear both his Trojan blood and the blood of Lavinia, his Italian wife-to-be.
[15]Caesar Augustus was the great-nephew and adopted son of Julius Caesar, who had been declared a god after his death.

Aeneas himself was half divine; his mother was Venus, the goddess of love.
[16]The region surrounding Rome, where the Latin people lived.
[17]According to Roman tradition, the Golden Age of Saturn was a primeval era of purity and simplicity — virtues that made Rome great. Saturn, originally an Italian god of agriculture, was deposed by his son Jupiter, king of the gods. Thereupon, Saturn fled to Latium, where he became its king, establishing a society that lacked weapons, money, walled cities, and all similar corrupting influences. During this era the fruits of the soil were gained without toil.
[18]A people of northeast Africa.
[19]Beyond the known world.
[20]The Parthian Empire ruled the region around the Caspian Sea.
[21]A reference to the steppe peoples north of the Black Sea.
[22]The Nile Delta.
[23]A reference to his victory over the forces of Cleopatra VII and Marc Antony at Actium.
[24]Another name for the legendary hero Hercules. Like Hercules, Augustus performed civilizing tasks and was a mortal who was destined to become a god.

still hesitate to assert our valor by action, or does fear forbid our settling on Italian soil?[25]

▷ Anchises returns to a chronological description of the shades of future Roman heroes, beginning with Numa, an ancient king of Rome and its first lawgiver. After pointing out Fabius Maximus, whose delaying tactics saved Rome in the dark days of the Second Punic War, Anchises sums up the essence of Rome's unique genius.

[25]These two questions are directed to Aeneas: After seeing Augustus, can he have any hesitation as to following his destiny?

"Others,[26] for so I believe, shall hammer out more delicately breathing likenesses from bronze and draw forth living faces from marble. Others shall plead their causes better, plot with a gauge the movement of the heavens, and describe the rising of the stars. But, Roman, remember that you must rule nations by your dominion. These will be your arts: to crown peace with civilization, to show mercy to the conquered, and to tame the proud by war."

[26]Namely, the Greeks.

Han China

As we survey Eurasia around the turn of the millennium, we see two massive empires of about equal size and population at the ends of this great landmass. For the next two centuries, Han China and Rome dominated their respective regions, and although each experienced periods of crisis, each also offered its subjects fairly stable government and a degree of prosperity.

The Han Dynasty reigned during one of China's golden ages. It expanded China's influence into Korea and Vietnam and across the reaches of Central Asia. It presided over a general economic upswing, in spite of its expansionist policies, and witnessed a period of rich cultural productivity. Han China flourished for close to four centuries, but in the end, like the Roman Empire, the dynasty and its empire collapsed, the victim of internal instabilities and invasions.

The age of Han was not one period, but two. From 202 B.C.E. to 9 C.E., the Former, or Western, Han ruled China. Following an interlude in which the imperial throne was temporarily wrested from the Han family, the dynasty returned to power in the form of the Later, or Eastern, Han (25–220 C.E.). After the first century C.E., however, domestic and frontier conditions deteriorated. From 88 C.E. onward, the family was plagued by a series of ineffective rulers.

By 220, when the Han Dynasty formally came to an end, local lords and invaders from the steppes ruled over a fragmented China. The stability and unity of earlier Han was only a memory as China was plunged into a social, economic, and political chaos that lasted for more than 350 years. The centuries of disruption following the collapse of Han have often been likened to the so-called Dark Ages that ensued after the disintegration of Roman imperial unity in the West, but the differences between the two are more significant than any superficial parallels.

Two Views on How to Deal with Empire

▼▼▼

28 ▼ *Huan Kuan,*
DISCOURSES ON SALT AND IRON

The *First Chinese Empire* can be said to have begun with the triumph of the Qin Dynasty in 221 B.C.E. and continued until the collapse of the Han Dynasty in 220 C.E. The two dynasties experienced setbacks and disasters, but, by and large, China was *the* imperial power in East and Central Asia during these 441 years.

The reign of Emperor *Han Wudi* (r. 141–87 B.C.E.) was pivotal in China's drive toward empire. In 124 B.C.E. the emperor decreed that proven knowledge of one of the *Confucian Classics* would be a basis for promotion into the imperial civil service, and he created a rudimentary imperial academy for educating aspiring scholar-officials in the various fields of Confucian learning. By this act he set in motion a process whereby Confucianism was set on the road to become, centuries later, the empire's ideological framework. However, although the principles of Confucius and his followers provided the Han Empire with a façade of moralism and conformity to the ways of the past, its policies were Legalist.

The policies that Han Wudi pursued during his fifty-four-year reign were pragmatic and expansionistic. Beginning in 121, his armies began driving a fierce pastoral people, whom the Chinese called the *Xiongnu*, out of the Gansu (or Hexi) Corridor, a narrow defile bordered by desert and mountains that ran northwest for about 600 miles from the Han capital of Chang'an (present-day Xi'an) in north-central China. Once the Chinese gained control of the corridor, their armies, administrators, settlers, and merchants could begin moving farther west into the heart of Central Asia. The result was an empire whose influence stretched all the way to the Ferghana Valley in what is today eastern Uzbekistan. It also meant that the Silk Road, the network of caravan routes linking China with India and the Mediterranean, entered its first age of efflorescence.

Empire and long-distance trade have their rewards and their costs. Armies along an expanded western frontier demanded large outlays of money, and to raise sufficient funds Han Wudi's government turned the manufacture of two basic necessities, salt and iron, into government monopolies. It also placed liquor production under government supervision and taxed it heavily. All three were enterprises that previously had brought great wealth to private entrepreneurs. The government also took large-scale commerce in grain and other staple food products, another source of huge profits, out of the hands of individuals and turned it into a function of the state. Governmental control of food distribution, known as *equable marketing*, was designed to stabilize prices and to prevent famines by buying grain and similar commodities where and when they were plentiful and cheap and selling them at fair prices in places and times of scarcity. But it also turned the government into a market speculator.

In 81 B.C.E. Confucian scholars who disagreed with these policies were invited by Emperor Han Zhaodi (r. 87–74) to debate the issue with Sang Hongyang, the emperor's chief economic minister. Sometime between 74 and 49 B.C.E., an otherwise unknown scholar by the name of Huan Kuan preserved at least the essential elements of this debate in his *Discourses on Salt and Iron*. To his credit, although his sympathies lay with the Confucian critics, Huan Kuan impartially reported both sides of the debate. Because both parties put forth their best arguments in these discourses, we have a privileged insight into the differences that separated Confucians and Legalists in this age of empire.

QUESTIONS FOR ANALYSIS

1. What was the Confucian position? Was it consistent with the principles articulated in the Analects (source 20)?
2. Can you discover any Daoist principles (source 19) in the Confucians' arguments? What do you infer from your answer?
3. What was the Legalist position?
4. Consider the styles and methods of argumentation employed by each side. Were they different or similar? What do you infer from your answer?
5. What does this document allow us to infer about the state of the Han Empire and its economy in the early first century B.C.E.? Be specific.

It so happened that . . . an Imperial edict directed the Chancellor and the Lord Grand Secretary[1] to confer with the recommended Worthies and Literati,[2] and to enquire of them as to the rankling grievances among the people.

The Literati responded as follows: It is our humble opinion that the principle of ruling men lies in nipping in the bud wantonness and frivolity, in extending wide the elementals of virtue, in discouraging mercantile pursuits, and in displaying benevolence and righteousness. Let profit never be paraded before the eyes of the people; only then will enlightenment flourish and folkways improve.

But now, with the system of the salt and iron monopolies, the liquor excise, and *equable marketing* established . . . , the Government has entered into financial competition with the people, undermining their native honesty and simplicity and promoting selfishness and greed. As a result few among our people take up the fundamental pursuits of life,[3] while many flock to the nonessential.[4] Now sturdy natural qualities decay as artificiality thrives, and rural values decline when industrialism flourishes. When industrialism is cultivated, the people become frivolous; when the values of rural life are developed, the people are simple and unsophisticated. The people being unsophisticated, wealth will abound; when the people are extravagant, cold and hunger will follow. We pray that the salt, iron and liquor monopolies and the system of *equable marketing* be abolished so that the rural pursuits may be encouraged, people be deterred from entering

[1] Sang Hongyang, the son of a shopkeeper, who rose to high office in 110 B.C.E. because of his mathematical abilities.
[2] Two grades of Confucian scholars.
[3] Agriculture.

[4] The Confucians considered manufacture and trade nonessential (or branch) pursuits in the sense that they were secondary in importance to agriculture.

the secondary occupations, and agriculture be materially and financially benefited.

The Lord Grand Secretary said: When the Xiongnu rebelled against our authority and frequently raided and devastated the frontier settlements, to be constantly on the watch for them was a great strain upon the soldiery of the Middle Kingdom;[5] but without measures of precaution being taken, these forays and depredations would never cease. The late Emperor,[6] grieving at the long suffering of the frontier settlers who live in fear of capture by the barbarians, caused consequently forts and signal stations[7] to be built, where garrisons were held ready against the nomads. When the revenue for the defense of the frontier fell short, the salt and iron monopoly was established, the liquor excise and the system of *equable marketing* introduced; goods were multiplied and wealth increased so as to furnish the frontier expenses.

Now our critics here, who demand that these measures be abolished, at home would have the hoard of the treasury entirely depleted, and abroad would deprive the border of provision for its defense; they would expose our soldiers who defend the barriers and mount the walls to all the hunger and cold of the borderland. How else do they expect to provide for them? It is not expedient to abolish these measures!

The Literati: Confucius observed that *the ruler of a kingdom or the chief of a house is not concerned about his people being few, but about lack of equitable treatment, nor is he concerned about poverty, but over the presence of discontentment.*[8] Thus the Son of Heaven should not speak about *much and little*, the feudal lords should not talk about *advantage and detriment*, ministers about *gain and loss*, but they should cultivate benevolence and righteousness, to set an example to the people, and extend wide their virtuous conduct to gain the people's

confidence. Then will nearby folk lovingly flock to them and distant peoples joyfully submit to their authority. . . . Cultivate virtue in the temple and the hall, then you need only to show a bold front to the enemy and your troops will return home in victory. The Prince who practices benevolent administration should be matchless in the world; for him, what use is expenditure?

The Lord Grand Secretary: The Xiongnu, savage and wily, boldly push through the barriers and harass the Middle Kingdom, massacring the provincial population and killing officers and officials along the northern frontier. They long deserve punishment for their unruliness and lawlessness. But Your Majesty[9] graciously took pity on the insufficiency of the multitude and did not allow his officials and soldiers to be exposed in the desert plains, yet unflinchingly You cherish the purpose of raising strong armies and driving the Xiongnu before You to their original haunts in the north. I again assert that the proposal to do away with the salt and iron monopoly and *equable marketing* would grievously diminish our frontier supplies and impair our military plans. I can not consider favorably a proposal so heartlessly dismissing the frontier question.

The Literati: The ancients held in honor virtuous methods and discredited resort to arms. Thus Confucius said: *If remoter people are not submissive, civil culture and virtue are to be cultivated to attract them to be so; and when they have been so attracted, they must be made contented and tranquil.*[10] Now these virtuous principles are discarded and reliance put on military force; troops are raised to attack the enemy and garrisons are stationed to make ready for him. It is the long drawn-out service of our troops in the field and the ceaseless transportation for the needs of the commissariat that cause our soldiers on the marches to suffer from hunger and cold abroad, while the common

---

[5]China.
[6]Han Wudi.
[7]These forts and signal towers, some of which were linked by steep but not very high earthen berms to hinder the progress of the nomads and their flocks of animals, constituted the original Great Wall of China. The massive stone wall that tourists visit today was largely built by the Ming Dynasty (1368–1644).
[8]A quotation from the *Analects* (source 20).
[9]Apparently the emperor was present at the debate.
[10]Another quotation from the *Analects*.

people are burdened with labor at home. The establishment of the salt and iron monopoly and the institution of finance officials to supply the army's needs were not permanent schemes; it is therefore desirable that they now be abolished.

The Lord Grand Secretary: The ancient founders of this country made open the ways for both fundamental and branch industries and facilitated equitable distribution of goods. Markets and courts were provided to harmonize various demands; there people of all classes gathered together and all goods collected, so that farmer, merchant, and worker could each obtain what he desired; the exchange completed, everyone went back to his occupation. *Facilitate exchange so that the people will be unflagging in industry* says the Book of Changes.[11] Thus without artisans, the farmers will be deprived of the use of implements; without merchants, all prized commodities will be cut off. The former would lead to stoppage of grain production, the latter to exhaustion of wealth. It is clear that the salt and iron monopoly and *equable marketing* are really intended for the circulation of amassed wealth and the regulation of the consumption according to the urgency of the need. It is inexpedient to abolish them.

The Literati: Lead the people with virtue and the people will return to honest simplicity; entice the people with gain, and they will become vulgar.[12] Vulgar habits would lead them away from duty to follow after gain, with the result that people will swarm on the road and throng at the markets. . . . Hence the true King promotes rural pursuits and discourages branch industries; he checks the people's desires through the principles of propriety and duty and provides a market for grain in exchange for other commodities, where there is no place for mer-

chants to circulate useless goods, and for artisans to make useless implements. The purpose of merchants is to circulate and of artisans to provide tools; they should not become a major concern of the government. . . .

The Lord Grand Secretary: The worthies and the sages did not found their families by means of one room,[13] nor did they enrich the state through one way. . . . If one must resort to agriculture alone to make a living and found a family, then Shun[14] would not have had to make pottery and Yi Yin[15] would not have had to be a cook. Hence, the Empire Builder acts according to the principle: *I honor what the whole world despises and value what the whole world slights.*[16] He would exchange the non-essential for the fundamental and secure the substantial with his own emptiness. . . . Thus, a piece of Chinese plain silk can be exchanged with the Xiongnu for articles worth several pieces of gold and thereby reduce the resources of our enemy. Mules, donkeys and camels enter the frontier in unbroken lines; horses, dapples and bays and prancing mounts, come into our possession. The furs of sables, marmots, foxes and badgers, colored rugs and decorated carpets fill the Imperial treasury, while jade and auspicious stones, corals and crystals, become national treasures. That is to say, products keep flowing in, while our wealth is not dissipated. Novelties flowing in, the government has plenty. National wealth not being dispersed abroad, the people enjoy abundance. So the Book of Poetry describes it: *Those hundred houses being full, the wives and children have a feeling of repose.*[17]

The Literati: In ancient times merchants circulated goods without premeditation, artisans got their price without cheating. Therefore when the true gentleman farmed, hunted or fished he was in reality doing but one thing. Trade promotes

---

[11]The *Yijing*, a book of divination and one of the *Confucian Classics.* Today it is quite popular in the West among New Agers.
[12]See the *Analects* (source 20).
[13]They were polygamists who had many wives and bedrooms.
[14]One of the legendary Five Sage Emperors who preceded the Xia Dynasty.

[15]A legendary minister of the Shang Dynasty. See source 5.
[16]A quotation from the *Guanzi*, a book of Legalist-Daoist essays on society and politics compiled between the mid fourth and mid second centuries B.C.E.
[17]Also known as the *Book of Songs.* See source 6.

dishonesty. Artisans provoke disputes. They lie in wait for their chance without a scruple. Thus avaricious men become cheats and honest men avaricious. . . . Now mules and donkeys are not as useful as cattle and horses. Sable and marmot furs, wool and felt goods do not add substance to silk. Beautiful jades and corals come from Mount Kun.[18] Pearls and ivory are produced in Gui Lin.[19] These places are more than ten thousand *li* distant from Han.[20] Calculating the labor for farming and silk raising and the costs in material and capital, it will be found that one article of foreign import costs a price one hundred times its value,[21] and for one handful, ten thousand weight of grain are paid. As the rulers take delight in novelties, extravagant clothing is adopted among the masses. As the rulers treasure the goods from distant lands, wealth flows

outward. Therefore, a true King does not value useless things, so to set an example of thrift to his subjects; does not love exotic articles, so to enrich his country. Thus the principle of administering the people lies only in carefulness in expenditure, in honoring the primary occupation, and in distribution of land according to the "well tithe."[22]

The Lord Grand Secretary: From the capital,[23] east, west, north and south across the mountains and rivers and throughout the provinces and the demesnes, you will find that all of the prosperous, rich and great municipalities have streets extending in all directions, where the merchants gather and all commodities are exposed. Thus, the Sage utilizes nature's seasons and the Wise utilizes the wealth of the land. Superior men acquire through others. The mediocre burden their own bodies.

---

[18]A mountain far to the west.
[19]The Kunlun Mountains, which lay far to the west of the heart of Han China. See the next note.
[20]A *li* is usually computed as roughly one-third of a mile, but evidence suggests that a li at this time was about one-fifth of a mile. About 2,000 miles is a pretty good estimate.
[21]Compare this with a similar statement by Pliny the Elder (Multiple Voices III, source 1).

[22]According to legend, in China's earliest days agricultural fields were divided into nine equal squares. Eight were given out to tenant farmers, who paid for their one-eighth portions by working together in the ninth portion, which belonged to the lord.
[23]From Chang'an.

A Woman's Place as Viewed by a Female Confucian

▼▼▼

29 ▼ *Ban Zhao, LESSONS FOR WOMEN*

Education in the *Confucian Classics* increasingly became one of several avenues to a position of social and political power in Han China. Confucian doctrine, however, did not accord women a status equal to that of men. In fact, the *Confucian Classics* say little about women, and this silence suggests how little they mattered in the scheme of Confucian values. Most Confucians accepted women's subservience to men as natural and proper. In their view, failure to maintain a proper relationship between two such obviously unequal persons as husband and wife or brother and sister would result in a breakdown of all the rules of propriety and lead to social disharmony.

Yet this was only part of the story. Confucian doctrine and Chinese society at large accorded women, as both mothers and mothers-in-law, a good deal of honor, and with that honor came power within the family structure. Moreover, there is plenty of evidence of literate, educated women of high status during the Han and Tang eras (202 B.C.E.–907 C.E.). Indeed, a handful of extraordinary women managed to acquire advanced literary educations and achieve positions of far-ranging influence and authority despite social constraints. The foremost female Confucian of the Age of Han was *Ban Zhao* (ca. 45–116 C.E.), sister of the court historian Ban Gu (32–92). Upon Gu's death Zhao served as imperial historian and completed the *Han Annals,* a history of the Former Han Dynasty begun by her father and continued but left unfinished by her brother. She probably composed fully one-quarter of what is regarded as one of China's historical masterpieces. She also served as advisor on state matters to Empress Deng, who assumed power as regent for her infant son in 106.

Madame Ban was the daughter of the widely respected writer and administrator Ban Biao (3–54) and received her elementary education from her literate mother. She married at the age of fourteen and bore children. Her husband died young, and Ban Zhao never remarried, devoting herself instead to literary pursuits and acquiring a reputation for scholarship and stylistic grace that brought her to the imperial court, where she was accorded the title "Learned One."

Among her many literary works, Ban Zhao composed a commentary on the popular *Lives of Admirable Women* by Liu Xiang (77–6 B.C.E.) and later in life produced her most famous work, the *Nü Jie,* or *Lessons for Women,* which purports to be an instructional manual on feminine behavior and virtue for her daughters. In fact, she intended it for a much wider audience. Realizing that Confucian texts contained little in the way of specific and practical guidelines for a woman's everyday life, Ban Zhao sought to fill that void.

QUESTIONS FOR ANALYSIS

1. What does Ban Zhao tell us about the status of daughters-in-law? What does she mean when she states, "Now and hereafter, . . . I know how to escape from such fears"?
2. This essay contains several clues regarding a woman's role in maintaining a beneficial relationship with the family's ancestors. Find and comment on them. How significant, if at all, do you find this role?
3. What does Ban Zhao consider the principal duty of a husband? Of a wife? How and why are they complementary parts of the natural order of the universe?
4. According to Ban Zhao, what rules of propriety should govern a marriage?
5. Why does Ban Zhao advocate that women be educated? Do her stated reasons strike you as her true motives? Be specific in defending your answer.
6. What was there about Ban Zhao's essay that caused it to be so highly regarded by male Confucian scholars over the following centuries?

I, the unworthy writer, am unsophisticated, un-enlightened, and by nature unintelligent, but I am fortunate both to have received not a little favor from my scholarly father, and to have had a cultured mother and instructresses upon whom to rely for a literary education as well as for training in good manners. More than forty years have passed since at the age of fourteen I took up the dustpan and the broom in the Cao family.[1] During this time with trembling heart I feared constantly that I might disgrace my parents, and that I might multiply difficulties for both the women and the men of my husband's family. Day and night I was distressed in heart, but I labored without confessing weariness. Now and hereafter, however, I know how to escape from such fears.

Being careless, and by nature stupid, I taught and trained my children without system. . . . I do grieve that you, my daughters, just now at the age for marriage, have not at this time had gradual training and advice; that you still have not learned the proper customs for married women. I fear that by failure in good manners in other families you will humiliate both your ancestors and your clan. I am now seriously ill, life is uncertain. As I have thought of you all in so untrained a state, I have been uneasy many a time for you. At hours of leisure I have composed . . . these instructions under the title, "Lessons for Women." In order that you may have something wherewith to benefit your persons, I wish every one of you, my daughters, each to write out a copy for yourself.

From this time on every one of you strive to practice these lessons.

HUMILITY

On the third day after the birth of a girl the ancients observed three customs: first to place the baby below the bed; second to give her a potsherd[2] with which to play; and third to an-nounce her birth to her ancestors by an offering. Now to lay the baby below the bed plainly indicated that she is lowly and weak, and should regard it as her primary duty to humble herself before others. To give her potsherds with which to play indubitably signified that she should practice labor and consider it her primary duty to be industrious. To announce her birth before her ancestors clearly meant that she ought to esteem as her primary duty the continuation of the observance of worship in the home.

These three ancient customs epitomize a woman's ordinary way of life and the teachings of the traditional ceremonial rites and regulations. Let a woman modestly yield to others; let her respect others; let her put others first, herself last. Should she do something good, let her not mention it; should she do something bad, let her not deny it. Let her bear disgrace; let her even endure when others speak or do evil to her. Always let her seem to tremble and to fear. When a woman follows such maxims as these, then she may be said to humble herself before others.

Let a woman retire late to bed, but rise early to duties; let her not dread tasks by day or by night. Let her not refuse to perform domestic duties whether easy or difficult. That which must be done, let her finish completely, tidily, and systematically. When a woman follows such rules as these, then she may be said to be industrious.

Let a woman be correct in manner and upright in character in order to serve her husband. Let her live in purity and quietness of spirit, and attend to her own affairs. Let her love not gossip and silly laughter. Let her cleanse and purify and arrange in order the wine and the food for the offerings to the ancestors. When a woman observes such principles as these, then she may be said to continue ancestral worship.

No woman who observes these three fundamentals of life has ever had a bad reputation or has fallen into disgrace. If a woman fails to observe them, how can her name be honored; how can she but bring disgrace upon herself?

---

[1] The family into which she married.

[2] A piece of broken pottery.

HUSBAND AND WIFE

The Way of husband and wife is intimately connected with *Yin* and *Yang*,[3] and relates the individual to gods and ancestors. Truly it is the great principle of Heaven and Earth, and the great basis of human relationships. . . .

If a husband is unworthy, then he possesses nothing by which to control his wife. If a wife is unworthy, then she possesses nothing with which to serve her husband. If a husband does not control his wife, then the rules of conduct manifesting his authority are abandoned and broken. If a wife does not serve her husband, then the proper relationship between men and women and the natural order of things are neglected and destroyed. . . .

Now examine the gentlemen of the present age. They only know that wives must be controlled, and that the husband's rules of conduct manifesting his authority must be established. They therefore teach their boys to read books and study histories. But they do not in the least understand that husbands and masters must also be served, and that the proper relationship and the rites should be maintained.

Yet only to teach men and not to teach women — is that not ignoring the essential relation between them? . . . [I]t is the rule to begin to teach children to read at the age of eight years, and by the age of fifteen years they ought then to be ready for cultural training. Only why should it not be that girls' education as well as boys' be according to this principle?

RESPECT AND CAUTION

As *Yin* and *Yang* are not of the same nature, so man and woman have different characteristics. The distinctive quality of the *Yang* is rigidity; the function of the *Yin* is yielding. Man is honored for strength; a woman is beautiful on account of her gentleness. Hence there arose the common saying: "A man though born like a wolf may, it is feared, become a weak monstrosity; a woman though born like a mouse may, it is feared, become a tiger."

Now for self-culture nothing equals respect for others. To counteract firmness nothing equals compliance. Consequently it can be said that the Way of respect and acquiescence is woman's most important principle of conduct. . . . Those who are steadfast in devotion know that they should stay in their proper places; those who are liberal and generous esteem others, and honor and serve them.

If husband and wife have the habit of staying together, never leaving one another, and following each other around within the limited space of their own rooms, then they will lust after and take liberties with one another. From such action improper language will arise between the two. This kind of discussion may lead to licentiousness. Out of licentiousness will be born a heart of disrespect to the husband. Such a result comes from not knowing that one should stay in one's proper place. . . .

If wives suppress not contempt for husbands, then it follows that such wives rebuke and scold their husbands. If husbands stop not short of anger, then they are certain to beat their wives. The correct relationship between husband and wife is based upon harmony and intimacy, and conjugal love is grounded in proper union. Should actual blows be dealt, how could matrimonial relationship be preserved? Should sharp words be spoken, how could conjugal love exist? If love and proper relationship both be destroyed, then husband and wife are divided.

WOMANLY QUALIFICATIONS

A woman ought to have four qualifications: (1) womanly virtue; (2) womanly words; (3) womanly bearing; and (4) womanly work. Now what is

---

[3]See *The Yellow Emperor's Classic of Internal Medicine* (Multiple Voices II, source 1).

called womanly virtue need not be brilliant ability, exceptionally different from others. Womanly words need be neither clever in debate nor keen in conversation. Womanly appearance requires neither a pretty nor a perfect face and form. Womanly work need not be work done more skillfully than that of others.

To guard carefully her chastity; to control circumspectly her behavior; in every motion to exhibit modesty; and to model each act on the best usage, this is womanly virtue.

To choose her words with care; to avoid vulgar language; to speak at appropriate times; and not to weary others with much conversation, may be called the characteristics of womanly words.

To wash and scrub filth away; to keep clothes and ornaments fresh and clean; to wash the head and bathe the body regularly; and to keep the person free from disgraceful filth, may be called the characteristics of womanly bearing.

With whole-hearted devotion to sew and to weave; to love not gossip and silly laughter; in cleanliness and order to prepare the wine and food for serving guests, may be called the characteristics of womanly work.

These four qualifications characterize the greatest virtue of a woman. No woman can afford to be without them. In fact they are very easy to possess if a woman only treasure them in her heart. . . .

IMPLICIT OBEDIENCE

Whenever the mother-in-law says, "Do not do that," and if what she says is right, unquestionably the daughter-in-law obeys. Whenever the mother-in-law says, "Do that," even if what she says is wrong, still the daughter-in-law submits unfailingly to the command.

Let a woman not act contrary to the wishes and the opinions of parents-in-law about right and wrong; let her not dispute with them what is straight and what is crooked. Such docility may be called obedience which sacrifices personal opinion. Therefore the ancient book, "A Pattern for Women," says: "If a daughter-in-law who follows the wishes of her parents-in-law is like an echo and a shadow, how could she not be praised?"

India in the Age of Empires

Between the third century B.C.E. and the sixth century C.E., India witnessed the rise of two native empires, each of which participated in the general interchange of goods, ideas, and peoples that characterized this age of Afro-Eurasian interchange.

The first was the *Mauryan Empire* (ca. 315–183 B.C.E.), which controlled all but the most southern portions of the subcontinent. Centuries later the *Gupta Empire* (320–ca. 550 C.E.) arose, centered on the Ganges River in the northeast but exercising authority over most of northern and central India. Although neither equaled the Han and Roman empires in size, military power, or longevity, both Indian empires provided peace and general prosperity based, at least in part, on energetic administration and benign social intervention. At the height of the Gupta Empire under Chandragupta II (r. ca. 376–415), India was possibly the most prosperous and peaceful society in the Afro-Eurasian World. China was then immersed in an interdynastic time of troubles; Greco-Roman civilization was undergoing severe stresses at every level; and the Sassanian Empire of Persia was embroiled in internal religious turmoil and wars on its frontiers.

Between these two homebred imperial periods, India underwent a series of invasions from the northwest that resulted in portions of northern India falling under the domination of alien rulers and being joined to important Central Asian kingdoms and empires. First came Greeks from Bactria (source 26), who arrived in the early second century B.C.E. and established a number of competing kingdoms in northern India. The Greco-Bactrians soon gave way to various nomadic invaders from East and Central Asia, whose lives had been disrupted by the emergence of Chinese imperialism in the late third and second centuries B.C.E. and also by intertribal conflicts.

The most significant of the new invaders were a nomadic people the Chinese knew as the *Yuezhi,* who created the *Kushan Empire* toward the end of the first century B.C.E. The Kushans, whose imperial focus was always Central Asia, lasted into the late third century C.E., and during their centuries of empire, they provided India with connections to Southwest Asia, the Mediterranean, and China (see Multiple Voices III). Much of that interaction was the peaceful exchange of goods and ideas, but Chinese annals also tell how General Ban Chao, brother of the historians Ban Gu and Ban Zhao (source 29), destroyed a Yuezhi army in 90 C.E. when the Kushan emperor launched a retaliatory strike against the Chinese after he was refused the hand of a Han princess.

The Softening Effects of Dharma
▼▼▼
30 ▾ *Asoka, ROCK AND PILLAR EDICTS*

As Alexander the Great and his Macedonian generals pulled back from northwest India, a local lord, Chandragupta Maurya (r. ca. 315–281 B.C.E.), began forming what would become the greatest of India's ancient empires. Under the founder and his son, Bindusara, the empire expanded and functioned with brutal efficiency. Around 269 B.C.E. Bindusara's son *Asoka* (r. ca. 269–232) inherited the throne and initially continued his family's tradition of foreign aggression and domestic repression.

In the eighth year of his reign, however, he underwent a spiritual conversion when he beheld the bloodshed and misery that resulted from his conquest of the land of Kalinga, along India's southeastern coast. As a consequence, Asoka embraced the teachings of the Buddha and embarked on a new policy of government. Inspired by the public monuments of the kings of Persia, Asoka publicized his change of heart and new imperial policies in a series of engraved rock and pillar inscriptions scattered throughout his lands. More than thirty still exist, located in present-day India, Nepal, Pakistan, and Afghanistan.

QUESTIONS FOR ANALYSIS

1. Is there any evidence in this source that Asoka promoted Buddhist missionary activities? Be specific.
2. What was Asoka's attitude and policy toward all non-Buddhist religions and ceremonies?

3. Following his conversion, what did Asoka consider to be the purpose of good government? What structures and policies did he institute to achieve his vision?

4. Asoka saw himself as a follower of the Buddha's Law of Righteousness (*Dharma*). Review sources 15 and 16. Based on your understanding of these two lessons by the Buddha, respond to the following questions: Would the Buddha agree with any of Asoka's policies and beliefs? If so, which ones? Would the Buddha disagree with any of Asoka's policies and beliefs? If so, which ones? What would be the Buddha's overall evaluation of Asoka's understanding of Buddhist teachings?

5. Imagine that three Chinese travelers — a Confucian, a Legalist, and a Daoist — read these inscriptions. What would be their reactions?

ROCK EDICT XIII

The Kalinga country was conquered by King Priyadarsi,[1] Beloved of the Gods, in the eighth year of his reign. One hundred and fifty thousand persons were carried away captive, one hundred thousand were slain, and many times that number died.

Immediately after the Kalingas had been conquered, King Priyadarsi became intensely devoted to the study of Dharma,[2] to the love of Dharma, and to the inculcation of Dharma.

The Beloved of the Gods, conqueror of the Kalingas, is moved to remorse now. For he has felt profound sorrow and regret because the conquest of a people previously unconquered involves slaughter, death, and deportation.

But there is a more important reason for the King's remorse. The Brahmanas[3] and Sramanas[4] as well as the followers of other religions and householders — who all practiced obedience to superiors, parents, and teachers, and proper courtesy and firm devotion to friends, acquaintances, companions, relatives, slaves, and servants — all suffer from the injury, slaughter, and deportation inflicted on their loved ones. Even

those who escaped calamity themselves are deeply afflicted by the misfortunes suffered by those . . . for whom they feel an undiminished affection. Thus all men share in the misfortune, and this weighs on King Priyadarsi's mind. . . .

King Priyadarsi now thinks that even a person who wrongs him must be forgiven for wrongs that can be forgiven.

King Priyadarsi seeks to induce even the forest peoples[5] who have come under his dominion to adopt this way of life and this ideal. He reminds them, however, that he exercises the power to punish, despite his repentance, in order to induce them to desist from their crimes and escape execution.

For King Priyadarsi desires security, self-control, impartiality, and cheerfulness for all living creatures.

King Priyadarsi considers moral conquest the most important conquest. He has achieved this moral conquest repeatedly both here and among the peoples living beyond the borders of his kingdom, even as far away as six hundred *yojanas*,[6] where the Yona [Greek] king Antiyoka[7] rules, and even beyond Antiyoka in the realms of

---

[1] Asoka's throne name, it means "one who sees to the good of others."
[2] Source 15 provides a definition of Buddhist *Dharma*.
[3] Hindu ascetics who were members of the Brahmin, or priestly, caste. They were divided into many sects.
[4] Another group of ascetics. In the context of this edict, *Brahmanas and Sramanas* means all Hindu and Buddhist holy people.

[5] The primitive, largely uncivilized folk of the southern jungle.
[6] About 3,000 miles.
[7] Antiochus II Theos (r. 261–246 B.C.E.), a member of the Macedonian family of Seleucus and king of Syria.

the four kings named Turamaya, Antikini, Maka, and Alikasudara,[8] and to the south among the Cholas and Pandyas[9] as far as Ceylon.[10] . . .

Even in countries which King Priyadarsi's envoys have not reached, people have heard about Dharma and about his Majesty's ordinances and instructions in Dharma, and they themselves conform to Dharma and will continue to do so.

Wherever conquest is achieved by Dharma, it produces satisfaction. Satisfaction is firmly established by conquest by Dharma. Even satisfaction, however, is of little importance. King Priyadarsi attaches value ultimately only to consequences of action in the other world.

This edict on Dharma has been inscribed so that my sons and great-grandsons who may come after me should not think new conquests worth achieving. If they do conquer, let them take pleasure in moderation and mild punishments. Let them consider moral conquest the only true conquest.

This is good, here and hereafter. Let their pleasure be pleasure in morality. For this alone is good, here and hereafter.

PILLAR EDICT VII

King Priyadarsi, the Beloved of the Gods, speaks as follows: . . .

How can the people be induced to follow Dharma strictly? How can progress in morality be increased sufficiently? How can I raise them up by the promotion of Dharma? . . . To this end I have issued proclamations on Dharma, and I have instituted various kinds of moral and religious instruction.

My highest officials, who have authority over large numbers of people, will expound and spread the precepts of Dharma. I have instructed the provincial governors, too, who are in charge of many hundred thousand people, concerning how to guide people devoted to Dharma. . . .

My officers charged with the spread of Dharma are occupied with various kinds of services beneficial to ascetics and householders, and they are empowered to concern themselves with all sects. I have ordered some of them to look after the affairs of the Sangha,[11] some to take care of the brahmin . . . ascetics, some to work among the Nirgranthas,[12] and some among the various other religious sects. Different officials are thus assigned specifically to the affairs of different religions, but my officers for spreading Dharma are occupied with all sects. . . .

These and many other high officials take care of the distribution of gifts from myself as well as from the queens. They report in various ways . . . worthy recipients of charity. . . . I also ordered some of them to supervise the distribution of gifts from my sons and the sons of other queens, in order to promote noble deeds of Dharma and conformity to the precepts of Dharma. These noble deeds and this conformity consist in promoting compassion, liberality, truthfulness, purity, gentleness, and goodness. . . .

Whatever good deeds I have done the people have imitated, and they have followed them as a model. In doing so, they have progressed and will progress in obedience to parents and teachers, in respect for elders, in courtesy to priests and ascetics, to the poor and distressed, and even to slaves and servants. . . .

The people can be induced to advance in Dharma by only two means, by moral prescriptions and by meditation. Of the two, moral prescriptions are of little consequence, but meditation is of great importance. The moral prescriptions I have promulgated include rules making certain animals inviolable,[13] and many others. But even in the case of abstention from injuring

---

[8]Ptolemy II Philadelphus of Egypt (r. 285–247 B.C.E.); Antigonos Gonatas of Macedonia (r. 278–239 B.C.E.); Magos of Cyrene in North Africa (r. 300–258 B.C.E.); and Alexander of Epirus in northwest Greece (r. ca. 272–258 B.C.E.).

[9]People of the southern tip of India who lived outside of his empire.

[10]The major island off the southeast coast of India; today it is the nation of Sri Lanka.

[11]Buddhist monastic groups.

[12]Jain ascetics, who followed the teachings of the *Mahavira*, a rough contemporary of the Buddha who taught a doctrine of extreme asceticism and absolute nonviolence.

[13]Certain animals are not to be harmed.

and from killing living creatures, it is by meditation that people have progressed in Dharma most.

This edict on Dharma has been inscribed in order that it may endure and be followed as long as my sons and great-grandsons shall reign and as long as the sun and moon shall shine. For one who adheres to it will attain happiness in this world and hereafter. . . .

This edict on morality should be engraved wherever stone pillars or stone slabs are available, in order that it may endure forever.

PILLAR EDICT II

King Priyadarsi says:

Dharma is good. But what does Dharma consist of? It consists of few sins and many good deeds, of kindness, liberality, truthfulness, and purity.

I have bestowed even the gift of spiritual insight on men in various ways. I have decreed many kindnesses, including even the grant of life, to living creatures, two-footed and four-footed as well as birds and aquatic animals. I have also performed many other good deeds.

I have ordered this edict on Dharma to be inscribed in order that people may act according to it and that it may endure for a long time. And he who follows it completely will do good deeds.

ROCK EDICT IX

King Priyadarsi, the Beloved of the Gods, says:

People perform various ceremonies. Among the occasions on which ceremonies are performed are sicknesses, marriages of sons or daughters, children's births, and departures on journeys. Women in particular have recourse to many diverse, trivial, and meaningless ceremonies.

For I desire that, when the period of respite has expired, they may attain happiness in the next world, and that various ways of practicing Dharma by self-control and the distribution of gifts may be increased among the people.

Gupta India Through Chinese Buddhist Eyes
▼▼▼

31 ▼ *Faxian, TRAVELS*

As Buddhism expanded in China (see Chapter 9, Multiple Voices VI), devotees of the new religion, particularly monks, avidly sought to add to the available body of Buddhist literature, which meant tracking down various Buddhist holy books, or *sutras,* in India and translating them into Chinese. They also desired to journey to pilgrimage sites, to acquire more authentic images of the Buddha, and to bring home relics, if they could be acquired. The result was a small but steady stream of Chinese travelers to India during the age of the Gupta Empire and thereafter.

The earliest known Chinese pilgrim to travel to India and return with sacred books and images was the monk Faxian, who set out from North China in 399 along a difficult overland route. Once in India, he confined himself to areas in the north sacred to the memory of the Buddha, although he did sail south to Ceylon on his homeward journey (see Multiple Voices III, source 2). In 414 he returned home, where he spent the rest of his days translating the texts he had obtained in India.

In addition to the translations, Faxian left behind a record of his travels, in which he described northern Indian society in the reign of Chandragupta II. Although he was mainly concerned with pilgrimage sites and holy books rather than with providing a detailed description of Indian culture, his travelogue gives us an outsider's view of northern India at the height of Gupta prosperity.

QUESTIONS FOR ANALYSIS

1. How well or poorly did Hindu and Buddhist communities interact? What conclusion follows from your answer?
2. Consider the Buddha's original teaching, which refused to deal with such questions as the existence of spirits and gods (source 16) and rejected all ritual. How had Buddhism evolved by Faxian's day?
3. Describe in detail the social and political situation in Gupta India as reported by Faxian.
4. Is there any evidence whatsoever that Buddhist principles might have influenced the social practices and values of Gupta India, whose rulers were Hindu?
5. Play a bit of historical fantasy: Compose Asoka's commentary on Gupta India.

From this place they[1] traveled southeast, passing by a succession of very many monasteries, with a multitude of monks, who might be counted by myriads. After passing all these places, they came to a . . . river on the banks of which, left and right, there were twenty monasteries, which might contain three thousand monks; and here the Law of Buddha was still more flourishing. Everywhere, from the Sandy Desert,[2] in all the countries of India, the kings had been firm believers in that Law. When they make their offerings to a community of monks, they take off their royal caps, and along with their relatives and ministers, supply them with food with their own hands. That done, the king has a carpet spread for himself on the ground, and sits down on it in front of the leader of the monastery; — they dare not presume to sit on couches in front of the community. The laws and ways, according to which the kings presented their offerings when Buddha was in the world, have been handed down to the present day.

All south from this is named the Middle Kingdom.[3] In it the cold and heat are finely tempered, and there is neither hoarfrost nor snow. The people are numerous and happy; they have not to register their households, or attend to any magistrates and their rules; only those who cultivate the royal land have to pay a portion of the gain from it. If they want to go, they go; if they want to stay on, they stay. The king governs without decapitation or other corporal punishments. Criminals are simply fined, lightly or heavily, according to the circumstances of each case. Even in cases of repeated attempts at wicked rebellion, they only have their right hands cut off. The king's bodyguards and attendants all have salaries. Throughout the whole country the people do not kill any living creature, nor drink intoxicating liquor, nor eat onions or garlic. The only exception is that of the Kandalas.[4] That is the name for those who are held to be wicked men, and live apart from others. When they enter the gate of a city or a market-place, they strike a piece of wood to make themselves known, so that men know and avoid them, and do not come into contact with them. In that country they do not keep pigs and fowls, and do not sell live cattle; in the markets there are no butchers' shops and no dealers in intoxicating drink. . . . Only the Kandalas are fishermen and hunters, and sell flesh meat.

[1]Faxian and his fellow pilgrims.
[2]The Thar Desert in the northwest.
[3]*Majhimadesa* in Pali — the Middle Country. An Indian term that refers to north-central India, the region of the Buddha's early activities.
[4]The lowest group of untouchables.

After Buddha attained to pari-nirvana[5] the kings of the various countries and the heads of the Vaisyas[6] built viharas[7] for the monks, and endowed them with fields, houses, gardens, and orchards, along with the resident populations and their cattle, the grants being engraved on plates of metal, so that afterwards they were handed down from king to king, without any one daring to annul them, and they remain even to the present time.

The regular business of the monks is to perform acts of meritorious virtue, and to recite their Sutras and sit wrapt in meditation. When stranger monks arrive at any monastery, the old residents meet and receive them, carry for them their clothes and alms-bowl, give them water to wash their feet, oil with which to anoint them, and the liquid food permitted out of the regular hours.[8] When the stranger has enjoyed a very brief rest, they further ask the number of years that he has been a monk, after which the receives a sleeping apartment with its appurtenances, according to his regular order, and everything is done for him which the rules prescribe.

Where a community of monks resides, they erect stupas[9] to Sariputtra, to Mahamaudgalyayana, and to Ananda,[10] and also stupas in honor of the Abhidharma, the Vinaya, and the Sutras.[11] A month after the annual season of rest, the families which are looking out for blessing stimulate one another to make offerings to the monks, and send round to them the liquid food which may be taken out of the ordinary hours. All the monks come together in a great assembly, and preach the Law; after which offerings are presented at the stupa of Sariputtra, with all kinds of flowers and incense. All through the night lamps are kept burning, and skillful musicians are employed to perform. . . .

Having crossed the river, and descended south . . . the travelers came to the town of Pataliputtra,[12] in the kingdom of Magadha,[13] the city where king Asoka ruled. . . .

By the side of the stupa of Asoka, there has been made a Mahayana monastery, very grand and beautiful; there is also a Hinayana[14] one; the two together containing six hundred or seven hundred monks. The rules of demeanor and the scholastic arrangements in them are worthy of observation.

Shamans[15] of the highest virtue from all quarters, and students, inquirers wishing to find out truth and the grounds of it, all resort to these monasteries. There also resides in this monastery a Brahmin teacher, whose name also is Manjusri,[16] whom the shamans of greatest virtue in the kingdom, and the Mahayana bhikshus[17] honor and look up to.

The cities and towns of this country are the greatest of all in the Middle Kingdom. The inhabitants are rich and prosperous, and vie with one another in the practice of benevolence and righteousness. Every year on the eighth day of the second month they celebrate a procession of images. They make a four-wheeled car, and on it erect a structure of five stories by means of bamboos tied together. This is supported by a king-post, with poles and lances slanting from it, and is rather more than twenty cubits high, having the shape of a stupa. White and silk-like cloth of hair is wrapped all round it, which is then painted in various colors. They make figures of devas[18] with

---

[5]The Buddha's release from the bonds of matter — his final death.
[6]The caste of merchants and prosperous farmers.
[7]A hermitage for a recluse or a little house built for a holy person.
[8]Solid food was prohibited between sunrise and noon.
[9]A *stupa* is a large, domed structure built to house a relic of the Buddha or of one of his early disciples.
[10]Three of the Buddha's principal disciples.
[11]The *Tipitaka*, or "Three Baskets" — the three major collections of Buddhist scripture. See the introduction to source 15.
[12]Present-day Patna.

[13]The kingdom in northeastern India, which served as the nucleus of the Mauryan Empire.
[14]*Hinayana* (the Small Vehicle), or, more correctly, *Theravada* (the Way of the Elders), was one of the two major branches of Buddhism at this time. It and *Mahayana* (the Great Vehicle) are treated in Chapter 6.
[15]He probably means Hindu holy persons.
[16]Manjusri is the name of one of the most popular Mahayana Bodhisattvas (see Chapter 6, sources 32–33). Hence, Faxian points out that this Hindu "also" bears that name.
[17]Buddhist monks.
[18]Gods and goddesses.

gold, silver, and lapis lazuli grandly blended and having silken streamers and canopies hung out over them. On the four sides are niches, with a Buddha seated in each, and a Bodhisattva[19] standing in attendance on him. There may be twenty cars, all grand and imposing, but each one different from the others. On the day mentioned, the monks and laity within the borders all come together; they have singers and skillful musicians; they pay their devotions with flowers and incense. The Brahmins come and invite the Buddhas to enter the city. These do so in order, and remain two nights in it. All through the night they keep lamps burning, have skillful music, and present offerings. This is the practice in all the other kingdoms as well. The heads of the Vaisya families in them establish in the cities houses for dispensing charity and medicines. All the poor and destitute in the country, orphans, widowers, and childless men, maimed people and cripples, and all who are diseased, go to those houses, and are provided with every kind of help, and doctors examine their diseases. They get the food and medicines which their cases require, and are made to feel at ease; and when they are better, they go away of themselves.

---

[19]See Chapter 6, sources 32–33.

Multiple Voices III   ▼▼▼
Sea Routes and Silk Roads

BACKGROUND

At the beginning of the first millennium C.E., two major trade networks, one by water and the other by land, linked the First Afro-Eurasian Ecumene, making it possible for commodities and ideas (as well as diseases) to circulate from Southeast to Southwest Asia, from China to the Greco-Roman Mediterranean, and from India to all of the above.

A series of sea routes extended from China and the lands of Southeast Asia in the east and from the Red Sea and the Persian Gulf in the west to India, which served as a central meeting point for merchants from both directions. There, for example, merchants from the Mediterranean exchanged gold for pepper and other spices, jewels, and muslin cloth, as well as for Chinese manufactured commodities, such as porcelains, lacquered boxes, ironware, and silk. The Hellenistic geographer Strabo (ca. 64 B.C.E.–25 C.E.) claimed that in his day 120 vessels made the annual voyage from Egypt to India. There is even a record of a group of supposedly Roman merchants (probably Syrians or Egyptians) who sailed from India to south China in the mid second century C.E., but such adventures were rare. For most merchant mariners, India was the main terminus and marketplace where East met West.

The other network connecting the East with the West was the *Silk Road* (or Silk Roads), a series of linked caravan routes that ran on its east-west axis from northwestern China to the eastern shores of the Mediterranean, a distance of more than 4,000 miles, and on its north-south axis from China to India, by way of Afghanistan. As the name implies, Chinese silk was a major commodity along these roads, but many other trade items, including Central Asian horses and Baltic amber, moved along these overland routes. Although their lands were linked by this vast complex of routes, very few Mediterraneans traveled all the way to China, and fewer Chinese ventured even to the borders of the Roman Empire. Instead, a series of merchant intermediaries passed along the silk, cotton, brocades, spices, plants and animals, manufactured goods, gold, ideas, and even killing diseases that traveled from one end of this great network to the other.

THE SOURCES

The first source comes from the *Natural History* of Pliny the Elder (23–79 C.E.), the greatest Roman scholar of his day. Completed in the year 77, the work covers a wide range of natural phenomena. He claimed to present 20,000 items of importance carefully culled from the works of 100 selected authors, as well as his own observations. The excerpts that appear here discuss Central Asia, the land of the Seres (China), Roman trade with India, and a wondrous people who lived at the far eastern end of Asia. Combined, they illustrate the extent and limitations of the Roman World's participation in long-distance Afro-Eurasian commerce during the first century C.E. and allow insight into the Roman view of the world beyond its imperial borders.

The second source is from a traveler we have already encountered, Faxian (source 31), who describes his homeward voyage from Ceylon (present-day Sri Lanka). Faxian's plan was to reach the southern Chinese port of Guangzhou (Canton), but, as we shall see, when he finally set foot on Chinese soil, he found himself far up the northeast coast in Shandong Province, which lies across the Yellow Sea from Korea. His adventures on this voyage shed light on the interesting nature of early-fifth-century C.E. oceanic travel between India and China. Indeed, the source suggests why overland travel was often preferred at this time.

The third source is four sculptures, which collectively illustrate the transit of artistic motifs and styles across the Silk Road. As we saw in source 26, Hellenistic sculptors employed the elements of expressive faces, drapery that defined the body, and *contrapposto* (the turning of the hip and leg away from the shoulders and the head) to impart a sense of drama, motion, and reality to their work. As the heirs and continuators of Hellenistic culture, artists throughout the Roman Empire employed these same techniques, thereby creating an empire-wide style known as Greco-Roman.

The first sculpture, crafted in 136 C.E., portrays *Vibia Sabina*, wife of the Roman emperor Hadrian. This particular statue was probably not seen outside of Italy, but significant numbers of miniature bronze statues of similar style were exported beyond the boundaries of the Greco-Roman World, especially to imperial Rome's immediate neighbor to the east — Parthia.

The second sculpture — a woman in Southwest Asian dress — comes from the Parthian city of Hatra in northern Mesopotamia and dates from the second or early third century C.E. It is a votive offering, given by the unknown noblewoman it portrays to an equally unknown deity.

The third statue portrays the Buddha. Toward the end of the first century C.E., artists in the Kushan province of *Gandhara*, which today comprises Afghanistan and northwest Pakistan, began representing the Buddha as a human. The sculpture of the standing Buddha that appears here is typical of the many carvings that have survived from this period and place. The setting is the Buddha's first sermon on the Law of Righteousness. Many of the features are distinctively Buddhist. The knot on the top of the Buddha's head is known as the *ushnisha* and represents his cosmic consciousness, and it probably has no connection whatsoever with the stylish twist worn by Vibia Sabina. His pierced, distended earlobes symbolize his former royal life; the garment he wears is the *sanghati*, or monk's robe; the *halo*, or solar disk, that frames his head is typical of all Gandharan statues of the Buddha and represents his sanctity. His missing right hand probably was raised palm outward in the gesture of blessing. The lotuses, or water lilies, carved into the base of the statue are a Buddhist symbol of purity and peace, therefore Nirvana. Despite all of these Indian-Buddhist features, it is the general consensus of scholars that the style and majesty of the Greco-Roman imperial sculpture that emanated from the workshops of the Mediterranean deeply influenced the creators of the early Gandharan statues of the Buddha.

The fourth sculpture depicts the Buddha standing on a lotus flower. Composed of gilded bronze, it was crafted in 477 in the region of China ruled by the Northern Wei Dynasty (386–535). The Northern Wei, Turkic invaders who had conquered and unified northern China, had adopted the trappings of Chinese aristocratic culture but added a new element. They were deeply devoted to Mahayana Buddhism (see Chapter 6) and patronized its rapid spread throughout northern China. The statue, missing only its original, attached halo, deals largely with the same theme and setting as the Gandharan Buddha, but artistically it is somewhat different.

QUESTIONS FOR ANALYSIS

1. How well did Pliny understand the peoples and lands of Central and East Asia? What do you infer from your answer?
2. How might one best characterize mercantile travel and trade between India and the Mediterranean in the first century C.E.?
3. Based on Faxian's experiences, describe the state of sea travel between India and Southeast Asia and India and China in the early fifth century C.E.
4. When host societies receive foreign elements, they usually adapt them to fit into the framework of their own cultures. This process of adaptive adoption is often termed *syncretism*. How, if at all, do the four sculptures exhibit this phenomenon at work across the early Silk Road?
5. Based on these three sources, how would you characterize the extent, level, and significance of long-distance communication and exchange across the Afro-Eurasian Ecumene during this era?

I ▼ *Pliny the Elder, NATURAL HISTORY*

TRAVEL TO THE LAND OF THE SERES[1]

From the Caspian Sea and the Scythian Ocean,[2] our course bends toward the Morning Star, as the coast turns toward the east. The first part of the coast after the Scythian Promontory[3] is uninhabitable because of snow, and the neighboring region is uncultivated because of the savagery of its people. Here the Scythian cannibals live who feast on human bodies.[4] Consequently, the lands adjacent are vast wastelands inhabited by multitudinous wild beasts that lie in wait for humans who are no less bestial than the beasts themselves. Then we come to more Scythians and to more deserts teeming with beasts, until we come to a mountain range that runs up to the sea and is called Tabis.[5] It is not until we have traversed almost half the length of the coast that faces northeast that we come to a region that is inhabited. The first people we encounter are called the Seres. They are famous for the wool that is found in their forests.[6] After soaking it in water, they comb the white strands of the leaves and so give our women the double task of unraveling the threads and reweaving them again.[7] Such is the substantial labor involved and from such a distant part of the globe is this material fetched — all so that a Roman matron might wear a transparent garment in public. Although the Seres are certainly a gentle people, they are like wild animals insofar as they flee the company of the rest of humanity and wait for trade to come to them.

COMMERCE WITH INDIA

It is appropriate to explain the entire journey from Egypt now that reliable knowledge of it is available for the first time. It is a worthy subject because in no year does India draw off less than fifty million sesterces[8] from our empire, sending back merchandise that is sold to us at one hundred times its original price.

Two miles from Alexandria[9] there is the town of Juliopolis. From there one sails up[10] the Nile to Coptos, a journey of 309 miles that takes twelve days when the midsummer trade winds blow. From Coptos the journey is made with camels, with watering stations located along the way. The first, located twenty-two miles along the way, is called Hydreuma.[11] The second is in the mountains, a day's journey away. The third is in another place called Hydreuma, eighty-five miles from Coptos. The next is in the mountains. Then we come to Apollo's Hydreuma, 184 miles from Coptos. Again there is one in the mountains. Then we get to New Hydreuma, 230 miles from Coptos. There is also another old Hydreuma, which is called Trogodyticum, where a garrison keeps watch over a caravansary[12] that can accommodate 2,000 travelers. It lies seven

---

[1]This subtitle and the two that follow are editorial creations for the readers' ease of comprehension. They do not appear in any manuscript copies of the text.

[2]Pliny and geographers before him imagined that a great northern ocean, here called the Scythian Ocean, bordered Asia just a few degrees north of the Caspian Sea. Its shores were the presumed place of origin of the Scythians, a nomadic steppe people who inhabited the region north of the Black Sea, essentially present-day Ukraine and southern Russia, in the sixth and fifth centuries B.C.E.

[3]Probably an imaginary place, but possibly Siberia or northern Russia.

[4]Herodotus, a Greek historian of the mid fifth century B.C.E., reported that the Scythians allied with a tribe of cannibals in their fight against an invading Persian army. There probably was no truth to that statement.

[5]Possibly Tibet.

[6]Probably Chinese silk.

[7]The Romans reworked Chinese silk, unraveling and reweaving it.

[8]The basic coin of the empire, made from either bronze or silver.

[9]A port city on Egypt's Mediterranean coast.

[10]Sails south. Because the Nile flows north, upriver lies to the south.

[11]Literally, "watering-place" in Greek.

[12]A place of refuge for caravans.

miles from New Hydreuma. Then comes the town of Berenice, where there is a port on the Red Sea, 257 miles from Coptos. Because the major part of the journey is done at night on account of the heat and days are spent at the stations, the entire journey from Coptos to Berenice takes twelve days.

Sea travel begins in midsummer before the Dog Star[13] rises or immediately after its rising. After about thirty days they arrive at Ocelis or else at Cane in the incense-producing region of Arabia.[14] There is also a third port named Muza, which is not called at on the voyage to India, not unless they are merchants trading in the incense and perfumes of Arabia. In the interior there is a town, the residence of the local king, which is called Sapphar. And there is another called Save.

The most advantageous route, however, for those intent on reaching India is to set out from Ocelis. If the Hippalus[15] is blowing, sailing time is forty days to the first trading station in India, Muziris, an undesirable port of call because of the pirates in the neighborhood who occupy a place called Nitrias. It is also not rich in trade articles. Furthermore, the place where ships anchor is located far from shore, and cargoes are brought in and ferried out in little boats. The person ruling there as I wrote this was Caelobothras. There is another, more serviceable port which is called Becare and belongs to the Neacyndi people. Pandion ruled there and dwelled in a town called Modura, which is located far inland, a long way from the market place. The region from which they transport pepper to Becare in boats made from a single tree is called Cottonara. All of these names of peoples or ports or towns are not to be found in the work of earlier authors, which suggests that local conditions are changing. Those sailing home from India begin in the Egyptian month of Tybis (our December) or, at the latest, before the sixth day of the Egyptian Mechir, which works out to before our January 13. This makes it possible for them to return home in the same year. They set sail from India with a southeast wind and after entering the Red Sea, continue with a southwest or south wind.

THE PEOPLE OF THE FAR EAST

To the east, at the far end of the borders of India near the source of the Ganges, Megasthenes[16] places the Astomi,[17] a people who have no mouth and a body that is totally covered in hair. They dress in wool made from leaves[18] and subsist only by breathing and through the scent that they draw in through their nostrils. They have no food or drink except for the various aromas of the roots, flowers, and wild apples that they carry with them on their longer journeys, lest they lack a supply of scent. He writes that they can easily be killed by an odor that is a bit stronger than usual.

---

[13]Sirius, or the Dog Star, the brightest star in the heavens, rises and sets with the sun from early July to early September.

[14]Yemen, in the southwestern corner of the Arabian Peninsula.

[15]The wind from the west.

[16]Megasthenes (ca. 350–290 B.C.E.), a Greek diplomat and scholar, served for ten years as ambassador to the Mauryan court in India (source 30), representing the interests of Seleucus I, king of Hellenistic Syria. Megasthenes' *Indica*, a firsthand account of the geography, people, governments, religions, legends, and history of India, is lost, but fragments survive in the writings of later authors, such as Pliny.

[17]Literally, "mouthless" in Greek.

[18]Silk. See note 6.

2 ▾ Faxian, TRAVELS

Faxian abode in this country[1] two years. . . . Having obtained these Sanskrit works,[2] he took passage in a large merchantman, on board of which there were more than 200 men, and to which was attached by a rope a smaller vessel, as a provision against damage or injury to the large one from the perils of the navigation. With a favorable wind, they proceeded eastwards for three days, and then they encountered a great wind. The vessel sprang a leak and the water came in. The merchants wished to go to the smaller vessel; but the men on board it, fearing that too many would come, cut the connecting rope. The merchants were greatly alarmed, feeling their risk of instant death. Afraid that the vessel would fill, they took their bulky goods and threw them into the water. Faxian also took his pitcher and washing-basin, with some other articles, and cast them into the sea; but fearing that the merchants would cast overboard his books and images, he could only think with all his heart of Guanshiyin,[3] and commit his life to [the protection of] the Buddhist congregation of the land of Han,[4] [saying in effect], "I have traveled far in search of our Law. Let me, by your dread and supernatural [power], return from my wanderings, and reach my resting place!"

In this way the tempest continued day and night, till on the thirteenth day the ship was carried to the side of an island, where, on the ebbing of the tide, the place of the leak was discovered, and it was stopped, on which the voyage was resumed. On the sea [hereabouts] there are many pirates, to meet with whom is speedy

death. The great ocean spreads out, a boundless expanse. There is no knowing east or west; only by observing the sun, moon, and stars was it possible to go forward. If the weather were dark and rainy, [the ship] went as she was carried by the wind, without any definite course. In the darkness of the night, only the great waves were to be seen, breaking on one another, and emitting a brightness like that of fire, with huge turtles and other monsters of the deep [all about]. The merchants were full of terror, not knowing where they were going. The sea was deep and bottomless, and there was no place where they could drop anchor and stop. But when the sky became clear, they could tell east and west, and [the ship] again went forward in the right direction. If she had come on any hidden rock, there would have been no way of escape.

After proceeding in this way for rather more than ninety days, they arrived at a country called Java-dvipa,[5] where various forms of error and Brahminism are flourishing,[6] while Buddhism in it is not worth speaking of. After staying there for five months,[7] [Faxian] again embarked in another large merchantman, which also had on board more than 200 men. They carried provisions for fifty days, and commenced the voyage on the sixteenth day of the fourth month.

Faxian kept his retreat on board the ship. They took a course to the north-east, intending to reach Guangzhou. After more than a month, when the night-drum sounded the second watch, they encountered a black wind and tempestuous rain, which threw the merchants and

---

[1]Ceylon.
[2]Four sutras to add to those he had collected in India.
[3]Literally, "Perceiver of the World's Sounds" or "One Who Hears the Cries of the World," this Bodhisattva is better known as *Guanyin*. (See Chapter 6, sources 32–33, for a fuller treatment of this Mahayana Buddhist intermediary.)
[4]The Han Dynasty had collapsed in 220 C.E., but the Chinese still referred to China as the "land of Han."
[5]The island of Java (see note 6), which lies to the east of Sumatra. If Faxian wanted a direct voyage home, Java was

off course, and his putting in there was probably an unforeseen consequence of the storm. Sumatra, which forms the southern coast of the narrow Strait of Malacca, makes more sense as an intermediary stopping point. The strait connects the Indian Ocean with the South China Sea.
[6]As part of "Greater India," Java had already been deeply influenced by Hindu culture. Indeed, its name, *Jawadwip*, is Sanskrit in origin (meaning island shaped like a barley corn) and was given it by Indian navigators.
[7]Probably waiting for favorable trade winds.

passengers into consternation. Faxian again with all his heart directed his thoughts to Guanshiyin and the monkish communities of the land of Han; and, through their awesome and mysterious protection, was preserved to daybreak. After daybreak, the Brahmins[8] deliberated together and said, "It is having this Sramana[9] on board that has occasioned our misfortune and brought us this great and bitter suffering. Let us land the bhikshu[10] and place him on some island-shore. We must not for the sake of one man allow ourselves to be exposed to such imminent peril." A patron of Faxian, however, said to them, "If you land the bhikshu, you must at the same time land me; and if you do not, then you must kill me. If you land this Sramana, when I get to the land of Han, I will go to the emperor, and inform against you. The emperor also reveres and believes the Law of Buddha, and honors the bhikshus." The merchants hereupon were perplexed, and did not dare immediately to land Faxian.

At this time the sky continued very dark and gloomy, and the sailing-masters looked at one another and made mistakes. More than seventy days passed [from their leaving Java], and the provisions and water were nearly exhausted. They used the salt-water of the sea for cooking, and carefully divided the [fresh] water, each man getting two pints. Soon the whole was nearly gone, and the merchants took counsel and said, "At the ordinary rate of sailing we ought to have reached Guangzhou, and now the time is passed by many days; — must we not have held a wrong course?" Immediately they directed the ship to the northwest, looking out for land; and after sailing day and night for twelve days, they reached the shore on the south of mount Lao,[11] . . . and immediately got good water and vegetables. They had passed through many perils and hardships, and had been in a state of anxious apprehension for many days together; and now suddenly arriving at this shore, . . . they knew indeed that it was the land of Han.

---

[8]He might mean all Hindus on board, not just members of the Brahmin caste.
[9]A Buddhist monk.

[10]Another term for a Buddhist monk.
[11]On the Shandong Peninsula.

3 ▾ *FOUR ROBED STATUES*

1

2

Vibia Sabina

Parthian Noblewoman

3

4

Gandharan Buddha   *Northern Wei Buddha*

Part Two

Faith, Devotion, and Salvation: Great World Religions to 1500

BY ABOUT 200 B.C.E., two overarching religious traditions had taken shape in Eurasia. Indian civilization produced a wide variety of cults and religions, most important of which were Buddhism and Brahminical Hinduism. Regardless of differences, all of India's homegrown religions denied the reality of this world and sought release from it. And in Southwest Asia, two faiths emerged — Judaism and Zoroastrianism — each of which focused on a single God of righteousness, whose believers saw themselves as agents in the transformation of the world according to moral precepts decreed by their God.

During the next 1,500 years, all four religions underwent significant changes. Zoroastrianism largely disappeared after the ninth century C.E., except for remnant communities in Iran, India, Central Asia, and China. Before it passed away as a major religion, Zoroastrianism had a profound impact on the teachings of several new faiths: Christianity, *Manichaeism*, and *Islam*. Judaism, which also exhibited Zoroastrian influences, survived, continued its historical evolution, and served as a major source for two new religions: Christianity and Islam. Meanwhile, one school of Buddhist thought, the *Mahayana* sect, evolved into a faith that offered its believers personal salvation. Mainstream Brahminical Hinduism never developed a clearly articulated doctrine of heavenly salvation as it is understood in the religious traditions of Christianity and Islam, but it did evolve a form of worship centered on an intensely personal and deeply emotional devotion to a single, select deity.

Four faiths — Buddhism (largely in its Mahayana form), Christianity, Manichaeism, and Islam — became *universal religions*. That is, they found homes in a wide variety of cultural settings and claimed to offer salvation to all humanity. Of the four, Buddhism was the most regional, confined largely to the vast, heavily populated lands of South, Central, and East Asia. Islam became the most global, at least until around 1500. Islamic communities dominated the east coast of Africa and the trading empires of interior West Africa. Islam stretched across the entire breadth of North Africa, Southwest Asia, and the northern and central portions of India. It spread through much of Central Asia, the island and coastal regions of Southeast Asia and touched many parts of China. It even penetrated Europe. Islamic rulers controlled much of the

Iberian Peninsula from the early eighth to the early thirteenth century, and it was not until 1492 that Christian powers were able to conquer the final Islamic state in Spain. Meanwhile, during the fourteenth century Islam arrived in Europe's Balkan region, where it has remained a vital force down to today.

Christianity in its various forms found homes in Ethiopia and Nubia, in the lands that bordered the eastern rim of the Mediterranean, in Armenia and Georgia in the southern Caucasus, among the Slavs of Eastern and Central Europe, and throughout Western Europe. In addition, small groups of Christians inhabited portions of Central Asia, northern and western China, and the western shores of India. With the new age of European transoceanic explorations, which got under way in the fifteenth century, Westerners transplanted Christianity throughout the Americas, along the Atlantic and Indian Ocean coasts of Africa, and, in a limited way, in various parts of East and South Asia. Manichaeism, which had its origins in third-century Babylonia, penetrated the Roman and Chinese empires but was never more than a minority movement in either area. Persecutions led to its ultimate disappearance in Southwest Asia and the Roman World, but it remained a vital force in Central Asia for a millennium more.

Meanwhile, Judaism and Hinduism also expanded beyond the confines of their ethnic and geographic origins. The most notable example of conversion to Judaism was when the ruling families of the *Khazars*, a Turkic people inhabiting the upper Volga region between the Black and Caspian seas, embraced Judaism toward the middle of the eighth century, possibly under the influence of Jewish refugees from Persia. Yet conversions of this sort were rare in Jewish history, and generally Jews did not attempt to spread their religion beyond their ethnic boundaries. Indian merchants and Brahmin teachers were more active disseminators of culture and religion than their Jewish counterparts. As we saw in Chapter 5, Indians traveled in significant numbers across the waters of the Bay of Bengal, bringing Hindu culture, particularly that of southern India, to the coastal regions of Southeast Asia. The cults of *Shiva* and *Vishnu* were welcomed and patronized by local rulers in these lands across the sea, but in the process the cults were modified to fit their new host cultures. Despite this expansion, however, both Judaism and Hinduism remained far less universal in scope or appeal than Buddhism, Christianity, and Islam, and maybe even Manichaeism.

❖ Chapter 6 ❖

New Developments in Three Ancient Religions

URING THE FIRST AGE of Afro-Eurasian interchange, Buddhism, Hinduism, and Judaism all experienced profound changes. The most far-reaching from the perspective of world history was a new form of Buddhist belief and devotion — the *Mahayana* sect, which offered the promise of salvation through the intermediacy of divine saviors. The message attracted many people suffering from the chaos of the breakdown of the first Afro-Eurasian Ecumene. During the first century B.C.E., Mahayana Buddhist ideas began to enter China from Central Asian lands as far away as Iran, and in the centuries that followed the Mahayana Doctrine swept through East Asia, becoming the dominant form of Buddhism in China, Tibet, Mongolia, Korea, and Japan.

Within Hinduism a new movement known as *bhakti*, or the Way of Devotion, challenged the caste system, not surprisingly because it sprang up and was strongest in India's Tamil regions of the south, which were far less touched by the Indo-Aryan castes that had originated in the north. Likewise, it was this new form of Hindu religion, not the caste system, that South Indian merchants transplanted among the emerging civilizations of Southeast Asia in the early centuries C.E. Without the Way of Devotion, Hinduism probably would not have spread significantly beyond the Indian subcontinent.

Hinduism and Judaism have historically been family religions in the sense that each has been largely confined to the heirs of a single civilization. Normally, their adherents are born into these religious-social complexes and are not converts. At the same time, both religions have occasionally reached out beyond their cultural matrices. This was so in the case of *Rabbinical Judaism* because of the *Diaspora*, or Great Dispersion, which scattered Jewish communities over much of the civilized Afro-Eurasian World. While Jews remained conscious of being a people apart from their *gentile*, or non-Jewish, neighbors, Jewish communities could not avoid cultural interchange with the societies within which they were settled.

Mahayana Buddhism:
A Religion of Infinite Compassion

Around the turn of the first millennium — the first century B.C.E. and the first century C.E. — a new form of Buddhism, *Mahayana*, or the Great Vehicle, emerged. The title is metaphorical: Mahayana sectarians picture their form of Buddhism as a great ferry which, under the guidance of enlightened pilots known as *Bodhisattvas*, carries all of humanity simultaneously across the river of life and suffering to salvation on the opposite shore.

Conversely, Mahayanists term the older, more traditional form of Buddhism *Hinayana*, or the Small Vehicle. The image is of a one-person raft because Hinayana Buddhism centers on the single *arahat*, or perfected disciple, who individually attains Enlightenment and Nirvana through solitary meditation, normally within a monastic setting. Followers of this form of Buddhism — which today predominates in the island nation of Sri Lanka and several countries of mainland Southeast Asia, especially Burma and Thailand — dislike the term *Hinayana*, because it implies inferiority, and call their sect *Theravada* (the Teaching of the Elders), maintaining that their form of Buddhism preserves the faith's earliest traditions.

Evidence indicates that Mahayana Buddhism emerged in northwest India, far from the Buddha's homeland and the regions in which he had taught, and quite possibly it was influenced by ideas regarding savior deities emanating from Hellenistic Southwest Asia and Parthia. According to Mahayana belief, the historical *Shakyamuni Buddha* (Siddhartha Gautama, who came from the Shakya clan) was not unique. There have been many cosmic Buddhas who lived before and after Gautama and who now preside over countless heavens that serve as way stations to Nirvana. Additionally, there are infinite numbers of Bodhisattvas. The title *Bodhisattva* means "an enlightened being." Although they have attained Enlightenment, these compassionate perfected beings delay Buddhahood and Nirvana in order to lead all humanity to salvation, drawing upon the countless merits they accumulated in their perfect lives of selflessness to achieve this task. Those whom they save become, in turn, Bodhisattvas, who then delay their entry into Nirvana in order to help others. Through this pyramid of selfless compassion, ultimately all humanity will cross together into Nirvana, a state of perfect bliss. This comforting, nonexclusive doctrine was destined to become the basis of a world religion, and during the first millennium of the Common Era it spread throughout most of Central and East Asia.

Perceiver of the World's Sounds: A Bodhisattva for All Emergencies

▼▼▼

32 ▼ *TALES OF GUANSHIYIN*

When faced with disaster on the high seas, the Chinese monk Faxian sought the protection of *Guanshiyin* (see Multiple Voices III, source 2). Guanshiyin was the Chinese version of the Indian Bodhisattva *Avalokitesvara*, whose name in both Sanskrit and Chinese translation means "Perceiver of the World's Sounds," the sounds being both cries and prayers. The cult of Avalokitesvara/Guanshiyin entered China as early as 255 C.E. thanks to an early Chinese translation of the *Lotus Sutra*. In this Mahayana scripture, the Shakyamuni Buddha promises that because of his infinite compassion and merit, Perceiver of the World's Sounds will miraculously intervene on behalf of anyone in distress who simply utters his name.

In the age of turmoil that followed the collapse of the Han regime, this doctrine proved quite comforting, and devotion to Guanshiyin spread throughout China and beyond into Tibet, Korea, and Japan. In China, scriptures relating to him, such as the *Lotus Sutra* and the later *Guanshiyin Sutra*, were far and away the most popular of all Buddhist texts, and paintings of Guanshiyin's saving people from every sort of danger covered the walls of Buddhist shrines.

The period from the late fourth century to the late sixth century was particularly hard on the people of northern China. Various non-Chinese nomads, whom the Chinese called *caitiffs* (base and despicable people), invaded and exploited the region north of the Yangzi River. To make matters worse, periodic floods, famines, and plagues devastated the land, and rebellions and civil wars were endemic throughout all of China. In the midst of this chaos, a small number of pious monks and laypeople began to collect and record stories of Guanshiyin's miraculous interventions. They believed that by so doing they would earn merit by spreading the cult of a Bodhisattva who was available to all who called upon him.

Roughly 470 such stories exist in known manuscripts produced before the seventh century. The following four tales are part of that devotional literature.

QUESTIONS FOR ANALYSIS

1. What are the criteria for Guanshiyin's bestowing his mercy on a recipient? In other words, what does a person have to be or do?
2. What inferences do you draw from your answer to question 1?
3. What happened to Wang Tao after he had been saved by Guanshiyin? What insight do you reach based on your answer?

4. Buddhism faced a good deal of opposition from Chinese traditionalists during these centuries (see Multiple Voices VI). Does knowing that help you place these stories into a fuller context? Explain your answer.

THE WIDOW LI

There was a widow surnamed Li who lived in Liang Province.[1] Her family had long been Buddhist; they faithfully kept every fast day and attended meetings. Each time she would listen to sutra readings; as soon as they were over, she could recite the sutra herself. Later, a [Chinese] woman who had been made a princess among the caitiffs suddenly [showed up and] sought refuge in Li's home. It was a moonless night, and Li could not bear to send her away. Soon officials came to register Li [on the population list], and their report stated that she was harboring a rebellious female slave.[2] Once this register was submitted [to the authorities], Li was jailed. Then with a perfect mind she recited the *Guanshiyin Sutra* and was able to keep reciting it continuously for over ten days.

Suddenly in the middle of the day she saw Guanshiyin. He asked her why she did not leave [her cell]; she replied that it was impossible. He then said: "Just get up." On doing so she found that her shackles were already unfastened, and then she quickly found herself back at home. The warden and the guards were all completely unaware of her departure. Later when the caitiffs learned of her escape, they sent someone to question her and find out how she had managed to return home. She told them everything that had happened. She was not rearrested.

TWO REBELS

Formerly, when the bandit Sun [En] stirred up rebellion,[3] many people living near the coast, both aristocrats and commoners, fled the destruction. A group of a dozen or so people were about to be executed in the eastern marketplace. Only one among them respected the Dharma, and this man began chanting [the name of] Guanshiyin with perfect sincerity. Another man who was sitting with him asked him what he was doing. He replied: "I have heard that the scriptures of the Buddha's Dharma mention a Bodhisattva Guanshiyin who saves people from distress. So I am taking refuge in him." The other man then followed his example. When the hour of execution arrived, the official list [of those to be executed] was found to be lacking just the names of these two people. This created shock and panic in the crowd, and everyone fled in different directions. These two men followed the crowd and were thus able to escape execution.

THE BIRTH OF A SON

Sun Daode, who lived during the Song, was a Daoist and a libationer.[4] He still had no son even after passing the age of fifty. In the year 423 a [Buddhist] monk who lived in a monastery nearby told Daode: "If you are determined to have a son, you must respectfully and with a per-

---

[1] Modern Gansu Province along China's northwestern border. The Gansu Corridor is a narrow defile between mountains and desert that served as an avenue of incursion for invading nomads from the western steppes.
[2] A rebel against the non-Chinese lords who controlled the area.

[3] Sun En led a Daoist-inspired peasant rebellion in 399–400.
[4] He was a leader for communal affairs and rituals of a Daoist religious movement known as the *Way of the Celestial Masters*. This particular cult traced its origin to the prophet Zhang Daoling, who in 142 claimed a revelation from the Most High Lord Lao — the now-deified Laozi (source 19).

fect mind recite the *Guanshiyin Sutra*. You may then hope for success." Daode then gave up serving the Dao; with single-minded sincerity he took refuge in Guanshiyin. Within a few days he had a dream-response. His wife was indeed pregnant, and subsequently she gave birth to a boy.[5]

A CONVERSION

Wang Tao came from the Zhaodu district of the capital. He was by nature violent and cruel, and in his youth he was leader of a band of young toughs. After reaching the age of thirty he settled down in a forest. Once he encountered a tiger eating its captured prey. He drew his bow and shot it, and it fled, injured; but there was

another tiger that chased him down and crushed both his arms with its fangs, and still would not let him go. Tao suddenly remembered having once heard a monk speak of Guanshiyin, so he now took refuge in and meditated on [the Bodhisattva] with a perfect mind. The tiger at once let him go, and he was able to get up. But it was still angry and resentful, roaring as it circled around him. Tao once more tempered his heart and perfected his thoughts. The tiger then finally went away. Tao returned home and swore that if he did not die from his wounds he would revere the Buddha and undertake the [lay] precepts.[6] He soon recovered and so in the end became a devout man.

[5]Guanshiyin became increasingly associated with fertility and childbirth and slowly metamorphosed into a female Bodhisattva. See source 33.

[6]He would live as a devout Buddhist layman. The precepts he vowed to follow included refraining from killing all living beings. (See source 15, note 8.)

Images of Compassion
▼▼▼
33 ▼ *THREE BODHISATTVAS*

Mahayana Buddhism developed a strong tradition of spreading the word through every available medium, which in China included mass printing of the sacred texts, beginning in the era of the Tang Dynasty (618–907). The oldest extant printed book known today is a Chinese copy of the *Diamond Sutra*, which dates from 868. But sutras were not enough. People, especially the illiterate, needed artistic representations of the Bodhisattvas to whom they prayed. Statues and paintings of Bodhisattvas became fixtures wherever the Mahayana Doctrine took root, and as the following three statues demonstrate, images of the Bodhisattvas took many different forms.

The first statue is of Perceiver of the World's Sounds, whom we encountered in source 32. Called *Avalokitesvara* in India, the home of his origin, this Bodhisattva took several different forms, one of which was an androgynous young man, and he carried that image to China, where he was initially known as *Guanshiyin*, but as time went on he became more commonly called *Guanyin*. In China, Perceiver of the World's Sounds also underwent a sex change. This probably was due to two main factors. In the *Lotus Sutra*, the primary scriptural source for the cult of Avalokitesvara/Guanyin, the Buddha notes that this Bodhisattva will assume any form whatsoever in order to save a devotee. In China, Guanyin assumed the dual functions of making women fertile (especially so that they could bear male children) and protecting them in childbirth. Consequently, a few artists began, as early as the late sixth century, to portray this Bodhisattva as a woman. The two images, male and female, coexisted for quite a while, but the female was dominant by the beginning of the twelfth century and totally won out by the sixteenth century. Whether called Guanyin or *Kannon*, her Japanese name, she became the most widely beloved and prayed-to Bodhisattva in East Asia. A pure and benevolent spirit, she was the gateway to the Pure Land, or Western Paradise, a heavenly way station of bliss on the road to Nirvana that the *Amitaba Buddha*, one of the great cosmic Buddhas, presided over.

This particular Guanyin is a gilded bronze statuette from the early years of the Sui Dynasty (589–618). Standing on a lotus blossom and wearing an ornate gown, jewelry, and a tasseled crown, she holds a flask of heavenly dew in her right hand. In her left hand, Guanyin bears a willow sprig. A touch of the willow sprinkled with the dew cures all physical and spiritual disorders. The lotus, or water lily, which has iconographic origins in ancient Egyptian art, where it symbolized eternity, is one of the most common Buddhist symbols of Nirvana, chosen because this flower, rooted in mud, rises through stagnant water to free itself in purity and beauty.

The second statue comes from the *Khmer* kingdom (802–1406), located in the Southeast Asian land of Cambodia. The temple complexes in the Khmer capital at Angkor, which reached their heights of splendor in the twelfth and thirteenth centuries, show the profound influence of Hindu culture, but they also display strong Mahayanist elements. This statue is a late-twelfth-century representation of the Bodhisattva *Hevajra* and displays the worldview of a branch of Mahayana Buddhism known as *Tantrism*. Tantrism, which originated in Hindu beliefs and practices, emphasizes magic and esoteric rituals. Beyond that it stresses the doctrine of *non-dualism*, a rejection of the notion that apparently contradictory elements — such as life and death, female and male, goodness and evil — are truly opposed to one another. Tantric Buddhism is particularly prevalent in Tibet, and this statue is markedly Tibetan in its overall form, but its Indian influences are equally apparent. Here we see an eight-faced Hevajra, with four legs (only seven faces and two legs are visible in the picture) and sixteen arms. In each hand he holds a skull, and he dances above a corpse. Significantly, that corpse lies on a lotus blossom.

The third statue, carved in 1343, is of *Arapacana* and comes from the island of Java in Southeast Asia. He sits in the lotus position of meditation (see source 7, seal 6) on a giant lotus flower. Wielding the sword of interior knowledge above his tiered crown, he clutches in his left hand the book of wisdom (the *Sutra of the Perfection of Insight*). Surrounding him are more lotuses and four lesser Bodhisattvas, who serve as his constant companions.

QUESTIONS FOR ANALYSIS

1. Consider Guanyin's dress, posture, facial expression, and implements. What do they combine to tell us about this Bodhisattva?
2. Review source 32. Is this statue true to the spirit and message of those tales of Guanshiyin? If so, how?

3. What do Hevajra's multiple limbs and faces seem to connote?
4. In what specific ways does the statue of Hevajra convey the doctrine of non-dualism?
5. Consider Arapacana. What does he appear to be doing? In answering this, consider his posture, his facial expression, his special sword, and the book that he holds.
6. Compare the three Bodhisattvas. What do their similarities and differences suggest about Mahayana beliefs and devotion?

Guanyin   *Hevajra*

Arapacana

Bhakti: The Way of Devotion

In one of the *Bhagavad Gita*'s most famous scenes (which does not appear in the excerpt quoted in source 14), Krishna, an incarnation of the god Vishnu, teaches Arjuna that *bhakti*, or unconditional devotion to a god, is one of several *yogas*, or paths of selfless, god-focused action, by which a person can win release from the cycle of rebirth. Such a path to liberation appealed to many low-caste and casteless persons (as well as many women), who found strict and selfless conformity to the laws of dharma (the *Yoga of Action*) unattractive. It likewise appealed to persons who lacked the temperament or leisure to attain release from the shackles of matter through asceticism, study of the sacred scriptures, and meditation (the *Yoga of Knowledge*). The *Yoga of Devotion*, in which one passionately adores a savior god, offered a promise of immediate liberation to everyone.

In the Gupta Age (320–ca. 550 c.e.) and thereafter, there was an increasing tendency among many Hindus to reduce the myriad divine personifications of Brahman, the One, to three: *Brahma* the Creator, *Vishnu* the Preserver, and *Shiva* the Destroyer. Of this trinity, Brahma (not to be confused with Brahman) was the least widely worshiped because he was perceived as a remote kingly god who, after completing the process of creation, had retired from worldly affairs. However, Hindus, especially in South India, widely adored Vishnu and Shiva, and they became two of the great gods of Asia. The exported cult of Shiva was especially popular in Southeast Asia, where he merged with several local native deities and was adopted even by some Buddhist sects.

Hindus who concentrated their worship on Vishnu or Shiva did not deny the existence of the many other divine and semidivine personalities who were part of the traditional pantheon of India. They simply chose Shiva or Vishnu as gods of special devotion because each, in his way, was a loving personification of the totality of Divine Reality. Vishnu's worshipers, for example, believed that he had selflessly blessed and taught humanity on a number of critical occasions in descents (*avataras*) from Heaven. On each occasion he took on either human or animal form and intervened on behalf of the forces of goodness to redress the equilibrium between good and evil. In fact, Vishnu's worshipers regarded the Buddha as one of Vishnu's nine chief avataras. Of all his various incarnations, however, the warriors Krishna and Rama enjoyed the widest devotional popularity. As Lord Krishna exemplified in the *Bhagavad Gita*, Vishnu's emergence into this world provided humanity with a model of divine perfection. By offering exclusive and unqualified devotion to such a god, a worshiper hoped to share in that perfection.

The development of bhakti, which met so many of the needs of members of India's lower castes and social levels, helped Hinduism to counter successfully the challenge of Buddhism, especially that of the Mahayana school. Faxian, whom we saw in source 31, reported that Buddhist monasteries and festivals were an integral part of the cultural landscape of early-fifth-century India. A millennium later all that had changed. By 1500 c.e. Buddhism, as a religion with an identity separate from Hinduism, had largely disappeared from the land of its origin. Many factors contributed to its disappearance, but one important reason was a Hindu Renaissance during the Gupta Age that began and was strongest in the Tamil area of southern India. Tamil religious teachers and poets taught and sang about devotion to either Vishnu or Shiva, and their teachings and hymns traveled throughout India and across the waters of the Bay of Bengal to the coastal regions of Southeast Asia.

The Way of Supreme Love
▼▼▼

34 ▼ *Narada, THE BHAKTI SUTRA*

Between approximately 300 and 1000 C.E., many authors gave literary voice to
bhakti in tracts, stories, and poems. The following sutra was composed at some unknown time by an anonymous author or authors but is ascribed to *Narada*, a legendary sage who was said to have sprung from the forehead of Brahman (much as
the Hellenic goddess of wisdom, Athena, sprang from Zeus's head). As you read the
sutra, do not be misled by its reference to God. The author does not mean God as
understood by Jewish, Christian, or Muslim monotheists. In this context, it means a
god who encompasses in himself the fullness of Brahman — Divine Reality.

QUESTIONS FOR ANALYSIS

1. How does this sutra define bhakti?
2. How does one achieve bhakti?
3. What are the consequences of bhakti?
4. In what ways, if any, is bhakti consonant with the traditions and teachings of
   Brahminical Hinduism? To answer this question, review sources 13 and 14.
5. In what ways was bhakti a Hindu answer to Mahayana Buddhism?

Now then, we shall expound devotion. Devotion
consists of supreme love for God. It also consists
of immortality. On obtaining that, man has
achieved everything, he becomes immortal,[1] he
is completely satisfied. Having got it, he desires
nothing else, he grieves not, he hates nothing, he
delights not in anything else, he strives for nothing; having realized which, man becomes as if
intoxicated, and benumbed; he delights in his
own intrinsic bliss.

Devotion is not like ordinary passion, as it is
the suppression of all other preoccupations. This
suppression of preoccupations is the giving up of
the activities of the world as well as those [ritu-
als] ordained by the Vedas.

Devotion is complete and exclusive absorption
in God and indifference to things opposed to
Him. Completeness or exclusiveness of devotion
to Him means the abandoning of anything else

or anybody else as one's prop and support. And
indifference to things opposed to Him means
the doing and observance of only those things in
the world or the Vedas which are conducive to
devotion towards Him.

One may observe the scriptural ordinances
after one's faith in God has been firmly established, for otherwise the devotee may be deemed
to have fallen off from the standard of ordained
conduct. Similarly, worldly activities, like taking food, should be kept up by the devotee only
to the extent needed for keeping his body. . . .

[D]evotion . . . [is] . . . dedication of all acts to
God and the intense anguish when one slips
from his absorption in God. . . .

Devotion is superior to action, knowledge, or
yogic contemplation; for devotion is itself its
fruit,[2] and God loves the meek and dislikes those
who are proud [of their attainments]. . . .

---

[1]The person has thrown off the shackles of matter and rebirth
and has achieved Moksha (release) and Brahma-Nirvana.

[2]Devotion is its own good karma.

Now, the means of acquiring devotion are set forth by teachers: 1) renunciation of sense pleasures and mundane associations; 2) ceaseless adoration of the Lord; 3) even when one is with others, engaging oneself in the listening to and the singing of the glory of the Lord; 4) chiefly the grace of the great souls[3] or a particle of divine grace itself.

The association of the great souls is hard to acquire, hard to be had completely, but is always fruitful. For gaining even that association, one requires God's blessing; for between God and His men there is no difference. So try to acquire the company of the holy souls; strive for that.

And, by all means, shun evil company; for that is responsible for passion, wrath, delusion, loss of the thought of the Lord, the loss of knowledge, in fact all kinds of loss; these evil traits swell up like an ocean by reason of bad company.

Who crosses over the illusion of phenomenal existence? He who gives up evil association, who waits upon the high-souled ones, who becomes freed of the ego; he who resorts to a secluded spot, uproots worldly bondage, . . . and stops worrying himself about acquiring something or safeguarding something acquired; he who abandons the fruit of actions, renounces all action[4] and thereby transcends the pairs of joy and sorrow, gain and loss, and so on;[5] he who lays aside even scriptures and cultivates solely uninterrupted love for God. He saves himself and becomes also the savior of the world.[6]

Devotion is something indescribable; it is like the taste that a dumb man enjoys. But it is occasionally revealed when there is somebody deserving of it. It is absolute, not vitiated by desire for anything, multiplying every minute of its existence, and is uninterrupted; it is a highly sublime form of experience. One who has it looks at it only, listens to it alone, and thinks of nothing else. . . .

Compared to other paths, devotion is easiest. It stands in need of no external proof and it is its own proof; for it is of the very form of tranquility and supreme bliss.

The devotee should have no anxiety if the world slips away from him; for has he not surrendered himself, the world, and the scriptures to the Lord? However, even when one is established in devotion, one should not voluntarily give up normal activities, but he should certainly give up the fruits of his actions and learn how to give them up.

The devotee should not listen to accounts of women's beauty, riches, and what unbelievers say; should cast away pride and vanity. Offering up all his activities to God, he should show his desire or pride only in activities on His behalf. . . .

[O]ne should develop that love which consists of continuous service and is like the yearning of a beloved for her lover. Those who are exclusive lovers are the chief devotees; with choked voices and streaming eyes, they commune among themselves; they are the souls who sanctify our homes and the world; they make holy spots holy, sanctify acts, and render scriptures sacred. For they are full of God. . . .

Among such devotees there is no distinction of birth, learning, appearance, pedigree, wealth, or profession;[7] for they belong to God.

A devotee should not get involved in discussion about God; for reasoning cuts in anyway and there is no finality about it. Texts which speak of devotion should be honored and the acts taught therein followed. Anxious to gain a time free from the preoccupation of pleasure or pain, desire or gain, one should not waste even a split second. One should observe nonviolence, truth, purity, compassion, faith, and other virtues.

---

[3]The saints, or *mahatman*, whose perfection brings grace and blessings to those whom they teach and with whom they come into contact.

[4]On the Way of Action, see source 14.

[5]The illusion that dualities — such as joy and sorrow — are real. See Hevajra (source 33).

[6]Compare this with the doctrine of Mahayana Buddhism (sources 32–33).

[7]Caste distinctions.

Ever and with all heart, devotees should, without any other thought, worship only the Lord. When He is sung of, He hastens to present Himself and bestow on devotees His experience. Devotion to God is true for all times and is superior to everything else; it is superior. . . .

Devotion, which is really one, yet takes eleven forms: attachment to the greatness of the Lord's qualities, to His form; being engrossed in His worship, and His thought; attachment to Him as a servant, as a friend, as a child or as toward a child, and as a beloved; surrendering oneself unto Him; seeing Him everywhere; and inability to bear the separation from Him.

So do they declare in one voice, without fear of what people say, the teachers of the path of devotion. . . . He who has faith in this wholesome teaching that Narada has given gains devotion and gains that most beloved object [God]; indeed he gains that Dearest Thing.

Shiva, Auspicious Destroyer

▼▼▼

35 ▼ *SHIVA NATARAJA*

Many people, especially those whose religions spring from the Southwest Asian tradition of ethical monotheism, might find it hard to accept the notion that a god whose primary function is destruction and death is regarded as a loving deity. Yet *Shiva,* the name of the Hindu god of destruction, means "auspicious." Indeed, contradiction is central to the cult of Shiva. He is celebrated as the divine patron of holy persons and is often portrayed as *Mahayogi* (the Great Ascetic) — deep in meditation, with matted hair and covered with ashes, all of which are signs of those who have renounced the pleasures of the world. At the same time, he is celebrated as a deity with an insatiable sexual appetite and is often portrayed as a sensuous lover.

The artifact illustrated here is a bronze statue of *Shiva Nataraja* (Lord of the Dance) from the Chola kingdom of southern India (ca. 850–1250), an area of fervent devotion to Shiva. The statue represents the god engaged in an ecstatic cosmic dance by which he brings to an end one of the cosmos's cycles of time and ushers in a new era. The statue's symbols offer numerous clues to how Shiva's worshipers perceive him. Here he is dancing within a circle of fire, but his face presents a countenance of absolute equanimity. His hair is piled up in a crownlike style; flowing from the sides of his head are strands of hair intertwined with flowers and forming the shape of wings. His upper-left hand holds a devouring flame; his upper-right hand clasps a drum for beating out the endless rhythm of the universe, for he is also Lord of Time. The lower-right arm is entwined by a cobra, but the hand is raised in the silent "fear not" *mudra,* or hand gesture. The lower-left hand points to his raised left foot as a sign of release from the bonds of the material world. The other foot is planted firmly on the writhing body of *Apasamara,* the demon of ignorance and heedlessness.

Shiva Nataraja

QUESTIONS FOR ANALYSIS

1. What double function does fire serve, especially in an agricultural society?
2. Keeping in mind your answer to question 1 and also the fact that Shiva uses a drum to beat out the rhythm of the universe, what do you think the circle of fire and the flame in his left hand represent?
3. If fire presents a double message, what other symbols in this statue give a similar double message?
4. Consider Shiva's hair. According to one tradition, the sacred River Ganges, the Mother of India and the source of all life, flows from Shiva's head. What do this tradition and the manner in which the god's hair is represented suggest about this deity?
5. Why do you think the artist has depicted Shiva with four arms instead of the standard two?
6. One of the primary doctrines of the bhakti movement is that a chosen savior god, Vishnu or Shiva, exercises all of the primary functions of the Godhead — creation, destruction, regeneration, preservation, and release. Can you find the appropriate symbols in this statue that illustrate this belief?
7. Consider the demon of ignorance. How would an ignorant person regard death? What do you think Shiva's triumph over this demon represents?
8. Compare *Shiva Nataraja* and *Hevajra* (source 33). Which are more striking, the similarities or the differences? Be specific in addressing this issue. Now, what do you conclude from your answer?

Rabbinical Judaism

In 66 C.E. the Jews of Palestine broke out in general rebellion against Roman occupation, and it took the Roman armies seven bloody years to root out the last vestiges of insurgency. In the process, Jerusalem and its Temple were destroyed in the year 70. Again in 132 another Jewish revolt against Roman authority flared up, and when it was finally suppressed in 135, the rebuilt remnants of ancient Jerusalem had been transformed into a Roman military camp that was closed to Jewish habitation. Long before the destruction of the Temple and their sacred city, Jews had established prosperous communities throughout the Greco-Roman, Persian, and Arabic worlds. After these two unsuccessful rebellions, however, the Jewish flight from Palestine reached the proportions of a folk migration, and the vast majority of Jews now resided outside of their ancestral lands. The Great Dispersion, or *Diaspora*, was under way.

Regardless, Judaism survived as a living faith and culture because wherever Jews settled, they remained faithful to the memory of their special Covenant with God and their dream of returning to the Promised Land. Moreover, despite its innate conservatism, born of a need to maintain contact with the ways of the past, Judaism continued to be flexible. Jews proved adaptable to a variety of alien settings, and over the centuries Judaism continued its historical development in response to the needs of its various scattered communities.

The primary agents responsible for cementing dispersed Jewish communities together and keeping alive Judaism's distinctive traditions were its religious teachers, or *rabbis*. The destruction of the Temple in Jerusalem occasioned a shift in religious emphasis and leadership. The old priesthood that had performed Temple sacrifices lost its primacy, giving way to rabbis who presided over congregations that met to pray and study in *synagogues* (places of assembly). Unlike the priests of old, rabbis did not inherit their positions by birth; they achieved prominence because of their reputations for piety and mastery of the Law. During the first six centuries of the Common Era, rabbis, especially groups of them residing in Palestine and Babylon, articulated a vision of Judaism that recognized only prayer and righteous conduct as legitimate forms of communication with the Divine. There were no heavenly saviors and no magical rituals. This was to become the core of mainstream Judaism down to the present.

A Defense of the Law

▼▼▼

36 ▼ *Flavius Josephus, AGAINST APION*

Joseph ben Matthias (37 or 38–ca. 100), known to his Roman patrons as *Flavius Josephus*, is the most important eyewitness to the history of the Jewish people during the first century C.E. Born into a distinguished priestly family in Jerusalem, Josephus received a sound education in Jewish traditions and Greek culture. At the outbreak of the revolt against Roman occupation in 66, Josephus became leader of the Jewish forces in the north. Following an early defeat and capture at the hands of the Romans, Josephus went over to the enemy and became an advisor to two successive Roman generals, Vespasian and his son Titus. Vespasian became emperor in 69, leaving the final stages of the siege and capture of Jerusalem to Titus. After conquering and destroying Jerusalem, Titus succeeded his father as emperor in 79. Following the war, Josephus was brought to Rome, where he was granted citizenship, lodged in the private household of his imperial patron, and provided with a generous pension. It was in this setting that he wrote, in Greek, a history of the Jewish War, a work flattering to the Romans but one that also attempted to present a sympathetic account of Jewish suffering and heroism. Following Titus's death in 81, Josephus found another Roman patron and continued to write on Jewish history and tradition. His *Jewish Antiquities* traces the story of his people from Creation to the eve of the rebellion. More so than his earlier work, the *Antiquities* clearly rests on the argument that Judaism deserves an honored place within the Greco-Roman Ecumene. Josephus's last work was a spirited defense of Judaism entitled *Against Apion*. Written in the last decade of the first century, the work answered the anti-Jewish slanders made by many Greco-Roman critics, especially an Alexandrian grammarian named Apion. In the following excerpt, which appears at the end of his tract, Josephus expounds on the Law of Moses. That Law is the body of religious regulations contained within the first five books of the Bible, books ascribed to the authorship of Moses and known collectively as the *Torah* (the Law).

QUESTIONS FOR ANALYSIS

1. How does Josephus compare the Law of Moses with Greek law and philosophy? What is his point? What is his apparent purpose?
2. What is his apparent reason for stating that Judaism is a *theocracy*?
3. According to Josephus, what role does the Law play in a Jew's life?
4. "Josephus compared the particularism of the Greeks with the universalism of the Jews, thereby implicitly arguing that Jews, more than Greeks, were true citizens of the Roman Commonwealth." Comment on and evaluate this statement.

Now, I maintain that our legislator[1] is the most ancient of all legislators in the record of the whole world. Compared with him, you Lycurguses[2] and Solons,[3] . . . and all who are held in such high esteem by the Greeks appear to have been born but yesterday. Why, the very word "law" was unknown in ancient Greece. Witness Homer, who nowhere employs it in his poems. In fact, there was no such thing in his day; the masses were governed by maxims not clearly defined and by the orders of royalty, and continued long afterwards the use of unwritten customs, many of which were from time to time altered to suit particular circumstances. On the other hand, our legislator, who lived in the remotest past (that, I presume, is admitted even by our most unscrupulous detractors), proved himself the people's best guide and counselor; and after framing a code to embrace the whole conduct of their life, induced them to accept it, and secured, on the firmest footing, its observance for all time. . . .

There is endless variety in the details of the customs and laws which prevail in the world at large. To give but a summary enumeration: some peoples have entrusted the supreme political power to monarchies, others to oligarchies,[4] yet others to the masses. Our lawgiver, however, was

attracted by none of these forms of polity, but gave to his constitution the form of what — if a forced expression be permitted — may be termed a "theocracy," placing all sovereignty and authority in the hands of God. To Him he persuaded all to look, as the author of all blessings, both those which are common to all mankind, and those which they had won for themselves by prayer in the crises of their history. He convinced them that no single action, no secret thought, could be hid from Him. He represented Him as One, uncreated and immutable to all eternity; in beauty surpassing all mortal thought, made known to us by His power, although the nature of His real being passes knowledge.

That the wisest of the Greeks learned to adopt these conceptions of God from principles with which Moses supplied them, I am not now concerned to urge; but they have borne abundant witness to the excellence of these doctrines, and to their consonance with the nature and majesty of God. In fact, Pythagoras, Anaxagoras, Plato, the Stoics[5] who succeeded him, and indeed nearly all the philosophers appear to have held similar views concerning the nature of God. These, however, addressed their philosophy to the few, and did not venture to divulge their true beliefs to the masses who had their own preconceived opinions;

[1]Moses (see source 12).
[2]Lycurgus was the ninth-century B.C.E. lawgiver of Sparta.
[3]Solon (ca. 638–ca. 559 B.C.E.) was an Athenian constitutional reformer.
[4]Governments ruled by small factions.

[5]Pythagoras was a Greek philosopher and mathematician of the sixth century B.C.E. Anaxagoras (ca. 500–428 B.C.E.) was a Greek philosopher and astronomer. For Plato, see source 24. The Stoics were a Hellenistic school of philosophy founded in Athens by Zeno (ca. 335–ca. 263 B.C.E.). All had expressed ideas regarding some sort of Universal Spirit.

whereas our lawgiver, by making practice square with precept, not only convinced his own contemporaries, but so firmly implanted his belief concerning God in their descendants to all future generations that it cannot be moved. The cause of his success was that the very nature of his legislation made it [always] far more useful than any other; for he did not make religion a department of virtue,[6] but the various virtues — I mean, justice, temperance, fortitude, and mutual harmony in all things between the members of the community — departments of religion. Religion governs all our actions and occupations and speech; none of these things did our lawgiver leave unexamined or indeterminate. . . .

Starting from the very beginning with the food of which we partake from infancy and the private life of the home, he left nothing, however insignificant, to the discretion and caprice of the individual. What meats a man should abstain from, and what he may enjoy; with what persons he should associate; what period would be devoted respectively to strenuous labor and to rest — for all this our leader made the Law the standard and rule, that we might live under it as under a father and master, and be guilty of no sin through willfulness or ignorance.

For ignorance he left no pretext. He appointed the Law to be the most excellent and necessary form of instruction, ordaining, not that it should be heard once for all or twice or on several occasions, but that every week men should desert their other occupations and assemble to listen to the Law and to obtain a thorough and accurate knowledge of it, a practice which all other legislators seem to have neglected. . . .

To this cause above all we owe our admirable harmony. Unity and identity of religious belief, perfect uniformity in habits and customs, produce a very beautiful concord in human character. Among us alone will be heard no contradictory statements about God, such as are common among other nations, not only on the lips of ordinary individuals under the impulse of some passing mood, but even boldly propounded by philosophers; some putting forward crushing arguments against the very existence of God, others depriving Him of His providential care for mankind. Among us alone will be seen no difference in the conduct of our lives. With us all act alike, all profess the same doctrine about God, one which is in harmony with our Law and affirms that all things are under His eye. Even our womenfolk and dependents would tell you that piety must be the motive of all our occupations in life. . . .

Our earliest imitators were the Greek philosophers, who, though ostensibly observing the laws of their own countries, yet in their conduct and philosophy were Moses' disciples, holding similar views about God, and advocating the simple life and friendly communion between man and man. But that is not all. The masses have long since shown a keen desire to adopt our religious observances; and there is not one city, Greek or barbarian, nor a single nation, to which our custom of abstaining from work on the seventh day has not spread, and where the fasts and the lighting of lamps and many of our prohibitions in the matter of food are not observed. Moreover, they attempt to imitate our unanimity, our liberal charities, our devoted labor in the crafts, our endurance under persecution on behalf of our laws. The greatest miracle of all is that our Law holds out no seductive bait of sensual pleasure,[7] but has exercised this influence through its own inherent merits; and, as God permeates the universe, so the Law has found its way among all mankind. Let each man reflect for himself on his own country and his own household, and he will not disbelieve what I say. It follows, then, that our accusers must either condemn the whole world for deliberate malice in being so eager to adopt the bad laws of a foreign country in preference to the good laws of their own, or else give up their grudge against us.

---

[6]For many within the Greco-Roman World, religion was a civic virtue, honoring the deities who protected the state.
[7]Jews and Christians alleged that pagan religious festivals were occasions for drinking, excessive eating, and sexual license. There was truth to the charge, especially in some forms of bacchic worship (but see source 23) and in fertility rites.

A Commentary on the Law
▼▼▼
37 ▾ *THE BABYLONIAN TALMUD*

The *Talmud*, which means "instruction" or "learning," is a collection of post-biblical laws, customs, moral teachings, and edifying stories compiled in Jerusalem and Mesopotamia during the first six centuries C.E. As far as Rabbinical Judaism is concerned, it is second in authority only to the Tanakh, or Bible. Indeed, the Talmud *is* Rabbinical Judaism, inasmuch as it preserves the oral law and traditions of the early synagogues, where learned sages interpreted the Law of Moses in ways that accorded with changing circumstances. Thus, the Talmud became and remains the basis for interpreting a living law that regulates all aspects of Jewish life. Rather than being the final word on a legal question, it is the starting point for learned debate.

The Talmud consists of two major divisions. The *Mishnah* (Repetition or Study), which was edited around 200 C.E. in Palestine, is a compendium of rabbinical teachings regarding aspects of the Law. The *Gemara* (Explanation or Teaching) consists of two separate collections of commentaries on the Mishnah. An earlier, shorter, and less authoritative edition was completed in Palestine sometime before 400 C.E. A larger and richer edition was completed sometime before 600 C.E. in Babylonia, the Mesopotamian region of the Sassanid Empire. When combined with the Mishnah, the former is known as the *Palestinian Talmud*, and the latter is known as the *Babylonian Talmud*.

Our selection, which comes from the Babylonian Talmud, illustrates the type of debate that Talmudic scholars engaged in. The issue under consideration here is the duty of every Jew to marry and raise a family. The Mishnah sets out the problem by first stating the traditional Jewish understanding of this obligation and its biblical foundation. It then informs the reader of how the two major schools of early rabbinical thought, the Beit Shammai and the Beit Hillel, interpreted the obligation. It then presents a third opinion — that of Rabbi Yohanan ben Beroka, an early rabbinical sage. Following this comes the commentary of the Gemara.

QUESTIONS FOR ANALYSIS

1. Rabbi Nathan's citation of the opinions of the Beit Shammai and the Beit Hillel, as set down in the Gemara, seems to contradict the opinions of those two schools as they appear in the Mishnah. Why do you think the Gemara includes this apparent error or contradiction? What does your answer suggest about the Gemara and its sources?
2. Likewise, the Gemara cites Rabbi Joshua's opinion, with which the Mishnah does not agree. Why do you think Rabbi Joshua's opinion appears here? What does your answer suggest about the nature and purpose of the Gemara?
3. What does the story about Ben Azzai suggest, and why do you think it was preserved?

4. How do these rabbis use Scripture to support their arguments? What does your answer suggest about their view of the Bible?
5. What is the main weight of opinion regarding marriage and procreation, and what does this suggest about Judaism?

A person should not abstain from carrying out the obligation to "be fruitful and multiply"[1] unless he already has two children. The Beit Shammai[2] ruled: This means two sons, and the Beit Hillel[3] ruled: A son and a daughter, because it is written: "Male and female He created them."[4] The duty of procreation applies to a man, but not to a woman. R. Yohanan b. Beroka said: Concerning both it is written: "And God blessed them and said to them: Be fruitful and multiply."[5]

MISHNAH

This means that if he has children he may abstain from the duty of procreation but he may not abstain from the duty of living with a wife. This supports the view of R. Nahman who reported a ruling in the name of Samuel,[6] that even though a person has many children, he may not remain without a wife, as it is written: "It is not good for a man to be alone."[7] Others held the view that if he had children, he may abstain from the duty of procreation and he may also abstain from the duty of living with a wife. Shall we say that this contradicts what was reported by R. Nahman in the name of Samuel? No. If he has no children, he is to marry a woman capable of having a child, but if he already has children, he may marry a woman who is incapable of having children.

Elsewhere it was taught: R. Nathan said: According to the Beit Shammai, a person satisfies the obligation to "be fruitful and multiply" if he has a son and a daughter, and according to the Beit Hillel if he has a son or a daughter. Said Rava: What is the reason for the view of the Beit Hillel? It is written: "He created it not to be a waste, He formed it to be inhabited,"[8] and [by having a son or a daughter] he has already contributed to making it a place of habitation.

It was started: If a person had children while he was an idolator, and was later converted [to Judaism], R. Yohanan said that he has already fulfilled the duty of procreation but Resh Lakish said that he has not fulfilled it, because when a person is converted he is like a born-again child.

The Mishnah does not agree with the view of R. Joshua, for it was taught that R. Joshua stated: If a person married in his youth he is also to marry in his old age; if he had children in his youth, he is also to have children in his old age, for it is written: "Sow your seed in the morning and do not withdraw your hand in the evening, for you do not know which will prosper, this or that, or whether both alike will be good."[9]

Said R. Tanhum in the name of R. Hanilai: A person who is without a wife is without joy, without blessing, without good. Without joy — as it is written: "You shall rejoice, you and your household";[10] without blessing — as it is written: "That a blessing may rest on your house"[11] ["house" in such a context has generally been

---

[1]The Bible, Genesis 1:28.
[2]Literally, "the House of Shammai," namely the school that followed the teachings of Rabbi Shammai, a teacher who lived at the turn of the millennium — the late first century B.C.E. and the early first century C.E.
[3]Along with Shammai, Hillel (ca. 70 B.C.E.–ca. 10 C.E.) was the dominant interpreter of the Torah, or Law, of his day. Like Shammai, he had a school of disciples.
[4]The Bible, Genesis 5:2.

[5]The Bible, Genesis 1:28.
[6]A prophet of the eleventh century B.C.E. Citing Samuel as the source gives the opinion greater authority.
[7]The Bible, Genesis 2:18.
[8]The Bible, Isaiah 45:18.
[9]The Bible, Ecclesiastes 11:6.
[10]The Bible, Deuteronomy, 14:26.
[11]The Bible, Ezekiel 44:30.

interpreted to mean one's wife]; without good —
as it is written: "It is not good for a man to be
alone."[12] In Palestine they said: He is without
Torah,[13] and without protection [from the ravages of life]. Without Torah — as it is written:
"In truth, I have no one to help me [a wife], and
sound wisdom [Torah] is driven from me";[14]
without protection — as it is written: "A
woman protects a man."[15] R. b. Ila said: He is
without peace — as it is written: "And you shall
know that your tent [when presided over by
one's wife] is at peace, and you will visit your
habitation and you will not sin."[16] . . .

The rabbis taught: When one loves his wife as
himself, and honors her more than himself, and
trains his sons and daughters in the right path
and arranges for their marriage at a young age —
concerning such a person does the verse say:
"And you shall know that your tent is at peace."

Said R. Eleazar: A man without a wife is not a
complete man, as it is written: "Male and female
created He them, and He called their name
adam, 'man.'"[17] . . .

It was taught: R. Eliezer said: A person who
does not share in propagating the race is as
though he were guilty of bloodshed, for it is

written: "Whoever sheds the blood of a person,
by man shall his blood be shed,"[18] and following
this is the verse "and you be fruitful and multiply."[19] R. Jacob said: It is as though he diminished the divine image, for it is written: "For in
the image of God He made man."[20] Ben Azzai
said: It is as though he shed blood, and diminished the divine image, for after both the reference to bloodshed and the divine we have the
admonition: "And you be fruitful and multiply."
They said to Ben Azzai [who was unmarried]:
Some preach well and practice well, some act
well but do not preach well, but you preach well
but do not act well. Ben Azzai answered them:
What can I do, I am addicted to the study of the
Torah. The continuity of the world can be assured through others.

Other Sages say: He causes the divine presence
to depart from Israel. Thus it is written: "[I will
keep my covenant] to be God to you and to your
descendants after you."[21] When there are descendants after you, the divine presence will be with
them, but when there are not descendants after
you, with whom will the divine presence be?
With sticks and stones?

---

[12]The Bible, Genesis 2:18.
[13]The Law, the first five books of the Bible, ascribed to
Moses (see source 36).
[14]The Bible, Job 6:13.
[15]The Bible, Jeremiah 31:22.
[16]The Bible, Job 5:24.

[17]The Bible, Genesis 5:2.
[18]The Bible, Genesis 9:6.
[19]The Bible, Genesis 9:7.
[20]The Bible, Genesis 9:7.
[21]The Bible, Genesis 17:7.

❖ Chapter 7 ❖

Christianity
Conquering the World for Christ

J UDAISM'S SPECIAL COVENANT with God bound it body and soul to the Lord of the Universe. Most Jews, therefore, believed that the Lord had given them, His Chosen People, a sanctified homeland, and when they were dispossessed of that inheritance and scattered among the gentiles, they believed it was because of their sins. They further believed that should they reform their ways and observe their holy Covenant with God, they would regain sovereign possession of Palestine. For it was by divine mandate that this Holy Land and its Chosen People be ruled according to the Law given through Moses (source 12).

Not all Jewish sects, however, accepted this interpretation of the Covenant. One dissident element was a small body of religious Jews who gathered around a prophet from Nazareth called *Joshua*, or, in Greek, *Jesus* (ca. 4 B.C.E.–ca. 30 C.E.). The heart of Jesus' message was that the promised messianic Kingdom of God was at hand. The *Messiah* (the Anointed One) — God's promised deliverer — was generally expected to be a political and military leader, who would re-establish Israel as a free state. Jesus, to the contrary, expanding upon themes in the teachings of Second Isaiah (source 18), preached that the Messiah would usher in a spiritual age of judgment and redemption.

As his ministry developed, Jesus became convinced that he was the Messiah. Although he claimed, "My kingdom is not of this Earth," local Roman and Jewish authorities were disquieted by the apparent threat to the establishment posed by Jesus and his followers, and they collaborated to execute him by crucifixion. Jesus' followers believed, however, that he rose from the dead, appeared to a number of his friends, and then ascended to Heaven with the promise of returning soon to sit in judgment of all humanity. Believing that his resurrection proved Jesus' messiahship, his disciples proceeded to spread the *Gospel* (Good News) of redemption.

Initially the disciples preached only to Palestinian Jews. Soon, however, they began to spread the faith throughout the Roman Empire and beyond, welcoming Jew and gentile alike to receive the *New Covenant* proclaimed by Jesus. Before the end of the first century C.E., *Christians* (called so because of Jesus' title *Christos*, which is Greek for *Messiah*) had established the faith in every major city of the Roman Empire and had penetrated the Parthian Empire, non-Roman Africa, Arabia, and the west coast of India. In the early fourth century, Christianity was adopted as the state religion in Armenia, Ethiopia, and Georgia; became the favored religion of the Roman emperor Constantine I (r. 306–337); and took root among a number of German tribes beyond the northeast borders of the Roman Empire. In the seventh century, a group of dissident Christians known as *Nestorians* established themselves in western China. This otherworldly faith was waging a successful campaign of spiritual conquest in a fair portion of the Afro-Eurasian World.

The Foundations of Christianity

During Christianity's first century, its adherents had to define the religion to which they gave their allegiance. Just as important, they had to confront the issue of what Christianity *was not*. Were they Jews? Were they something else? If something else, what set their religion apart from Judaism and all of the other religions that flourished within the Greco-Roman World? In essence, what did they believe, and how should they organize themselves?

In resolving these issues, Christians had the guidance of several great teachers. First and foremost was Jesus himself. His call for spiritual perfection was the foundation of the Christian faith and has remained so for almost 2,000 years. Following Jesus' departure from the world, his followers had to grapple with many unresolved questions: Who was Jesus? What was his relationship with God and humanity? What was the nature of the community he had left behind? Among the many leaders who tried to answer these questions, none was more influential than *Paul of Tarsus.*

Becoming Spiritually Perfect
▼▼▼
38 ▼ THE GOSPEL OF SAINT MATTHEW

Tradition ascribes authorship of the *Gospels*, the four major accounts of Jesus of Nazareth's life and teachings, to authors known as Matthew, Mark, Luke, and John. The early Christian Church believed that Matthew had been one of Jesus' *Twelve Apostles*, or major companions, and accepted his Gospel as the authoritative remembrances of a divinely inspired author. Modern scholarship dates the work to the period around 85 or 90, or approximately fifty-five to sixty years after Jesus' ministry. Its author appears to have been a Christian of Antioch in Syria and possibly a disciple of the Apostle Matthew, but probably not the apostle himself. The author clearly was trained in the rabbinical tradition (source 37) but was equally comfortable with the Greek language and Hellenistic culture, and he seems to have addressed his Gospel to a cosmopolitan Christian community composed of former Jews and gentiles.

The central theme of the Gospel of Matthew is that Jesus is the Messiah, the fulfillment of the promises made by God through Abraham, Moses, and the prophets. For Matthew, Second Isaiah was the greatest of the prophets, the one who had most clearly foretold Jesus' mission of salvation and who had preached that the universal reign of the Lord was imminent. In the following selection, Matthew presents what is commonly known as the *Sermon on the Mount*. Here Jesus instructs his followers about what the *Kingdom of God* requires of all its members. In all likelihood, this is not a verbatim account of a specific sermon that Jesus delivered on some mountainside but a distillation of Jesus' core moral and theological teachings. As you read this excerpt, keep in mind that Jesus lived in the fluid environment that produced Rabbinical Judaism and was, himself, considered a rabbi, or teacher.

QUESTIONS FOR ANALYSIS

1. In what ways does Jesus emphasize the spiritual relationship of each believer to God?
2. How does Jesus regard Judaism and especially the Law of Moses? In what ways does he claim that his teachings complete, or perfect, the Law of Moses?
3. To whom would Jesus' message especially appeal?
4. Compare the message and spirit behind the Sermon on the Mount with that of the Buddha's first sermon, "Setting in Motion the Wheel of the Law" (source 15). Which strike you as more pronounced, their differences or similarities? What do you conclude from your answer?

Seeing the crowds, he went up on the mountain, and when he sat down his disciples came to him. And he opened his mouth and taught them, saying:

"Blessed are the poor in spirit, for theirs is the kingdom of Heaven.

"Blessed are those who mourn, for they shall be comforted.

"Blessed are the meek, for they shall inherit the Earth.

"Blessed are those who hunger and thirst for righteousness, for they shall be satisfied.

"Blessed are the merciful, for they shall obtain mercy.

"Blessed are the pure in heart, for they shall see God.

"Blessed are the peacemakers, for they shall be called sons of God.

"Blessed are those who are persecuted for righteousness' sake, for theirs is the kingdom of Heaven.

"Blessed are you when men revile you and persecute you and utter all kinds of evil against you falsely on my account. Rejoice and be glad, for your reward is great in Heaven, for so men persecuted the prophets who were before you. . . .

"Think not that I have come to abolish the law and the prophets; I have come not to abolish them but to fulfill them. For truly, I say to you, till Heaven and Earth pass away, not an iota, not a dot, will pass from the law until all is accomplished. Whoever then relaxes one of the least of these commandments and teaches men so, shall be called least in the kingdom of Heaven; but he who does them and teaches them shall be called great in the kingdom of Heaven. For I tell you, unless your righteousness exceeds that of the scribes and the Pharisees,[1] you will never enter the kingdom of Heaven.

"You have heard that it was said to the men of old, 'You shall not kill; and whoever kills shall be liable to judgment.' But I say to you that every one who is angry with his brother shall be liable to judgment; whoever insults his brother shall be liable to the council,[2] and whoever says, 'You fool!' shall be liable to the hell of fire. So if you are offering your gift at the altar, and there remember that your brother has something against you, leave your gift there before the altar and go; first be reconciled to your brother, and then come and offer your gift. . . . You have heard that it was said, 'An eye for an eye and a tooth for a tooth.' But I say to you, Do not resist one who is evil. But if any one strikes you on the right cheek, turn to him the other also. . . . You have heard that it was said, 'You shall love your neighbor and hate your enemy.' But I say to you, Love your enemies and pray for those who persecute you, so that you may be sons of your Father who is in Heaven; for he makes his sun rise on the evil and on the good, and sends rain on the just and on the unjust. For if you love those who love you, what reward have you? . . . You, therefore, must be perfect, as your heavenly Father is perfect. . . .

"And in praying do not heap up empty phrases as the Gentiles do; for they think that they will be heard for their many words. Do not be like them, for your Father knows what you need before you ask him. Pray then like this:

Our Father who art in Heaven.
Hallowed be thy name.
Thy kingdom come,
Thy will be done,
    On Earth as it is in Heaven.
Give us this day our daily bread;
And forgive us our debts,
    As we also have forgiven our debtors
And lead us not into temptation,
    But deliver us from evil.

For if you forgive men their trespasses, your heavenly Father also will forgive you; but if you do not forgive men their trespasses, neither will your Father forgive your trespasses. . . .

[1]The *scribes* were nonpriestly professionals who copied, interpreted, and applied the oral traditions that supplemented written biblical Law. The *Pharisees* were members of a Jewish religious party who stressed that all of this nonscriptural, oral law had to be observed as equally and as fully as the written Law of Moses. Eventually this *Oral Torah*, as it was often called, became codified in the *Talmud* (source 37). [2]The *Sanhedrin*, Judaism's chief religious and judicial body.

"Do not lay up for yourselves treasures on Earth, where moth and rust consume and where thieves break in and steal, but lay up for yourselves treasures in Heaven, where neither moth nor rust consumes and where thieves do not break in and steal. For where your treasure is, there will your heart be also. . . . Therefore do not be anxious, saying, 'What shall we eat?' or 'What shall we drink?' or 'What shall we wear?'

For the Gentiles seek all these things; and your heavenly Father knows that you need them all. But seek first his kingdom and his righteousness, and all these things shall be yours as well. . . .

"Judge not, that you be not judged. For with the judgment you pronounce you will be judged, and the measure you give will be the measure you get."

The Path to Righteousness: The Law or Faith?

▼▼▼

39 ▼ Saint Paul, EPISTLE TO THE ROMANS

Our earliest Christian sources are not the Gospels but rather the *epistles*, or letters, that Saint Paul (ca. 3 B.C.E.–64 or 67 C.E.) wrote to a number of Christian communities. Paul, or to give him his Hebrew name, *Saul*, was a Hellenized Jew and rabbinical scholar from Tarsus in Asia Minor and has often been called *the second founder of Christianity*. Prior to his becoming a Christian, Paul was a member of the Jewish elite of the eastern Mediterranean. Moreover, he was a Roman citizen, which was rare for Jews of his day. Converted dramatically to Christianity by a blinding revelation while traveling to Damascus in Syria in the pursuit of Christians whom he was persecuting, Paul became the leading opponent of Jewish-Christian conservatives who wished to keep Christianity within the boundaries of Judaism. From roughly 47 to his death in Rome in either 64 or 67 (ancient authorities differ on the date), Paul was an indefatigable missionary, converting gentiles and Jews alike in many of the major cities of the eastern Mediterranean. Most important of all, Paul transformed Jesus' messianic message into a faith centering on Jesus as Lord and Savior.

Paul developed his distinctive theology in his epistles, his only extant writings. Although each epistle was addressed to a specific group of Christians and often dealt with local issues, they were revered as authoritative pronouncements of general interest for all believers. As a result, copies were circulated, and in time some of his letters (as well as some Paul never composed but that were ascribed to him) were incorporated into the body of scriptural books known to Christians as the *New Testament*, the *Old Testament* being the pre-Christian, or Jewish, portion of the Bible. (See Multiple Voices IV for sources relating to the process through which the books of the New Testament were established.)

Around 57, probably while residing in Corinth, Greece, Paul planned to establish a mission in Spain and decided to make Rome his base of operations. In preparation, he wrote to the Christians at Rome to inform them of his plans and to instruct them in the faith. The result was the *Epistle to the Romans*, the most fully articulated expression of Paul's theology of salvation.

QUESTIONS FOR ANALYSIS

1. According to Paul, who was Jesus?
2. For Paul, how can gentiles also be called the Children of Abraham?
3. This epistle centers on the issue of how one becomes righteous in the eyes of God. According to Paul, can the Law of Moses or any other body of law put one right with God? Why or why not? What role does faith play in putting one right with God? Faith in what or whom?
4. Compare this epistle with the Sermon on the Mount. Do they agree, disagree, or complement each another? Be specific.
5. What do you infer from the evidence about the role of women in the early Church?
6. What parallels can you discover between Christian devotion to Jesus, as taught by Paul, and similar contemporary forms of piety and belief in the Hindu and Buddhist traditions? In answering this question, consider the sources in Chapter 6.

Paul, a servant of Jesus Christ, called to be an apostle,[1] set apart for the Gospel of God which he promised beforehand through his prophets in the holy scriptures, the Gospel concerning his Son, who was descended from David[2] according to the flesh and designated Son of God in power according to the Spirit of holiness by his resurrection from the dead, Jesus Christ our Lord, through whom we have received grace and apostleship to bring about obedience to the faith for the sake of his name among all the nations, including yourselves who are called to belong to Jesus Christ;

To all God's beloved in Rome, who are called to be saints: . . . I am eager to preach the Gospel to you also who are in Rome.

For I am not ashamed of the Gospel: it is the power of God for salvation to every one who has faith, to the Jew first and also to the Greek.[3] For in it the righteousness of God is revealed through faith for faith; as it is written, "He who through faith is righteous shall live." . . . For we hold that a man is justified[4] by faith apart from works of law.[5] Or is God the God of Jews only? Is he not the God of gentiles also? Yes, of gentiles also, since God is one; and he will justify the circumcised[6] on the ground of their faith and the uncircumcised because of their faith. . . . The promise to Abraham[7] and his descendants, that they should inherit the world, did not come through the Law but through the righteousness of faith. . . . That is why it depends on faith, in order that the promise may rest on grace and be guaranteed to all his descendants — not only to the adherents of the law but also to those who share the faith of Abraham, for he is the father of us all, as it is written, "I have made you the father of many nations." . . .

---

[1]Paul claimed apostolic status because he believed he had been miraculously called and converted by the Risen Christ, who appeared to him in a vision. Some of the close friends and earliest followers of Jesus were reluctant to recognize Paul as an apostle.
[2]The prophetic tradition maintained that the Messiah would be descended from the line of King David. Consequently, Christian Jews stressed Jesus' Davidic lineage.
[3]*Greek* means any non-Jew, or gentile, because Greek was the common tongue of educated people in the eastern half of the Roman Empire.
[4]Made just, or righteous, in the eyes of God.
[5]The Law of Judaism.
[6]The Law of Moses prescribes circumcision for all Jewish males; gentiles are, therefore, *the uncircumcised.*
[7]The ancient patriarch from whom all Jews were descended and with whom YHWH entered into a covenant.

Therefore, since we are justified by faith, we have peace with God through our Lord Jesus Christ. Through him we have obtained access to this grace in which we stand, and we rejoice in our hope of sharing the glory of God. . . . God shows his love for us in that while we were yet sinners Christ died for us. Since, therefore, we are now justified by his blood, much more shall we be saved by him from the wrath of God. For if while we were enemies we were reconciled to God by the death of his Son, much more, now that we are reconciled, shall we be saved by his life. . . . There is therefore now no condemnation for those who are in Christ Jesus. For the law of the Spirit of life in Christ Jesus has set me free from the law of sin and death. . . .

If you confess with your lips that Jesus is Lord and believe in your heart that God raised him from the dead, you will be saved. For man believes with his heart and so is justified, and he confesses with his lips and so is saved. . . . For there is no distinction between Jew and Greek; the same Lord is Lord of all and bestows his riches upon all who call upon him. For, "every one who calls upon the name of the Lord will be saved." . . .

I appeal to you therefore, brethren, by the mercies of God, to present your bodies as a living sacrifice, holy and acceptable to God, which is your spiritual worship. . . . Let love be genuine; hate what is evil, hold fast to what is good; love one another with brotherly affection; outdo one another in showing honor. Never flag in zeal, be aglow with the Spirit, serve the Lord. Rejoice in your hope, be patient in tribulation, be constant in prayer. Contribute to the needs of the saints, practice hospitality.

Bless those who persecute you; bless and do not curse them. Rejoice with those who rejoice, weep with those who weep. Live in harmony with one another; do not be haughty, but associate with the lowly; never be conceited. Repay no one evil for evil, but take thought for what is noble in the sight of all. If possible, so far as it depends upon you, live peaceably with all. Beloved, never avenge yourselves, but leave it to the wrath of God; for it is written, "Vengeance is mine, I will repay, says the Lord." No, "if your enemy is hungry, feed him; if he is thirsty, give him drink; for by so doing you will heap burning coals upon his head." Do not be overcome by evil, but overcome evil with good. . . .

Owe no one anything, except to love one another; for he who loves his neighbor has fulfilled the Law. The commandments, "You shall not commit adultery, You shall not kill, You shall not steal, You shall not covet," and any other commandment, are summed up in this sentence, "You shall love your neighbor as yourself." Love does no wrong to a neighbor; therefore love is the fulfilling of the Law. . . .

I commend to you to our sister Phoebe, a deaconess of the church at Cenchreae,[8] that you may receive her in the Lord as befits the saints, and help her in whatever she may require from you, for she has been a helper of many and of myself as well.

Greet Prisca and Aquila,[9] my fellow workers in Christ Jesus, who risked their necks for my life, to whom not only I but also all the churches of the gentiles give thanks; greet also the church in their house.

---

[8]A community in the Greek Peloponnesus. *Deaconesses* and their male counterparts, *deacons*, were assistants to the *presbyters* (elders) who supervised the various churches. The duties of these assistants consisted of baptizing, preaching, and dispensing charity.

[9]A married couple of Hellenized Jewish-Christians who figured prominently in the Christian community of Rome. Prisca was the wife; Aquila the husband.

▼▼▼

Christianity and the Roman World

Roman authorities were generally tolerant of the deities and religious practices of the empire's subjects and tried to foster loyalty to the empire by merging these gods and goddesses into the Roman *pantheon*, or assemblage of recognized deities. Normally all that Rome required was that the various cults and their devotees not threaten public order or morality and that each religion help guarantee the gods' continued favor toward the state. Because, however, Roman officials perceived that Bacchism (source 23) violated all norms of decent social behavior and the Celts' Druid priests threatened the stability of Roman rule in Gaul and Britain, they acted vigorously to suppress both cults. The same was true of Christianity. As far as many Romans were concerned, Christianity was a threat to the state and civil order because of its uncompromising monotheism and its extreme sense of exclusivity. Although Judaism shared those characteristics, it enjoyed the status of being the legally recognized religion of one of Rome's subject peoples. Once Christianity separated itself from Jewish synagogues, it lost whatever protection it had enjoyed by reason of its Judaic heritage.

We possess no official state pronouncement concerning Christianity before the second century, but it appears that the first imperial persecution of Christians took place in Rome under Emperor Nero (r. 54–68) around the year 64. Our source is the historian and moralist Tacitus (ca. 55–after 116). Writing more than four decades later, Tacitus noted that, following a massive fire that devastated the city, Christians became convenient targets of attack because they were "hated for their abominations." Because of those putative abominations, Christianity became a prohibited cult, and adherence to it was technically a capital offense.

As the following three sources indicate, this was not the whole story. Indeed, the story of relations between Christianity and the Roman Empire is one of world history's most interesting and historically significant sagas.

Persecution and Deliverance
▼▼▼

40 ▼ *Eusebius of Caesarea,* ECCLESIASTICAL HISTORY

Although some Christians were jailed and executed by Roman authorities, between roughly the mid first and mid third centuries persecution of Christians was sporadic, local, and often halfhearted. When persecutions occurred, it was usually when provincial governors found themselves forced to bow to local sentiment in order to keep a discontented populace quiet. Crop failures and other natural disasters often seemed to demand a few Christian victims as propitiation to the gods, the theory being that the Christians were atheists and had angered the gods by their refusal to worship them. This policy of overlooking the Christians' supposed atheism and immorality changed around the year 250, when Emperor Decius embarked on a short but bitter empire-wide attack on Christians.

In 303 the empire launched its last and greatest persecution of Christianity; the attack continued until 311, when Emperor Galerius, in the grips of a frightening disease, decided to strike a bargain with the Christian god. His edict of toleration granted Christians freedom of worship, in exchange for their prayers for him. A few days after issuing the edict, Galerius was dead.

The following year, *Constantine I* (r. 306–337), a claimant to the imperial throne, was campaigning in Italy against a rival. According to a Christian source, prior to the battle Constantine had a vision in which the Christian god promised him victory. Shortly thereafter he won a decisive victory, thereby becoming uncontested emperor in the West. In 313 a grateful Constantine and his coemperor, Licinius, who ruled the eastern half of the empire, granted freedom of worship to all persons in the empire and recognized the full legal status of each local Christian church. Christianity had weathered the storm of Roman persecution.

Constantine never wavered in his patronage of Christianity, and the consequences were momentous for the empire, for Christianity, and for the subsequent civilizations of western Eurasia. A faith that commanded the belief of only about 10 percent of the empire's population in 313 was, by century's end, the religion of the vast majority of eastern Mediterranean urban dwellers and was making rapid advances among the region's rural populations. In the western half of the empire, the progress of conversion was slower but steady.

The most important eyewitness to the revolution initiated by Constantine is Eusebius (ca. 260–339 or 340), leader, or *bishop*, of the church of Caesarea in Palestine. Bishop Eusebius was a prolific writer, but his single enduring work is the *Ecclesiastical History*, which traces the fortunes of the Christian Church from its earliest days to the early fourth century.

Eusebius's history is the most complete and coherent account that we possess of the early Church's first three centuries, but its author's careful scholarship did not negate the *Ecclesiastical History*'s apologetical tone and theological message. Within its pages history is a cosmic contest between the forces of God and those of the Devil. On one side are patriarchs, prophets, saints, and martyrs; on the other are pagans, persecutors, latter-day Jews, and *heretical*, or wrong-believing, Christians. Although the Devil and his minions always lose, the righteous suffer considerably as they struggle against evil.

More than simply a scholar, Eusebius was active in the affairs of the early-fourth-century Church and suffered in the process. He had been imprisoned during the era of the Great Persecution and had seen many of his friends tortured and martyred. But he also lived to see the miracle of the Emperor Constantine's conversion to Christianity after the emperor's victory in 312. Following Eusebius's elevation to the bishopric of Caesarea around 313, he came to enjoy the Christian emperor's patronage and friendship.

Earlier, before the onslaught of the Great Persecution, Eusebius had begun a detailed history of the Church down to his own day, completing the work in seven books, or volumes, around 303. The events of 312 and following, however, necessitated that he update his work. Consequently, he enlarged the *Ecclesiastical History*

184   *Faith, Devotion, and Salvation*

to ten books in order to include the history of Christian fortunes down to 324, thereby demonstrating the manner in which Divine Providence had once again triumphed over the forces of evil.

The following two excerpts come from an appendix to Book 8, entitled "The Martyrs of Palestine," and Book 10, which recounts the consequences of Constantine's sudden patronage of Christianity and his subsequent victory over his pagan coemperor, Licinius, in 324, thereby making him the single ruler of an empire that now overtly favored the Christian religion.

QUESTIONS FOR ANALYSIS

1. Why do you think Eusebius dwells on the punishments that Christian confessors bore?
2. What does his description of the heroism of the two female martyrs suggest about Christian notions of the place of women in the Church?
3. Compare your answer to the question above with your answer to question 5 of source 39. What conclusions do you reach?
4. Some see a dramatic difference in tone and message between what Eusebius writes in the first excerpt and what he writes in the second. Do you see a difference? If so, how do you explain it?

THE MARTYRS OF PALESTINE

Up to the sixth year[1] the storm had been incessantly raging against us. Before this time there had been a very large number of confessors[2] of religion in the so-called Porphyry quarry in Thebais.[3] . . . Of these, one hundred men, lacking three, together with women and infants, were sent to the governor of Palestine. When they confessed the God of the universe and Christ, Firmilianus, who had been sent there as a governor. . . , directed, in accordance with the imperial command, that they should be maimed by burning the sinews of the ankles of their left feet, and that their right eyes with the eyelids and pupils should first be cut out, and then destroyed by hot irons to the very roots. And he

then sent them to the mines in the province to endure hardships with severe toil and suffering.[4]

But it was not sufficient that these only who suffered such miseries should be deprived of their eyes, but those natives of Palestine also, who were mentioned just above as condemned to pugilistic combat,[5] since they would neither receive food from the royal storehouse nor undergo the necessary preparatory exercises. Having been brought on this account not only before the overseers, but also before Maximinus himself,[6] and having manifested the noblest persistence in confession by the endurance of hunger and stripes, they received like punishment with those whom we have mentioned, and with them other confessors in the city of Caesarea. Immediately afterwards others who were gathered to

[1]The sixth year of the persecution, which began in the spring of 303.
[2]Those who confess, or proclaim and live, the faith in a heroic manner.
[3]The region around Thebes in Egypt.
[4]Slave labor in stone quarries and mines, which usually ended in an early death, was a common criminal penalty.
[5]They were condemned to fight as boxing gladiators in the circus.
[6]Maximin Daia, emperor in the East from 305 to 313.

hear the Scriptures read, were seized in Gaza,[7] and some endured the same sufferings in the feet and eyes; but others were afflicted with yet greater torments and with most terrible tortures in the sides. One of these, in body a woman, but in understanding a man, would not endure the threat of rape, and spoke directly against the tyrant who entrusted the government to such cruel judges. She was first scourged and then raised aloft on the stake, and her sides lacerated. As those appointed for this purpose applied the tortures incessantly and severely at the command of the judge, another, with mind fixed, like the former, on virginity as her aim, — a woman who was altogether mean in form and contemptible in appearance, but, on the other hand, strong in soul, and endowed with an understanding superior to her body, — being unable to bear the merciless and cruel and inhuman deeds, with a boldness beyond that of the combatants famed among the Greeks,[8] cried out to the judge from the midst of the crowd: "And how long will you thus cruelly torture my sister?" But he was greatly enraged and ordered the woman to be immediately seized. Thereupon she was brought forward and having called herself by the august name of the Savior, she was first urged by words to sacrifice, and as she refused she was dragged by force to the altar. But her sister continued to maintain her former zeal, and with intrepid and resolute foot kicked the altar, and overturned it with the fire that was on it. Thereupon the judge, enraged like a wild beast, inflicted on her such tortures in her sides as he never had on any one before, striving almost to glut himself with her raw flesh. But when his madness was satiated, he bound them both together, this one and her whom she called sister, and condemned them to death by fire. It is said that the first of these was from the country of

Gaza; the other, by name Valentina, was of Caesarea, and was well known to many.

BOOK 10

Thanks for all things be given unto God the Omnipotent Ruler and King of the universe, and the greatest thanks to Jesus Christ the Savior and Redeemer of our souls, through whom we pray that peace may be always preserved for us firm and undisturbed by external troubles and troubles of the mind. Since in accordance with your wishes, my most holy Paulinus,[9] we have added the tenth book of the Church History to those which have preceded, we will inscribe it to you, proclaiming you as the seal of the whole work; and we will fitly add in a perfect number[10] the perfect panegyric upon the restoration of the churches, obeying the Divine Spirit which exhorts us in the following words: "Sing unto the Lord a new song, for he hath done marvelous things. His right hand and his holy arm hath saved him. The Lord hath made known his salvation, his righteousness hath he revealed in the presence of the nations."[11] And in accordance with the utterance which commands us to sing the new song, let us proceed to show that, after those terrible and gloomy spectacles which we have described, we are now permitted to see and celebrate such things as many truly righteous men and martyrs of God before us desired to see upon Earth and did not see, and to hear and did not hear. But they, hastening on, obtained far better things, being carried to Heaven and the paradise of divine pleasure. But, acknowledging that even these things are greater than we deserve, we have been astonished at the grace manifested by the author of the great gifts, and rightly do we admire him, worshiping him with the whole power of our souls, and testifying to

---

[7]The southern coastal region of Palestine.
[8]Professional wrestlers and boxers. See source 26.
[9]The bishop of Tyre, whom Eusebius especially admired.

[10]According to Pythagorean numerology, 10 is the perfect number because it is the sum of the four principal geometric numbers: 1, 2, 3, and 4.
[11]The Bible, Psalms 98:1–2.

the truth of those recorded utterances, in which it is said, "Come and see the works of the Lord, the wonders which he hath done upon the earth; he removeth wars to the ends of the world, he shall break the bow and snap the spear in sunder, and shall burn the shields with fire."[12] Rejoicing in these things which have been clearly fulfilled in our day, let us proceed with our account.

The whole race of God's enemies was destroyed in the manner indicated, and was thus suddenly swept from the sight of men. . . . And finally a bright and splendid day, overshadowed by no cloud, illuminated with beams of heavenly light the churches of Christ throughout the entire world. And not even those outside our communion[13] were prevented from sharing in the same blessings, or at least from coming under their influence and enjoying a part of the benefits bestowed upon us by God.

All men, then, were freed from the oppression of the tyrants, and being released from the former ills, one in one way and another in another acknowledged the defender of the pious to be the only true God. And we especially who placed our hopes in the Christ of God had unspeakable gladness, and a certain inspired joy bloomed for all of us, when we saw every place which shortly before had been desolated by the impieties of the tyrants reviving as if from a long and death-fraught pestilence, and temples again rising from their foundations to an immense height, and receiving a splendor far greater than that of the old ones which had been destroyed. But the supreme rulers also confirmed to us still more extensively the munificence of God by repeated ordinances in behalf of the Christians; and personal letters of the emperor were sent to the bishops, with honors and gifts of money. . . .

To him, therefore, God granted, from Heaven above, the deserved fruit of piety, the trophies of victory over the impious, and he cast the guilty one with all his counselors and friends prostrate at the feet of Constantine. For when Licinius[14] carried his madness to the last extreme, the emperor, the friend of God, thinking that he ought no longer to be tolerated, acting upon the basis of sound judgment, and mingling the firm principles of justice with humanity, gladly determined to come to the protection of those who were oppressed by the tyrant, and undertook, by putting a few destroyers out of the way, to save the greater part of the human race. For when he had formerly exercised humanity alone and had shown mercy to him who was not worthy of sympathy, nothing was accomplished; for Licinius did not renounce his wickedness, but rather increased his fury against the people that were subject to him, and there was left to the afflicted no hope of salvation, oppressed as they were by a savage beast. Wherefore, the protector of the virtuous, mingling hatred for evil with love for good, went forth with his son Crispus,[15] a most beneficent prince, and extended a saving right hand to all that were perishing. Both of them, father and son, under the protection, as it were, of God, the universal King, with the Son of God, the Savior of all, as their leader and ally, drew up their forces on all sides against the enemies of the Deity and won an easy victory; God having prospered them in the battle in all respects according to their wish. Thus, suddenly, and sooner than can be told, those who yesterday

[12]Psalms 46:8–9.
[13]Non-Christians and Christian heretics.
[14]Licinius had been coemperor since 308. In 313 he and Constantine allied, with Constantine taking the western half of the empire. In 316 Constantine attacked Licinius's lands, on the pretext that Licinius was persecuting Christians, and confiscated a major portion of the eastern half of the empire. In 324 Constantine returned to complete the job, on the same pretext. After capturing Licinius and uniting the entire empire under his control, Constantine had his former colleague murdered within a year. Circumstances thus forced Eusebius to excise earlier complimentary allusions to Licinius from his last edition of the *Ecclesiastical History*.
[15]Crispus was Constantine's eldest son and had held the title of *Caesar* (deputy emperor) since 317. He served with distinction in the war of 324, commanding Constantine's naval forces. For reasons unknown, Constantine ordered his execution in 326.

and the day before breathed death and threatening were no more, and not even their names were remembered, but their inscriptions and their honors suffered the merited disgrace. And the things which Licinius with his own eyes had seen come upon the former impious tyrants he himself likewise suffered, because he did not receive instruction nor learn wisdom from the chastisements of his neighbors, but followed the same path of impiety which they had trod, and was justly hurled over the same precipice. Thus he lay prostrate.

But Constantine, the mightiest victor, adorned with every virtue of piety, together with his son Crispus, a most God-beloved prince, and in all respects like his father, recovered the East which belonged to them; and they formed one united Roman empire as of old, bringing under their peaceful sway the whole world from the rising of the sun to the opposite quarter, both north and south, even to the extremities of the declining day. All fear therefore of those who had formerly afflicted them was taken away from men, and they celebrated splendid and festive days. Everything was filled with light, and those who before were downcast beheld each other with smiling faces and beaming eyes. With dances and hymns, in city and country, they glorified first of all God the universal King, because they had been thus taught, and then the pious emperor with his God-beloved children. There was oblivion of past evils and forgetfulness of every deed of impiety; there was enjoyment of present benefits and expectation of those yet to come. Edicts full of clemency and laws containing tokens of benevolence and true piety were issued in every place by the victorious emperor. Thus after all tyranny had been purged away, the empire which belonged to them was preserved firm and without a rival for Constantine and his sons alone. And having obliterated the godlessness of their predecessors, recognizing the benefits conferred upon them by God, they exhibited their love of virtue and their love of God, and their piety and gratitude to the Deity, by the deed which they performed in the sight of all men.

The Christian Empire
▼▼▼
41 ▼ *THE THEODOSIAN CODE*

All Roman emperors from Constantine I (the Great) onward were baptized Christians, and most were generous patrons of the Church. It was almost an anticlimax when Theodosius I (r. 379–395) and his two coemperors declared Catholic Christianity the state religion in 380.

In 429 Theodosius II (r. 408–450), ruler of the eastern half of the empire, commissioned a panel of jurists to arrange systematically all imperial edicts from the reign of Constantine I to his time. In 438 they produced *The Theodosian Code*. The code's laws span the period from 313 to 437, thereby providing a panoramic view of the first century of imperial Christianity.

QUESTIONS FOR ANALYSIS

1. According to the edicts of February 380 and May 391, what is the status of heretical Christians, namely those who do not accept the *orthodox* (correctly thought) form of Christianity?
2. Compare the legal status of Jews, pagans, and heretics. Ranking them from 1 to 3, 1 being "not tolerated" and 3 "most tolerated," what ranking would you give each? Cite the evidence to support each ranking.

3. Skip ahead to Multiple Voices IV. After reading those sources in the light of these edicts, explain why the Christian empire adopted the policies that it did regarding religious conformity.

4. How did the emperors treat the Christian clergy? Can you think of any reasons for this policy?

5. Compare Asoka's edicts (source 30) with these laws. What does this exercise lead you to infer about the two societies?

THE IMPERIAL CHURCH

Edict to the people of the Constantinopolitan city.

All peoples, whom the moderation of our Clemency rules, we wish to be engaged in that religion, which the divine Peter,[1] the apostle, is declared — by the religion which has descended even to the present from him — to have transmitted to the Romans and which, it is clear the pontiff[2] Damasus[3] and Peter, bishop of Alexandria,[4] a man of apostolic sanctity, follow: this is, that according to apostolic discipline[5] and evangelic doctrine[6] we should believe the sole Deity of the Father and of the Son and of the Holy Spirit under an equal Majesty and under a pious Trinity.[7]

We order those following this law to assume the name of Catholic[8] Christians, but the rest, since we judge them demented and insane, to sustain the infamy of heretical dogma and their conventicles[9] not to take the name of churches, to be smitten first by divine vengeance, then also by the punishment of our authority; which we have claimed in accordance with the celestial will.

[February 28, 380]

HERETICS

Those who shall have betrayed the holy faith and shall have profaned holy baptism[10] should be segregated from all persons' association, should be debarred from testifying,[11] should not have . . . the making of a will, should succeed to no one in an inheritance, should be written by no one as heirs.

And these also we should have commanded to be banished to a distance and to be removed rather far away, if it has not seemed to be a greater penalty for them to dwell among men and to lack men's approbation.

But they never shall return to their previous status, the shame of their conduct shall not be obliterated by penitence and shall not be concealed by any shade of elaborate defense or protection, since things which are fabricated and fashioned cannot protect indeed those who have polluted the faith which they had vowed to God and who, betraying the divine mystery,[12] have turned to profanations. And indeed for the lapsed[13] and the errant[14] there is help, but for the lost — that is, the profaners of holy baptism —

---

[1]Peter (d. ca. 64 or 67), the leader of the apostles and presumed first bishop of Rome.

[2]A title reserved for bishops and their superiors.

[3]Damasus I, bishop of Rome (r. 366–384).

[4]Peter II (r. 373–381). Like the bishops of Rome, the patriarchs of Alexandria were (and are) accorded the title *papa* (father), or pope.

[5]According to the practices of the apostles.

[6]According to the faith as revealed in the Gospels.

[7]Theodosius I and his coemperors rejected the teaching of the *Arian* Christians, who maintained that Jesus was God only by adoption, being God the Father's First Creation, which meant that Jesus was not coeternal with God the Father or his equal in majesty or nature. The imperial Church eventually rejected this as heresy and postulated instead the doctrine of the *Holy Trinity*, which recognizes three separate and equal divine persons in a single, indivisible God: God

the Father, the Creator; God the Son (Jesus), the Redemer; God the Holy Spirit, the Sanctifier. See the Creed of Nicaea in Multiple Voices IV. Compare the Hindu Trinity of Brahma, Vishnu, and Shiva (sources 32 and 33).

[8]*Catholic*, which means "universal," refers here to the official Church of the entire empire.

[9]Secret religious meeting places.

[10]It is not clear if this condemnation extended to all heretics, who profaned their baptism (the rite through which they were initiated into the Church) by their heresy, or only those heretics who insisted on rebaptizing persons who had previously been baptized as orthodox Catholic Christians.

[11]In a court of law.

[12]Baptism.

[13]Those who no longer practice the religion but are not heretics.

[14]Non-Christians.

there is no aid through any remedy of penitence, which is wont to be available for other crimes.

[May 11, 391]

We order the heretics' polluted contagions to be driven from cities, to be ejected from villages, and the communities not at all to be available for any meetings, lest in any place a sacrilegious company of such persons should be collected. Neither public meeting places to their perversity nor more hidden retreats to their errors should be granted.

[May 19, 391]

PAGANS

We ordain that none may have the liberty of approaching any shrine or temple whatever or of performing abominable sacrifices at any place or time whatever.

[August 7, 391]

JEWS

Governors of provinces should forbid Jews, in a certain ceremony of their festival Aman[15] for remembrance of a former punishment, to ignite and to burn for contempt of the Christian faith with sacrilegious mind a simulated appearance of the Holy Cross[16] lest they should connect our faith's sign with their sports; but they should retain their rites without contempt of the Christian law,[17] because without doubt they shall lose privileges previously permitted to them, unless they shall have abstained from illicit acts.

[May 29, 408]

No one, on the ground that he is a Jew, when he is innocent, should be condemned nor any religion whatsoever should cause a person to be exposed to contumely.[18]

Their synagogues or habitations should not be burned indiscriminately or should not be damaged wrongfully without any reason, since, moreover, even if anyone should be implicated in crimes, yet the vigor of the law-courts and the protection of the public law appear to have been established in our midst, lest anyone should have the power to venture on vengeance for himself.

But as we desire this to be provided for the persons of the Jews, so we decree also that the following warning ought to be made: that Jews perchance should not become insolent and, elated by their own security, should not commit anything rash against reverence for the Christian worship.

[August 6, 412 or 418]

THE CLERGY

Pursuant to his own duty a judge shall be bound to observe that, if there should be an appeal to an episcopal court,[19] silence should be applied[20] and that, if anyone shall have wished to transfer a matter to the Christian law and to observe that sort of court, he should be heard, even if the matter has been begun before the judge. . . .

[June 23, 318]

Whoever devote to divine worship the services of religion, that is, those who are called clergymen, should be excused entirely from all public services, lest through certain persons' sacrilegious malice they should be diverted from divine services.

[October 21, 319]

---

[15]The feast of Purim, which commemorates the deliverance of Persian Jews from the evil designs of Haman, a fifth-century B.C.E. Persian official.
[16]Haman was hanged for his machinations. In celebrating the feast, Jews burned an effigy of Haman suspended from a gallows that vaguely resembled a cross.
[17]The Christian religion.
[18]Abuse.
[19]A bishop's court.
[20]The civil judge cannot object.

The Imperial Christ

▼▼▼

42 ▼ *CHRIST MILITANT*

Early Christian artists usually depicted Jesus either as a lamb or as the youthful and beardless Good Shepherd. When Christianity became the emperor's religion, new iconographical images were needed in order to incorporate Christ into Roman imperial culture.

This *mosaic* (a mural composed of pieces of colored stone, glass, and precious metal), which dates from around the year 500, is located in the archbishop's chapel at Ravenna, a city in northeast Italy that served as the western imperial capital from 402 to 476 and thereafter continued to be Italy's most important political center into the eighth century. During the fifth century, the archbishops of Ravenna, who were often imperial appointees, rivaled the popes of Rome in power and prestige.

Here *Christ the Redeemer of the World* is dressed in the military uniform of a Roman emperor — golden armor, a purple cloak with a shoulder clasp bearing three pendants to signify imperial rank, and campaign boots. Underneath his feet are a lion and a snake, representing two biblical passages. The Book of Palms declares, "You shall tread on the lion and the adder; the young lion and the dragon you shall trample under foot." In the Gospel of Luke, Jesus tells his disciples, "Behold, I have given you the power to tread on snakes and scorpions and to overcome all the power of the Enemy." The open book, symbolizing either the Gospels or the Book of Life, which contains the names of all the redeemed, reads, "I am the Way, the Truth, and Life," a statement ascribed to Jesus in the Gospel of John.

QUESTIONS FOR ANALYSIS

1. Consider elements not commented on in the introduction. Is the way in which Christ carries his cross significant? If so, how do you interpret it? What about his facial expression?
2. What is the overall message of this mosaic?
3. Review source 40, and then compose Eusebius of Caesarea's commentary on the mosaic.
4. Compare this mosaic with Shiva Nataraja (source 35) and Hevajra (source 33). What common triumph do these three savior deities claim, and what do their parallel victories suggest?

Christ the Redeemer of the World

Beyond the Roman World

In the Gospel of Mark, composed probably sometime between 65 and 75 C.E. and written with a gentile, or non-Jewish, audience in mind, the Risen Jesus instructs his followers to "go out into the whole world and proclaim the Good News to all creation" (Mark 16:15–16).

According to tradition, the apostles divided up the known world by lot and went forth to preach. Thomas, for example, went to India and Matthew to Ethiopia. Regardless of the historicity of this legend, given the steady commerce from the Roman Empire to the Horn of East Africa, southern Arabia, and India (see Multiple Voices III), it is more than likely that before the first century ended, Christian missionaries had followed the monsoon trade winds into the Indian Ocean. Likewise, the land routes of the so-called Silk Road that connected Han China with the Mediterranean World allowed missionaries to move east from

Roman Syria and Anatolia into the heartland of the Parthian Empire and beyond. The Christian Church of the Anatolian city of Edessa (present-day Sanliurfa in Turkey), situated at the crossroads of two major trade routes and on the border between the Roman and Persian worlds, played a major role in the transmission of Christianity into the Caucasus, Mesopotamia, western Central Asia, and northern India by at least the end of the second century and maybe quite a bit earlier.

As the following two sources show, this was just the beginning. The first source deals with the acceptance of Christianity as a state religion by a people of the Caucasus known as *Georgians*; the second source illustrates how Christianity traveled to China in the early seventh century. During the fourth and fifth centuries, missionaries also carried several different forms of Christianity to Celtic and Germanic peoples who lived outside of the Roman Empire.

Georgia Becomes a Christian State
▼▼▼
43 ▼ *Rufinus of Aquileia, CHURCH HISTORY*

Christian gravesites in the Caucasus region — the area between the Black and Caspian seas that today includes southwest Russia, Azerbaijan, Armenia, and Georgia — date from as early as the second and third centuries. It was only in the fourth century, however, that two of its peoples, the Armenians and the Georgians, accepted the faith as a state religion. Indeed, the fourth century was pivotal in this regard. Early in the century, Constantine I accepted Christianity as the new Roman imperial cult, and the Ethiopian kingdom of Axum adopted Christianity as the new religion of its kings sometime around 333, if traditional dates can be accepted. Armenia seems to have accepted Christianity as its official religion around 300. Neighboring Georgians, a people who speak a language that is unrelated to any known tongue of Eurasia, followed probably sometime between 325 and 355, during a period when Eastern Roman influence penetrated their land.

The earliest account of the Georgians' acceptance of Christianity was composed by Tyrannius Rufinus (ca. 345–410/411), a Christian Roman from Aquileia in northeast Italy. Rufinus resided, from 373 to 397, in the eastern Mediterranean, the home- and heartland of Christianity. Following his return to Italy, Rufinus undertook to translate Eusebius of Caesarea's *Ecclesiastical History* from Greek into Latin around the year 402. In that year Visigothic warriors marched into Italy and laid siege to Milan. Eusebius's history, which had been completed in 325, presented a triumphalist vision of Christian history, and the consolation that it offered the Christians of Italy in this time of trials was sorely needed. In 402 or 403, Rufinus completed an abridged translation of Eusebius's history, with two additional books of his own composition that brought the story down to 395.

Rufinus's history is also triumphalist, ending on an upbeat note with the reception into Heaven of the pious emperor Theodosius I (r. 379–395) and the Christian Roman Empire established on a firm foundation. Unhappily for Rufinus, he lived long enough to learn of the sack of the city of Rome by the Visigoths in 410.

QUESTIONS FOR ANALYSIS

1. Which elements in this story have the ring of pious legend, and which have the ring of authenticity? Defend your choices.
2. What might we infer from this story about gender roles in fourth-century Georgia?
3. What does this story suggest about Roman-Georgian relations in the fourth century?
4. Based on clues contained within this story, what factors and motives do you think were behind the Georgian royal family's acceptance of Christianity? Support your inferences with specific reference to the evidence.

It was at this time[1] too that the Georgians, who dwell in the region of Pontus,[2] accepted the word of God and faith in the kingdom to come. The cause of this great benefit was a woman captive[3] who lived among them and led such a faithful, sober, and modest life, spending all of her days and nights in sleepless supplications to God, that the very novelty of it began to be wondered at by the barbarians. Their curiosity led them to ask what she was about. She replied with the truth: that in this manner she simply worshiped Christ as God. This answer made the barbarians wonder only at the novelty of the name, although it is true, as often happens, that her very perseverance made the common women wonder if she were deriving some benefit from such great devotion.

Now it is said that they have the custom that, if a child falls sick, it is taken around by its mother to each of the houses to see if anyone knows of a proven remedy to apply to the illness. And when one of the women had brought her child around to everyone, according to custom, and had found no remedy in any of the houses, she went to the woman captive as well to see if she knew of anything. She answered that she

knew of no human remedy, but declared that Christ her God, whom she worshiped, could give it the healing despaired of by humans. And after she had put the child on her hair shirt[4] and poured out above it her prayer to the Lord, she gave the infant back to its mother in good health. Word of this got around to many people, and news of the wonderful deed reached the ears of the queen, who was suffering from a bodily illness of the gravest sort and had been reduced to a state of absolute despair. She asked for the woman captive to be brought to her. She declined to go, lest she appear to pretend to more than was proper to her sex. The queen ordered that she herself be brought to the captive's hovel. Having placed her likewise on her hair shirt and invoked Christ's name, no sooner was her prayer done than she had her stand up healthy and vigorous, and taught her that it was Christ, God and Son of God most high, who had conferred healing upon her, and advised her to invoke him whom she should know to be the author of her life and well-being, for he it was who allotted kingdoms to kings and life to mortals. She returned joyfully home and disclosed the affair to her husband,[5] who wanted to know the reason

[1]The establishment of a Christian Church in India during the reign of Constantine I. Contrary to the more popular tradition, Rufinus does not credit the Apostle Thomas with bringing Christianity to India in the first century. Rather, he credits Frumentius, a captive-turned-missionary, with having planted the seeds of Christianity in India in the early fourth century.

[2]The Black Sea.
[3]A later Georgian tradition accords her the name Nino.
[4]A shirt worn as penance because of the discomfort it causes.
[5]Legend identifies him as Mirian, and he is usually identified with King Meribanes, a contemporary of Emperor Constantine I.

for this sudden return to health. When he in his joy at his wife's cure ordered gifts to be presented to the woman, she said, "O king, the captive deigns to accept none of these things. She despises gold, rejects silver, and battens on fasting as though it were food. This alone may we give her as a gift, if we worship as God the Christ who cured me when she called upon him."

But the king was not then inclined to do so and put it off for the time, although his wife urged him often, until it happened one day when he was hunting in the woods with his companions that a thick darkness fell upon the day, and with the light removed there was no longer any way for his blind steps through the grim and awful night. Each of his companions wandered off a different way, while he, left alone in the thick darkness which surrounded him, did not know what to do or where to turn, when suddenly there arose in his heart, which was near to losing hope of being saved, the thought that if the Christ preached to his wife by the woman captive were really God, he might now free him from this darkness so that he could from then on abandon all the others and worship him. No sooner had he vowed to do so, not even verbally but only mentally, than the daylight returned to the world and guided the king safely to the city. He explained directly to the queen what had happened. He required that the woman captive be summoned at once and hand on to him her manner of worship, insisting that from then on he would venerate no god but Christ. The captive came, instructed him that Christ is God, and explained, as far as it was lawful for a woman to disclose such things,[6] the ways of making petition and offering reverence. She advised that a church be built and described its shape.

The king therefore called together all of his people and explained the matter from the beginning, what had happened to the queen and him, taught them the faith, and before even being ini-

tiated into sacred things became the apostle of his nation. The men believed because of the king, the women because of the queen, and with everyone desiring the same thing a church was put up without delay. The outer walls having quickly been raised, it was time to put the columns in place. When the first and second had been set up and they came to the third, they used all the machines and the strength of men and oxen to get it raised halfway up to an inclined position, but no machine could lift it the rest of the way, not even with efforts repeated again and again; with everyone exhausted, it would not budge. Everyone was confounded, the king's enthusiasm waned, and no one could think what to do. But when nightfall intervened and everyone went away and all mortal labors ceased, the woman captive remained inside alone, passing the night in prayer. And when the worried king entered in the morning with all his people, he saw the column, which so many machines and people had been unable to move, suspended upright just above its base: not placed upon it, but hanging about one foot in the air. Then indeed all the people looking on glorified God and accepted the witness of the miracle before them that the king's faith and the captive's religion were true. And behold, while everyone was still in the grip of wonder and astonishment, before their very eyes the column, with no one touching it, gradually and with perfect balance settled down upon its base. After that the remaining columns were raised with such ease that all that were left were put in place that day.

Now after the church had been magnificently built and the people were thirsting even more deeply for God's faith, on the advice of the captive an embassy of the entire people was sent to the emperor Constantine,[7] and what had happened was explained to him. They implored him to send priests who could complete God's work begun among them. He dispatched them with all joy and honor, made far happier by this than

---

[6]In other words, she was not a (male) priest.

[7]Rufinus tended to ascribe to Constantine and his time events that actually took place during the reign of his son Constantius II (r. 337–361).

if he had annexed to the Roman empire un-known peoples and kingdoms. That this hap-pened was related to us by that most faithful man Bacurius, the king of that nation who in our realm held the rank of *comes domesticorum*[8] and

whose chief concern was for religion and truth; when he was *dux limitis*[9] in Palestine he spent some time with us in Jerusalem in great concord of spirit.[10]

---

[8]Overseer of household attendants — he was in charge of the imperial court garrison.
[9]General of the frontier — he commanded troops in a fron-tier district.

[10]The Roman historian Ammianus Marcellinus places Bacarius at the disastrous Battle of Adrianople of 378, where he commanded Roman archers and lightly armed foot soldiers.

Christianity Comes to China
▼▼▼
44 ▼ *Bishop Adam, THE CHRISTIAN MONUMENT*

The Silk Road provided missionaries with a convenient route into the heart of China. During the early years of the Tang Dynasty (618–907), roughly down to 750, China was open to the outside world and its influences (see Chapter 9). As ev-idence of that, in 635 a *Nestorian* Christian bishop from Persia named Aluoben (Abraham?) arrived in Chang'an, China's capital city.

In the fifth century, the Nestorian Christians of Syria, who drew a sharp distinc-tion between the human and divine natures of Jesus, had been declared heretics by the imperial Roman Church. The charges of heresy were motivated more by political considerations than theological doctrine, but the result was no less devas-tating. Moving east, the Nestorians found a home in the Sassanid Empire of Per-sia. From Persia, Nestorian Christian ideas traveled farther east to the Turkic peoples of Inner Asia and finally to China. Bishop Aluoben was not the first Nestorian to reach China, but he is the first of whom we have any record.

Aluoben was fortunate that he arrived in the reign of *Tang Taizong* (r. 626–649), who was open to novelties from the western steppes and beyond, including Bud-dhism, Manichaeism, and Nestorian Christianity. Under the emperor's protection, Aluoben established a monastery, which initially housed twenty-one monks, probably all of them Persians.

In 781 a scholar-bishop named Adam, who also bore the Chinese name Jing Jing, composed a short history of the early fortunes of the Nestorian Church in China. Under the patronage of a prominent Chinese-born Nestorian of Persian de-scent named Yazdbozid, whose Chinese name was Yisi, Adam's history was then inscribed on a nine-foot-high stone memorial that bears the heading "A Monu-ment Commemorating the Propagation of the Daqin {Syrian} Luminous Religion in the Middle Kingdom {China}." Interestingly, Yazdbozid, who apparently was Adam's father, was an assistant bishop in the Nestorian Church and had formerly served as a high-ranking general in the Chinese army and an imperial civil official. The career of this Christian priest, warrior, and civil servant of Persian heritage nicely illustrates the cosmopolitanism of early Tang, in which non-Chinese were called to the imperial service. Yazdbozid is also a symbol of the Nestorian

Church's eighth-century political connections, which gave it a measure of influence in Tang China.

That good fortune did not last. By tying its fortunes to the patronage of the Tang emperors, this minor foreign religion suffered irreversible losses when the empire waged an assault on foreign religions between 840 and 846 (see Multiple Voices VI). Although some small communities possibly survived, Nestorian Christianity essentially disappeared in China by the late tenth century. It reappeared, however, in the twelfth and thirteenth centuries, brought in from Central Asia by various Turkic tribes that had adopted the faith. But it suffered a second eclipse in the fourteenth century with the rise of the antiforeign Ming Dynasty.

Regardless of future reverses, the Nestorian community's *Christian Monument* celebrates an age when China was open to foreign innovations, including this faith from Southwest Asia.

QUESTIONS FOR ANALYSIS

1. Review source 19. How does Adam borrow Daoist imagery and terms to describe Nestorian Christianity? Why do you think he does so?
2. Can you find any Buddhist and Confucian overtones in this memorial? How and why does Adam use them?
3. What reasons did Emperor Tang Taizong give for allowing this new religion into his empire? What does your answer suggest about the man and his reign?
4. This and the preceding source show us how Christian missionaries used monarchs and their families in their attempts to propagate the faith. What were the advantages and disadvantages of that tactic?

"The *Way*" would not have spread so widely had it not been for the Sage,[1] and the Sage would not have been so great were it not for "The *Way*." Ever since the Sage and "The *Way*" were united . . . then the world became refined and enlightened.

When the accomplished Emperor Taizong began his magnificent career in glory and splendor . . . and ruled his people with intelligence, he proved himself to be a brilliant Sage.

And behold there was a highly virtuous man named Aluoben in the Kingdom of Daqin.[2] Auguring (of the Sage, i.e., Emperor) from the azure sky,[3] he decided to carry the true Sutras[4] (of the True Way) with him, and observing the course of the winds, he made his way (to China) through difficulties and perils. Thus in the ninth year of the period named Zhenguan (635 C.E.) he arrived at Chang'an.[5] The Emperor dispatched his Minister, Duke Fang Xuanling, with a guard of honor, to the western suburb to meet the visitor and conduct him to the Palace. The Sutras (Scriptures) were translated in the Imperial Library. (His Majesty) investigated "The *Way*" in his own forbidden apartments,[6] and being deeply convinced of its correctness and truth, he gave special orders for its propagation.

---

[1] Emperor Tang Taizong.
[2] Syria. We should not take it literally. Aluoben came from the west with a religion that was shaped in Syria. Thus, Iran, Mesopotamia, and Syria are all lumped together under this term.
[3] He discovered in the heavens signs of the Sage Emperor.

[4] The Bible.
[5] Tang China's capital, Chang'an (present-day Xi'an), was probably the largest and richest city in the world in the seventh century.
[6] The private imperial chambers.

In the twelfth year of the Zhenguan Period (638 C.E.) . . . , the following Imperial Rescript was issued: —

"'The Way' had not, at all times and in all places, the selfsame name; the Sage had not, at all times and in all places, the selfsame human body. (Heaven) caused a suitable religion to be instituted for every region and clime so that each one of the races of mankind might be saved. Bishop Aluoben of the kingdom of Daqin, bringing with him the Sutras and Images,[7] has come from afar and presented them at our Capital. Having carefully examined the scope of his teaching, we find it to be mysteriously spiritual and of silent operation. Having observed its principal and most essential points, we reached the conclusion that they cover all that is most important in life. . . . This Teaching is helpful to all creatures and beneficial to all men. So let it have free course throughout the Empire."

Accordingly, the proper authorities built a Daqin monastery . . . in the Capital and twenty-one priests were ordained and attached to it. The virtue of the honored House of Zhou had died away;[8] (the rider on) the black chariot had ascended to the West.[9] But (virtue revived) and "The *Way*" was brilliantly manifested again at the moment when the Great Tang began its rule, whilst the breezes of the Luminous (Religion) came eastward to fan it.[10] Immediately afterwards, the proper officials were again ordered to take a faithful portrait of the Emperor, and to

have it copied on the walls of the monastery. The celestial beauty appeared in its variegated colors, and the dazzling splendor illuminated the Luminous "portals" (i.e., congregation). The sacred features (thus preserved) conferred great blessing (on the monastery), and illuminated the Church for evermore. . . .

The great Emperor Gaozong (650–683 C.E.) succeeded most respectfully to his ancestors; and giving the True Religion the proper elegance and finish, he caused monasteries of the Luminous Religion to be founded in every prefecture. Accordingly, he honored Aluoben by conferring on him the office of the Great Patron and Spiritual Lord of the Empire. The Law (of the Luminous Religion) spread throughout the ten provinces, and the Empire enjoyed great peace and concord. Monasteries were built in many cities, whilst every family enjoyed the great blessings (of Salvation).

During the period of Shengli (698–699 C.E.),[11] the Buddhists, taking advantage of these circumstances, and using all their strength raised their voices (against the Luminous Religion) in the Eastern Zhou,[12] and at the end of the Xiandian Period (712 C.E.)[13] some inferior scholars[14] ridiculed and derided it, slandering and speaking against it. . . . But there came the Headpriest (or Archdeacon) Luohan,[15] Bishop Jilie,[16] and others, as well as Noblemen from the "Golden" region[17] and the eminent priests who had forsaken all worldly interests. All these men

---

[7]Artistic representations, or *icons*, of Jesus and the saints.

[8]Rule by virtue, as established in the early Zhou Dynasty and later taught by Confucius, had departed long before the rise of Tang.

[9]According to one tradition, when the Eastern Zhou Dynasty (770–256 B.C.E.) lost its virtue, Laozi, the founder of Daoism, abandoned China in disgust. He went west (or ascended to the Western Heaven) in a chariot drawn by a black ox, thereby leaving China without a moral guide. The Tang Dynasty shared Laozi's family name, Li, and claimed descent from him.

[10]Laozi had gone west (note 9); now the Way was returning from that direction.

[11]One of several periods in the reign of Empress Wu, who ruled the empire in her own name from 690 to 705. She gained effective control over the state around 654 but at first used several puppet emperors to mask her power.

[12]Empress Wu changed the name of her short-lived dynasty to *Zhou* and moved her primary capital east to Luoyang, the capital city of the ancient Eastern Zhou Dynasty (770–256 B.C.E.). She declared Buddhism the official state religion in 691 and seems to have encouraged persecution of Christianity, although persecution did not become an articulated state policy. In 698 a mob sacked the Nestorian church in Luoyang.

[13]The last year of disorder following Empress Wu's retirement in 705.

[14]Probably Confucians, but possibly Daoists. Maybe both.

[15]Abraham.

[16]Gabriel?

[17]From the West, the source of so much gold and silver that flowed into Tang China by virtue of China's favorable balance of trade across the Silk Road.

co-operated in restoring the great fundamental principles and united together to re-bind the broken ties.

The Emperor Xuanzong,[18] who was surnamed "the Perfection of the Way," ordered the Royal prince, the King of Ningguo and four other Royal princes to visit the blessed edifices (i.e., monastery) personally and to set up altars therein. Thus the "consecrated rafters," which had been temporarily bent, were once more straightened and strengthened, whilst the sacred foundation-stones which for a time had lost the right position were restored and perfected. In the early part of the period Tianbao (742 C.E.) he gave orders to his general Gao Lishi to carry the faithful portraits of the Five Emperors[19] and to have them placed securely in the monastery, and also to take the Imperial gift of one hundred pieces of silk with him. Making the most courteous and reverent obeisance to the Imperial portraits, we feel as though "we were in a position to hang on to the Imperial bow and sword, in case the beard of the Dragon should be out of reach."[20] . . .

In the third year of the same period (744 C.E.) there was a priest named Jihe[21] in the Kingdom of Daqin. Observing the stars, he decided to engage in the work of conversion; and looking to-ward the sun (i.e., eastward), he came to pay court to the most honorable Emperor. The Imperial orders were given to the Head-priest (Archdeacon) Luohan, priest Pulun[22] and others, seven in all, to perform services to cultivate merit and virtue with this Bishop Jihe in the Xingqing Palace. Thereupon the monastery-names, composed and written by the Emperor himself, began to appear on the monastery gates; and the front-tablets to bear the Dragon-writing (i.e., the Imperial hand-writing).[23] The monastery was resorted to by (visitors) whose costumes resembled the shining feathers of the king-fisher bird whilst all (the buildings) shone forth with the splendor of the sun. The Imperial tablets hung high in the air and their radiance flamed as though vying with the sun. The gifts of the Imperial favor are immense like the highest peak of the highest mountains in the South, and the food of its rich benevolence is as deep as the depths of the Eastern sea.

There is nothing that "The *Way*" cannot effect (through the Sage); and whatever it effects, it is right of us to define it as such (in eulogy). There is nothing that the Sage cannot accomplish (through "The *Way*"); and whatever He accomplishes, it is right we should proclaim it in writing (as the Sage's work).

---

[18]In the reign of Emperor Xuanzong (r. 712–756), Tang China reached the heights of its greatness and prosperity but also began its precipitous decline.
[19]The legendary Five Sage Emperors, who established the foundations of Chinese civilization in predynastic times.
[20]Although the emperor (the dragon) might be far away, his power extends to the monastery.
[21]George.
[22]Paul?
[23]The emperor composed an inscription to be fixed above the monastery's door. Almost all public buildings in China had similar inscriptions.

Multiple Voices IV ▼▼▼
One Christianity or Many Christianities?

BACKGROUND

During the first five centuries C.E., Christians found themselves grappling with a number of basic doctrinal issues as they endeavored to establish a *canon*, or standard set, of beliefs that fully and correctly articulated the teachings of Jesus and his apostles. It was not easy. Indeed, the road to establishing an *orthodoxy* (correct thinking) that could be embraced by a majority of Christians was filled with pitfalls.

One of the major issues that early Christians had to deal with was the legitimacy or error of a way of envisioning the spiritual and physical worlds that is known as *Gnosticism*. Gnosticism is an all-encompassing term for a widespread, Hellenistic religious philosophy based on the belief that salvation is attainable through a secret, mystical knowledge, which is called *gnosis* in Greek. Gnosticism predated Christianity and manifested itself in numerous varieties. There were many different Gnostic sects, most of which were pagan, but there were also Jewish Gnostics, and likewise Gnosticism made deep inroads into early Christianity.

As they faced the necessity of defining the True Faith, Christian theologians of every stripe found themselves identifying and excoriating *heresies* as opposed to correct doctrines. The word *heresy*, which is Greek, means "choice," the presumption being that heretics willfully choose error over truth. Needless to say, one Christian's orthodoxy was another's heresy.

In like manner, there were different Christian views of the proper relationship between the Old and New Testaments, between Judaism and Christianity, and Christians also differed on which texts they considered to be inspired holy scripture — all of this depending on which forms of Christian belief they endorsed.

All of these differences needed some sort of official resolution, especially once Christianity became the favored religion of the Roman state, as happened under Constantine I (r. 306–337).

THE SOURCES

The first source is the *Gospel of Thomas*. Recent publication of the long-lost *Gospel of Judas* has awakened many readers of the popular press to the fact that *Gnostic* forms of Christianity flourished in the early centuries C.E. Gnostic Christians, of whom there were many varieties, produced their own scriptures. One of the best preserved is the Gospel of Thomas. Probably written originally in Greek, the Gospel of Thomas exists today in a Coptic translation, the language of late ancient Egypt. The papyrus on which it was written was discovered at Nag Hammadi in Upper Egypt in 1945.

Ascribed to Jesus' presumed twin brother, the Apostle Judas Thomas, it was composed during the second century or earlier. The Gospel of Thomas has no narrative; it consists simply of 113 sayings of Jesus. The reader who knows the four canonical, or officially recognized, Gospels of Matthew, Mark, Luke, and John will see some familiar passages. Many of the sayings, however, will seem foreign, possibly even strange. Cumulatively, the sayings portray Jesus as a purely spiritual, noncorporeal savior who imparts to a select few a secret wisdom that will enable them to discover within themselves the divine spark of heavenly light.

The second source is from a treatise, commonly known as *Against Heresies*, by Irenaeus (ca. 125?–ca. 200?). A Greek-speaking Christian from western Anatolia, Irenaeus became bishop of Lyons in Gaul, and it was there that he penned this work around the year 180. Its original title, *Refutation and Overthrow of the Falsely Called Knowledge*, clearly indicates its purpose. In this excerpt he attacks the teachings of Marcion (d. ca. 160), who like Irenaeus was born in Anatolia but moved west. Marcion established himself in Rome, where his doctrines were condemned by the church of Rome in the year 144. However, Marcionite Christianity spread outward from the imperial capital and continued to flourish into the fifth century, especially in the eastern regions of the empire.

The third source, the *Homilies of Clement*, purports to be a set of discourses composed by Clement, believed to be the third bishop of Rome (r. ca. 91–ca. 101), and sent to James the Apostle, bishop of Jerusalem. In reality, this work was crafted by an unknown author probably in the late third century.

The fourth source is from Eusebius of Caesarea's *Ecclesiastical History* (see source 40), in which the bishop-historian lists, in two separate passages, the scriptural texts that the early-fourth-century Church generally accepted as canonical elements of the New Testament.

The last source is the *creed*, or statement of faith, articulated by the Council of Nicaea of 325. Held at the Anatolian city of Nicaea, not far from Constantinople, this gathering of largely Eastern Christian church leaders, assembled at the invitation and under the patronage of Emperor Constantine I, is recognized as the first *Ecumenical*, or *General, Council* of the Church. Convened to settle several doctrinal controversies, the council was believed (by those who accepted its authority) to speak infallibly for the entire Church. Brief confessions of faith were commonly used in liturgical services, especially baptisms, by the mid second century, but they followed no standard form. The Council of Nicaea witnessed the first attempt to craft an official creed for the entire Church that clearly separated orthodox from *heterodox* (different-thinking) doctrine. The Creed of Nicaea was not universally accepted (the two bishops at Nicaea who refused to sign their names to it were exiled by the emperor) and did not end doctrinal controversies immediately, but it did signal the beginning of a clearly articulated orthodox faith that enjoyed imperial patronage. An amplified form of this creed, which subsequently became known as the Nicene Creed, was approved and reaffirmed by the next two ecumenical councils — Constantinople (381) and Chalcedon (451) — thereby firmly establishing it as the definitive statement of True Belief. Eventually, other forms of Christian belief that deviated from the Nicene Creed and the proclamations of the Seven Ecumenical Councils (325–787) were driven to the margins of the Roman Empire and its successor states.

QUESTIONS FOR ANALYSIS

1. What were the beliefs of the Gnostic Christians who revered the Gospel of Thomas as divinely revealed truth?
2. What were Marcion's core doctrines? Was Irenaeus correct in terming him a Gnostic? Why or why not?
3. Compare the first two sources with the *Upanishads* (source 13). What conclusions follow from this comparative analysis?
4. How does the theology of the *Homilies of Clement* differ radically from the teachings of both Marcion and St. Paul's Epistle to the Romans (source 39)? What do you conclude from your answer?
5. Compare a modern New Testament to Eusebius's lists of "recognized," "disputed," "spurious," and "heretical" books. What does this suggest about the process of establishing the canon of the New Testament?
6. Some elements in the Creed of Nicaea were aimed at rejecting Arianism (see source 41, note 7). Where do you find those elements? Which elements were aimed at countering Gnostic teachings?
7. Based on these five sources, compose an essay on "The State of Christian Belief During Its First Three Centuries."

---

1 ▾ THE GOSPEL OF THOMAS

Prologue

These are the secret sayings that the living Jesus[1] spoke and Judas Thomas the Twin[2] recorded.

Saying 1

He said, "Whoever finds the interpretation of these sayings will not taste death." . . .

Saying 3

Jesus said, "If your leaders say to you, 'Behold, the kingdom is in the sky,' then the birds in the sky will get there before you. If they say to you, 'It is in the sea,' then the fish will get there before you.

"Rather, the kingdom is inside you and outside you.[3] When you know yourselves, then you will be known, and will understand that you are children of the living Father. But if you do not know yourselves, then you live in poverty, and embody poverty." . . .

Saying 22

Jesus saw some babies nursing. He said to his disciples, "These nursing babies are like those who enter the kingdom."[4]

They said to him, "Then shall we enter the kingdom as babies?"

Jesus said to them,

"When you make the two into one,
when you make the inner like the outer
and the outer like the inner,
and the upper like the lower,

---

[1]Jesus who offered the life of *gnosis*.
[2]According to a Syriac Christian tradition, Jesus had a twin brother, Judas Thomas.
[3]The Kingdom of God begins with knowledge of self and of God.

[4]Compare this with Matthew 18:1–5, Mark 9:33–37, and Luke 9:46–48; also compare Matthew 19:13–15, Mark 10:13–16, and Luke 18:15–17.

when you make male and female into a single one,
   so that the male will not be male
   and the female will not be female,[5]
when you make eyes replacing an eye,
   a hand replacing a hand,
   a foot replacing a foot,
   and an image replacing an image,
then you will enter the kingdom." . . .

Saying 49

Jesus said,
   "Blessed are those who are alone and chosen:
     you will find the kingdom.[6]
   For you have come from it, and you will
     return there again."

Saying 50

Jesus said, "If some say to you, 'Where have you come from?' say to them, 'We have come from the light,
   where the light came into being by itself,
   established itself,
   and appeared in an image of light.'
"If they say to you, 'Are you the light?' say,
   'We are its children,
   and we are the chosen of the living Father.'
"If they ask you, 'What is the evidence of your Father in you?' tell them,
'It is motion and rest.'" . . .

Saying 70

Jesus said,
   "If you bring forth what is within you,
     what you have will save you.
   If you do not have that within you,
     what you do not have within you will kill
     you." . . .

Saying 75

Jesus said,
   "I am the light that is over all things.
   I am all:
     all came forth from me,
     and all attained to me.
   Split a piece of wood,
     and I am there.
   Pick up a stone,
     and you will find me there." . . .

Saying 113

Simon Peter[7] said to them, "Let Mary[8] leave us, because women are not worthy of life."

Jesus said, "Behold, I shall guide her so as to make her male, that she too may become a living spirit like you men.[9] For every woman who makes herself male will enter the kingdom of heaven."

---

[5]Compare the statues *Hevajra* and *Shiva Nataraja* (sources 33 and 35).
[6]Compare this with the Sermon on the Mount (source 38).
[7]The Apostle Peter. Prior to being given the name *Peter* (Greek for "rock") by Jesus, his name was Simon.

[8]Several of Jesus' closest and most loyal female friends were named Mary. This probably refers to *Mary Magdalene*, one of Jesus' inner circle of followers.
[9]The male (heavenly) principle must replace totally the female (earthly) principle.

2 ▾ *Irenaeus,* AGAINST HERESIES

A certain Cerdo, who had taken his fundamental ideas from those who were with Simon[1] and who was in Rome in the time of Hyginus, who held the ninth place from the Apostles in the episcopa succession,[2] taught that the God who was preached by the law and the prophets is not the Father of our Lord Jesus Christ. For the former is known, but the latter is unknown; and the former is righteous, but the other is good.

And Marcion of Pontus succeeded him and developed a school, blaspheming shamelessly Him who is proclaimed as God by the law and the prophets; saying that He is maker of evils and a lover of wars, inconstant in purpose and inconsistent with Himself. He said, however, that Jesus came from the Father, who is above the God who made the world, into Judea in the time of Pontius Pilate, the procurator of Tiberius Caesar, and was manifested in the form of a man to those who were in Judea,[3] destroying the prophets and the law, and all the works of that God who made the world and whom he[4] also called Cosmocrator.[5] In addition to this, he mutilated the Gospel which is according to Luke, and removed all that refers to the generation of the Lord, removing also many things from the teaching in the Lord's discourses, in which the Lord is recorded as very plainly confessing that the founder of this universe is His Father; and thus Marcion persuaded his disciplines that he himself is truer than the Apostles who delivered the Gospel; delivering to them not the Gospel but a part of the Gospel. But in the same manner he also mutilated the epistles of the Apostle Paul, removing all that is plainly said by the Apostle concerning that God who made the world, to the effect that He is the Father of our Lord Jesus Christ, and all that the Apostle taught by quotation from the prophetical writings which foretold the coming of the Lord.

He taught that salvation would be only of the souls of those who should receive his doctrine, and that it is impossible for the body to partake of salvation, because it was taken from the earth.

---

[1]Simon the Magician. He appears in the *Acts of the Apostles* (8:9–24) as a convert who offers money to Peter and John in order to learn the secret of bestowing the Holy Spirit by the laying on of hands. He is rebuked and apparently repents, but in later Christian tradition he reappears as the father of all heresy and a devilish wizard.

[2]Thought to have been bishop of Rome from around 138 to ca. 142.
[3]He appeared suddenly in Judea as an *apparent* (not real in any physical sense) full-grown man.
[4]Marcion.
[5]Greek for "Ruler of the Universe."

---

3 ▾ HOMILIES OF CLEMENT

"For even the Hebrews who believe in Moses . . . are not saved unless they abide by what has been said to them.

"For their believing in Moses lies not with a decision of their own will but with God who said to Moses. 'Behold, I come to you in a pillar of cloud that the people may hear me speaking to you and believe for ever!'[1] Since then it is granted to the Hebrews and to them that are called from the Gentiles to believe the teachers of truth, while it is left to the personal decision of each individual whether he will perform good deeds, the reward rightly falls to those who do well.

---

[1]Exodus 19:9.

"For neither Moses nor Jesus would have needed to come if of themselves people had been willing to perceive the way of discretion. . . .

"Therefore is Jesus concealed from the Hebrews who have received Moses as their teacher, and Moses hidden from those who believe Jesus.

"For since through both one and the same teaching becomes known, God accepts those who believe in one of them. . . .

"Thus the Hebrews are not condemned because they did not know Jesus . . . provided only they act according to the instructions of Moses and do not injure him whom they did not know.

"And again the offspring of the Gentiles are not judged, who. . . . have not known Moses, provided only they act according to the words of Jesus and thus do not injure him whom they did not know.

"Also it profits nothing if many describe their teachers as their lords, but do not do what it befits servants to do.

"Therefore our Lord Jesus said to one who again and again called him Lord, but at the same time did not abide by any of his commands. 'Why call me Lord and not do what I say?'[2] For it is not speaking that can profit any one, but doing.

"In all circumstances goods works are needed; but if a person has been considered worthy to know both teachers as heralds of a single doctrine, then that one is counted rich in God. . . ."

---

[2]Matthew 7:21; Luke 6:46.

---

4 ▾ *Eusebius of Caesarea,* ECCLESIASTICAL HISTORY

Of Peter, one epistle, that which is called his first, is admitted, and the ancient presbyters[1] used this in their own writings as unquestioned, but the so-called second Epistle we have not received as canonical, but nevertheless it has appeared useful to many, and has been studied with other Scriptures. On the other hand, of the Acts bearing his name, and the Gospel named according to him and Preaching called his and the so-called Revelation,[2] we have no knowledge at all in Catholic tradition,[3] for no orthodox writer of the ancient time or of our own has used their testimonies. As the narrative proceeds I will take pains to indicate successively which of the orthodox writers in each period used any of the doubtful books, and what they said about the canonical and accepted Scriptures and what about those which are not such. Now the above are the books bearing the name of Peter, of which I recognize only one as genuine and admitted by the presbyters of old. And the fourteen letters of Paul are obvious and plain, yet it is not right to ignore that some dispute the Epistle to the Hebrews, saying that it was rejected by the church of Rome as not being by Paul. . . . Nor have I received his so-called Acts among undisputed books.[4] But since the same Apostle in the salutations at the end of Romans has mentioned among others Hermas, whose, they say, is the Book of the Shepherd, it should be known that this also is rejected by

---

[1]Elders of the Church.

[2]The *Acts of Peter* contains a number of charming, often humorous stories regarding his contests with the satanic Simon Magus (see Irenaeus above). Only fragments of the *Gospel of Peter* are known today, and those pieces show it to be quite anti-Jewish. Today the *Preaching of Peter* exists only in a few fragmentary quotations recorded by some early Christian author. Probably composed in the early second century, it was a popular defense of Christianity and one of the earliest written for that purpose. Today there are three different surviving Apocalypses, or Books of Revelation, ascribed to Peter.

[3]*Catholic* here means the universal Church.

[4]According to Tertullian (ca. 160–after 220), the forger of this work was caught in the act and admitted he had written it, "for love of Paul." Large fragments of it exist today.

some, and for their sake should not be placed among accepted books, but by others it has been judged most valuable, especially to those who need elementary instruction. For this reason we know that it has been used in public in churches, and I have found it quoted by some of the most ancient writers.[5] Let this suffice for the establishment of the divine writings which are undisputed, and of those which are not received by all.

▼▼▼

At this point it seems reasonable to summarize the writings of the New Testament which have been quoted. In the first place should be put the holy tetrad[6] of the Gospels. To them follows the writing of the Acts of the Apostles. After this should be reckoned the Epistles of Paul. Following them the Epistle of John called the first, and in the same way should be recognized the Epistle of Peter. In addition to these should be put, if it seem desirable, the Revelation of John, the arguments concerning which we will expound at the proper time. These belong to the Recognized Books. Of the Disputed Books which are nevertheless known to most are the Epistle called of James, that of Jude, the second Epistle of Peter, and the so-called second and third Epistles of John which may be the work of the evangelist or of some other with the same name.[7] Among the books which are not genuine must be reckoned the Acts of Paul, the work entitled the Shepherd, the Apocalypse of Peter, and in addition to

them the letter called of Barnabas[8] and the so-called Teachings of the Apostles.[9] And in addition, as I said, the Revelation of John, if this view prevail. For as I said, some reject it, but others count it among the Recognized Books. Some have also counted the Gospel according to the Hebrews in which those of the Hebrews who have accepted Christ take a special pleasure. These would all belong to the disputed books, but we have nevertheless been obliged to make a list of them, distinguishing between those writings which, according to the tradition of the Church, are true, genuine, and recognized, and those which differ from them in that they are not canonical but disputed, yet nevertheless are known to most of the writers of the Church, in order that we might know them and the writings which are put forward by heretics under the name of the apostles containing gospels such as those of Peter, and Thomas, and Matthias,[10] and some others besides, or Acts such as those of Andrew and John and the other apostles.[11] To none of these has any who belonged to the succession of the orthodox ever thought it right to refer in his writings. Moreover, the type of phraseology differs from apostolic style, and the opinion and tendency of their contents is widely dissonant from true orthodoxy and clearly shows that they are the forgeries of heretics. They ought, therefore, to be reckoned not even among spurious books but shunned as altogether wicked and impious.

[5]The *Shepherd*, written apparently by Hermas, brother of Pius, bishop of Rome (r. ca. 142–ca. 155), was popular through the fourth century. The oldest surviving manuscript of the entire New Testament, the fourth-century *Codex Sinaiticus*, included the *Shepherd*. Eventually, however, it was excluded from the New Testament because its authorship was not ascribed to an apostle. The work consists of a number of allegorical visions supposedly experienced by Hermas.

[6]The quartet of Matthew, Mark, Luke, and John.

[7]When the official canon of the New Testament was finally fixed in the late fourth century, it included seven non-Pauline epistles: James; I and II Peter; I, II, and III John; and Jude.

[8]The Letter of Barnabus almost made it into the New Testament. It was included in the *Codex Sinaiticus* (note 5) but was later dropped from the canon.

[9]Composed around 100 C.E., *The Teaching of the Twelve Apostles to the Nations* was a church manual consisting of sets of rules regarding moral living and proper liturgical practices, and it further offered practical advice on how to keep itinerant, often free-loading preachers and prophets under control.

[10]The Gospel of Matthias, which is known only from a few quotations by early Christian writers, appears to have been quite Gnostic.

[11]The Acts of Andrew was a third-century list of miracles. Only a summary of it survives. The Acts of John, dating from the late second century, contains amusing stories of the Apostle John's ministry. It also contains apparent Gnostic undertones.

5 ▾ THE CREED OF NICAEA

We believe in one God, the Father Almighty, Maker of all things visible and invisible: — and in our Lord Jesus Christ, the Son of God, the only begotten of the Father, that is of the substance of the Father; God of God and Light of light; true God of true God; begotten, not made, consubstantial[1] with the Father: by whom all things were made, both which are in heaven and on earth: who for the sake of us men, and on account of our salvation, descended, became incarnate, and was made man; suffered, arose again the third day, and ascended into the heavens, and will come again to judge the living and the dead. We also believe in the Holy Spirit.[2] But the holy Catholic and Apostolic Church anathematizes those who say that there was a time when the Son of God was not, and that he was not before he was begotten, and that he was made from that which did not exist; or who assert that he is of other substance or essence than the Father, or that he was created, or is susceptible of change.[3]

---

[1] Of the same essence as the Father.
[2] See source 41, note 7.

[3] This creed was preserved in the *Church History* of Socrates (ca. 380–450), who composed a continuation of Eusebius's history of the Church, carrying the story from 306 to 439.

▲▲▲

❖ Chapter 8 ❖

Islam
Universal Submission to God

*T*HE LAST OF THE GREAT MONOTHEISTIC FAITHS to arise in Southwest Asia was Islam, which emerged in Arabia during the early seventh century. *Islam* means "submission" in Arabic, and a *Muslim* is anyone who submits to the Will of God.

The Prophet of Islam was a merchant of Mecca known as *Muhammad ibn (son of) Abdullah* (ca. 571–632), who around 610 began to receive visions in which he was called to be the Messenger of *Allah* — a divinity whose Arabic name (al-Llah) means "*the* God." Muhammad's mission was to preach the Oneness of God ("there is no god but the God"), the imminence of the Resurrection of the Dead, the coming of a divine Day of Judgment, and the existence of an all-consuming hellfire for the unjust and unbelievers and a paradise of bliss for the faithful. Muhammad believed that, just as Jews and Christians had their divine revelations from God, now the Arabs were receiving the full and final word of God through him, the last and greatest of the prophets. Abraham, Moses, and Jesus had been earlier messengers of God. Muhammad was the *seal* of these forerunners.

Most Meccans were initially unmoved by Muhammad's message, so in 622 he and the majority of his small band of converts journeyed over 200 miles northeast to an oasis settlement that would become known as *Medinat al-Nabi* (City of the Prophet) or, more simply, *Medina*. By this act, known as the *hijra* (breaking of ties), these first Muslims abandoned their tribal bonds — bonds that defined traditional Arabic society — and opted for membership in an Islamic community of faith, or *umma*. This migration was so pivotal in the history of Islam that Muslims later designated it as the starting point of the Islamic Era — the Year 1 of the Islamic calendar.

Circumstances at Medina forced Muhammad to add the duties of statesman and warrior to that of prophet, and he proved successful at all three. After more than seven years of struggle, Muhammad and a reputed 10,000 followers were able to enter Mecca in triumph in January 630. The Messenger of Allah was now the most powerful chieftain in Arabia, and most of the tribes of the peninsula soon were united under his leadership. When Muhammad died in 632, his closest friend, *Abu Bakr*, assumed the title and office of *caliph* (deputy of the Prophet), thereby accepting leadership over the family of Islam. Abu Bakr, however, did not claim to be a prophet; God's revelation had ceased with Muhammad's death. Thanks to Abu Bakr's efforts at destroying secessionist elements that arose after Muhammad's death, Islam under his stewardship (632–634) remained a unified community ready to explode out of its homeland, which it did under the second caliph, Umar (r. 634–644).

Both the Sassanian Persian and Byzantine empires had exhausted each other in a series of wars from 503 to 627. In addition, the Byzantine Empire was rent by ethnic and religious dissension. So, when Muslims began raiding the territories of these neighboring empires, they discovered lands ripe for conquest. Before Umar's death the Byzantines had lost all of Syria-Palestine and Egypt to Islam, and the Arab conquest of the Sassanian Empire was virtually completed. By the year 750, lands under Islamic domination reached from the Pyrenees and Atlantic Coast in Spain to the Indus Valley of India and to China's far-western borders.

Originally, Muslim Arabs had little or no interest in sharing Islam with their non-Arab subjects, but several factors combined to attract large numbers of converts. These included Islam's uncompromising monotheism and the straightforwardness of its other central doctrines; its attractive ethical code; the psychic and social security offered by membership in a totally integrated Muslim community, where one's entire life is subject to God's Word; and the desire to escape the second-class status of Islam's non-Muslim subjects. When the Abbasid caliphs (r. 750–1258) established their court at Baghdad on the Tigris in 762, they claimed dominion over a multiethnic ecumene bound together by one of the fastest-growing religions in the history of humanity. The culture of this world community was a combination of many elements, of which the most important were Arabic, Persian, and Hellenistic.

Later other peoples, especially the Turks, would convert to Islam and carry it farther afield, especially into the heart of India and deep into Central Asia. Arab and Persian merchants would bring Islam to East Africa's Swahili Coast, and still later, East African and Arab merchants would transport the faith across the Indian Ocean to the ports of Southeast Asia. Berbers and Arabs from North Africa would introduce Islam into western sub-Saharan Africa. In brief, by 1450 Islam was the fastest-growing and most extensively spread religion on the face of the Earth.

▼▼▼

The Foundations of Islamic Life

Like the Buddha and Jesus, Muhammad was a teacher who spoke rather than wrote his message, but also like Buddhism and Christianity, following its Messenger's death, Islam quickly became a religious culture centered on a body of sacred texts, and it has remained so to the present. Islam's text without equal is *al-Quran* (the Recitations), which Muslims believe contains, word for word, absolutely everything that God revealed to Muhammad and nothing else. In Muslim eyes the Quran is the full and final revelation of God and coeternal with Him. Its verses, each a poetically perfect proclamation from Heaven, are both doctrine and law, governing every aspect of a Muslim's life. Islam without the Quran is unimaginable.

A second source of guidance for most Muslims is *al-Hadith* (Tradition), a vast body of transmitted stories and sayings attributed to the Prophet and his Companions. Unlike the Quran, these stories, individually known as *hadiths* (tales or instructions), are not assembled in a single, absolutely accepted text. Rather, there are many collections of Hadith, some more authoritative than others. The majority of Muslims believe that authentic hadiths enshrine the *sunna* (the beaten track), or valid traditions, of the Prophet and the first Islamic community at Medina and thereby provide perfect models for behavior in all aspects of life, especially those not expressly covered in the precepts of the Quran.

A third source that provides inspiration and guidance is the earliest extant biography of the Prophet of God. Because Muslims regard Muhammad as only a man, Islam has no Gospels in the sense that Christianity does — divinely inspired and infallible accounts of its Teacher's miracles and salvific deeds. Islam does have, however, the recorded remembrances of the Messenger of God's Companions from Mecca and his earliest converts at Medina, which document portions of Muhammad's life and actions. Collected and arranged into a coherent biography in eighth-century Baghdad, this work has served through the centuries as a model for devout Muslims who desire to follow the path of Allah's perfect servant.

Like the Jewish Torah, the Quran provides its believers with a total way of life. The dichotomy between church and state that the European West developed has no meaning in Islam, at least as it emerged in the seventh century. Indeed, Islam has no Church in the Christian sense, and it has no separate secular polity — at least in the ideal. In the ideal, there is only God's *umma*, which is governed by God's Holy Law, or *Sharia*. The study and application of Sharia is one of the highest callings in Islamic life and stands at the center of its civilization.

The Word of God

▼▼▼

45 ▼ THE QURAN

As long as the Prophet was alive, there was no compelling reason to set his messages down in some definitive form. However, following Muhammad's death in 632, Caliph Abu Bakr ordered one of the Prophet's Companions, Zayd ibn Thabit, to collect from both oral and written sources all of Muhammad's inspired utterances. Subsequently, Caliph Uthman (r. 644–656) promulgated an official collection of these Recitations and ordered all other versions destroyed.

This standard text became the basis of every pious Muslim's education. As Islam spread beyond Arab ethnic boundaries, Muslims all over the world continued to learn Arabic in order to study and recite (usually from memory) the sacred *surahs* (chapters) of this holy book. Because of the Quran's centrality to Islam, Arabic literacy became the hallmark of Muslims from sub-Saharan West Africa to Southeast Asia.

The following excerpts come from the second of the Quran's 114 surahs. Known as "The Cow" (*al-Baqarah*) because portions of it tell the story of how the ancient Israelites sacrificed a cow to God, this surah dates to the first year after the *hijra* from Mecca to Medina, or around 623. The following selections illustrate several of Islam's major doctrinal tenets, religious obligations, and moral principles and also shed light on the connections between Islam and the faiths of Judaism and Christianity.

QUESTIONS FOR ANALYSIS

1. How does the Quran portray Jews and Christians, and what is Islam's relationship with these two faiths?
2. What are the basic tenets of faith enjoined on all Muslims?
3. What are a Muslim's basic moral obligations?
4. What specific religious rites and practices must every observant Muslim perform?
5. How are Muslims to deal with those who attack them?
6. "For members of the Islamic community, there is no distinction between what one believes and the manner in which one lives and conducts one's affairs." After reading these passages from the Quran, do you agree or disagree that this is a central Islamic principle?
7. Compare these passages with the Sermon on the Mount (source 38). Which strike you as more significant, the similarities or the differences in message and tone? What do you conclude from your answer?

Those unbelievers of the People of the Book[1]
and the idolaters[2] wish not that any good
should be sent down upon you from your Lord;
but God singles out for His mercy whom he will;
   God is of bounty abounding. . . .

Many of the People of the Book wish they might
restore you as unbelievers, after you have believed,
in the jealousy of their souls, after the truth
has become clear to them; yet do you pardon
and be forgiving, till God brings His command;
truly God is powerful over everything.
And perform the prayer,[3] and pay the alms;[4]
whatever good you shall forward to your souls'
   account,
you shall find it with God; assuredly God sees
   the things you do.
And they say, "None shall enter Paradise
except that they be Jews or Christians."
Such are their fancies. Say: "Produce your proof,
   if you speak truly."
Nay, but whosoever submits his will to God,
being a good-doer, his wage is with his Lord,
and no fear shall be on them, neither shall they
   sorrow. . . .

Children of Israel,[5] remember My blessing
wherewith I blessed you, and that I have
   preferred you above all beings. . . .

And when his Lord tested Abraham[6]
with certain words, and he fulfilled them.
He said, "Behold, I make you a leader
for the people." Said he, "And of my seed?"
He said, "My covenant shall not reach the
   evildoers."[7]
And when We appointed the House[8] to be
a place of visitation for the people, and a
   sanctuary,
and: "Take to yourselves Abraham's station
for a place of prayer." And We made covenant
with Abraham and Ishmael,[9] "Purify
My House[10] for those that shall go about it
and those that cleave to it, to those who bow
   and prostrate themselves."[11] . . .

When his Lord said to him, "Surrender,"
he said, "I have surrendered me to the Lord of
   all Being."
And Abraham charged his sons with this
and Jacob[12] likewise: "My sons, God has chosen
   for you the religion;
see that you die not save in surrender."[13]

Why, were you witnesses, when death came
to Jacob? When he said to his sons,
"What will you serve after me?" They said,
"We will serve thy God and the God of thy
   fathers

---

[1]People who have their own sacred scriptures from God through such prophets as Moses and Jesus. Elsewhere, this surah identifies three such peoples: Jews, Christians, and Sabeans (a Gnostic sect with Jewish and Christian roots that inhabited the borderlands of Syria, Iraq, and Iran; see Multiple Voices IV for Gnosticism).

[2]Pagans who worship idols.

[3]The ritual prayer performed five times daily by all observant Muslims. See source 47.

[4]The *zakat*, or obligatory alms-payment, which supports the poor within the Islamic community.

[5]Jews — the offspring of Israel, or Jacob, the son of Isaac and the grandson of Abraham (see note 6).

[6]According to both Arabic and Jewish traditions, Abraham (ca. 1800 B.C.E.) was the father of both the Arabic and Jewish people, through, respectively, his sons Ishmael and Isaac.

[7]Jews who have abandoned God's Word and are not submissive to the Divine Will.

[8]The Kaaba, a cube-shaped shrine at the heart of the Great Mosque of Mecca (see note 11 and source 47).

[9]See notes 6 and 10.

[10]According to this surah, Abraham and his elder son, Ishmael, were commanded by God to cleanse the Kaaba of its idols, whose worship Muslims consider to be the worst of all possible sins. Muhammad cleansed the same sanctuary of idols following his triumphant reentry into Mecca in 630.

[11]Associated with Adam, Abraham, and Ishmael, the Kaaba is the focal point of a Muslim's daily prayer and the sacred spot around which pilgrims on *hajj* (see note 21) circumambulate in a series of ritual ceremonies.

[12]See notes 5 and 6.

[13]By surrendering to God, Abraham and his sons and grandsons were Muslims.

Abraham, Ishmael, and Isaac, One God; to Him
　　we surrender."
That is a nation that has passed away;[14]
there awaits them that they have earned,
and there awaits you that you have earned;
you shall not be questioned concerning the
　　things they did.

And they say, "Be Jews or Christians and
you shall be guided." Say thou: "Nay, rather
the creed of Abraham, a man of pure faith; he
　　was no idolater."
Say you: "We believe in God, and
in that which has been sent down on us
and sent down on Abraham, Ishmael,
Isaac and Jacob, and the Tribes,[15]
and that which was given to Moses and Jesus
and the Prophets, of their Lord; we
make no division between any of them, and to
　　Him we surrender."
And if they believe in the like of that you
believe in, then they are truly guided; but if
they turn away, then they are clearly in schism;[16]
God will suffice you for them; He is the All-
　　hearing, the All-knowing;
the baptism of God; and who is there
that baptizes fairer than God?[17] Him we are
　　serving.
Say: "Would you then dispute with us
concerning God, who is our Lord
and your Lord? Our deeds belong to us,
and to you belong your deeds; Him we serve
　　sincerely. . . .

It is not piety, that you turn your faces to the
　　East and to the West.[18]
　　　True piety is this:
to believe in God, and the Last Day,
the angels, the Book, and the Prophets,
to give of one's substance, however cherished, to
　　kinsmen, and orphans,
the needy, the traveler, beggars, and to ransom
　　the slave,
to perform the prayer, to pay the alms.
And they who fulfill their covenant
when they have engaged in a covenant, and
　　endure with fortitude misfortune, hardship,
　　and peril,
these are they who are true in their faith, these
　　are the truly godfearing. . . .

O believers, prescribed for you is
the Fast,[19] even as it was prescribed for
those that were before you — haply you will be
　　godfearing —
for days numbered; and if any of you
be sick, or if he be on a journey,
then a number of other days. . . .

And fight in the way of God with those
who fight with you, but aggress not: God loves
　　not the aggressors.
And slay them wherever you come upon them,
and expel them from where they expelled you;
persecution is more grievous than slaying.
But fight them not by the Holy Mosque[20]
until they should fight you there;
then, if they fight you, slay them —

---

[14]Jews (the progeny of Jacob) who surrender to God, and are Muslims by reason of that submission, no longer exist.
[15]The Twelve Tribes of the Israelites whom Moses led out of Egypt.
[16]*Schism* means "separation." They have separated themselves from Islam.
[17]Here the Quran juxtaposes the Christian sacrament of baptism, the ceremony of initiation into the Christian faith, with God's baptism of the Word.

[18]In prayer.
[19]The annual fast during the month of *Ramadan*, when observant Muslims refrain from all food, drink, and other physical pleasures from sunrise to sunset.
[20]The Great Mosque of Mecca (see note 8).

such is the recompense of unbelievers —
but if they give over, surely God is
All-forgiving, All-compassionate.
Fight them, till there is no persecution
and the religion is God's; then if they
give over, there shall be no enmity save for
    evildoers.
The holy month for the holy month;
holy things demand retaliation.
Whoso commits aggression against you,
do you commit aggression against him
like as he has committed against you;
and fear you God, and know that God is with
    the godfearing.

And expend in the way of God;
and cast not yourselves by your own hands
into destruction, but be good-doers; God loves
    the good-doers.

Fulfill the Pilgrimage[21] and the Visitation
unto God; but if you are prevented,
then such offering as may be feasible. . . .
And when you have performed your holy rites
remember God, as you remember your fathers
or yet more devoutly. . . .
    God
there is no god but He, the
Living, the Everlasting.
Slumber seizes Him not, neither sleep; to Him
    belongs
all that is in the heavens and the earth.
Who is there that shall intercede with Him save
    by His leave?
He knows what lies before them and what is
    after them,
and they comprehend not anything of His
    knowledge save such as He wills.

His Throne comprises the heavens and earth;
the preserving of them oppresses Him not;
He is the All-high, the All-glorious.

No compulsion is there in religion.
Rectitude has become clear from error.
So whosoever disbelieves in idols
and believes in God, has laid hold of
the most firm handle, unbreaking; God is All-
    hearing, All-knowing.

God is the Protector of the believers;
He brings them forth from the shadows into the
    light. . . .

Those who believe and do deeds of righteousness,
and perform the prayer, and pay the alms —
their wage awaits them with their Lord,
and no fear shall be on them, neither shall they
    sorrow. . . .
God charges no soul save to its capacity;
standing to its account is what it has earned,
and against its account what it has merited.
    Our Lord,
take us not to task
if we forget, or make mistake.
    Our Lord,
charge us not with a load such
as Thou didst lay upon those before us.
    Our Lord,
do Thou not burden us
beyond what we have the strength to bear.
    And pardon us,
    and forgive us,
    and have mercy on us;
    Thou art our Protector.
And help us against the people
    of the unbelievers.

---

[21]All adult Muslims who are able to make the journey must embark on the *hajj*, or pilgrimage to Mecca, at least once before death. See source 50.

The Tales of Tradition

▼▼▼

46 ▼ *Abu Abdullah ibn Ismail al-Bukhari,* THE AUTHENTIC [TRADITIONS]

Early Muslims collected stories about the Prophet, but it was not until about two centuries after Muhammad's death that Muslim scholars began to catalogue systematically the traditions that circulated about the Prophet and his Companions. The first and most important individual in this effort was the Persian scholar al-Bukhari (810–870), a native of Bukhara (located in present-day Uzbekistan), who reportedly collected some 600,000 tales (many were variations of common themes) and memorized more than 200,000 of them. From this vast body of material, he identified as authentic a few more than 7,000 tales, which he then preserved in a work titled *Al-Sahih* (*The Authentic*). The following excerpts suggest the variety and types of hadiths that became enshrined in *Sunni*, or mainstream, Islamic tradition. *Shia* hadiths and the Shia-Sunni schism are dealt with in source 49.

QUESTIONS FOR ANALYSIS

1. Which virtues do these selections emphasize?
2. What gives Hadith its authority, since, unlike the Quran, Muslims do not regard it as the literal word of God?
3. Explain the reasoning behind the order of *Al-Sahih*'s first four books, or chapters: "How Revelation Began," "Faith," "Knowledge," and "Ablution."

BOOK 1: HOW REVELATION BEGAN[1]

H. 2. Aisha[2] reported that Harith Ibn Hisham[3] asked the Messenger of Allah, O Messenger of Allah! How does revelation come to thee? The Messenger of Allah [Peace and blessings of Allah be upon him] said: "Sometimes it comes to me like the ringing of a bell, and that is the hardest on me, then he (the Angel) departs from me and I retain in memory from him what he says, and sometimes the Angel comes to me in the like-ness of a man and he speaks to me and I retain in memory what he says" Aisha said:

And "I saw him when revelation came down upon him on a severely cold day, then it departed from him and his forehead dripped with sweat."

BOOK 2: FAITH

H. 24. Abu Huraira[4] reported that the Messenger of Allah [Peace and blessings of Allah be upon him] was questioned as to what deed was

---

[1]These headings are the chapter titles (chapters are known as "books" in this context) of the *Al-Sahih*.
[2]Aisha bint (daughter of) Abu Bakr (ca. 613–ca. 678). Muhammad's favorite (and youngest) wife, she was present for many of the Prophet's revelations. She was the source of many Sunni hadiths, but Shia Muslims reject her testimony (see note 4).

[3]He converted to Islam after the Prophet took possession of Mecca in 630.
[4]One of the major sources of hadiths, Abu Huraira (d. 678) was a constant companion of Muhammad during the last two years of the Prophet's life. Many Shia Muslims accuse him and Aisha of having perverted Islam and reject their testimony.

the most excellent? He said: "Faith in Allah and His Messenger."[5]

It was said, What after that? He said: "Jihad in the way of Allah."

It was said, What after that? He said: "A Pilgrimage that is acceptable (to Allah)." . . .

H. 36. Abu Huraira reported that the Prophet [Peace and blessings of Allah be upon him] said, "Verily, religion is easy and no one becomes severe in the matter of religion, but it overpowers him, so be upright and adopt moderation and be of good cheer and seek the help (of Allah) in the morning and in the evening and during a part of night." . . .

H. 38. Abu Said al-Khudri[6] reported that he heard the Messenger of Allah [Peace and blessings of Allah be upon him] say: "When a servant of Allah adopts Islam and his Islam becomes beautiful, Allah will remove from him all the evils which he may have acquired, and retribution[7] comes after that, the retribution of a good deed is from ten to seven hundred times of it and that of an evil deed is equal to it, except that Allah overlooks it." . . .

H. 40. Anas[8] reported that the Prophet [Peace and blessings of Allah be upon him] said: "Whosoever says that there is no object of worship except Allah and in his heart there is goodness of the weight of a grain of barley, will come out of the fire, and whoever says that there is no object of worship except Allah and in his heart there is goodness of the weight of a grain of wheat, will come out of the fire, and whoever says that there is no object of worship except Allah and in his heart there is goodness of the weight of an atom, will come out of the fire."

BOOK 3: KNOWLEDGE

H. 72. Anas reported, The Messenger of Allah [Peace and blessings of Allah be upon him] said: "Verily among the signs of the Hour, is that knowledge will be lifted up and ignorance will be established and intoxicating liquors will be drunk and fornication will prevail."

H. 73. Anas reported, "I am narrating a hadith which no one will narrate to you after me; I heard the Messenger of Allah [Peace and blessings of Allah be upon him] say, verily among the signs of the Hour is that knowledge will dwindle and ignorance will be widespread and fornication and women will preponderate in number and men will be small in number so much so that for fifty women there will be one supporter."[9] . . .

H. 85. Ibn Abbas[10] reported, "I bear witness that the Prophet [Peace and blessings of Allah be upon him] came out and with him was Bilal[11] and he thought that women did not hear (his sermon), so he preached to them and enjoined upon them charity; so the women began to throw earrings and rings and Bilal began to collect them in a part of his garment."

BOOK 4: ABLUTION

H. 141. Aisha reported, "The Prophet [Peace and blessings of Allah be upon him] loved to start with the right side in wearing shoes, in combing his hair and in washing himself and in every affair of his." . . .

H. 193. Aisha reported on the authority of the Prophet [Peace and blessings of Allah be upon

---

[5]Muhammad.
[6]One of the major sources for Sunni hadiths. Shia Muslims do not automatically reject al-Khudri's testimony (see note 4), but they use it cautiously.
[7]In the sense of payment.
[8]Anas ibn al-Malik (d. 710), the longest living of the Prophet's Companions. He was the source for 128 hadiths, which are revered by Sunni Muslims and largely dismissed by Shia Muslims.

[9]Most men will have been killed in wars.
[10]Abd-Allah ibn Abbas (d. 686–687) was Muhammad's cousin and is revered by Shias and Sunnis alike because of that relationship.
[11]A slave of Ethiopian descent, he was purchased by Muhammad's closest friend, Abu Bakr, and freed because of his faith. He accompanied Muhammad to Medina and there was appointed the first *muezzin*, the person who calls the Faithful to prayer.

him] "Every drink that gives intoxication is forbidden." . . .

   H. 198. Bara ibn Azib[12] reported that the
Prophet [Peace and blessings of Allah be upon
him] said, "When you go to your bed make
ablution like the one you do for prayer, then lie
on your right side, then say, 'O Allah, I submit
myself in obedience to Thee and I make Thee

my object of reliance for the sake of Thy love and
fear, there is no refuge nor rescue excepting with
Thee, O Allah! I believe in Thy book which
Thou hast revealed and Thy Prophet, whom
Thou hast sent.' Then if you die in that night
you are in the (religion of) nature (Islam), and
make it the last thing which you utter."

---

[12]Al-Bara ibn Azib was one of the Prophet's Companions.

Muhammad's Night Journey and Ascent to Heaven
▼▼▼

47 ▼ *Muhammad ibn Ishaq,*
THE LIFE OF THE MESSENGER OF GOD

An ambiguous passage in the Quran proclaims: "Glory be to Him who carried His
servant by night from the sacred shrine to the distant shrine, whose surroundings
We have blessed, that We might show him some of Our signs" (Surah 17:1). Most
Muslims interpret the *sacred shrine* to mean Mecca's *Kaaba*, a temple sacred to the
pre-Islamic polytheists of Arabia and, once Muhammad cleansed it of its 360
idols, a shrine that has remained a focal point of Islamic devotion down to our
day. Many Muslims further interpret the *distant shrine* to signify Jerusalem's *Temple Mount*, the site of the destroyed Jewish Temple. According to a tradition not
specifically recorded in the Quran, one night, around the year 620, while asleep
within the Kaaba's stone porch, Muhammad was transported to Jerusalem and
from there to Heaven on a mythical beast known as *Buraq*. Actually, the tradition
is not and never was that simple. Many variations of the story existed (and exist)
side by side, even in the Prophet's own day. Apparently, Muhammad had a mystical vision that he was reluctant or unable to discuss in detail.

   Around the mid eighth century, Muhammad ibn Ishaq (ca. 704–ca. 767), the author of the first and most influential biography of the Prophet, faced the problem
of trying to reconcile the often contradictory stories that he had collected regarding the Messenger of God's Night Journey. What follows is his attempt to balance
and evaluate these variant accounts.

QUESTIONS FOR ANALYSIS

1. Where does Ibn Ishaq seem to stand on the question of whether Muhammad's Night Journey was a physical one or a purely spiritual one?
2. How do these various accounts use the Night Journey to explain some of
   Islam's values, practices, and attributes? Be specific.

3. Compare this story with Hadith (source 46). What conclusions follow from this comparative analysis?

4. Compare this account of Heaven and Hell with the other visions of the Afterworld that we saw in *The Epic of Gilgamesh* (source 1), the *Odyssey* (source 10), and the *Aeneid* (source 27). What conclusions follow from this comparative analysis?

Then the apostle was carried by night from the mosque at Mecca to the Masjid al-Aqsa,[1] which is the temple of Aelia.[2] . . .

The following account reached me from Abdullah ibn Masud[3] and Abu Said al-Khudri,[4] and Aisha the prophet's wife,[5] and Muaiya ibn Abu Sufyan,[6] and al-Hasan ibn Abul-Hasan al-Basri,[7] and Ibn Shihab al-Zuhri[8] and Qatada[9] and other traditionists.[10] . . . It is pieced together in the story that follows, each one contributing something of what he was told about what happened when he was taken on the night journey. The matter of the place of the journey and what is said about it is a searching test and a matter of God's power and authority wherein is a lesson for the intelligent; and guidance and mercy and strengthening to those who believe. It was certainly an act of God by which He took him by night in what way He pleased to show him His signs which He willed him to see so that he witnessed His mighty sovereignty and power by which He does what He wills to do.

According to what I have heard Abdullah b. Masud used to say: Buraq, the animal whose every stride carried it as far as its eye could reach on which the prophets before him used to ride was brought to the apostle[11] and he was mounted on it. His companion[12] went with him to see the wonders between Heaven and Earth, until he came to Jerusalem's temple. There he found Abraham the friend of God, Moses, and Jesus assembled with a company of prophets, and he prayed with them. Then he was brought three vessels containing milk, wine, and water respectively. The apostle said: "I heard a voice saying when these were offered to me: If he takes the water he will be drowned and his people also; if he takes the wine he will go astray and his people also; and if he takes the milk he will be rightly guided and his people also. So I took the vessel containing milk and drank it. Gabriel said to me, You have been rightly guided and so will your people be, Muhammad."[13] I was told that al-Hasan said that the apostle said: "While I was sleeping in the Hijr[14] Gabriel came and stirred me with his foot. I sat up but saw nothing and lay down again. He came a second time and stirred me with his foot. I sat up but saw noth-

---

[1]The Farther Shrine. The Mosque of al-Aqsa, which stands on Jerusalem's Temple Mount, is believed by many Muslims to be the location from which Muhammad physically rose to Heaven.

[2]The Roman name for Jerusalem.

[3]Abdullah ibn Masud (d. ca. 652) was an early and close Companion of the Prophet.

[4]See source 46, note 6.

[5]See source 46, note 2.

[6]Better known as Muawiyah I (r. 661–680), founder of the Umayyad Dynasty of caliphs (661–750).

[7]His father had been one of Muhammad's Helpers (Medinans who supported the immigrant Meccan Muslims). Al-Hasan (642–737) became a noted theologian at Basra and is deemed to have been an early Sufi saint (see source 51).

[8]Muhammad ibn Muslim ibn Zuhri (d. 742), one of the initial compilers of hadiths at the instruction of Caliph Umar II (r. 717–720).

[9]Qatada ibn al-Numan, a Medinan Helper (see note 7) and Companion of the Prophet. He was the source of many hadiths.

[10]Traditionists, of which Ibn Ishaq was one, held that Islamic law should be inferred from hadiths, without significant recourse to reason (see source 48, passim).

[11]Muhammad.

[12]Archangel Gabriel.

[13]Many Islamic commentators interpret this as meaning that Muhammad rejected the extremes of asceticism (water) and hedonism (wine). See source 46.

[14]The Kaaba's stone porch.

ing and lay down again. He came to me the third time and stirred me with his foot. I sat up and he took hold of my arm and I stood beside him and he brought me out to the door of the mosque and there was a white animal, half mule, half donkey, with wings on its sides with which it propelled its feet, putting down each forefoot at the limit of its sight and he mounted me on it. Then he went out with me keeping close to me. . . ."

In his story al-Hasan said: "The apostle and Gabriel went their way until they arrived at the temple at Jerusalem. There he found Abraham, Moses, and Jesus among a company of the prophets. The apostle acted as their imam[15] in prayer. Then he was brought two vessels, one containing wine and the other milk. The apostle took the milk and drank it, leaving the wine. Gabriel said: 'You have been rightly guided to the way of nature and so will your people be, Muhammad. Wine is forbidden you.'[16] Then the apostle returned to Mecca and in the morning he told Quraysh[17] what had happened. Most of them said, 'By God, this is a plain absurdity! A caravan takes a month to go to Syria and a month to return and can Muhammad do the return journey in one night?' Many Muslims gave up their faith; some went to Abu Bakr[18] and said, 'What do you think of your friend now, Abu Bakr? He alleges that he went to Jerusalem last night and prayed there and came back to Mecca.' He replied that they were lying about the apostle; but they said that he was in the mosque at that very moment telling the people about it. Abu Bakr said, 'If he says so then it is true. And what is so surprising in that? He tells me that communications from God from Heaven to Earth come to him in an hour of a day or night and I believe him, and that is more extraordinary than that at which you boggle!' He then went to the apostle and asked him if these reports were

true, and when he said they were, he asked him to describe Jerusalem to him." Al-Hasan said that he was lifted up so that he could see the apostle speaking as he told Abu Bakr what Jerusalem was like.[19] Whenever he described a part of it he said, "That's true. I testify that you are the apostle of God" until he had completed the description, and then the apostle said, "And you, Abu Bakr, are the *Siddiq*."[20] This was the occasion on which he got this honorific. . . .

One of Abu Bakr's family told me that Aisha the prophet's wife used to say: "The apostle's body remained where it was but God removed his spirit by night." Yqub b. Utba b. al-Mughira b. al-Akhnas told me that Muawiya b. Abu Sufyan when he was asked about the apostle's night journey said, "It was a true vision from God." What these two latter said does not contradict what al-Hasan said, seeing that God Himself said, "We made the vision which we showed thee only for a test to men"; nor does it contradict what God said in the story of Abraham when he said to his son, "O my son, verily I saw in a dream that I must sacrifice thee,"[21] and he acted accordingly. Thus, as I see it, revelation from God comes to the prophets waking or sleeping.

I have heard that the apostle used to say, "My eyes sleep while my heart is awake." Only God knows how revelation came and he saw what he saw. But whether he was asleep or awake, it was all true and actually happened. . . .

One whom I have no reason to doubt told me on the authority of Abu Said al-Khudri: "I heard the apostle say, 'After the completion of my business in Jerusalem a ladder was brought to me finer than any I have ever seen. It was that to which the dying man looks when death approaches. My companion mounted it with me until we came to one of the gates of Heaven called the Gate of the Watchers. An angel called

---

[15]Prayer leader.
[16]See source 46.
[17]The dominant tribe of Mecca, which controlled the city's commerce. Although Muhammad was of that tribe, most of its members rejected his prophecies at this time.

[18]Muhammad's closest friend, the first caliph (r. 632–634), and father of Aisha (see source 46, note 2).
[19]Al-Hasan was a child at the time in which he witnessed this.
[20]Testifier to the Truth.
[21]Surah 37:10.

Ismail was in charge of it, and under his command were twelve thousand angels each of them having twelve thousand angels under his command.' As he told this story the apostle used to say, 'and none knows the armies of God but He.' When Gabriel brought me in, Ismail asked who I was, and when he was told that I was Muhammad he asked if I had been given a mission, and on being assured of this he wished me well. . . ."

In his tradition Abu Said al-Khudri said that the apostle said: "When I entered the lowest heaven I saw a man sitting there with the spirits of men passing before him. To one he would speak well and rejoice in him saying: 'A good spirit from a good body' and of another he would say 'Faugh!' and frown, saying: 'An evil spirit from an evil body.' In answer to my question Gabriel told me that this was our father Adam reviewing the spirits of his offspring; the spirit of a believer excited his pleasure, and the spirit of an infidel excited his disgust so that he said the words just quoted.

"Then I saw men with lips like camels; in their hands were pieces of fire like stones which they used to thrust into their mouths and they would come out of their posteriors. I was told that these were those who sinfully devoured the wealth of orphans. . . .

"Then I saw men with good fat meat before them side by side with lean stinking meat, eating of the latter and leaving the former. These are those who forsake the women which God has permitted and go after those he has forbidden.

"Then I saw women hanging by their breasts. These were those who had fathered bastards on their husbands." . . .

To continue the tradition of Said al-Khudri: "Then I was taken up to the second heaven and there were the two maternal cousins Jesus, Son of Mary, and John, son of Zakariah.[22] Then to the third heaven and there was a man whose face was as the moon at the full. This was my brother Joseph, son of Jacob. Then to the fourth heaven and there was a man called Idris.[23] And we have exalted him to a lofty place. Then to the fifth heaven and there was a man with white hair and a long beard, never have I seen a more handsome man than he. This was the beloved among his people Aaron son of Imran.[24] Then to the sixth heaven, and there was a dark man with a hooked nose. . . . This was my brother Moses, son of Imran. Then to the seventh heaven and there was a man sitting on a throne at the gate of the immortal mansion. Every day seventy thousand angels went in not to come back until the resurrection day. Never have I seen a man more like myself. This was my father Abraham.[25] Then he took me into Paradise and there I saw a damsel with dark red lips and I asked her to whom she belonged, for she pleased me much when I saw her, and she told me 'Zayd b. Haritha.' The apostle gave Zayd the good news about her."[26]

From a tradition of Abdullah b. Masud from the prophet there has reached me the following: When Gabriel took him up to each of the heavens and asked permission to enter he had to say whom he had brought and whether he had received a mission and they would say "God grant him life, brother and friend!" until they reached the seventh heaven and his Lord. There the duty of fifty prayers a day was laid upon him.

The apostle said: "On my return I passed by Moses and what a fine friend of yours he was! He asked me how many prayers had been laid upon me and when I told him fifty he said, 'Prayer is a weighty matter and your people are weak, so go back to your Lord and ask him to reduce the

---

[22]Known to Christians as John the Baptist.
[23]Known to Jews and Christians as Enoch, the father of Methuselah.
[24]Islam reveres the memory of two men named *Imran*: the father of the Prophet Moses and Moses' brother Aaron; and the father of Mary, the mother of Jesus. Clearly, the reference is to the former Imran.

[25]See source 45, notes 6, 10, 11, and 13.
[26]Zayd was a former slave whom Muhammad freed and then received into his house as a foster son. Muhammad arranged the marriage between Zayd and the beautiful Zaynab bint Jahsh. Later, when Zayd divorced Zaynab, Muhammad married her.

number for you and your community.' I did so and He took off ten. Again I passed by Moses and he said the same again; and so it went on until only five prayers for the whole day and night were left. Moses again gave me the same advice. I replied that I had been back to my Lord and asked him to reduce the number until I was ashamed, and I would not do it again. He of you who performs them in faith and trust will have the reward of fifty prayers."

Rules Regarding Jihad
▼▼▼

48 ▼ *Abu al-Walid Muhammad ibn Ahmad ibn Muhammad ibn Rushd, THE DISTINGUISHED JURIST'S PRIMER*

Muslims believe that Allah imparted to His community of believers a body of revelation that encompasses every aspect of their being. Therefore, the study and application of Sacred Law, or *Sharia*, became and remains one of Islam's most revered religious professions. Among *Sunni* Muslims, four major schools of interpretive jurisprudence, or *fiqh*, emerged: *Maliki* (see note 4), *Hanafi* (see note 12), *Shafii* (see note 15), and *Hanbali* — each named after an early master of the law.

The schools differ in some matters of juristic interpretation and emphasis, but they agree on fundamental legal principles and are largely divided along regional, rather than ideological, lines. All four recognize "the four roots of jurisprudence." Foremost is the *Quran*. Second is the *sunna*, or correct pathway, of the Prophet and his Companions as preserved in *Hadith* (source 46). Third is the consensus and tradition (also the sunna) of the *umma*, or universal body of Muslims, which cannot err because it is God's community. Finally, there is a measure of personal interpretation based on analogy, reason, and good sense.

Jurists belonging to the *Shia* branch of Islam revere the same Quran but have their own, distinctive collections of Hadith and reject the consensus of the majority Sunni community as a valid root of the law because they view Sunni Muslims as misguided. They rely, instead, on the infallible teachings of their *imams*, or religious teachers. For more on these imams and the Shia-Sunni schism, see source 49.

One of the leading Muslim intellectuals of the twelfth century was Ibn Rushd (1126–1198), known to thirteenth-century Western Europeans who studied his commentaries on Aristotle as *Averroës*. Ibn Rushd was a noted physician, theologian, philosopher, mathematician, and astronomer, but his main claim to fame within *Dar al-Islam* (The House of Islam) was as a jurist of the Maliki tradition. He served as a *qadi*, or judge, in his native Córdoba, Spain, as well as in Seville. In a single year, 1167, he composed the bulk of his *Bidayat al-Mujtahid* (*The Distinguished Jurist's Primer*). The following excerpt focuses on the issue of jihad. Jihad, which means "struggle," has many levels of meaning within Islam (see source 51), but in this source it means solely Jihad of the Sword, or holy war. Ibn Rushd's learned commentary, which draws upon legal traditions extending back to at least the eighth century, indicates the extent to which Islamic jurisprudence had developed rules governing holy warfare by the twelfth century.

QUESTIONS FOR ANALYSIS

1. Are all questions resolved in this treatise, or does the author leave some questions open? Be specific.
2. How does Ibn Rushd use quranic verses, hadiths, the consensus of the umma, and legal opinions to establish his legal edifice? Be specific by citing examples of each.
3. Based on this excerpt, describe the legal parameters of Jihad of the Sword in Ibn Rushd's day.
4. Compare this treatise with the Babylonian Talmud (source 37). Leaving aside the fact that the excerpts focus on radically different issues, which strike you as more significant, so far as their methods of presentation and analysis are concerned, their similarities or their differences? What conclusions follow from your answer?

Par. 1. The Legal Qualification of This Activity and the Persons Obliged to Take Part in It.

Scholars agree that the jihad is a collective not a personal obligation. Only Abd Allah Ibn al-Hasan[1] professed it to be a recommendable act. According to the majority of scholars, the compulsory nature of the jihad is founded on [2:216]: *"Prescribed for you is fighting, though it be hateful to you."*[2] That this obligation is a collective and not a personal one, i.e. that the obligation, when it can be properly carried out by a limited number of individuals, is cancelled for the remaining Muslims, is founded on [9:122]: *"It is not for the believers to go forth totally,"* on [4:95]: *"Yet to each God has promised the reward most fair"* and, lastly, on the fact that the Prophet never went to battle without leaving some people behind. All this together implies that this activity is a collective obligation. The obligation to participate in the jihad applies to adult free men who have the means at their disposal to go to war and who are healthy, that is, not ill or suffering from chronic diseases. There is absolutely no controversy about the latter restriction because of [48:17]: *"There is no fault in the blind,*

and there is no fault in the lame, and there is no fault in the sick" and because of [9:91]: *"There is no fault in the weak and the sick and those who find nothing to expend."* Nor do I know of any dissentient views as regards the rule that this obligation applies only to free men. Nearly all scholars agree that this obligation is conditional on permission granted by the parents. Only in the case that the obligation has become a personal one, for instance because there is nobody else to carry it out, can this permission be dispensed with. This prerequisite of permission is based on the following authentic Tradition: *"Once a man said to the Messenger of God: 'I wish to take part in the jihad.' The Messenger said to him: 'Are both your parents still alive?' When he answered in the affirmative, the Messenger said: 'Then perform the jihad for their sake.'"* Scholars are not agreed whether this permission is also required of parents who are polytheists. There is controversy, too, about the question whether the creditor's permission has to be asked when a person has run into debt. An argument in favor of this can be found in the following Tradition: *"A man said to the Prophet: 'Will God forgive me my sins if I shall sacrifice myself patiently and shall be killed in the way of God (i.e. by taking part in the jihad)?' The*

---

[1]Al-Hasan (d. 762) was an early *traditionist* (see source 47, note 10).

[2]A quotation from the Quran: the second surah, verse 216. All subsequent citations of quranic verses appear in this form.

Prophet said: 'Yes, with the exception of your debts. This Jibril[3] has told me before.'" The majority of scholars do not consider it obligatory, especially not when the debtor leaves enough behind to serve as payment for his debts.

Par. 2. The Enemy.

Scholars agree that all polytheists should be fought. This is founded on [8:39]: *"Fight them until there is no persecution and the religion is God's entirely."* However, it has been related by Malik[4] that it would not be allowed to attack the Ethiopians and the Turks on the strength of the Tradition of the Prophet: *"Leave the Ethiopians in peace as long as they leave you in peace."* Questioned as to the authenticity of this Tradition, Malik did not acknowledge it, but said: "People still avoid attacking them."

Par. 3. The Damage Allowed to Be Inflicted upon the Different Categories of Enemies.

Damage inflicted upon the enemy may consist in damage to his property, injury to his person or violation of his personal liberty, i.e. that he is made a slave and is appropriated. This may be done . . . to all polytheists: men, women, young and old, important and unimportant. Only with regard to monks do opinions vary; for some take it that they must be left in peace and that they must not be captured, but allowed to go unscathed and that they may not be enslaved. In support of their opinion they bring forward the words of the Prophet: *"Leave them in peace and also that to which they have dedicated themselves,"* as well as the practice of Abu Bakr.[5]

Most scholars are agreed that, in his dealings with captives, various policies are open to the Imam [head of the Islamic state, caliph]. He may pardon them, enslave them, kill them, or release them either on ransom or as *dhimmi*,[6] in which latter case the released captive is obliged to pay poll-tax.[7] Some scholars, however, have taught that captives may never be slain. According to al-Hasan Ibn Muhammad al-Tamimi,[8] this was even the *Consensus* of the *Sahaba*.[9] This controversy has arisen because, firstly, the Quran-verses contradict each other in this respect; secondly, practice [of the Prophet and the first caliphs] was inconsistent; and lastly, the obvious interpretation of the Quran is at variance with the Prophet's deeds. The obvious interpretation of [47:4]: *"When you meet the unbelievers, smite their necks, then, when you have made wide slaughter among them, tie fast the bonds"* is that the Imam is only entitled to pardon captives or to release them on ransom. On the other hand, [8:67]: *"It is not for any Prophet to have prisoners until he make wide slaughter in the land,"* as well as the occasion when this verse was revealed[10] would go to prove that it is better to slay captives than to enslave them. The Prophet himself would in some cases slay captives outside the field of battle, while he would pardon them in others. Women he used to enslave. Abu Ubayd[11] has related that the Prophet never enslaved male Arabs. After him, the *Sahaba* reached unanimity about the rule that the People of the Book, both male and female, might be enslaved. Those who are of the opinion that the verse which prohibits slaying

---

[3]The Arabic name of Archangel Gabriel, the intermediary through whom the Prophet received his revelations.

[4]Malik ibn Anas (d. ca. 795), the first significant Sunni jurist to set his hand to codifying *Sharia* and the person after whom the Maliki School, which predominates in western North Africa and was also the dominant tradition in Muslim Spain (*al-Andalus*) before 1492, is named. His masterwork, which was largely compiled by his students from his lectures, is *Al-Muwatta (The Smoothed Path).* He rejected the strict traditionist position (see note 1) and opted instead for law based on the actual practices of the Muslims of Medina. When Hadith and the common practices of the umma of Medina conflicted, he opted usually for the latter. He also did not hesitate to use reason to clarify or resolve knotty issues.

[5]See source 47, note 18.

[6]Subject non-Muslims. See Multiple Voices V.

[7]Known as the *jizya*, it was paid by male non-Muslim subjects as a token of submission to the authority of the Islamic state and as payment for protection. See Multiple Voices V.

[8]A traditionist.

[9]The Companions of Muhammad.

[10]The Battle of Badr: a key victory on March 17, 624, which proved to be a turning point in the struggle against the Meccan enemies of Islam. Although some prominent Meccan prisoners were executed, most were spared.

[11]Abu Ubayd Sad ibn Ubayd al-Zuhri (d. 716), a prominent traditionist.

[47:4] abrogates the Prophet's example, maintain that captives may not be slain. Others profess, however, that this verse does not concern itself with the slaughter of captives and that it was by no means intended to restrict the number of policies possible with regard to captives. On the contrary, they say, the fact that the Prophet used to slay captives adds a supplementing rule to the verse in question [47:4] and thus removes the occasion for the complaint that he omitted to kill the captives of Badr. These, now, do profess that the killing of captives is allowed. . . .

As regards injury to the person, that is, the slaying of the enemy, the Muslims agree that in times of war, all adult, able-bodied, unbelieving males may be slain. As to the question whether the enemy may also be slain after he has been captured, there is the above-mentioned controversy. There is no disagreement about the rule that it is forbidden to slay women and children, provided that they are not fighting, for then women, in any case, may be slain. This rule is founded on the fact that, according to authoritative Traditions, the Prophet prohibited the slaughter of women and children and once said about a woman who had been slain: *"She was not one who would have fought."*

There is controversy about the question whether it is allowed to slay hermits who have retired from the world, the blind, the chronically ill and the insane, those who are old and unable to fight any longer, peasants, and serfs. Malik professes that neither the blind, nor the insane, nor hermits may be slain and that of their property not all may be carried off, but that enough should be left for them to be able to survive. Nei-

ther is it allowed, according to him, to slay the old and decrepit. Of the same opinion are Abu Hanifa[12] and his pupils. Thawri[13] and Awzai,[14] however, have taught that of these groups, only the aged may not be slain. On the other hand, Awzai had also taught that this prohibition is also valid with regard to peasants. According to the most authoritative opinion of Shafii,[15] all of these categories may be slain. The source of this controversy is to be found in the fact that in a number of Traditions, rules are given which are at variance with the general rule from the Book [i.e. the Quran] as well as with the general rule of the authentic Tradition: *"I have been commanded to fight the people until they say: 'There is no God but God.'"* [9:5]: *"Then, when the sacred months are drawn away, slay the idolaters wherever you find them"* as well as the above-mentioned Tradition give as a general rule that every polytheist must be slain, whether he is a monk or not. Nevertheless, the following Traditions, among others, are brought forward in support of the prescription that the lives of the categories mentioned must be saved: 1. Dawud Ibn al-Hasin[16] has related on the authority of Ikrima[17] on the authority of Ibn Abbas[18] that the Prophet used to say, whenever he sent out his armies: *"Do not slay hermits."* 2. On the authority of Anas Ibn Malik[19] it has been related that the Prophet said: *"Do not slay the old and decrepit, children, or women. Do not purloin what belongs to the spoils."* Abu Dawud[20] included this Tradition in his compilation. 3. Malik has related that Abu Bakr said: *"You will find people who will profess that they have dedicated themselves entirely to God. Leave them in peace and also that to which they have dedicated themselves."* 4. *"Do not slay women,*

---

[12]Abu Hanifa al-Numan (d. 767), the lawyer after whom the Hanafi School is named. The Hanafi School, the largest of the four schools, counting about 50 percent of all Sunnis, is preeminent in many lands that were formerly part of the Ottoman and Mughal empires and in Central Asia and China.

[13]Sufyan al-Thawri (d. 778), a traditionist.

[14]Al-Awazai (d. 774), founder of a school of legal thought that was superseded after a few centuries.

[15]Al-Shafii (d. 820), the first to systematize the study of sources and the scholar from whom the Shafii School traces its origins. The most conservative of the four schools, and the second largest, today it predominates throughout most

of the lands of the Indian Ocean, including Yemen, East Africa, southwest India and Sri Lanka, and Southeast Asia; in western Arabia (the *Hejaz*), Egypt, Lebanon, and Syria; and among the Kurds and Chechens.

[16]Dawud ibn al-Hasin (d. 752–753), a noted traditionist.

[17]Ikrima (d. 723–724), a noted traditionist. He transmitted and gave authority to many hadiths.

[18]See source 46, note 10.

[19]See source 46, note 8.

[20]Abu Dawud (d. 888–889) compiled one of the *Six Authentic Compilations* of Hadith. Al-Bukhari (see source 46) compiled the first of the six.

nor infants, nor those worn with age." However, it seems to me that the chief source for the controversy about this question is that [2:190]: *"And fight in the way of God with those who fight you, but aggress not: God loves not the aggressors"* is in conflict with [9:5]: *"Then, when the sacred months are drawn away, slay the idolaters wherever you find them."* Some maintain that 9:5 has abrogated 2:190, because at the outset it was only allowed to slay people who were able-bodied. Consequently, the latter take it that 9:5 gives a rule without exceptions. Others are of the opinion that 2:190 has not been abrogated and that it is valid with regard to all those categories which do not take part in the fighting. According to these, 2:190 gives an exceptive regulation as regards 9:5. Shafii, in support of his interpretation, argues that it has been related on the authority of Sumra that the Prophet commanded: *"Slay the polytheists but spare their children."* The only motive why the enemy should be put to death, according to him, is their unbelief. This motive, then, goes for all unbelievers. Those who maintain that peasants are not to be slain argue that Zayd Ibn Wahb[21] has related: *"We received a letter from Umar,[22] saying: Do not purloin what belongs to the spoils, do not act perfidiously, do not slay babies and be god-fearing with regard to peasants."* The prohibition to slay polytheist serfs is based on the Tradition of Rabah Ibn Rabia:[23] *"Once, when Rabah Ibn Rabia sallied forth with the Messenger of God, he and (the) companions of the Prophet passed by a woman who had been slain. The Messenger halted and said: 'She was not one who would have fought.' Thereupon he looked at the men and said to one of them: 'Run after Khalid Ibn al-Walid[24] (and tell him) that he must not slay children, serfs or women.'"* Basically, however, the source of their controversy is to be found in their divergent views concerning the motive why the enemy may be slain. Those who think that this is because they are unbelieving do not make exceptions for any polytheist. Others, who are of the opinion that this motive consists in their capacity for fighting, in view of the prohibition to slay female unbelievers, do make an exception for those who are unable to fight or who are not as a rule inclined to fight, such as peasants and serfs. Enemies must not be tortured nor must their bodies be mutilated. The Muslims agree that they may be slain with weapons. Controversy exists, however, concerning the question whether it is allowed to burn them by fire. Some consider it reprehensible to burn or to assail them with fire. This is also the opinion of Umar. It has been related that Malik held a similar view. Sufyan al-Thawri, on the other hand, considered it admissible. Others allow it only in case the enemy has started it. The source of this controversy is again in the fact that a general rule and a particular rule are at variance. The general rule is given by [9:5]: *"Slay the idolaters wherever you find them."* This does not preclude any manner of slaying. The particular rule is founded on an authoritative Tradition, according to which the Prophet said to a certain man: *"If ye should seize him, then slay him, yet do not burn him. No one is free to punish by means of fire, save the Lord of the (Hell) fire (i.e. God)."* Most scholars agree that fortresses may be assailed with mangonels[25] no matter whether there are women and children within them or not. This is based on the fact that the Prophet used mangonels against the population of al-Taif.[26] Some, among whom is Awzai, have taught that mangonels should not be resorted to when Muslim captives or children are within the [walls of the] fortress. Layth, on the other hand, considered it admissible. The argument of those who do not allow it, reads [48:25] *"Had they been separated clearly, then We would have chastised the unbelievers among them with a painful chastisement."* Those who do allow it do so, as it were, with a view to the general interest. So much for the extent to which injury may be inflicted upon the person of the enemy.

---

[21]Zayd ibn Wahb (d. 714–715), a famous traditionist.
[22]Umar I (r. 634–644), the second caliph, under whose guidance Islam began its imperial conquests in earnest.
[23]A Companion of the Prophet.

[24]Early Islam's greatest general, Khalid ibn al-Walid (d. 642) is known as "the Drawn Sword of Allah."
[25]A torsion catapult that hurls stones and burning material.
[26]A city that the Muslims unsuccessfully besieged in 630. In 631 the city found itself isolated and accepted Islam peacefully.

Variety and Unity Within Islam

Ideally, Islam is a single community united in submission and service to God. In fact, however, as is true of every world religion, almost from its origins it has fragmented into a wide variety of sects and schools. The single greatest split within the community of Islam is the division between *Sunnis* and *Shias*, which we shall explore in source 49. The schism between these two branches has often been bitter and violent, as events in contemporary Iraq and other nations of the Islamic Middle East bear witness.

For every act of animosity, however, one can find many instances of understanding and solidarity binding together members of the various factions of Islam. Certainly the centrality of the Quran in the life of every practicing Muslim, regardless of sect, plays a large role in this regard. So also does the fact that almost all Muslims accept as basic religious obligations the Five Pillars of Islam: affirmation of the Oneness of God and Muhammad as His Messenger; prayer five times daily; almsgiving (*zakat*); fasting during the month of Ramadan; and pilgrimage to Mecca. Of these, the *hajj*, or pilgrimage to Mecca, has served as the single most important vehicle for bringing Muslims of every identity together in a common religious exercise of transcendental importance. Source 50 provides further insight into the ways in which the hajj has helped unify Muslims from all corners of the umma.

Two major purposes behind the hajj are reconciliatory: to reconcile Muslims with God and with one another. Another phenomenon within Islam that has served these same ends is *Sufi* mysticism. Sunnis and Shias alike have had and continue to have their Sufi saints, and despite sectarian differences, both sets of Sufi teachers have preached the primacy of love. Source 51 introduces us to the great thirteenth-century Sufi mystic, *al-Rumi*, a poet whose voice is as alive today as it was seven centuries ago.

God's Martyrs: The Party of Ali

▼▼▼

49 ▾ *Ibn Babawayh al-Saduq,* CREED CONCERNING THE IMAMS

The Six Authentic Compilations preserve traditions sacred to *Sunni* Muslims, who claim to follow the correct path (*sunna*) of tradition as it evolved from the day of the Prophet and his Companions to the present. Underlying the Sunni self-image is the belief that God's community cannot fall into error. Consequently, the practices and institutions of mainstream Islam are always correct. Another major faction of Islam, which claims its own Hadith as the authentic record of the words and actions of the Prophet and his closest Companions, is the *Shiat Ali* (Party of Ali). Members of this branch of Islam, known popularly as *Shias*, today comprise almost all of Iran's population, are the overwhelming majority in Iraq, and also inhabit portions of Syria, Lebanon, and the Indian subcontinent.

The Shia break with other Muslims dates back to the mid seventh century. Partisans of Ali, Muhammad's cousin and son-in-law, managed to have him installed as fourth caliph (r. 656–661) following the murder of Caliph Uthman (r. 644–656). Many of Uthman's followers did not recognize Ali, however, and civil war ensued. The result was Ali's assassination in 661, establishment of the rival *Umayyad Dynasty* in the caliphate (r. 661–750), and the martyrdom of Ali's son, *al-Husayn*, the Prophet's sole surviving grandson, in 680 at the Battle of Karbala in Iraq. Supporters of the family of Ali, who included many of the original Muslims of the first Islamic community at Medina, refused to accept the Umayyads as rightful successors of the Prophet. Following the patriarchal traditions of the desert, they claimed that only a member of Muhammad's family could succeed him as *imam*, or religious leader, of Islam. The result was a schism in Islam, and to this day, the twice-yearly pilgrimage of Shias to al-Husayn's tomb and shrine at Karbala is marked by sorrow and penance.

Often persecuted as religious dissidents and driven underground, the Shias evolved a theology of history. They traced the rightful succession of leadership over the community of Islam from Muhammad and Ali through a number of subsequent imams, whom the Sunnis did not accept as legitimate, and they also developed the notion of a messianic *hidden imam*, or *Mahdi* (the Guided One). According to this religious vision, the imams who followed Muhammad were infallible and perfect teachers appointed by God, who spoke with the same authority as the Prophet. (To the contrary, Sunnis believe that divine revelation ended with Muhammad's death and that the caliphs were simply men — fallible deputies of the Prophet who ruled over the earthly umma.) For Shias, this line of earthly imams ended at an early point in time (here the various Shia sects disagree as to who was the last visible imam). The imamate, however, was not destroyed. Rather, the last visible imam had, through the power of God, withdrawn from human sight into a state of *occultation*, or spiritual concealment. There he would remain until some future time when he would reappear as the Mahdi to gather his faithful, persecuted followers around him, usher in an Islamic holy age, and herald the Last Judgment.

The largest of all Shia sects is the *Twelver Shia*, which developed around the year 900. These Shias, who predominate in Iran, accept a line of twelve infallible imams, divinely appointed from birth, and believe that the twelfth and last of these visible imams disappeared in the late ninth century.

The following selection from the creed, or statement of belief, of Muhammad ibn Ali ibn Babawayh, known as *Sheik al-Saduq* (d. 991), one of the greatest of the early Twelver theologians, illustrates several major Twelver beliefs.

QUESTIONS FOR ANALYSIS

1. Who is Muhammad al-Qaim, and what will he accomplish?
2. What happened to the Prophet Muhammad and each of the first eleven imams?

3. What is *taqiya*, and why is it obligatory for a Shia? In what ways does a follower of the imams follow the model of al-Qaim by practicing taqiya?
4. Can you find any suggestion that Shias believe they possess a secret religious truth denied to Sunnis? What is the source of the truth?
5. Shias are said to see themselves as the persecuted, righteous remnant of Islam. Is there any evidence to support such a conclusion in this document? Explain your answer.
6. Will this persecution end? If so, how?
7. How does al-Saduq view Sunnis? Please be specific.

It is necessary to believe that God did not create anything more excellent than Muhammad and the Imams. . . . After His Prophet,[1] the proofs of God for the people are the Twelve Imams. . . .

We believe that the Proof of Allah in His earth and His viceregent among His slaves in this age of ours is the Upholder [*al-Qaim*] [of the law of God], the Expected One, Muhammad ibn al-Hasan al-Askari.[2] He it is concerning whose name and descent the Prophet was informed by God, and he it is WHO WILL FILL THE EARTH WITH JUSTICE AND EQUITY JUST AS IT IS NOW FULL OF OPPRESSION AND WRONG. He it is whom God will make victorious over the whole world until from every place the call to prayer is heard and religion will belong entirely to God, exalted be He. He is the rightly guided *Mahdi* about whom the prophet gave information that when he appears, Jesus, son of Mary, will descend upon the earth and pray behind him.[3] We believe there can be no other *Qaim* than him; he may live in the state of occultation[4] (as long as he likes); were it the space of the existence of this world, there would be no *Qaim* other than him.

Our belief concerning prophets, apostles, Imams, and angels is that they are infallible . . . and do not commit any sin, minor or major. . . . [H]e who denies infallibility to them in any matter . . . is a *kafir*, an infidel. . . .

Our belief concerning the Prophet [Muhammad] is that he was poisoned by Jews during the expedition to Khaybar. The poison continued to be noxious until he died of its effects.

1. Imam: And the Prince of Believers [Ali], on whom be peace, was murdered by . . . Ibn Muljam al-Muradi, may God curse him, and was buried in Ghari.
2. Imam: Hasan ibn Ali,[5] on whom be peace, was poisoned by his wife Jada bint Ashath of Kinda, may God curse her and her father.
3. Imam: Husayn ibn Ali[6] was slain at Karbala. His murderer was Sinan ibn-Anal al-Nakhai, may God curse him and his father. . . .

▷   Al-Saduq then lists the fourth through eleventh imams and identifies the murderer of each.

And verily the Prophet and Imams, on whom be peace, had informed the people that they would be murdered. He who says that they were not has given them the lie and has imputed falsehood to God the Mighty and Glorious.

Our belief concerning *taqiya* [permissible dissimulation of one's true beliefs] is that it is obligatory, and he who forsakes it is in the same position as he who forsakes prayer. . . . Now until the time when the Imam al-Qaim appears,

---

[1]The Prophet Muhammad.
[2]The twelfth imam. Al-Hasan al-Askari, the eleventh imam, died around January 1, 874. Twelvers believe that he was succeeded by a young son, Muhammad ibn (son of) al-Hasan al-Askari, known as *al-Qaim* (the Upholder [of God's Law]), who went into concealment around 878.

[3]Sunni and Shia Muslims believe that the return to Earth in Jerusalem of the prophet and Messiah Jesus will signal the Last Judgment.
[4]Invisible to earthly eyes.
[5]Hasan, the elder son of Ali and Fatima, the Prophet's daughter and sole surviving offspring.
[6]Al-Husayn, Ali and Fatima's younger son.

taqiya is obligatory and it is not permissible to dispense with it. He who does . . . has verily gone out of the religion of God. And God has described the showing of friendship to unbelievers as being possible only in the state of *taqiya*.

And the Imam Jafar[7] said, "Mix with enemies openly but oppose them inwardly, so long as authority is a matter of question."[8] . . . And he said, "He who prays with hypocrites [Sunnis], standing in the first row, it is as though he prayed with the Prophet standing in the first row." And he said, "Visit their sick and attend their funerals and pray in their mosques." . . .

Our belief concerning the Alawiya [descendants of Ali] is that they are the progeny of the Messenger of God and devotion to them is obligatory.

---

[7]The sixth imam.

[8]As long as there are Sunni rulers.

An African Pilgrim to Mecca
▼▼▼

50 ▼ *Mahmud Kati,*
THE CHRONICLE OF THE SEEKER

Despite differences, all Muslims accept certain basic beliefs, such as the Oneness of God, and perform a number of common religious obligations that serve as powerful forces for Islamic unification. Among them is the pilgrimage, or *hajj*, to Mecca. Every Muslim adult is expected, unless it is impossible, to travel once in a lifetime to Mecca, arriving during the sacred month of *Dhu-al-Hijja*, and join a vast multitude of other pilgrims in a mass celebration of devotional activities. Here Muslims of all sects, races, and social levels mingle without distinction and join in affirming the unity of the family of Islam.

The following document describes the famous pilgrimage that Mansa (King) Musa (Moses) of Mali (r. 1312–1327) made to Mecca in 1324–1325. The sheer size of Mansa Musa's entourage and the generosity this king of sub-Saharan West Africa exhibited to Muslims along the route guaranteed that the memory of his pilgrimage would not be lost. Several written accounts exist. This particular record is ascribed to the family of Mahmud Kati (1468?–1593), a scholar and Islamic judge of Timbuktu. Kati, who according to tradition lived for 125 years, began to compose his history around 1519 and continued it until his death almost 75 years later. His sons and grandsons carried on his labors, bringing the story of Islam in West Africa down to 1655. As was the case with all contemporary writers in that region of the world, Kati and his family composed the work in Arabic.

QUESTIONS FOR ANALYSIS

1. What does Mansa Musa's alleged reason for undertaking the pilgrimage suggest about the hajj and pilgrimages in general?
2. How did his going on pilgrimage make Mansa Musa a better Muslim? What does this suggest about the role of hajj?
3. Is there any evidence in this story to suggest that Islam, though a world religion, still retained strong Arabic connections and flavor? Please explain your answer.

4. What impact did Mansa Musa's hajj have on the traditions and shared historical memory of Mali?
5. What role did oral tradition apparently play in sub-Saharan West African society?

We shall now relate some of what we have been able to discover about the history of the Mali-koy Kankan Musa.[1]

This Mali-koy was an upright, godly, and devout sultan.[2] His dominion stretched from the limits of Mali as far as Sibiridugu, and all the peoples in these lands, Songhay[3] and others, obeyed him. Among the signs of his virtue are that he used to emancipate a slave every day, that he made the pilgrimage to the sacred house of God,[4] and that in the course of his pilgrimage he built the great mosque of Timbuktu[5] as well as the mosques of Dukurey, Gundam, Direy, Wanko, and Bako.

His mother Kankan was a native woman, though some say she was of Arab origin. The cause of his pilgrimage was related to me as follows by the scholar Muhammad Quma, may God have mercy on him, who had memorized the traditions of the ancients. He said that the Mali-koy Kankan Musa had killed his mother, Nana Kankan, by mistake. For this he felt deep regret and remorse and feared retribution. In expiation he gave great sums of money in alms and resolved on a life-long fast.

He asked one of the ulama[6] of his time what he could do to expiate this terrible crime, and he replied, "You should seek refuge with the Prophet of God, may God bless and save him. Flee to him, place yourself under his protection, and ask him to intercede for you with God, and

God will accept his intercession. That is my view."

Kankan Musa made up his mind that very day and began to collect the money and equipment needed for the journey. He sent proclamations to all parts of his realm asking for supplies and support and went to one of his shaykhs[7] and asked him to choose the day of his departure. "You should wait," said the shaykh, "for the Saturday which falls on the twelfth day of the month. Set forth on that day, and you will not die before you return safe and sound to your residence, please God."

He therefore delayed and waited until these two coincided, and it was not until nine months later that the twelfth of the month fell on a Saturday. He set forth when the head of his caravan had already reached Timbuktu, while he himself was still in his residence in Mali.

Since that time travelers of that people believe it is lucky to set out on a journey on a Saturday which falls on the twelfth of a month. It has become proverbial that when a traveler returns in a bad state, they say of him, "Here is one who did not set out on the Mali-koy's Saturday of departure!"

Kankan Musa set out in force, with much money and a numerous army. A scholar told me that he heard from our shaykh, the very learned qadi[8] Abul-Abbas Sidi Ahmad ibn Ahmad ibn Anda-ag-Muhammad, may God have mercy on

---

[1] Titles meaning "King of Mali, Lord Musa."
[2] An Arabic term meaning "one who wields authority."
[3] Songhay lay to the east of Mali and centered on the trading city of Gao. Mansa Musa's armies conquered Gao around 1325, and Mali maintained control over Songhay until about 1375. By the late fifteenth century, Songhay had replaced Mali as West Africa's major sub Saharan trading kingdom and held this position of primacy until it was conquered in 1591 by invaders from Morocco.
[4] The *Kaaba* in Mecca, Islam's holiest site. See source 47.

[5] Timbuktu was the major trading city of the kingdom of Mali from 1325 to 1433. Its madrasa, or mosque school, became the chief center of Islamic learning in sub-Saharan West Africa.
[6] A term that means "the Learned." Islam has no priests, but, very much like Rabbinical Judaism, its religious authorities attain and hold their position by virtue of their learning.
[7] An Arabic title of respect meaning "elder."
[8] An Islamic judge who interprets and administers Sharia.

him and be pleased with him, that on the day when the pasha[9] Ali ibn al-Qadir[10] left for Twat, announcing that he was going on the pilgrimage to Mecca, he asked how many persons were going with him and was told that the total number of armed men the pasha had with him was about eighty. "God is great! Praise be to God!," said the qadi. "Everything in the world grows less. When Kankan Musa left here to go on pilgrimage he had with him 8,000 men. The Askia Muhammad[11] made the pilgrimage later with 800 men, that is, one-tenth of that. Third after them came Ali ibn Abd al-Qadir, with 80 men, one-tenth of 800." And he added, "Praise be to God, other than Whom there is no God! Ali ibn Abd al-Qadir did not even achieve his purpose."

Kankan Musa went on his journey, about which there are many stories. Most of them are untrue and the mind refuses to accept them. One such story is that in every town where he stopped on Friday between here and Egypt he built a mosque on that very day. It is said that the mosques of Gundam and Dukurey were among those he built. Both at lunch and at dinner, from when he left his residence until he returned, he ate fresh fish and fresh vegetables.

I was told that his wife, called Inari Konte, went with him, accompanied by 500 of her women and serving women.

Our shaykh, the Mori Bukar ibn Salih, . . . may God have mercy on him, told me that Kankan Musa took forty mule-loads of gold with him when he went on his pilgrimage and visited the tomb of the Prophet.[12]

It is said that he asked the Shaykh of the noble and holy city of Mecca, may Almighty God protect it, to give him two, three, or four *sharifs*[13] of the kin of the Prophet of God, may God bless him and save him, to go with him to his country, so that the people of these parts might be blessed by the sight of them and by the blessing of their footsteps in these lands. But the shaykh refused, it being generally agreed that such things should be prevented and refused out of respect and regard for the noble blood of the *sharifs* and for fear lest one of them fall into the hands of the infidels and be lost or go astray. But he persisted in his request and urged them very strongly, until the shaykh said, "I will not do it, but I will neither command nor forbid it. If anyone wishes, let him follow you. His fate is in his own hands, I am not responsible."

The Mali-koy then sent a crier to the mosques to say, "Whoever wishes to have a thousand *mithqals*[14] of gold, let him follow me to my country, and the thousand is ready for him." Four men of the tribe of Quraysh[15] came to him, but it is claimed that they were freedmen[16] of Quraysh and not real Qurayshis. He gave them 4,000, 1,000 each,[17] and they followed him, with their families, when he returned to his country.

When the Mali-koy reached Timbuktu on his way back, he collected ships and small boats on which he transported their families and luggage, together with his own women, as far as his country, for the riding animals were too exhausted to use. When the ships, carrying the *sharifs* from Mecca, reached the town of Kami, the Dienne-koy[18] . . . attacked the ships and plundered all that they contained. They took the *sharifs* ashore and revolted against the Mali-koy. But when the people of the ships told them about the *sharifs* and informed them of their high station, they attended them, and installed them in a nearby place called Shinshin. It is said that the *sharifs* of the town of Kay are descended from them.

---

[9]A Turkish title meaning "chief."
[10]Governor of Timbuktu, 1628–1632.
[11]Askia (Emperor) Muhammad Ture the Great (r. 1492–1528), Lord of Songhay. The askia undertook his pilgrimage in 1495–1496, accompanied by Mahmud Kati, who was one of his chief advisors.
[12]The Prophet's tomb is in Medina.
[13]An Arabic title meaning "exalted one."

[14]A weight of precious metal that varied by region.
[15]The tribe of the Prophet.
[16]Freed former slaves, therefore Qurayshis by adoption, not birth.
[17]He gave each of four men 1,000 mithqals of gold.
[18]The lord of Dienne, technically one of Mansa Musa's vassals.

This is the end of the story of the pilgrimage of the Mali-koy Kankan Musa. . . .

As for Mali, it is a vast region and an immense country, containing many towns and villages. The authority of the Sultan of Mali extends over all with force and might. We have heard the common people of our time say that there are four sultans in the world, not counting the supreme sultan,[19] and they are the Sultan of Baghdad,[20] the Sultan of Egypt, the Sultan of Bornu,[21] and the Sultan of Mali.

---

[19]The Ottoman sultan of Constantinople. As early as the reign of Mehmed II (r. 1451–1481), the Ottoman sultans occasionally used the title "caliph," thereby claiming supremacy over the Community of Islam (see source 49).

[20]The last Abbasid caliph of Baghdad died in 1258.

[21]A West African trading rival of Songhay located in the region of Lake Chad, along the border of present-day Chad and Nigeria.

The Sufi Jihad

▼▼▼

51 ▼ *Jalaluddin al-Rumi, SPIRITUAL COUPLETS*

Islam enjoins all its faithful to live a life centered on God. Those who have taken this injunction most literally, to the point of seeking mystical union with the Divine, are known as *Sufis*. The term might derive from the rough wool (*suf*) clothes worn by many Sufis; it could also refer to the reputed purity (*safa*) of their lives. Whatever the origin of their name, Sufis have been an important force within Islam from its early days.

Despite their emphasis on interior spirituality, Sufis accept the dogmas, rituals, traditions, and practices of Islam, all of which emphasize a balanced, moderate life and worship within a community of believers. This means that although Sufis form themselves into religious brotherhoods, or orders, devoted to prayer and study, most opt not to cut themselves off from the world. Rather, after initiation into an order, most Sufis return to the world to marry, earn a livelihood, and serve the community. At the same time, the movement has produced numerous saints and teachers who have given their entire lives to finding God and leading all who would listen to that Divine Reality. While alive, these Sufi masters have enjoyed widespread popularity among the masses, and in death their tombs serve as sites of pilgrimage.

One of the most popular Sufi pilgrimage sites for more than 700 years has been the mausoleum raised over the body of *Mevlana Jalaluddin al-Rumi* (1207–1273) in Konya, a city in Turkey. *Al-Rumi*, as he is generally known in the West, has enjoyed widespread popularity outside of the Islamic World during the past half century because of his poetry, which has been translated out of Persian into a wide variety of modern languages. Sufism has produced many great poets, but none is more beloved than al-Rumi, whose passionate, even eccentric style of ecstatic lyricism has struck respondent chords in millions of Muslims and non-Muslims alike.

Born in Balkh, Afghanistan, the son of a renowned religious teacher, the young Jalaluddin (Keeper of the Faith) left in advance of the Mongol destruction of the city. After wandering from city to city for sixteen years, during which time Jalaluddin married, the young man and his father reached Konya in 1226, where they settled down for life. Konya, the capital of the Seljuk Turkish state of Rum (Rome), so called because it was carved out of Anatolian lands that had once been part of the East Roman, or Byzantine, Empire, gave Jalaluddin not only a home but also an identity. He became al-Rumi, "the man from Rum."

Thirteenth-century Konya was a richly cosmopolitan city, with a large Jewish community and a Christian population that outnumbered its resident Muslims. Under its Turkish sultan, the city was also noted for its arts, letters, and religious scholarship. For two years, until his death in 1228, Jalaluddin's father served as the city's leading Islamic teacher. Upon his father's death, the young Jalaluddin continued his studies for an additional eleven years, until, at the age of thirty-two, he was ready to take his place as Konya's preeminent religious teacher. As such, he earned the title *Mevlana* (Our Master).

During the years that followed, until his death on December 17, 1273, al-Rumi wrote and taught prolifically, becoming his city's most revered figure, honored in life and mourned in death by Muslims, Jews, and Christians alike. His brand of Sufi mysticism inspired the founding of the *Mevlevi Order of Sufis*, which takes its name from his honorific title — Mevlana. Today this order is popularly known in the West as the Whirling Dervishes. The term *dervish* is a Turkish variant of the Persian word *darvish*, which means "the sill of a door" and is used to describe someone on the threshold of reaching God. The term *whirling* refers to this brotherhood's distinctive devotional dance, in which members whirl about rhythmically to the accompaniment of music while they utter over and over in prayer the name "Allah." Through this dance and prayer, they reach a state of transcendence whereby, they believe, they are able to leave behind all earthly concerns and to touch the Divine.

What follows is an excerpt from al-Rumi's greatest literary achievement, the *Masnavi* (*Spiritual Couplets*), a massive work in six books that contains more than 25,000 rhymed couplets. In source 48, we saw a twelfth-century legal commentary on rules governing Jihad of the Sword. In this excerpt, al-Rumi takes a well-known hadith, which states that following a battle the Prophet informed his followers that they were returning from the Lesser Jihad to the Greater Jihad, and uses it as a launching point for his exploration of the Muslim's true victory.

QUESTIONS FOR ANALYSIS

1. *Jihad* means "struggle." What struggle does al-Rumi celebrate here?
2. How is victory achieved in that struggle?
3. Compose a commentary by a Sufi follower of al-Rumi on one of the following: Ibn Ishaq's treatment of the Prophet's Night Journey; Ibn Rushd's commentary on jihad; al-Saduq's treatise on the Shia.
4. Sufis proved to be effective messengers of Islam in India after around the year 1000. What was there about Sufis and their approach to religion that might have made it easy for some Indians to convert to Islam?

Commentary on (the Tradition) "We have returned from the lesser Jihad to the greater Jihad."

O kings, we have slain the outward enemy; there remains within a worse enemy than he.

To slay this is not the work of reason and intelligence: the inward lion is not subdued by the hare.

This carnal self is Hell, and Hell is a dragon {the fire of} which is not diminished by oceans.

It would drink up the Seven Seas, and still the blazing of that consumer of all creatures would not become less.

Stones and stony-hearted infidels enter it, miserable and shamefaced,

Still it is not appeased by all this food, until there comes to it from God this call —

"Art thou filled, art thou filled?" It says, "Not yet; lo, here is the fire, here is the glow, here is the burning!"

It made a mouthful of and swallowed a whole world, its belly crying aloud, "*Is there any more?*"

God, from where place is not, sets His foot on it: then it subsides at [the command] *Be, and it was.*

Inasmuch as this self of ours is a part of Hell, and all parts have the nature of the whole,

To God (alone) belongs this foot[1] to kill it: who, indeed, but God should draw its bow [vanquish it]?

Only the straight arrow is put on the bow; this bow [of the self] has arrows bent back and crooked.

Be straight, like an arrow, and escape from the bow, for without doubt every straight [arrow] will fly from the bow [to its mark].

When I turned back from the outer warfare, I set my face towards the inner warfare.

We have returned from the lesser Jihad, we are engaged along with the Prophet in the greater Jihad.

I pray God to grant me strength and aid and [the right of] boasting,[2] that I may root up with a needle[3] this mountain of Qaf.[4]

Deem of small account the lion who breaks the ranks [of the enemy]: the [true] lion is he that breaks himself.

---

[1]Power.
[2]Success that entitles me to boast that I have conquered.

[3]Slowly and painfully.
[4]A mythical mountain that encircles the world.

Multiple Voices V   ▼▼▼
Islam and Unbelievers

BACKGROUND

The Quran reminds Muslims of the heritage that they share with *People of the Book*. Yet it also threatens eternal hellfire for all who perversely refuse to become Muslims. For those who embrace Islam, there is God's peace because they reside in *Dar al-Islam*, the *House of Submission* (or Peace). Yet Hadith also enjoins jihad, or holy struggle, against unbelievers who do not belong to that community but who reside, rather, in *Dar al-Harb*, the *House of Chaos* (or War), namely lands that have not accepted the rule of Islam. Most classical Islamic jurists from the late eighth century onward agreed that while there might be momentary truces between Muslims and those who reside in the House of Chaos, the two Houses could never be permanently at peace with each other.

But what about unbelievers, or *infidels*, who submit to Islam's secular authority but remain outside of the community of Muslim faithful? How should and, more important, *did* Islamic rulers deal with their non-Muslim subjects, both People of the Book and those outside of the Judeo-Christian tradition?

The Quran expressly forbids forced conversion, and the Prophet's actions underscored that prohibition. In 628 Muhammad entered into a contract, or *dhimma*, with an Arabic Jewish tribe at the oasis of Khaybar, whereby he guaranteed to defend them and to respect their religious practices in return for their submission, assistance, and payment of tribute. This contract of protection became the paradigm for Islam's generals and statesmen as Arab armies exploded out of the peninsula, but the manner in which Muslims understood and applied the dhimma differed from age to age, place to place, and ruler to ruler. The following documents show us varieties of the dhimma and also reflect some of the ways that the pact tended to change over time.

THE SOURCES

The first document records a pact of peace offered to the Christian inhabitants of the city of Tiflis (present-day Tbilisi in Georgia) around 653 by Habib ibn Muslama (617–662), the military commander responsible for the conquest of the region between the Black and Caspian seas south of the Caucasus Mountains. This pact with the Christians of Tiflis is a good example of the earliest form of the dhimma.

The second document purports to be the pact of peace offered by Caliph Umar I (r. 634–644) to the Christians of Syria around 637, but it is a later creation, crafted probably in the early ninth century when the new Abbasid Dynasty of caliphs (r. 750–1258) was occupied with crushing local revolts and needed historical support for policies that were more repressive than those of the earlier Umayyad caliphs (r. 661–750).

However their pacts of protection might differ, the non-Muslims who lived under these compacts were known as *dhimmis* and paid a *jizya*, or poll tax (a tax levied on persons rather than on property), as a token of their submission to the authority of Islam.

The third document is the account of Benjamin ben Jonah of Tudela. Around 1159 he departed his native northern Spain and spent the next thirteen or fourteen years visiting Jewish communities possibly as far east as India, seeking to discover places where Jews lived in peace and prospered.

In this excerpt Benjamin describes the quality of life for Jews under Islamic rule in Baghdad, the capital of the Abbasid caliphate. Despite what Benjamin implies, the twelfth-century caliphs exercised no real civil or military power, having surrendered those powers in the eleventh century to a variety of *sultans* and other so-called subordinates. What is more, the lands that owed the caliphs even nominal obedience had shrunk dramatically in number and size from the days of Abbasid greatness in the early ninth century. By exaggerating the position of the caliph, Benjamin might have also exaggerated the position of the *Exilarch* (the leader of the Jewish Community in Exile). Benjamin's book of travels falls into a special genre of Jewish writing known as *consolation literature*. His purpose was to offer his coreligionists the consolation of hope by showing them that, regardless of the Diaspora, the Jewish people prospered because they remained faithful to the Covenant. Given such faithful service, the day of their return to Israel was not far away. If he wanted to highlight Jewish prosperity and strict adherence to the Law, where would be a better place than in the capital of Islam?

This purpose and the possible exaggerations that followed from it do not mean that Benjamin's account is so distorted as to be worthless. Other portions of his book strongly suggest that he attempted to give a true account of Jewish fortunes as he discovered them. He noted that the Jewish community of Christian Constantinople suffered constant public humiliation from the city's inhabitants. Presumably he visited both Constantinople and Baghdad and was able to compare the relative situations of the Jewish populations in these two imperial capitals — the two richest cities in the world, according to Benjamin.

As the armies of Islam moved out of Arabia, they came into contact with cultures that practiced religions other than Judaism and Christianity, such as Zoroastrianism and Buddhism in Iran and Hinduism and Buddhism in India. Around the year 1000, Turkish Muslims out of Afghanistan began pushing into northwest India, where they set up a base of operations in Lahore (in present-day Pakistan). Around the year 1200, another Islamic-Turkish group of warlords, also out of Afghanistan, swept through north-central India. In the course of the next 150 years, this second wave of Turks established the *Sultanate of Delhi*. At its height in the early fourteenth century, this Islamic state controlled, in varying degrees, almost the entire Indian subcontinent, except for the southernmost areas.

Firuz Shah Tughluq, who reigned from 1351 to 1388, enjoyed the reputation of being the most pious, humane, and generous of the sultans of Delhi. Toward the end of his life, he prepared an account of the accomplishments in which he took the greatest pride. In our excerpts from that account, he details the manner in which he carried out his duties toward his subjects, of whom only a minority were Muslims.

QUESTIONS FOR ANALYSIS

1. When the armies of Islam initially conquered regions that formerly had been part of the Sassanian and Roman empires, Muslims were a small minority in seas of Christians, Jews, and Zoroastrians. Over the centuries that followed, large numbers of non-Muslims converted to Islam. What evidence is there in the two pacts, or dhimmas, to support the first statement and to help explain the second?
2. The introduction to Benjamin of Tudela's account suggests that Benjamin might have had reason to exaggerate the position and status of the Jews of Baghdad. Which elements in his account strike you as believable? Which strike you as unbelievable or suspicious? In addressing these two questions, analyze Benjamin's account in light of the other three sources.
3. Compare Firuz Shah's treatment of Hindus with the way in which he dealt with Shias. What conclusions follow from this analysis?
4. Compose an essay on the issue "Islam and Its Dhimmis over the Centuries." Always cite specific evidence to support your conclusions, and do not neglect to consider the ambiguities, tones of gray, and complexities of this or any other historical phenomenon.

I ▾ THE PACT OF IBN MUSLAMA

In the name of Allah, the compassionate, the merciful. This is a statement from Habib ibn-Muslama to the inhabitants of Tiflis, . . . securing them safety for their lives, churches, convents,[1] religious services and faith, provided they acknowledge their humiliation and pay tax to the amount of one *dinar* on every household.[2] You are not to combine more than one household into one in order to reduce the tax, nor are we to divide the same household into more than one in order to increase it. You owe us counsel and support against the enemies of Allah and his Prophet to the utmost of your ability, and are bound to entertain the needy Muslim for one night and provide him with that food used by "the people of the Book" and which it is legal for us to partake of.[3] If a Muslim is cut off from his companions and falls into your hands, you are bound to deliver him to the nearest body of the "Believers," unless something stands in the way. If you return to the obedience of Allah and observe prayer, you are our brethren in faith, otherwise poll-tax is incumbent on you. In case an enemy of yours attacks and subjugates you while the Muslims are too busy to come to your aid, the Muslims are not held responsible, nor is it a violation of the covenant with you. The above are your rights and obligations to which Allah and his angels are witness and it is sufficient to have Allah for witness.

[1]Places that house religious communities, such as monks.
[2]The *jizya*.
[3]Islam prohibits the consumption of certain foods and drink, most notably pork and alcohol.

2 ▾ THE PACT OF UMAR

In the name of God, the Merciful, the Compassionate! This is a writing to Umar from the Christians of *such and such a city*. When you[1] marched against us,[2] we asked of you protection for ourselves, our posterity, and our co-religionists; and we made this stipulation with you that we will not erect in our city or the suburbs any new monastery, church, cell, or hermitage;[3] that we will not repair any of such buildings that might fall into ruins, or renew those that might be situated in the Muslim quarters of the town; that we will not refuse the Muslims entry into our churches either by night or by day; that we will open the gates wide to passengers and travelers; that we will receive any Muslim traveler into our houses and give him food and lodging for three nights; that we will not harbor any spy in our churches or houses or conceal any enemy of the Muslims.

That we will not teach our children the Quran; that we will not make a show of the Christian religion or invite anyone to embrace it; that we will not prevent any of our kinsmen from embracing Islam, if they so desire. That we will honor the Muslims and rise up in our assemblies when they wish to take their seats; that we will not imitate them in our dress, either in the cap, turban, sandals, or parting of the hair; that we will not make use of their expressions of speech[4] or adopt their surnames; that we will not ride on saddles or gird on swords or take to ourselves arms or wear them or engrave Arabic inscriptions on our rings; that we will not sell wine; that we will shave the front of our heads; that we will keep to our own style of dress, wherever we might be; that we will wear belts around our waists.[5]

That we will not display the cross[6] upon our churches or display our crosses or our sacred books in the streets of the Muslims or in their marketplaces; that we will strike the clappers in our churches lightly;[7] that we will not recite our services in a loud voice when a Muslim is present; that we will not carry palm-branches[8] or our images in procession in the streets; that at the burial of our dead we will not chant loudly or carry lighted candles in the streets of the Muslims or their marketplaces; that we will not take any slaves who have already been in the possession of Muslims or spy into their houses; and that we will not strike any Muslim.

All this we promise to observe, on behalf of ourselves and our co-religionists, and receive protection from you in exchange; and if we violate any of the conditions of this agreement, then we forfeit your protection and you are at liberty to treat us as enemies and rebels.

---

[1]Muslims.

[2]The Christians of Syria.

[3]The dwelling of a Christian hermit or monk.

[4]Muslims greet one another with certain quranic verses and other affirmations of their faith.

[5]Dhimmis wore leather or cord belts; Muslims wore silk and other types of cloth belts.

[6]Although they greatly revere Jesus as the Messiah, Muslims deny he died on the cross.

[7]Christian churches could not ring bells; the faithful were summoned to prayer by wooden clappers.

[8]On Palm Sunday, the Sunday that precedes Easter. This public procession commemorates Jesus' triumphal entry into Jerusalem.

3 ▼ Benjamin of Tudela, BOOK OF TRAVELS

Baghdad [is] . . . the royal residence of the Caliph Emir al-Muminin al-Abbasi[1] of the family of Muhammad.[2] He is at the head of the Muslim religion, and all the kings of Islam obey him; he occupies a similar position to that held by the pope over the Christians.[3] . . . [H]e is kind unto Israel, and many belonging to the people of Israel are his attendants; he knows all languages, and is well versed in the Law of Israel. He reads and writes the holy language [Hebrew]. . . . He is truthful and trusty, speaking peace to all men. . . .

In Baghdad there are about forty thousand Jews, and they dwell in security, prosperity, and honor under the great Caliph, and among them are great sages, the heads of Academies engaged in the study of the Law.[4] In this city there are ten Academies. . . . And at the head of them all is Daniel the son of Hisdai, who is styled "Our Lord the Head of the Captivity of all Israel." He possesses a book of pedigrees going back as far as David, King of Israel.[5] The Jews call him "Our Lord, Head of the Captivity," and the Muslims call him "Saidna ben Daoud,"[6] and he has been invested with authority over all the congregations of Israel at the hands of the Emir al-Muminin, the Lord of Islam. For thus Muhammad[7] commanded concerning him and his descendants; and he granted him a seal of office over all

the congregations that dwell under his rule, and ordered that every one, whether Muslim or Jew, or belonging to any other nation in his dominion, should rise up before him and salute him, and that any one who should refuse to rise up should receive one hundred stripes.[8]

And every fifth day when he goes to pay a visit to the great Caliph, horsemen, gentiles as well as Jews, escort him, and heralds proclaim in advance, "Make way before our Lord, the son of David, as is due unto him." . . . He is mounted on a horse, and is attired in robes of silk and embroidery with a large turban on his head. . . . Then he appears before the Caliph and kisses his hand, and the Caliph rises and places him on a throne which Muhammad had ordered to be made for him, and all the Muslim princes who attend the court of the Caliph rise up before him. And the Head of the Captivity is seated on his throne opposite to the Caliph, in compliance. . . . The authority of the Head of the Captivity extends over all the communities of Shinar,[9] Persia, Khurasan[10] and Sheba which is El-Yemen,[11] and Diyar Kalach[12] and the land of Aram Naharaim,[13] and over the dwellers in the mountains of Ararat[14] and the land of the Alans.[15] . . . His authority extends also over the land of Siberia,[16] and the communities in the land of the Togarmim[17] unto the mountains of Asveh and the

[1]Also known as *al-Mustanjid* (r. 1160–1170).
[2]The Abbasids claimed descent from the Prophet's uncle Abbas.
[3]The bishop of Rome who served as head of the Latin Christian Church in the West. See Chapter 10.
[4]Academies for the study of Scripture and the Talmud (source 37). These scholars served as the rabbis, or religious teachers and judges, of their community.
[5]King of Israel around 1000 B.C.E.
[6]The Lord son of David.
[7]Not the Prophet Muhammad but possibly al-Abbasi's predecessor, Muhammad el-Moktafi.
[8]A public flogging in which the person receives 100 blows.
[9]Southern Mesopotamia (ancient Sumer and Akkad).
[10]Northeastern Iran.

[11]Southern Arabia, the presumed land of the tenth-century B.C.E. queen of Sheba, who visited Israel's King Solomon (the Bible, 1 Kings 10:1–13).
[12]Anatolia (present-day Asian Turkey).
[13]Northern Mesopotamia (present-day northern Syria).
[14]Armenia.
[15]An Indo-European people inhabiting the southern Caucasus Mountain region of Georgia.
[16]He probably means *Iberia*, not Siberia. If the reference is to Iberia, he does not mean the Iberian Peninsula, where the present-day nations of Spain and Portugal are located, but rather the land that today roughly corresponds to the nation of Georgia (source 43).
[17]One of a number of people of the central Euphrates in biblical times (the Bible, Genesis 10:3).

land of Gurgan, the inhabitants of which . . . follow the Christian religion.[18] Further it extends to the gates of Samarkand,[19] the land of Tibet, and the land of India. In respect of all these countries the Head of the Captivity gives the communities power to appoint Rabbis and Ministers who come unto him to be consecrated and to receive his authority. They bring him offerings and gifts from the ends of the earth. He owns hospices, gardens, and plantations in Babylon,[20] and much land inherited from his fathers, and no one can take his possessions from him by force. He has a fixed weekly revenue arising from the hospices of the Jews, the markets and the merchants, apart from that which is brought to him from far-off lands. The man is very rich, and wise in the Scriptures as well as in the Talmud,[21] and many Israelites dine at his table every day.

At his installation, the Head of the Captivity gives much money to the Caliph, to the Princes, and to the Ministers. On the day that the Caliph performs the ceremony of investing him with authority, he rides in the second of the royal carriages, and is escorted from the palace of the Caliph to his own house with timbrels and fifes. The Exilarch[22] appoints the Chiefs of the Academies by placing his hand upon their heads, thus installing them in their office. The Jews of the city are learned men and very rich.

In Baghdad there are twenty-eight Jewish Synagogues. . . . The great synagogue of the Head of the Captivity has columns of marble of various colors overlaid with silver and gold, and on these columns are sentences of the Psalms[23] in golden letters. And in front of the ark are about ten steps of marble; on the topmost step are the seats of the Head of the Captivity and of the Princes of the House of David.

[18]Apparently he means the African Christian civilizations of Nubia (present-day Sudan) and Ethiopia. Gihon was one of the four biblical rivers of the Garden of Eden and usually refers to the Nile. The Girgashites were one of the seven people who inhabited Canaan before its conquest by the Hebrews under Joshua.

[19]A major commercial city that today is located in Uzbekistan, in Central Asia.
[20]The region around Baghdad.
[21]See source 37.
[22]The ruler of the exile — Daniel, the son of Hisdai.
[23]Sacred hymns that constitute one of the books of the Bible.

4 ▾ *THE DEEDS OF SULTAN FIRUZ SHAH*

Praises without end, and infinite thanks to that merciful Creator who gave to me his poor abject creature Firuz. . . . His impulse for the maintenance of the laws of His religion, for the repression of heresy, the prevention of crime, and the prohibition of things forbidden; who gave me also a disposition for discharging my lawful duties and my moral obligations. . . . First I would praise Him because when irreligion and sins opposed to the Law prevailed in Hindustan,[1] and

men's habits and dispositions were inclined towards them, and were averse to the restraints of religion, He inspired me His humble servant with an earnest desire to repress irreligion and wickedness, so that I was able to labor diligently until with His blessing the vanities of the world, and things repugnant to religion, were set aside, and the true was distinguished from the false.

In the reigns of former kings[2] the blood of many Muslims had been shed, and many vari-

[1]The north-central region of India inhabited largely by Hindus.

[2]Muhammad ben Tughluq (r. 1325–1351), his predecessor, had been noted for his cruelty.

eties of torture employed. . . . The great and merciful God made me, His servant, hope and seek for His mercy by devoting myself to prevent the unlawful killing of Muslims, and the infliction of any kind of torture upon them or upon any men. . . .

By God's help I determined that the lives of Muslims and true believers should be in perfect immunity, and whoever transgressed the Law should receive the punishment prescribed by the book[3] and the decrees of judges. . . .

The sect of Shias . . . had endeavored to make proselytes.[4] They wrote treatises and books, and gave instruction and lectures upon the tenets of their sect, and traduced and reviled the first chiefs of our religion (on whom be the peace of God!). I seized them all and I convicted them of their errors and perversions. On the most zealous I inflicted punishment, and the rest I visited with censure and threats of public punishment. Their books I burnt in public, and so by the grace of God the influence of this sect was entirely suppressed. . . .

The Hindus and idol-worshipers had agreed to pay the money for toleration, and had consented to the poll tax, in return for which they and their families enjoyed security. These people now erected new idol temples in the city and the environs in opposition to the Law of the Prophet which declares that such temples are not to be tolerated. Under Divine guidance I destroyed these edifices, and I killed those leaders of infidelity who seduced others into error, and the lower orders I subjected to stripes and chastise-

ment, until this abuse was entirely abolished.[5] . . . I forbade the infliction of any severe punishment on the Hindus in general, but I destroyed their idol temples, and instead thereof raised mosques. . . . Where infidels and idolaters worshiped idols, Muslims now, by God's mercy, perform their devotions to the true God. Praises of God and the summons to prayer are now heard there, and that place which was formerly the home of infidels has become the habitation of the faithful, who there repeat their creed and offer up their praises to God. . . .

I encouraged my infidel subjects to embrace the religion of the Prophet, and I proclaimed that every one who repeated the creed[6] and became a Muslim should be exempt from the jizya, or poll-tax. Information of this came to the ears of the people at large, and great numbers of Hindus presented themselves, and were admitted to the honor of Islam. Thus they came forward day by day from every quarter, and, adopting the faith, were exonerated from the jizya, and were favored with presents and honors. . . .

My object in writing this book has been to express my gratitude to the All-bountiful God for the many and various blessings He has bestowed upon me. Secondly, that men who desire to be good and prosperous may read this and learn what is the proper course. There is this concise maxim, by observing which, a man may obtain God's guidance: Men will be judged according to their works, and rewarded for the good that they have done.

---

[3]Sharia according to the dictates of the Quran.
[4]Converts.
[5]Compare this with the *Pact of Umar*.

[6]"There is no god but *the* God; Muhammad is the Messenger of God."

Part Three

Continuity, Change, and Interchange: 500–1500

H INDUISM, BUDDHISM, CONFUCIANISM, imperial systems of government and bureaucracy, Christianity, and many other major world traditions were firmly in place by 500 C.E., and despite vicissitudes, they remained integral elements of global history for the next 1,000 years and beyond. The continuity of culture, especially in China and India, is one of the major features of the period 500–1500. A Chinese of the Han Dynasty would find much that was familiar in *Ming* China (1368–1644), and even while Islam was making a deep impact on northern India after 1000, Hindu culture continued to flourish and develop along lines that reached back at least to Indo-Aryan antiquity. At the same time, this millennium witnessed radical changes from which even the essentially conservative societies of China and India were not immune.

Many of the changes were a result of the movement and interchange of peoples. Germans and other fringe groups infiltrated the Roman Empire and became a major factor in the radical transformation of society in the empire's western regions. The rise and spread of Islam in the seventh and eighth centuries created a new cultural bloc that stretched from western North Africa and Spain to Central Asia. The later movements of Turkish and Mongol nomads out of Central Asia resulted in empires that severely strained but also richly cross-pollinated almost all of Eurasia's older civilized societies. Hindu, Chinese, and Arab merchants deeply influenced the development of civilization in Southeast Asia, their common meeting ground. It is almost impossible to exaggerate the impact that China had on the development of Korean and Japanese cultures, but regardless of their debts to China, both evolved distinctive cultures that were anything but slavish copies of Chinese civilization. The Byzantine World, centered on Constantinople, became the model and civilizer of Eastern and Southern Slavs, most notably the Russians and the Serbs. Western (or Latin) Christian Europe expanded into Ireland, Germany, Scandinavia, Iceland, Greenland, the lands of the Baltic Sea, Poland, and Hungary. It even established a brief presence in North America around the year 1000 and, more significantly, set up overseas colonies in the eastern Mediterranean and Black Sea during the Age of the Crusades. By 1500 Christianity, in its Latin and

Byzantine forms, provided spiritual direction to Europeans from Iceland to the Volga. Well before 1500, major portions of sub-Saharan Africa had become integral parts of the Islamic World, and toward the end of the fifteenth century, Europeans were making their presence known along the African coast.

Of all of Eurasia's civilizations, Western Europe underwent the most radical changes during this 1,000-year period. Out of the chaos that ensued following the collapse of Roman society in the West, a new civilization emerged: Western Christian Europe. By 1100 it was an aggressive, expansionistic power, as the crusades bear witness. Despite a number of crises in the fourteenth century, which occasioned a momentary retrenchment, Western Europe never abandoned its spirit of expansion. In 1492 it was ready to resume explorations across the Atlantic. One consequence of this transoceanic expansion was the virtual destruction of almost all Amerindian cultures and their absorption into the fabric of Western European civilization.

❖ Chapter 9 ❖

Asia
Change in the Context of Tradition

ASIA WAS HOME to the world's oldest and most complex civilizations, and as such, its deeply rooted cultures were the most tradition bound. Even Asia's newer civilizations, such as Japan, exhibited an innate conservatism, in part because they had borrowed so heavily from their well-established neighbors.

Change, of course, comes to all societies, old and new, and Asia was no exception. Occasionally, it arrived in dramatic fashion, as in the destruction of the Abbasid caliphate in 1258 or the establishment of the hated *Yuan* Dynasty (1264–1368) in China. More often than not, however, change arrived clothed in the guise of tradition. Even *Khublai Khan*, Mongol emperor of China (r. 1260–1294), adopted a Chinese name for his dynasty, performed the Confucian imperial rites, and tried to re-establish the civil service examination system. When in 1192 Minamoto Yoritomo (1147–1199) transferred all real political and military power to himself as *shogun*, he left Japan's imperial court and structure in place and allowed local lords to retain a good measure of their old feudal autonomy.

A reverence for tradition did not mean a lack of dynamism. The great urban centers of Asia — Baghdad, Cambay, Chang'an, Delhi, Hangzhou, Nara — were prosperous and cosmopolitan. China in the eleventh century had several cities with populations of a million or more, and the volume of commerce in those urban centers eventually necessitated the creation of imperially guaranteed paper money. Economic prosperity also meant artistic patronage, and as a result artistic expression flourished from Southwest Asia to Japan. As European travelers learned, the riches of Asia were no empty fable.

▼▼▼

Japan: Creating a Distinctive Civilization

Composed of four main islands, the Japanese archipelago's closest continental neighbor is Korea, which at its closest point is about 120 miles away across a stretch of often tempestuous water. This insularity has benefited Japan to the point that it is close enough to the East Asian mainland to receive the stimulation of foreign ideas but far enough away to be free to choose what it wished to adopt from abroad.

Around the end of the fourth century B.C.E., agriculture based on rice cultivation arrived in Japan from South China, probably by way of Korea. Given Korea's relative proximity, the peninsula proved to be a major conduit for cultural imports from mainland East Asia. Around 200 C.E. the Japanese were working iron, a Chinese process received from Korea. The Japanese were illiterate until, as the story goes, a Korean scribe arrived in 405 C.E. to offer instruction in Chinese script. The Japanese quickly adapted the script to their own language, which is unrelated to Chinese but distantly related to Korean. In the mid sixth century, a Chinese form of Mahayana Buddhism made its way to Japan from Korea, and in 646 it was officially acknowledged as the religion of the aristocracy. The coming of Buddhism sharpened the desire of Japan's leaders to adopt Chinese culture, and during the seventh and eighth centuries, the imperial court of Japan dispatched numerous sons of noblemen to China's imperial court at *Chang'an*, where they could observe firsthand the governmental system of the *Tang Dynasty* (618–907) before returning home to assume important official positions. These visitors to Chang'an brought back with them not only the forms of Chinese government but also some of the spirit that infused Chinese culture. Confucianism, Buddhism, and Daoism were woven into the fabric of Japanese civilization during these centuries of tutelage. What is more, many Chinese tastes, artistic styles, and artifacts were adopted as well.

Never, however, did these Chinese influences destroy native Japanese culture. *Shinto* (the way of the gods), Japan's original animistic religion, remained a vital force within Japanese culture despite attempts by some Japanese leaders to suppress it as a backward religion. Just as important, clan descent and inherited status remained vital social and political determinants in Japan. Unlike China, whose tightly organized government was increasingly in the hands of a professional class of scholars, Japan's society and government remained in the control of feudal clan lords and hereditary aristocrats. Japan experimented with but chose not to adopt the Chinese civil service examinations.

In 794 Emperor Kammu moved his capital from *Heijo* (present-day *Nara*), which had been modeled physically on the Tang capital at Chang'an, to *Heian-kyo* (present-day *Kyoto*) in order to end what seemed to him to be a slavish imitation of everything Chinese. Tang China was now in turmoil, and it was a good time to modify and even discard some aspects of Chinese culture that earlier Japanese Sinophiles (lovers of all things Chinese) had adopted so enthusiastically. During the *Heian Period* (794–1185), the culture of the imperial court soared to unprecedented levels of refinement, and Japanese civilization reached a level of mature independence it would never relinquish. The Japanese became more selective in their assimilation of Chinese influences and increasingly discovered inspiration for creative expression in their own land and people.

The Constitution of Prince Shotoku
▼▼▼
52 ▼ CHRONICLES OF JAPAN

A single imperial dynasty has reigned over Japan and its people for the past 1,700 years. Known as the *Sun Line*, the family claims descent from the sun-goddess Ameterasu through her great-great-grandson *Jimmu Tennu* (Divine Warrior), the mythic first emperor of Japan who, according to legend, began to rule in 660 B.C.E. The historical truth is less grand. The *Yamato* clan, which became the Sun Line, seems to have established its hegemony over the western regions of the island of Honshu no earlier than the third century C.E. The range of the Yamato clan's authority grew in the course of its first several centuries of state building, thanks to fortunate alliances, conquests, and the development of a literate bureaucracy. By the sixth century, Yamato emperors and empresses had become living symbols of Japanese religious and cultural unity. However, even though it claimed divine origins, the Yamato family could not control several of Japan's powerful clan chieftains. Indeed, the opposite was more the case. Several powerful clans vied to control the imperial family.

One of the most powerful late-sixth-century clans, or *uji*, was the *Soga family*, headed by *Soga no Umako*. In addition to struggling successfully against rivals for influence over the imperial court, Soga no Umako also supported the policy of actively welcoming Chinese influences on a massive scale into Japan as a way of extending the authority of the imperial family that it controlled and increasing the overall prosperity and power of the island empire.

After engineering the assassination of one emperor, Soga no Umako chose *Empress Suiko* (r. 592–628) as nominal ruler. To guide her along lines that he considered correct, Soga designated an imperial prince to serve as regent. Under the direction of this crown prince, known as *Shotoku* (Sovereign Moral Power), Japan embarked on a course of deliberate cultural borrowing that was unprecedented in history. In 604 Prince Shotoku issued the *Constitution of Seventeen Articles*, which laid out the ideological basis for the reforms that he, Empress Suiko, and Soga no Umako were championing.

Our knowledge of Shotoku's constitution comes from the *Nihongi* (*Chronicles of Japan*), one of Japan's two oldest collections of legend and history. Composed in its final form in 720, the *Nihongi* traces the history of Japan back to the mythological age of the gods. By the time the *Nihongi* reaches the sixth century C.E., its narrative has largely left the realm of myth and become more reliable history.

QUESTIONS FOR ANALYSIS

1. What kind of constitution is this? Is it a code of institutional rules and regulations, or is it something else? What does your answer suggest?
2. What does this constitution allow you to infer about Shotoku's ideals and goals?
3. Review sources 5–6, 19–21, and 28–29. What Confucian principles do you find in this document? Can you find any Daoist ideas? What about Legalist elements?
4. What native, or non-Chinese, elements do you find in this document? What do they suggest about Japanese society?

The Prince Imperial in person prepared for the first time laws. There were seventeen clauses as follows: —

1. Harmony is to be valued, and an avoidance of wanton opposition to be honored. All men are influenced by class-feelings, and there are few who are intelligent. Hence there are some who disobey their lords and fathers, or who maintain feuds with the neighboring villages. But when those above are harmonious and those below are friendly, and there is concord in the discussion of business, right views of things spontaneously gain acceptance. Then what is there which cannot be accomplished!

2. Sincerely reverence the three treasures. The three treasures: the Buddha, the Law, and the Priesthood,[1] are the final refuge . . . and are the supreme objects of faith in all countries. What man in what age can fail to reverence this law? Few men are utterly bad. They may be taught to follow it. But if they do not go to the three treasures, how shall their crookedness be made straight?

3. When you receive the Imperial commands, fail not scrupulously to obey them. The lord is Heaven, the vassal is Earth.[2] Heaven overspreads, and Earth upbears. When this is so, the four seasons follow their due course, and the powers of Nature obtain their efficacy. If the Earth attempted to overspread, Heaven would simply fall in ruin. Therefore is it that when the lord speaks, the vassal listens; when the superior acts, the inferior yields compliance. Consequently when you receive the Imperial commands, fail not to carry them out scrupulously. Let there be a want of care in this matter, and ruin is the natural consequence.

4. The Ministers and functionaries should make decorous behavior their leading principle, for the leading principle of the government of the people consists in decorous behavior. If the superiors do not behave with decorum, the inferiors are disorderly: if inferiors are wanting in proper behavior, there must necessarily be offenses. Therefore it is that when lord and vassal behave with propriety, the distinctions of rank are not confused: when the people behave with propriety, the Government of the Commonwealth proceeds of itself. . . .

6. Chastise that which is evil and encourage that which is good. This was the excellent rule of antiquity. Conceal not, therefore, the good qualities of others, and fail not to correct that which is wrong when you see it. Flatterers and de-

---

[1]The Buddha, the Law of Dharma, and the Sangha, or order of male and female monks, are the three treasures, or key elements, of Buddhism.

[2]Lord and vassal mean in this context not just emperor and subject but local clan chieftains and their retainers.

ceivers are a sharp weapon for the overthrow of the State, and a pointed sword for the destruction of the people. Sycophants are also fond, when they meet, of speaking at length to their superiors on the errors of their inferiors; to their inferiors, they censure the faults of their superiors. Men of this kind are all wanting in fidelity to their lord, and in benevolence toward the people. From such an origin great civil disturbances arise.

7. Let every man have his own charge, and let not the spheres of duty be confused. When wise men are entrusted with office, the sound of praise arises. If unprincipled men hold office, disasters and tumults are multiplied. In this world, few are born with knowledge: wisdom is the product of earnest meditation. In all things, whether great or small, find the right man, and they will surely be well managed: on all occasions, be they urgent or the reverse, meet but with a wise man, and they will of themselves be amenable. In this way will the State be lasting and the Temples of the Earth and of Grain[3] will be free from danger. Therefore did the wise sovereigns of antiquity seek the man to fill the office, and not the office for the sake of the man. . . .

10. Let us cease from wrath, and refrain from angry looks. Nor let us be resentful when others differ from us. For all men have hearts, and each heart has its own leanings. Their right is our wrong, and our right is their wrong. We are not unquestionably sages, nor are they unquestionably fools. Both of us are simply ordinary men. How can any one lay down a rule by which to distinguish right from wrong? For we are all, one with another, wise and foolish, like a ring which has no end. Therefore, although others give way to anger, let us on the contrary dread our own faults, and though we alone may be in the right, let us follow the multitude and act like them.

11. Give clear appreciation to merit and demerit, and deal out to each its sure reward or punishment. In these days, reward does not attend upon merit, nor punishment upon crime. You high functionaries who have charge of public affairs, let it be your task to make clear rewards and punishments. . . .

15. To turn away from that which is private, and to set our faces toward that which is public — this is the path of a Minister. Now if a man is influenced by private motives, he will assuredly feel resentments, and if he is influenced by resentful feelings, he will assuredly fail to act harmoniously with others. If he fails to act harmoniously with others, he will assuredly sacrifice the public interest to his private feelings. When resentment arises, it interferes with order, and is subversive of law. . . .

16. Let the people be employed [in forced labor] at seasonable times. This is an ancient and excellent rule. Let them be employed, therefore, in the winter months, when they are at leisure. But from Spring to Autumn, when they are engaged in agriculture or with the mulberry trees,[4] the people should not be so employed. For if they do not attend to agriculture, what will they have to eat? If they do not attend to the mulberry trees, what will they do for clothing?

17. Decisions on important matters should not be made by one person alone. They should be discussed with many. But small matters are of less consequence. It is unnecessary to consult a number of people. It is only in the case of the discussion of weighty affairs, when there is a suspicion that they may miscarry, that one should arrange matters in concert with others, so as to arrive at the right conclusion.

---

[3]Shinto shrines dedicated to the *kami*, or spirits, of agriculture — probably a metaphor for prosperity in this context.

[4]The cultivation of silkworms that ate mulberry leaves. The technique of silk production was an import from China.

Lives and Loves at the Heian Court
▼▼▼
53 ▼ *Sei Shonagon, THE PILLOW BOOK*

The centralized administrative system modeled on Tang China's imperial structure that Japanese reformers tried to establish during the seventh and eighth centuries failed to function as intended. By the mid ninth century, true power in the provinces rested in the hands of local clan chiefs and a new element, Buddhist monasteries (see source 54). The imperial government continued to appoint provincial governors, who theoretically administered their regions in the name of the emperor, but most governors resided in the imperial court at *Kyoto*, far away from their areas of nominal responsibility. The court itself became an increasingly elegant setting for emperors and empresses, who were regarded as sacred beings and theoretically stood at the summit of all power. The elaborate ceremony that surrounded these people, who claimed to rule the world, masked, at least at close hand, the fact that effective power lay elsewhere.

While the imperial court was increasingly losing touch with the center of political authority, a group of aristocratic women at court were developing Japan's first native literature. Unlike Japan's male Confucian scholars, who continued to study the Chinese classics along fairly rigid lines established a millennium earlier in a foreign land, the court women gave free play in their prose and poetry to their imaginations, emotions, and powers of analysis.

Among Japan's great female literary artists of the Heian Period, *Sei Shonagon* (ca. 965–after 1000), a lady-in-waiting to Empress Sadako (r. 990–1000), deserves a special place of honor. Her masterpiece is *The Pillow Book*, a collection of observations that she began while serving at the imperial court. The title probably derives from the fact that the author composed miscellaneous notes at night, after retiring to her room, on paper that she kept in a drawer of her wooden pillow. Although the book appears to be a hodgepodge of random observations that lack order and cohesion, it is a carefully polished work of literature that the author began around 994 and continued to refine well after 1000, when she left the court following the young empress's death.

Many of the imperial ladies-in-waiting at Heian composed memoirs and diaries with an eye toward publication, but Sei Shonagon's contribution to this genre is special because of the beauty of her prose and the human face that she puts on upper-class Heian society, with all its virtues, foibles, and flaws. Although we know almost nothing about the details of her life, even the casual reader comes away from *The Pillow Book* feeling that Sei Shonagon has revealed her complex personality in an especially intimate way.

QUESTIONS FOR ANALYSIS

1. Consider the role of ceremony at the Heian court. How significant does it appear to have been? What do you infer from your answer?
2. *The Pillow Book* has been said to be a complex collection of apparently contradictory elements. What are those apparently contradictory strands, and

what do they suggest to you about life and values at the late-tenth-century Heian court?

3. How well or poorly does Sei Shonagon measure up to the stereotype of East Asian women? Be specific. What do you infer from your answer?
4. Compose a commentary on *The Pillow Book* by Ban Zhao (source 29).

ESPECIALLY DELIGHTFUL IS THE FIRST DAY

Especially delightful is the first day of the First Month, when the mists so often shroud the sky. Everyone pays great attention to his appearance and dresses with the utmost care. What a pleasure it is to see them all offer their congratulations to the Emperor and celebrate their own new year![1]

I also enjoy the seventh day. . . . This is the day when members of the nobility who live outside the Palace arrive in their magnificently decorated carriages to admire the blue horses.[2] As the carriages are drawn over the ground-beam of the Central Gate, there is always a tremendous bump, and the heads of the women passengers are knocked together; the combs fall out of their hair, and may be smashed to pieces if the owners are not careful. I enjoy the way everyone laughs when this happens. . . .

The fifteenth day is the festival of the full-moon gruel,[3] when a bowl of gruel is presented to His Majesty. On this day all the women of the house carry gruel-sticks, which they hide carefully from each other. It is most amusing to see them walking about, as they await an opportunity to hit their companions. Each one is careful not to be struck herself and is constantly looking over her shoulder to make sure that no one is stealing up on her. Yet the precautions are useless, for before long one of the women manages

to score a hit. She is extremely pleased with herself and laughs merrily. Everyone finds this delightful — except, of course, the victim, who looks very put out. . . .

Sometimes when the women are hitting each other the men also join in the fun. The strange thing is that, when a woman is hit, she often gets angry and bursts into tears; then she will upbraid her assailant and say the most awful things about him — most amusing. Even in the Palace, where the atmosphere is usually so solemn, everything is in confusion on this day, and no one stands on ceremony.

▼▼▼

WHEN I MAKE MYSELF IMAGINE

When I make myself imagine what it is like to be one of those women who live at home, faithfully serving their husbands — women who have not a single exciting prospect in life yet who believe that they are perfectly happy — I am filled with scorn. Often they are of quite good birth, yet have had no opportunity to find out what the world is like. I wish they could live for a while in our society . . . so that they might come to know the delights it has to offer.

I cannot bear men who believe that women serving in the Palace are bound to be frivolous and wicked. Yet I suppose their prejudice is understandable. After all, women at Court do not

[1]In the Japanese lunar calendar (borrowed from China), New Year's Day is a movable date, falling between January 21 and February 19 in the Western, or Gregorian, calendar. New Year's Day is also a sort of birthday; on that day the Japanese add a year to their age.
[2]In the early eighth century, Japan imported from Tang China the annual ceremony of parading twenty-one steel-

gray (blue) horses before the emperor. Because such horses are rare and white is the color of purity in Shinto rituals, white horses were substituted in the tenth century, even though the ceremony's name remained unchanged.
[3]In the Japanese lunar calendar, the fifteenth is the day of the full moon. At the full moon of the First Month, a special gruel was eaten.

spend their time hiding modestly behind fans and screens, but walk about, looking openly at people they chance to meet. Yes, they see everyone face to face, not only ladies-in-waiting like themselves, but even Their Imperial Majesties (whose august names I hardly dare mention), High Court Nobles, senior courtiers, and other gentlemen of high rank. In the presence of such exalted personages the women in the Palace are all equally brazen, whether they be the maids of ladies-in-waiting, or the relations of Court ladies who have come to visit them, or housekeepers, or latrine-cleaners, or women who are of no more value than a roof-tile or a pebble. Small wonder that the young men regard them as immodest! Yet are the gentlemen themselves any less so? They are not exactly bashful when it comes to looking at the great people in the Palace. No, everyone at Court is much the same in this respect.

Women who have served in the Palace, but who later get married and live at home, are called Madam and receive the most respectful treatment. To be sure, people often consider that these women, who have displayed their faces to all and sundry during their years at Court, are lacking in feminine grace. How proud they must be, nevertheless, when they are styled Assistant Attendants, or summoned to the Palace for occasional duty, or ordered to serve as Imperial envoys during the Kamo Festival![4] Even those who stay at home lose nothing by having served at Court. In fact they make very good wives. For example, if they are married to a provincial governor and their daughter is chosen to take part in the Gosechi dances,[5] they do not have to disgrace themselves by acting like provincials and asking other people about procedure. They themselves are well versed in the formalities, which is just as it should be.

▾▾▾

[4]The main Shinto festival, observed in the middle of the Fourth Month.

HATEFUL THINGS

One is in a hurry to leave, but one's visitor keeps chattering away. If it is someone of no importance, one can get rid of him by saying, "You must tell me all about it next time"; but, should it be the sort of visitor whose presence commands one's best behavior, the situation is hateful indeed. . . .

A man who has nothing in particular to recommend discusses all sorts of subjects at random as though he knew everything. . . .

I hate the sight of men in their cups who shout, poke their fingers in their mouths, stroke their beards, and pass on the wine to their neighbors with great cries of "Have some more! Drink up!" They tremble, shake their heads, twist their faces, and gesticulate like children who are singing, "We're off to see the Governor." I have seen really well-bred people behave like this and I find it most distasteful. . . .

One is just about to be told some interesting piece of news when a baby starts crying. . . .

An admirer has come on a clandestine visit, but a dog catches sight of him and starts barking. One feels like killing the beast.

One has been foolish enough to invite a man to spend the night in an unsuitable place — and then he starts snoring. . . .

One is in the middle of a story when someone butts in and tries to show that he is the only clever person in the room. Such a person is hateful, and so, indeed, is anyone, child or adult, who tries to push himself forward.

One is telling a story about old times when someone breaks in with a little detail that he happens to know, implying that one's own version is inaccurate — disgusting behavior! . . .

Some children have called at one's house. One makes a great fuss of them and gives them toys to play with. The children become accustomed to this treatment and start to come regularly,

[5]Court dances performed in the Eleventh Month by four young girls from high-ranking families.

forcing their way into one's inner rooms and scattering one's furnishings and possessions. Hateful! . . .

A man with whom one is having an affair keeps singing the praises of some woman he used to know. Even if it is a thing of the past, this can be very annoying. How much more so if he is still seeing the woman! (Yet sometimes I find that it is not as unpleasant as all that.)

A person who recites a spell himself after sneezing.[6] In fact I detest anyone who sneezes except the master of the house.

Fleas, too, are very hateful. When they dance about under someone's clothes, they really seem to be lifting them up. . . .

I cannot stand people who leave without closing the panel behind them. . . .

I hate people whose letters show that they lack respect for worldly civilities, whether by discourtesy in the phrasing or by extreme politeness to someone who does not deserve it. This sort of thing is, of course, most odious if the letter is for oneself, but it is bad enough even if it is addressed to someone else.

As a matter of fact, most people are too casual, not only in their letters but in their direct conversation. Sometimes I am quite disgusted at noting how little decorum people observe when talking to each other. It is particularly unpleasant to hear some foolish man or woman omit the proper marks of respect when addressing a person of quality; and, when servants fail to use honorific forms of speech in referring to their masters, it is very bad indeed. No less odious, however, are those masters who, in addressing their servants, use such phrases as "When you were good enough to do such-and-such" or "As you so kindly remarked." No doubt there are some masters who, in describing their own actions to a servant, say, "I presumed to do so-and-so"!

Sometimes a person who is utterly devoid of charm will try to create a good impression by using very elegant language; yet he only succeeds in being ridiculous. No doubt he believes this refined language to be just what the occasion demands, but, when it goes so far that everyone bursts out laughing, surely something must be wrong. . . .

A lover who is leaving at dawn announces that he has to find his fan and his paper.[7] "I know I put them somewhere last night," he says. Since it is pitch dark, he gropes about the room, bumping into the furniture and muttering, "Strange! Where on earth can they be?" Finally he discovers the objects. He thrusts the paper into the breast of his robe with a great rustling sound; then he snaps open his fan and busily fans away with it. Only now is he ready to take his leave. What charmless behavior! "Hateful" is an understatement.

Equally disagreeable is the man who, when leaving in the middle of the night, takes care to fasten the cord of his headdress. This is quite unnecessary; he could perfectly well put it gently on his head without tying the cord. And why must he spend time adjusting his cloak or hunting costume? Does he really think someone may see him at this time of night and criticize him for not being impeccably dressed?

A good lover will behave as elegantly at dawn as at any other time. He drags himself out of bed with a look of dismay on his face. The lady urges on: "Come, my friend, it's getting light. You don't want anyone to find you here." He gives a deep sigh, as if to say that the night has not been nearly long enough and that it is agony to leave. Once up, he does not instantly pull on his trousers. Instead he comes close to the lady and whispers whatever was left unsaid during the night. Even when he is dressed, he still lingers, vaguely pretending to be fastening his sash.

---

[6]Saying the equivalent of "Bless you" or "Gesundheit" to counter the evil omen that sneezing represents.

[7]Colored paper that gentlemen carried in the folds of their robe for notes and use as tissue.

Presently he raises the lattice, and the two lovers stand together by the side door while he tells her how he dreads the coming day, which will keep them apart; then he slips away. The lady watches him go, and this moment of parting will remain among her most charming memories.

Indeed, one's attachment to a man depends largely on the elegance of his leave-taking. When he jumps out of bed, scurries about the room, tightly fastens his trouser-sash, rolls up the sleeves of his Court cloak, over-robe, or hunting costume, stuffs his belongings into the breast of his robe and then briskly secures the outer sash — one really begins to hate him.

▼▼▼

EMBARRASSING THINGS

While entertaining a visitor, one hears some servants chatting without any restraint in one of the back rooms. It is embarrassing to know that one's visitor can overhear. But how to stop them?

A man whom one loves gets drunk and keeps repeating himself.

To have spoken about someone not knowing that he could overhear. This is embarrassing even if it be a servant or some other completely insignificant person.

To hear one's servants making merry. This is equally annoying if one is on a journey and staying in cramped quarters or at home and hears the servants in a neighboring room.

Parents, convinced that their ugly child is adorable, pet him and repeat the things he has said, imitating his voice.

An ignoramus who in the presence of some learned person puts on a knowing air and converses about men of old.

A man recites his own poems (not especially good ones) and tells one about the praise they have received — most embarrassing.

Lying awake at night, one says something to one's companion, who simply goes on sleeping.

In the presence of a skilled musician, someone plays a zither just for his own pleasure and without tuning it.

A son-in-law who has long since stopped visiting his wife runs into his father-in-law in a public place.

The Ideal Samurai
▼▼▼
54 ▼ *CHRONICLE OF THE GRAND PACIFICATION*

While imperial court women at Kyoto devoted their talents to crafting new forms of literature, Japan's warlords engaged their energies in carving out independent principalities backed by the might of their private armies of *samurai* (they who serve). Between 1180 and 1185, a conflict known as the *Gempei War* devastated the heartland of the main island of Honshu as the mighty Taira and *Minimoto* clans fought for control of the imperial family and its court. In 1185 the Minimoto house destroyed the Taira faction and thereby became the supreme military power in Japan.

Rather than seizing the imperial office for himself, the Minimoto leader accepted the title of *shogun*, or imperial commander in chief, and elected to rule over a number of military governors from his remote base at *Kamakura*, while a puppet emperor reigned at Kyoto. This feudal system, known as the *bakufu* (tent headquarters), shaped the politics and culture of Japan for centuries to come.

Toward the early fourteenth century, the *Kamakura Shogunate* began to show signs of weakening, which encouraged *Emperor Go-Daigo* (r. 1318–1336) to lead a coup in an attempt to destroy the shogunate and re-establish the primacy of the emperor. This rebel emperor became the nucleus of a full-scale feudal uprising by a wide number of dissatisfied warlords, samurai, and warrior-monks. The warrior-monks were members of great landholding Buddhist monasteries, which had been for centuries independent political, economic, and military powers. The rebellion resulted in the destruction of Kamakura and the death of its last shogun.

Go-Daigo's victory was brief, however. Within a few years, he was deposed by another warlord, who installed his own emperor and received back from him the title of shogun, thereby establishing the *Ashikaga Shogunate* (1338–1573). Japanese government and society, therefore, continued to be dominated by its feudal warriors.

The story of the last several years of the Kamakura Shogunate is recorded in the pages of the *Taiheiki*, or *Chronicle of the Grand Pacification*. Composed by a number of largely anonymous Buddhist monks between about 1333 and maybe as late as 1370, the chronicle recounts the battles and intrigues of the period 1318–1333. Its title refers to Go-Daigo's momentarily successful attempt to destroy, or "pacify," the shogunate.

The following excerpt tells the story of the defense in 1331 of Akasaka castle by *Kusunoki Masashige*, one of the emperor's most fervent supporters. The emperor, along with many followers, had recently been captured at Kasagi, a fortified monastic temple. The imperial cause needed a victory, even a moral one, and this heretofore obscure warrior was about to provide new hope with his inspired defense of this stronghold.

Killed in 1333 in a battle he knew he could not win, Masashige has been revered through the centuries as a paragon of samurai virtues. The *kamikaze* (divine wind) suicide pilots whom Japan launched against the U.S. Navy in 1945 were called "chrysanthemum warriors" in reference to the Kusunoki family's flowered crest.

QUESTIONS FOR ANALYSIS

1. Why do the warriors assaulting Akasaka hope that Kusunoki will be able to hold out for at least one day? What does your answer suggest?
2. Bravery is expected of all warriors, but which other samurai virtues does Kusunoki Masashige exemplify?
3. Which samurai virtues do his foes exhibit? In what ways did they show themselves to be less than ideal warriors?
4. Thinking their enemy dead, the shogun's warriors pause to remember Kusunoki Masashige. What does this suggest?
5. Based on this account, what picture emerges of the ideals and realities of fourteenth-century Japanese feudal warfare?

No man of the mighty host from the distant eastern lands was willing to enter the capital, so sorely were their spirits mortified because Kasagi castle had fallen.[1] . . . All took their way instead toward Akasaka castle, where Kusunoki Hyoe Masashige was shut up. . . .

When these had passed beyond the Ishi River, they beheld the castle. Surely this was a stronghold of hasty devising! The ditch was not a proper ditch, and there was but a single wooden wall, plastered over with mud. Likewise in size the castle was not more than one hundred or two hundred yards around, with but twenty or thirty towers within, made ready in haste. Of those who saw it, not one but thought:

"Ah, what a pitiable spectacle the enemy presents! . . . Let us hope that in some strange manner Kusunoki will endure for at least a day, that by taking booty and winning honor we may obtain future rewards."

Drawing near, the three hundred thousand riders[2] got down from their horses, one after another, jumped into the ditch, stood below the towers, and competed to be the first to enter the castle.

Now by nature Masashige was a man who would "scheme in his tent to defeat an enemy a thousand leagues distant," one whose counsels were as subtle as though sprung from the brain of Chenping or Zhang Liang.[3] Wherefore had he kept two hundred mighty archers within the castle, and had given three hundred riders to his brother Shichiro and Wada Goro Masato outside in the mountains. Yet the attackers, all unwitting, rushed forward together to the banks of the ditch on the four sides, resolved to bring down the castle in a single assault.

Then from tower tops and windows the archers shot furiously with arrowheads aligned together, smiting more than a thousand men in an instant. And greatly amazed, the eastern warriors said:

"No, no! From the look of things at this castle, it will never fall in a day or two. Let us take time before going against it, that we may establish camps and battle-offices and form separate parties."

They drew back from the attack a little, took off their horses' saddles, cast aside their armor, and rested in their camps.

In the mountains Kusunoki Shichiro and Wada Goro said, "The time is right." They made two parties of the three hundred horsemen, came out from the shelter of the trees on the eastern and western slopes with two fluttering banners, whereon were depicted the chrysanthemum and water crest of the Kusunoki house, and advanced quietly toward the enemy, urging their horses forward in the swirling mist. . . .

Then suddenly from both sides the three hundred attacked, shouting, in wedge-shaped formations. They smote the center of the three hundred thousand horsemen spread out like clouds or mist, broke into them in all directions, and cut them down on every side. And the attackers' hosts were powerless to form to give battle, so great was their bewilderment.

Next within the castle three gates opened all together, wherefrom two hundred horsemen galloped forth side by side to let fly a multitude of arrows from bows pulled back to the utmost limits. Although the attackers were a mighty host, they were confounded utterly by these few enemies, so that they clamored aloud. Some mounted tethered horses and beat them with their stirrups, seeking to advance; others fixed arrows to unstrung bows and tried vainly to shoot. Two or three men took up a single piece of armor and disputed it, pulling against each other. Though a lord was killed, his vassals knew nothing of it; though a father was killed, his sons aided him not, but like scattered spiders they retreated to the Ishi River. For half a league along their way there was no space where a foot

---

[1]This force of Kamakura supporters from the east was dispirited because it had arrived too late to participate in the capture of Kasagi.

[2]The *Taiheiki* grossly exaggerates the number of pro-Kamakura fighters.

[3]Two ministers of the first Han emperor of China. The quotation is from Ban Gu and Ban Zhao's *History of the Former Han Dynasty*.

might tread, by reason of their abandoned horses and arms. To be sure, great gains came suddenly to the common folk of Tojo district![4]

Perhaps the proud eastern warriors thought in their hearts that Kusunoki's strategy could not be despised, since blundering unexpectedly they had been defeated in the first battle. For though they went forth against Handa and Narahara,[5] they did not seek to attack the castle again quickly, but consulted together and made a resolution, saying:

"Let us remain awhile in this place, that led by men acquainted with the home provinces we may cut down trees on the mountains, burn houses, and guard thereby against warriors waiting in reserve to fall upon us. Then may we attack the castle with tranquil spirits."

But there were many . . . who had lost fathers and sons in the fighting. These roused themselves up, saying:

"What is the use of living? Though we go alone, let us gallop forth to die in battle!"

And thereupon all the others took heart as well, and galloped forward eagerly.

Now Akasaka castle might not be attacked easily on the east, where terraced rice fields extended far up the mountainside. But on three sides the land was flat; likewise there was but a single ditch and wall. All the attackers were contemptuous, thinking, "No matter what demons may be inside, it cannot be much of an affair." When they drew near again, they went forward quickly into the ditch to the opposite bank, pulled away the obstacles and made ready to enter. Yet within the castle there was no sound.

Then the attackers thought in their hearts:

"As it was yesterday, so will it be today. After wounding many men with arrows to confuse us, they will send other warriors to fight in our midst."

They counted out a hundred thousand riders to go to the mountains in the rear, while the remaining two hundred thousand compassed the castle round about like thickly growing rice,

hemp, bamboo, or reeds. Yet from within the castle not an arrow was released, nor was any man seen.

At last the attackers laid hold of the wall on the four sides to climb over it, filled with excitement. But thereupon men within the castle cut the ropes supporting that wall, all at the same time, for it was a double wall, built to let the outside fall down. More than a thousand of the attackers became as though crushed by a weight, so that only their eyes moved as the defenders threw down logs and boulders onto them. And in this day's fighting more than seven hundred of them were slain.

Unwilling to attack again because of the bitterness of the first two days of fighting, for four or five days the eastern hosts merely besieged the castle from camps hard by. Truly were they without pride, to watch thus idly from a nearby place! How mortifying it was that men of the future would make a mock of them, saying, "Although the enemy were no more than four or five hundred persons shut up in a flatland castle not five hundred yards around, the hosts of the eight eastern provinces would not attack them, but shamefully laid down a siege from a distance!"

At last the attackers spoke among themselves, saying:

"Previously we attacked in the fierceness of our valor, not carrying shields or preparing weapons of assault, wherefore we suffered unforeseen injury. Let us go against them now with a different method."

All commanded the making of shields with toughened hide on their faces, such as might not be smashed through easily, and with these upheld they went against the castle once more, saying:

"There can be no difficulty about jumping across to the wall, since the banks are not high, nor is the ditch deep. Yet will not this wall also drop down upon us?"

They spoke with fearful hearts, reluctant to seize upon the wall lightly. All went down into the water of the ditch, laid hold upon the wall

[4]Commoners scavenged battlefields.

[5]Settlements near Akasaka.

with grapnels, and pulled at it. But when the wall was about to fall, those within the castle took ladles with handles ten or twenty feet long, dipped up boiling water, and poured it onto them. The hot water passed through the holes in their helmet tops, ran down from the edges of their shoulder-guards, and burned their bodies so grievously that they fled panic-stricken, throwing down their shields and grapnels. How shameful it was! Although no man of them was slain, there were as many as two or three hundred persons who could not stand up from the burns on their hands and feet, or who lay down with sick bodies.

So it was that whenever the attackers advanced with new devisings, those within the castle defended against them with changed stratagems. Wherefore in consultation together the attackers said, "From this time on, let us starve them, for we can do no other." They forbore utterly to do battle, but only built towers in their camps, lined up obstacles, and laid down a siege.

Soon the warriors in the castle grew weary of spirit, since there was no diversion for them. Nor was their food sufficient, since Kusunoki had built the castle in haste. The battle having begun and the siege commenced, within twenty days the stores were eaten up; nor did food remain for more than four or five days.

Then Masashige spoke a word to his men, saying:

"In various battles of late have we overreached the foe, whose slain are beyond counting, but these things are as nothing in the eyes of so mighty a host. Moreover, the castle's food is eaten up, and no other warriors will come to deliver us.

"Assuredly I will not cherish life in the hour of need, from the beginning having been steadfast for His Majesty's sake. . . . But the true man of courage 'is cautious in the face of difficulties, and deliberates before acting.'[6] I will flee this castle for a time, causing the enemy to believe that I have taken my life, so that they may go away rejoicing. When they are gone I will come forward to fight; and if they return I will go deep into the mountains. When I have harassed the eastern hosts four or five times in this manner, will they not grow weary? This is a plan for destroying the enemy in safety. What are your views?"

All agreed, "It ought to be so."

Then quickly within the castle they dug a mighty hole seven feet deep, filling it with twenty or thirty bodies of the slain . . . , whereon they piled up charcoal and firewood. And they awaited a night of pouring rain and driving wind.

Perhaps because Masashige had found favor in the sight of Heaven, suddenly a harsh wind came raising the sand, accompanied by a rain violent enough to pierce bamboo. The night was exceedingly dark, and all the enemy in their camps were sheltered behind curtains. This indeed was the awaited night!

Leaving a man in the castle to light a blaze when they were fled away safely five or six hundred yards, the defenders cast off their armor, assumed the guise of attackers, and fled away calmly by threes and fives, passing in front of the enemy battle-offices and beside enemy sleeping places.

It came about that the eyes of an enemy fell upon Masashige. . . . The man challenged him, saying, "What person passes before this battle-office in stealth, not announcing himself?"

In haste Masashige passed beyond that place, calling back, "I am a follower of the grand marshal who has taken the wrong road."

"A suspicious fellow indeed!" thought the man. "Assuredly he is a stealer of horses! I shall shoot him down."

He ran up close and shot Masashige full in the body. But although the arrow looked to have driven deep at the height of the elbow-joint, it turned over and flew back again without touching the naked flesh.

---

[6]A quotation from Confucius's *Analects*.

Later, when that arrow's track was observed, men saw that it had struck an amulet wherein was preserved the *Kannon Sutra*,[7] which Masashige had trusted and read for many years. Its arrowhead had stopped in the two-line poem, "Wholeheartedly praising the name."[8] How strange it was!

When in this manner Masashige had escaped death from a certain-death arrowhead, he fled to a safe place more than half a league distant. And looking back he saw that the warrior had lighted fires in the castle's battle-offices, faithful to his covenant.

The hosts of the attackers were seized with amazement at the sight of the flames.

"Aha! The castle has fallen!" they shouted exultantly. "Let no man be spared! Let none escape!"

When the flames died away, they saw a mighty hole inside the castle, piled up with charcoal, wherein lay the burned bodies of many men. And then not a man of them but spoke words of praise, saying:

"How pitiful! Masashige had ended his life! Though he was an enemy, his was a glorious death, well befitting a warrior."

---

[7] Known in its Chinese original as the *Guanshiyin Sutra*, this Buddhist holy book was dedicated to the Bodhisattva Guanyin (sources 32 and 33), who in Japan was known as *Kannon*.

[8] Compare this with the miracle stories in the *Tales of Guanshiyin* (source 32).

▼▼▼

China: The Ages of Tang and Song

The period from 500 to 1500 witnessed a variety of momentous developments in China: renewed imperial greatness, philosophical and technological innovation, economic expansion and a rapidly growing population, new modes of artistic expression, rebellions, invasions by various nomadic peoples, conquest by Mongol invaders, and recovery and retrenchment. Through it all, Chinese civilization managed to retain its basic institutions and way of life.

The Time of Troubles that followed the fall of the House of Han was over by the end of the sixth century, and under the *Tang Dynasty* (618–907) China was again a great imperial power, with a restored Confucian civil service in power. At the end of the seventh century, China's borders reached to Korea and Manchuria in the northeast, to Vietnam in the south, and to the Aral Sea in the western regions of Central Asia, where China met and was checked by the new Islamic Empire at the Battle of the Talas River in 751. The almost simultaneous creation of these two massive empires, which together once again connected the Atlantic with the Pacific, resulted in a dramatic increase of traffic along the Silk Road and through the waters of South Asia. Foreign goods, precious metals, peoples, and ideas flowed into China's cities. As a consequence, Tang China enjoyed the richest, most cosmopolitan culture on the face of the Earth, until its empire began to deteriorate after the mid eighth century. Between 755 and 763, China was torn apart by rebellion. In the wake of the devastation, Tang imperial strength rapidly disintegrated, and with it went an earlier openness of spirit to outside influences. Fifty-three years of disunity followed Tang's official collapse in 907, but, in fact, the previous half century of nominal Tang rule had been equally anarchic.

In 960 the *Song Dynasty* (960–1279) reunited most of China, which it ruled over from its northern capital at Kaifeng. In 1126, however, Kaifeng, along with all of North China, fell to invaders from the steppes. A younger brother to the Song emperor escaped to the south, where he re-established a truncated Song Empire centered on the port city of *Hangzhou*.

For almost one-half of its more than 300-year-long reign, the Song Dynasty was cut off from the Yellow River. Despite this, Song Era China reached and maintained levels of economic prosperity, technological advancement, and cultural maturity unequaled anywhere else on Earth at the time. By the mid eleventh century, the production of printed books had become such an important industry that artisans were experimenting with movable type — 400 years before the introduction of a similar printing process in Europe. The thousands of books and millions of pages printed in Song China before and after 1126/1127 are evidence that a remarkably high percentage of its population was literate.

In addition to this dramatic rise in basic literacy, there were significant developments in advanced philosophy. Intellectuals reinvigorated Confucian thought by injecting into it metaphysical concepts borrowed from Buddhism and Daoism. This new Study of the Way, or *Neo-Confucianism*, provided fresh philosophical insights clothed in traditional forms and enabled Confucianism to topple Buddhism from its position of intellectual preeminence.

The fine arts also reached new levels of achievement. Landscape painting, particularly during the era of Southern Song, expressed in two dimensions the mystical visions of Daoism and Chan Buddhism. On a three-dimensional plane, the craft of porcelain-making became a high art, and large numbers of exquisitely delicate pieces of fine ceramic-ware were traded from Japan to East Africa.

Advanced ships and navigational aids enabled Chinese traders to take to the sea in unprecedented numbers, especially in the direction of Southeast Asia, thereby transforming China into the greatest merchant marine power of its day. Rapid-maturing strains of rice, introduced from Champa in Southeast Asia, made it possible to feed a population that exceeded 100 million, about double that of the Age of Tang. Although most of this massive population was engaged in traditional, labor-intensive agriculture, some Chinese were employed in industries, primarily mining, iron and steel production, and textile manufacture, that used advanced technologies unequaled anywhere else in the world.

Song's age of greatness was brought to a close by *Mongol* invaders, who by 1279 had joined all of China to the largest land empire in world history. Mongol rule during what is known as the *Yuan Dynasty* (1264–1368) was unmitigated military occupation. Both the Mongols and the many foreigners whom they admitted into their service exploited and oppressed the Chinese. Although the Mongols encouraged agriculture and trade, few Chinese benefited from a prosperity that was largely confined to a small circle of landlords.

By the mid fourteenth century, China was in rebellion, and in 1368 a commoner, Zhu Yuanzhang, re-established native rule in the form of the *Ming Dynasty* (1368–1644). This new imperial family restored Chinese prestige and influence in East Asia to levels enjoyed under Tang and provided China with stability and prosperity until the late sixteenth century. Under the Ming traditional

Chinese civilization attained full maturity. Toward the middle of the Age of Ming, however, China reluctantly established relations with seaborne Western European merchants and missionaries, and the resultant challenge of the West would result, centuries later, in major transformations in Chinese life.

Chapters 12 and 13 will deal with the Yuan and Ming eras. In this chapter we will concentrate on the Tang and Song eras.

Imperial Greatness and Disaster in Eighth-Century China
▼▼▼

55 ▼ *Du Fu, POEMS*

The first half of the eighth century was dominated by the seesaw reign of Emperor *Tang Xuanzong* (r. 713–756), known popularly as *Tang Ming Huang* (Brilliant Emperor of Tang). In these forty-three years, China's empire went from heights of grandeur to debasement and disaster. A gifted artist and generous patron of the arts, he created a court known for refined elegance. Continuing the expansionistic policies of his predecessors, he drove his armies to overextension along China's far western and southwestern frontiers. His passionate love for a young concubine, *Yang Guifei*, finally led him to neglect imperial duties. One result was the rebellion of General *An Lushan* in 755 and the seizure and sacking of the capital cities of Luoyang and Chang'an. In the confusion that followed, the grieving emperor was forced to order his lover's death, and shortly thereafter he abdicated, a broken man. Although An Lushan was killed in 757, the rebellion continued to rage across China. Tang rule was nominally restored in 763, but for the next 144 years Tang power remained weak.

One witness to these events was *Du Fu* (712–770), a Confucian man of letters who is generally regarded as China's greatest poet. Born a year before Xuanzong assumed the throne, Du Fu enjoyed the peace and prosperity of an apparently successful empire during his youth. By the late 740s and early 750s, however, Du Fu became increasingly aware of the cracks and imperfections in the imperial system. The Great Rebellion, which broke the back of Tang power, brought numerous hardships to Du Fu and his family. Despite intermittent impoverishment, constant wandering in search of employment and security, and poor health, he composed some of his greatest poems during this time of trials. Far from home, he died in late 770, but not before leaving behind works of poetry that provide vivid insights into the vicissitudes of fortune that China experienced during his eventful life.

Our first selection was composed around 741. The second poem, written around 750, describes the consequences of China's border conflicts with such peoples as the Tibetans and the Uighurs (see source 56). The third poem was composed in the autumn of 756, when Du Fu was detained in Chang'an after it had been captured by rebel forces. The last poem was composed in 759.

QUESTIONS FOR ANALYSIS

1. What are the tone and message of "Officer Fang's Barbarian Steed"?
2. The "Ballad of the War Wagons" deals with the conscription of peasants to fight Emperor Xuanzong's border wars. What are its tone and message?
3. Who is the prince in "Pitying the Prince," and what does he represent?
4. Compare "Pitying the Prince" with "Officer Fang's Barbarian Steed." What are the tone and overall message of the latter poem? Has Du Fu lost all hope?
5. "Lovely Lady" might describe the situation of a particular woman whom Du Fu met, but it is certainly also an extended metaphor. Who is the lady? Who is the husband? Who is the "new girl"?

OFFICER FANG'S BARBARIAN STEED

Barbarian steed, pride of Ferghana,[1]
all jags and angles, well-knit bones;
two ears cocked, like bamboo tubes split
  sideways;
four hoofs fleet, as though buoyed on the wind.
Wherever headed, no distance too challenging,
fit indeed for a life-or-death charge.
With a mount superlative as this,
ten-thousand-mile sorties are at your command![2]

BALLAD OF THE WAR WAGONS

Rumble-rumble of wagons,
horses whinnying,
war-bound, bow and arrows at each man's waist,
fathers, mothers, wives, children running
  alongside,
dust so thick you can't see Xianyang Bridge,[3]
snatching at clothes, stumbling, blocking the
  road, wailing,
wailing voices that rise straight up to the clouds.
From the roadside, a passer-by, I question the
  recruits;

all they say is, "Again and again men drafted!
Some sent north at fifteen to guard the Yellow
  River,
at forty still manning garrison farms out west.
When they set out, the village headman tied
  their turbans for them;
they come home white-haired and draw border
  duty again!
Border posts washed in blood, enough to make a
  sea,
but the Martial Sovereign's not yet done
  'expanding his borders.'[4]
You've never seen them?
Our Han land's two hundred districts east of the
  mountains,
a thousand villages, ten thousand hamlets gone
  to thorns and brambles!
Sturdy wives can handle plow and mattock,
but the rows of grain never come up quite right.
What's worse, we men of Qin,[5] renowned as
  tough fighters,
they herd us into the ranks like dogs and
  chickens!
You, sir, ask these questions,
but recruits like us hardly dare grumble out
  loud.

---

[1]The Ferghana Valley, in what is today Uzbekistan and adjacent lands, was the breeding ground for the most highly prized horses out of Central Asia.

[2]Tang China had an absolute love affair with the superior horses of the Ferghana Valley — horses that the Chinese called "heavenly horses." Horses and equestrian sports (including polo, a game that came into China from Central Asia in the Tang Era) were favorite subjects of Tang artists, particularly its ceramic sculptors.

[3]A bridge that spans the Wei River. The Wei had been the ancient boundary between the heartland of China and the untamed "Western Lands." The troops are on their way to a western border.

[4]Here Tang Xuanzong is identified with Han Wudi (r. 141–87 B.C.E.), the "Martial Emperor of Han," whose aggressive policies expanded the First Chinese Empire deep into Central Asia.

[5]Men from the capital area around Chang'an.

Still, in winter this year,
troops from here, West of the Pass,[6] not yet
    disbanded,
officials started pressing for taxes —
tax payments — where would they come from?
Now you know why it's no good to have sons,
much better have daughters instead!
Sire a daughter, you can marry her to a neighbor;
sire a son and he ends buried under a hundred
    grasses.
You've never seen what it's like in Koko Nor?[7]
Years now, white bones no one gathers up,
new ghosts cursing fate, old ghosts wailing,
skies dark, drizzly rain, the whimpering,
    whimpering voices."

PITYING THE PRINCE

Over Chang'an city walls white-headed crows[8]
fly by night, crying above Greeting Autumn
    Gate.
Then they turn to homes of the populace,
    pecking at great mansions,
mansions where high officials scramble to flee
    the barbarians.
Golden whips broken, royal steeds dropping
    dead,
even flesh and blood of the ruler can't all get
    away in time.
How pathetic — costly disc of green coral at his
    waist,
this young prince standing weeping by the
    roadside!
I ask, but he won't tell me his name or surname,
says only that he's tired and in trouble, begs me
    to make him my servant.
A hundred days now, hiding in brambles and
    thorns,

not a spot on his body where the flesh is untorn.
Sons and grandsons of the founder all have high-
    arched noses;
heirs of the Dragon line[9] naturally differ from
    plain people.
"Wild cats and wolves in the city, dragons in the
    wilds,
prince, take care of this body worth a thousand
    in gold![10]
I dare not talk for long, here at the crossroads,
but for your sake, prince, I stay a moment
    longer.
Last night, east winds blew rank with the smell
    of blood,
from the east came camels[11] crowding the old
    Capital.[12]
Those Shuofang troops, good men all —
why so keen, so brave in the past, so ineffectual
    now?[13]
I've heard the Son of Heaven has relinquished
    his throne,
but in the north his sacred virtue has won the
    Uighur khan to our side.[14]
The Uighurs slash their faces,[15] beg to wipe out
    our disgrace.
Take care, say nothing of this — others wait in
    ambush!
I pity you, my prince — take care, do nothing
    rash!
Auspicious signs over the five imperial graves
    never for a moment cease."[16]

LOVELY LADY

Lovely lady, fairest of the time,
hiding away in an empty valley;
daughter of a good house, she said,
fallen now among grasses of the wood.

---

[6]Another term for the area around Chang'an.
[7]A lake on the border between China and Tibet. Tibet at this time was an enemy and competitor for hegemony over major routes of the Silk Road.
[8]White-headed crows are harbingers of evil.
[9]The Tang family. The dragon is a symbol of imperial power.
[10]As ransom, should he be captured.
[11]The rebels used Bactrian camels as transport animals.

[12]Chang'an.
[13]Troops from north of Chang'an who had fought successfully against the Tibetans but were defeated by the rebels in 756.
[14]Emperor Tang Suzong had recently concluded an alliance with the Uighurs. See source 56.
[15]A sign of Uighur sincerity. See source 56.
[16]Omens of good fortune still linger around the gravesites of Emperor Tang Suzong's greatest imperial ancestors.

"There was tumult and death within the passes
     then;
my brothers, old and young, all killed.
Office, position — what help were they?
I couldn't even gather up my brothers' bones!
The world despises you when your luck is down;
all I had went with the turn of the flame.
My husband was a fickle fellow,
his new girl as fair as jade.
Blossoms that close at dusk keep faith with the
     hour,
mandarin ducks will not rest apart;

but he could only see the new one laughing,
never hear the former one's tears —"
Within the mountain the stream runs clear;
out of the mountain it turns to mud.
Her maid returns from selling a pearl,
braids vines to mend their roof of thatch.
The lady picks a flower but does not put it in
     her hair,
gathers juniper berries, sometimes a handful.
When the sky is cold, in thin azure sleeves,
at dusk she stands leaning by the tall bamboo.

The Bartered Bride:
China and the Uighurs in an Age of Civil War
▼▼▼
56 ▼ *THE OLD TANG HISTORY*

Following the collapse of the Tang Dynasty, China passed into a period of turmoil known as the Era of the Five Dynasties (907–960). Even in the midst of troubles, what passed for an imperial court took pains to recover and record the past. In 941 Emperor Gaozu, a non-Chinese, Turkic adventurer, ordered the compilation from extant records of the history of the previous Tang Era. Completed in 945, the work eventually became known as *The Old Tang History*, to distinguish it from a later version, *The New Tang History*, which was compiled in the Song Era.

In the story excerpted here, we learn about relations between the short-lived but important Uighur Empire (744–840) and Tang China. The time period is 758–759, and China is torn apart by rebellion. In desperation, Emperor Tang Su-zong (r. 756–762) turns to the *Uighurs*, a Turkic people who dominated the Mongolian steppes and had recently emerged as the major force along China's northwestern border. Traditionally pastoral nomads, the Uighurs were in the process of settling down as agriculturalists and establishing several cities, but they maintained much of their nomadic culture, especially their warrior traditions. Until recently, in fact, they had been at war with the Chinese.

The story begins in June 758 with the arrival of an embassy at the capital city of Chang'an, which imperial forces, with the help of a Uighur detachment of about 4,000 cavalry, had reoccupied in November 757. Indeed, Uighurs had been fighting alongside loyalist Chinese forces since December 756.

QUESTIONS FOR ANALYSIS

1. What did each side, the Chinese and the Uighur, hope to gain by this marriage alliance? Were the goals achieved?
2. This story is told from a Chinese perspective. How did the Chinese interpret or explain their relations with the Uighurs?

3. Retell the story from the Uighur perspective.
4. Retell it from the princess's perspective.
5. What does this story suggest about China's relations with the nomadic peoples along its borders?

On . . . the first day of the fifth month of the first year of Qianyuan (June 11, 758), eighty Uighur envoys . . . and six Abbasid Arab chiefs[1] . . . came simultaneously to court to have an audience. When they arrived at the pavilion gate, they argued over who should go in first. The visitors-and-audience officials separated them into right and left and they entered at the same time through the east and west gates.

In the sixth month, on the day *wuxu* (July 7, 758), there was a banquet in honor of some Uighur envoys in front of the Zichen Hall.[2]

In the autumn, on the day *dinghai* of the seventh month (August 25, 758), the emperor issued an edict that one of his young daughters[3] should be installed as the Princess of Ningguo and that she should go out and be married [to the Uighur khaghan].[4] On the day of her departure for the Uighur territory, the emperor's younger cousin on his father's side, who was the Prefectural Prince of Hanzhong, Yu, . . . was to hold temporarily the rank of President of the Censorate, and was to fill the office of Commissioner Who Appoints and Names "Brave and Warlike, Aweing the Distant Lands, the Turkic Khaghan.". . .

On the day *guiwu* (August 31, 758), the emperor appointed and set up "Brave and Warlike, Aweing the Distant Lands, the Turkic Khaghan of the Uighurs." He (the emperor) sat in the Grand Audience Hall, and the Prince of

Hanzhong received from him the imperial diploma [of appointment].

On the day *jiawu* (September 1, 758), the Emperor Suzong, escorting the Princess of Ningguo, arrived at the Cimen Postal Station in Xianyang.[5] The princess wept and spoke to him saying, "The affairs of our state are serious. Even should I die, I shall not regret going." The emperor shed tears and returned.

When Yu reached his royal camp, the Turkic khaghan, dressed in a yellow-ocher robe[6] and a barbarian hat, was sitting in his tent on a bed. His insignia and body-guards were extremely abundant. They led Yu before him, standing outside the tent. The khaghan spoke to Yu saying, "Prince, what relation are you to the Heavenly Khaghan?"[7] Yu said, "I am the cousin of the Son of Heaven of Tang." . . .

Everybody was in his proper place. But Yu would not bow and remained standing. The khaghan declared thus, "The leaders, nobility and subjects of both our states observe a rite. How can you not bow?" Yu said, "The Son of Heaven of Tang considered you, the khaghan, to have merit, and therefore he is having his daughter brought here and given to you in marriage. He is tying together a friendship through this marriage with you, the khaghan. Recently the women whom China has given to outside barbarians as wives have in all cases been [merely] daughters of members of the imperial clan and

---

[1]The Abbasids, who had seized the caliphate from the Umayyads in 750, had beaten Chinese forces rather badly at the Battle of the Talas River in 751, which meant a loss of China's westernmost areas of influence and the beginning of the Tang Dynasty's downward slide. Despite these earlier hostilities, the Arab ambassadors were in Chang'an to discuss rendering military assistance in the fight against the rebels.
[2]A hall in the heart of the imperial palace complex, which was known as the Daming Palace.

[3]The second of Emperor Tang Suzong's seven daughters. She had been married previously.
[4]Moyanchuo (r. 747–759), second *khaghan*, or leader, of the Uighur confederation. He consolidated the empire and built the Uighur capital city and palace.
[5]A city about twenty miles northwest of Chang'an.
[6]In China yellow was reserved for the imperial family.
[7]Emperor Tang Suzong. The Uighurs also used this title for their own khaghan.

have been named 'princesses.' The present Princess of Ningguo is the true daughter of the Son of Heaven.[8] Also she has talents and a becoming appearance and has come 10,000 *li*[9] to be married to the khaghan. The khaghan is to be the son-in-law of the Son of Heaven of the Tang family. He should know the differences in grades of the rites. How can he conceivably remain seated on his bed while receiving the diploma of such an edict?" At that the khaghan stood up to take the edict and immediately received the imperial diploma of his appointment.

The following day the princess was appointed the khatun.[10] The barbarian chief rejoiced over it and said, "The Son of Heaven of the Tang state is most high and has had his true daughter brought here." The state seals, the silken fabrics, the multi-colored clothes and garments and the gold and silver dishes which Yu had brought, the khaghan distributed down to the last one among his officials, chiefs and others. When Yu was on the point of going home, the khaghan presented him with 500 horses and 100 pieces of sable fur.

In the eighth month,[11] the Uighurs sent their prince, Prince Guchuo, and their Chief Minister, Dide, and other brave men at the head of 3,000 troops to help China in her fight against the rebels. Suzong commended them for having come from so far, and gave them a banquet. He ordered that they be attached to the Expeditionary Camps of the Shuofang Army and made Pugu Huaien[12] supervise them. On the day *jiashen* of the ninth month (October 21, 758), the Uighurs sent the great chief, General Gai, and others to give thanks for the granting of the

Princess [of Ningguo] in marriage. At the same time a memorial was set up to the effect that they had destroyed [an army of] 50,000 Kirghiz.[13]

There was a banquet in the Zichen Hall and the emperor gave gifts according to rank.

On the day *jiazi* of the twelfth month (January 29, 759?), the Uighurs sent three ladies to give thanks for the marriage of the Princess of Ningguo. The emperor gave them a banquet in the Zichen Hall.

In the second year of Qianyuan (759), the Uighurs, Prince Guchuo and others led their armies, following Guo Ziyi[14] and the nine military governors to [positions] outside the walls of Xiangzhou. There was a battle,[15] [the outcome of which] was not favorable [for government forces]. . . . [T]he Uighur prince, Prince Guchuo, the Chief Minister, Dide, and thirteen others fled from Xiangzhou to the Western Capital.[16] Suzong gave them a banquet in the Zichen Hall and rewarded them according to rank.

On the day *gengyin* of the same month (April 25, 759), the Uighur prince took his farewell and was about to take home his expeditionary camps. The emperor gave them a banquet in the Zichen Hall and made presentations according to rank.

▷   After receiving several imperial offices and titles, the prince and his troops return home.

In the summer, in the fourth month (May 2–30, 759), the Uighur Turkic khaghan died.[17] . . .

---

[8]The princess was the first daughter of a Tang emperor to be married to a foreign ruler.

[9]Later one *li* was about one-third of a mile, but evidence (as well as measurement of the distance from Chang'an to the heart of Mongolia) suggests that one *li* in the Tang Era was about one-fifth of a mile.

[10]Wife of the khaghan.

[11]The period from September 7 through October 6, 758.

[12]One of Tang China's leading generals, he was a member of the Turkic Pugu tribe, which was one of the nine tribes that made up the Uighur confederation.

[13]In an unrelated battle. The Kirghiz, a Turkic enemy of the Uighurs, eventually destroyed the Uighur Empire in 840.

[14]China's most successful general of the time, he was responsible, more than anyone else, for suppressing the rebellion and defending China from two Tibetan invasions.

[15]On April 7, 759.

[16]Chang'an. They arrived on April 19, 759.

[17]Sometime between May 2 and May 30, word arrived in Chang'an of his death. It had occurred a bit earlier.

When the Turkic khaghan died, his court officials, governors-general and others had wanted the Princess of Ningguo to be buried with him. The princess said, "In our Chinese law, when a woman's husband dies, she immediately observes mourning. She weeps in the morning and evening, and for a period approaching three years she dons mourning clothes. That [the khaghan of] the Uighurs took me as his wife must mean that he admired the rites of the Middle Kingdom. If he had still been following the laws of his own country, why was it necessary for him to marry a wife from 10,000 *li* away?" However, the princess also observed Uighur custom by slashing her face and weeping loudly. Finally, since she had no sons, she obtained permission to go home, and in the autumn . . . , the Princess of Ningguo came back from Uighur territory to China.[18] There was an edict that all the officials should welcome her outside the Mingfeng Gate.

---

[18]She arrived on September 18, 759.

The Dao of Agriculture in Song China

▼▼▼

57 ▼ *Chen Pu, THE CRAFT OF FARMING*

During the Song Era, China met the challenge of producing an adequate supply of food with reasonable success, despite the fact that its population of probably 50 to 60 million in the early 700s grew to about 120 million by about 1200. This success was partially due to an activist agenda by the central government, which encouraged land reclamation through tax incentives and published illustrated handbooks that promoted up-to-date agricultural technology. The following selections from a popular treatise written in 1149 by the otherwise unknown Chen Pu provide insight into the manner in which Song China approached the problem of feeding itself adequately.

QUESTIONS FOR ANALYSIS

1. What does Chen Pu assume is more scarce, and consequently more valuable, labor or land? What do you infer from your answer?
2. Chen Pu focuses on several key elements that contributed to Song China's success in feeding its people. What were they?
3. According to Chen Pu, which qualities set the superior farmer apart from all others?
4. In what ways is this treatise a combination of agricultural science, folk wisdom, Confucian learning, and Daoist ideology? Can you find any Legalist elements in the essay?

FINANCE AND LABOR

In the farming business, which is the most difficult business to manage, how can you afford not
to calculate your financial and labor capacities
carefully? Only when you are certain that you
have sufficient funds and labor to assure success
should you launch an enterprise. Anyone who
covets more than he can manage is likely to fall
into carelessness and irresponsibility. . . . Thus,
to procure more land is to increase trouble, not
profit.

On the other hand, anyone who plans carefully, begins with good methods, and continues
in the same way can reasonably expect success
and does not have to rely on luck. The proverb
says, "Owning a great deal of emptiness is less
desirable than reaping from a narrow patch of
land." . . . For the farmer who is engaged in the
management of fields, the secret lies not in expanding the farmland, but in balancing finance
and labor. If the farmer can achieve that, he can
expect prosperity and abundance. . . .

PLOWING

Early and late plowing both have their advantages. For the early rice crop,[1] as soon as the
reaping is completed, immediately plow the
fields and expose the stalks to glaring sunlight.
Then add manure and bury the stalks to nourish
the soil. Next, plant beans, wheat, and vegetables to ripen and fertilize the soil so as to mini-
mize the next year's labor. In addition, when the
harvest is good, these extra crops can add to the
yearly income. For late crops, however, do not
plow until spring. Because the rice stalks are soft
but tough, it is necessary to wait until they have
fully decayed to plow satisfactorily. . . .

---

[1]Rice became a central part of the Chinese diet in the Song
Era, thanks to the introduction of early-ripening, drought-
resistant strains from Southeast Asia. These new seeds made
it possible to grow the crop in areas that previously had
been unsuitable for rice cultivation.

THE SIX KINDS OF CROPS

There is an order to the planting of different
crops. Anyone who knows the right timing and
follows the order can cultivate one thing after
another, and use one to assist the others. Then
there will not be a day without planting, nor a
month without harvest, and money will be coming in throughout the year. How can there then
be any worry about cold, hunger, or lack of
funds?

Plant the nettle-hemp in the first month.
Apply manure in intervals of ten days and by the
fifth or sixth month it will be time for reaping.
The women should take charge of knotting and
spinning cloth out of the hemp.

Plant millet in the second month. It is necessary to sow the seeds sparsely and then roll cart
wheels over the soil to firm it up; this will make
the millet grow luxuriantly, its stalks long and
its grains full. In the seventh month the millet
will be harvested, easing any temporary financial
difficulties.

There are two crops of oil-hemp. The early
crop is planted in the third month. Rake the
field to spread out the seedlings. Repeat the rak-
ing process three times a month and the hemp
will grow well. It can be harvested in the seventh or the eighth month.

In the fourth month plant beans. Rake as with
hemp. They will be ripe by the seventh month.

In mid-fifth month plant the late oil-hemp.
Proceed as with the early crop. The ninth month
will be reaping time.

After the 7th day of the seventh month, plant
radishes and cabbage.

In the eighth month, before the autumn sacrifice to the god of the Earth, wheat can be
planted. It is advisable to apply manure and re-

move weeds frequently. When wheat grows from the autumn through the spring sacrifices to the god of the Earth, the harvest will double and the grains will be full and solid.

The *Book of Poetry*[2] says, "The tenth month is the time to harvest crops." You will have a large variety of crops, including millet, rice, beans, hemp, and wheat and will lack nothing needed through the year. Will you ever be concerned for want of resources? . . .

FERTILIZER

At the side of the farm house, erect a compost hut. Make the eaves low to prevent the wind and rain from entering it, for when the compost is exposed to the moon and the stars, it will lose its fertility. In this hut, dig a deep pit and line it with bricks to prevent leakage. Collect waste, ashes, chaff, broken stalks, and fallen leaves and burn them in the pit; then pour manure over them to make them fertile. In this way considerable quantities of compost are acquired over time. Then, whenever sowing is to be done, sieve and discard stones and tiles, mix the fine compost with the seeds, and plant them sparsely in pinches. When the seedlings have grown tall, again sprinkle the compost and bank it up against the roots. These methods will ensure a double yield.

Some people say that when the soil is exhausted, grass and trees will not grow; that when the *qi*[3] is weak, all living things will be stunted; and that after three to five years of continuous planting, the soil of any field will be exhausted. This theory is erroneous because it fails to recognize one factor: by adding new, fertile

soil, enriched with compost, the land can be reinforced in strength. If this is so, where can the alleged exhaustion come from?

WEEDING

The *Book of Poetry* says, "Root out the weeds. Where the weeds decay, there the grains will grow luxuriantly." The author of the *Record of Ritual* also remarks, "The months of midsummer are advantageous for weeding. Weeds can fertilize the fields and improve the land."[4] Modern farmers, ignorant of these principles, throw the weeds away. They do not know that, if mixed with soil and buried deep under the roots of rice seedlings, the weeds will eventually decay and the soil will be enriched; the harvest, as a result, will be abundant and of superior quality. . . .

CONCENTRATION

If something is thought out carefully, it will succeed; if not, it will fail; this is a universal truth. It is very rare that a person works and yet gains nothing. On the other hand, there is never any harm in trying too hard.

In farming it is especially appropriate to be concerned about what you are doing. Mencius[5] said, "Will a farmer discard his plow when he leaves his land?" Ordinary people will become idle if they have leisure and prosperity. Only those who love farming, who behave in harmony with it, who take pleasure in talking about it and think about it all the time will manage it without a moment's negligence. For these people a day's work results in a day's gain, a year's work in a year's gain. How can they escape affluence?

---

[2]Also known as the *Book of Songs* (source 6).
[3]Vital energy, or material force. *Qi* was a construct of *Neo-Confucian* philosophers during the Song Era. They envisioned a cosmos in which all entities are composed of *li* (an infinite Moral Principle) and *qi* (its driving force). See Multiple Voices VI.

[4]Also known as the *Classic of Rites* (*Liji*), it is one of the five Confucian Classics.
[5]Mencius (*Mengzi*), a fourth-century B.C.E. philosopher, is considered the greatest Confucian after Confucius himself.

▼▼▼

Southwest Asia:
Crossroads of the Afro-Eurasian World

Of all the significant developments that took place in Southwest Asia during the 1,000-year period from 500 to 1500, the two most far-reaching were the rise and spread of Islam and the arrival of Turkish, European, and Mongol invaders after the year 1000. By approximately 750 Islam was firmly in control of most of Southwest Asia, except for the Anatolian Peninsula, which remained the heart of the East Roman, or *Byzantine*, Empire until late in the eleventh century, when Islamic Turkish forces began the process of transforming this land into Turkey. Seljuk and Ottoman Turks, European crusaders, Mongols, and the armies of *Timur the Lame*, or *Tamerlane* (see Chapter 12, source 86), would invade and contest Southwest Asia for much of the period from 1000 to 1500.

Around the early sixteenth century, a clear pattern emerged. Most of Europe's Christian crusaders had been expelled from the eastern Mediterranean, except for their precarious possession of a handful of island strongholds, such as Cyprus and Crete; the Mongol empire was only a fading memory; and Timur the Lame's empire had crumbled upon his death in 1405. Two Turkish Islamic empires dominated Southwest Asia — the Shia Safavids of Persia and the Sunni Ottomans, whose base of power was Anatolia, but who also controlled Syria-Palestine, Egypt, and western Arabia and were driving deeply into Europe's Balkan Peninsula. Although these two empires would quarrel viciously for control of Islam, and Sunnis and Shias would continue to shed each other's blood, Turkish domination of Southwest Asia was secure for the foreseeable future. European attempts to counter the Turkish menace by launching new crusades in the eastern Mediterranean generally proved feeble, and the Ottomans' and Safavids' pastoral cousins on the steppes of Inner Asia were becoming less of a threat to the stability of Eurasia's civilizations.

The Arrival of the Turks
▼▼▼

58 ▼ Al-Jahiz,
THE MERITS OF THE TURKS AND
OF THE IMPERIAL ARMY AS A WHOLE

Early in the ninth century, the caliphs of Baghdad addressed the problem of creating a loyal army by enlisting foreign slaves and mercenaries, many of whom came from various tribes of Turkic-speaking, pastoral peoples across the frontier in the steppes of Inner Asia. As aliens, the Turks theoretically had no ties to the various factions that threatened the caliph's power. In a short time, however, these Turkish warriors converted to Islam and became powers behind the throne. As early as the mid ninth century, some Turkish officers were playing important roles in the selection of caliphs. From that point on, the caliphs and their ministers became increasingly dependent on various Turkish elements in the army, and it was almost an anticlimax when Tughril-Beg, leader of a tribe of Turks known as the *Seljuks*, entered Baghdad on December 19, 1055, to be recognized formally as *sultan* (governor) and to have his name mentioned in Friday prayers after that of the caliph. Civil and military authority now lay in the hands of Turkish sultans, and the caliph retained only religious and ceremonial functions. Under the Seljuks, Islam quickly expanded into Byzantine Anatolia, thereby precipitating a Western Christian response — the crusades.

Two centuries earlier, a resident of the port city of Basra in southern Iraq, Abu Uthman Amr ibn Bahr (776–869) — better known by his nickname *al-Jahiz* (the Goggle-Eyed) — composed a study of the Turks, in which he attempted to place these recent converts to Islam in a favorable light. Many cultivated Arabs and Persians despised the Turks, whom they considered to be barbarians, and resented their growing power. Al-Jahiz, one of the most popular and gifted essayists of his day and always a voice of reason and moderation, attempted to counter those attitudes.

QUESTIONS FOR ANALYSIS

1. What does al-Jahiz's essay tell us about the equestrian and military qualities of the Turks and, by extension, of other pastoral peoples from Central Asia? Does this portrait help explain the role played in Eurasian history by the horse nomads?
2. How, according to the essayist, do the Turks resemble the Arabs of the Prophet's day?
3. Given these qualities, what special value do the Turks offer Islamic society?
4. How, if at all, does this essay reveal the cosmopolitan perspective of ninth-century Iraq?

THE TURK AS A HORSEMAN

A Kharijite[1] at close quarters relies entirely on his lance. But the Turks are as good as the Kharijites with the lance, and in addition, if a thousand of their horsemen are hard-pressed they will loose all their arrows in a single volley and bring down a thousand enemy horsemen. No body of men can stand up against such a test.

Neither the Kharijites nor the Bedouins[2] are famous for their prowess as mounted bowmen.

But the Turk will hit from his saddle an animal, a bird, a target, a man, a couching animal, a marker post or a bird of prey stooping on its quarry. His horse may be exhausted from being galloped and reined in, wheeled to right and left, and mounted and dismounted: but he himself goes on shooting, loosing ten arrows before the Kharijite has let fly one. He gallops his horse up a hillside or down a gully faster than the Kharijite can make his go on the flat.

---

[1]One of the earliest sects to break off from the main body of Islam, the Kharijites were noted as fierce warriors.

[2]Arab nomads of Arabia, North Africa, and the eastern Mediterranean.

The Turk has two pairs of eyes, one at the front and the other at the back of his head. . . .

They train their horsemen to carry two or even three bows, and spare bowstrings in proportion. Thus in the hour of battle the Turk has on him everything needful for himself, his weapon and the care of his steed. As for their ability to stand trotting, sustained galloping, long night rides and cross-country journeys, it is truly extraordinary. In the first place the Kharijite's horse has not the staying-power of the Turk's pony; and the Kharijite has no more than a horseman's knowledge of how to look after his mount. The Turk, however, is more experienced than a professional farrier,[3] and better than a trainer at getting what he wants from his pony. For it was he who brought it into the world and reared it from a foal; it comes when he calls it, and follows behind him when he runs. . . .

If the Turk's daily life were to be reckoned up in detail, he would be found to spend more time in the saddle than on the ground.

The Turk sometimes rides a stallion, sometimes a brood mare. Whether he is going to war, on a journey, out hunting or on any other errand, the brood mare follows behind with her foals. If he gets tired of hunting the enemy he hunts waterfowl. If he gets hungry, jogging up and down in the saddle, he has only to lay hands on one of his animals. If he gets thirsty, he milks one of his brood mares. If he needs to rest his mount, he vaults on to another without so much as putting his feet to the ground.

Of all living creatures he is the only one whose body can adapt itself to eating nothing but meat. As for his steed, leaves and shoots are all it needs; he gives it no shelter from the sun and no covering against the cold.

As regards ability to stand trotting, if the stamina of the border fighters, the posthorse outriders,[4] the Kharijites and the eunuchs[5] were all combined in one man, they would not equal a Turk.

The Turk demands so much of his mount that only the toughest of his horses is equal to the task; even one that he had ridden to exhaustion, so as to be useless for his expeditions, would outdo a Kharijite's horse in staying power, and no Tukhari pony could compare with it.

The Turk is at one and the same time herdsman, groom, trainer, horse-dealer, farrier and rider: in short, a one-man team.

When the Turk travels with horsemen of other races, he covers twenty miles to their ten, leaving them and circling around to right and left, up on to the high ground and down to the bottom of the gullies, and shooting all the while at anything that runs, crawls, flies or stands still. The Turk never travels like the rest of the band, and never rides straight ahead. On a long, hard ride, when it is noon and the halting-place is still afar off, all are silent, oppressed with fatigue and overwhelmed into weariness. Their misery leaves no room for conversation. Everything round them crackles in the intense heat, or perhaps is frozen hard. As the journey drags on, even the toughest and most resolute begin to wish that the ground would open under their feet. At the sight of a mirage or a marker post on a ridge they are transported with joy, supposing it to be the halting-place. When at last they reach it, the horsemen all drop from the saddle and stagger about bandy-legged like children who have been given an enema, groaning like sick men, yawning to refresh themselves and stretching luxuriously to overcome their stiffness. But your Turk, though he has covered twice the distance and dislocated his shoulders with shooting, has only to catch sight of a gazelle or an onager[6] near the halting-place, or put up a fox or a hare, and he is off again at a gallop as though he had only just mounted. It

---

[3]A blacksmith.
[4]Mounted attendants who rode alongside a carriage and, as needed, exchanged horses at post stations along the route.

[5]Castrated slaves who performed domestic services. According to ninth-century Arab folklore, eunuchs endured long horse rides especially well — possibly as a consequence of their mutilation.
[6]A speedy wild ass of Central Asia.

might have been someone else who had done that long ride and endured all that weariness.

At the gully the band bunches together at the bridge or the best crossing-place; but the Turk, digging his heels into his pony, is already going up the other side like a shooting star. If there is a steep rise, he leaves the track and scrambles straight up the hillside, going where even the ibex[7] cannot go. To see him scaling such slopes anyone would think he was recklessly risking his life: but if that were so he would not last long, for he is always doing it. . . .

NATIONAL CHARACTERISTICS

Peoples of varying habits of thought, different opinions and dissimilar characters cannot attain perfection unless they fulfill the conditions needed to carry on an activity, and have a natural aptitude for it. Good examples are the Chinese in craftsmanship, the Greeks in philosophy and literature, the Arabs in fields that we mean to deal with in their proper place . . . and the Turks in the art of war. . . .

The Chinese for their part are specialists in smelting, casting and metalworking, in fine colors, in sculpture, weaving and drawing; they are very skillful with their hands, whatever the medium, the technique or the cost of the materials. The Greeks are theoreticians rather than practitioners, while the Chinese are practitioners rather than theoreticians; the former are thinkers, the latter doers.

The Arabs, again, were not merchants, artisans, physicians, farmers — for that would have degraded them —, mathematicians or fruit-farmers — for they wished to escape the humiliation of the tax; nor were they out to earn or amass money, hoard possessions or lay hands on other people's; they were not of those who make their living with a pair of scales; . . . they were not poor enough to be indifferent to learning, pursued neither wealth, that breeds foolishness, nor good fortune, that begets apathy, and never tolerated humiliation, which was dishonor and death to their souls. They dwelt in the plains, and grew up in contemplation of the desert. They knew neither damp nor rising mist, neither fog nor foul air, nor a horizon bounded by walls. When these keen minds and clear brains turned to poetry, fine language, eloquence and oratory, to physiognomy and astrology, genealogy, navigation by the stars and by marks on the ground, . . . to horse-breeding, weaponry and engines of war, to memorizing all that they heard, pondering on everything that caught their attention and discriminating between the glories and the shames of their tribes, they achieved perfection beyond the wildest dreams. Certain of these activities broadened their minds and exalted their aspirations, so that of all nations they are now the most glorious and the most given to recalling their past splendors.

It is the same with the Turks who dwell in tents in the desert and keep herds: they are the Bedouins of the non-Arabs. . . . Uninterested in craftsmanship or commerce, medicine, geometry, fruit-farming, building, digging canals or collecting taxes, they care only about raiding, hunting, horsemanship, skirmishing with rival chieftains, taking booty and invading other countries. Their efforts are all directed towards these activities, and they devote all their energies to these occupations. In this way they have acquired a mastery of these skills, which for them take the place of craftsmanship and commerce and constitute their only pleasure, their glory and the subject of all their conversation. Thus have they become in the realm of warfare what the Greeks are in philosophy, the Chinese in craftsmanship, and the Arabs in the fields we have enumerated.

---

[7]An Asiatic mountain goat.

Muslims and Franks in the Crusader States
▼▼▼

59 ▼ Ibn Jubayr, TRAVELS

In 1095 Pope Urban II (r. 1088–1099) set in motion a movement that became known as the *crusades* — close to 500 years of Western Christian involvement in the lands of the *Levant*, or eastern Mediterranean. Between March 1098 and July 1109, the armies of the *First Crusade* (1096–1099) and adventurers building upon the gains of their predecessors carved out four *crusader states* in lands that had recently been under Muslim domination: the *county of Edessa* (1098–1150); the *principality of Antioch* (1098–1268); the *kingdom of Jerusalem* (1099–1291); and the *county of Tripoli* (1109–1289). In some respects they were Europe's first overseas colonies, but each was a state answerable to no mother country in Europe.

Western European settlers, known as *Franj*, or *Franks*, to the natives of the region, were a decided minority in the land they called *Outremer* (the land across the sea). Edessa had a large Armenian Christian majority, and Antioch's population was dominated by Greek (Byzantine) and Syrian Christians. Both states also had significant Muslim minorities who probably outnumbered the resident Franks several times over. Probably 80 percent or more of the populations of Tripoli and Jerusalem were divided about equally between Muslims and Eastern Christians of various sorts, with Western, or *Latin*, Christian settlers constituting the remainder — no more than 20 percent and probably far less. The only places where Franks probably outnumbered indigenous Eastern Christians and Muslims were key coastal towns, such as Acre, and the holy city of Jerusalem. These realities meant that the Frankish lords of the crusader states had to find ways of governing the indigenous populations of their states that took into account this overall numerical imbalance.

In 1184 Abu al-Husayn Muhammad ibn Ahmad ibn Jubayr, a native of Valencia in Muslim Spain, on his way home after having completed the *hajj* to Mecca, spent thirty-two days in crusader territory. Throughout his two-year journey from Spain to the East and back, Ibn Jubayr kept an almost-daily journal of his travels, which provides us with vivid pictures of late-twelfth-century life and culture in Egypt, Iraq, Arabia, Syria-Palestine, and other stopping places along the way.

QUESTIONS FOR ANALYSIS

1. Does Ibn Jubayr like the Franks? Support your answer.
2. What does he think is the worst aspect of Frankish rule?
3. What arguments can you adduce to support the proposition that Ibn Jubayr's testimony is solid and trustworthy?
4. What counterarguments can you adduce that cast doubt on his testimony?
5. Where do you stand on the issue? Be specific in explaining your position.
6. Based on your study of this source, what do you conclude you can say with some degree of certainty about Frankish-Muslim relations in the Latin kingdom of Jerusalem around 1184?

We left Damascus[1] on the evening of Thursday . . . , which was the 13th of September, in a large caravan of merchants traveling with their merchandise to Acre. One of the strangest things in the world is that Muslim caravans go forth to Frankish lands, while Frankish captives enter Muslim lands. . . . We ourselves went forth to Frankish lands at a time when Frankish prisoners were entering Muslim lands.[2] Let this be evidence enough to you of the temperateness of the policy of Saladin.[3] . . . We left, on the morning of Saturday, for the city of Banyas. Halfway on the road, we came upon an oak-tree of great proportions and with widespreading branches. We learnt that it is called "The Tree of Measure," and when we inquired concerning it, we were told that it was the boundary on this road between security and danger, by reason of some Frankish brigands who prowl and rob thereon. He whom they seize on the Muslim side, be it by the length of the arms or a span, they capture; but he whom they seize on the Frankish side at a like distance, they release. This is a pact they faithfully observe and is one of the most pleasing and singular conventions of the Franks.

A Note on the City of Banyas {Belinas}

God Most High defend it

This city is on the frontier of the Muslim territories. It is small, but has a fortress below the walls

of which winds a river that flows out from one of the gates of the city. A canal leading from it turns the mills. The city had been in the hands of the Franks, but Nur al-Din[4] — may God's mercy rest upon his soul — recovered it [in 1165]. It has a wide tillage in a contiguous vale. It is commanded by a fortress of the Franks called Hunin[5] three parasangs[6] distant from Banyas. The cultivation of the vale is divided between the Franks and the Muslims, and in it there is a boundary known as "The Boundary of Dividing." They apportion the crops equally, and their animals are mingled together, yet no wrong takes place between them because of it.

We departed from Banyas. . . . We . . . came to one of the biggest fortresses of the Franks, called Tibnin.[7] At this place customs dues are levied on the caravans. It belongs to the sow known as Queen[8] who is the mother of the pig who is the Lord of Acre[9] may God destroy it.[10]

We camped at the foot of this fortress. The fullest tax was not exacted from us. . . . No toll was laid upon the merchants, since they were bound for the place of the accursed king [Acre], where the tax is gathered.[11] The tax there is a qirat in every dinar[12] (worth of merchandise), the dinar having twenty-four qirat.[13] The greater part of those taxed were Maghribis,[14] those from all other Muslim lands being unmolested. This was because some earlier Maghribis had annoyed

---

[1]Damascus was the center of Islamic power in southern Syria.
[2]The several thousand Franks who had been captured and enslaved during the successful campaign of 1184 against the crusader city of Nablus and its environs, which had been conducted by Saladin, sultan of Egypt and Syria.
[3]Ibn Jubayr seems to be arguing here that Saladin's reputation for fair-dealing and temperate behavior, even with the Franks, made this commerce possible.
[4]Nur al-Din, Turkish ruler of Syria (r. 1146–1174), initiated the first real *jihad* against the crusader states. Saladin continued his religious war, but both Nur al-Din and Saladin were willing to enter into periodic but time-limited truces with the Franks when it suited their needs.
[5]Better known to the Franks as *Chastel Neuf*, the fortress commanded the headwaters of the Jordan River and the fertile plain around Banyas, which is located in the Upper Galilee (present-day northern Israel).
[6]An ancient Persian unit of measurement — about 3.5 miles.
[7]Better known as *Toron*, this was one of the strongest crusader castles in the Galilee.

[8]Queen Agnes of Courtenay, widow of King Amalric. In a state noted for its powerful and strong-willed women, Agnes was one of the Latin kingdom of Jerusalem's most powerful and controversial queens.
[9]King Baldwin IV (r. 1174–1185).
[10]Acre, a city on the Bay of Haifa in northern Israel, was the kingdom of Jerusalem's premier port. Initially captured by crusaders in 1104, it was recaptured by Saladin in 1187. The armies of the Third Crusade retook the city in 1191, and it remained in Frankish hands until 1291, when the Mamluk sultan of Egypt captured and razed the city's defenses. With its fall, crusader presence along the Mediterranean coast of Southwest Asia was essentially ended.
[11]The laws of the kingdom of Jerusalem specified 111 items on which tax was due at Acre.
[12]A gold coin weighing 4.72 grams.
[13]A *qirat* was one-twenty-fourth of anything. In this case, of a dinar.
[14]Muslims from the western Mediterranean, either western North Africa or *al-Andalus* (Muslim Spain).

the Franks. A gallant company of them had attacked one of their strongholds with Nur al-Din — may God have mercy upon him — and by its taking they had become manifestly rich and famous. The Franks punished them by this tax, and their chiefs enforced it. Every Maghribi therefore paid this dinar for his hostility to their country. The Franks declared: "These Maghribis came and went in our country and we treated them well and took nothing from them. But when they interfered in the war, joining with their brother Muslims against us, we were compelled to place this tax upon them." In the payment of this tax, the Maghribis are pleasingly reminded of their vexing of the enemy, and thus the payment of it is lightened and its harshness made tolerable.

We moved from Tibnin — may God destroy it[15] — at daybreak on Monday. Our way lay through continuous farms and ordered settlements, whose inhabitants were all Muslims,[16] living comfortably with the Franks. God protect us from such temptation. They surrender their crops to the Franks at harvest time, and pay as well a poll-tax[17] of one and five qirat for each person. Other than that, they are not interfered with, save for a light tax on the fruits of trees. Their houses and all their effects are left to their full possession. All the coastal cities occupied by the Franks are managed in this fashion, their rural districts, the villages and farms, belonging to the Muslims. But their hearts have been seduced, for they observe how unlike them in ease and comfort are their brethren in the Muslim regions under their (Muslim) governors. This is one of the misfortunes afflicting the Muslims. The Muslim community bewails the injustice of a landlord of its own faith, and applauds the con-

duct of its opponent and enemy, the Frankish landlord, and is accustomed to justice from him. He who laments this state must turn to God. . . .

On the same Monday, we alighted at a farmstead a parasang distant from Acre. Its headman is a Muslim, appointed by the Franks to oversee the Muslim workers in it. He gave generous hospitality to all members of the caravan, assembling them, great and small, in a large room in his house, and giving them a variety of foods and treating all with liberality. We were amongst those who attended this party, and passed the night there. On the morning of Tuesday . . . , which was the 18th of September, we came to the city of Acre — may God destroy it. We were taken to the custom-house, which is a khan[18] prepared to accommodate the caravan. Before the door are stone benches, spread with carpets, where are the Christian[19] clerks of the Customs with their ebony ink-stands ornamented with gold. They write Arabic, which they also speak. Their chief is the Sahib al-Diwan [Chief of the Customs], who holds the contract to farm the customs.[20] . . . All the dues collected go to the contractor for the customs, who pays a vast sum [to the Government]. The merchants deposited their baggage there and lodged in the upper story. The baggage of any who had no merchandise was also examined in case it contained concealed [and dutiable] merchandise, after which the owner was permitted to go his way and seek lodging where he would. All this was done with civility and respect, and without harshness and unfairness. We lodged beside the sea in a house which we rented from a Christian woman, and prayed God Most High to save us from all dangers and help us to security.

---

[15]Toron held out until 1291.
[16]Frankish, Eastern Christian, and Muslim farmers normally inhabited villages separate from one another.
[17]A head tax. This was a Frankish variation on the *jizya*, or poll tax, that Islamic law prescribed for *dhimmis*, or tolerated People of the Book (see Multiple Voices V). Under Frankish law, Muslims were now the dhimmis.

[18]Another term for *caravanserai* — a place set aside for caravan traffic.
[19]Syrian Christians whose native language was Arabic.
[20]As Ibn Jubayr makes clear below, a person who farms taxes pays the state a set fee for the contract. Whatever is collected in excess of the payment is profit.

A Note on the City of Acre

May God exterminate (the Christians in) it and restore it (to the Muslims)

Acre is the capital of the Frankish cities in Syria[21] . . . and a port of call for all ships. In its greatness it resembles Constantinople. It is the focus of ships and caravans, and the meeting-place of Muslim and Christian merchants from all regions. Its roads and streets are choked by the press of men, so that it is hard to put foot to ground. Unbelief and unpiousness there burn fiercely, and pigs[22] and crosses abound. It stinks and is filthy, being full of refuse and excrement. The Franks ravished it from Muslim hands in the first decade of the sixth century,[23] and the eyes of Islam were swollen with weeping for it; it was one of its griefs. Mosques became churches and minarets bell-towers, but God kept undefiled one part of the principal mosque, which remained in the hands of the Muslims as a small mosque where strangers could congregate to offer the obligatory prayers. Near its mihrab[24] is the tomb of the prophet Salih[25] — God bless and preserve him and all the prophets. God protected this part (of the mosque) from desecration by the unbelievers for the benign influence of this holy tomb.

To the east of the town is the spring called Ayn al-Baqar [the Spring of the Cattle], from which God brought forth the cattle for Adam[26] — may God bless and preserve him. The descent to this spring is by a deep stairway. Over it is a mosque of which there remains in its former state only the mihrab, to the east of which the Franks have built their own mihrab,[27] and Muslim and infidel assemble there, the one turning to his place of worship, the other to his. In the hands of the Christians its venerableness is maintained, and God has preserved in it a place of prayer for the Muslims.

Two days we tarried at this place, and then, on Thursday . . . the 20th of September, we set forth across country to Sur [Tyre].[28] . . . We lodged in a khan in the town prepared for the reception of pilgrims.

A Note on the City of Sur {Tyre}

May God Most High destroy it

This city has become proverbial for its impregnability, and he who seeks to conquer it will meet with no surrender or humility.[29] The Franks prepared it as a refuge in case of unforeseen emergency, making it a strong point for their safety. Its roads and streets are cleaner than those of Acre. Its people are by disposition less stubborn in their unbelief, and by nature and habit they are kinder to the Muslim stranger. Their manners, in other words, are gentler. Their dwellings are larger and more spacious. The state of the Muslims in this city is easier and more peaceful. Acre is a town at once bigger, more impious, and more unbelieving. But the strength and impregnability of Tyre is more marvelous. . . . The beauty of the site of this port is truly wonderful. Acre resembles it in situation and description, but cannot take the large ships, which must anchor outside, small ships only being able to enter. The port of Tyre is more complete, more beautiful, and more animated. Eleven days we tarried in the city, entering it on Thursday, and

---

[21]It only became the capital of the kingdom of Jerusalem upon its recapture by Christian forces in 1191 (see note 10) because Jerusalem, the former capital, had been captured by Saladin in 1187. This anachronism might suggest later editing. More likely, it is due to Ibn Jubayr's misunderstanding, but see note 29.

[22]The pig is the most unclean of animals in Islamic tradition. Here he uses the term to mean Christians. See his characterizations of Queen Agnes and King Baldwin IV.

[23]Actually, the last decade of the fifth century of the Islamic calendar (March 24, 1104).

[24]The decorated niche in the mosque that indicates the direction of Mecca.

[25]A prophet and messenger (*rasul*) of God who is mentioned only in the Quran (7:73 and following). Like the biblical Jonah, he was sent to warn an errant people.

[26]The Quran, 20:115.

[27]Probably an altar niche facing Jerusalem.

[28]Tyre (in present-day Lebanon) was held continuously by the Franks from 1124 to 1291. It was the northernmost and deepest of the kingdom of Jerusalem's ports.

[29]Either this is prophetic, or it was composed after Saladin failed to take the city — one of his few failures — during his campaign of 1187–1188, when he almost (momentarily) swept the Franks out of Syria-Palestine. See note 21.

leaving it on Sunday . . . , which was the last day of September; this was because the ship in which we had hoped to sail we found to be too small, so that we were unwilling to set forth in it.

An alluring worldly spectacle deserving of record was a nuptial procession which we witnessed one day near the port in Tyre. All the Christians, men and women, had assembled, and were formed in two lines at the bride's door. Trumpets, flutes, and all the musical instruments, were played until she proudly emerged between two men who held her right and left as though they were her kindred. She was most elegantly garbed in a beautiful dress from which trailed, according to their traditional style, a long train of golden silk. On her head she wore a golden diadem covered by a net of woven gold, and on her breast was a like arrangement. Proud she was in her ornaments and dress, walking with little steps of half a span, like a dove, or in the manner of a wisp of cloud. God protect us from the seduction of the sight. Before her went Christian notables in their finest and most splendid clothing, their trains falling behind them. Behind her were her peers and equals of the Christian women, parading in their richest apparel and proud of bearing in their superb ornaments. Leading them all were the musical instruments. The Muslims and other Christian onlookers formed two ranks along the route, and gazed on them without reproof. So they passed along until they brought her to the house of the groom; and all that day they feasted. We thus were given the chance of seeing this alluring sight, from the seducement of which God preserve us.

We then returned by sea to Acre and landed there on the morning of Monday . . . , being the first day in October. We hired passages on a large ship, about to sail to Messina on the island of Sicily. My God Most High, in His power and strength, assure the easing and lightening (of our way).

During our stay in Tyre we rested in one of the mosques that remained in Muslim hands. One of the Muslim elders of Tyre told us that it[30] had been wrested from them . . . after a long siege and after hunger had overcome them. We were told that it had brought them to such a pass — we take refuge in God from it — that shame had driven them to propose a course from which God had preserved them. They had determined to gather their wives and children into the Great Mosque and there put them to the sword, rather than that the Christians should possess them. They themselves would then sally forth determinedly, and in a violent assault on the enemy, die together. But God made His irreversible decree, and their jurisprudents[31] and some of their godly men prevented them. They thereupon decided to abandon the town, and to make good their escape. So it happened, and they dispersed among the Muslim lands. But there were some whose love of native land impelled them to return and, under the conditions of a safeguard which was written for them, to live amongst the infidels. . . .

There can be no excuse in the eyes of God, for a Muslim to stay in any infidel country, save when passing through it, while the way lies clear in Muslim lands. They will face pains and terrors such as the abasement and destitution of the capitation and more especially, amongst their base and lower orders, the hearing of what will distress the heart in the reviling of him [Muhammad] whose memory God has sanctified, and whose rank He has exalted; there is also the absence of cleanliness, the mixing with the pigs, and all the other prohibited matters too numerous to be related or enumerated. Beware, beware of entering their lands. May God Most High grant His beneficent indulgence for this sin into which (our) feet have slipped, but His forgiveness is not given save after accepting our penitence. Glory to God, the Master. There is no Lord but He. . . .

[30]The city.

[31]*Qadis*, or Islamic jurists.

By an unhappy chance, from the evils of which we take refuge in God, we were accompanied on our road to Acre from Damascus by a Maghribi. . . . In one of his patron's caravans he had come to Acre, where he had mixed with the Christians, and taken on much of their character. The devil increasingly seduced and incited him until he renounced the faith of Islam, turned unbeliever, and became a Christian in the time of our stay in Tyre. We left to Acre, but received news of him. He had been baptised and become unclean, and had put on the girdle of a monk, thereby hastening for himself the flames of hell, verifying the threats of torture, and exposing himself to a grievous account and a long-distance return (from hell). We beg Great and Glorious God to confirm us in the true word in this world and the next, allowing us not to deviate from the pure faith and letting us, in His grace and mercy, die Muslims. . . .

On Saturday . . . , being the 6th of October, with the favor of God towards the Muslims, we embarked on a large ship, taking water and provisions. The Muslims secured places apart from the Franks. Some Christians called "bilghriyin"[32] came aboard. They had been on the pilgrimage to Jerusalem, and were too numerous to count, but were more than two thousand. May God in His grace and favor soon relieve us of their company and bring us to safety with His hoped-for assistance and beneficent works; none but He should be worshipped. So, under the will of Great and Glorious God, we awaited a favoring wind and the completion of the ship's stowing.

---

[32]From the Italian *pellegrini* — pilgrims.

Sinbad's First Voyage

▼▼▼

60 ▼ *A THOUSAND AND ONE ARABIAN NIGHTS*

Many would-be empire builders and invaders marched across this crossroad of the Afro-Eurasian World, and in the process they destroyed and altered much. Notwithstanding these invasions, villages, towns, and cities prospered in large numbers, fed by the productive activities of peasants, artisans, and merchants alike. Farming, craft production, and even large-scale industrial manufacture contributed to a healthy economy, but all these activities paled in comparison with the economic impact of commerce, particularly transit trade. Evidence suggests that Southwest Asian production of commodities for export declined from the eleventh century onward, whereas trade in manufactured goods produced elsewhere, primarily China, India, and Western Europe, rose appreciably. Added to this was a booming trade in the raw materials of Africa and Southeast Asia, including slaves, ivory, and gold from Africa and exotic woods and spices from the eastern islands of the Indian Ocean. Merchants who engaged in long-distance commerce could become rapidly wealthy and rise to positions of eminence within their cities.

This was especially the case with the merchants of Iraq. One ninth-century Arab geographer described Iraq as "the center of the world, the navel of the Earth." Iraq's centrality, and its consequent prosperity, was a function of its location at the head of the Persian Gulf, which afforded the merchants of Baghdad and Basra access to the rich markets of the Indian Ocean and the South China Sea. The potential for wealth was great for any Iraqi merchant who was enterprising, courageous, skilled, and lucky. Danger, however, lay around every corner, as the following tale from *A Thousand and One Arabian Nights* suggests.

A Thousand and One Arabian Nights, one of the most celebrated collections of stories in the world, is a rich pastiche of Persian, Arabic, Greco-Roman, Indian, and Egyptian fables and legends. Its core is a now-lost ancient Persian collection known as *A Thousand Tales*. This Persian work served as the matrix around which numerous anonymous Arab storytellers wove additional tales, especially out of the rich folk traditions of Iraq and Egypt, to create, by the fourteenth century, *The Arabian Nights* as we more or less know it today.

A major Arab addition to this constantly changing treasury of tales was the Sinbad cycle — seven stories that related the merchant voyages of one of literature's most celebrated adventurers. In the course of his seven voyages into the Indian Ocean, Sinbad narrowly escaped death at the hands of pirates and cannibals, monster birds and huge serpents, storms and whirlpools, and the murderous one-eyed Cyclops and the Old Man of the Sea. In his travels he discovered such fabled places as the valley of diamonds, the land where people were buried alive with their deceased spouses, and the ivory-rich elephant burying ground. Not only did he survive to tell his tales, but each voyage left him wealthier than before.

Doubtless the professional storytellers who recounted the adventures of this fictional merchant-sailor deliberately employed hyperbolic flights of fancy because their purpose was to present thrilling entertainment. Yet the more fantastic elements within the stories also hint at some of the ways in which the world of the Indian Ocean was viewed from the perspective of Iraq.

QUESTIONS FOR ANALYSIS

1. How did an Arab merchant of modest means undertake the expense of outfitting a ship and filling it with cargo?
2. What do the goods that Sinbad brought back with him suggest about the nature of commerce in the Indian Ocean?
3. Consider the wonders that Sinbad reported. What do they suggest about the level of Arab knowledge of the more distant regions of the Indian Ocean? What do they suggest about Arab attitudes toward the eastern Indian Ocean?
4. It has been said that this tale illustrates the ambivalence of the Iraqi World toward the vast region of the Indian Ocean. Do you agree? Why or why not?
5. What might we infer from this story about the role and status of merchants in Arab society?

I dissipated the greatest part of my paternal inheritance in the excesses of my youth; but at length, seeing my folly, I became convinced that riches were not of much use when applied to such purposes as I had employed them in; and I moreover reflected that the time I spent in dissipation was of still greater value than gold, and that nothing could be more truly deplorable than poverty in old age. I recollected the words of the wise Solomon, which my father had often repeated to me, that it is better to be in the grave than poor. Feeling the truth of all these reflections, I resolved to collect the small remains of my patrimony and to sell my goods by auction. I then formed connections with some merchants who had negotiations by sea, and consulted those who appeared best able to give me advice. In short, I determined to employ to some profit the small sum I had remaining, and no sooner was this resolution formed than I put it into execution. I went to Basra,[1] where I embarked with several merchants in a vessel which had been equipped at our united expense.

We set sail and steered toward the East Indies by the Persian Gulf, which is formed by the coast of Arabia on the right, and by that of Persia on the left, and is commonly supposed to be seventy leagues[2] in breadth in the widest part; beyond this gulf the Western Sea, or Indian Ocean, is very spacious, and is bounded by the coast of Abyssinia,[3] extending in length four thousand five hundred leagues to the island of Vakvak.[4] I was at first rather incommoded with what is termed sea-sickness, but I soon recovered my health; and from that period I have never been subject to that malady. In the course of our voyage we touched at several islands, and sold or exchanged our merchandise. One day, when in full sail, we were unexpectedly becalmed before a small island appearing just above the water, and which, from its green color, resembled a beautiful meadow. The captain ordered the sails to be lowered, and gave permission to those who wished it to go ashore, of which number I formed one. But during the time that we were regaling ourselves with eating and drinking, by way of relaxation from the fatigues we had endured at sea, the island suddenly trembled, and we felt a severe shock.

They who were in the ship perceived the earthquake in the island, and immediately called to us to re-embark as soon as possible, or we should all perish, for what we supposed to be an island was no more than the back of a whale. The most active of the party jumped into the boat, whilst others threw themselves into the water to swim to the ship: as for me, I was still on the island, or, more properly speaking, on the whale, when it plunged into the sea, and I had only time to seize hold of a piece of wood which had been brought to make a fire with. Meantime the captain, willing to avail himself of a fair breeze which had sprung up, set sail with those who had reached his vessel, and left me to the mercy of the waves. I remained in this situation the whole of that day and the following night; and on the return of morning I had neither strength nor hope left, when a breaker happily dashed me on an island. The shore was high and steep, and I should have found great difficulty in landing, had not some roots of trees, which fortune seemed to have furnished for my preservation, assisted me. I threw myself on the ground, where I continued, more than half dead, till the sun rose.

Although I was extremely enfeebled by the fatigues I had undergone, I tried to creep about in search of some herb or fruit that might satisfy my hunger. I found some, and had also the good luck to meet with a stream of excellent water, which contributed not a little to my recovery. Having in a great measure regained my strength, I began to explore the island, and entered a beautiful plain, where I perceived at some distance a horse that was grazing. I bent my steps that way, trembling between fear and joy, for I could not ascertain whether I was advancing to safety or perdition. I remarked, as I approached, that it was a mare tied to a stake: her beauty attracted my attention; but whilst I was admiring her, I heard a voice underground of a man, who shortly after appeared, and coming to me, asked me who I was. I related my adventure to him; after which he took me by the hand and led me into a cave, where there were some other persons, who were not less astonished to see me than I was to find them there.

---

[1]Basra, located at the northern tip of the Persian Gulf and connected to Baghdad by the Tigris River, is Iraq's entryway to the Persian Gulf and Indian Ocean.
[2]A league is three miles.

[3]The horn of Africa — the region of present-day Ethiopia and Somalia.
[4]Possibly a reference to Sumatra.

I ate some food which they offered me; and having asked them what they did in a place which appeared so barren, they replied that they were grooms to King Mihrage, who was the sovereign of that isle, and that they came every year about that time with some mares belonging to the king, for the purpose of having a breed between them and a sea-horse which came on shore at that spot. They tied the mares in that manner, because they were obliged almost immediately, by their cries, to drive back the sea-horse, otherwise he began to tear them in pieces. As soon as the mares were with foal they carried them back, and these colts were called sea-colts, and set apart for the king's use. To-morrow, they added, was the day fixed for their departure, and if I had been one day later I must certainly have perished, because they lived so far off that it was impossible to reach their habitations without a guide.

Whilst they were talking to me, the horse rose out of the sea as they had described, and immediately attacked the mares. He would then have torn them to pieces, but the grooms began to make such a noise that he let go his prey, and again plunged into the ocean.

The following day they returned to the capital of the island with the mares, whither I accompanied them. On our arrival, King Mihrage, to whom I was presented, asked me who I was, and by what chance I had reached his dominions; and when I had satisfied his curiosity, he expressed pity at my misfortune. At the same time, he gave orders that I should be taken care of and have everything I might want. These orders were executed in a manner that proved the king's generosity, as well as the exactness of his officers.

As I was a merchant, I associated with persons of my own profession. I sought, in particular, such as were foreigners, as much to hear some intelligence of Baghdad, as with the hope of meeting with some one whom I could return with;

for the capital of King Mihrage is situated on the sea-coast, and has a beautiful port, where vessels from all parts of the world daily arrive. I also sought the society of the Indian sages, and found great pleasure in their conversation; this, however, did not prevent me from attending at court very regularly, nor from conversing with the governors of provinces, and some less powerful kings, tributaries of Mihrage, who were about his person. They asked me a thousand questions about my country; and I, on my part, was not less inquisitive about the laws and customs of their different states, or whatever appeared to merit my curiosity.

In the dominions of King Mihrage there is an island called Cassel. I had been told that in that island there was heard every night the sound of cymbals, which had given rise to the sailors' opinion, that al-Dajjal[5] had chosen that spot for his residence. I felt a great desire to witness these wonders, and during my voyage I saw some fish of one and two hundred cubits in length,[6] which occasion much fear, but do no harm; they are so timid that they are frightened away by beating on a board. I remarked also some other fish that were not above a cubit long, and whose heads resembled that of an owl.

After I returned, as I was standing one day near the port, I saw a ship come toward the land; when they had cast anchor, they began to unload its goods, and the merchants, to whom they belonged, took them away to their warehouses. Happening to cast my eyes on some of the packages, I saw my name written, and, having attentively examined them, I concluded them to be those which I had embarked in the ship in which I left Basra. I also recollected the captain; but as I was persuaded that he thought me dead, I went up to him, and asked him to whom those parcels belonged. "I had on board with me," replied he, "a merchant of Baghdad, named Sinbad. One day, when we were near an island, at least such it

---

[5]The *deceiver*, or *impostor*, al-Dajjal is the false messiah who, according to Islamic belief, will appear shortly before Jesus returns to Earth to usher in the end of time. Jesus will destroy al-Dajjal, and the Day of Judgment will follow.

[6]A cubit varies from seventeen to twenty-two inches.

appeared to be, he, with some other passengers, went ashore on this supposed island, which was no other than an enormous whale, that had fallen asleep on the surface of the water. The fish no sooner felt the heat of the fire they had lighted on its back, to cook their provisions, than it began to move and flounce about in the sea. The greatest part of the persons who were on it were drowned, and the unfortunate Sinbad was one of the number. These parcels belonged to him, and I have resolved to sell them, that, if I meet with any of his family, I may be able to return them the profit I shall have made of the principal." "Captain," said I then, "I am that Sinbad, whom you supposed dead, but who is still alive, and these parcels are my property and merchandise."

When the captain of the vessel heard me speak thus, he exclaimed, "Great God! whom shall I trust? There is no longer truth in man. I with my own eyes saw Sinbad perish; the passengers I had on board were also witnesses of it; and you have the assurance to say that you are the same Sinbad? what audacity! At first sight you appeared a man of probity and honor, yet you assert an impious falsity to possess yourself of some merchandise which does not belong to you." "Have patience," replied I, "and have the goodness to listen to what I have to say." "Well," said he, "what can you have to say? speak, and I will attend." I then related in what manner I had been saved, and by what accident I had met with King Mihrage's grooms, who had brought me to his court.

He was rather staggered at my discourse, but was soon convinced that I was not an impostor; for some people arriving from his ship knew me, and began to congratulate me on my fortunate escape. At last he recollected me himself, and embracing me, "Heaven be praised," said he, "that you have thus happily avoided so great a danger; I cannot express the pleasure I feel on the occasion. Here are your goods, take them, for they are yours, and do with them as you like." I thanked him, and praised his honorable conduct, and by way of recompense I begged him to accept part of the merchandise, but that he refused.

I selected the most precious and valuable things in my bales, as presents for King Mihrage. As this prince had been informed of my misfortunes, he asked me where I had obtained such rare curiosities. I related to him the manner in which I had recovered my property, and he had the complaisance to express his joy on the occasion; he accepted my presents, and gave me others of far greater value. After that, I took my leave of him, and re-embarked in the same vessel, having first exchanged what merchandise remained with that of the country, which consisted of aloes and sandal-wood,[7] camphor,[8] nutmegs, cloves, pepper, and ginger. We touched at several islands, and at last landed at Basra, from whence I came here, having realized about a hundred thousand dinars.[9] I returned to my family, and was received by them with the joy which a true and sincere friendship inspires. I purchased slaves of each sex, and bought a magnificent house and grounds. I thus established myself, determined to forget the disagreeable things I had endured, and to enjoy the pleasures of life. . . .

I had resolved after my first voyage, to pass the rest of my days in tranquility at Baghdad. . . . But I soon grew weary of an idle life; the desire of seeing foreign countries, and carrying on some negotiations by sea returned: I bought some merchandise, which I thought likely to answer in the traffic I meditated; and I set off a second time with some merchants, upon whose probity I could rely. We embarked in a good vessel, and having recommended ourselves to the care of the Almighty, we began our voyage. . . .

▷ And so the second voyage begins.

---

[7]Both are woods noted for their aromatic and medicinal properties.

[8]A medicinal drug and aromatic made from camphor wood.
[9]A gold coin weighing 4.72 grams.

India: Continuity and Change

Invasions from Central Asia by a nomadic people known as the *Hunas*, or White Huns, precipitated the collapse of the Gupta Empire around the middle of the sixth century. Northern India was again politically fragmented, but Indian culture, having reached maturity in the Gupta Age, continued to develop vigorously. Hinduism took on new vitality, thanks in large part to the bhakti movement out of southern India (sources 34 and 35), and Buddhism was still a significant force, although it was steadily losing ground to a Hindu Renaissance. Although transcendental spirituality has always been a primary concern of Indian culture, India's cultural developments were not confined to religion. There was a significant literary revival both in the sacred language of Sanskrit and in such vernacular tongues as Pali and Tamil, and Indian comic drama emerged as a major art form. Music, dance, sculpture, and painting all flowered. In astronomy and mathematics, India was second to none. Indian astronomers borrowed and built upon Greek observations and theories, and Indian mathematicians formulated the principle of *zero* as a positive numerical value. India's Arab neighbors happily adopted the base-ten concept, turned it into a tool of the marketplace, and passed it on. For that reason, Indian decimal mathematics became mistakenly known as the Arabic system of numeration in the European West. If India received scant or no recognition for its cultural brilliance in the Far West, the same was not true of Asia, especially South and East Asia. Just as merchants from elsewhere in Asia and from East Africa flocked to its markets, so scholars and religious persons sought out its schools, monasteries, and temples.

It is no exaggeration to say that the history of classical India is largely the story of cultural continuity and evolution, in which political events and their chronology, although important, are less central to the story. The one significant exception to this rule in the period 500–1500 was the coming of Islam. Its impact was profound and permanent.

Early in the eighth century, Arabs conquered the northwest corner of the Indian subcontinent, a region known as *Sind*, but advanced no farther. While Hindu civilization moved to its own rhythms, neighboring Muslims traded with it and freely borrowed whatever they found useful and nonthreatening to their Islamic faith.

Islam did not make a significant impact on Indian life until the appearance of the Turks. These recent converts to the faith, whose origins lay in Central Asia, conducted a series of raids out of Afghanistan between 986 and 1030. After a respite of about 150 years, they turned to conquest. In 1192 the army of *Muhammad of Ghor* crushed a coalition of Indian princes, and the whole Ganges basin lay defenseless before his generals. By 1206 the Turkish *sultanate of Delhi* dominated all of northern India, and by 1327 it had extended its power over almost the entire peninsula. Although these Turkish sultans lost the south to the Hindu state of *Vijayanagar* (1336–1565), they controlled India's northern and central regions until the arrival of other Islamic conquerors: first, *Timur the Lame*'s (Tamerlane's) plundering horde in 1398; then *Babur*, who established the great *Mughal Dynasty* (1526–1857), which ruled most of India until the mid eighteenth century.

As the present-day Islamic states of Pakistan and Bangladesh bear witness, Islam became an important element in Indian society, but in the end Hinduism, in its almost countless forms, prevailed as the way of life for the majority of the Indian subcontinent's people. The coming and going of armies all but destroyed Buddhism in mainland India by 1400. Many factors contributed to the decline of Buddhism in its homeland since the Gupta Era, but Islamic armies delivered the final blow. Its monasteries, the heart of Buddhism, were easy targets for marauders, especially Muslim raiders out to destroy every visible vestige of polytheism. At the same time, because Ceylon (Sri Lanka) escaped the ravages of Islamic attack, Buddhism continued to flourish there, as it does today. Despite similar attacks on Hindu shrines on the mainland, no amount of destruction could root out the hold that the many varieties of Hindu belief and custom had on Indian life. In the final analysis, Hinduism is rooted not in temples and not in any class of specially trained clerics, but in family traditions and practices.

Islam and Hindu Civilization: Cultures in Conflict
▼▼▼

61 ▼ *Abul Raihan al-Biruni,* DESCRIPTION OF INDIA

At the end of the tenth century, Sultan Mahmud of Ghazana (r. 998–1030), who bore the titles *Sword of Islam* and *Image Breaker*, began a series of seventeen raids into India from his base just south of Kabul in present-day Afghanistan. This Turkish lord made no serious attempt at conquering all of India, but he incorporated into his lands part of the subcontinent's northwestern region of Punjab (an area that today is part of the Islamic state of Pakistan). For a century and a half after Mahmud's death, Islam penetrated no farther into India, but the precedent of Islamic jihad against infidel Hindus had been established.

The riches that Mahmud accumulated from his plunder and destruction of Hindu temples (he is reputed to have carried off six and a half tons of gold from one expedition alone) enabled him to turn his otherwise remote, mountain-ringed capital of Ghazana into a major center of Islamic culture. Scholars and artists gathered at Mahmud's court. Many came willingly; others were forced to come. In 1017 Mahmud conquered the Central Asian Islamic state of Khwarazm, located west of Ghazana and just south of the Aral Sea. The conqueror brought back many of Khwarazm's intellectuals and artisans to his capital, including the Iranian scholar *Abul Raihan al-Biruni* (973–ca. 1050).

Known to subsequent generations as *al-Ustadh* (the Master), al-Biruni was primarily an astronomer, mathematician, and linguist, but his wide-ranging interests and intellect involved him in many other fields of inquiry. For thirteen years following his capture, al-Biruni served Mahmud, probably as court astrologer, and traveled with him into India's Punjab region. Shortly after his lord's death in 1030, al-Biruni completed his *Description of India*, an encyclopedic account of Indian civilization, especially Hindu science. The following excerpts come from the book's opening pages, in which the author deals with the essential differences that separate Hindus from Muslims.

QUESTIONS FOR ANALYSIS

1. According to al-Biruni, what separates Muslims from Hindus?
2. What impact did eighth-century Islam have on India?
3. What impact did Mahmud and his father have on India?
4. Al-Biruni presents a critique of Hindu science and compares it with Greek science (and implicitly with Islamic science). In so doing, he faults Hindu scientists for certain basic failings. What are they?
5. What basic Hindu vision of reality might have influenced a scientific tradition that followed a path different from that of the Greeks and the Muslims?
6. What is the general tone of this entire excerpt, and what do you infer from it?

ON THE HINDUS IN GENERAL, AS AN INTRODUCTION TO OUR ACCOUNT OF THEM

Before entering on our exposition, we must form an adequate idea of that which renders it so particularly difficult to penetrate to the essential nature of any Indian subject. The knowledge of these difficulties will either facilitate the progress of our work, or serve as an apology for any shortcomings of ours. For the reader must always bear in mind that the Hindus entirely differ from us in every respect, many a subject appearing intricate and obscure which would be perfectly clear if there were more connection between us. The barriers which separate Muslims and Hindus rest on different causes.

First, they differ from us in everything which other nations have in common. And here we first mention the language, although the difference of language also exists between other nations. . . .

Secondly, they totally differ from us in religion, as we believe in nothing in which they believe, and *vice versa*. On the whole, there is very little disputing about theological topics among themselves; at the utmost, they fight with words, but they will never stake their soul or body or their property on religious controversy. On the contrary, all their fanaticism is directed against those who do not belong to them —

against all foreigners. They call them *mleccha, i.e.* impure, and forbid having any connection with them, be it by intermarriage or any other kind of relationship, or by sitting, eating, and drinking with them, because thereby, they think, they would be polluted. . . . They are not allowed to receive anybody who does not belong to them,[1] even if he wished it, or was inclined to their religion. This, too, renders any connection with them quite impossible, and constitutes the widest gulf between us and them.

In the third place, in all manners and usages they differ from us to such a degree as to frighten their children with us, with our dress, and our ways and customs, and as to declare us to be devil's breed, and our doings as the very opposite of all that is good and proper. . . .

But then came Islam;[2] the Persian empire perished, and the repugnance of the Hindus against foreigners increased more and more when the Muslims began to make their inroads into their country; for Muhammad Ibn al-Qasim entered Sind[3] . . . and conquered the cities of Bahmanwa and Mulasthana. . . . He entered India proper, and penetrated even as far as Kanauj, marched through the country of Gandhara, and on his way back, through the confines of Kashmir,[4] sometimes fighting sword in hand, sometimes gaining his ends by treaties, leaving to the people their ancient belief, except in the case of

---

[1]Here al-Biruni describes Hindu caste separation and purity.
[2]The initial rise of Islam in the seventh century.
[3]In 711.

[4]The mountainous northwestern region that separates present-day Pakistan and India and which today is disputed territory.

those who wanted to become Muslims. All these events planted a deeply rooted hatred in their hearts.

Now in the following times no Muslim conqueror passed beyond the frontier of Kabul and the river Sind until the days of the Turks, when they seized the power in Ghazna . . . and the supreme power fell to the lot of Sabuktagin. This prince chose the holy war as his calling, and therefore called himself *al-Ghazi*.[5] In the interest of his successors he constructed, in order to weaken the Indian frontier, those roads on which afterwards his son Mahmud marched into India during a period of thirty years and more. God be merciful to both father and son! Mahmud utterly ruined the prosperity of the country, and performed there wonderful exploits, by which the Hindus became like atoms of dust scattered in all directions, and like a tale of old in the mouth of the people. Their scattered remains cherish, of course, the most inveterate aversion towards all Muslims. This is the reason, too, why Hindu sciences have retired far away from those parts of the country conquered by us, and have fled to places which our hand cannot yet reach, to Kashmir, Benares,[6] and other places. And there the antagonism between them and all foreigners receives more and more nourishment both from political and religious sources.

In the fifth place, there are other causes, the mentioning of which sounds like satire — peculiarities of their national character, deeply rooted in them, but manifest to everybody. We can only say, folly is an illness for which there is no medicine, and the Hindus believe that there is no country but theirs, no nation like theirs, no kings like theirs, no religion like theirs, no science like theirs. They are haughty, foolishly vain, self-conceited, and stolid. They are by nature stingy in communicating that which they know, and they take the greatest possible care to withhold it from men of another caste among their own people, still much more, of course, from any

foreigner. According to their belief, there is no other country on earth but theirs, no other race of man but theirs, and no created beings besides them have any knowledge of science whatsoever. . . . If they traveled and mixed with other nations, they would soon change their mind, for their ancestors were not as narrow-minded as the present generation is. One of their scholars, Varahamihira,[7] in a passage where he calls on the people to honor the Brahmins, says: *"The Greeks, though impure, must be honored, since they were trained in sciences and therein excelled others. What, then, are we to say of a Brahmin, if he combines with his purity the height of science?"* In former times, the Hindus used to acknowledge that the progress of science due to the Greeks is much more important than that which is due to themselves. But from this passage of Varahamihira alone you see what a self-lauding man he is, while he gives himself airs as doing justice to others. . . .

The heathen Greeks, before the rise of Christianity, held much the same opinions as the Hindus; their educated classes thought much the same as those of the Hindus; their common people held the same idolatrous views as those of the Hindus. Therefore I like to confront the theories of the one nation with those of the other simply on account of their close relationship, not in order to correct them. For that which is not *the truth*[8] does not admit of any correction and all heathenism, whether Greek or Indian, is in its heart and soul one and the same belief, because it is only a deviation *from the truth*. The Greeks, however, had philosophers who, living in their country, discovered and worked out for them the elements of science, not of popular superstition, for it is the object of the upper classes to be guided by the results of science, while the common crowd will always be inclined to plunge into wrong-headed wrangling, as long as they are not kept down by fear of punishment. Think of Socrates when he opposed the crowd of his na-

---

[5]The holy warrior.
[6]A city on the Ganges River in central northeast India, it is a sacred site of both Hindu and Buddhist pilgrimage.

[7]An astronomer and astrologer of the early sixth century (ca. 505), he was one of Gupta India's greatest scientists.
[8]The true faith of Islam.

tion as to their idolatry and did not want to call the stars gods! At once eleven of the twelve judges of the Athenians agreed on a sentence of death, and Socrates died faithful to the truth.[9]

The Hindus had no men of this stamp both capable and willing to bring sciences to a classical perfection. Therefore you mostly find that even the so-called scientific theorems of the Hindus are in a state of utter confusion, devoid of any logical order, and in the last instance always mixed up with the silly notions of the crowd, *e.g.* immense numbers, enormous spaces of time, and all kinds of religious dogmas, which the vulgar belief does not admit of being called into question. . . . I can only compare their mathematical and astronomical literature, as far as I know it, to a mixture of pearl shells and sour dates, or of pearls and dung, or of costly crystals and common pebbles. Both kinds of things are equal in their eyes, since they cannot raise themselves to the methods of a strictly scientific deduction.[10]

---

[9]Al-Biruni's facts regarding the trial of Socrates are not correct. For a description of the trial, see Plato's *Apologia*.
[10]That is, logical argumentation, especially according to the system created by Aristotle, a Greek scientist-philosopher of the fourth century B.C.E. Aristotle's logic, which had a profound impact on both Islamic and Western science and philosophical thought, was based on the *principle of contradiction*: An entity either *is* or *is not*; it cannot simultaneously be both. The spiritual principle of *non-dualism* (sources 33 and 35) rejects the principle of contradiction.

A Sati's Sacrifice

▼▼▼

62 ▼ *VIKRAMA'S ADVENTURES*

One of the many myths regarding premodern Indian history is that a majority of widows performed ritual suicide by self-immolation on their late husbands' funeral pyres and that those who refused to go willingly to their deaths were forced into the flames. In point of fact, it was rare for widows to join their recently deceased husbands in death in ancient India. It was only during the Gupta Era, when female remarriage began to be discouraged and even prohibited, that the practice began to become something of a tradition. Even then, death by burning was not the fate of the vast majority of widows in that or any subsequent period. There were, however, enough incidents of widow suicide and murder to shock British colonial administrators, who took over direct management of India in the mid nineteenth century and managed to suppress the practice fairly effectively.

Another myth shared by Western observers is that Indians call this practice *suttee*. There is no such word. *Suttee* is a British misunderstanding and mispronunciation of *sati*, which means "a virtuous woman." According to the social-religious traditions that supported the practice of widow burning, a widow, no matter her caste, could not remarry, for this would entail her breaking her marriage vow and endangering her husband's spiritual welfare. She was expected to live out her life in severe austerity, shunned by all but her children, in the hope of remarrying her husband in some future incarnation. If she were especially virtuous, she would choose to join her deceased husband sooner rather than later and end her present life on his funeral day. Undoubtedly some satis committed suicide willingly. Probably far more were forced by their husbands' relatives, for social and economic reasons, to perform this ultimate act of loyalty.

The following selection, which sheds some light on this act of sacrifice, comes from an anonymous collection of stories recounting the adventures and wisdom of the semi-legendary King Vikrama, or Vikramaditya, who might have lived around 58 B.C.E. The stories, as we have received them, were probably collected between the eleventh and thirteenth centuries.

QUESTIONS FOR ANALYSIS

1. Can a widow who refuses to immolate herself achieve *moksha* (release)?
2. What proprietary interest do the families to which the sati belongs have in her sacrifice?
3. What impact does her act have on her husband's soul? On her own?
4. What social and psychological factors make suicide appear so attractive?
5. "By her perfect selflessness, a sati perfects and redeems her husband." What does this anonymous statement mean? How, if at all, does this story illustrate that attitude?
6. Some commentators have argued that this story is predicated on the assumption that a wife and husband fulfill each other and that without the other each is incomplete. Do you agree with this analysis? Why or why not?

Once King Vikrama, attended by all his vassal princes, had ascended his throne. At this time a certain magician came in, and blessing him with the words "Live forever!" said: "Sire, you are skilled in all the arts; many magicians have come into your presence and exhibited their tricks. So today be so good as to behold an exhibition of my dexterity." The king said: "I have not time now; it is the time to bathe and eat. Tomorrow I will behold it." So on the morrow the juggler came into the king's assembly as a statcly man, with a mighty beard and glorious countenance, holding a sword in his hand, and accompanied by a lovely woman; and he bowed to the king. Then the ministers who were present, seeing the stately man, were astonished, and asked: "O hero, who are you, and whence do you come?" He said: "I am a servant of Great Indra;[1] I was cursed once by my lord, and was cast down to Earth; and now I dwell here. And this is my wife. Today a great battle has begun between the gods and the Daityas [demons], so I am going

thither. This King Vikramaditya treats other men's wives as his sisters, so before going to the battle I wish to leave my wife with him." Hearing this the king also was greatly amazed. And the man left his wife with the king and delivered her over to him, and sword in hand flew up into Heaven. Then a great and terrible shouting was heard in the sky: "Ho there, kill them, kill them, smite them, smite them!" were the words they heard. And all the people who sat in the court, with upturned faces, gazed in amazement. After this, when a moment had passed by, one of the man's arms, holding his sword and stained with blood, fell from the sky into the king's assembly. Then all the people, seeing it, said: "Ah, this great hero has been killed in battle by his opponents; his sword and onc arm have fallen." While the people who sat in the court were even saying this, again his head fell also; and then his trunk fell too. And seeing this his wife said: "Sire, my husband, fighting on the field of battle, has been slain by the enemy. His head, his arm, his sword,

---

[1]See source 9.

and his trunk have fallen down here. So, that this my beloved may not be wooed by the heavenly nymphs, I will go to where he is. Let fire be provided for me." Hearing her words the king said: "My daughter, why will you enter the fire? I will guard you even as my own daughter; preserve your body." She said: "Sire, what is this you say? My lord, for whom this body of mine exists, has been slain on the battlefield by his foes. Now for whose sake shall I preserve this body? Moreover, you should not say this, since even fools know that wives should follow their husbands. For thus it is said:

1. Moonlight goes with the moon, the lightning clings to the cloud, and women follow their husbands; even fools know this. And so, as the learned tradition has it:

2. The wife who enters into the fire when her husband dies, imitating Arundhati [a star, regarded as the wife of one of the Seven Rishis (the Dipper), and as a typical faithful spouse] in her behavior, enjoys bliss in Heaven.

3. Until a wife burns herself in the fire after the death of her husband, so long that woman can in no way be permanently freed from the body.

4. A woman who follows after her husband shall surely purify three families: her mother's, her father's, and that into which she was given in marriage.

And so:

5. Three and a half crores[2] is the number of the hairs on the human body; so many years shall a wife who follows her husband dwell in Heaven.

6. As a snake-charmer powerfully draws a snake out of a hole, so a wife draws her husband upward [by burning herself] and enjoys bliss with him.

7. A wife who abides by the law of righteousness [in burning herself] saves her husband, whether he be good or wicked; yes, even if he be guilty of all crimes.

Furthermore, O king, a woman who is bereft of her husband has no use for her life. And it is said:

8. What profit is there in the life of a wretched woman who has lost her husband? Her body is as useless as a banyan tree in a cemetery.

9. Surely father, brother, and son measure their gifts; what woman would not honor her husband, who gives without measure?

Moreover:

10. Though a woman be surrounded by kinsfolk, though she have many sons, and be endowed with excellent qualities, she is a miserable, poor wretched creature, when deprived of her husband.

And so:

11. What shall a widow do with perfumes, garlands, and incense, or with manifold ornaments, or garments and couches of ease?

12. A lute does not sound without strings, a wagon does not go without wheels, and a wife does not obtain happiness without her husband, not even with a hundred kinsfolk.

13. Woman's highest refuge is her husband, even if he be poor, vicious, old, infirm, crippled, outcast, and stingy.

14. There is no kinsman, no friend, no protector, no refuge for a woman like her husband.

15. There is no other misery for women like widowhood. Happy is she among women who dies before her husband.

Thus speaking she fell at the king's feet, begging that a fire be provided for her. And when the king heard her words, his heart being tender with genuine compassion, he caused a pyre to be erected of sandalwood and the like, and gave her leave. So she took leave of the king, and in his presence entered the fire together with her husband's body.

---

[2]One *crore* is 10 million; therefore, 35 million.

Multiple Voices VI ▼▼▼
Buddhism in China: Acceptance, Rejection, and Accommodation

BACKGROUND

Following branches of the Silk Road out of northwest India, Buddhism traveled through Central Asia and into the heartland of northern China, reaching the Middle Kingdom at least as early as the first century C.E. Initially, Buddhism made little progress in China because some of its principles and practices ran counter to key Chinese values. In the time of troubles that followed the collapse of Later Han in 220, however, Buddhism, especially in its Mahayana form, achieved its own place in China as a religious doctrine offering comfort in the face of affliction. Even though it became an imperially sponsored religion in the first two centuries of the Tang Dynasty (618–906) and its monasteries became major centers of economic and political power, Buddhism did not lack detractors and enemies. Eventually, they were successful in orchestrating an attack on Buddhist monasteries in the mid ninth century that resulted in the shutting down of thousands of these centers of worship and the secularization of numerous monks and nuns.

As severe as this blow was, Buddhist beliefs and practices were not eradicated. The religion remained strong at the popular level, especially in a form of Mahayana devotion known as the *Pure Land Sect*, which centered on devotion to *Amitabha*, the Buddha of Infinite Light, who presided over the Western Paradise, and his chief Bodhisattva, Guanyin (sources 32 and 33). Moreover, Buddhism increasingly merged with folk magic, Daoism, and Confucianism to become part of a uniquely Chinese religious complex. In essence, China assimilated Buddhism's basic concepts, deities, rituals, artistic motifs, and festivals into its everyday culture and even into the ways of thought and behavior of its educated elites and in the process made these once-alien elements fully Chinese. Indeed, under the Ming emperors (1368–1644), Chinese Buddhism would enjoy a new era of imperial patronage. But that is another story.

THE SOURCES

Our first source, contained in a collection of sixty-five biographies of eminent Buddhist nuns who lived between the fourth and sixth centuries, illustrates the inherent tension between traditional Chinese social principles and Buddhist beliefs. It also shows us how Buddhist missionaries were able to accommodate Mahayana Buddhism to China's prevailing values.

The nun *An Lingshou* lived 200 years before Shi Baochang completed his work in or around 516. Because of the time gap and because of the compiler's avowed purpose to offer these holy women as models of Buddhist virtue, we would be naive if we did not wonder about the authenticity of the story, or at least the truth of its details. Yet there are aspects of the story that ring true. Even if the reported debate between An Lingshou and her father never took place, it certainly reflects opinions that were voiced during this era of Buddhist infiltration.

Chinese Buddhism reached its first high point of popularity and influence during the early years of the Tang Dynasty. However, because so many aspects of Buddhism were at variance with the traditional culture of China, especially Confucian values, conflict was almost inevitable. One of the leaders in the Confucian counterattack on Buddhism was the classical prose stylist and poet Han Yu (768–824), who in 819 composed a polemic against Buddhism, which is presented as our second source. Offered as a memorandum, or *memorial*, to Emperor Tang Xianzong (r. 805–820) on the subject of the emperor's veneration of a relic of the Buddha's finger, Han Yu's elegant and witty essay so enraged the emperor that initially he wanted to execute the author. Eventually, the emperor contented himself with banishing his impudent civil servant to a frontier outpost.

A champion of rationalism, Han Yu wished to suppress not only Buddhism but also Daoism, which had evolved into an organized religion that promised physical immortality through magic. Ironically, it was due to the influence of Daoist priests that Emperor Tang Wuzong (r. 840–846) initiated a policy of state suppression of a number of foreign religious establishments in 842, culminating with his *Proclamation Ordering the Destruction of Buddhist Monasteries* in 845, our third source. The emperor died seven months after issuing the order, and with his death the full force of the edict was relaxed. But substantial damage had already been done to the institutional structures of Buddhism, and Chinese Buddhism never fully recovered the economic and political power that it had enjoyed under the early Tang emperors, but it did not die out.

Through an already centuries-long process of adaptive adoption, which we call *syncretism*, Buddhist beliefs and values had increasingly become deeply embedded in Chinese society — too deeply to be rooted out — but the story did not end there. Beginning in the eleventh century, a school of moral philosophy, which was later known as *Neo-Confucianism*, fashioned a cosmology that offered intellectuals a metaphysical *alternative* to Buddhist transcendentalism, even as it borrowed from Buddhist spirituality. In essence, Neo-Confucians placed humanity into a full spiritual and cosmological context while simultaneously rejecting all notions of human immortality and salvation. Neo-Confucians asserted that there is an infinite Moral Principle (*li*) that pervades and energizes the universe and everything and everyone within it, but that Principle is knowable and intimately connected to physical reality.

The greatest and most influential Neo-Confucian was *Zhu Xi* (1130–1200), who created a body of thought that became the basis of the entire educational system of China in the fourteenth century and remained so into the early twentieth century. This philosophy traveled to Korea and also found a home in Japan. Early in the seventeenth century, Ieyasu, the first Tokugawa shogun, adopted and patronized Neo-Confucianism as an ideology to buttress his reorganization of Japanese society.

Long before Zhu Xi's teachings were canonized into official state orthodoxies in China and Japan, his students wrote down and collected their master's conversations. In 1270 Li Jingde compiled and published the *Conversations of Master Zhu, Arranged Topically*. Our fourth source, which is taken from that book, presents a sampling of Master Zhu's statements regarding how one is to read and use books.

QUESTIONS FOR ANALYSIS

1. According to the story of An Lingshou, what was the classic Chinese objection to Buddhism? How did Buddhists answer this objection?
2. What was there about Buddhism, and maybe especially its Mahayana forms, that attracted women and provided support for female monasticism?
3. In Han Yu's mind, what are the social, cultural, and political dangers of Buddhism?
4. Compose Han Yu's rejoinder to the story of the nun An Lingshou.
5. On what ideological basis did Emperor Wuzong order the suppression of monasteries and temples? Is there any evidence to suggest that there might also have been political and economic reasons for closing down and confiscating these establishments?
6. Whereas many Buddhists hoped to reach Enlightenment through the Holy Eightfold Path (source 16) and, if they were Mahayanists, through the agency of Bodhisattvas, Neo-Confucians sought the Moral Principle through study. Notwithstanding that difference, do you find anything in Zhu Xi's educational theory that suggests Buddhist influence?
7. Using these sources as fully as possible, compose an essay titled "Buddhism in China: Acceptance, Rejection, and Accommodation."

---

1 ▼ Shi Baochang, LIVES OF THE NUNS

An[1] Lingshou's secular surname was Xu. Her family was originally from Donghuan.[2] Her father Xu Chong served the non-Chinese dynasty of Latter Zhao[3] as an undersecretary of the provincial forces.

When she was young, Lingshou was intelligent and fond of study.[4] Her speech was clear and beautiful; her nature modest and unassuming. Taking no pleasure in worldly affairs, she was at ease in secluded quiet. She delighted in the Buddhist teachings and did not wish for her parents to arrange her betrothal.

Her father said, "You ought to marry. How can you be so unfilial?"

Lingshou said, "My mind is concentrated on the work of religion, and my thought dwells exclusively on spiritual matters. Neither blame nor praise moves me; purity and uprightness are sufficient in themselves. Why must I submit three times before I am considered a woman of propriety?"[5]

Her father said, "You want to benefit only one person — yourself. How can you help your father and mother at the same time?"

---

[1] Her religious surname, An, indicates that she traced her spiritual lineage back to a Parthian Buddhist missionary.
[2] In northeastern China.
[3] Literally, "the illegitimate dynasty of Latter Zhao." Between 304 and 431, sixteen kingdoms, largely dominated by foreigners of Mongol and Turkic ethnicity, emerged and vied with one another in northern China. Latter Zhao,

which lasted from 319 to 350, instituted a reign of terror (see notes 12–14).
[4] High-born women in Han and for centuries thereafter tended to be well educated.
[5] Submit first to her father and elder brother, then to her husband, and after his death to her son.

Lingshou said, "I am setting myself to cultivate the Way exactly because I want to free all living beings from suffering. How much more, then, do I want to free my two parents!"

Xu Chong consulted the Buddhist magician monk[6] from Kucha,[7] Fotudeng,[8] who said, "You return home and keep a vegetarian fast, and after three days you may come back to see me again." Xu Chong obeyed him. At the end of the three days, Fotudeng spread Xu Chong's palm with the oil of sesame ground together with safflower. When he ordered Xu Chong to look at it, Chong saw a person who resembled his daughter dressed in Buddhist monastic robes preaching the Buddhist teachings in the midst of a large assembly.

When he told all of this to Fotudeng, the monk said, "This is a former incarnation of your daughter, in which she left the household life and benefited living beings — such were her deeds. If you consent to her plan, she indeed shall raise her family to glory and bring you blessings and honor; and she shall guide you [to Nirvana] on the far shore of the great ocean of suffering known as the incessant round of birth and death."

Xu Chong returned home and permitted his daughter to become a nun.[9] Lingshou thereupon cut off her hair, discarded secular ornaments, and received the rules of monastic life from Fotudeng and the nun Jingjian.[10] She established Founding of Wisdom Convent, and Fotudeng presented her with a cut-flower embroidered vestment, a seven-strip monastic robe,[11] and an elephant-trunk-shaped water ewer that Shiluo, first emperor of the Latter Zhao Dynasty, had given him.[12]

Lingshou widely perused all kinds of books, and, having read a book through only once, she was always able to chant it by heart. Her thought extended to the depths of the profound; her spirit intuited the subtle and divine. In the religious communities of that time there was no one who did not honor her. Those who left the household life because of her numbered more than two hundred. Furthermore, she built five or six monastic retreats. She had no fear of hard work and brought her projects to completion.

The Emperor Shihu,[13] nephew of the late Emperor Shiluo,[14] honored her and promoted her father Xu Chong to the official court position of undersecretary of the Yellow Gate and administrator of the Qinghe Commandery.

---

[6]A number of Buddhist missionary monks in China enjoyed reputations as healers, magicians, seers, interpreters of dreams, and miracle workers.

[7]An oasis city that was the center of a Central Asian kingdom along the Silk Road.

[8]Zhu Fotudeng (232–348) was a Central Asian of Indian ancestry who arrived in northern China in 310. His disciples are considered the founding parents of Chinese Buddhism.

[9]Buddhist monastic rules mandated parental consent for minors and young women who wished to enter the *Sangha*, or monastic community.

[10]The subject of the first biography in this collection, Zhu Jingjian (ca. 292–ca. 361), whose secular name was Zhong

Lingyi, was a well-educated widow. She is credited with founding China's first female Buddhist monastery, Bamboo Grove Convent, in 317 in the city of Chang'an.

[11]Traditionally, a garment made out of rags and scraps that symbolized rejection of worldly wealth.

[12]Shiluo reigned 319–333. Fotudeng's magical powers gained him entry to the court of Latter Zhao, and he was able to use his influence to ameliorate somewhat its brutality (see note 3).

[13]Reigned 335–349, he had a reputation for psychopathic viciousness.

[14]Shihu gained the throne by killing off Shiluo's son.

---

2 ▼ Han Yu, *MEMORIAL ON BUDDHISM*

Your servant submits that Buddhism is but one of the practices of barbarians which has filtered into China since the Later Han. In ancient times there was no such thing. . . . In those times the empire was at peace, and the people, contented

and happy, lived out their full complement of years. . . . The Buddhist doctrine had still not reached China, so this could not have been the result of serving the Buddha.

The Buddhist doctrine first appeared in the time of the Emperor Ming[1] of the Han Dynasty, and the Emperor Ming was a scant eighteen years on the throne. Afterwards followed a succession of disorders and revolutions, when dynasties did not long endure. From the time of the dynasties Song, Qi, Liang, Chen, and Wei,[2] as they grew more zealous in the service of the Buddha, the reigns of kings became shorter. There was only the Emperor Wu of the Liang who was on the throne for forty-eight years. First and last, he thrice abandoned the world and dedicated himself to the service of the Buddha. He refused to use animals in the sacrifices in his own ancestral temple. His single meal a day was limited to fruits and vegetables. In the end he was driven out and died of hunger. His dynasty likewise came to an untimely end. In serving the Buddha he was seeking good fortune, but the disaster that overtook him was only the greater. Viewed in the light of this, it is obvious that the Buddha is not worth serving.

When Gaozu[3] first succeeded to the throne of the Sui,[4] he planned to do away with Buddhism, but his ministers and advisors were shortsighted men incapable of any real understanding of the Way of the Former Kings, or of what is fitting for past and present; they were unable to apply the Emperor's ideas so as to remedy this evil, and the matter subsequently came to naught — many the times your servant has regretted it. I venture to consider that Your Imperial Majesty, shrewd and wise in peace and war, with divine wisdom and heroic courage, is without an equal through the centuries. When first you came to the throne, you would not permit laymen to become monks or nuns or Daoist priests, nor would you allow the founding of temples or cloisters. It constantly struck me that the intention of Gaozu was to be fulfilled by Your Majesty. Now even though it has not been possible to put it into effect immediately, it is surely not right to remove all restrictions and turn around and actively encourage them.

Now I hear that by Your Majesty's command a troupe of monks went to Fengxiang[5] to get the Buddha-bone, and that you viewed it from a tower as it was carried into the Imperial Palace; also that you have ordered that it be received and honored in all the temples in turn. Although your servant[6] is stupid, he cannot help knowing that Your Majesty is not misled by this Buddha, and that you do not perform these devotions to pray for good luck. But just because the harvest has been good and the people are happy, you are complying with the general desire by putting on for the citizens of the capital this extraordinary spectacle which is nothing more than a sort of theatrical amusement. How could a sublime intelligence like yours consent to believe in this sort of thing?

But the people are stupid and ignorant; they are easily deceived and with difficulty enlightened. If they see Your Majesty behaving in this fashion, they are going to think you serve the Buddha in all sincerity. All will say, "The Emperor is wisest of all, and yet he is a sincere believer. What are we common people that we still should grudge our lives?" Burning heads and searing fingers by the tens and hundreds, throwing away their clothes and scattering their money, from morning to night emulating one another and fearing only to be last, old and young rush about, abandoning their work and place; and if restrictions are not immediately imposed, they will increasingly make the rounds of temples and some will inevitably cut off their arms and slice their flesh in the way of offerings. Thus to violate decency and draw the ridicule of the whole world is no light matter.

---

[1]Han Mingdi (r. 57–75 C.E.).
[2]Five fairly short-lived dynasties of the troubled fourth through sixth centuries. The Wei, who were foreign conquerors, apparently used Buddhism's universal message as an ideological buttress for their rule.
[3]Literally "high (or great) ancestor," an honorific title bestowed posthumously on several Chinese emperors. This high ancestor was Li Yuan, the first Tang emperor.
[4]The Sui Dynasty (581–618) reunited China in 589 and began a period of expansion that some characterize as the *Second Chinese Empire* (589–ca. 755).
[5]A western city.
[6]Han Yu.

Now the Buddha was of barbarian origin. His language differed from Chinese speech; his clothes were of a different cut; his mouth did not pronounce the prescribed words of the Former Kings,[7] his body was not clad in the garments prescribed by the Former Kings. He did not recognize the relationship between prince and subject, nor the sentiments of father and son. Let us suppose him to be living today, and that he come to court at the capital as an emissary of his country. Your Majesty would receive him courteously. But only one interview in the audience chamber, one banquet in his honor, one gift of clothing, and he would be escorted under guard to the border that he might not mislead the masses.

How much the less, now that he has long been dead, is it fitting that his decayed and rotten bone, his ill-omened and filthy remains, should be allowed to enter in the forbidden precincts of the Palace? Confucius said, "Respect ghosts and spirits, but keep away from them."[8] The feudal lords of ancient times, when they went to pay a visit of condolence in their states, made it their practice to have exorcists go before with rush-brooms and peachwood branches to dispel un-

lucky influences. Only after such precautions did they make their visit of condolence. Now without reason you have taken up an unclean thing and examined it in person when no exorcist had gone before, when neither rush-broom nor peachwood branch had been employed. But your ministers did not speak of the wrong nor did the censors call attention to the impropriety; I am in truth ashamed of them. I pray that Your Majesty will turn this bone over to the officials that it may be cast into water or fire, cutting off for all time the root and so dispelling the suspicions of the empire and preventing the befuddlement of later generations. Thereby men may know in what manner a great sage acts who a million times surpasses ordinary men. Could this be anything but ground for prosperity? Could it be anything but a cause for rejoicing?

If the Buddha has supernatural power and can wreak harm and evil, may any blame or retribution fittingly fall on my person. Heaven be my witness: I will not regret it. Unbearably disturbed and with the utmost sincerity I respectfully present my petition that these things may be known.

Your servant is truly alarmed, truly afraid.

---

[7]The legendary predynastic Sage Emperors.

[8]From the *Analects* (source 20).

---

3 ▼ PROCLAMATION ORDERING THE DESTRUCTION OF THE BUDDHIST MONASTERIES

We learn that there was no such thing as Buddhism prior to the Three Dynasties, i.e., Xia, Yin, and Zhou.[1] After the dynasties of Han and Wei, the Image-Teaching[2] gradually began to flourish. And once established in that degenerate age, this strange custom prevailed far and wide, and now the people are soaked to the bone with it. Just now the national spirit begins to be

spoiled unconsciously by it; and, leading the heart of the people astray, it has put the public in worse condition than ever. In the country — throughout the nine provinces, and among the mountains and fields as well as in both the capitals[3] — the number of priests is daily increasing and the Buddhist temples are constantly winning support.

---

[1]China's first three dynasties (see Chapter 1). *Yin* is another name for the latter years of the Shang Dynasty.
[2]Buddhism, which used statues and images for veneration and instruction (see source 33).

[3]The main capital was Chang'an (present-day Xi'an); the auxiliary, or eastern, capital was Dongdu (present-day Luoyang).

Wasting human labor in building, plundering the people's purse by golden decorations, neglecting both husband and wife by their vigil-keeping, no teaching is more harmful than this Buddhism. In breaking the laws of the country and injuring the people, none can surpass this Buddhism. Moreover, if a farmer neglects his field, many suffer the pangs of starvation from his negligence; if a woman neglects her silk-worm culture, many suffer the calamity of being frozen to death through her negligence. Now there are at present so many monks and nuns that to count them is almost impossible. They all depend on farming for their food, and upon silk-worms for their clothing!

"The public monastaries and temples, as well as private chapels and shrines, are innumerable; and all of them so gigantic and imposing that they vie with the Imperial Palace in splendor! In Dynasties Jin (317–420 C.E.) and Song (420–476 C.E.), Qi (479–501 C.E.), and Liang (502–557 C.E.), the resources of this Empire were exhausted and the country gradually declined, while its manners and customs became flippant and insincere, solely because of this Buddhism.[4]

"Our Imperial ancestor Taizong[5] put an end to confusion and disorder by his arms, and built up the glorious Middle Kingdom and governed his people by his accomplished learning and culture. The right of 'the pen' (i.e., peaceful rule or civic administration) and 'the sword' (i.e., war) belongs to the State, and they are the two weapons wherewith to govern the Empire. How dare the insignificant Teaching of the Western Lands compete with ours? During the periods of Zhenguan and Gaiyuan,[6] things were bettered once for all, but the remnants were smouldering, and poverty began to grow bigger and wider and threatened to set the country ablaze!

"After closely examining the examples set by our Imperial predecessors, We have finally decided to put an end to such conspicuous evils. Do you, Our subjects at home and abroad, obey and conform to Our sincere will. If you send in a Memorial[7] suggesting how to exterminate these evils which have beset Us for many Dynasties, We shall do all We can to carry out the plan. Know that We yield to none in fulfilling the laws of Our predecessors and in trying to be helpful to Our people and beneficial to the public.

"Those 4,600 monasteries supported by the Government shall be confiscated and, at the same time, 260,500 nuns and priests shall return to the secular life so that they may be able to pay the taxes. We shall also confiscate 40,000 private temples with the fertile and good lands amounting to several tens of millions of acres; and emancipate 150,000 slaves and make them into free, tax-paying people. Examining into the teaching from the foreign lands in the Empire, We have discovered that there are over 3,000 monks from Daqin[8] and Muhufu;[9] and these monks also shall return to the lay life. They shall not mingle and interfere with the manners and customs of the Middle Kingdom.

"More than a hundred thousand idle, lazy people and busy bodies have been driven away, and numberless beautifically decorated useless temples have been completely swept away. Hereafter, purity of life shall rule Our people and simple and non-assertive rules prevail, and the people of all quarters shall bask in the sunshine of Our Imperial Influence. But this is only the beginning of the reforms. Let time be given for all, and let Our will be made known to every one of Our subjects lest the people misunderstand Our wish."

---

[4]Compare Han Yu's charges against Buddhism.
[5]Tang Taizong (r. 626–649), the second Tang emperor and the true founder of Tang imperial power. He actually became a generous patron of Buddhism after 645.
[6]The throne names of Tang Taizong (see note 5) and Tang Xuanzong (r. 712–756), the dynasty's two greatest rulers.

[7]Memorandum.
[8]Syria — a reference to Nestorian Christianity (see source 44).
[9]Persia — a reference to Zoroastrians and Manichaeans.

4 ▾ *Zhu Xi, CONVERSATIONS OF MASTER ZHU, ARRANGED TOPICALLY*

4.2. Book learning is of secondary importance. It would seem that Moral Principle[1] is originally complete in man,[2] the reason he must engage in book learning is that he hasn't experienced much. The sages experienced a great deal and wrote it down for others to read. Now in book learning we must simply apprehend the many manifestations of Moral Principle. Once we understand them, we'll find that all of them were complete in us from the very beginning, not added to us from the outside.

4.3. Learning is to focus on what is of vital importance to our selves (i.e., Moral Principle) — book learning itself is of secondary importance. Moral Principle is complete in us, not something added from the outside. Thus when sages tell people that they must engage in book learning, it's because even though they might possess Moral Principle they must experience it if it is to have any effect. What the sages speak about is what they have exprienced of it.

4.4. In teaching others, the sages and worthies explained the way of learning quite clearly. Generally speaking, in their reading students should probe to the limit. "The pursuit of learning" is an important matter, for one has to understand Moral Principle to become fully human. Ordinarily, in reading a book we must read and reread it, appreciating each and every paragraph, each and every sentence, each and every word. Furthermore, we must consult the various annotations, commentaries, and explanations so that our understanding is complete. In this way Moral Principle and our own minds will be in perfect accord. Only then will our reading be effective. . . .

4.6. It's best to take up the books of the sages and read them so that you understand their ideas. It's like speaking with them face to face.

4.7. You must frequently take the words of the sages and worthies and pass them before your eyes, roll them around and around in your mouth, and turn them over and over in your mind.

4.8. When you begin reading, you become aware that you're unlike the sages and worthies — how can you not urge yourself on?

4.9. There is layer upon layer {of meaning} in the words of the sages. In your reading of them, penetrate deeply. If you simply read what appears on the surface, you will misunderstand. Steep yourself in the words; only then will you grasp their meaning. . . .

4.13. In reading a text, you must be full of vigor. Arouse your spirits, keep your body alert, and don't let yourself grow weary — as if a sword were at your back. You must pierce through each passage. "Strike the head, the tail responds; strike the tail, the head responds."[3] Only then have you read it right. You cannot open a book and fix your mind on it then close it and forget about it. Nor can you when reading the commentary forget about the text or when reading the text forget about the commentary. You must pierce through one passage and only then go on to later ones. . . .

4.16. In reading, to understand Moral Principle the mind must be open, unobstructed, and bright. You musn't be calculating beforehand the gain you'll get from the reading. For once you think about gain,[4] you'll become distressed. And if you're distressed, trivial things will

---

[1]*Li.*

[2]This idea is very close to the Platonic notion of the inherent knowledge of Real Ideas that must be discovered through philosophy. Whether there was any Platonic influence on Neo-Confucian thought is impossible to say. See source 24 for an introduction to Plato.

[3]By reading one part intensively, the rest will make sense.

[4]A Confucian pun. Confucius juxtaposed *propriety* (or right behavior or the proper rites) and *profit*, both characters pronounced as *li* (see *Analects* 4:16 in source 20). Zhu Xi juxtaposes the Moral Principle (also *li*) and profit, or gain.

gather in the mind and won't leave. Now you should put aside unimportant matters, stop engaging in idle thought, and concentrate the mind in order to get a real sense of moral principle. In this way the mind will become sharp, and once the mind's sharp, it'll become intimately familiar with Moral Principle.

4.17. In reading, open wide the mind and Moral Principle will appear. If the mind is anxious and under pressure, Moral Principle ultimately will have no way of appearing.

4.18. Your reading will be successful only if you understand the spot where everything interconnects — east and west meet at this pivotal point. Simply dedicate yourself to what you're doing at the moment, don't think about the past or the future, and you'll naturally get to this point. But now you say that you've never been able to do it (i.e., read properly), that you fear you're too slow, or fear that you're not up to doing it, or fear that it is difficult, or fear that you're stupid, or fear that you won't remember what you've read — all this is idle talk. Simply dedicate yourself to what you're doing at the moment, don't be concerned whether you're slow or fast, and soon you will naturally get there. Because you have never done it before, exert the right effort now, and make up for past failures. Don't look to your front or back, don't think about east or west, or soon you'll have wasted a lifetime without realizing that you've grown old. . . .

▲▲▲

Chapter 10

Two Christian Civilizations

Byzantium and Western Europe

THE ROMAN EMPIRE was a Mediterranean civilization that encompassed the coastlands and peoples of three continents: Africa, Asia, and Europe. Given this fact, it is best to think of it as the last and greatest of the Hellenistic empires, with all of the cultural variety that the term connotes.

During the period from roughly 235 to 600, the Mediterranean World underwent a transformation. Many historians have characterized it as "the decline and fall of the Roman Empire," but the phrase and all that it implies misses the mark. Rome and its empire did not suddenly collapse. What happened was more subtle and profound. The lands of the empire, which embraced the cultures of so many diverse peoples, metamorphosed over a period of centuries into three new civilizations: Byzantium; Western, or Latin, Europe; and Islam.

Islam originated in Arabia, a land beyond Roman imperial boundaries, and in the mid eighth century it established its capital at Baghdad, in the heart of the former Sassanian Empire of Persia. Nevertheless, by conquering the lands of Syria-Palestine, all of North Africa, and most of the Iberian Peninsula, Islam inherited a good deal of Hellenistic culture, including Greek science and philosophy, and in that sense it was an heir of the Roman Empire. We studied Islam in Chapters 8 and 9, and it needs no further comment here. Byzantium and Latin Europe, Rome's two Christian heirs, are another matter. It is to these civilizations that we now turn.

The civilization that we term *Byzantium* receives its name from the eastern Mediterranean city of that name (*Byzantion* in Greek; *Byzantium* in Latin), which Emperor Constantine the Great transformed into the capital of the newly Christianized Roman Empire in 330. The fact that Constantine chose to locate *New Rome*, as he styled the city, in the East is testimony to the increasing unimportance of the West to the fourth-century empire. Although the city came to be called *Constantinople* (Constantine's city), modern scholars have favored using the older name — Byzantium — to delineate the civilization that centered on this Eastern Roman capital. Actually, the Byzantines never called themselves anything other than *Romaioi* (Romans). From the early fourth century to 1453, when the city and its empire finally succumbed to the Ottoman Turks, Constantinople was the center of an empire and a civilization whose members viewed it as the legitimate heir of Roman imperial traditions. In fact, however, already by the late sixth century, Byzantium had become a distinctive civilization — a Greek-speaking civilization that retained many Hellenistic qualities but which also developed many new forms of expression and organization.

Byzantine civilization resulted from the fusion of three key elements. First there were the traditions of the Late Roman Empire in which the emperor had been transformed into an autocratic ruler along the lines of the Persian *shahs*, or emperors. Then there was *Eastern Orthodox Christianity*. As we saw in Multiple Voices IV, *orthodox* is a Greek term that means "correct thinking," and in this context it means the time-honored, officially sanctioned traditions of Eastern Mediterranean Christianity, which included folk practices as well as the teachings of theologians and church councils. The third element was the cultural heritage of the Hellenistic past, itself a fusion of Greek, western Asian, and Egyptian elements.

Although Byzantium was an empire, with frontiers that expanded and contracted over the centuries, as a civilization it transcended political boundaries. Byzantine traditions deeply influenced the cultures of a number of neighboring peoples. In a real sense, even after the Byzantine Empire collapsed in the face of Ottoman Turkish assaults, its civilization lived on, in somewhat altered forms, among such Orthodox Christian cultures as Bulgaria, Romania, Russia, Serbia, and Ukraine.

The story in the western half of the Roman Empire was different. Continuities were less evident, and dramatic changes were more the norm. Whereas the empire's eastern half evolved somewhat gently into a new cultural synthesis, the western half experienced a painful process of political breakdown and sweeping cultural transformation.

Toward the end of the fourth century C.E., pressures on Rome's western frontiers had become intolerable, and the western portion of the empire rapidly slid toward its unforeseen end, defeated and transformed by fringe peoples who came from beyond the borders of the Rhine and Danube rivers. By the end of the sixth century, precious little of the western half of the Roman World was ruled by imperial Roman authority. More profoundly, these newcomers played a key role in transforming culture in the West, thereby helping to usher out the old Greco-Roman order and to lay the basis for a new civilization that many historians call *Western Europe*, or *Latin Europe*.

One of the enduring clichés favored by writers of history textbooks is that Latin Europe emerged out of a fusion of three elements: the remnants of Greco-Roman civilization; Latin, or Western, Christianity; and the culture and vigor of the fringe peoples who migrated into the western regions of the late Roman Empire. As is true of so many commonplace notions, there is a good deal of truth to this statement, but it is not the complete story. These three elements differed radically from one another in many essential ways, and it took centuries for them to fuse into something resembling a coherent civilization. Even when they had achieved a level of integration, their differences continued to infuse into an emerging European civilization tensions that became identifying characteristics of the new order developing in the West. That dynamism eventually drove Europe into competition with Islam and Byzantium — a competition that had global consequences.

▼▼▼

Justinian the Great:
The First Byzantine Emperor

Some eighteenth-century European historians regarded Byzantine civilization as an unoriginal and degenerate fossilization of late antiquity, but nothing could be farther from the truth. Although the Byzantines saw their state as a living continuation of the Roman Empire, by the late sixth century Constantinople had become the matrix of a new civilization that persisted and largely flourished down to 1453, when the city finally fell to Ottoman Turkish forces.

The history of Byzantium is one of peaks and troughs. The pattern of triumph, decline, and recovery repeated itself continuously until Byzantium's collapse in the mid fifteenth century. One key to understanding this cycle is the power invested in the emperor (and occasionally the empress). Rarely does an individual single-handedly alter in a radical way the historical course of an empire or any other large institution, but autocratic monarchs could and did play inordinately important roles in the unfolding of Byzantine fortunes. The following sources shed light on the person and reign of Justinian the Great (r. 527–565), arguably the Eastern Roman Empire's first Byzantine emperor, and of Isaac I Comnenus (r. 1057–1059).

Two Imperial Portraits: Justinian and Theodora
▼▼▼
63 ▼ *THE MOSAICS OF SAN VITALE*

The age of Justinian I (r. 527–565) was pivotal in the history of the Eastern Roman Empire. The last of the emperors of Constantinople to speak Latin as his native tongue, Justinian attempted to reconquer the West from the various Germanic tribes that had divided it into competing kingdoms. Justinian's forces invaded Italy in 535 in order to wrest it from the Ostrogoths, who had controlled the peninsula since the late fifth century. The war that ensued was protracted and destructive. When fighting finally ceased in 553, the Ostrogoths had been eliminated as a recognizable culture, and Rome's aristocratic families likewise had disappeared from the historical record. Cities, towns, and countryside alike were in ruin. Fifteen years later, in 568, new Germanic invaders, the Lombards, carved out states in northern Italy and in parts of central and southern Italy, thereby denying Byzantium control over the entire peninsula. In effect, Justinian's attempt at reconquest enjoyed only limited, short-term success. Its major accomplishment was transforming Rome and much of Italy into a war-ravaged backwater and stripping the eastern empire of much-needed resources. After Justinian's age, the Greek-speaking emperors and people of Constantinople were forced to look less to the West and more toward their eastern, southern, and northern borders, thereby accelerating the impact of Asian influences on Byzantium's cultural development.

For all of his large-scale miscalculations, however, Justinian ranks as one of Byzantium's greatest emperors; indeed, he often is referred to as *Justinian the Great*, the last Roman and first Byzantine emperor. A measure of that greatness is seen in the portrait mosaics of Justinian and Empress Theodora at the Church of San Vitale in Ravenna, Italy.

Created in 548 following the capture of Ravenna by imperial troops, the two mosaics flank the altar of the church. High above the altar is a mosaic of *Christ in Glory*. Below and to Christ's right is Justinian's mosaic; opposite and to Christ's left is Theodora's mosaic. In Justinian's mosaic we see the crowned emperor, his head surrounded by a *nimbus*, or *halo*, a sign of sacred power. He wears imperial purple and gold and carries, as an offering, the eucharistic bread, which a priest will transform at Mass into the Body of Christ. On his left are four individuals: three churchmen and what appears to be a court official (the person in the background). The clerics are Maximian, archbishop of Ravenna (his name appears over his head, he holds a cross, and he wears around his shoulders an archbishop's *pallium*, a long white cloth with an embroidered cross), and two priests. One priest holds a book of Gospels (every Mass has a Gospel reading from the same side of the altar on which Justinian's mosaic is located); the other holds an incense burner. On the emperor's right stand two high-ranking imperial officials and six members of the imperial bodyguard. One of the guardsmen displays a shield with the *chi-rho* monogram: the Greek letters *X* (chi) and *P* (rho), which when combined represent the word *Christos* (Christ). Empress Theodora, Justinian's wife, also appears with a crown, imperial purple and gold robes, and a halo. The hem of her robe has an image of the Three Kings bearing gifts to the Christ child. In her hands is a golden, bejeweled cup containing the eucharistic wine, which a priest will transform at Mass into the Blood of Christ. On her left are seven court ladies, in descending order of rank; the one closest to her wears the purple of the imperial family. Two high-ranking civil officials stand on her right. One pulls back a curtain to reveal a baptismal font, the fountain in which persons are baptized into the Church.

QUESTIONS FOR ANALYSIS

1. Theodora's mosaic places her into a definite space: an imperial palace (or possibly a church). Justinian's mosaic lacks any spatial points of reference. Does this seem significant? If so, how do you interpret the emperor's lack of specific place?

2. Based on these two mosaics, describe the place that Empress Theodora apparently held within the empire. What was her theoretical position? What do you think were her actual powers? As always, be as specific as possible.

3. "The Byzantine emperor was acknowledged as the living icon, or image, of God on Earth, insofar as his imperial majesty was a pale reflection of the Glory of God. As such, he was the link between the Roman Christian people and their God." In light of these mosaics, comment in depth on this anonymous statement.

4. Two titles borne by the emperor of Constantinople were *isapostolos* (peer of the apostles) and *autokrator* (sole ruler of the world). Does the San Vitale mosaic of Justinian symbolize either or both of these titles? Please be specific in your answer.

Emperor Justinian and His Court

Empress Theodora and Her Court

The Relationship of Emperor and Patriarch in Byzantium
▼▼▼
64 ▼ *Michael Psellus, CHRONOGRAPHIA*

Late in the eleventh century, Michael Psellus (1018–after 1081?), a monk, scholar, and politician, composed the *Chronographia* (*Chronicle*), a series of imperial character sketches covering the period 976–1077. The underlying thesis of Psellus's work was that the empire's history was driven by the ways in which emperors and empresses responded to the challenges and temptations of office.

In the following excerpt, Psellus describes Emperor Isaac I Comnenus's attempted deposition of a popular patriarch of Constantinople, Michael I Cerularius (r. 1043–1058). As the metropolitan archbishop, or chief priest, of the imperial capital, the patriarch of Constantinople had borne the title "Ecumenical Patriarch" since the late sixth century. The title meant that the patriarch was "first among equals" within the ecclesiastical hierarchy in lands governed directly by the emperor. Emperor Isaac had ordered Cerularius's arrest in late 1058 for reasons that are unclear, especially in light of the fact that Isaac owed his accession to the throne to Cerularius's support in 1057. When the patriarch refused to abdicate, Isaac drew up a long list of charges against him, including accusations of heresy and treason. When Cerularius died on his way to trial at a church synod, or council, the emperor secured the succession of Constantine III (r. 1059–1063) to the patriarchate. Ironically, Isaac himself, for reasons that are also unclear, abdicated the imperial throne that same year — 1059 — and retired to a monastery. In death, Michael, who in 1054 had vigorously resisted charges by legates, or emissaries, of Pope Leo IX (r. 1049–1054) that the Church of Constantinople had lapsed into error (see Multiple Voices VII), was revered as a saint by the people of Constantinople.

QUESTIONS FOR ANALYSIS

1. Most historians infer that the quarrel between Cerularius and Emperor Isaac centered on (1) the patriarch's interference in imperial matters of state, (2) the patriarch's desire to establish a church that was independent of imperial control, or (3) both issues. What evidence is there in this account to support any or all of these theories?
2. The term *caesropapism* (a caesar, or emperor, acting as a pope) is often used to describe the authority of Byzantine emperors in the realm of church affairs. Does such a term adequately describe the emperor's role? Does it adequately describe the patriarch's position in Byzantine society? Cite specific evidence from this and the previous source to support your inferences.

Once he had taken the government on his own shoulders — from the moment of his coronation indeed — and once he had, by his coronation, legalized his position as emperor, his policy was radically opposed to that of the aged Michael.[1] Donations which Michael had given,[2] Isaac took away; wherever Michael had done something of note, Isaac destroyed it. Then, becoming gradually more bold, he went too far in his reforms, and here too he wiped out and rescinded much of Michael's work. Quite a number of his measures he completely annulled. . . . He classed under one heading the acts of his predecessors, thus attacking all and bringing all into discredit at once. In pursuit of such a policy it was inevitable that he should add to his other victims the priests of the Church. Indeed, he cut off the greater part of the monies set apart for their sacred buildings, and having transferred these sums to the public funds, he estimated the bare necessities for the clergy, thereby making the name "place of meditation" really appropriate. He did this with the insouciance of a man picking up a grain of sand from the seashore. He just set his hand to the task, and it was all done without the slightest commotion. Indeed, I never saw any man on earth so deliberate in his reasoning, or so quiet in the execution of vast ideas. . . .

. . . If this emperor had chosen the proper time for his reforms; if he had condemned one practice, shall we say, and allowed another to stand for the time being, destroying it at some later date; if, after the amputation, he had rested before attempting another operation; if he had advanced thus, step by step, in his extermination of evil, quietly and without attracting attention . . . he . . . would have introduced real harmony into the affairs of state. . . . But if Isaac did not complete his whole task in a *single* day, he reckoned the failure intolerable, such was the excessive zeal with which he tried to accomplish his purpose. Nothing on earth restrained him, no prof-

fering of wiser counsels, no fear for the future, no hatred of the mob, none of the other factors which, in normal men, curb vanity or check mighty ambition. Had some rein kept him under control, he would have overrun the whole inhabited world, country by country. . . . But lack of restraint, refusal to accept reason as his guide, these were the ruin of his noble character. . . .

. . . Being a man of great pride, he had a horror of being rebuked, whether openly or subtly.

An example of this is found in his treatment of the Patriarch Michael. The latter had spoken frankly to him on a certain occasion, using language that was somewhat bold. At the time the emperor passed it over and checked his anger, but he cherished resentment deep in his heart. It broke out unexpectedly, and in the belief that he was following a precedent he expelled Michael from the city. He was condemned to exile in a circumscribed area, and it was there that he died. However, I will not explain how this came about now, for it is a long story. If anyone cares to examine the quarrel between these two, he will blame the one for the start of it, the other for its ending, when the emperor cast the patriarch off as if he were a load on his shoulders. One point here that I almost forgot: a messenger returning from a distant mission brought to him the news of the patriarch's death, with the air of a man who was freeing him from all trouble in the future, but Isaac, when he heard of it, his heart immediately touched, bewailed loudly — an unusual thing for him — and mourned him deeply. He was sorry for the way he had treated the patriarch and often tried to propitiate his soul. As if to justify himself, or rather to appease the dead man, he at once granted to Michael's family the privilege of speaking freely in his presence, and they were allowed to join his immediate retinue. As Michael's successor in the sacred office, he presented to God and honored with high rank one whom his previous life had

---

[1]Emperor Michael VI (r. 1056–1057). Isaac Comnenus, who commanded Byzantium's Asian army, forced Emperor Michael from the throne (with, ironically, the approval of Patriarch Michael).

[2]Gifts, largely to the nobility, which exhausted the imperial treasury.

shown to be blameless, one whose eloquence had left him without a rival, even among the most eminent scholars.

▼▼▼

This gentleman was none other than the famous Constantine, who in the past had on more than one occasion restored peace to a storm-tossed Empire and had been much sought after by many of the emperors.[3] The crowning-point of his career came with his elevation to the Patriarchate. All other candidates for the office yielded to his claims. All were agreed that he had pre-eminent qualities which fitted him for the duty above the rest. And to the glorification of this dignity he dedicated all his efforts, a man who lived the life of a priest, yet possessed qualities of statesmanship and great public spirit. . . .

. . . He played either rôle, churchman or politician, without deviating one iota from his natural habits. As a politician, he impressed his interrogators by his priestly dignity, yet when you approached him in his capacity of Patriarch, even if you stood in considerable awe of him and trembled a bit, he still appeared human, with the graceful manners of a diplomat, a man of sturdy character and smiling gravity. His whole life inspired confidence: on the one side, his military and political career, on the other, his great dignity, his courtesy. It was natural, even before this appointment, that I should often predict for him promotion to the Church's highest offices. His manner of life taught me what to expect in the future, and now, after he has actually become High Priest, I still see in him a gentleman of the noblest character.[4]

By appointing such a man as Michael's successor, therefore, the emperor paid a compliment to the late Patriarch.

---

[3]Constantine Leichudes, who became Patriarch Constantine III, had served as prime minister to Emperor Constantine IX (r. 1042–1055) and was a member of the Senate, as well as a priest.

[4]There is reason to believe that Psellus produced his *Chronographia* at the urging of his friend and fellow scholar, Constantine Leichudes (see note 3).

▼▼▼

Charles the Great: Latin Europe's First Emperor

Although Byzantine cultural influences spread beyond the territorial limits of the Eastern Roman Empire, Byzantium was largely a civilization centered on a single empire. In the West, to the contrary, a new civilization arose that was not identified with any single political entity, even though the West created its own empire in the year 800 and then recreated it in 962. Despite having its own *Holy Roman Empire*, as it was later called, Latin European civilization was politically pluralistic and was never tied to any single state.

In many respects, youthful, dynamic Europe was an ever-expanding culture in the period from roughly 500 to 1500. Yet this dynamism was not obvious during the early centuries in which Western European civilization was taking shape. With the passing of Roman imperial order, Western Europeans were thrown back on their own resources and forced to create new social and political structures and a new civilization. In fashioning this civilization, Westerners melded together three elements: the vestiges and memories of Roman civilization, the moral and organizational leadership of the Roman Church, and the vigor and culture of the various fringe peoples who carved out kingdoms in Europe from the fifth century onward. The single act that most vividly symbolizes the new order that emerged from that fusion was Pope Leo III's coronation of Charles the Great as Roman emperor on Christmas Day, 800. The following sources shed light on the person and reign of Charlemagne, a man whom the West styled *Roman emperor* but who was both less and much more than that.

A Papal Portrait: Leo III and Charles the Great

▼▼▼

65 ▼ *POPE LEO III'S LATERAN MOSAIC*

In 476 the western half of the Roman Empire lost its last resident Roman emperor. Theoretically, the emperors at Constantinople remained rulers of the western, as well as the eastern, regions of the Roman Empire; in reality, the West was divided into a number of Germanic kingdoms — a process that had begun well before 476. If any single entity commanded the loyalties of all or most Europeans, it was the *Roman Church*, which centered on the person and office of the *pope* of Rome. The pope, whose title means "father" in Latin, was bishop of the city of Rome and claimed authority over all of Christendom, not just the Western Church, by virtue of being the heir of Saint Peter. According to arguments first put forward in the fourth century, Christ had given Saint Peter, the leader of the apostles, "the keys of the Kingdom of Heaven" and, therefore, authority over the entire Church. Peter later became the first bishop of Rome, and it was as bishop of Rome that he exercised his God-given authority over Christendom. When he died in office, all his power passed to his successor, and it continued to be handed on to each successive bishop of Rome. This vision of church history, which received a fair amount of acceptance in the West, failed to convince Christians in the East, including those who looked to Constantinople for spiritual guidance.

Although the Western Church considered the bishop of Rome to be the successor of Saint Peter and, therefore, the *holy father*, the actual power that popes exercised over Western Christendom was severely limited, especially before the twelfth century. Certainly Pope Leo III (r. 795–816), a contemporary of Charles the Great, had a vision of papal authority that far exceeded the bounds of political and even ecclesiastical reality. In point of fact, he had very little authority outside of Rome and its environs, and even in Rome he was beset by enemies, some of whom plotted his deposition and even his assassination.

In search of a protector, Leo III turned to the most powerful man of the day, Charles, king of the Franks and of the Lombards, whose lands covered much of western continental Europe by the late eighth century. Protection, however, usually comes with a price, and perhaps Pope Leo had that in mind when he commissioned the mosaic that appears here.

One of Leo's building projects was adding two state reception halls to the papal residence known as the *Lateran Palace*. In the fashion of the day, the interiors of each hall were covered with mosaics. One of the mosaics pictured a seated Saint Peter flanked by two kneeling figures: Pope Leo and King Charles. Inasmuch as

Lateran Palace Mosaic

the mosaic was completed sometime between 798 and April 799, Charles undoubtedly saw this artistic interpretation of papal-Frankish relations on his last
visit to Rome in 800/801, when the pope crowned him emperor. One can only
wonder what Charles thought of the mosaic.

Time badly deteriorated the mosaic. What we see in this mid-eighteenth-century
replacement copy is Saint Peter, with the keys to the Kingdom of Heaven on his
lap, handing a *pallium* (see source 63) to Pope Leo and a lance with attached battle
standard to King Charles. The pallium that Leo receives is the sign of authority
worn by popes and archbishops. Note that Peter, who is dressed in clerical robes,
wears one. Both the pope and the king have square nimbuses, or haloes, conventional signs that they are especially sanctified or powerful people who are still living; Peter has a round nimbus, a sign of sainthood. The four Latin inscriptions

read, from top to bottom and left to right as we view the mosaic: "Saint Peter"; "Most Holy Lord Pope Leo"; "To Lord King Charles"; and "Blessed Peter, You Give Life to Pope Leo and You Give Victory to King Charles."

QUESTIONS FOR ANALYSIS

1. Is there anything significant about Leo's position on Saint Peter's right and Charles's position on his left? Explain your answer.
2. What do you make of the fact that it is *Peter* who gives Charles the lance and not Jesus or some other manifestation of God?
3. What is the message of this mosaic?
4. Review sources 63 and 64. Now compose a Byzantine commentary on the mosaic.

A Carolingian Vision of Reality
▼▼▼

66 ▼ Charles the Great, *THE CAPITULARY ON SAXONY and A LETTER TO POPE LEO III*

Charlemagne ruled a major portion of continental Europe for close to half a century (768–814). During his lifetime Charles's efforts to expand the boundaries of Christendom and impose an order based on his understanding of Christian principles won him a reputation that extended all the way to the court of Caliph Harun al-Rashid in Baghdad. His *Carolingian* (the family of Charles) successors, however, were less fortunate and probably less able. In 843 Charles's three grandsons divided the empire into three kingdoms, signaling continental Europe's return to political pluralism — a pluralism that proved permanent and one of the major driving forces in European history.

Before the collapse of the Carolingian Empire, however, Charlemagne established at least a sense of order and unity, if not its total reality, that served as an inspiration for many of Europe's later emperors and kings. These included the king of Germany, Otto I, who laid the basis for the Germanic *Holy Roman Empire* with his imperial coronation in 962, and Napoleon, who in the early nineteenth century attempted to create a pan-European empire centered on France.

The following two sources, both composed in Charlemagne's name by his counselors and secretaries, illustrate the ideals of Charles's court and the realities that faced it. The first document is a *capitulary*, so called because it consists of a number of regulatory chapters (*capitula* in Latin), which King Charles issued in 785. Known as the *Capitulary on Saxony*, it set down regulations regarding the Saxons and the Christian Church of Saxony that Charles was attempting to establish. From 772 to 804, Charles's armies waged a series of campaigns of conquest against the Saxons, a pagan Germanic people who lived just beyond the Franks' northeastern frontier. Although the Saxons resisted Charles's attempts to impose Carolingian order and Christianity upon them, in the end Charles's tenacity won out. By 804 all resistance had collapsed. Saxony was incorporated into the Carolingian Empire, and the Saxons were at least nominal Christians. The second document is a letter to Pope Leo III written in 796, shortly after King Charles received word of the pope's accession to the papal throne — some four years before Charles's imperial coronation.

QUESTIONS FOR ANALYSIS

1. Consider the Capitulary on Saxony. What tactics does Charles employ to win over the Saxons to Christianity?
2. Does the Capitulary on Saxony distinguish between crimes and sins? Does it punish one type of infraction more than another? If yes, what type of infractions are most severely punished? What inferences do you draw from your answers?
3. Consider Charles's letter to Pope Leo III. What role(s) does Charles claim for himself? What role(s) does he assign the pope?
4. After a careful reading of both documents, what do you infer was Charles's vision of his duties as king?
5. On one of his campaigns in Italy, King Charles visited the Church of San Vitale and viewed the mosaic of Justinian (source 63). He subsequently constructed a palace chapel at Aachen, his favorite residence, which was roughly modeled on San Vitale. Compose King Charles's commentary on the mosaic of Justinian.
6. Compose Charles's commentary on Pope Leo III's *Lateran Mosaic* (source 65).

CAPITULARY ON SAXONY

First, concerning the greater chapters[1] it has been enacted:

1. It is pleasing to all that the churches of Christ, which are now being built in Saxony and consecrated to God, should not have less, but greater and more illustrious honor than the shrines of the idols have had.

2. If any one shall have fled to a church for refuge, let no one presume to expel him from the church by violence, but he shall be left in peace until he shall be brought to the judicial assemblage; and on account of the honor due to God and the saints, and the reverence due to the church itself, let his life and all his members be granted to him. Moreover, let him plead his cause as best he can and he shall be judged; and so let him be led to the presence of the lord king, and the latter shall send him where it shall seem fitting to his clemency.

3. If any one shall have entered a church by violence and shall have carried off anything in it by force or theft, or shall have burned the church itself, let him be punished by death.

4. If any one, out of contempt for Christianity, shall have despised the holy Lenten fast[2] and shall have eaten flesh, let him be punished by death. But, nevertheless, let it be taken into consideration by a priest lest perhaps any one from necessity has been led to eat flesh.

---

[1]The greater chapters concerned offenses that involved capital punishment; the lesser chapters dealt with noncapital offenses.

[2]The forty-day fast preceding Easter during which meat and many other foods were prohibited.

5. If any one shall have killed a bishop or priest or deacon[3] let him likewise be punished capitally.

6. If any one, deceived by the devil, shall have believed, after the manner of the pagans, that any man or woman is a witch and eats men, and on this account shall have burned the person, or shall have given the person's flesh to others to eat, or shall have eaten it himself, let him be punished by a capital sentence. . . .

8. If any one of the race of the Saxons hereafter, concealed among them, shall have wished to hide himself unbaptized, and shall have scorned to come to baptism, and shall have wished to remain a pagan, let him be punished by death.

9. If any one shall have sacrificed a man to the devil, and, after the manner of the pagans, shall have presented him as a victim to the demons, let him be punished by death.

10. If any one shall have formed a conspiracy with the pagans against the Christians, or shall have wished to join with them in opposition to the Christians, let him he punished by death; and whosoever shall have consented fraudulently to this same against the king and the Christian people, let him be punished by death. . . .

14. If, indeed, for these mortal crimes secretly committed any one shall have fled of his own accord to a priest, and after confession[4] shall have wished to do penance, let him be freed by the testimony of the priest from death.[5] . . .

18. On the Lord's day no meetings or public judicial assemblages shall be held, unless perchance in a case of great necessity, or when war compels it, but all shall go to church to hear the word of God, and shall be free for prayers or good works. Likewise, also, on the special festivals they shall devote themselves to God and to the services of the Church, and shall refrain from secular assemblies.

19. Likewise, it has been pleasing to insert in these decrees that all infants shall be baptized within a year; we have decreed this, that if any one shall have refused to bring his infant to baptism within the course of a year, without the advice or permission of the priest, if he is a noble he shall pay 120 *solidi*[6] to the treasury; if a freeman, 60; if a *litus*,[7] 30. . . .

21. If any one shall have made a vow at springs or trees or groves,[8] or shall have made an offering after the manner of the heathen and shall have partaken of a repast in honor of the demons, if he shall be a noble, 60 *solidi*; if a freeman, 30; if a *litus*, 15. If, indeed, they have not the means of paying at once, they shall be given into the service of the Church[9] until the *solidi* are paid.

22. We command that the bodies of Saxon Christians shall be carried to the church cemeteries, and not to the mounds of the pagans.

23. We have ordered that diviners and soothsayers shall be handed over to the churches and priests.

A LETTER TO POPE LEO III

Charles, by the grace of God king of the Franks[10] and Lombards,[11] and patrician of the Romans,[12]

---

[3]A Greek term meaning "minister" or "administrator." A deacon ranked just below a priest and performed such functions as preaching and dispensing alms.

[4]The sacrament in which a person confesses sins to a priest and receives absolution and a penance.

[5]From this point on the capitulary deals with lesser chapters.

[6]A weight, not a coin, a *solidus* (plural *solidi*) was 1/72 of a pound of gold.

[7]A *litus*, or *leet*, was someone whose class was midway between a free person and a slave.

[8]Places sacred to Saxon deities. Pagan Germans believed in the sacredness of nature and conducted all of their religious rites in the open air, having no enclosed temples.

[9]As indentured servants.

[10]In 768 Charles and his brother Carloman had divided the kingdom of the Franks between them upon the death of their father, King Pepin. When Carloman died in 771, Charles seized his deceased brother's half of the kingdom.

[11]In 774 Charles seized control of the Lombard Kingdom in northern and central Italy. The Lombards, a Germanic people, had invaded Italy in 568.

[12]A title bestowed on King Pepin and his sons Charles and Carloman by Pope Stephen II in 754.

to his holiness, Pope Leo, greeting. . . . Just as I entered into an agreement with the most holy father, your predecessor,[13] so also I desire to make with you an inviolable treaty of mutual fidelity and love; that, on the one hand, you shall pray for me and give me the apostolic benediction,[14] and that, on the other, with the aid of God I will ever defend the most holy seat[15] of the holy Roman Church. For it is our part to defend the holy Church of Christ from the attacks of pagans and infidels[16] from without, and within to enforce the acceptance of the Catholic faith. It is your part, most holy father, to aid us in the good fight by raising your hands to God as Moses did,[17] so that by your intercession the Christian people under the leadership of God may always and everywhere have the victory over the enemies of His holy name, and the name of our Lord Jesus Christ may be glorified throughout the world. Abide by the canonical law[18] in all things and obey the precepts of the Holy Fathers always, that your life may be an example of sanctity to all, and your holy admonitions be observed by the whole world, and that your light may so shine before men that they may see your good works and glorify your father who is in Heaven.[19] May omnipotent God preserve your holiness unharmed through many years for the exalting of His holy Church.

---

[13]Pope Hadrian I (r. 772–795).
[14]The blessing of the pope, the *apostolic* successor of Saint Peter, prince of the apostles, whom each pope claims as his predecessor and the source of papal authority.
[15]The *see*, or church, where the pope resides — this is a metaphor for the papacy itself.
[16]The unfaithful who do not believe in the teachings of the Church.
[17]The Bible, Exodus 17:11.
[18]*Canon law* is the law of the Church; the word *canon* means "standard of measurement" in Greek.
[19]The Bible, Matthew 5:16.

Byzantium and the West in the Age of Otto the Great

Internal weaknesses, irresistible tendencies toward the creation of regional power blocs, and multiple invasions by non-Christians precipitated the collapse of Carolingian unity during the later ninth century. We would be mistaken, however, if we viewed the 800s and the following two centuries as an era of unmitigated disasters, unremitting invasions, universal political fragmentation, and total social dislocation. Between roughly 850 and 1050, Western Europe rose to the challenge of meeting its crises and emerged quite the stronger for it.

The power that took the lead in this effort was Germany, led by its Saxon kings. The Saxons, whom Charles the Great had violently introduced to Christianity, became the new champions of Western Christendom and inheritors of the imperial crown.

During the early tenth century, the imperial title died out in the West for lack of anyone strong enough to claim it, but on February 2, 962, Pope John XII (r. 955–964) anointed the Saxon king of Germany, *Otto I* (r. 936–973), as emperor, thereby resurrecting the Western imperial office. Like Charlemagne, upon whom he modeled himself, Otto was the most powerful monarch of his day in Western Europe and was remembered by posterity as worthy of the title "the Great," but unlike Charles the Great, Otto carved out an empire in Germany and Italy that lived on for centuries after his death.

Under Otto and his son and grandson, Germany pushed out the boundaries of Latin Christianity as it subjugated and colonized Slavic lands to its immediate east and converted its new subjects in the process. What is more, imperially sponsored missionaries ranged into Poland, Bohemia, Croatia, and Hungary — all of which officially accepted Latin forms of the Christian faith by the year 1000. Meanwhile, Anglo-Saxon England was taking the lead in the conversion of Scandinavia, especially Denmark and Norway.

At the same time that Western Europe was extending its cultural boundaries, Byzantium's missionaries were bringing Byzantine forms of Christian culture to the Bulgars, Serbs, and Rus' in the Balkans and Eastern Europe. By 1000 the Rus' of Kiev, a people of mixed Slavic and Scandinavian origin, had officially accepted the ecclesiastical leadership of the Church of Constantinople, and the foundations for the Russian and Ukrainian Orthodox Churches had been laid. Farther south in the Balkans, Latin Christian Croats lived alongside Byzantine Christian Serbs.

At times the Churches of Rome and Constantinople cooperated in these missionary ventures; at times they competed. This ambivalent spirit of a shared Christianity tempered by a realization of their differences and competing claims was also manifested in their religious art and diplomatic exchanges, as the following two sources indicate.

A Western Ambassador to Constantinople

▼▼▼

67 ▼ *Liudprand of Cremona,*
A REPORT ON THE EMBASSY TO CONSTANTINOPLE

In 968 Emperor Otto I endeavored to lessen tensions with Byzantium, after an unsuccessful attack on Byzantine lands south of Rome, by arranging a marriage alliance between his son and heir, the future Otto II, and a Byzantine princess. His natural choice of ambassador to the court of Emperor Nicephorus II Phocas was Liudprand, bishop of Cremona (ca. 920–972), in northern Italy. Not only did Liudprand speak and read Greek, but he had already served as an ambassador to Constantinople for King Berengar II in 949 and possibly also visited Constantinople for Otto as recently as 960.

Liudprand had gained an appreciation for the imperial city and its people, as he showed in his *Antapodosis* (*Tit-for-Tat*), an early work in which he stated that Constantinople's inhabitants surpassed all of their Eastern neighbors in wealth and wisdom. His experiences in 968–969 changed that opinion.

Liudprand's embassy was a failure, and, even worse, he felt insulted by the way he and other Westerners were treated by the Byzantines. Before leaving the city, Liudprand witnessed a tiff between the emperor and envoys from Pope John

XIII. The envoys arrived in Constantinople bearing a papal letter addressed to the "emperor of the Greeks," and for that unintentional provocation, they were tossed into prison. Liudprand also had to endure the indignity of having precious purple cloth that he had secured and tried to carry back home confiscated by Byzantine authorities who deemed it wrong for foreigners to wear this imperial color. If we can believe Liudprand, he retorted that at home such garments were worn by prostitutes and magicians.

Following his return to the West, the bishop composed the *Report on the Embassy to Constantinople*, in which he vented his anger. When reading the following excerpt, we should keep Liudprand's indignation in mind; he was not an objective reporter.

Despite his bitterness, Liudprand returned to Constantinople in 971 and was successful on that occasion, returning with the princess Theophano as wife for the future Otto II (r. 973–983).

This excerpt from Liudprand's account of his misadventures in Byzantium begins with his being ill and feeling quite mistreated by the emperor, with whom he has dined and exchanged insults (if we can believe that the bishop had the courage to do so). In that mood, he was banished to his lodgings, from which he wrote to the emperor's brother, Leo, threatening to go home.

QUESTIONS FOR ANALYSIS

1. Emperor Otto I secured the deposition of two popes (John XII and Benedict V) and arranged the appointment of three other popes, including the current John XIII. Despite this close imperial control over the Roman papacy, how does Liudprand view and treat the papal office?
2. How do the Byzantines view the pope? Other churchmen?
3. Does Liudprand consider the Byzantines to be fellow Christians in communion with the West?
4. How do the Byzantines look upon the Western Church?
5. What was the real reason that the Bulgarian envoy was accorded more honor than Liudprand? (Hint: Locate the land of the Bulgars on a map.) What does your answer to this question suggest about cultural-political realities at this time?
6. What does the emperor imply by his remark concerning the synod of Saxony?
7. How does Liudprand answer these charges, and what does his answer imply?
8. What does this excerpt suggest about Western-Byzantine relations toward the end of the tenth century?

Leo read my letter and gave me an audience four days later. In accordance with their rule, their wisest men . . . sat with him to discuss your request, namely Basil the chief chamberlain, the chief secretary, the chief master of the wardrobe, and two other dignitaries. They began their discourse as follows: "Tell us, brother, the reason that induced you to take the trouble to come here." When I told them that it was on account of the marriage which was to be the ground for a lasting peace, they said: "It is unheard of that a daughter born in the purple of an emperor born in the purple[1] should contract a foreign marriage. Still, great as is your demand, you shall have what you want, if you give what is proper: Ravenna,[2] namely, and Rome with all the adjoining territories from thence to our possessions. If you desire friendship without the marriage, let your master permit Rome to be free,[3] and hand over to their former lord[4] the princes of Capua and Benevento,[5] who were formerly slaves of our holy empire and are now rebels."

To this I answered: "Even you cannot but know that my master rules over Slavonian princes[6] who are more powerful than Peter, king of the Bulgarians, who has married the daughter of the emperor Christopher."[7] "Ah," said they, "but Christopher was not born in the purple."[8]

"As for Rome," I went on, "for whose freedom you are so noisily eager; who is her master? To whom does she pay tribute? Was she not formerly enslaved to harlots? And while you were sleeping, nay powerless, did not my master the august emperor free her from that foul servitude?[9] Constantine, the august emperor who founded this city and called it after his name, as ruler of the world made many offerings to the holy Roman apostolic Church, not only in Italy but in almost all the western kingdoms, as well as those in the east and south, in Greece, Judaea, Persia, Mesopotamia, Babylonia, Egypt, Libya, as his own special regulations testify that are preserved in our country. In Italy, in Saxony, in Bavaria, and in all my master's realms, every-

thing that belongs to the Church of the blessed apostles has been handed over to the vicar of those holy apostles.[10] And if my master has kept back a single city, farm, vassal or slave, then I have denied God. Why does not your emperor do the same? Why does he not restore to the apostolic Church what lies in his kingdoms and thereby himself increase the richness and freedom that it already owes to my master's exertions and generosity?"

"He will do so," said the chief chamberlain Basil, "when Rome and the Roman Church shall be so ordered as he wishes." Then said I: "A certain man having suffered much injury from another, approached God with these words: 'Lord, avenge me upon my adversary.' To whom the Lord said: 'I will do so on the day when I shall render to each man according to his works.' 'How late that day will be!' the man replied."

At that everyone except the emperor's brother burst into laughter. Then they broke off the discussion and ordered me to be taken back to my detestable dwelling place and to be carefully guarded until the day of the apostles, a feast that all religious persons duly observe.[11] At the ceremony the emperor commanded me, though I was very ill at the time, together with the Bulgarian envoys who had arrived the day before, to meet him at the Church of the Holy Apostles.[12] After some verbose chants had been sung and mass celebrated, we were invited to table, where I found placed above me on my side of the long narrow board the Bulgarian envoy. He was a fel-

---

[1]The daughter of a reigning emperor (who wore purple, the imperial color), who himself was born the son of a reigning emperor.

[2]See sources 42 and 63. Ravenna had been the seat of Byzantine power in Italy until it was captured by the Lombards (Liudprand's ancestors) in the eighth century.

[3]From Otto's control.

[4]Emperor Nicephorus.

[5]Lordships in south-central Italy.

[6]In the northern Balkans, where both empires clashed.

[7]In 927 King Peter (r. 927–969) married Maria, daughter of Christopher, the eldest son and crowned coemperor of Romanus I (r. 920–944). Christopher died in 931 before he could assume the imperial throne on his own.

[8]When Christopher was born, his father, Romanus, was not a member of the imperial family. Romanus I rose from humble origins.

[9]According to the Ottonian vision of history, Rome had been under the control of immoral men and women, including the evil Pope John XII, until Otto I liberated the city and the papacy from this scourge.

[10]The pope is the vicar, or deputy, of Saint Peter, prince of the apostles.

[11]One of the many holy days shared by the Churches of Constantinople and Rome.

[12]The Church of the Holy Apostles was one of the city's grandest structures and served as the model for many Byzantine-style churches in the East and the West (e.g., San Marco in Venice and Saint Basil's Cathedral in Moscow).

low with his hair cut in the Hungarian[13] fashion, girt about with a brazen chain and, as I fancy, just admitted into the Christian faith. The preference given to him over me was plainly meant as an insult to you, my august masters.[14] On your account I was despised, rejected, and scorned. . . . However, my masters, I considered that the insult was done to you, not to me, and I therefore left the table. I was just going indignantly away when Leo, the emperor's brother and marshal of the court, and Simeon, the chief secretary, came after me, howling: "When Peter, king of the Bulgarians, married Christopher's daughter, a mutual agreement was sworn to on both sides to the effect that envoys of the Bulgarians should with us be preferred, honored, and esteemed above the envoys of all other nations. What you say is true: the Bulgarian envoy over there has his hair cut short, he has not washed himself, and his girdle consists of a brass chain. But nevertheless he is a patrician, and we are definitely of the opinion that it would be wrong to give a bishop, especially a Frankish[15] bishop, preference over him. We have noticed your show of indignation, and we are not going to allow you to return to your lodgings, as you suppose; we shall force you to take food with the emperor's servants in an inn."

My mental anguish was so unparalleled that I could not answer them back but did what they ordered, judging that table no fit place for me, seeing that a Bulgarian envoy was preferred, I will not say to myself personally, that is, to Bishop Liudprand, but to your representative. . . .

When eight days had passed and the Bulgarians had left the city, Nicephorus, thinking that I esteemed his table highly, compelled me, in spite of my ill health, to dine with him again in the same place. The patriarch[16] with several other bishops was present, and before them he propounded to me many questions concerning the Holy Scriptures, which, under the inspiration of the Holy Spirit, I elegantly answered. Finally, wishing to make merry of you, he asked which synods[17] we recognized. Those of Nicaea, Chalcedon, Ephesus, Carthage, Antioch, Ancyra, and Constantinople,[18] I replied. "Ha, ha," he said, "you have forgotten to mention Saxony.[19] If you ask me, the reason why our books do not mention it either is that the Christian faith there is too young. . . ."[20]

I answered: "On that member of the body where the malady has its seat a cautery must be used. All the heresies have emanated from you and among you have flourished; by our Western peoples they have been either strangled or killed. . . . As for the Saxon people, ever since they received holy baptism and the knowledge of God, they have not been stained by any heresy which rendered a synod necessary for its correction; of heresies we have had none. You declare that our Saxon faith is young, and I agree. Faith in Christ is always young and not old among people whose faith is seconded by works. Here faith is old, not young; works do not accompany it, and by reason of its age it is held in light esteem like a worn-out garment. I know for certain of one synod held in Saxony where it was enacted and decreed that it was more seemly to fight with the sword than with the pen, and better to face death than to fly before a foe. Your own army is finding that out now." And in my own mind I said: "May it soon find out by experience how warlike our men are."

---

[13]The Hungarians, whom Otto I had crushed in battle in 955, were still considered barbaric pagans. Their leader, Duke Vajik (renamed Stephen upon his conversion), accepted Latin Christianity and was crowned as their first king on Christmas Day 1000 with a crown sent him by Pope Sylvester II (r. 999–1003).

[14]Otto I and his son.

[15]All Westerners were *Franks* to the Byzantines.

[16]Polyeuctus, patriarch of Constantinople (r. 956–970).

[17]Here he means ecumenical councils of the Church, not local synods (see Multiple Voices IV). The Byzantine Church recognized seven as ecumenical: Nicaea (325); I Constantinople (381); Ephesus (431); Chalcedon (451); II Constantinople (553); III Constantinople (680–681); II Nicaea (787).

[18]A rather strange list.

[19]Saxony, the northern German homeland of Emperor Otto I, was never the site of a major church council.

[20]As we saw in source 66, Christianity came to Saxony around the year 800 with the conquering armies of Charlemagne.

Two Representations of the Virgin
▼▼▼
68 ▼ *A BYZANTINE ICON OF THE KOIMESIS and A DORMITION MINIATURE*

By the year 1000, Eastern and Western Christians disagreed over a number of issues, but they equally regarded Mary, the mother of Jesus, as the most lovable and loving of all God's saints. Both Byzantine and Latin Christians revered Mary as the fully human yet sinless Mother of God who served as advocate for all humanity before her Son's throne.

The cult of Mary resulted in a massive volume of religious artwork in East and West centering on the Virgin Mother. One of the more popular themes, which originated in Byzantium (possibly influenced by somewhat similar representations of the Buddha's *parinirvana*, or passing into Nirvana at death), was the "Falling Asleep" of Mary, known in Greek as the *Koimesis*. According to a tradition equally accepted in the East and the West, when Mary died, her incorruptible body was assumed into Heaven. With body and soul reunited, she was crowned Queen of Heaven. In the West, the same moment in sacred history was referred to as the *Dormition*. By whichever name they knew it, Byzantines and Western Christians celebrated the event as one of the holiest feast days in the religious calendar.

The following two images depict the *Falling Asleep*. The first is a carved icon, or sacred image, from Byzantium, dating from the second half of the tenth century. Here we see the sleeping Virgin, who could not die because she was sinless. She is surrounded by mourning apostles and disciples, including Mary Magdalene (in the far left corner covering her lower face with a veil). Saint Paul stands at the foot of her bed, and Saint Peter is at the head, incensing her body. Her son, Jesus, has taken her soul in his hands, and two angels prepare to receive it into Heaven. The second illustration is a miniature (a small manuscript painting) from the German monastery at Reichenau. This work, which dates to around 1000, varies somewhat from the Byzantine icon. Saint Paul is still at the foot of the bed, but Saint Peter has been replaced at the head of the bed to stand just behind the beardless Saint John, to whom Jesus commended the care of his mother as he was dying on the cross. (In the Byzantine icon, John is half hidden behind Peter's censer and has his hand on the Virgin's bed.)

As you study these two masterpieces, see if you can find any iconographical and artistic connections between them.

QUESTIONS FOR ANALYSIS

1. List all of the similarities and dissimilarities between these two works of art.
2. The artistic motif of the Virgin's Falling Asleep originated in the East, where popular veneration of Mary was deep and widespread. What do the similarities in these two works of art suggest to you?

3. Discuss the dissimilarities. Do they suggest anything about the differences between these two Christian cultures?
4. Which seem to you the more significant, the similarities or the dissimilarities? Why? Be specific in your answer.

A Byzantine Icon of the Koimesis

A Dormition Miniature

Imperium Versus Sacerdotium: The Tensions Between Secular Rulers and Priests

As we saw with Pope Leo III and Charlemagne (see sources 65 and 66), there was an inherent tension in Latin Europe between those who held royal or imperial power (*imperium*) and those who exercised priestly authority (*sacerdotium*). Note that we have avoided terming this a conflict between church and state because that would be anachronistic. In the eleventh century, most theorists and persons in power in both Byzantium and the West envisioned a single Christian body that, like the human body, had both corporeal and spiritual functions but only one head. The question was, who was that head: the God-anointed emperor or king or the chief priest, be he pope or patriarch? In Byzantium, as we saw in source 64, emperors generally were able to appoint and control the patriarchs of Constantinople, thereby making the Byzantine Church a deeply venerated but largely controlled instrument of the state. The situation was different in the Latin West.

Charles the Great and his Carolingian successors, as well as the emperors of various dynasties who followed for the next 500 years, claimed that the emperor was *the* God-appointed defender of righteousness, the punisher of the wicked, the defender and overseer of the Church, and the champion of orthodox Christian doctrine and practice. And they acted accordingly. Otto the Great and his successors went so far as to depose unworthy popes and to appoint those who they believed were suitable for that holy office. Since at least the early fifth century, however, most of the popes of Rome disagreed with this worldview, even when they were dependent on the favor, goodwill, and patronage of various rulers, be they emperors (whom the popes generally crowned), kings, or local Italian princes.

In the last quarter of the eleventh century, these inherent tensions and contradictions sparked a half-century-long struggle between the Western Roman Empire (it was not yet called the Holy Roman Empire) and the papacy, known as the *Investiture Controversy*. A peace treaty in 1122, known as the Concordat of Worms, resolved some of their peripheral differences but never addressed the core issue: Who is the God-appointed head of Christendom, the emperor or the pope? For the next two centuries, this question continued to set off struggles between popes and emperors and popes and kings.

The fact that neither popes nor monarchs were ever able to overwhelm the other proved ultimately fruitful. Slowly, ever so slowly, in the course of these disputes some theorists began to articulate a revolutionary idea.

Three Views of Right Order in Christian Society

▼▼▼

69 ▾ *DICTATUS PAPAE; Henry IV, LETTER TO HILDEBRAND; John of Paris, A TREATISE ON ROYAL AND PAPAL POWER*

The Investiture Controversy, which raged from 1075 to 1122, began as a contest between Pope Gregory VII (r. 1073–1085) and Henry IV, king of Germany and emperor-elect (r. 1056–1106), for authority over the right to *invest*, or appoint and install, clerics in church offices in Germany and Italy, but it soon turned into an ideological struggle for control over the Church and Christian society. The controversy outlived both men and spread elsewhere into Western Europe, far beyond the boundaries of the empire, which encompassed only Germany and portions of Italy. When finally, in 1122, Pope Calixtus II and Emperor Henry V agreed to a compromise regarding imperial rights over appointments to church offices within the empire, the core ideological issue remained unresolved.

Our first two documents, one from the camp of Pope Gregory and one from Henry IV's side, lay out the two positions. Gregory's contribution is known as the *Dictatus Papae* (*The Pope's Proclamation*). Composed in March 1075 under the heading "What is the power of the Roman Pontiffs?" it was inserted into the pope's *register*, or official collection of his correspondence. It consists simply of twenty-seven assertions regarding papal authority, but despite its sketchiness, it provides clear insight into Gregory VII's mindset and program. King Henry IV's letter of January 24, 1076, undoubtedly written on his behalf by a clerical supporter, lays out the royal-imperial position, which many churchmen in Europe also subscribed to at this time. One consequence of the many bitter and protracted struggles that followed on the heels of the Investiture Controversy was the growing opinion among some observers that there were two powers that had valid but different claims on a subject's loyalty. The clearest medieval articulator of this revolutionary notion was John of Paris, a French priest and theologian, who articulated his ideas around 1302. Although his was still a minority voice, it foreshadows what would become, many centuries later, the Western ideal of separation of church and state.

QUESTIONS FOR ANALYSIS

1. The *Dictatus Papae* and King Henry IV's letter reveal two views of how the earthly Church functions. What were those views?
2. In what way, if at all, did John of Paris offer a third view?
3. Compose a commentary on all three documents by one Byzantine and one Latin Christian from the following list: Justinian I; Michael Psellus; Leo III; Charles the Great; Liudprand of Cremona.

DICTATUS PAPAE

1. That the Roman Church was established by God alone.

2. The only the Roman Pontiff is, by right, called universal.[1]

3. That only he has the power to depose and reinstate bishops. . . .

8. That he alone may use the imperial insignia.[2]

9. That all princes shall kiss the foot of only the pope. . . .

12. That he has the power to depose emperors. . . .

16. That no Ecumenical Council may be called without his ordering it.

17. That no action of a synod [council] and no book shall be regarded as canonical without his authority.

18. That his decree can be annulled by no one, and that he can annul the decrees of anyone.

19. That he can be judged by no one. . . .

22. That the Roman Church has never erred and will never err to all eternity, according to the testimony of Holy Scripture. . . .

24. That by his command or permission subjects may accuse their rulers. . . .

26. That no one can be regarded as Catholic who does not agree with the Roman Church.

27. That he has the power to release subjects from their oaths of fidelity to wicked rulers.

LETTER OF HENRY IV
TO HILDEBRAND

Henry, king not by usurpation, but by the holy ordination of God, to Hilderband,[3] not pope, but false monk.

This is the salutation which you deserve, for you have never held any office in the Church without making it a source of confusion and a curse to Christian men instead of an honor and a blessing. To mention only the most obvious cases out of many, you have not only dared to touch the Lord's anointed, the archbishops, bishops, and priests; but you have scorned them and abused them, as if they were ignorant servants not fit to know what their master was doing. This you have done to gain favor with the vulgar crowd. You have declared that the bishops know nothing and that you know everything; but if you have such great wisdom you have used it not to build but to destroy. . . . All this we have endured because of our respect for the papal office, but you have mistaken our humility for fear, and have dared to make an attack upon the royal and imperial authority[4] which we received from God. You have even threatened to take it away, as if we had received it from you, and as if the empire and kingdom were in your disposal and not in the disposal of God. Our Lord Jesus Christ has called us to the government of the empire, but he never called you to the rule of the Church. This is the way you have gained advancement in the Church: through craft you have obtained wealth; through wealth you have obtained favor; through favor, the power of the sword; and through the power of the sword, the papal seat, which is the seat of peace,[5] and then from the seat of peace you have expelled peace. For you have incited subjects to rebel against their prelates by teaching them to despise the bishops, their rightful rulers. You have given to laymen the authority over priests, whereby they condemn and depose those whom the bishops have put over them to teach them.[6] You have

---

[1]The pope (Roman Pontiff) alone has universal authority over all churches.
[2]A claim based on an eighth-century forgery known as *The Donation of Constantine*. It purported to be a grant from Constantine I to Pope Sylvester I that ceded to the pope the right to wear all imperial insignia and bestowed on him and his successors dominion over Rome, Italy, and the "western regions."

[3]Gregory VII's name before he became pope.
[4]Actually, Henry had not yet been crowned emperor. He was king of Germany and emperor-elect.
[5]Henry claims Hildebrand had usurped the papal throne.
[6]Gregory and the other radical reformers within the papal party called on Europe's laity to reject sinful priests and bishops. See source 70, note 3.

attacked me, who, unworthy as I am, have yet been anointed to rule among the anointed of God, and who, according to the teaching of the fathers, can be judged by no one save God alone, and can be deposed for no crime except infidelity. . . . St. Peter himself said: "Fear God, honor the king" [1 Pet. 2:17]. But you, who fear not God, have dishonored me, whom He has established. . . . Come down, then, from that apostolic seat which you have obtained by violence; for you have been declared accursed . . . for your false doctrines and have been condemned by us and our bishops for your evil rule. Let another ascend the throne of St. Peter, one who will not use religion as a cloak of violence, but will teach the life-giving doctrine of that prince of the apostles. I, Henry, king by the grace of God, with all my bishops, say unto you: "Come down, come down, and be accursed through all the ages."

A TREATISE ON ROYAL AND PAPAL POWER

A kingdom is ordered to this end, that an assembled multitude may live virtuously, . . . and it is further ordered to a higher end which is the enjoyment of God; and responsibility for this end belongs to Christ, whose ministers and vicars are the priests. Therefore the priestly power is of greater dignity than the secular and this is commonly conceded. . . .

But if the priest is greater in himself than the prince and is greater in dignity, it does not follow that he is greater in all respects. For the lesser secular power is not related to the greater spiritual power as having its origin from it or being derived from it. . . . The relationship is rather like that of a head of a household to a general of armies, since one is not derived from the other but both from a superior power. And so the secular power is greater than the spiritual in some things, namely in temporal affairs, and in such affairs it is not subject to the spiritual power in any way because it does not have its origin from it but rather both have their origin immediately from the one supreme power, namely the divine. Accordingly the inferior power is not subject to the superior in all things but only in those where the supreme power has subordinated it to the greater. A teacher of literature or an instructor in morals directs the members of a household to a nobler end, namely the knowledge of truth, than a doctor who is concerned with a lower end, namely the health of bodies, but who would say therefore the doctor should be subjected to the teacher in preparing his medicines? For this is not fitting, since the head of the household who established both in his house did not subordinate the lesser to the greater in this respect. Therefore the priest is greater than the prince in spiritual affairs and, on the other hand, the prince is greater in temporal affairs.

A Byzantine Perspective on the Investiture Controversy
▼▼▼
70 ▼ *Anna Comnena, THE ALEXIAD*

Anna Comnena (1083–after 1148), daughter of Emperor Alexius I (r. 1081–1118), undertook to write the history of her father's eventful reign sometime after 1137. The fact that she entitled the work the *Alexiad*, in imitation of Homer's epic poem the *Iliad*, clearly indicates the view she held of her father's place in history.

In this selection Anna comments on the first years of the *Investiture Controversy*, a struggle that provided the background to the First Crusade, which figured so prominently in her father's reign (see Multiple Voices VII) and in her book. Although she was far removed in space and time from the opening salvos exchanged by Gregory and Henry, her perspective, her knowledge of the affair, and even her misinformation are equally revealing.

QUESTIONS FOR ANALYSIS

1. Review source 69. How well informed was Anna of these events? What do you conclude from your answer?
2. Compose Anna Comnena's commentary on the three documents in source 69.

An event occurred which is worth relating, as it, too, contributed to this man's [Emperor Alexius] reputation and good fortune. . . . Now it happened that the pope of Rome had a difference with Henry, king of Germany. . . . The pope is a very high dignitary, and is protected by troops of various nationalities. The dispute between the king and the pope was this: the latter accused Henry of not bestowing livings[1] as free gifts, but selling them for money,[2] and occasionally entrusting archbishoprics to unworthy recipients,[3] and he also brought further charges of a similar nature against him. The king of Germany on his side indicted the pope of usurpation, as he had seized the apostolic chair without his consent.[4] Moreover, he had the effrontery to utter reckless threats against the pope, saying that if he did not resign his self-elected office, he should be expelled from it. . . . When these words reached the pope's ears, he vented his rage upon Henry's ambassadors;[5] first he tortured them inhumanly, then clipped their hair with scissors, and sheared their beards with a razor, and finally committed a most indecent outrage upon them, which transcended even the insolence of barbarians, and so sent them away. My womanly and princely dig-

nity forbids my naming the outrage inflicted on them, for it was not only unworthy of a high priest, but of anyone who bears the name of a Christian. I abhor this barbarian's idea, and more still the deed, and I should have defiled both my pen and my paper had I described it explicitly.[6] But as a display of barbaric insolence, and a proof that time in its flow produces men with shameless morals, ripe for any wickedness, this alone will suffice, if I say, that I could not bear to disclose or relate even the tiniest word about what he did. And this was the work of a high priest. Oh, justice! The deed of the supreme high priest! nay, of one who claimed to be the president of the whole world, as indeed the Latins assert and believe, but this, too, is a bit of their boasting. For when the imperial seat was transferred from Rome hither to our native Queen of Cities, and the senate, and the whole administration, there was also transferred the arch-hieratical primacy.[7] And the emperors from the very beginning have given the supreme right to the episcopacy[8] of Constantinople, and the Council of Chalcedon emphatically raised the bishop of Constantinople to the highest position, and placed all the dioceses of the inhabited world

---

[1]A *living* was the income a cleric received to support him in his clerical office and duties.
[2]The papacy claimed that lay rulers, such as Henry, were guilty of the sin of *simony* (named for the sin of Simon Magus [the Magician]: see Multiple Voices IV) — the selling of sacred clerical offices and other holy items.
[3]According to the papal reformers, this was another abuse of lay investiture, and some radical reformers, such as Gregory VII, called on pious laypeople to throw out unworthy clerics who had been invested in their offices by lay rulers.

[4]By tradition, the pope-elect applied for imperial approval of his election.
[5]There is no evidence for the abuse that she recounts in the account that follows.
[6]Anna seems to imply that Gregory had the envoys castrated.
[7]Chief *patriarch* of the universal Church (see note 8).
[8]The question was: Who was the chief patriarch of the Church — the bishop of Rome or the bishop of Constantinople?

under his jurisdiction.[9] There can be no doubt that the insult done to the ambassadors was aimed at the king who sent them; not only because he scourged them, but also because he was the first to invent this new kind of outrage. For by his actions, the pope suggested, I think, that the power of the king was despicable, and by

this horrible outrage on his ambassadors that he, a demi-god, as it were, was treating with a demi-ass! The pope consequently, by wreaking his insolence on the ambassadors, and sending them back to the king in the state I have mentioned, provoked a very great war.

---

[9]Wrong. The Ecumenical Council of Chalcedon of 451 stipulated in canon (regulation) 28 that the bishop of Constantinople enjoyed a primacy of honor second only to that of the bishop of Rome because Constantinople was the *New Rome.*

Multiple Voices VII ▼▼▼
Byzantium and the West in the Age of the Crusades: The Dividing of Christendom?

BACKGROUND

Many books continue to perpetuate the myth that the Churches of Constantinople and Rome entered into clear and permanent *schism*, or separation, in 1054 when Patriarch Michael I Cerularius (see source 64) and legates of Pope Leo IX hurled mutual curses of damnation and excommunication at each other's Church. Nothing of the sort happened. It is true that, following a heated argument, several papal envoys laid a sentence of excommunication on the patriarch and his supporters. But they did so on their own initiative, and their attack was essentially aimed at only Patriarch Michael. It is also true that Byzantine church officials responded in kind by excommunicating the offending Western churchmen. But the Byzantine Church officially refused to believe that the legates were true representatives of the pope or the Western Church. The point is that this celebrated incident of 1054 was not the *cause* of a visible rift between these two branches of Christendom. It was, however, one of many *symptoms* of a growing alienation between the two Christian cultures.

The factors that led to the division between the Churches of Catholic Rome and Orthodox Constantinople were rooted in centuries of political separation and cultural estrangement. The process began as early as the fourth century and accelerated as time went on. Not until the latter half of the eleventh century, however, when the papacy promoted an agenda of transforming Christian society under papal leadership (see source 69), did the differences between the Byzantine and Western visions of the world and the Church begin to become apparent.

One expression of the new papal self-confidence was its attempt to marshal the military vigor of the West in a series of holy wars known as the *crusades*. As early as 1074, news of Seljuk Turkish victories over Byzantine forces moved Pope Gregory VII to propose publicly that he lead an army of 50,000 volunteers to rescue Eastern Christians. The Investiture Controversy prevented him from realizing this dream, but the papacy never forgot the project. His successor once-removed, Pope Urban II, responded to overtures from Emperor Alexius I for help in raising troops for the Byzantine army by calling on the warrior class of the West to march eastward to rescue fellow Christians and to liberate Jerusalem from the infidel. The pope's appeal, enunciated for the first time on November 27, 1095, provided the impetus for the First Crusade (1096–1099).

By transforming this simple request from Emperor Alexius for assistance in raising soldiers for the imperial army into a call for a mass expedition of holy warriors, Pope Urban unleashed the vigor of emerging Europe on an unsuspecting Eastern Mediterranean World.

What began as an idealistic call for warriors to oppose a Muslim threat to Eastern Christendom and to liberate the Holy Land grew into complex series of holy wars fought on many fronts and against a variety of perceived enemies in Southwest Asia, North Africa, Europe, the Indian Ocean, and even the Americas over hundreds of years and at least into the late sixteenth century. Our focus here, however, is limited to the impact that crusading had on Byzantine-Latin relations between 1095 and 1204.

THE SOURCES

The first document comes from the pen of a monk, Baldric of Dol, who had been at the Council of Clermont in 1095 when Pope Urban called for the liberation of Jerusalem. In his history of the First Crusade, composed around 1108, Baldric presents his version of Pope Urban's sermon.

We have no transcript of the sermon. Rather, five versions exist, each contained in one of five early-twelfth-century histories of the First Crusade. Although they contain some similarities, their differences are striking. And this should not surprise us. Each author felt free to exercise his rhetorical skills in crafting his version of the pope's sermon, and each emphasized those aspects of the speech that most captivated or interested him. Clearly, all of the authors were influenced by the crusade's success and wrote from a post-crusade perspective, which influenced how they remembered Urban's speech. Moreover, as was the case with Baldric, several of them tried to place the crusade sermon into a theological context. Nevertheless, despite the fact that we will never know exactly what Urban II said that day, it seems clear that Baldric and the other four chroniclers did a pretty good job, individually and collectively, in conveying the major points that the pope made in one of the most significant speeches in world history.

That speech, and the sermons of numerous other preachers across Europe, unleashed a massive folk movement. Between 1096 and 1099, probably well over 100,000 men, women, and children trekked or sailed east on crusade in several waves. Probably no more than 10 percent of them were professional warriors, and the death rate from disease, accidents, and combat was possibly higher than 70 percent. Yet, despite the losses and long odds, the crusaders managed to capture Jerusalem on July 15, 1099. But before they reached the Holy Land, they had to travel through Byzantine territory. In the second excerpt, Anna Comnena, whom we encountered in source 70, describes the first great wave, the misnamed Peasants' Crusade of the summer of 1096. It is misnamed because the various elements of this first wave, which ended in disastrous defeat, contained a fair number of professional soldiers and even some lords and their retinues. Regardless, most of its elements were poorly led and ill supplied, and some of its members were guilty of attacks on Latin and Byzantine Christians, as well as Jews, along their routes of march.

In evaluating Anna's testimony, be aware that the armies of her father had several clashes with some crusader groups and that Emperor Alexius fell into disfavor with a number of crusade leaders when he failed to send them a relief force when they were in desperate straits at Antioch in 1098.

The misunderstandings and animosities engendered by the First Crusade paled in comparison to those of the Fourth Crusade (1202–1204). A force made up largely of French warriors and Venetian sailors planned to strike at Islam through a seaborne assault on Alexandria in Egypt. Unforeseen circumstances, however, led the crusaders to Constantinople, where they became embroiled in a dynastic power struggle between rival imperial claimants. Further circumstances and misadventures finally drove the crusaders to attempt to capture the city for themselves. They breached the city's walls on April 12, 1204, and captured it the following day. After three days of looting, the Westerners settled down to enjoy the fruits of conquest and established the Latin Empire of Constantinople, which enjoyed a precarious existence down to 1261. Although the Byzantines regained their capital city fifty-seven years after having lost it, both the city and the empire were by then largely shadows of their former selves. As our third, fourth, and fifth sources suggest, the Fourth Crusade had a profound effect on Byzantine-Latin relations.

The first of these three Fourth Crusade sources is an eyewitness account by Robert of Clari, a French knight who participated in the crusade and returned home to tell of it. This excerpt, taken from an account that he narrated sometime after 1205, describes preparations that the crusaders made following their initial, unsuccessful attack against the city on April 9.

The next source comes from the pen of Nicetas Choniates (ca. 1155–ca. 1216), a Byzantine nobleman, court official, and historian. His account is especially telling inasmuch as he was an eyewitness to and victim of the crusaders' capture and pillage of Constantinople. Our selection begins early on the morning of April 13. The day before, after bloody and bitter fighting, the crusaders had managed to penetrate the walls of the city and set up a small armed camp within hostile territory. With the situation still in doubt, they spent a sleepless night, wondering what the morning would bring.

The last source consists of excerpts from two letters of Pope Innocent III (r. 1198–1216) to the crusaders. Innocent had prohibited and attempted, without success, to prevent the diversion to Constantinople, but once he learned of the crusaders' apparently miraculous capture of the city, he changed his tune. Soon thereafter, however, he was forced to recant his earlier jubilation. Despite this change of mood, the pope never considered for a moment not supporting the Latin Empire of Constantinople and not demanding obedience to papal authority by the captive Byzantine Church.

QUESTIONS FOR ANALYSIS

1. Consider how Baldric presents Pope Urban's reasons for calling for this holy war. If order of presentation and emphasis mean anything, what was, according to our chronicler, the pope's chief motive?
2. Consider also the myth of 1054 mentioned previously. How does Urban (or at least Baldric) envision the Christians of the East?
3. Despite Urban II's hopes and idealism, the Age of the Crusades witnessed a growing estrangement between the societies of Western Europe and Byzantium. Judging from Anna's account, what do you think contributed to that rift?
4. How did the clergy of the Fourth Crusade endeavor to convince the crusaders that they were engaged in a just war against the Byzantines? And why was it necessary to bring forward these arguments?
5. Innocent III had attempted to stop the diversion to Constantinople. Then how do you explain his letter to the crusade clergy on November 1204?
6. Compare Innocent III's letter of August/September 1205 with Nicetas's account. What conclusions do you reach?
7. Compose Baldric of Dol's commentary on Nicetas's account and Innocent's two letters.

---

1 ▼ Baldric of Dol, THE JERUSALEM HISTORY

"We have heard, most beloved brethren, and you have heard what we cannot recount without deep sorrow — how, with great hurt and dire sufferings our Christian brothers, members in Christ, are scourged, oppressed, and injured in Jerusalem, in Antioch,[1] and the other cities of the East. Your own blood-brothers, your companions, your associates (for you are sons of the same Christ and the same Church) are either subjected in their inherited homes to other masters, or are driven from them, or they come as beggars among us; or, which is far worse, they are flogged and exiled as slaves for sale in their own land. Christian blood, redeemed by the blood of Christ, has been shed, and Christian flesh, akin to the flesh of Christ, has been subjected to unspeakable degradation and servitude. Everywhere in those cities there is sorrow, everywhere misery, everywhere groaning (I say it with a sigh). The churches in which divine mysteries

---

[1]The major city of northern Syria, most of its population was Byzantine Christian. In 1084 it was lost to the Seljuk Turks.

were celebrated in olden times are now, to our sorrow, used as stables for the animals of these people! Holy men do not possess those cities; nay, base and bastard Turks hold sway over our brothers. The blessed Peter first presided as bishop at Antioch;[2] behold, in his own church the Gentiles[3] have established their superstitions, and the Christian religion, which they ought rather to cherish, they have basely shut out from the hall dedicated to God! The estates given for the support of the saints and the patrimony of nobles set aside for the sustenance of the poor are subject to pagan tyranny, while cruel masters abuse for their own purposes the returns from these lands. The priesthood of God has been ground down into the dust. The sanctuary of God (unspeakable shame!) is everywhere profaned. Whatever Christians still remain in hiding there are sought out with unheard of tortures.

"Of holy Jerusalem, brethren, we dare not speak, for we are exceedingly afraid and ashamed to speak of it. This very city, in which, as you all know, Christ Himself suffered for us, because our sins demanded it, has been reduced to the pollution of paganism and, I say it to our disgrace, withdrawn from the service of God. Such is the heap of reproach upon us who have so much deserved it! Who now serves the church of the Blessed Mary in the valley of Josaphat, in which church she herself was buried in body?[4] But why do we pass over the Temple of Solomon,[5] nay of the Lord, in which the barbarous nations placed their idols[6] contrary to law, human and divine?

Of the Lord's Sepulcher[7] we have refrained from speaking, since some of you with your own eyes have seen to what abominations it has been given over. The Turks violently took from it the offerings which you brought there for alms in such vast amounts, and, in addition, they scoffed much and often at your religion. . . . With what afflictions they wronged you who have returned and are now present, you yourselves know too well, you who there sacrificed your substance and your blood for God.[8]

"This, beloved brethren, we shall say, that we may have you as witness of our words. More suffering of our brethren and devastation of churches remains than we can speak of one by one, for we are oppressed by tears and groans, sighs and sobs. . . . Woe unto us, brethren! We who have already become a reproach to our neighbors, a scoffing, and derision to them round about us, let us at least with tears condone and have compassion upon our brothers! We who have become the scorn of all peoples, and worse than all, let us bewail the most monstrous devastation of the Holy Land! This land we have deservedly called holy in which there is not even a footstep that the body or spirit of the Savior did not render glorious and blessed; which embraced the holy presence of the mother of God, and the meetings of the apostles, and drank up the blood of the martyrs shed there. . . . The children of Israel, who were led out of Egypt, and who prefigured you in the crossing of the Red Sea, have taken that land by their arms, with Jesus[9] as leader; they have driven out the

---

[2]According to tradition, Peter, prince of the apostles, had been initially bishop of Antioch before moving to Rome.
[3]Muslim Turks.
[4]The Church of Mary, believed to be the site where her body was laid before her Assumption into Heaven (see source 68), lies just outside the walls of Jerusalem.
[5]The site that Christians identified as the place on which the Temple of Solomon once stood was now occupied by the Mosque of al-Aqsa (see source 47, note 1).
[6]The misperception that Muslims are idol worshipers was rampant in the West at this time.
[7]The empty tomb of Jesus. Christendom's holiest site, it lies within the Church of the Holy Sepulcher in Jerusalem.

[8]The traffic in pilgrimages to the Holy Land from Europe picked up appreciably in the eleventh century, despite widespread rumors in the West that some Christian pilgrims were abused by various Muslim groups. There is some evidence of attacks on pilgrim parties, but how typical and frequent those attacks were is impossible to say.
[9]Joshua, who led the Israelites across the Jordan and into Canaan after Moses' death. Jesus is the Greek version of the name Joshua, and the medieval Church saw Joshua as a prefiguration of Jesus the Savior, who led humanity to salvation. During the era of the crusades, the biblical Joshua served as an archetype of the God-directed crusader.

Jebusites[10] and other inhabitants and have themselves inhabited earthly Jerusalem, the image of celestial Jerusalem.[11]

"What are we saying? Listen and learn! You, girt about with the badge of knighthood, are arrogant with great pride; you rage against your brothers and cut each other in pieces. This is not the [true] soldiery of Christ which rends asunder the sheepfold of the Redeemer. The Holy Church has reserved a soldiery for herself to help her people, but you debase her wickedly to her hurt. Let us confess the truth, whose heralds we ought to be; truly, you are not holding to the way which leads to life. You, the oppressors of children, plunderers of widows; you, guilty of homicide, of sacrilege, robbers of another's rights; you who await the pay of thieves for the shedding of Christian blood — as vultures smell fetid corpses, so do you sense battles from afar and rush to them eagerly. Truly, this is the worst way, for it is utterly removed from God! If you wish to be mindful of your souls, either lay down the belt of such knighthood, or advance boldly, as knights of Christ, and rush as quickly as you can to the defense of the Eastern Church. For she it is from whom the joys of your whole salvation have come forth, who poured into your mouths the milk of divine wisdom, who set before you the holy teachings of the Gospels.[12] We say this, brethren, that you may restrain your murderous hands from the destruction of your brothers, and in behalf of your relatives in the faith oppose yourselves to the Gentiles. Under Jesus Christ, our Leader, may you struggle for your Jerusalem, in Christian battle-line, most invincible line,

even more successfully than did the sons of Jacob[13] of old — struggle, that you may assail and drive out the Turks, more execrable than the Jebusites, who are in this land, and may you deem it a beautiful thing to die for Christ in that city in which He died for us. But if it befall you to die this side of it, be sure that to have died on the way is of equal value, if Christ shall find you in His army. God pays with the same coin, whether at the first or eleventh hour.[14] You should shudder, brethren, you should shudder at raising a violent hand against Christians; it is less wicked to brandish your sword against Saracens. It is the only warfare that is righteous, for it is charity to risk your life for your brothers. That you may not be troubled about the concerns of tomorrow, know that those who fear God want nothing, nor those who cherish Him in truth. The possessions of the enemy, too, will be yours, since you will make spoil of their treasures and return victorious to your own; or empurpled with your own blood, you will have gained everlasting glory. For such a Commander you ought to fight, for One who lacks neither might nor wealth with which to reward you. Short is the way, little the labor, which, nevertheless, will repay you with the crown that fadeth not away. . . . Gird yourselves, everyone of you, I say, and be valiant sons; for it is better for you to die in battle than to behold the sorrows of your race and of your holy places. Let neither property nor the alluring charms of your wives entice you from going; nor let the trials that are to be borne so deter you that you remain here."

---

[10]One of several groups of people living in Canaan when the Israelites invaded.
[11]Earthly Jerusalem prefigures the Heavenly Jerusalem.
[12]Christianity was born in the East.
[13]The Israelites.
[14]A reference to Jesus' parable of the workers in the vineyard: Matthew 20:1–16.

2 ▾ *Anna Comnena,* THE ALEXIAD

Before he[1] had enjoyed even a short rest, he heard a report of the approach of innumerable Frankish[2] armies. Now he dreaded their arrival for he knew their irresistible manner of attack, their unstable and mobile character and all the peculiar natural and concomitant characteristics which the Frank retains throughout; and he also knew that they were always agape for money, and seemed to disregard their truces readily for any reason that cropped up. For he had always heard this reported of them, and found it very true. However, he did not lose heart, but prepared himself in every way so that, when the occasion called, he would be ready for battle. And indeed the actual facts were far greater and more terrible than rumor made them. For the whole of the West and all the barbarian tribes which dwell between the further side of the Adriatic and the pillars of Heracles,[3] had all migrated in a body and were marching into Asia through the intervening Europe, and were making the journey with all their household. . . . And they were all so zealous and eager that every highroad was full of them. And those Frankish soldiers were accompanied by an unarmed host more numerous than the sand or the stars, carrying palms and crosses on their shoulders; women and children, too, came away from their countries. And the sight of them was like many rivers streaming from all sides, and they were advancing towards us . . . with all their hosts. . . .

The incidents of the barbarians' approach followed in the order I have described, and persons of intelligence could feel that they were witnessing a strange occurrence. The arrival of these multitudes did not take place at the same time nor by the same road (for how indeed could such masses starting from different places have crossed the straits of Lombardy all together?). Some first, some next, others after them and thus successively all accomplished the transit, and then marched through the continent. Each army was preceded, as we said, by an unspeakable number of locusts; and all who saw this more than once recognized them as forerunners of the Frankish armies.

[1]Emperor Alexius.
[2]*Frank* was a term used in the eastern Mediterranean to refer to any Westerner (see source 59).

[3]The Strait of Gibraltar.

3 ▾ *Robert of Clari,* THE CAPTURE OF CONSTANTINOPLE

After the barons returned and debarked from their ships, they met and were greatly troubled, saying that their sins were the cause of their not being able to do better at the city. Finally the bishops and other clergy of the army consulted among themselves and judged that the battle was a righteous one and that they were right in attacking the Greeks. For in the remote past the citizens of the city had been obedient to the rule of [the Church of] Rome, but now they disobeyed it, saying that the law of Rome counted for nothing and all who believed in it were dogs. The bishops further said that for this reason they [the crusaders] were right in attacking them, and it was not at all a sin. Rather, it was a righteous deed.

Then it was announced throughout the camp that all should attend a sermon on Sunday morning. . . . And so they did. Then the bishops preached throughout the camp . . . and showed the pilgrims[1] that the battle was righteous, for those whom they opposed were traitors and murderers and disloyal . . . and they were worse than the Jews. And the bishops said they would absolve of their sins all who should attack them, in the name of God and by papal authority. Then the bishops commanded all the pilgrims to make good confessions of their sins and to take communion and not to fear attacking the Greeks, for they were the enemies of God. And

it was ordered that all prostitutes be sought out, expelled from the camp, and be sent far away. And so they put them all on a ship and sent them far away from the camp.

Then, after the bishops had preached, showing the pilgrims that the battle was a righteous one, they all made good confessions and were given communion. When Monday morning [April 12] arrived, all of the pilgrims made themselves ready and armed themselves right well.

[1]Because the Earthly and the Heavenly Jerusalems were always the dual ultimate goals of the crusades, crusaders were often called "pilgrims."

4 ▾ Nicetas Choniates, ANNALS

The enemy, who had expected otherwise, found no one openly venturing into battle or taking up arms to resist; they saw that the way was open before them and everything there for the taking. . . . The populace, moved by the hope of propitiating them, had turned out to greet them with crosses and venerable icons[1] of Christ as was customary during festivals of solemn processions. But their disposition was not at all affected by what they saw, nor did their lips break into the slightest smile, nor did the unexpected spectacle transform their grim and frenzied glance and fury into a semblance of cheerfulness. Instead, they plundered with impunity and stripped their victims shamelessly. . . . Not only did they rob them of their substance but also the articles consecrated to God. . . .

What then should I recount first and what last of those things dared at that time by these murderous men? O, the shameful dashing to earth of the venerable icons and the flinging of the relics[2]

of the saints, who had suffered for Christ's sake, into defiled places! How horrible it was to see the Divine Body and Blood of Christ[3] poured out and thrown to the ground! These forerunners of Antichrist,[4] chief agents and harbingers of his anticipated ungodly deeds, seized as plunder the precious chalices and patens;[5] some they smashed, taking possession of the ornaments embellishing them, and they set the remaining vessels on their tables to serve as bread dishes and wine goblets. Just as happened long ago, Christ was now disrobed and mocked, his garments were parted, and lots were cast for them by this race; and although his side was not pierced by the lance, yet once more streams of Divine Blood poured to the earth.

The report of the impious acts perpetrated in the Great Church[6] are unwelcome to the ears. The table of sacrifice[7] . . . was broken into pieces and divided among the despoilers, as was the lot of all the sacred church treasures, countless in

[1]Sacred pictures.
[2]Highly revered body parts and other items associated with the lives of saints and of Jesus.
[3]Consecrated eucharistic bread and wine, which both Western and Eastern Christians believed was the actual body and blood of Jesus.

[4]An evil false Christ who will momentarily reign prior to Jesus' Second Coming.
[5]Vessels used in the sacrifice of the Mass.
[6]The Church of Hagia Sophia, Constantinople's patriarchal church.
[7]The high altar.

number and unsurpassed in beauty. They found it fitting to bring out as so much booty the all-hallowed vessels and furnishings which had been wrought with incomparable elegance and craftsmanship from rare materials. In addition, in order to remove the pure silver which overlay the railing of the bema,[8] the wondrous pulpit and the gates, as well as that which covered a great many other adornments, all of which were plated with gold, they led to the very sanctuary of the temple itself mules and asses with pack-saddles; some of these, unable to keep their feet on the smoothly polished marble floors, slipped and were pierced by knives so that the excrement from the bowels and the spilled blood defiled the sacred floor. Moreover, a certain silly woman laden with sins . . . the handmaid of demons, the workshop of unspeakable spells and reprehensible charms, waxing wanton against Christ, sat upon the synthronon[9] and intoned a song, and then whirled about and kicked up her heels in dance.

It was not that these crimes were committed in this fashion while others were not, or that some acts were more heinous than others, but that the most wicked and impious deeds were perpetrated by all with one accord. Did these madmen, raging thus against the sacred, spare pious matrons and girls of marriageable age or those maidens who, having chosen a life of chastity, were consecrated to God? Above all, it was a difficult and arduous task to mollify the barbarians with entreaties and to dispose them kindly towards us, as they were highly irascible and bilious and unwilling to listen to anything. Everything incited their anger, and they were thought fools and became a laughingstock. He who spoke freely and openly was rebuked, and often the dagger would be drawn against him who expressed a small difference of opinion or who hesitated to carry out their wishes.

The whole head was in pain. There were lamentations and cries of woe and weeping in the narrow ways, wailing at the crossroads, moaning in the temples, outcries of men, screams of women, the taking of captives, and the dragging about, tearing in pieces, and raping of bodies heretofore sound and whole. They who were bashful of their sex were led about naked, they who were venerable in their old age uttered plaintive cries, and the wealthy were despoiled of their riches. Thus it was in the squares, thus it was on the corners, thus it was in the temples, thus it was in the hiding places; for there was no place that could escape detection or that could offer asylum to those who came streaming in. . . .

Such then, to make a long story short, were the outrageous crimes committed by the Western armies against the inheritance of Christ. Without showing any feelings of humanity whatsoever, they exacted from all their money and chattel, dwellings and clothing, leaving to them nothing of all their goods. . . . More to blame were the learned and wise among men, they who were faithful to their oaths, who loved the truth and hated evil, who were both more pious and just and scrupulous in keeping the commandments of Christ than we "Greeks."[10] Even more culpable were those who had raised the cross to their shoulders, who had time and again sworn by it and the sayings of the Lord to cross over Christian lands without blood-letting, neither turning aside to the right nor inclining to the left, and to take up arms against the Saracens and to stain red their swords in their blood; they who had sacked Jerusalem, and had taken an oath not to marry or to have sexual intercourse with women as long as they carried the cross on their shoulders, and who were consecrated to God and commissioned to follow in his footsteps.

---

[8]The sanctuary where Mass is performed.
[9]The patriarch's throne.

[10]A sarcastic reference to Western clerics who maintained that they were better Christians than these degenerate *Greeks.*

In truth, they were exposed as frauds. Seeking to avenge the Holy Sepulcher,[11] they raged openly against Christ and sinned by overturning the Cross with the cross they bore on their backs,[12] not even shuddering to trample on it for the sake of a little gold and silver. By grasping pearls, they rejected Christ, the pearl of great price, scattering among the most accursed of brutes the All-Hallowed One. The sons of Ismael[13] did not behave in this way, for when the Latins overpowered Sion[14] the Latins showed no compassion or kindness to their race.[15] Neither did the Ismaelites neigh after Latin women, nor did they turn the cenotaph of Christ[16] into a common burial place of the fallen, nor did they transform

the entranceway of the life-bringing tomb into a passageway leading down into Hades. . . . Rather, they allowed everyone to depart in exchange for the payment of a few gold coins; they took only the ransom money and left to the people all their possessions, even though these numbered more than the grains of sand. Thus the enemies of Christ dealt magnanimously with the Latin infidels, inflicting upon them neither sword, nor fire, nor hunger, nor persecution, nor nakedness, nor bruises, nor constraints. How differently, as we have briefly recounted, the Latins treated us who love Christ and are their fellow believers, guiltless of any wrong against them.

---

[11]The Tomb of Christ. See Baldric of Dol.
[12]Each crusader wore a cross on his or her clothing, and by 1200 the term *crucesignatus* (one signed with a cross) was a term commonly applied to crusaders.
[13]Muslims. Arabs claim descent from Abraham through his son Ishmael. In what follows, Nicetas contrasts Saladin's reported treatment of the defeated Latins, after he captured

Jerusalem in 1187, with the crusaders' actions when they captured Jerusalem in 1099 and in 1204 in Constantinople.
[14]Jerusalem.
[15]The army of the First Crusade captured Jerusalem in a bloodbath in July 1099.
[16]A funerary monument — a reference to the Church of the Holy Sepulcher.

---

5 ▾ *Innocent III, LETTERS TO THE CRUSADERS*

To the bishops, abbots, and other clerics residing with the army of the crusaders at Constantinople [November 13, 1204].

We read in the Prophet Daniel that it is God in Heaven who reveals mysteries; it is He who changes times and transfers kingdoms.[1] Moreover, in our age we see this in the kingdom of the Greeks, and we rejoice in its accomplishment because He, who has dominion in the kingdom of humanity and who will give it to whom He might wish, has transferred the empire of Constantinople from the proud to the humble, from the disobedient to the obedient, from schismatics[2] to Catholics, namely from the

Greeks to the Latins. Surely this was done by the Lord and is wondrous in our eyes. This is truly a change done by the right hand of the Most High . . . so that He might exalt the most holy Roman Church while He returns the daughter to the mother, the part to the whole, and the member to the head.

▾▾▾

To the nobleman, the marquis of Montferrat[3] [ca. August 15–September 15, 1205]

Although you vowed, in obedience to the Crucified One, to liberate the Holy Land from the hands of the pagans and although you were forbidden

---

[1]The Bible, Daniel 2:21–22 and 2:28.
[2]A schismatic is someone who is separated from a rightful authority. Ever since the time of the reformed papacy of the mid eleventh century and following (see source 69), the Roman Church increasingly claimed that all Christians who

did not accept papal authority, but who were not outright heretics, were schismatics.
[3]Boniface of Montferrat was the leader of the Fourth Crusade army.

under threat of excommunication to attempt to invade or violate the lands of Christians, unless, perchance, either they should wickedly impede your journey or another just and necessary cause should present itself to you that would allow you to act otherwise in accordance with the guidance offered by our legate, all of you, having no jurisdiction or power over the Greeks, appear to have rashly turned away from the purity of your vow when you took up arms not against Saracens but Christians, not aiming to recover Jerusalem but to occupy Constantinople, preferring earthly wealth to celestial treasure. And, more seriously, it is known far and wide that some showed no mercy for reasons of religion, age, or sex but committed acts of fornication, adultery, and lewdness in the sight of all, and they exposed not only married women and widows but even matrons and virgins dedicated to God to the filth of the lowborn. It was not enough to empty the imperial treasuries and to plunder alike the spoils of princes and lesser folk, but rather you extended your hands to church treasuries and, what was more serious, to their possessions, ripping away silver tablets from altars and violating sacristies, carrying away crosses, icons, and relics. The result is that the Greek Church, afflicted to some degree by persecutions, disdains returning to obedience to the Apostolic See. It has seen in the Latins nothing other than an example of affliction and the works of Hell, so that now it rightly detests them more than dogs.

▲▲▲

❖ Chapter 11 ❖

Africa and the Americas

TOWARD THE END of the first century B.C.E., the dominant
civilizations of Eurasia and North Africa were loosely
linked through a series of trade networks and imperialistic
adventures. The result was the first *Afro-Eurasian Ecumene*,
the heyday of which extended down to about 200 C.E. The
term itself is misleading, however, because most of Africa
south of the Sahara lay outside of this first ecumene of the so-
called Old World.

The cultures of the so-called New World — the Americas
— also did not participate in that first age of Afro-Eurasian
linkage, nor in the second, which peaked between 1250 and
1350. Granted all of this, the question remains: Were there
any meaningful contacts between the Eastern and Western
Hemispheres before 1492?

A few adventurers and lost sailors from Africa and Eurasia
undoubtedly reached the Americas prior to Columbus. That
certainly was the case with a handful of Norse who set up a
short-lived colony in northern Newfoundland around 1000 C.E.
but departed without having made any appreciable impact
on the culture of the native peoples whom they encountered.
We can only speculate how many other ancient mariners
made it all the way to the Americas alive. Did any of them
leave behind cultural footprints? Several sober specialists
have pointed to certain striking similarities between the classic 260-day calendar of Mesoamerica and the lunar zodiacs of
East Asia and have suggested that coincidence does not adequately explain the parallels. One scholar has studied the
tools and means used to fashion bark paper all around the Pacific Basin and concluded that the technique traveled from
Indonesia to Mesoamerica at an early date. There is even better evidence for one east-to-west exchange. Botanical evidence shows that the sweet potato, which became a staple in
the diet of Oceania, originated in South America and made its
way across the ocean by unknown means. Whatever those
means, what the Quecha-speaking people of the Andes called
kumar became known as *kumara* by the Polynesians of Easter

Island. These clues, as well as some interesting parallels in certain artistic styles and motifs around the Pacific Basin (for example, both Polynesians and the American Indians of the Northwest carved wooden totems), suggest that there was some cultural exchange across the Pacific before 1492, but to what extent is uncertain.

Even if we grant these exchanges, we still are left with the conclusion that no American Indian culture was a derivative of any culture from across the oceans. At the most, a few ideas and techniques probably made their way across the waters, but once in the Americas they were grafted onto essentially indigenous cultures and civilizations. The fact that American Indian agriculture was based on fruits, vegetables, and cereals unknown in the Old World seems evidence enough of that. Moreover, the fact that European and African diseases caused such massive depopulation in the Americas after 1492 is convincing evidence that occasional pre-Columbian visitors established no meaningful or long-term links between the Americas and the outside world.

Isolated though they might have been from the rest of the world before 1492, most American Indian peoples were linked, although loosely, in an *American Ecumene* that made possible the spread of goods and cultural influences over vast expanses. Maize, for example, initially domesticated as early as 5000 B.C.E. in the highlands of south-central Mexico, had spread to Peru by 2000 B.C.E. or earlier and to Canada by 1000 C.E.

Sub-Saharan Africa also had its early cultural and trade networks, which made possible a widespread diffusion of such technologies as agriculture and iron metallurgy and such ideas as the faith of Islam. Moreover, despite the continued growth of the Sahara from around 2500 B.C.E. to the present, interior Africa has never been totally cut off from the rest of the Afro-Eurasian World, even in the most ancient times. However, the volume of traffic across the Sahara began to achieve significant proportions only after the introduction into North Africa of the Arabian, or single-humped, camel as a beast of burden during the early centuries C.E. Conquest of western North Africa by Muslim Arabs in the seventh century provided another major boost to trans-Saharan trade, so by about 1000 C.E. four major commercial routes connected the north with western sub-Saharan Africa. Gold, more than any other single item, drew the camel caravans of Berber and Arab traders to the inland kingdoms of West Africa's grasslands, but large numbers of slaves were also sold for transportation northward to markets throughout the Mediterranean and beyond.

In return, western sub-Saharan Africans received salt, raw copper, fine horses, and manufactured goods such as tempered steel and even glassware from Venice.

Trade and the development of trade-based Islamic states in the western sub-Saharan grasslands constitute a major chapter in Africa's history, but they are not the whole story of what was happening during the millennium 500–1500 C.E. in this richly diverse continent. East Africa, especially its coastal region from Somalia to Tanzania, was linked to a shipping network of monsoon-driven vessels that sailed throughout the Indian Ocean and its adjacent waters — all the way to China. Commodities such as ivory and gold made their way from the interior of East Africa to ports on the Indian Ocean, where they joined coastal raw materials such as ambergris (a resin used in the production of perfumes) and mangrove timber. At these emporia, which dotted the islands off the eastern coast, East Africa's goods were exchanged for ceramics from China, glassware, and Indian textiles. In addition, captives taken in war and by raiding parties were brought to the coast, where they were sold to Arab slavers for exportation to the mines and plantations of Iraq. For better and for worse, Africa was increasingly linked to the Eurasian World between 500 and 1500.

▼▼▼

Africa

During the millennium from 500 to 1500, Africa witnessed a number of important historical developments. Chief among them were the last stages of the *Bantu Expansion*, the coming of Islam, the creation of trade empires in the western Sudan, the rise of a *Swahili* culture in East Africa, and the arrival of Europeans toward the end of this period.

The approximately 450 languages belonging to the *Bantu* linguistic family that are spoken today throughout most of the southern half of the continent are traceable to a common place of origin in West Africa, probably in present-day eastern Nigeria. Bantu speakers probably began spreading out of their ancestral homeland as early as 3,000 or 4,000 years ago, aided by their skills in fishing and agriculture. In its later stages, this slow, almost imperceptible movement was aided by their ironworking skills. As they spread east and south, the Bantu-speaking peoples introduced wherever they settled the crafts of farming and iron metallurgy. By the early centuries C.E., Bantu speakers had pushed as far south as the region today occupied by the nation of Zimbabwe, where by the late thirteenth century they constructed a gold-trade civilization centered on the now famous Great Zimbabwe stone citadel, from which the modern state took its name in 1979.

Another great migration that profoundly influenced Africa's history was the influx of Islam in the wake of the conquering Arab armies that swept through North Africa in the seventh century. These conquests and the conversions that followed transformed what had been Christian North Africa into an integral part of the Islamic World, thereby wrenching it out of the orbits of Constantinople and Rome and tying it culturally to Mecca, Damascus, and Baghdad.

From North Africa the faith and culture of Islam penetrated into the trade empires of the western grassland states south of the Sahara after 1000 C.E. The empires of *Ghana*, *Mali*, and *Songhai* became progressively more Islamic and, therefore, more closely tied to North Africa and the greater Islamic World beyond Africa by reason of a shared religious culture, as well as by commercial interests.

On the east coast of Africa, a similar phenomenon was at work. In the ninth and tenth centuries, Arab sailor-merchants established trading settlements far down the coast of East Africa. The culture that emerged from the interchange between the Arab and East African peoples who traded and intermarried here is known as *Swahili* (from the Arabic word for "coast" — *sahil*). Like *Kiswahili*, the language of the region, Swahili culture was a coastal trade culture consisting of an indigenous Bantu base with strong Arabic influences. From about 1200 to the early sixteenth century, the port city of *Kilwa*, today located in the nation of Tanzania, served as the Swahili coast's main emporium.

Kilwa's commercial prominence along Africa's eastern shore ended with its sack and destruction by the Portuguese in 1505. With the arrival in force of the Portuguese, first on Africa's west coast in the fifteenth century and then on the east coast in the early sixteenth century, the age of direct European contact with sub-Saharan Africa had begun, with all of the consequences that would follow from that interchange.

Despite the impact of Islam and Europe on Africa south of the Sahara, older ways of life proved usually resilient to influences from outside. *Ethiopia*, for example, successfully resisted Islamic and later Portuguese attempts at conquest and conversion, retaining its autonomy and ancient Christian culture. Likewise, the coastal states of West Africa retained their core cultural features, even as their leaders accepted the faith of Islam. Moreover, they maintained autonomy, extensive political authority, and widespread economic interests, even in the face of the European presence along their coastline.

The Land of Zanj: Tenth-Century East Africa
▼▼▼

71 ▼ *Abul-Hasan Ali al-Masudi,*
MEADOWS OF GOLD

The Arabs who traded along the coast of East Africa knew it as the *Land of Zanj*, a name that survives in *Zanzibar*, an island that is part of present-day Tanzania. Following the monsoon winds of the Indian Ocean, which blow toward East Africa between November and March, Arab merchants sailed from Oman and other regions of the Arabian Peninsula and visited trading ports that stretched southward from Mogadishu in Somalia to Sofala, which is located in present-day Mozambique. At these trading centers, they met sailors from India and the islands of Southeast Asia, as well as Arab and Iranian colonists, many of whom had intermarried with Africans. Because of the presence of Arabic speakers along this coast, Arab merchants had little difficulty in conducting commerce, apart from the normal hazards of venturing long distances across treacherous ocean waters in small vessels. After acquiring the desired raw materials, Arab merchants either returned home or sailed to India, driven by monsoon winds that blow northeastward between April and October.

One of the earliest Arabic accounts of East African society and its trade comes from the pen of Abul-Hasan Ali al-Masudi (ca. 890–956), who visited the region in 915/916. In his masterwork of history and geography, *Meadows of Gold*, which he composed in 943, al-Masudi informs his readers of the Indian Ocean trade network into which the Land of Zanj was interwoven and of the people of interior East Africa, who fed that trade. How much of what he tells us about the people of Zanj is fact and how much is the stuff of distorted legend is open to question. What is clear and undisputed is the picture that al-Masudi draws of the importance of Africa's east coast to foreign merchants.

QUESTIONS FOR ANALYSIS

1. What evidence does al-Masudi provide of the evolving Swahili culture of this region?
2. What does al-Masudi tell us about the culture of the Bantu people of the interior? Which elements seem the most believable? Why? Which seem the least believable? Why?
3. Review the story of Sinbad (source 60). Does al-Masudi's account place the story into a clearer context?
4. The Indian Ocean has been described as the heart of the Afro-Eurasian World. To what extent does al-Masudi's account support or call into question that judgment? Cite specific evidence to support your conclusion.

The pilots of Oman[1] pass by the channel [of Berbera] to reach the island of Kanbalu,[2] which is in the Zanj sea.[3] It has a mixed population of Muslims and Zanj idolaters.[4] . . . The aforesaid Kanbalu is the farthest point of their voyages on the Zanj sea, and the land of Sofala and the Waqwaq,[5] on the edge of the Zanj mainland and at the end of this branch of the sea. The people of Siraf[6] also make this voyage, and I myself have sailed on this sea, setting off from Sanjar, the

---

[1]The region of southeast Arabia that stretches along the entrance to the Persian Gulf.
[2]The island of Pemba.
[3]The region of the Indian Ocean that washes the central portion of Africa's eastern coast.
[4]Worshipers of idols. People who follow traditional religions.

[5]Arabs normally used this term to refer only to the people of Malaysia, who speak a language that is related to the Malagasy tongue of Madagascar. Madagascar is a large island off the coast of East Africa and opposite Sofala; Malaysia is across the Indian Ocean in Southeast Asia (see note 15). In the present context, however, the term seems to refer to the people of interior Africa.
[6]A port on the Iranian shore of the Persian Gulf.

capital of Oman, in company with a number of Omani shipowners, among whom were Muhammad ibn al-Zaidbud and Jawhar ibn Ahmad surnamed Ibn Sirah, who was later lost at sea with his ship. My last voyage from Kanbalu to Oman was in A.H. 304[7] on the ship belonging to Ahmad and Abd al-Samad, who were the brothers of Abd al-Rahim ibn Jafar al-Sirafi. . . . They were both lost at sea with all their goods later on. . . . I have sailed much on the seas, . . . but I do not know of one more dangerous than that of the Zanj. . . .

The land of Zanj produces wild leopard skins. The people wear them as clothes, or export them to Muslim countries. They are the largest leopard skins and the most beautiful for making saddles. . . . They also export tortoise-shell for making combs, for which ivory is likewise used. . . . In the same way that the sea of China ends with the land of Japan, the sea of Zanj ends with the land of Sofala and the Waqwaq, which produces gold and many other wonderful things. It has a warm climate and is fertile. The Zanj capital is there[8] and they have a king called the *Mfalme*. This is the ancient name of their kings, and all the other Zanj kings are subject to him: he has 300,000 horsemen. The Zanj use the ox as a beast of burden, for they have no horses, mules or camels in their land, and do not know of their existence. . . . They do not know of snow or hail. Some of their tribes sharpen their teeth and are cannibals. . . . The villages stretch for 700 parasangs[9] and the same distance inland: the country is cut up into valleys, mountains and stony deserts. There are many wild elephants but no tame ones. The Zanj do not use them for war

or anything else, but only hunt and kill them. When they want to catch them, they throw down the leaves, bark and branches of a certain tree which grows in their country: then they wait in ambush until the elephants come to drink. The water burns them and makes them drunk. They fall down and cannot get up: their limbs will not articulate. The Zanj rush upon them armed with very long spears, and kill them for their ivory. It is from this country that come tusks weighing fifty pounds and more. They usually go to Oman, and from there are sent to China and India. This is the chief trade route, and if it were not so, ivory would be common in Muslim lands.

In China the kings and military civil officers use ivory palanquins:[10] no officer or notable dares to come into the royal presence in an iron palanquin, and ivory alone can be used. Thus they seek after straight tusks in preference to the curved, to make the things we have spoken of. They also burn ivory before their idols and cense their altars with it, just as Christians use the Mary incense[11] and other perfumes. The Chinese make no other use of the elephant, and consider it unlucky to use it for domestic purposes or war. This fear has its origin in a tradition about one of their most ancient military expeditions. In India ivory is much sought after.[12] It is used for the handles of daggers called *harari* or *harri* in the singular: and also for the curved sword-scabbards called *kartal*, in the plural *karatil*, but the chief use of ivory is making chessmen and backgammon pieces. . . . It is only in the land of Zanj and in India that elephants reproduce. . . .

---

[7]A.H. is an abbreviation for a Latin term that translates as *in the year of the Hijra*. Muhammad's *hijra* from Mecca to Medina, which took place in 622, is the starting point of the Islamic calendar. Because the Islamic year is lunar, one cannot simply subtract 622 years from a date in the common calendar to arrive at its equivalent in the Islamic calendar. A.H. 304 equates to 915/916 C.E.
[8]Probably the site, far up the Sabi River Valley, where the Shona state would construct the massive enclosures of Great Zimbabwe between 1200 and 1450.
[9]A *parasang*, an ancient Persian unit of measurement, was roughly three and a half miles.

[10]A covered litter carried on the shoulders of two or four persons.
[11]Incense (also known as *frankincense*) was a fragrant resin from Yemen, in the southwestern corner of the Arabian Peninsula, that Christians, Muslims, Jews, Zoroastrians, and many others burned in their places of worship. Here the author seems to refer to a particular grade of incense that was burned in Christian churches in honor of Mary, the mother of Jesus.
[12]Despite the presence of elephants in India, Indian artisans preferred African ivory because of its texture and size.

Now let us return to . . . the Zanj, the description of their country and of the other peoples of Abyssinia.[13] The Zanj, although always busied hunting the elephant and collecting its ivory, make no use of it for domestic purposes. They use iron instead of gold and silver, just as they use oxen, as we said before, both for beasts of burden and for war. These oxen are harnessed like a horse and run as fast. . . .

To go back to the Zanj and their kings, these are known as *Wafalme*,[14] which means son of the Great Lord, since he is chosen to govern them justly. If he is tyrannical or strays from the truth, they kill him and exclude his seed from the throne; for they consider that in acting wrongfully he forfeits his position as the son of the Lord, the King of Heaven and Earth. They call God *Maliknajlu*, which means Great Lord.

The Zanj have an elegant language and men who preach in it. One of their holy men will often gather a crowd and exhort his hearers to please God in their lives and to be obedient to him. He explains the punishments that follow upon disobedience, and reminds them of their ancestors and kings of old. These people have no religious law: their kings rule by custom and by political expediency.

The Zanj eat bananas,[15] which are as common among them as they are in India; but their staple food is millet[16] and a plant called *kalari* which is pulled out of the earth like truffles. It is plentiful in Aden[17] and the neighboring part of Yemen[18] near to the town. It is like the cucumber of Egypt and Syria. They also eat honey and meat. Every man worships what he pleases, be it a plant, an animal or a mineral. They have many islands where the coconut grows: its nuts are used as fruit by all the Zanj peoples. One of these islands, which is one or two days' sail from the coast, has a Muslim population and a royal family. This is the island of Kanbalu of which we have already spoken.

---

[13]Usually the term refers only to Ethiopia, but al-Masudi uses it to refer to a substantial portion of the northeastern coast of Africa.

[14]Apparently these are the kings mentioned earlier in this excerpt who are subordinate to the *Mfalme*.

[15]Migrants from Malaysia in Southeast Asia settled in Madagascar around the first century C.E. (see note 5) and brought with them plants and seeds from their homeland, including the banana. From Madagascar the banana traveled into the tropical rainforests of continental Africa, where it flourished as a domesticated crop.

[16]A cereal.

[17]An Arabian port city that commands the entrance to the Red Sea.

[18]See note 11.

The Land of Ghana: Eleventh-Century Western Sudan

▼▼▼

72 ▼ *Abu Ubaydallah al-Bakri,* *THE BOOK OF ROUTES AND REALMS*

South of the Sahara is a broad expanse of grasslands, or *savanna*, that stretches from the Atlantic Ocean to the Red Sea. To the Arabs this region was *Bilad al-Sudan* (the Country of the Blacks). Arab and Berber merchants were keenly interested in West Africa's Sudan because its inhabitants were advantageously located between the markets of North Africa and cultures farther south toward the tropical rainforests of the coast. From the southern peoples of the Niger and Senegal river valleys the inhabitants of the savanna obtained gold and slaves, which they traded for manufactured goods, horses, and salt with Berber and Arab merchants, who arrived in camel caravans from the north. Over time, this trans-Saharan commerce stimulated development of a series of large trading states in the region that connected West Africa's gold fields with the cities of Mediterranean North Africa.

One of the earliest important trading empires to emerge was *Ghana* (not to be confused with its present-day namesake, the nation of Ghana), which was located essentially in territory encompassed today by the nations of Mauritania and Mali. The origins of Ghana as an organized entity are lost in the shadows of the past but go back at least as far as the fifth century C.E., when the introduction of the *dromedary*, or single-humped Arabian camel, made it easier for outsiders to penetrate across the Sahara into the land of the *Soninke* people. Coming as traders and as raiders, the *Berber* people of the western Sahara apparently helped stimulate the formation of a Soninke kingdom organized for commerce and defense. Eventually, that kingdom became known as *Ghana* — a term that originated as a royal title. During the course of the eighth and ninth centuries, Arab merchants inhabiting the coastal cities of North Africa began to enter the lucrative trans-Saharan trading system, thereby gaining direct access to the region they called the *land of gold* — a land then dominated by the well-established state of Ghana.

In 1067/1068 Abu Ubaydallah al-Bakri (d. 1094), a resident of Córdoba in Muslim Spain, composed a detailed description of this fabled region. Although he never traveled to nearby Africa, al-Bakri provides one of the most important sources for the early history of the western Sudan. As was accepted practice among Islamic geographers of his era, he drew heavily from the writings of predecessors, many of whose works are now otherwise lost, and he also interviewed merchants who had traveled to the area. These interviews made it possible for al-Bakri to present up-to-date information on Ghana at a crucial moment in its history.

During the latter portion of the eleventh century, the rulers and leading families of Ghana were increasingly adopting the faith and culture of Islam. However, Muslims from the north not only brought the peaceful message of universal submission to the Word of God, they also brought war. A fundamentalist Islamic group of Berbers from Morocco, known as the *Almoravids*, waged holy war, or *jihad*, against the Soninke of Ghana. It is unclear whether the Almoravids prevailed in this war, but apparently the conflict disrupted trade and weakened Ghana's economic base. In addition, the heartland of Ghana was becoming far less able to support its population due to an environmental crisis brought about by overfarming and excessive grazing. Large numbers of farmers and townspeople were forced to move away. With these combined losses, the recently converted monarchs of Ghana lost their ability to hold together their loosely organized and still predominantly non-Islamic empire. By the early thirteenth century, Ghana had disintegrated. Hegemony over the markets of the western Sudan passed briefly to the kingdom of *Sosso* and then to the state of *Mali*, which reached its greatest territorial extent under Mansa Musa (r. 1312–1327), whom we saw in source 50. We shall see Mali again in Chapter 12.

QUESTIONS FOR ANALYSIS

1. Describe the city of Ghana. What does its physical environment, especially its two centers, suggest about eleventh-century Ghanaian culture?
2. How would you characterize the authority and sources of power of the rulers of Ghana?
3. What role did Islam play in Ghanaian society? What does your answer suggest about the way in which Islam entered the western Sudan?
4. What does the story of the conversion of the king of Malal suggest about the process of Islamization in the western Sudan?

Ghana is a title given to their kings; the name of the region is Awkar, and their king today . . . is Tunka Manin. . . . The name of his predecessor was Basi and he became their ruler at the age of 85. He led a praiseworthy life on account of his love of justice and friendship for the Muslims. . . . Basi was a maternal uncle of Tunka Manin. This is their custom and their habit, that the kingship is inherited only by the son of the king's sister. He has no doubt that his successor is a son of his sister, while he is not certain that his son is in fact his own, and he is not convinced of the genuineness of his relationship to him. This Tunka Manin is powerful, rules an enormous kingdom, and possesses great authority.

The city of Ghana consists of two towns situated on a plain.[1] One of these towns, which is inhabited by Muslims, is large and possesses twelve mosques, in one of which they assemble for the Friday prayer. There are salaried imams and muezzins,[2] as well as jurists and scholars. In the environs are wells with sweet water, from which they drink and with which they grow vegetables. The king's town is six miles distant from this one and bears the name of Al-Ghaba.[3] Between these two towns there are continuous habitations. The houses of the inhabitants are of stone and acacia wood. The king has a palace and a number of domed dwellings all surrounded with an enclosure like a city wall. In the king's town, and not far from his court of justice, is a mosque where the Muslims who arrive at his court pray. Around the king's town are domed buildings and groves and thickets where the sorcerers of these people, men in charge of the religious cult, live. In them too are their idols and the tombs of their kings. These woods are guarded and none may enter them and know what is there. In them also are the king's prisons. If somebody is imprisoned there no news of him is ever heard. The king's interpreters, the official in charge of his treasury and the majority of his ministers are Muslims. Among the people who follow the king's religion[4] only he and his heir apparent (who is the son of his sister) may wear sewn clothes. All other people wear robes of cotton, silk, or brocade, according to their means. All of them shave their beards, and women shave their heads. The king adorns himself like a woman, wearing necklaces round his neck and bracelets on his forearms, and he puts on a high cap decorated with gold and wrapped in a turban of fine cotton. He sits in audience or to hear grievances against officials in a domed pavilion

---

[1] The city consisted of two separate walled towns connected by a long, unwalled strip of private dwellings. Known as *Koumbi-Saleh*, its ruins are located in the southern region of the present-day nation of Mauritania. At its eleventh-century height, this double city probably held some 20,000 people.

[2] *Imams* are religious teachers and prayer leaders; *muezzins* are the chanters who ascend the minarets, or towers, of mosques and call the faithful to prayer five times daily.

[3] The term means "the forest" and refers to the sacred grove mentioned later in this source.

[4] The king, who was not a Muslim, followed the ancient religious ways of the Soninke people.

around which stand ten horses covered with gold-embroidered materials. Behind the king stand ten pages holding shields and swords decorated with gold, and on his right are the sons of the vassal kings[5] of his country wearing splendid garments and their hair plaited with gold. The governor of the city sits on the ground before the king and around him are ministers seated likewise. . . . When people who profess the same religion as the king approach him they fall on their knees and sprinkle dust on their heads, for this is their way of greeting him. As for the Muslims, they greet him only by clapping their hands.

Their religion is paganism and the worship of idols. When their king dies they construct over the place where his tomb will be an enormous dome of wood. Then they bring him on a bed covered with a few carpets and cushions and place him beside the dome. At his side they place his ornaments, his weapons, and the vessels from which he used to eat and drink, filled with various kinds of food and beverages. They place there too the men who used to serve his meals. They close the door of the dome and cover it with mats and furnishings. Then the people assemble, who heap earth upon it until it becomes like a big hillock and dig a ditch around it until the mound can be reached at only one place.

They make sacrifices to their dead and make offerings of intoxicating drinks.

On every donkey-load of salt when it is brought into the country their king levies one golden dinar,[6] and two dinars when it is sent out. From a load of copper the king's due is five mithqals,[7] and from a load of other goods ten mithqals. The best gold found in his land comes from the town of Ghiyaru, which is eighteen days' traveling distant from the king's town over

a country inhabited by tribes of the Sudan whose dwellings are continuous.

The nuggets found in all the mines of his country are reserved for the king, only this gold dust being left for the people. But for this the people would accumulate gold until it lost its value. The nuggets may weigh from an ounce to a pound. It is related that the king owns a nugget as large as a big stone. . . .

The king of Ghana, when he calls up his army, can put 200,000 men[8] into the field, more than 40,000 of them archers. . . .

On the opposite bank of the Nil[9] is another great kingdom, stretching a distance of more than eight days' marching, the king of which has the title of *Daw*. The inhabitants of this region use arrows when fighting. Beyond this country lies another called Malal,[10] the king of which is known as *al-musulmani*.[11] He is thus called because his country became afflicted with drought one year following another; the inhabitants prayed for rain, sacrificing cattle till they had exterminated almost all of them, but the drought and the misery only increased. The king had as his guest a Muslim who used to read the Quran and was acquainted with the Sunna.[12] To this man the king complained of the calamities that assailed him and his people. The man said: "O King, if you believed in God (who is exalted) and testified that He is One, and testified as to the prophetic mission of Muhammad (God bless him and give him peace) and if you accepted all the religious laws of Islam, I would pray for your deliverance from your plight and that God's mercy would envelop all the people of your country and that your enemies and adversaries might envy you on that account." Thus he continued to press the king until the latter accepted Islam and became a sincere Muslim. The man

[5]Subordinate kings, or lords.
[6]A standard gold coin in the Islamic world that weighed 4.72 grams, or one *mithqal* (see note 7).
[7]A standard of weight equaling 4.72 grams.
[8]An apparent exaggeration. There was no regular standing Ghanaian army; the various districts of the empire sent warriors as the occasion warranted.

[9]Islamic geographers of this era mistakenly believed that the Niger River was the western source of the Nile.
[10]A *Mandike* kingdom that was the nucleus of the later empire of Mali.
[11]"The Muslim."
[12]The traditions of Islam.

made him recite from the Quran some easy passages and taught him religious obligations and practices which no one may be excused from knowing. Then the Muslim made him wait till the eve of the following Friday,[13] when he ordered him to purify himself by a complete ablution, and clothed him in a cotton garment which he had. The two of them came out towards a mound of earth, and there the Muslim stood praying while the king, standing at his right side, imitated him. Thus they prayed for a part of the night, the Muslim reciting invocations and the king saying "Amen." The dawn had just started to break when God caused abundant rain to descend upon them. So the king ordered the idols to be broken and expelled the sorcerers from his country. He and his descendants after him as well as his nobles were sincerely attached to Islam, while the common people of his kingdom remained polytheists. Since then their rulers have been given the title of *al-musulmani*.

---

[13]The beginning of the Islamic day of rest and community worship.

The Land of Seyon: Fourteenth-Century Ethiopia

▼▼▼

73 ▼ *ETHIOPIAN ROYAL CHRONICLE*

Ethiopia, a kingdom to the southeast of ancient Kush (or Nubia) in Africa's northeast highlands, looks out across the Red Sea to Yemen, the southwestern portion of the Arabian Peninsula. Settlers from Yemen, known as the *Sabeans*, crossed these waters, perhaps as early as the seventh century B.C.E., and mixed with the indigenous inhabitants to produce a hybrid civilization whose language, *Geez*, was essentially Semitic but contained significant Kushitic elements. Because of its strategic location astride a trade route that linked Egypt and the Mediterranean World with the markets of East Africa, Arabia, and India, Ethiopia flourished. A Greek shipping manual of the first century C.E. notes that Adulis, Ethiopia's port on the Red Sea, was northeast Africa's premier center for the ivory trade.

The Ethiopian Church claims that Christianity came to the land and its people in the first century C.E., at the time of the apostles. Given Ethiopia's commercial importance, this is credible, but Christianity did not become the state-sponsored religion of Ethiopia until the early fourth century. Under the influence of Egyptians and Nubians to their north, Ethiopians embraced a type of Christianity known as *Monophysitism* (from the Greek words for "one nature"). This form of Christian belief centered on a doctrine that deemphasized Jesus' humanity to the point of maintaining that he had a single, divine nature. When the Churches of Constantinople and Rome condemned Monophysite teachings as heresy in 451, the Ethiopian Church was doctrinally cut off from these two Mediterranean centers of Christianity. The Arab-Muslim conquest of Egypt in the 640s further cut Ethiopia off from its Christian coreligionists in Byzantium and the West. In time, most of previously Christian Egypt converted to Islam, although its native Christians, known as *Coptic Christians*, remained a significant minority, as they are today. Egypt, the land that had introduced Christianity to Nubia and Ethiopia, was now an Islamic stronghold. On their part, Nubians and Ethiopians vigorously fought to retain their political autonomy and Christian identity in the face of Islamic pressure from Egypt. After the mid thirteenth century, however, Nubian resistance to Islam weakened. By the mid fourteenth century, Nubia no longer had an independent Christian monarchy, and the Christian faith was fast losing out to Islam. By the sixteenth century, Nubia's Christian population was a minority and would remain so down to the present. (Nubia today is the nation of Sudan.)

Farther to the south, Ethiopia, fairly secure in its mountain strongholds, continued to hold out against Islam. The following document, a fourteenth-century royal chronicle, tells the story of how King *Amda Seyon I* (r. 1312–1342), whose throne name was *Gabra Masqal* (Servant of the Cross), resisted an invasion in 1329 by Sabr ad-Din, the ruler of Ifat, an Islamic emirate on the coast. More than simply a monarch on the defensive, Amda Seyon was a militant expansionist, who in his thirty-year reign undertook a series of offensive operations against neighboring Islamic states in his drive to control access routes to the Red Sea and the Gulf of Aden. Between 1320 and 1340, he managed to bring Ifat and other Islamic states of the highland plateau under the control of his expanding kingdom. As the chronicle points out, Sabr ad-Din was actually a tributary prince who revolted against Amda Seyon's authority.

QUESTIONS FOR ANALYSIS

1. What picture emerges of Muslim-Christian relations in fourteenth-century Ethiopia?
2. The Christian Ethiopian attitude toward Jews and Judaism has been characterized as ambivalent. Do you find in this source any evidence to support such a judgment? Please be specific in your answer.
3. Reread Eusebius of Caesarea's *Ecclesiastical History* (source 40). Do you see any parallels between the tone and message of that source and this document? What are they? What conclusions do you draw?

Let us write, with the help of our Lord Jesus Christ, of the power and the victory which God wrought by the hands of Amda Seyon king of Ethiopia. . . . Now the king of Ethiopia . . . heard that the king of the Rebels[1] had revolted, and in his arrogance was unfaithful to him, making himself great, like the Devil who set himself above his creator and exalted himself like the Most High. The king of the Rebels, whose name was Sabradin, was full of arrogance towards his lord Amda Seyon, and said, "I will be king over all the land of Ethiopia; I will rule the Christians according to my law, and I will destroy their churches." And having said this, he arose and set out and came to the land of the Christians, and killed some of them; and those who survived, both men and women, he took prisoner and converted them to his religion. . . .

---

[1]The word *elwan*, translated here as "rebels," can also be translated as "infidels," or nonbelievers.

But the feet cannot become the head, nor the Earth the sky, nor the servant the master. That perverse one, the son of a viper, of the seed of a serpent, the son of a stranger from the race of Satan, thought covetously of the throne of David[2] and said, "I will rule in Seyon,"[3] for pride entered into his heart, as into the Devil his father. He said, "I will make the Christian churches into mosques for the Muslims, and I will convert to my religion the king of the Christians together with his people, and I will nominate him governor of one province, and if he refuses to be converted to my religion I will deliver him to the herdsmen . . . that they make him a herder of camels. As for the queen Zan Mangesa, the wife of the king, I will make her work at the mill.". . .

Saying this, he collected all the troops of the Muslims, and chose from among them the ablest and most intelligent. These in truth were not able and intelligent, but fools, men full of error, impostors who foretell the future by means of sand and take omens from the sun and moon and stars of Heaven, who say, "We observe the stars," but they have knowledge only of evil, they have no knowledge of God, their knowledge is of men which fades and perishes, for as Saint Paul says, "God hath made foolish the wisdom of this world."[4]

Let us return to the original subject. This evil man then questioned the diviners, saying, "Now tell me, I pray you, shall we conquer when we fight with the king of the Christians?" And one of them rose, a prophet of darkness. . . .

When Sabradin the king of the Rebels examined him, this diviner answered him persuasively, saying, "Behold, the kingdom of the Christians is finished; it shall be given to us, and you shall reign in Seyon. Rise, make war on the king of the Christians, and conquering you shall rule him and his people." And all the diviners said likewise. So the Rebel king sent into all the lands of the Muslims and called together his troops, and formed them into three divisions: one division set out for the land of Amhara, another set out for the land of Angot, and he himself prepared for war and set out to invade Shoa where the king was, — the slave of slaves against the prince of princes, the tail of the dog against the head of the lion, trusting in the false prediction that the Christian kingdom was come to an end.

As for us, we have heard and we know from the Holy Scriptures that the kingdom of the Muslims, established for but seven hundred years, shall cease to be at the proper time. But the kingdom of the Christians shall continue till the second coming of the Son of God, according to the words of Holy Scripture; and above all we know that the kingdom of Ethiopia shall endure till the coming of Christ, of which David prophesied saying "Ethiopia shall stretch her hands unto God."[5]

The messengers whom the king had sent to that Rebel returned to him the whole answer of the renegade, that rebel against righteousness. Hearing the insults of the evil man, the king called together his commanders. . . . He sent them forth to war against the evil Sabradin on the 24th day of Yakatit,[6] saying to them, "May God give you strength and victory, and may He help you." . . . And they fought with him and forced him out of his residence; and he fled before them. And they defeated him through the power of God. . . . And they pursued him till

[2]The Ethiopian royal family, known as the *Solomonid Dynasty* (1270–1974), claimed descent from the union of the Queen of Sheba and King Solomon of Israel (r. ca. 962–922 B.C.E.), son of King David. See the Bible, 1 Kings 10:1–13 and 2 Chronicles 9:1–12, for an account of the queen's visit to King Solomon. According to Ethiopian tradition, *Menelik*, son of the Queen of Sheba and Solomon and the first king of Ethiopia, stole the Ark of the Covenant from Jerusalem and brought it to Ethiopia, where it is still revered as the country's most sacred relic.

[3]The Geez transliteration of *Zion*, one of Jerusalem's hills and a common symbolic term for Jerusalem and even the entire Holy Land. Here *Seyon* refers to Ethiopia because the Ethiopians claim partial Hebraic descent (see note 2). *Amda Seyon* means "Pillar of Zion."
[4]The Bible, 1 Corinthians 1:20.
[5]The Bible, Psalms 68:31.
[6]February 18, 1329.

sunset; but he escaped them, going by a different road. God threw him down from his glory. . . .

Then the army of the king set forth and attacked the camp of the Rebel. They looted the rebel king's treasure houses and took gold and silver and fine clothes and jewels without number. They killed men and women, old men and children; the corpses of the slain filled a large space. And those who survived were made prisoners, and there were left none but those who had escaped with that evil man. But the soldiers could not find a place to camp because of the foul smell of the corpses; and they went to another place and made their camp there. . . .

The king, hearing that the Rebel had escaped, went into the tabernacle[7] and approached the altar; seizing the horns of the altar[8] he implored mercy of Jesus Christ saying, "Hear the petition of my heart and reject not the prayer of my lips, and shut not the gates of Thy mercy because of my sins, but send me Thy good angel to guide me on my road to pursue mine enemy who has set himself above Thy sheep and above Thy holy name." And having said this, he gave an offering to the church of colored hangings for the altar, and went out. Then he sent other troops, . . . cavalry and foot-soldiers, strong and skilled in war, powerful without comparison in warfare and battle; he sent their commander . . . to make war in the land of the renegades who are like Jews, the crucifiers.[9] . . . Because like the Jews, the crucifiers, they denied Christ, he sent troops to destroy and devastate them and subject them to the rule of Christ. . . .

The Rebel was filled with fear, and not knowing where to turn, for fear had taken possession of him, he sent to the queen[10] saying, "I have done wrong to my lord the king, I have wrought injustice against him, and it is better that I fall into his hands than into the hands of a stranger. I will come myself and surrender to him, that he may do what he will to me." Thereupon the queen went to tell the king the whole of the message from that Rebel Sabradin, whose acts, like his name "broken judgment,"[11] consist of insults, mad rage, errors, contentions, and arrogance. When the king heard this message which the Rebel had sent to the queen, he was exceedingly angry, and said to the queen, "Do you send him a message and say: 'If you come, or if you do not come, it will not trouble me; but if you go to a distant country I will pursue you through the power of God. And if you go into a cave, or if you just run away, I will not leave you alone nor will I return to my capital till I have taken you.'"

Now when he received this message, Sabradin set out and came to the king, and stood before him. And the king asked him, saying, "Why have you behaved thus to me? The gifts which you formerly sent to me you have given to your servants; and the multitude of goods of silver and gold which I gave to the poor you have taken away. Those who traded with me you have bound in chains; and what is worse, you have aspired to the throne of my kingdom, in imitation of the Devil your father who wished to be the equal of his creator." When that Rebel heard these words of the king he was at a loss for an answer in the greatness of his fear, for he was afraid of the king's presence; and he answered, "Do with me according to your will." And immediately the soldiers who were on the left and right of the king stood forth in anger and said, "This man is not worthy of life, for he has burnt the churches of God, he has slain Christians, and those whom he did not kill he has compelled to accept his religion. Moreover he desired to ascend the high mountain of the kingdom." And

---

[7]A tent used as a chapel in the king's camp.

[8]As was the fashion in ancient Israel, Ethiopian altars had horns on all four corners. Suppliants would grasp one while praying.

[9]The *Falashas*, or Ethiopian Jews, are a Kushitic people whose ancestors had intermarried with Jewish immigrants from Yemen. They are termed *crucifiers* here because of the notion that the Jews were responsible for Jesus' crucifixion.

[10]Queen Mangesa, wife of King Amda Seyon.

[11]A pun. In Geez *sabara* means "break" and *dayn* means "judgment." Actually, the Arabic name Sabr ad-Din means "Constant in the Faith."

some said, "Let us slay him with the edge of the sword"; others said, "Let us stone him to death"; and others again, "Let us burn him with fire that he may disappear from the Earth." And they said to the king, "Think not, O king, that he comes to you honestly and freely, for he trusts in his magic art." And so saying, they lifted from his bosom and arm a talisman and revealed the form of his magic. Then said the king, "Can your talismans deliver you from my hands in which God has imprisoned you?" And he gave orders for his two hands to be bound with iron chains; he did not wish him to be killed, for he is merciful and forbearing. Thus was taken the Rebel in the net which he himself had woven, and in the snare which he himself had set. . . . After this the king sent news to the capital of his kingdom. . . . "There is good news for you: with the help of your prayers I have defeated my enemy who is also the enemy of Christ."

A Yoruba Woman of Authority?

▼▼▼

74 ▼ SEATED FEMALE FIGURE

Like the Ethiopians, the *Yoruba*-speaking peoples of West Africa, who inhabit the forestlands that stretch from the edge of the savanna to the coast, trace their ancestry back to Southwest Asia, in this case Mecca. Such oral traditions are suspect as historical evidence and probably arose from a desire on the part of people converted to Islam well after 1200 to create for themselves an Arabic lineage. Whatever their origins, by the late fourteenth century the Yoruba people had established a number of independent kingdoms in a region encompassed today by the nations of Nigeria and Benin. One of the most important of these Yoruba kingdoms was *Oyo*. Although it reached its apogee as a regional power in the period 1600–1830, Oyo's foundations as a city-state go back much earlier. Its first capital city, Old Oyo, located near the Niger River, was founded sometime between 800 and 1000.

The Yoruba of Oyo and elsewhere were great artists as well as state builders. The town of Esie in Nigeria is the site of a collection of more than 1,000 soapstone carvings of human figures that have lain for centuries in a grove (see source 72 for a description of Ghana's sacred groves). Each carving is an individual portrait, and it seems reasonable to infer that each represents a prominent, probably deceased, individual. The sculptures date to somewhere between 1100 and 1500 and seem to have come from either Old Oyo or the equally powerful Yoruba city-state of *Ife*.

The sculpture pictured here is twenty-six inches high and represents a seated woman holding a cutlass that rests against her right shoulder. Note her elaborate hairstyle, whose height equals that of her face, the three-stringed necklace, and the scarification of her face. This arrangement of scars is found equally on male and female effigies in the collection. The figure probably represents an *Iyalode* (mother in charge of external affairs), an important officer among the Yoruba. Although the specific functions of Iyalodes differed from kingdom to kingdom and from era to era, it is clear that they enjoyed wide-ranging political, social, economic, and even military powers. Simply stated, the Iyalode was a chief in her own right and one of the monarch's main lieutenants.

QUESTIONS FOR ANALYSIS

1. List and comment on all of the clues that lead us to infer that this figurine represents a woman of authority. What do you think each symbol of authority represents?
2. Compare this statue with the four statues in Multiple Voices III. What do all five statues have in common? What do those common characteristics suggest about how authority is perceived and portrayed across cultures and time?

A Yoruba Woman of Authority?

The Americas

Recently reported genetic evidence based on a study of living Siberian and American Indian populations strongly suggests that migrants from East Asia reached the Western Hemisphere no more than 18,000 years ago. Datable artifacts in two widely separated archaeological sites, Cactus Hill in southeastern Virginia and Monte Verde in Chile, further indicate that hunter-gatherers inhabited both North and South America at least as far back as 15,000 years ago. The Monte Verde site is about 15,000 years old, and the earliest materials found at Cactus Hill are 15,000–17,000 years old. As the picture now stands, and it will likely be revised as new evidence comes in, the First Americans arrived in a series of waves, but of these, there were probably two periods of major migration. The first occurred sometime soon after 18,000 years ago when a landbridge, known as *Beringia*, connected Siberia and Alaska. Rising waters from melting glaciers toward the end of the last Ice Age wiped out that bridge about 11,000 years ago. The second major wave of migration probably occurred about 8,000 years ago as various newcomers traveled from northeastern Asia in small boats, stopping at various locations along the western shores of the Americas.

Whenever it began and however it occurred, the initial peopling of the Americas was an epochal event (or, better, series of events) rivaled in magnitude only by the demographic shifts that took place following the arrival in force of Europeans and Africans after 1492. With the advent of European and African peoples and their diseases, the whole population structure of the Americas underwent massive changes.

During the many years that separated these two eras, the Americas witnessed a variety of other only slightly less monumental developments. One of the most consequential was the indigenous development of agriculture based on the cultivation of more than 100 different crops unknown to the peoples of Africa and Eurasia. Chief among them were *maize* (*corn* in American English), potatoes, avocados, sweet potatoes, tomatoes, peanuts, manioc, and various types of beans, peppers (especially chilies), and squashes. By the time the Europeans arrived, agriculture was practiced from the woodlands of eastern North America to the rainforests of the Amazon tropics. As elsewhere, agriculture imposed restrictions on the behavior and social patterns of the cultivators and also produced enough food in a sufficiently regular manner to allow for the growth of dense populations. One result was the rise of civilizations, first in South America, Mexico, and Central America, and later in regions that are today part of the United States.

Three of the major civilizations of North America were the *Mississippian Mound Culture*, the *Hohokam*, and the *Anasazi*. Between 1050 and 1200 C.E., the Mississippian Mound Builders created the city of Cahokia at a site outside present-day East St. Louis, Illinois. At its height, Cahokia supported a population of at least 11,000 people and possibly as many as 30,000. The Hohokam (those who have vanished) of the Sonoran Desert produced a complex urban society based on their ability to construct and maintain some 300 miles of irrigation canals in the region of present-day Phoenix, Arizona. During the twelfth and thirteenth centuries, the Anasazi (the ancient ones) of the Four Corners region of the American Southwest built cities in Chaco Canyon, New Mexico, and at Mesa Verde in Colorado, which today stand as silent testimony of their engineering skills. All three civilizations participated in widespread trade networks and were influenced by the earlier civilizations of Mexico. All three also passed away as urban cultures long before the arrival of Europeans, who could only marvel at the ruins they left behind.

Because they left no written records behind and abandoned their urban centers so long ago, these North American civilizations remain largely mysterious, despite the considerable work of archaeologists over the past half century. Farther south, however, the *Maya, Mexica (Aztec)*, and *Inca* peoples were still identifiable cultures when European conquerors and missionaries arrived on the scene. Despite the best attempts of many Europeans to efface the presumed devilish cultures that they had discovered, the Maya, Aztec, and Inca civilizations would not be forgotten.

The sources that follow — the products of American Indian and European artisans and authors — combine to shed light on three important American cultures that flourished between 500 and 1500 C.E.

Mayan Faces and Figures
▼▼▼
75 ▼ *THREE MAYAN CERAMIC SCULPTURES*

The *Maya*, one of Ancient America's most brilliant civilizations, inhabited an area that today encompasses all of Mexico's Yucatán Peninsula and parts of the states of Tabasco and Chiapas, all of Guatemala and Belize, and the western regions of Honduras and El Salvador. The Maya, today more than 6 million strong, continue to inhabit these lands and to maintain their traditions and related but often mutually incomprehensible Mayan languages. Far from being a vanished people, they are a vital culture, despite often violent attempts since the sixteenth century and down to today to repress and acculturate them.

The Maya did not create the first civilization in pre-Spanish *Mesoamerica* (Mexico and Central America). That distinction belongs to a people we know as the *Olmec*, who formed a civilization around 1500 B.C.E. along Mexico's Gulf Coast and fashioned many of the distinguishing cultural characteristics shared by all Mesoamerican civilizations, including a complex calendar and massive ceremonial complexes.

A distinctive Mayan civilization began to flourish in what is known as the Late Preclassical Age (300 B.C.E.–250 C.E.), when the Maya constructed a number of monumental temple complexes. In the subsequent Classical Age (300–925), Mayan genius soared, but it was accompanied by turmoil and uneven fortunes.

Between around 800 to 925, Mayan civilization witnessed glory, tragic decline, and triumph as some areas of the Mayan World suffered profound political, social, and demographic dislocation. In the southern lowlands, thrones were toppled and cities abandoned, whereas in the Yucatán Peninsula, the northernmost area of Mayan civilization, there was prosperity. During the tenth century, however, there was a second Mayan collapse, and most cities in the Yucatán were abandoned, apparent victims of overpopulation and environmental degradation. Perhaps as a consequence of their own failings, the Maya of the north fell under the domination of the Toltecs from the highlands of central Mexico. Mayan civilization was not snuffed out, but its days of glory and independence were over.

Today's visitor to the lands of the Maya is awed by the recovered remains of their cities, such as Palenque. But Mayan artistic genius was not confined to the construction of great temples. The Maya excelled in all of the representational arts, including crafting ceramic figurines of human and divine beings. The following three ceramic pieces, all from Jaina, an island in the Bay of Campeche off the western shore of the Yucatán Peninsula, date from the Late Classical Period (700–925). The island was a religious sanctuary and necropolis (city of the dead), where important Mayans of the period were buried. All statuettes discovered there are hollow and fitted with whistles at their backs. We can only guess at their ceremonial use. Whatever their purposes, they are vivid portraits of flesh-and-blood Maya who lived more than 1,000 years ago, and they also provide us with some tantalizing clues regarding Mayan life, beliefs, and practices.

QUESTIONS FOR ANALYSIS

1. The first two statuettes depict ballplayers. One of the players is a captive who will be sacrificed at the end of the game. How do we know or infer that?
2. The other ballplayer is a Mayan aristocrat on the home team, as it were. How do we know or infer that?
3. The third piece, showing a woman and a man, has been variously interpreted. Some see it as the union of the moon-goddess and the sun-god. Others view it as evidence of the sophistication of Mayan society that could depict a common aspect of human life and love. What might that be? A third interpretation is that this is also a comic scene. What is the joke?
4. Based on these three statuettes, what do you conclude about Mayan interest in the human face and form? You might want to compare these works with the Hellenic and Hellenistic statues in sources 25 and 26.

Ballplayer

Ballplayer

A Woman and a Man

The Sacred Marketplace:
Mexica Commerce and Religion

▼▼▼

76 ▼ Diego Durán,
BOOK OF THE GODS AND RITES

Father Diego Durán (1537–1588) moved with his family to New Spain when he was a young boy. In 1556 he entered the Dominican Order in Mexico City and served as a priest throughout central and southern Mexico. Like a number of other Dominican and Franciscan friars, Durán became a strong advocate of the American Indians and a student of their history and culture. He mastered *Nahuatl*, the language of the Mexica (Aztecs), and explored indigenous beliefs and religious practices by talking with elders and studying available native records. As his studies progressed, he became increasingly convinced that apparent parallels between his own Catholic faith, moral code, and rituals and those of his native friends pointed to a diffusion of Judaism or Christianity or both into the New World at some unknown time or times in the past. He further concluded that the bloody human sacrifices that were an integral part of Mesoamerican religion were evidence of the intervention of the Devil, who had succeeded in perverting the True Religion among the Mesoamericans prior to the arrival of the Spaniards. He also believed that he and his fellow missionaries would never succeed in rooting out these erroneous beliefs and satanic practices until they first understood the ancient religion.

To aid this missionary work (and probably also because of his innate curiosity), Durán produced three books: the *Book of the Gods and Rites* (ca. 1576–1579), which is excerpted here; *The Ancient Calendar* (1579), which is a guide to the Mesoamerican calendar; and *The History of the Indies of New Spain* (1580?–1581), which traces the Mexica from their legendary origins in the ninth century up to the conquest of the Aztec Empire in 1521. The encyclopedic nature and apparent accuracy of his work places Durán, along with several other Spanish missionary-scholars, in the ranks of the pioneers of Mesoamerican ethnohistory, and his books are invaluable texts for modern students of both pre- and early post-Conquest Mexico. Much of the information he supplies is not found in any other extant documentary source, but quite a bit has been confirmed by archaeological evidence.

In the following excerpts, Durán deals with the intimate connections in Mesoamerican Indian society between commerce and religion and the manner in which the supposedly converted Mexicans of his day retained some of the old customs. Durán also drew or commissioned illustrations for his book, and one of those, a drawing of a market, accompanies these excerpts. Its overall composition suggests that it was copied from a pre-Conquest original.

QUESTIONS FOR ANALYSIS

1. Where did merchants fit into the Mesoamerican class system? How did they raise their status?
2. What religious and economic roles did the *tianguiz*, or local marketplace, play in pre-Conquest Mexico?
3. How did religious taboos help stimulate the Mesoamerican Indian economy?
4. What roles did slavery and human sacrifice play in the dynamics of the marketplace?
5. What religious functions did slavery and human sacrifice serve?
6. In what ways had the customs of the marketplace survived, despite the imposition of Christianity?
7. Based on Durán's description of a *tianguiz*, describe and explain all of the activities, persons, and elements in the accompanying illustration. Do not neglect to take into account the sexes of the nine people. If you wish, compose a short story or journalistic report revolving around this scene.

In this land in pagan times the ancient kings and princes took very special care and caution in rewarding and honoring the upright, the virtuous, and the brave so that the rest might find heart to imitate their strength, when they saw the reward given. . . . There were three established and honored ways in all the nations[1] [for obtaining these rewards]. The first and principal path which the kings designated was soldiery — to make oneself known in war through valiant feats, to be outstanding in killing, taking prisoners, to destroy armies and squadrons, to have directed these things. These [warriors] were given great honors, rewards, weapons, and insignia which were proof of their splendid deeds and valor. . . .

The second way in which men rose was through religion, entering the priesthood. After having served in the temples in a virtuous, penitential, and cloistered way of life, in their old age they were sent out to high and honorable posts (which exist to this day) in the different nations. They were given high-sounding names and titles, which in our language today, to judge by

the respect and reverence they enjoyed and still do, can be considered to have been the equivalent of counts, dukes, or marquises; bishops or archbishops; and so forth. They were present when the government councils were held, their opinions and advice were listened to, and they were part of the ruling boards and juntas. Without their council and opinion kings did not dare act. . . .

The third and least glorious manner of [rising in the world] was that of becoming a merchant or trader, that of buying and selling, going forth to all the markets of the land, bartering cloth for jewels, jewels for feathers, feathers for stones, and stones for slaves, always dealing in things of importance, of renown, and of high value. These [men] strengthened their social position with their wealth. We have seen many men of low birth and worse blood rise to a state which has permitted them to marry daughters of dukes, counts, and marquises and to form magnificent and rich family estates, mixing their humble blood with that of the highest of Spain. The same was true of these Indian merchants. They

---

[1]Not just the Mexica (Aztecs), but all tribes and states in pre-Conquest Mexico.

acquired wealth and obtained slaves to sacrifice to this their god.[2] And so they were considered among the magnates of the land, just as the valorous soldier brought sacrificial captives from war, gaining fame as a brave. He received people and prepared a banquet with the flesh of the man he had brought back as an offering to god, all the lords and chieftains granting him in return insignia and high privileges — the same was true of the merchants. They offered one or two sacrificial slaves with the usual ceremonies of eating and dancing, presenting gifts of mantles, breechcloths, and sandals to all the lords, preparing different dishes for all the guests. [These merchants] were given the title of noblemen and were honored with the same pomp as the warriors. [Each one] was given an appropriate name, different from the rest, which indicated the way in which he had gained his honors. . . .

The merchants celebrated the feast in honor of their god because their divine patron had been the most excellent, the richest merchant in his time, and possibly the one who gave them the patterns and rules of their trade. . . .

I wish to give warning that even today there is a diabolical custom among the natives, especially in Cholula,[3] where the god [Quetzalcoatl] was worshiped; peddlers will traffic for ten, twelve, and even twenty years, earning and saving up to two or three hundred pesos. And after all their toil, wretched eating and sleeping — without aim or reason — they offer a most lavish banquet. There they spend all their savings. What I most regret is that they follow the ancient custom of holding that memorial feast in order to celebrate their [ancient] titles and set themselves on high. This would not be wrong except that for their celebration they await the day on which the god [Quetzalcoatl] was honored. . . .

We have already dealt with all the main deities to whom men were sacrificed, with all the rites and ceremonies performed in their honor. Though briefly, in order not to be tiring, it is now timely and correct to tell something about the people who died as offerings to the gods, who were sacrificed and slain. Before we deal with this subject, though, first it will be necessary to say that in olden times there was a god of markets and fairs. This deity had his place upon a *momoztli*, which is like a roadside shrine or a pillory block. These were used in ancient times, and later we boys called them places of idle gossip. Many of these stood along the roads, on street corners, and in the market.

In the shrines at the market places were fixed round carved stones as large as shields, each one bearing a round figure like that of the sun with flowers and circles carved around it. Some were carved with other images, depending upon the feeling of the priests and the importance of the market place and the town. The gods[4] of these market places threatened terrible ills and made evil omens and auguries to the neighboring villages which did not attend their market places. There were clearly set limits regarding how many leagues[5] could be traveled to attend the markets to honor their gods. Also a law and commandment forced the people to attend unless excused by some just impediment. . . .

Thus they came from all parts, from two, from three, from four and more leagues away, to the market places. From all of this has survived the strange custom of attending the market before going to mass. Since the ancient custom of holding the market every five days still exists, occasionally this falls on Sunday, and no one hears mass in the area of the town where the market is held. . . .

---

[2]*Quetzalcoatl*, the feathered serpent, the chief deity of the *Choultecs*, or people of *Cholula*, a people noted for their mercantile skills and wealth. One of the gods of creation, as well as inventor of writing and the calendar, Quetzalcoatl also served as the god of all merchants. See note 3.

[3]A city in central Mexico noted for its commerce; it also served as an especially revered religious sanctuary because of its association with Quetzalcoatl's cult (see Multiple Voices VIII).
[4]In addition to Quetzalcoatl, the god of commerce, each marketplace had its local deity.
[5]A *league* is three miles.

The markets were so inviting, pleasurable, appealing, and gratifying to these people that great crowds attended, and still attend, them, especially during the big fairs, as is well known to all. I suspect that if I said to a market woman accustomed to going from market to market: "Look, today is market day in such and such a town. What would you rather do, go from here right to Heaven or to that market?" I believe this would be her answer: "Allow me to go to the market first, and then I will go to Heaven." She would be happier to lose those minutes of glory to visit the market place and walk about hither and thither without any gain or profit, to satisfy her hunger and whim to see the *tianguiz*.[6] . . .

The markets in this land were all enclosed by walls and stood either in front of the temples of the gods or to one side. Market day in each town was considered a main feast in that town or city. And thus in that small shrine where the idol of the market stood were offered ears of corn, chili, tomatoes, fruit, and other vegetables, seeds, and breads — in sum, everything sold in the *tianguiz*. Some say that [these offerings] were left there until they spoiled; others deny this, saying that all was gathered up by the priests and ministers of the temples.

But, to return to what I said about the market day being a feast day, the following is the truth. One day I was informed in a personal way, and now I shall tell what took place between me and a lord of a certain village.[7] When I begged him to finish a part of the church that was under construction, he answered: "Father, do you not know that tomorrow is a great feast in this town? How can you expect them to work? Leave it for another day." Then, very carefully, I looked at the calendar to see which saint's day it was, and I found none. Laughing at me, [the lord] said: "Do you not know that tomorrow is the feast of the *tianguiz* of this town? [Do you not know] that not a man or a woman will fail to pay

it its due honor?" From these words I realized [how important] a feast and solemnity the market is for them. . . .

Furthermore, a law was established by the state prohibiting the selling of goods outside the market place. Not only were there laws and penalties connected with this, but there was a fear of the supernatural, of misfortune, and of the ire and wrath of the god of the market. No one ventured, therefore, to trade outside [the market limits], and the custom has survived until these days. Many a time have I seen a native carry two or three hens or a load of fruit for sale in the market. On the road he meets a Spaniard who wants to buy them from him. The Spaniard offers the price which he would have received in the market. The native refuses and is unwilling to sell, even though he would save himself a league or two of walking. He begs the Spaniard to go to the market place to buy them there. . . . Even today, though they are Christians, the awe and fear of their ancient law is still strong. It must also be said that the planting of this awe and nonsense in these people brought a certain income from all that which was sold in the markets [in the form of taxes], which was divided between the lord and the community.

In this land the sovereigns had set up a regulation regarding the markets: they were to take the form of fairs or markets specializing in the selling of certain things. Some markets, therefore, became famous and popular for these reasons: it was commanded that slaves were to be sold at the fair in Azcapotzalco and that all the people of the land who had slaves for sale must go there and to no other place to sell. The same can be said of Itzocan. Slaves could be sold in these two places only. It was at these two fairs that slaves were sold so that those who needed them would go there and to no other place to buy. In other places, such as Cholula, it was ordered that the merchandise must consist of jew-

---

[6]The word means "marketplace."

[7]Probably a native lord, or local ruler, who was allowed to continue in office after the Conquest.

els, precious stones, and fine featherwork. At others, such as Tetzcoco, cloth and fine gourds were sold, together with exquisitely worked ceramics, splendidly done in the native way. . . .

I would like to say some things regarding the slaves sold in the two markets I have mentioned, Azcapotzalco and Itzocan. Some things worthy of remembering can be said about these slaves. In the first place, it should be known that in honor of the gods (as has been noted) men and women were slain on all the feast days. Some of these were slaves bought in the market place for the special purpose of representing gods. When they had performed the representation, when those slaves had been purified and washed — some for an entire year, others for forty days, others for nine, others for seven — after having been honored and served in the name of the god they impersonated, at the end they were sacrificed by those who owned them.

Captives of another type were those taken as prisoners in war. These served exclusively as sacrifices for the man who had impersonated the god whose feast was being celebrated.[8] Thus these were called the "delicious food of the gods." I do not have to deal with all of these, but only with the slaves who were sold in the market place for having broken the law or for the reasons I shall describe later. These were bought by rich merchants and by important chieftains, some to glorify their own names and others to fulfill their customary vows.[9]

The masters took the slaves to the *tianguiz*: some took men, others women, others boys or girls, so that there would be variety from which to choose. So that they would be identified as slaves, they wore on their necks wooden or metal collars with small rings through which passed

rods about one yard long. In its place I shall explain the reason for putting these collars on them. At the site where these slaves were sold (which stood at one side of the *tianguiz*, according to market regulations) the owners kept [the slaves] dancing and singing so that merchants would be attracted by the charm of their voices and their [dance] steps and buy them quickly. If one possessed this facility, therefore, he found a master immediately. This was not the case for those who lacked grace and were inept in these things. Thus they were presented many times at market places without anyone paying attention to them, though [occasionally] some bought them to make use of them [in some way],[10] since they were unfit to represent the gods. Singers and dancers were in demand because when they were garbed in the raiment of the gods they went about singing and dancing in the streets and the houses during the time of their impersonation. They entered [the houses] and the temples and [climbed to] the flat roofs of the royal houses and those of their masters. They were given all the pleasures and joys of the world — foods, drink, feasts — as if they had been the gods themselves. So it was that the merchants wished that, aside from being good dancers and singers, they were healthy, without blemish or deformity. . . . [These slaves] were therefore made to strip, and were examined from head to foot, member by member. They were forced to extend their hands and lift their feet [as is done today with] Negro [slaves], to determine whether they were crippled. If one was found healthy, he was bought; otherwise, no. For it was desired that the slaves to be purified to represent the gods (this ceremony belonging to their rites, religion, and precepts) were healthy and without

[8]Prisoners were sacrificed to the gods and to the impersonators of the gods. The feasts of important deities involved a sacrifice that assumed the level of death, ritual resurrection, and some sort of communion. Flawless slaves, as described later in the reading, became impersonators of the deity and lived a life of splendor and glory for a stipulated period of time. The impersonator of Quetzalcoatl served forty days. On the feast day, the impersonator was sacrificed. For some feasts the body was cooked and consumed in a ritual meal

(see note 9). For other feasts the body was flayed and the skin worn by a priest.
[9]Once when Durán asked why the people were not content to sacrifice animals, he was told that the sacrifice of humans was the honored offering of a great lord. For the feast of Quetzalcoatl, held on February 3, the merchants of Cholula purchased a slave without blemish to serve as the impersonator. Later they consumed his body.
[10]They were kept as domestic servants.

A Tianguiz, *or Marketplace*

blemish, just as we read in the Holy Writ about the sacrifices of the Old Testament which were to be without blemish. These slaves were not strangers or foreigners or prisoners of war, as some have declared, but were natives of the same town. . . .

▷   Durán then enumerates the reasons for which a person could be enslaved.

We have digressed from our theme (but not too far, because what we have told is related to the slaves and is worthy of note). Now that the way in which one became a slave has been described, it would be interesting to note how one was freed. It should be known that there was a law in this land of New Spain: whenever the masters of slaves took them out for sale, they were weighed down with collars and with rods one yard long across their backs. One reason [for these collars

and rods] was so that these [slaves] might be easily recognized; furthermore, if they tried to escape, the rod was an obstacle and hindrance to fleeing in a crowd. For it was decreed that if the slave could escape from his master in the *tianguiz* after having entered it and could pass the limits of the market before his master caught him, having passed these limits, he could step upon human excrement and in this way become free. Thus soiled, he went to the purifiers of slaves, showed himself to them, and said: "O lords, I was a slave, and, according to what your laws decree, I fled today from the market place, from the hands of my master! I escaped like a bird from a cage and stepped upon the offal as is the law. And so I have come to you to purify me and to free me from my servitude." The authorities removed the fetters, stripped him, and washed him from head to foot. Having washed him, they garbed him in new clothing and presented him to the lord; they told him that [this man] had been a slave but had been liberated according to law. The law praised him for his skill and enterprise and gave him complete freedom. Thenceforth he was to be honored and given insignia as a free and spirited man. Often he was kept in the palace as a servant of the house. . . .

Regarding the second [type of slaves], men captured in war, no more can be added to what has been said. It was certain and sure that such captives were to serve as victims in sacrifice (unless they escaped), because they had been brought exclusively to be sacrificed to the gods.

Governing the Inca Empire
▼▼▼
77 ▼ *Pedro de Cieza de León, CHRONICLES*

In addition to accounts composed by scholar-missionaries such as Diego Durán, we have written records, engraved on stone and written on parchment, from the hands of pre-Conquest Mesoamericans. Needless to say, they are invaluable for filling out our picture of the cultures of this region. The same is not true for South America.

Until recently, scholars believed that no indigenous civilization of South America produced a system of writing. A book published in 2003 challenges that notion and argues that the Inca Empire's *quipus*, knotted strings used for record keeping, constituted a highly complex system of three-dimensional writing that Spanish colonists (as well as almost all modern scholars) failed to recognize as more than just abacus-like devices that allowed Inca functionaries to perform numerical calculations. The failure by Spaniards and historians alike to look beyond the apparently obvious was due to their shared assumption that writing can only be two-dimensional. This new hypothesis needs further study and testing, especially through computer analysis of extant quipus, before it can be accepted or rejected. Whatever the truth, as the situation currently stands, even if the quipus were a form of writing, we cannot yet decipher them.

This absence of decipherable written records for the peoples of South America prior to the arrival of the Spaniards means that our only current sources for their pre-Conquest history are archaeological artifacts and accounts composed by sixteenth- and early-seventeenth-century American Indian and Spanish writers who labored to preserve the memory of a past in imminent danger of being lost forever.

One such ethnohistorian was Pedro de Cieza de León (1520–1554). In 1535 he arrived in the Americas as a teenage soldier-adventurer and spent the next seventeen years trekking throughout South America, falling increasingly under the spell of the continent and its native peoples. As he traveled and fought, he took detailed notes of all he observed and experienced. Believing, as he noted, that "we and the Indians have the same origin," Cieza wrote with great sympathy for the many different American Indian cultures he encountered, even though he seems never to have doubted the righteousness of the Spanish conquest and conversion of these peoples. Indeed, one of his primary reasons for recording his observations was that he considered it "right that the world know how so great a multitude of these Indians were brought into the sanctity of the Church."

Cieza's *Chronicles* describe many different native South American cultures, but their greatest value to modern historians is the wealth of detail they provide of the Inca Empire and the *Quechua* Indians who created it. Like the Mexica, the Quechuas were recent arrivals who fashioned a civilization that borrowed heavily from preceding cultures. Like the Aztec Empire, the Inca Empire was young, having taken shape during the reigns of Pachacuti (1438–1471) and Topac Yupanqui (1471–1493). As was also true in Mexico, the Inca Empire's life was prematurely cut short by *conquistadores*.

In the following selection, Cieza describes how the Inca monarchs governed an empire that covered about 500,000 square miles, stretched some 2,500 miles from end to end, and included anywhere from 6 to 13 million people of different ethnicities and languages.

QUESTIONS FOR ANALYSIS

1. What means did the Incas use to govern their vast empire?
2. From Cieza's perspective, what were the most admirable qualities of this empire?
3. What appear to have been the strengths of this empire? Can you perceive any weaknesses? Were the Incas aware of these shortcomings, and, if so, how did they attempt to counter them?
4. Consider the possibility that the quipus constituted a writing system. Does León's testimony seem to support or contradict this hypothesis? Be specific.

It is told for a fact of the rulers of this kingdom that in the days of their rule they had their representatives in the capitals of all the provinces, . . . for in all these places there were larger and finer lodgings than in most of the other cities of this great kingdom, and many storehouses. They served as the head of the provinces or regions, and from every so many leagues[1] around the tributes were brought to one of these capitals, and from so many others, to another. This was so well organized that there was not a village that did not know where it was to send its tribute. In all these capitals the Incas had temples of the sun, mints, and many silversmiths who did nothing but work rich pieces of gold or fair vessels of silver; large garrisons were stationed there, and, as I have said, a steward or representative who was in command of them all, to whom an accounting of everything that was brought in was made, and who, in turn, had to give one of all that was issued. And these governors could in no way interfere with the jurisdiction of another who held a similar post, but within his own, if there were any disorder or disturbance, he had authority to punish it[s perpetrators], especially if it were in the nature of a conspiracy or a rebellion, or failure to obey the Inca,[2] for full power resided in these governors. And if the Incas had not had the foresight to appoint them and to establish the *mitimaes*,[3] the na-

---

[1] One *league* is three miles.
[2] *Inca* means "sovereign lord." In its strictest sense, it should be used to refer only to this civilization's god-kings. Today, however, historians customarily use the term to refer to the entire Quechua people and their civilization and empire.
[3] Literally, "those moved from one land to another." This was the systematic practice of resettling groups from one area of

the empire to another. These resettled people served as a check on the loyalties of the natives of the region to which they had been transferred and, in turn, were kept in check by their new neighbors. This helped keep down rebellions and broke down regional and ethnic differences within the empire; it also was a means of cultivating land that needed settlers.

tives would have often revolted and shaken off the royal rule; but with the many troops and the abundance of provisions, they could not effect this unless they had all plotted such treason or rebellion together. This happened rarely, for these governors who were named were of complete trust, all of them *Orejones*,[4] and most of them had their holdings, or *chacaras*, in the neighborhood of *Cuzco*,[5] and their homes and kinfolk. If one of them did not show sufficient capacity for his duties, he was removed and another put in his place.

When one of them came to Cuzco on private business or to see the Inca, he left a lieutenant in his place, not one who aspired to the post, but one he knew would faithfully carry out what he was ordered to do and what was best for the service of the Inca. And if one of these governors or delegates died while in office, the natives at once sent word to the Inca how and of what he had died, and even transported the body by the post road if this seemed to them advisable. The tribute paid by each of these districts . . . and that was turned over by the natives, whether gold, silver, clothing, arms, and all else they gave, was entered in the accounts of . . . [those] who kept the *quipus* and did everything ordered by the governor in the matter of finding the soldiers or supplying whomever the Inca ordered, or making delivery to Cuzco; but when they came from the city of Cuzco to go over the accounts, or they were ordered to go to Cuzco to give an accounting, the accountants themselves gave it by the quipus, or went to give it where there could be no fraud, but everything had to come out right. Few years went by in which an accounting of all these things was not made. . . .

Realizing how difficult it would be to travel the great distances of their land where every league and at every turn a different language was

spoken, and how bothersome it would be to have to employ interpreters to understand them, these rulers, as the best measure, ordered and decreed, with severe punishment for failure to obey, that all the natives of their empire should know and understand the language of Cuzco, both they and their women. This was so strictly enforced that an infant had not yet left its mother's breast before they began to teach it the language it had to know. And although at the beginning this was difficult and many stubbornly refused to learn any language but their own, the Incas were so forceful that they accomplished what they had proposed, and all had to do their bidding. This was carried out so faithfully that in the space of a few years a single tongue was known and used in an extension of more than 1,200 leagues, yet, even though this language was employed, they all spoke their own [languages], which were so numerous that if I were to list them it would not be credited. . . .

As the city of Cuzco was the most important in all Peru, and the Incas lived there most of the time, they had with them in the city many of the leading men of the country, the most intelligent and informed of all, as their advisers. For all agree that before they undertook anything of importance, they discussed it with these counselors, and submitted their opinion to that of the majority. And for the administration of the city, and that the highways should be safe and nowhere should offenses or thefts be committed, from among the most highly esteemed of them he [the Inca] appointed those whose duty it was to punish wrongdoers, and to this end they were always traveling about the country. The Incas took such care to see that justice was meted out that nobody ventured to commit a felony or theft. This was to deal with thieves, ravishers of women, or conspirators against the Inca; however,

---

[4]Literally, "big ears." They were members of the ruling class, often of royal blood, who were distinguished by the large earplugs they wore. Earplugs can be seen in two of the Mayan figurines in source 75. Earplugs were a token of high status for many American Indian societies, from South America to the Mound Cultures of the Ohio Valley.

[5]The capital city of the empire.

there were many provinces that warred on one another, and the Incas were not wholly able to prevent this.

By the river that runs through Cuzco justice was executed on those who were caught or brought in as prisoners from some other place. There they had their heads cut off, or were put to death in some other manner which they chose. Mutiny and conspiracy were severely punished, and, above all, those who were thieves and known as such; even their wives and children were despised and considered to be tarred with the same brush. . . .

We have written how it was ordered by the Incas that the statues be brought out at their feasts, and how they selected from the wisest among their men those who should tell what the life of their kings had been and how they had conducted themselves in the rule of their kingdoms, for the purpose I have stated. It should also be known that, aside from this, it was the custom among them, and a rule carefully observed, for each of them to choose during his reign three or four old men of their nation, skilled and gifted for that purpose, whom they ordered to recall all that had happened in the province during the time of their reign, whether prosperous or adverse, and to make and arrange songs so that thereby it might be known in the future what had taken place in the past. Such songs could not be sung or proclaimed outside the presence of the Inca, and those who were to carry out this behest were ordered to say nothing referring to the Inca during his lifetime, but after he was dead, they said to his successor almost in these words: "Oh, mighty and powerful Inca, may the Sun and Moon, the Earth, the hills and trees, the stones and your forefathers guard you from misfortune and make you prosperous, happy, and blessed among all who have been born. Know that the things that happened to your predecessor were these." And saying this, with their eyes on the ground and heads hanging, with great humility they gave an account and report of all they knew, which they could do very well, for there were many among them of great memory, subtle wit, and lively intelligence, and abounding in knowledge, as those of us who are here and hear them can bear witness. After they said this, when the Inca had heard them, he sent for other of his old Indians whom he ordered to learn the songs the others bore in their memory, and to prepare new ones of what took place during the time of his reign, what was spent, what the provinces contributed, and put all this down in the quipus, so that after his death, when his successor reigned, what had been given and contributed would be known. And except on days of great celebration, or on the occasion of mourning and lament for the death of a brother or son of the Inca, for on such days it was permitted to relate their grandeur and their origin and birth, at no other time was it permitted to deal with this, for it had been forbidden by their lords, and if they did so, they were severely punished.

[The Indians] had a method of knowing how the tributes of food supplies should be levied on the provinces when the Lord-Inca came through with his army, or was visiting the kingdom; or, when nothing of this sort was taking place, what came into the storehouses and what was issued to the subjects, so nobody could be unduly burdened. . . . This involved the quipus, which are long strands of knotted strings, and those who were the accountants and understood the meaning of these knots could reckon by them expenditures or other things that had taken place many years before. By these knots they counted from one to ten and from ten to a hundred, and from a hundred to a thousand. On one of these strands there is the account of one thing, and on the other of another, in such a way that what to us is a strange, meaningless account is clear to them. In the capital of each province there were accountants whom they called *quipu-camayocs*, and by these knots they kept the account of the tribute to be paid by the natives of that district in silver, gold, clothing, flocks, down to wood and other more insignificant things, and by these same quipus at the end of a year, or ten, or twenty years, they gave a report to the one whose duty it was to check the account so exact that not even a pair of sandals was missing. . . .

The *Orejones* of Cuzco who supplied me with information are in agreement that in olden times, in the days of the Lord-Incas, all the villages and provinces of Peru were notified that a report should be given to the rulers and their representatives each year of the men and women who had died, and all who had been born, for this was necessary for the levying of the tributes as well as to know how many were available for war and those who could assume the defense of the villages. This was an easy matter, for each province at the end of the year had a list by the knots of the quipus of all the people who had died there during the year, as well as of those who had been born. At the beginning of the new year they came to Cuzco, bringing their quipus, which told how many births there had been during the year, and how many deaths. This was reported with all truth and accuracy, without any fraud or deceit. In this way the Inca and the governors knew which of the Indians were poor, the women who had been widowed, whether they were able to pay their taxes, and how many men they could count on in the event of war, and many other things they considered highly important.

As this kingdom was so vast, as I have repeatedly mentioned, in each of the many provinces there were many storehouses filled with supplies and other needful things; thus, in times of war, wherever the armies went they drew upon the contents of these storehouses, without ever touching the supplies of their confederates or laying a finger on what they had in their settlements. And when there was no war, all this stock of supplies and food was divided up among the poor and the widows. These poor were the aged, or the lame, crippled, or paralyzed, or those afflicted with some other diseases; if they were in good health, they received nothing. Then the storehouses were filled up once more with the tributes paid the Inca. If there came a lean year, the storehouses were opened and the provinces were lent what they needed in the way of supplies; then, in a year of abundance, they paid back all they had received. Even though the tributes paid to the Inca were used only for the aforesaid purposes, they were employed to advantage, for in this way their kingdom was opulent and well supplied.

No one who was lazy or tried to live by the work of others was tolerated; everyone had to work. Thus on certain days each lord went to his lands and took the plow in hand and cultivated the earth, and did other things. Even the Incas themselves did this to set an example, for everybody was to know that there should be nobody so rich that, on this account, he might disdain or affront the poor. And under their system there was none such in all the kingdom, for, if he had his health, he worked and lacked for nothing; and if he was ill, he received what he needed from the storehouses. And no rich man could deck himself out in more finery than the poor, or wear different clothing, except the rulers and headmen, who, to maintain their dignity, were allowed great freedom and privilege, as well as the *Orejones*, who held a place apart among all the peoples.

Part Four

Travel, Encounter, and Exchange:
1000–1700

EUROPE'S LATE-FIFTEENTH-CENTURY transoceanic explorations inaugurated a new age of global linkage. In many respects, however, the events of 1492 and following were a continuation of a process of long-range cultural exchange that had been gaining momentum throughout Eurasia and Africa since at least the opening of the Silk Road late in the second century B.C.E. The process had its periods of retreat and retrenchment, but the overall pattern was one of growing interchange. Between about 1000 and 1400 C.E., long-distance interchange received a boost from the travels and state-building of some newcomers — notably the Vikings, the Turks, the Franks of Western Europe, and the Mongols. To be sure, many of their travels and conquests were filled with wholesale destruction, yet these adventurers and empire builders also created new pathways for the transmission of cultures.

As important as these contacts were, none matched the historical significance of the transoceanic exchanges set in motion by Western Europe in the late fifteenth century. Earlier in that century, ships flying the flag of Portugal began to probe the waters of Africa's west coast in the hope of reaching the source of North Africa's sub-Saharan gold trade and of contacting *Prester John*, the legendary Christian king believed by some to live in Africa. Although the Portuguese made contact with the Christian civilization of Ethiopia, they failed to convert it to Catholicism, and their missionaries were expelled in 1633. Despite occasional setbacks, Portuguese commercial ventures along the African coastline and beyond proved to be enormously lucrative. Having reached India in 1498, the Malay coast in 1511, and China in 1513, the Portuguese were soon bringing back to Europe spices, silks, dyes, and other exotic items and reaping huge profits. Because of fierce state competition, other European nations sought routes by which they could sail to East and South Asia, a region that Europeans vaguely called *the Indies*. Columbus's voyage of 1492 was only the first of dozens of Spanish enterprises that established Spain as the dominant power not in Asia, as hoped, but in the Americas. The nations of northern Europe also joined in. The French, Dutch, English, Danes, and Swedes claimed lands in the Western Hemisphere, and the French, Dutch, and English successfully challenged and broke the early

Portuguese monopoly in African and Asian trade. By 1600, the European presence was beginning to be felt around the globe.

This initial burst of European expansion affected in radically different ways the various societies that Europeans encountered. It had little initial impact on the ancient centers of civilization in South and East Asia, whose rulers tolerated a limited amount of trade but were strong enough to prevent Europeans from undermining their political power or the cultural traditions of their subjects. In contrast, the civilizations of Meso- and South America were all but wiped out by Spanish military conquests, economic exploitation, missionary activity, and the introduction of deadly new diseases. In the Caribbean, the initial meeting point of American Indians and Spaniards, the story was even grimmer, if that was possible. Almost all of its peoples were eradicated by disease. The story north of the Rio Grande was more complex. Some North American cultures were obliterated soon after the first arrival of Europeans. Most of the American Indians of North America, however, faced similar threats of extinction only after 1600, when the French and English arrived in substantial numbers. Here the Native Americans' loss of territory and identity was generally not so sudden, but the process was no less painful, and the results were largely the same. In Africa, Europeans were unable to topple native rulers or impose their language and religion on most indigenous communities. Europeans largely remained on the coast, relying on Africans to bring them commodities for trade.

Tragically, in addition to gold and ivory, the commodities included slaves. Indeed, for the first several centuries of direct European–West African contact, the slave trade dominated coastal commerce along Africa's western shores. Initially, the Portuguese shipped their African slaves to Europe and various Atlantic islands, where they labored primarily on sugar plantations. Then, in ever-greater numbers, European entrepreneurs brought these workers-in-bondage to the plantations of the New World. There Africans replaced the large numbers of American Indian forced laborers who had died off and the far fewer numbers of transported European criminals and outcasts who had also succumbed to tropical diseases and abuse. Before it ended in the nineteenth century, the transatlantic slave trade robbed millions of human beings of their freedom, dignity, and lives.

❖ Chapter 12 ❖

Adventurers, Merchants, Diplomats, Pilgrims, and Missionaries
A Half Millennium of Travel and Encounter: 1000–1500

THE ERA FROM 1000 TO 1500 witnessed large-scale movements of individuals and peoples across much of the Afro-Eurasian Ecumene, and it also witnessed direct contacts between Europe and the Americas. The first of the recorded contacts between Europeans and Americans was a dead end; the second became an epochal event that set the history of the entire human community onto a new plane. Whereas the exploits of Scandinavian seafarers who reached the shores of North America around 1000 left no permanent imprint on either the Americas or Europe, the arrival of Spaniards in the Americas just before 1500 transformed both civilizations and, ultimately, the world.

Long before Columbus and his Portuguese counterparts set sail, however, the Old Afro-Eurasian World was well on its way toward becoming the home of an increasingly interconnected human community. Turks out of the steppes of Central Asia converted to Islam and then spread their faith and culture into India, the Balkan region of southeastern Europe, and deeper into their traditional Central Asian homeland as they carved out and expanded a variety of states. In Western Europe, Scandinavian adventurers (known as *Vikings, Norse,* and *Northmen*) first pillaged and then settled in Ireland, England, western France, Iceland, and various other places. With the exception of the Scandinavians who settled in Russia and accepted Byzantine Christianity, the Vikings converted to Western Christianity, and during the eleventh century these new members of the faith of Rome became a sharp cutting edge of militant, expansionistic Western Christendom. Norse who had settled in France and had become *Norman* French expanded the boundaries of European Christendom into the Mediterranean. During the last half of the eleventh century, Norman adventurers conquered and seized southern Italy from the Byzantine Empire and Sicily from its Islamic overlords. These same Normans assaulted the Balkan possessions of the emperor at Constantinople and became an integral part of medieval Western Europe's most energetic and protracted overseas colonial adventure — the crusades. Of all the catalysts of cultural exchange, the most explosive and important were the Mongols. In the course of the thirteenth century, they created a land empire that reached from the Pacific to Ukraine. After the initial shock of their conquests, they established a *Pax Mongolica* (Mongol Peace) that opened up lines of direct communication between East Asia and Western Europe. For about a century, people, goods, ideas, and even diseases traveled faster than ever before from one end of Eurasia to the other.

A number of factors combined by 1400 to sever most of the overland routes between Europe and China that had opened up in the mid thirteenth century. They included the onslaught of the Eurasian-wide pandemic of the Black Death in the mid fourteenth century; a massive economic depression that affected lands and peoples throughout Eurasia; the breakup of the Mongol Empire around the middle of the fourteenth century; the disruption of the ancient Silk Road routes of Inner Asia by the armies of the Turkish conqueror *Timur the Lame* (Tamerlane) between 1370 and 1405; the increasing antipathy toward foreigners and foreign adventure shown by China's *Ming* Dynasty (1368–1644); and the successes of the Ottoman Turks, who swept through Anatolia and the Balkans, finally capturing Constantinople in 1453.

To be sure, there was still a trickle of Western contact with Central, South, and East Asia in the early and mid fifteenth century. A handful of European merchants and adventurers even managed to reach the waters of the Indian Ocean by way of either the Red Sea or the Persian Gulf. Nevertheless, the heady days of regular mercantile and missionary contacts with the fabled land of *Cathay*, as China was called in the West, had ended — at least for the moment.

With most land routes blocked, it fell to the kingdoms of Europe's Iberian Peninsula that had ports on the Atlantic to attempt contact by way of the ocean. The results were extraordinary. Spain supported an enterprise that resulted in the European discovery of the Americas, and Portugal pushed into the Indian Ocean by way of Africa and also discovered Brazil.

The World Perceived

The Mongol Empire established an environment conducive to long-distance travel and cultural interchange by providing an avenue across Eurasia from the Pacific Ocean to the Black Sea. We would be wrong, however, to think that long-distance travel and cultural interaction occurred only as the result of conquest and state-building. Long before the rise of the Mongol Empire, hundreds of thousands, even millions, of anonymous men and women traveling as merchants, pilgrims, missionaries, diplomats, and curiosity seekers had already made long-distance travel and its consequent cultural exchanges an important historical phenomenon. This was especially true after 1000. Indian and Chinese merchants traveled to Southeast Asia, where they influenced the evolution of a hybrid culture that has been termed *Indo-Chinese*. Arabs and Berbers in camel caravans trekked across the desert to trade salt and manufactured goods for the gold, ivory, and slaves of sub-Saharan West Africa. Italian merchants established bases in the Black Sea on the western edge of Central Asia. African, Arab, Indian, Southeast Asian, Chinese, and even a few European sailors shared the waters of the Indian Ocean. Pilgrims of many different faiths often traveled great distances to worship at their holy sites. Islamic and Christian missionaries, motivated by devotion and love, labored among foreign people who they believed would be damned to Hell without spiritual guidance. Envoys in the service of princes and spiritual leaders regularly carried important messages to faraway potentates, and some states, such as Genoa and Venice, established resident ambassadors in distant lands. Then there were the curiosity seekers and adventurers, who traveled simply for the sheer joy and experience of it all. As the following three sources suggest, all of this travel and cross-cultural interchange had a profound impact on the ways in which people learned of and envisioned the world beyond their immediate frontiers.

A Chinese View of the World

▼▼▼

78 ▼ Zhau Rugua,
A DESCRIPTION OF FOREIGN PEOPLES

During the Age of Southern Song (1127–1279), China carried on extensive over-seas trade, especially in the Indian Ocean. Indeed, China was the world leader in naval technology, with ships that were larger and more seaworthy than those of any other culture. Chinese ships sailed as far west as the Arabian Peninsula and the northern regions of Africa's east coast, although most Chinese oceanic com-merce was conducted nearer to home in the port cities of Southeast Asia and India, where merchants from many lands traded for both local commodities and goods brought from points quite a bit farther away.

Toward the mid thirteenth century, a man named Zhau Rugua was appointed Inspector of Foreign Trade for the province of Fujian in South China. His chief duty was to levy and collect tariffs on imported goods at Quanzhou, the province's major port. About all we know of him is his name and the fact that he composed a descriptive catalogue of the various foreign peoples and products that China had come to know and know of through its trade networks. It is almost certain that none of his knowledge of overseas lands and cultures was firsthand. Rather, he borrowed liberally from an earlier handbook of this sort composed by Zhou Kufei in 1178. For the rest, Zhau Rugua appears to have gathered some of his informa-tion from Chinese merchants and sailors at Quanzhou, but most of it seems to have come from foreign merchants, especially Arabs. China's southern coastal cities, as well as its interior cities along the Silk Road, were home to large commu-nities of resident alien merchants, who were attracted by the enormous profit potential offered by commerce with the Middle Kingdom. It is no exaggeration to state that China was the engine that drove Eurasia's economy during this half millennium.

The lands that Zhau Rugua described extended from Spain and Morocco in the west to Borneo in the east, and the foreign commodities that he described in-cluded such exotics as rose water from Arabia and ambergris from the waters off East Africa. Throughout his catalogue Zhau Rugua makes clear the central role played by Arab merchant sailors, like Sinbad (see source 60), in carrying this high volume and variety of goods throughout the waters of the Indian Ocean and be-yond. Indeed, most of the foreign lands that Zhau Rugua catalogued were part of the expanding global community of Islam. For that reason, we turn to his descrip-tions of Arabia — a land he knew as the country of the *Dashi* — and southern Spain, which was still in Islamic hands.

QUESTIONS FOR ANALYSIS

1. Compare the late-twelfth-century voyage from Quanzhou to overseas lands with the voyage that Faxian made from Ceylon to China in the early fifth

century (see Multiple Voices III). What changed, and what remained the same? What conclusions follow from your answers?

2. How accurately does Zhau Rugua describe the climate, landscape, and culture of the land(s) of the Dashi? What conclusions follow from your answer?

3. Assuming that Zhau Rugua reflects an informed Chinese view of the land(s) of the Arabs, how would you characterize the way in which the Arabs' land, markets, and products were seen by the Chinese? What conclusions follow from your answer?

4. What do the products traded by the Arabs suggest about late-twelfth-century commerce in the Indian Ocean?

5. How accurate is Zhau Rugua's description of southern Spain and the regions to its north? What inferences follow from your answer?

THE LAND OF THE DASHI[1]

The Dashi are to the west and northwest of Quanzhou[2] at a very great distance from it, so that foreign ships find it difficult to make a direct voyage there. After these ships have left Quanzhou they arrive in some forty days at Lanli,[3] where they trade. The following year they go to sea again, when with the aid of the regular wind,[4] they take some sixty days to make the journey.

The products of the country[5] are for the most part brought to Sanfozi,[6] where they are sold to merchants who forward them to China.

This country of the Dashi is powerful and war-like. Its extent is very great, and its inhabitants are preeminent among all foreigners for their distinguished bearing. The climate throughout a large part of it is cold, snow falling to a depth of two or three feet; consequently rugs are much prized.

The capital of the country, called Maluoba,[7] is an important center for the trade of foreign peoples. . . . The streets are more than fifty feet broad; in the middle is a roadway twenty feet broad and four feet high for use of camels, horses, and oxen carrying goods about. On either side, for the convenience of pedestrians' business, there are sidewalks paved with green and bluish black flagstones of surpassing beauty. . . .

Very rich persons use a measure instead of scales in business transactions of gold or silver. The markets are noisy and bustling, and are filled with a great store of gold and silver damasks, brocades,[8] and similar wares. The artisans have the true artistic spirit.

The king, the officials, and all the people serve Heaven. They also have a Buddha by the name of Mahiawu.[9] Every seven days they cut their hair and clip their fingernails. At the New Year for a whole month they fast and chant prayers.[10] Daily they pray to Heaven five times.

---

[1]The Arabs.
[2]The Arabs knew this important port city as *Zayton* (as did Marco Polo).
[3]A port on the extreme northwestern coast of the island of Sumatra in Southeast Asia.
[4]The monsoon trade winds.
[5]Arabia. This sentence is confusing. The author has suddenly shifted his focus from merchants traveling by way of Sumatra to Arabia to merchants bringing their goods destined for China to Sumatra.

[6]The port of Palembang on the southeast coast of Sumatra.
[7]The coastal trading center of Merbat on the southwest corner of the Arabian Peninsula. Aden, which was located in the same region and was the Arabs' primary center for trade with Africa and India, is strangely not mentioned by name in this book.
[8]Both are richly patterned fabrics.
[9]Muhammad.
[10]The month of Ramadan.

The peasants work their fields without fear of floods or droughts; a sufficiency of water for irrigation is supplied by a river whose source is not known. During the season when no cultivation is in progress, the level of the river remains even with the banks; with the beginning of cultivation it rises day by day. Then it is that an official is appointed to watch the river and to await the highest water level, when he summons the people, who then plow and sow their fields. When they have had enough water, the river returns to its former level.[11]

There is a great harbor in this country, over two hundred feet deep, which opens to the southeast on the sea and has branches connecting with all quarters of the country.[12] On either bank of the harbor the people have their dwellings and here daily are held fairs, where boats and wagons crowd in, all laden with hemp, wheat, millet, beans, sugar, meal, oil, . . . fowl, sheep, geese, ducks, fish, shrimp, date cakes, grapes, and other fruits.

The products of the country consist of pearls, ivory, rhinoceros horns, frankincense, ambergris,[13] . . . cloves, nutmegs, benzoin,[14] aloes,[15] myrrh[16] dragon's blood,[17] . . . borax, opaque and transparent glass, . . . coral, cat's eyes,[18] gardenia flowers, rosewater, nutgalls,[19] yellow wax, soft gold brocades, camel's hair cloth, . . . and foreign satins.

The foreign traders who deal in these wares bring them to Sanfozi and to Foluoan[20] to barter. . . .

The country of Magia[21] is reached by traveling eighty days westward by land from the country of Maluoba. This is where the Buddha Mahiawu was born. In the House of the Buddha[22] the walls are made of jade stone of every color. Every year, when the anniversary of the death of the Buddha comes around,[23] people from all the countries of the Dashi assemble here, when they vie with each other in bringing presents of gold, silver, jewels, and precious stones. Then also is the House adorned anew with silk brocade.

Farther off there is the tomb of the Buddha.[24] Continually by day and night there is at this place such a brilliant radiance that no one can approach it; he who does is blinded. Whoever in the hour of his death rubs his breast with dirt taken from this tomb will, so they say, be restored to life again by the power of the Buddha.

MULANPI[25]

The country of Mulanpi is to the west of the Dashi country. There is a great sea, and to the west of this sea there are countless countries, but Mulanpi is the one country which is visited by the big ships of the Dashi. Putting to sea from Dobandi[26] in the country of the Dashi, after sailing due west for a full hundred days, one reaches this country. A single one of these ships of theirs carries several thousand men,[27] and on board they have stores of wine and provisions, as well as weaving looms. If one speaks of big ships, there are none so big as those of Mulanpi.

The products of this country are extraordinary. The grains of wheat are three inches long, the melons six feet round, enough for a meal for

---

[11]A reference to Egypt's Nile Valley.
[12]This seems to refer to Basra, located in southern Iraq at the head of the Persian Gulf.
[13]A waxy substance that sperm whales expel and which is added to perfumes.
[14]A tree resin used for medicine and perfume.
[15]A laxative drug processed from the juice of African aloe plants.
[16]An aromatic resin that was used for perfume and incense and also as a mild narcotic.
[17]Another aromatic tree resin.
[18]Semiprecious gems.
[19]Tree burls, or knots, formed by parasites. They are highly prized by woodcarvers because of their interesting shapes.

[20]Beranang, on the western coast of the Malay Peninsula.
[21]The city of Mecca.
[22]The Kaaba (see source 47).
[23]The hajj (see source 50) is not specifically connected to the anniversary of the Prophet's death, but Islam reveres the Prophet's last sermon, made while on his final pilgrimage.
[24]In Medina.
[25]Southern Spain, which was part of the Almohad Empire of western North Africa from around 1147 until the empire's disintegration after 1223 due to a bitter war of succession.
[26]Damietta in Egypt.
[27]A gross exaggeration.

twenty or thirty men. The pomegranates weigh five catties,[28] lemons over twenty catties, salad greens weigh over ten catties and have leaves three or four feet long. Rice and wheat are kept in silos for ten years without spoiling. Among the native products are foreign sheep that are several feet high and have tails as big as a fan.[29] In the springtime they slit open their bellies and take out some ten catties of fat, after which they sew them up again, and the sheep live on; if the fat were not removed, the animal would swell up and die.[30]

If one travels by land [from Mulanpi] two hundred days' journey, the days are only six hours long.[31] In autumn if the west wind arises, men and beasts must at once drink to keep alive, and if they are not quick enough about it they die of thirst.

---

[28]A *catty* was 600 grams, or about one and one-third pounds.
[29]These would be Ethiopian broad-tailed sheep, which were not to be found in Spain.

[30]This fantastic story might be based on the southern Spanish custom of slaughtering pigs in the springtime by cutting them lengthwise in this manner.
[31]The short winter days of northern Europe.

A European View of the World
▼▼▼
79 ▼ *THE BOOK OF JOHN MANDEVILLE*

If Zhau Rugua's catalogue illustrates a well-informed Chinese bureaucrat's vision of the world, a curious work by an otherwise unknown person who claimed to be *Sir John Mandeville*, an English knight of St. Alban's, illustrates the Western European view of the same globe. First appearing in Europe around 1360, *The Book of John Mandeville* purported to be the firsthand account of this knight's trans-Eurasian adventures between 1322 and 1356/1357, in which he claimed to have served the sultan of Egypt and the Mongol khan of China. There is every reason to conclude that this work is a fictional tour de force by a gifted author who masked his identity behind an assumed name and a fabricated place of origin. The author's name will likely never be known, and evidence from the book's manuscripts suggests that whoever he was, he probably came from northern France, not England. As far as his purported travels are concerned, scholarly consensus is that most of his expeditions were to libraries, where he discovered quite a few travel books from which he borrowed liberally. For example, the outline of Sir John's travelogue describing his supposed journey to India and China is lifted from the travel account of the Franciscan missionary Odoric of Pordenone (see source 83). Mandeville amplified Friar Odoric's rather spare story by adding fables and tales from many other authors, by giving free rein to his own fertile imagination and sardonic wit, and by spicing his story with an impressive array of geographic and astronomical theories, many of them based on borrowed Arabic science.

No matter the book's questionable authenticity, Mandeville's book, written originally in French, was widely hand-copied (about 300 manuscripts survive) and circulated in ten European languages by 1400. Between the late 1470s and 1515, it was mass-printed in eight languages. It became late medieval Europe's most popular travelogue in an age noted for its fascination with world travel. Even if "Sir

John" did not travel to the regions he claimed to have visited, his work is historically important because it illustrates the manner in which Europeans of the fourteenth and fifteenth centuries viewed the lands and peoples beyond their frontiers. Indeed, in many ways Mandeville was instrumental in shaping that vision of the outside world on the eve of Europe's overseas explorations.

In the first selection, Sir John deals with the shape and size of the Earth. Most people today are unaware that the notion that medieval European scholars believed the world was flat is a modern myth created, tongue in cheek, by the American humorist and writer Washington Irving in the nineteenth century. In the second selection, Mandeville shares his putative firsthand knowledge of the wondrous land of *Prester John*, descendant of the *Magi*, or the Three Wise Kings from the East, who had visited the Christ Child. Prester John (John the priest), whose existence was firmly accepted in the West from the mid twelfth century onward, was the mythic priestly emperor of some supposedly lost Christian people. The Prester John myth was born partly out of rumors of actual distant Christian cultures — such as the Ethiopians of Africa, the Nestorians of Central and East Asia, and the Saint Thomas Christians of India's west coast — and partly out of a crusading zeal to discover Christian allies in the war against Islam. As a consequence, European adventurers as late as the sixteenth century sought Prester John in Asia and Africa.

QUESTIONS FOR ANALYSIS

1. What was Sir John's view of the physical world? Be specific.
2. What do Mandeville's stories suggest about his attitudes toward alien customs and the world beyond Europe?
3. Many societies cherish a myth of a promised redeemer, or hero-to-come. How had the Christian West created in the mythic Prester John a person who represented the fulfillment of some of their deepest wishes?
4. In what ways, if at all, does Sir John seem to use these stories to point out his own society's flaws?
5. Reread the tale of Sinbad the Sailor (source 60) and Zhau Rugua's description of southern Spain. Leaving details aside, can you discover any common themes shared by these accounts and Mandeville's stories? What do those common motifs suggest to you?

OF THE FOUL CUSTOMS FOLLOWED IN THE ISLE OF LAMORY[1] AND HOW THE EARTH AND SEA ARE OF ROUND SHAPE, PROVED BY MEANS OF THE STAR ANTARCTIC

From India people go by the ocean sea by way of many islands and different countries, which it would be tedious for me to relate. Fifty-two days' journey from that land there is another large country called Lamory. That land is extremely hot, so that the custom there is for men and women to walk about totally naked, and they scorn foreigners who wear clothes. They say that God created Adam and Eve naked, and no person, therefore, should be ashamed to appear as God made him, because nothing that comes from nature's bounty is foul. They also say that people who wear clothes are from another world, or else they are people who do not believe in God. They say that they believe in God who created the world and made Adam and Eve and everything else. Here they do not marry wives, since all the women are common to all men, and no woman forsakes any man. They say that it is sinful to refuse any man, for God so commanded it of Adam and Eve and all who followed when he said: "Increase and multiply and fill the Earth."[2] Therefore, no man in that country may say: "This is my wife." No woman may say: "This is my husband." When they bear children, the women present them to whatever man they wish of those with whom they have had sexual relations. So also all land is held in common. What one man holds one year, another has another year, and everyone takes that portion which he desires. Also all the produce of the soil is held in common. This is true for grains and other goods as well. Nothing is held in private, nothing is locked up, and every person there takes what he wants without anyone saying "no." Each is as rich as the other.

There is, however, in that country an evil custom. They eat human flesh more happily than any other meat, this despite the fact that the land abounds in meats, fish, grains, gold, silver, and every other commodity. Merchants go there, bringing with them children to sell to the people of that country, and they purchase the children. If they are plump, they eat them immediately. If they are lean, they feed them until they fatten up, and then they eat them. They say this is the best and sweetest flesh in all the world.

In that land, and in many others beyond it, no one can see the Transmontane Star, known as the Star of the Sea, which is immoveable and stands in the north and is called the Lode Star.[3] They see, rather, another star, its opposite, which stands in the south and is called the Antarctic Star. Just as sailors here get their bearings and steer by the Lode Star, so sailors beyond those parts steer by the southern star, which we cannot see. So our northern star, which we call the Lode Star, cannot be seen there. This is proof that the Earth and sea are round in shape and form. For portions of the heavens that are seen in one country do not appear in another. . . . I can prove that point by what I have observed, for I have been in parts of Brabant[4] and seen, by means of an astrolabe, that the Transmontane Star is 53 degrees in elevation. In Germany and Bohemia it is 58 degrees; and farther north it is 62 degrees and some minutes high. I personally have measured it with an astrolabe. Understand that opposite the Transmontane Star is the other known as the Antarctic Star, as I have said. These two stars never move, and around them all the heavens revolve, just like a wheel about an axle. So those two stars divide the heavens into two equal parts, with as much above [the equator] as below. . . .

I say with certainty that people can encircle the entire world, below the equator as well as above,[5] and return to their homelands, provided

---

[1]Sumatra, which the Chinese called *Lanli* (see source 78).
[2]The Bible, Genesis 1:22.
[3]Polaris, or the North Star, which guides mariners.
[4]A region between present-day Belgium and the Netherlands.

[5]Here Mandeville refutes a notion, accepted by classical Greco-Roman geographers, that the *antipodes*, or lands south of the equator, are uninhabitable due to their extreme heat.

they have good company, a ship, and health. And all along the way one would find people, lands, and islands. . . . For you know well that those people who live right under the Antarctic Star are directly underneath, feet against feet, of those who dwell directly under the Transmontane Star,[6] just as we and those who dwell under us[7] are feet to feet. For every part of the sea and the land has its opposite, which balances it, and it is both habitable and traversable. . . . So people who travel to India and the foreign isles girdle the roundness of the Earth and the seas, passing under our countries in this hemisphere.

Something I heard as a youth has occurred to me often. A worthy man from our country departed some time ago to see the world. And so he passed through India and the islands beyond India, which number more than 5,000.[8] He traveled so far by sea and land and had so girdled the globe over the period of so many seasons that he found an island where he heard his own language being spoken. . . . He marveled at this, not knowing what to make of it. I conclude he had traveled so far by land and sea that he had encircled the entire globe, circumnavigating to the very frontier of his homeland. Had he traveled only a bit farther, he would have come to his own home. But he turned back, returning along the route by which he had come. And so he spent a great deal of painful labor, as he acknowledged, when he returned home much later. For afterwards he went to Norway, where a storm carried him to an island. While on that island he discovered it was the island where earlier he had heard his own language spoken.[9] . . .

That could well be true, even though it might seem to simple-minded persons of no learning that people cannot travel on the underside of the

world without falling off toward the heavens. That, however, is not possible, unless it is true that we also are liable to fall toward Heaven from where we are on the Earth. For whatever part of the Earth people inhabit, above or below [the equator], it always seems to them that they are in a more proper position than any other folk. And so it is right that just as it seems to us that they are under us, so it seems to them that we are beneath them. For if a person could fall from the Earth into the heavens, it is more reasonable to assume that the Earth and sea, which are more vast and of greater weight, should fall into the heavens. But that is impossible. . . .

Although it is possible for a person to circumnavigate the world, nonetheless, out of a 1,000 persons, one might possibly return home. For, given the magnitude of the Earth and the sea, a 1,000 people could venture forth and follow a 1,000 different routes. This being so, no person could plot a perfect route toward the place from where he left. He could only reach it by accident or the grace of God. For the Earth is very large and is some 20,425 miles in circumference, according to the opinion of wise astronomers from the past, whose words I am not going to contradict, even though it seems to me, with my limited understanding and with all due respect, that it is larger.[10]

OF THE ROYAL ESTATE OF PRESTER JOHN

This emperor, Prester John, commands a very large region and has many noble cities and fair towns in his realm, as well as many islands large and broad. For this land of India is divided into islands due to the great rivers that flow out of

[6]In other words, the South Pole is 180 degrees south of (or under) the North Pole.
[7]The place directly opposite on the globe.
[8]The islands of Southeast Asia.
[9]This story, especially in light of the passage that follows, seems to claim that the Englishman traveled south to India

and the islands of Southeast Asia and then continued south across the South Pole and up the far side of the globe across the North Pole to Scandinavia, and then he returned home by retracing his steps.
[10]Actually, it is closer to 25,000 miles.

Paradise, dividing the land into many parts.[11] He also has many islands in the sea. . . . This Prester John has many kings and islands and many different peoples of various cultures subject to him. And this land is fertile and wealthy, but not as wealthy as the land of the Great Khan. For merchants do not as commonly travel there to purchase merchandise as they do to the land of the Great Khan, for it is too far to travel to. Moreover, people can find in that other region, the Island of Cathay, every manner of commodity that people need — gold cloth, silk, spices, and every sort of precious item. Consequently, even though commodities are less expensive in Prester John's island, nonetheless people dread the long voyage and the great sea-perils in that region. . . . Although one must travel by sea and land eleven or twelve months from Genoa or Venice before arriving in Cathay, the land of Prester John lies many more days of dreadful journey away. . . .

The Emperor Prester John always marries the daughter of the Great Khan, and the Great Khan likewise marries Prester John's daughter.[12] For they are the two greatest lords under Heaven.

In Prester John's land there are many different things and many precious gems of such magnitude that people make vessels, such as platters, dishes, and cups, out of them. There are many other marvels there, so many, in fact, that it would be tiresome and too lengthy to put them down in a book . . . but I shall tell you some part.

This Emperor Prester John is Christian, as is a great part of his country as well. Yet they do not share all the articles of our faith. They believe fully in God, in the Son, and in the Holy Spirit. They are quite devout and faithful to one another, and they do not quarrel or practice fraud and deceit.

He has subject to him 72 provinces, and in every province there is a king. And these kings have kings under them, and all are tributaries to Prester John. And he has in his lordships many marvels. In his country is a sea that people call the Gravelly Sea.[13] It is all gravel and sand, without a drop of water, and it ebbs and flows in great waves, as other seas do, and never rests at any time. No one can cross that sea by ship or any other craft and, therefore, no one knows what land lies beyond that sea. Although it has no water, people find in it and on its banks plenty of good fish of a shape and size such as are found nowhere else, but they are tasty and delicious to eat. Three days journey from that sea are great mountains, out of which flows a great river that originates in Paradise. And it is full of precious stones, without a drop of water. . . . Beyond that river, rising toward the deserts, is a great gravel plain set between the mountains. On that plain everyday at sunrise small trees begin to grow, and they grow until mid-day, bearing fruit. No one dares, however, to eat the fruit, for it is like a deceptive phantom. After mid-day the trees decrease and reenter the Earth, so that by sunset they are no longer to be seen. And they do this every day. And that is a great marvel. In that desert are many wild people who are hideous to look at, for they are horned and do not speak but only grunt like pigs. . . .

When Emperor Prester John goes into battle against any other lord, he has no banners borne before him. Rather, he has three crosses of fine gold, which are massive and very tall and encrusted with precious stones. Each cross is set in a richly adorned chariot. To guard each cross, there is a detail of 10,000 mounted men at arms and 100,000 men on foot, . . . and this number is in addition to the main body of troops. . . . When he rides out in peace time with a private

---

[11]According to Mandeville, the *Terrestrial Paradise*, from which Adam and Eve had been expelled, lies far to the east of Prester John's country; four rivers — the Ganges, Nile, Tigris, and Euphrates — flow out of that paradise and divide the major lands of the Earth.

[12]This particular version of the Prester John myth seems to be a somewhat distorted reflection of the fact that many Mongol khans had Nestorian Christian wives.

[13]Apparently a garbled reference to the Gobi (Gravel) Desert of Central Asia.

entourage, he has borne before him only one wooden cross, unpainted and lacking gold, silver, or gems, as a remembrance that Jesus Christ suffered death on a wooden cross.[14] He also has borne before him a golden platter filled with earth, in token of the fact that his nobility, might, and flesh will all turn to earth. He also has borne before him a silver vessel full of great nuggets of gold and precious gems, as a token of his lordship, nobility, and might.

---

[14]Keep in mind that *crusade* means "to bear a cross." During the 1350s the Ottoman Turks were advancing in the Balkans and putting increasing pressure on Constantinople. Western European efforts to launch crusades to counter this menace in southeastern Europe and to save Byzantium were proving ineffective.

A Korean View of the World

▼▼▼

80 ▼ *THE KANGNIDO*

The most noteworthy world map from the period immediately preceding the European discovery of the Americas comes from Korea. Titled *Map of Integrated Regions and Terrains and of Historical Countries and Capitals*, but known more popularly as the *Kangnido*, the map was produced in 1402, early in the era of the Yi Dynasty (1392–1910), an age of vigorous cultural renewal. The cartographers who created this masterpiece borrowed freely from Chinese, Islamic, and Japanese maps to fashion an integrated map that included almost every known area of the world. Once one has become accustomed to the map's eccentricities, the modern viewer is astounded by its high degree of accuracy. To be sure, Japan is located directly south of Korea and farther away than it actually is. This might well represent a statement of supremacy over an age-old enemy by the Yi court. Also the image of Europe leaves much to be desired, but the fact remains that Europe is on the map!

The *Kangnido* was copied many times, so prominent was it to the Yi self-image and program of reform and regeneration. Although the original map is now lost, later-fifteenth-century copies are extant. The map that appears here dates from around 1470.

QUESTIONS FOR ANALYSIS

1. Locate Korea. What does its size relative to China and Japan suggest?
2. Where does the center of the map lie? What does that suggest to you?
3. What have the mapmakers done with China, India, and mainland Southeast Asia? What do you infer from this?
4. Locate the Arabian Peninsula and Africa. What strikes you as particularly significant about these two features? In answering this question, address their relative sizes and also the shape of Africa.
5. Locate Europe. Which areas are most recognizable? Which are most vague? What do your answers to these two questions suggest about the sources the Korean cartographers used for the Far West?

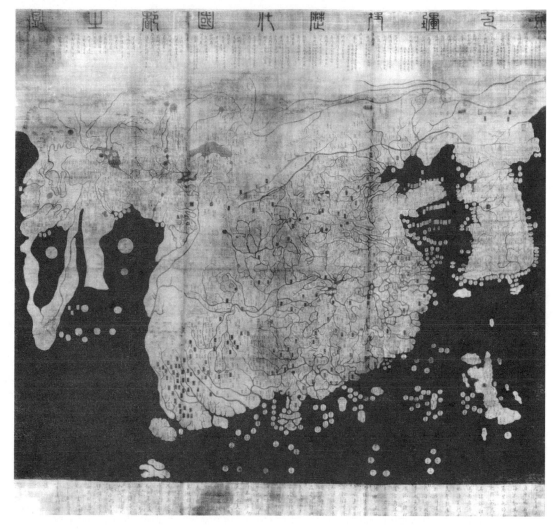

The Kangnido

Travel in the Age of the *Pax Mongolica*

Temujin (1167?–1227), the Mongol lord who assumed the title *Chinggis* (Genghis) *Khan* (Resolute Ruler) in 1206, believed he had a destiny to rule the world. He and his immediate successors, particularly his grandson *Khubilai* (1214–1294), actually came close to controlling all of Eurasia. Although the Mongols were stopped in Syria, in Southeast Asia, at the borders of India and Arabia, in Eastern Europe, and in the waters off Japan, by 1279 they had still managed to create the largest land empire in history.

Beginning around the time of the rule of Khubilai Khan (r. 1260–1294) and extending for more than half a century after his death, the Mongols ruled over their enormous empire in relative peace and good order. Mongol discipline and organization made it possible to travel between Europe and China with a fair degree of safety and speed, and large numbers of merchants, ambassadors, fortune seekers, missionaries, and other travelers journeyed in all directions across the Mongol Empire. This steppe landbridge between East Asia and Western Europe was severed after 1350, however, as the Mongol Empire broke up, and the opportunity for normal direct contact between the eastern and western extremities of Eurasia was lost for a century and a half.

The following four sources trace the Mongol Era and its travelers from the mid thirteenth century to the eve of the breakup of the Mongol Empire and the renewed fragmentation of the Silk Road.

Traveling Among the Mongols
▼▼▼

81 ▾ *William of Rubruck,*
JOURNEY TO THE LAND OF THE TARTARS

When the Mongols overran large portions of Christian Eastern Europe in a campaign that lasted from 1236 to 1242, the Latin West was forced to confront this new menace from the East. Fortunately for the West, the Mongols withdrew back to the Volga in 1242 due to the death of the Great Khan and the succession struggle that followed. This withdrawal took place, however, only after they destroyed a combined Polish and German army and, one day later, a Hungarian army.

Tales of horrendous atrocities convinced Western Europeans that these "Devil's horsemen" (see note 1) were demonic forces of the Antichrist who foreshadowed the Final Days as foretold in the Bible. In response, Pope Gregory IX called a crusade against the Mongols in 1241, and his successor, Pope Innocent IV, renewed it in 1243, but both were empty gestures. Most rulers in Western Europe were too caught up in struggles closer to home to rouse themselves against a foe that had retreated in 1242.

If a crusade was not an option, perhaps diplomacy was. Pope Innocent IV and King Louis IX of France dispatched a series of legations to the Khan of khans in Mongolia. The aim of the missions was threefold: to discover Mongol intentions; to convert these "enemies of God and friends of the Devil" to Christianity; and to enlist them in the West's crusade endeavors against Islam. These missions, which began in 1245 and lasted down to 1255, were conducted mainly by Franciscan friars, members of the religious order founded by Francis of Assisi in the early thirteenth century, and were met with Mongol indifference. To the Mongol mind, the West had only one option: submission.

The first mission, which left Europe in 1245 and returned late in 1247, failed to reach any accord with the Mongols but did produce an account of Mongol culture and battle tactics by the legation's leader, Brother John of Plano Carpini. A second, even more detailed account of Mongol life and customs resulted from another embassy to the Great Khan. Between May 1253 and June 1255, two Franciscan ambassadors, William of Rubruck and Bartholomew of Cremona, traveled from Constantinople to the court of Mongke Khan (r. 1251–1259) at *Karakorum* in Mongolia and returned to the eastern Mediterranean. The mission failed to convert the Great Khan, but Brother William of Rubruck's report of their adventures and his observations made the trip worthwhile (at least from our perspective). An observant individual, Brother William provides us with an exceptional account of mid-thirteenth-century Mongol society.

QUESTIONS FOR ANALYSIS

1. Many people think of nomads as wanderers who aimlessly travel about with their herds. What evidence does Rubruck provide to refute this misconception?
2. At this early date, some Mongol lords flirted with Buddhism, Daoism, and Islam, and several Mongol tribes professed Nestorian Christianity. Most, however, followed none of these faiths. Describe and categorize the Mongols' religious practices as reported by Rubruck.
3. How would you characterize the status of women relative to men? In addressing this issue, consider the respective tasks of women and men and Mongol marriage customs.
4. On the basis of this account, how would you characterize Mongol society in the mid thirteenth century?
5. Some commentators have argued that Rubruck displays a certain sensitivity toward and even sympathy for the Mongols he encountered. Based on these selections, do you agree or disagree? Please be specific in supporting your conclusion.

THE TARTARS[1] AND THEIR DWELLINGS

The Tartars have no abiding city. . . . Each captain, according to whether he has more or fewer men under him, knows the limits of his pasturage and where to feed his flocks in winter, summer, spring, and autumn, for in winter they come down to the warmer districts in the south, in summer they go up to the cooler ones in the north. They drive their cattle to graze on the pasture lands without water in winter when there is snow there, for the snow provides them with water.

The dwelling in which they sleep has as its base a circle of interlaced sticks, and it is made of the same material; these sticks converge into a little circle at the top and from this a neck juts up like a chimney; they cover it with white felt and quite often they also coat the felt with lime or white clay and powdered bone to make it a more gleaming white, and sometimes they make it black. The felt round the neck at the top they decorate with lovely and varied paintings. Before the doorway they also hang felt worked in multi-colored designs; they sew colored felt onto the other, making vines and trees, birds, and

[1]Westerners mistakenly called the Mongols *Tartars*, a corruption of *Tatars*, the name of a tribe of Turkic nomads who dwelled near the Mongols. Tartar seems to have been a deliberate pun. The classical Latin name for hell was *Tartarus*; hence, the Mongols were the "Devil's horsemen."

animals. They make these houses so large that sometimes they are thirty feet across. . . .

In addition they make squares to the size of a large coffer out of slender split twigs; then over it, from one end to the other, they build up a rounded roof out of similar twigs and they make a little entrance at the front end; after that they cover this box or little house with black felt soaked in tallow or ewes' milk so that it is rainproof, and this they decorate in the same way with multicolored handwork. Into these chests they put all their bedding and valuables; they bind them onto high carts which are drawn by camels so that they can cross rivers. These chests are never removed from the carts. When they take down their dwelling houses, they always put the door facing the south. . . .

The married women make for themselves really beautiful carts which I would not know how to describe for you except by a picture; in fact I would have done you paintings of everything if I only knew how to paint. A wealthy Mongol or Tartar may well have a hundred or two hundred such carts with chests. Baatu[2] has twenty-six wives and each of these has a large house, not counting the other small ones which are placed behind the large one and which are, as it were, chambers in which their attendants live; belonging to each of these houses are a good two hundred carts. When they pitch their houses the chief wife places her dwelling at the extreme west end and after her the others according to their rank, so that the last wife will be at the far east end, and there will be the space of a stone's throw between the establishment of one wife and that of another. And so the orda[3] of a rich Mongol will look like a large town and yet there will be very few men in it.

One woman will drive twenty or thirty carts, for the country is flat. They tie together the carts, which are drawn by oxen or camels, one after the other, and the woman will sit on the front one driving the ox while all the others follow in step. If they happen to come on a bad bit of track they loose them and lead them across it one by one. They go at a very slow pace, as a sheep or an ox might walk.

When they have pitched their houses with the door facing south, they arrange the master's couch at the northern end. The women's place is always on the east side, that is, on the left of the master of the house when he is sitting on his couch looking toward the south; the men's place is on the west side, that is, to his right.

On entering a house the men would by no means hang up their quiver in the women's section. Over the head of the master there is always an idol like a doll or little image of felt which they call the master's brother, and a similar one over the head of the mistress, and this they call the mistress's brother; they are fastened on to the wall. Higher up between these two is a thin little one which is, as it were, the guardian of the whole house. The mistress of the house places on her right side, at the foot of the couch, in a prominent position, a goatskin stuffed with wool or other material, and next to it a tiny image turned toward her attendants and the women. By the entrance on the women's side is still another idol with a cow's udder for the women who milk the cows, for this is the women's job. On the other side of the door toward the men is another image with a mare's udder for the men who milk the mares.

When they have foregathered for a drink they first sprinkle with the drink the idol over the master's head, then all the other idols in turn; after this an attendant goes out of the house with a cup and some drinks; he sprinkles thrice toward the south, genuflecting each time; this is in honor of fire; next toward the east in honor of the air, and after that to the west in honor of water; they cast it to the north for the dead. When the master is holding his cup in his hand

[2]Baatu or Batu (d. 1255/1256), grandson of Chinggis Khan and founder of the Golden Horde, the group of Mongols that conquered and ruled Russia.

[3]*Orda* is a Turkic word meaning "camp," from which we derive the word *horde*.

and is about to drink, before he does so he first pours some out on the Earth as its share. If he drinks while seated on a horse, before he drinks he pours some over the neck or mane of the horse. And so when the attendant has sprinkled toward the four quarters of the Earth he returns into the house; two servants with two cups and as many plates are ready to carry the drink to the master and the wife sitting beside him upon his couch. If he has several wives, she with whom he sleeps at night sits next to him during the day, and on that day all the others have to come to her dwelling to drink, and the court is held there, and the gifts which are presented to the master are placed in the treasury of that wife. Standing in the entrance is a bench with a skin of milk or some other drink and some cups.

In the winter they make an excellent drink from rice, millet, wheat, and honey, which is clear like wine. Wine, too, is conveyed to them from distant regions. In the summer they do not bother about anything except cosmos.[4] Cosmos is always to be found inside the house before the entrance door, and near it stands a musician with his instrument. Our lutes and viols I did not see there but many other instruments such as are not known among us. When the master begins to drink, then one of the attendants cries out in a loud voice "Ha!" and the musician strikes his instrument. And when it is a big feast they are holding, they all clap their hands and also dance to the sound of the instrument, the men before the master and the women before the mistress. After the master has drunk, then the attendant cries out as before and the instrument-player breaks off. Then they drink all round, the men and the women, and sometimes vie with each other in drinking in a really disgusting and gluttonous manner. . . .

---

[4]More correctly *qumiz*, the Mongols' favorite alcoholic drink, which they derived from mare's milk.

THE FOOD OF THE TARTARS

As for their food and victuals I must tell you they eat all dead animals indiscriminately and with so many flocks and herds you can be sure a great many animals do die. However, in the summer as long as they have any cosmos, that is mare's milk, they do not care about any other food. If during that time an ox or a horse happens to die, they dry the flesh by cutting it into thin strips and hanging it in the sun and the wind, and it dries immediately without salt and without any unpleasant smell. Out of the intestines of horses they make sausages which are better than pork sausages and they eat these fresh; the rest of the meat they keep for the winter. From the hide of oxen they make large jars which they dry in a wonderful way in the smoke. From the hind part of horses' hide they make very nice shoes.

They feed fifty or a hundred men with the flesh of a single sheep, for they cut it up in little bits in a dish with salt and water, making no other sauce; then with the point of a knife or a fork especially made for this purpose — like those with which we are accustomed to eat pears and apples cooked in wine — they offer to each of those standing round one or two mouthfuls, according to the number of guests. Before the flesh of the sheep is served, the master first takes what pleases him; and also if he gives anyone a special portion then the one receiving it has to eat it himself and may give it to no one else. But if he cannot eat it all he may take it away with him or give it to his servant, if he is there, to keep for him; otherwise he may put it away in his *captargac*, that is, a square bag which they carry to put all such things in: in this they also keep bones when they have not the time to give them a good gnaw, so that later they may gnaw them and no food be wasted

THE DUTIES OF THE WOMEN AND THEIR WORK

It is the duty of the women to drive the carts, to load the houses onto them and to unload them, to milk the cows, to make the butter and *grut*,[5] to dress the skins and to sew them, which they do with thread made out of tendons. They split the tendons into very thin threads and then twist these into one long thread. They also sew shoes and socks and other garments. They never wash their clothes, for they say that that makes God angry and that it would thunder if they hung them out to dry; they even beat those who do wash them and take them away from them. . . . They never wash their dishes, but when the meat is cooked, they wash out the bowl in which they are going to put it with some boiling broth from the cauldron which they afterwards pour back. The women also make the felt and cover the houses.

The men make bows and arrows, manufacture stirrups and bits and make saddles; they build the houses and carts, they look after the horses and milk the mares, churn the cosmos, that is the mares' milk, and make the skins in which it is kept, and they also look after the camels and load them. Both sexes look after the sheep and goats, and sometimes the men, sometimes the women, milk them. They dress skins with the sour milk of ewes, thickened and salted. . . .

As for their marriages, you must know that no one there has a wife unless he buys her, which means that sometimes girls are quite grown up before they marry, for their parents always keep them until they sell them. They observe the first and second degrees of consanguinity,[6] but observe no degrees of affinity;[7] they have two sisters at the same time or one after the other. No widow among them marries, the reason being that they believe that all those who serve them in this life will serve them in the next, and so of a widow they believe that she will always return after death to her first husband. This gives rise to a shameful custom among them whereby a son sometimes takes to wife all his father's wives, except his own mother; for the orda of a father and mother always falls to the youngest son[8] and so he himself has to provide for all his father's wives who come to him with his father's effects; and then, if he so wishes, he uses them as wives, for he does not consider an injury has been done to him if they return to his father after death.

And so when anyone has made an agreement with another to take his daughter, the father of the girl arranges a feast and she takes flight to relations where she lies hid. Then the father declares: "Now my daughter is yours; take her wherever you find her." Then he searches for her with his friends until he finds her; then he has to take her by force and bring her, as though by violence, to his house.

---

[5]A sour curd cheese.
[6]Siblings and first cousins are prohibited from marrying one another.

[7]One may wed any relative by marriage, such as a sister-in-law.
[8]The youngest son of his chief wife.

Traveling the Silk Road
▼▼▼

82 ▼ *Marco Polo, DESCRIPTION OF THE WORLD*

No chapter on trans-Eurasian travel in the Mongol Age would be complete without a selection from Marco Polo (ca. 1253–1324), a Venetian who spent twenty years in East Asia. A few scholars have questioned whether Marco Polo ever went to China, and some have even wondered whether he ever existed. Their conclusions, largely built on arguments from silence, in which they point to what Polo's account does not mention and to the absence of his name in all known Chinese records, have failed to win support within the academic community. As the issue currently stands, there is no good reason to doubt the basic historicity of Marco Polo's account of his years in China, even though the story, as we have received it, contains undoubted exaggeration and human error — error that was compounded by the manner in which Polo's story was transmitted to posterity.

Around 1260 Marco's father and uncle, Niccolò and Maffeo, both merchants from Venice, set sail for the Black Sea and from there made an overland trek to the court of Khubilai. When they were preparing to return home, the Great Khan requested that they visit the pope and ask him to send 100 missionary-scholars to Cathay (northern China). The Polos arrived at the crusader port of Acre (in present-day Israel) in 1269. In 1271 Pope Gregory X (r. 1271–1276), who had been elected pope while serving in Acre, commissioned them to return to China with two Dominican friars. The two friars, afraid of the dangers that awaited them, quickly abandoned the expedition, but Niccolò's seventeen-year-old son, Marco, was made of sterner stuff. The brothers Polo, now accompanied by young Marco, began the long trek back to northern China and the court of Khubilai, arriving there in 1274 or 1275. Here apparently Marco entered the service of the Great Khan, but we do not know what offices he held. Whatever Polo's position, it is clear that for close to two decades he traveled extensively over much of Khubilai's empire, and he probably functioned, at least occasionally, as one of the many foreign officials serving the Mongol, or *Yuan*, Dynasty (1264–1368).

In 1290 or 1292 the three men set sail for Europe by way of the Indian Ocean and arrived home in Venice in 1295. In 1298 Marco was captured in a war with Genoa and, while in custody, related his adventures to a writer of romances known as Rustichello of Pisa. Together they produced a rambling, often disjointed account of the sites, peoples, personalities, and events Marco had encountered in Asia.

Despite its literary flaws and a self-puffery that was obvious even to fourteenth-century contemporaries, the book was widely translated and distributed throughout late medieval Europe. Its popularity was due in part to Marco's eye for detail, as the book abounds with stories and descriptions of phenomena that Westerners found fascinatingly different.

In the following selection, Polo describes his journey to Cathay along the portion of the Silk Road that skirts the southern fringes of the forbidding *Taklamakan Desert*. The term *Silk Road* conjures up every sort of romantic notion in modern readers, but for the men and women who journeyed along its many routes it was anything but romantic, even though towns along the way offered pleasures and even exotic experiences. The fact that it took the Polos about three and a half years to travel from Acre to Shangdu, the summer palace of the Great Khan, suggests how arduous and dangerous the journey was.

QUESTIONS FOR ANALYSIS

1. What were the dangers for travelers along this portion of the Silk Road?
2. Despite the dangers, what made the journey possible and even bearable?

3. Why did people inhabit towns and cities along this route?
4. What dangers did these urban people encounter?
5. What impact did the Mongols have on this part of the Silk Road?

Let us turn next to the province of Yarkand,[1] five days' journey in extent. The inhabitants follow the law of Mahomet,[2] and there are also some Nestorian Christians.[3] They are subject to the Great Khan's nephew,[4] of whom I have already spoken. It is amply stocked with the means of life, especially cotton. But, since there is nothing here worth mentioning in our book, we shall pass on to Khotan,[5] which lies towards the east-northeast.

Khotan is a province eight days' journey in extent, which is subject to the Great Khan. The inhabitants all worship Mahomet.[6] It has cities and towns in plenty, of which the most splendid, and the capital of the kingdom, bears the same name as the province, Khotan. It is amply stocked with the means of life. Cotton grows here in plenty. It has vineyards, estates, and orchards in plenty. The people live by trade and industry; they are not at all warlike.

Passing on from here we come to the province of Pem, five days' journey in extent, towards the east-north-east. Here too the inhabitants worship Mahomet and are subject to the Great Khan. It has villages and towns in plenty. The most splendid city and the capital of the province is called Pem. There are rivers here in which are found stones called jasper and chalcedony[7] in plenty. There is no lack of the means

of life. Cotton is plentiful. The inhabitants live by trade and industry.

The following custom is prevalent among them. When a woman's husband leaves her to go on a journey of more than twenty days, then, as soon as he has left, she takes another husband, and this she is fully entitled to do by local usage. And the men, wherever they go, take wives in the same way.

You should know that all the provinces I have described, from Kashgar[8] to Pem and some way beyond, are provinces of Turkestan.[9]

I will tell you next of another province of Turkestan, lying east-north-east, which is called Charchan. It used to be a splendid and fruitful country, but it has been much devastated by the Tartars.[10] The inhabitants worship Mahomet. There are villages and towns in plenty, and the chief city of the kingdom is Charchan.[11] There are rivers producing jasper and chalcedony, which are exported for sale in Cathay and bring in a good profit; for they are plentiful and of good quality.

All this province is a tract of sand; and so is the country from Khotan to Pem and from Pem to here. There are many springs of bad and bitter water, though in some places the water is good and sweet. When it happens that an army passes through the country, if it is a hostile one, the

---

[1]Yarkand is on the southwestern border of the *Taklamakan Desert*, which is located in the *Tarim Basin*. The Taklamakan, whose name means "those who enter never return," cannot support human life. Travelers must decide whether to take the fork that skirts the northern edge of this 600-mile-long wilderness of sand (the Northern Tarim Route) or the southern fork (the Southern Tarim Route). Yarkand is the first major city on the Southern Tarim Route for those traveling from the west.
[2]Muhammad.
[3]Various Turkish and Mongolian tribes had adopted this form of Christianity.
[4]Kaidu.

[5]The next major city along this route.
[6]Many Western Christians thought *Mahomet* was a god whom Muslims worshiped. Centuries earlier, Khotan had been a Buddhist kingdom.
[7]Two highly valued quartz crystals.
[8]Kashgar, on the extreme western end of the Taklamakan, is where the northern and southern forks branch, for those traveling from the west.
[9]The region of Central Asia inhabited by Turkic peoples.
[10]Mongols, not Tatars. See source 81, note 1.
[11]Known to the Chinese as Shanshan, it was the next significant city along the Southern Tarim Route.

people take flight with their wives and children and their beasts two or three days' journey into the sandy wastes to places where they know that there is water and they can live with their beasts. And I assure you that no one can tell which way they have gone, because the wind covers their tracks with sand, so that there is nothing to show where they have been, but the country looks as if it had never been traversed by man or beast. That is how they escape from their enemies. But, if it happens that a friendly army passes that way, they merely drive off their beasts, because they do not want to have them seized and eaten; for the armies never pay for what they take. And you should know that, when they harvest their grain, they store it far from any habitation, in certain caves among these wastes, for fear of the armies; and from these stores they bring home what they need month by month.

After leaving Charchan, the road runs for fully five days through sandy wastes, where the water is bad and bitter, except in a few places where it is good and sweet; and there is nothing worth noting in our book. At the end of the five days' journey towards the east-north-east, is a city which stands on the verge of the Great Desert. It is here that men take in provisions for crossing the desert. Let us move on accordingly and proceed with our narrative.

The city I have mentioned, which stands at the point where the traveler enters the Great Desert, is a big city called Lop, and the desert is called the Desert of Lop.[12] The city is subject to the Great Khan, and the inhabitants worship Mahomet. I can tell you that travelers who intend to cross the desert rest in this town for a week to refresh themselves and their beasts. At the end of the week they stock up with a month's provisions for themselves and their beasts. Then they leave the town and enter the desert.

This desert is reported to be so long that it would take a year to go from end to end; and at the narrowest point it takes a month to cross it. It consists entirely of mountains and sand and valleys. There is nothing at all to eat. But I can tell you that after traveling a day and a night you find drinking water[13] — not enough water to supply a large company, but enough for fifty or a hundred men with their beasts. And all the way through the desert you must go for a day and a night before you find water. And I can tell you that in three or four places you find the water bitter and brackish; but at all the other watering-places, that is, twenty-eight in all, the water is good. Beasts and birds there are none, because they find nothing to eat. But I assure you that one thing is found here, and that a very strange one, which I will relate to you.

The truth is this. When a man is riding by night through this desert and something happens to make him loiter and lose touch with his companions, by dropping asleep or for some other reason, and afterwards he wants to rejoin them, then he hears spirits talking in such a way that they seem to be his companions. Sometimes, indeed, they even hail him by name. Often these voices make him stray from the path, so that he never finds it again. And in this way many travelers have been lost and have perished. And sometimes in the night they are conscious of a noise like the clatter of a great cavalcade of riders away from the road; and, believing that these are some of their own company, they go where they hear the noise and, when day breaks, find they are victims of an illusion and in an awkward plight. And there are some who, in crossing this desert, have seen a host of men coming towards them and, suspecting that they were robbers, have taken flight; so, having left the beaten track and not knowing how to return to it, they have gone hopelessly astray. Yes, and even by daylight men hear these

---

[12]On the eastern edge of the Taklamakan Desert is a salt-encrusted plain of hard-baked clay known as the Lop Nor (the Salt Sea) — the dried bed of an ancient sea.

[13]Streams from distant mountains, which long ago made this a great inland salt sea, create oases.

spirit voices, and often you fancy you are listening to the strains of many instruments, especially drums, and the clash of arms. For this
reason bands of travelers make a point of keeping very close together. Before they go to sleep
they set up a sign pointing in the direction in
which they have to travel. And round the necks
of all their beasts they fasten little bells, so that
by listening to the sound they may prevent them
from straying off the path.

That is how they cross the desert, with all the
discomfort of which you have heard. . . .

▾▾▾

Now I will tell you of some other cities, which
lie towards the north-west near the edge of this
desert.[14]

The province of Kamul, which used to be a
kingdom, contains towns and villages in plenty,
the chief town being also called Kamul.[15] The
province lies between two deserts, the Great
Desert and a small one three days' journey in extent.[16] The inhabitants are all idolaters[17] and
speak a language of their own. They live on the
produce of the soil; for they have a superfluity of
foodstuffs and beverages, which they sell to travelers who pass that way. They are a very gay folk,
who give no thought to anything but making
music, singing and dancing, and reading and
writing according to their own usage, and taking great delight in the pleasures of the body. I
give you my word that if a stranger comes to a
house here to seek hospitality he receives a very
warm welcome. The host bids his wife do every-

thing that the guest wishes. Then he leaves the
house and goes about his own business and stays
away two or three days. Meanwhile the guest
stays with his wife in the house and does what he
will with her, lying with her in one bed just as if
she were his own wife; and they lead a gay life
together. All the men of this city and province
are thus cuckolded by their wives; but they are
not the least ashamed of it. And the women are
beautiful and vivacious and always ready to
oblige.

Now it happened during the reign of Mongu
Khan,[18] lord of the Tartars, that he was informed
of this custom that prevailed among the men of
Kamul of giving their wives in adultery to outsiders. Mongu thereupon commanded them
under heavy penalties to desist from this form of
hospitality. When they received this command,
they were greatly distressed; but for three years
they reluctantly obeyed. Then they held a council and talked the matter over, and this is what
they did. They took a rich gift and sent it to
Mongu and entreated him to let them use their
wives according to the traditions of their ancestors; for their ancestors had declared that by the
pleasure they gave to guests with their wives and
goods they won the favor of their idols and multiplied the yield of their crops and their tillage.
When Mongu Khan heard this he said: "Since
you desire your own shame, you may have it." So
he let them have their way. And I can assure you
that since then they have always upheld this tradition and uphold it still.

[14]Polo now shifts to the Northern Tarim Route. He does not
claim that Kamul and the other cities that he describes in
this aside were on his route eastward. Indeed, the whole
tone of this section suggests he heard about these sites during his stay in China.
[15]The present-day city of Hami.
[16]This smaller desert has to be the edge of the Gobi Desert,
which is not a small desert and is not crossed in three days.
[17]Buddhists.
[18]Khubilai's older brother and Great Khan from 1251 to
1259.

A European Visitor to China

▼▼▼

83 ▼ *Odoric of Pordenone, REPORT*

After their defeat at the Battle of Ayn Jalut in 1260 at the hands of the Mamluks of Egypt, the Mongols reached a stalemate with Islam in Southwest Asia. Faced with this reality, the Mongol *il-khans* (subordinate khans) of Persia were now willing to discuss an alliance with the Christian West against the Mamluks, who controlled Egypt and Syria and were systematically dismantling the last of the crusader states. On its part, because of the crisis facing the crusader states in the Holy Land, the West was more than willing to make common cause with the Mongols.

In 1287 *Arghun*, il-khan of Persia (r. 1284–1291), a nephew of the Great Khan Khubilai, sent a Nestorian Christian monk, *Rabban* (Master) *Sauma*, to the West bearing letters for the pope, the kings of France and England, and the emperor of Constantinople, in which the Mongol prince offered to become a Christian in return for an alliance against the Mamluks.

In response to Rabban Sauma's appearance in Rome in 1289, Pope Nicholas IV dispatched a Franciscan friar, *John of Monte Corvino* (1247–ca. 1328), to the Mongols with letters for Arghun and other khans farther to the east, including the Khan of khans, Khubilai. In 1291 John was in Tauris (present-day Tabriz), Arghun's capital, but the il-khan died in March of that year, and his successor was on the verge of embracing Islam. Moreover, between May and July of the same year the last crusader strongholds in the Holy Land fell to Islamic forces. With nothing further to be accomplished in Persia, John set out for the court of the Great Khan in China. Due to delays, John arrived at the Mongol capital of *Khanbalik* (present-day Beijing) in 1294/1295, around or just after Khubilai's death. Making the best of his situation, John remained in China as a missionary, and in time he was joined by other Franciscans.

One of those assistants was Friar *Odoric of Pordenone* (ca. 1265–1331), who departed for the Far East in 1322. Brother Odoric, who had already served as a missionary in southern Russia for more than a decade and in Persia for eight years, sailed from the Persian Gulf to India, and from India sailed to the port of Guangzhou (Canton), arriving there around 1323–1324. For several years he served in China, where he assisted the aged Archbishop John of Monte Corvino, but departed for home before John's death (ca. 1328). Odoric's overland journey home finally got him to Venice in 1329. Soon thereafter he fell ill but managed to dictate his travel adventures in May 1330. He died on January 14, 1331.

Friar Odoric was not the first or the last medieval Catholic missionary to work in China. The mission probably survived, but barely so, the collapse of Mongol authority in China in 1368. It might well have limped along until around 1400. Although several missionaries communicated with the West through letters sent back by Italian merchants and other travelers, Odoric's *Report* is, by far, the best and most detailed account by any Western missionary in China at this time. Its excellence, in fact, attracted the plagiarizing eyes of John Mandeville (see source 79). In the following excerpts, Odoric describes Hangzhou, the former capital of the Southern Song Dynasty; the Great Khan's palace complex of *Dadu*; and his imperial court.

QUESTIONS FOR ANALYSIS

1. Does Friar Odoric's account seem to reach the level of unbelievable hyperbole at any point? Which parts of this account seem to be sober reporting of fact? Based on your answers to these questions, what is your overall evaluation of this source's worth?

2. How do we infer from this source that Marco Polo and Brother Odoric were only two of many Western Europeans who visited China in the late thirteenth and early fourteenth centuries?

3. Based on what Odoric tells us about Dadu and about the composition and character of the Great Khan's court, how would you characterize Mongol rule in China in the early fourteenth century?

4. Compare the picture that this source gives us of the Mongol court with the image of Mongol life that emerges from William of Rubruck's account (source 81). What has changed? To what do you ascribe those changes?

CONCERNING CANSAY, THE GREATEST CITY IN THE WORLD

I came to the city of Cansay,[1] which means "City of Heaven." This is the greatest city in the world and a good 100 miles in circumference. Within it there is not a square yard[2] of earth that is not heavily populated. Quite often one can find a residence that contains fully ten or twelve households. This city also has huge suburbs that contain a population larger than that of the city itself. The city has twelve principal gates, and extending out from each of these gates, for a distance of almost eight miles, are cities larger than Venice or Padua, so that one might journey six or seven days through one of these suburbs and it would seem as though he had traveled but a short distance.

This city is located on lagoons of standing and static water, like the city of Venice. It also has more than 12,000 bridges, on which are sta-

tioned guards who watch over this city for the Great Khan. Alongside the city flows a single river. Because the city is so situated, it finds itself in the same situation as Ferrara. That is, it is longer than it is wide.[3] I diligently inquired about this city and asked questions of Christians, Saracens,[4] idolaters,[5] and all others, and all said with one voice that it is fully 100 miles in circumference.

They also have an edict from their lord that each and every hearth[6] shall pay annually one *balis* to the Great Khan, that is five pieces of paper[7] that have an equivalent value in silk of one and a half *florins*.[8] They have a means of coping with this. Fully ten or twelve households will share a single hearth and so will pay for only a single hearth. Regardless, these hearths number eighty-five *tumans*, with an additional four *tumans* for the Saracens. Combined, they number eighty-eight.[9] One *tuman* is fully 10,000 hearths. Then there are the others: Christians, other mer-

---

[1]Hangzhou, the port city in southern China that had served as the capital of the Southern Song Dynasty (1127–1279). Marco Polo, who likewise reported on the marvels of the city, knew it as *Kinsai*, which he also translated as "Heavenly City."

[2]The Latin is *spansa*. It is not at all clear what Friar Odoric understood a "span" to be. Perhaps this comes close. See note 19.

[3]Like Ferrara along the Po, Hangzhou is stretched out along the contours of its river.

[4]Muslims.

[5]Buddhists, Daoists, and Mongol shamans.

[6]*Ignis*: literally, "fire."

[7]The Song Dynasty began printing and using paper currency in the 1120s.

[8]The *florin*, the official coin of Florence since 1252, was made from 3.53 grams of pure gold and was equal in value to a pound of silver.

[9]Someone's arithmetic is off. It should be eighty-nine.

chants, and other transients passing through the country. This being so, I marveled at how many human bodies could manage to inhabit the same space. Yet there is a great abundance of bread there, and of pork, and rice and wine. The wine is otherwise known as *vigim*, and is reputed to be a noble beverage. Indeed, an extraordinary abundance of every other sort of food is found there. . . .

If anyone should wish to tell of or report on the vastness of this city and the great marvels contained within it, a full quire of stationery could not contain all of these matters. Truly, this is the most noble and greatest city in the world for goods that are bought and sold. . . .

CONCERNING THE GREAT CITIES OF KHANBALIK AND TAYDO AND THE PALACE OF THE KHAN

I passed through many cities and lands on my way east before arriving at the noble city of Khanbalik,[10] an exceedingly old and ancient city in the famous province of Cathay.[11] The Tartars took the city and then built another one-half mile away, which they called Taydo.[12] This second city has twelve gates,[13] spaced two miles apart from one another. A large population resides between the two cities, and together the cities have a perimeter that extends more than forty miles.[14] The Great Khan resides in this city and has a great palace, the walls of which are a good four miles in circumference.[15] Within the Great Palace's enclosure there is a man-made hill on which has been constructed another palace, the most beautiful in the world. This entire hill has been planted over with trees, and for this reason it is called *Green Mount*. A lake has been created alongside the hill and an exceedingly beautiful bridge built over it. On this lake there are so many geese, ducks, and swans that one is struck in awe. For this reason, there is no need for that lord to leave home when he wishes to go hunting. Also within this palace enclosure are thickets filled with various sorts of wild animals so that he can take to the chase whenever he desires without ever leaving home.

For this palace in which he resides is vast and beautiful. Its ground floor is raised about two paces,[16] and inside there are twenty-four columns of gold. All of the walls are draped with red-leather, said to be the finest in the world. In the center of the palace there is a great cistern, more than two paces in height, totally fashioned out of a single precious stone called *merdacas*.[17] It is bound all around in gold, and in every corner there is a dragon[18] whose mouth threatens in a most menacing way. This cistern also has a hanging network of great pearls that fringe it, and these fringes of pearls are a good yard[19] wide. Drinking water for use in the royal court is dispensed through the cistern, which is fed by pipes. Nearby the cistern are many golden goblets from which those who desire to take a drink can drink. In that same palace there are also many peacocks made from gold. When one of the Tartars wishes to amuse his lord, one after another they clap their hands, upon which the

---

[10]Turkish for "city of the khan." This is the usual term that Western sources use for Beijing under the Mongols. But see note 12.

[11]Northern China, which received its name from the *Khitan Mongols*, who established the *Liao* state there in 907. They were replaced by the *Ruzhen* (Jurchen), who set up the *Jin* state in 1125, but the name *Cathay* stuck.

[12]In 1266 Khubilai Khan ordered the construction of a new capital slightly northeast of the *Jin* capital of *Zhongdu* (Central Capital). In 1272 the newly completed capital acquired the Chinese name *Dadu* (Great Capital), and to the Mongols it was known as *Daidu*. Khubilai mandated that the entire urban complex, namely both Dadu and the former Zhongdu, was to be called Dadu, but it seems likely that even the Mongols normally used the Turkish term *Khanba-*

lik when referring to this complex. Dadu later became the nucleus for the Ming (1369–1644) capital of *Beijing* (Northern Capital), which took shape under the Yongle Emperor (r. 1402–1424). Regarding the Yongle Emperor, see sources 86 and 87.

[13]Apparently it had only eleven gates.

[14]Dadu alone had a perimeter of 28,600 meters, or more than seventeen and a half miles.

[15]The palace complex had a perimeter of 3,480 meters, or a bit more than two miles.

[16]About six feet.

[17]Jade from the region of Khotan.

[18]The Latin is *serpens*, but dragon seems a better translation than "serpent."

[19]*Spansa*. See note 2.

peacocks flap their wings and appear to dance. Now this has to be done either through some diabolical art or by means of some underground engine.

CONCERNING THE LORD KHAN'S COURT

When that lord is seated on his imperial throne, the empress resides on his left, and one step below sit two of the other wives whom he keeps. At the bottom of the stairs are all the other women of his family. All of the women who are married have on their heads [something shaped like][20] a human foot, which is a good forearm and a half long. On the lower portion of the [so-called] foot are crane's feathers fashioned into a peak, and the entire "foot" is ornamented with great pearls. Whatever large and beautiful pearls there are in the world, they are to be found on the decorations of those ladies.

On the right-hand side of this king sits his first-born son, who is expected to reign after him. Beneath them are placed all who are of royal blood. There are also four scribes there who write down every word that the king utters. Before the khan stands an innumerable multitude of his barons. None of these dares to speak a word except if addressed by the great lord, except for the jesters, who might wish to amuse their lord. But even these jesters must not dare to do anything beyond the limits that the king has laid down for them. Before the gates of the palace stand baronial guards, on watch lest anyone tread on the threshold of the door. If they catch anyone doing that, they beat him soundly.

When this great lord desires to hold any sort of large entertainment, he has 14,000 crowned barons waiting on him at the festival, each of whom has a coat on his back whose pearls alone are worth more than 15,000 florins.

The court of this lord is well ordered, namely ranked into tens, hundreds, and thousands,[21] with all their assigned places and all answerable to one another lest any defect ever be found in the performance of their duties or in any other matter.

I, Brother Odoric, was there in this city of his for a good three years and often present at their festivals, for we Friars Minor[22] have an assigned place in his court, and it is always our duty to go and give him our blessing. So I took the opportunity to ask and inquire of Christians, Saracens, and all sorts of idolaters, as well as from those converts to our faith who are great barons in that court and who wait solely on the person of the king. They all said with one voice that of jesters alone there are easily thirteen *tumans*, of which one alone consists of 10,000 jesters. Moreover, when it comes to other groups: Of those who care for the dogs, wild beasts, and fowl, there are fully fifteen *tumans*; of physicians who care for the king's person, there are 400 idolaters, eight Christians, and one Saracen. All of these are supplied with everything that they need from the king's court. As for the rest of his household, it is beyond counting.

---

[20]Words in brackets are supplied by the translator.

[21]The Mongol army was organized along this decimal system, with troops organized into squadrons of tens, companies of ten tens, regiments of ten hundreds, and divisions of ten thousands.

[22]The official title of the Franciscans is the Order of Friars Minor (Lesser Brethren).

Advice for Merchants Traveling to Cathay

▼▼▼

84 ▼ Francesco Pegolotti, *THE PRACTICE OF COMMERCE*

Around 1340 *Francesco Balducci Pegolotti*, an agent of the Bardi banking house of Florence, composed a handbook of practical advice for merchants. Pegolotti, who served the Bardi family's mercantile interests from London to Cyprus, drew upon his years of experience to produce a work filled with lists of facts and figures on such items as local business customs, the taxes and tariffs of various localities, and the relative values of different standards of weights, measures, and coinage. In other words, the book contained just about everything a prudent merchant would want to know before entering a new market. In addition to these catalogues of useful data, Pegolotti included a short essay of advice for merchants bound for China.

QUESTIONS FOR ANALYSIS

1. What evidence is there that Pegolotti himself had not traveled to Cathay?
2. Considering that his advice is not based on firsthand experience, how knowledgeable does he appear to be on the subject, and what does this suggest?
3. Consider Pegolotti's advice regarding the types of interpreters the merchant will need. What language skills suffice to carry on this trans-Eurasian business enterprise? What does this suggest about the markets of Central Asia and northern China?
4. When and where could the trip be especially hazardous? What does this suggest about the *Pax Mongolica*?
5. Describe the type of merchant for whom this advice was written. Were these small-time traders? Big-time entrepreneurs? What inferences follow from your answer?
6. What overall impression does Pegolotti give us of this journey and its rewards?

THINGS NEEDFUL FOR MERCHANTS WHO DESIRE TO MAKE THE JOURNEY TO CATHAY

In the first place, you must let your beard grow long and not shave. And at Tana[1] you should furnish yourself with a dragoman.[2] And you must not try to save money in the matter of dragomen by taking a bad one instead of a good one. For the additional wages of the good one will not cost you so much as you will save by having him. And besides the dragoman it would be good to take at least two good manservants, who are acquainted with the Cumanian[3] tongue. And if the merchant likes to take a woman with him from Tana, he can do so; if he does not like to take one there is no obligation, only if he does take one he will be kept much more comfortably than if he does not take one. If he does take one, it would be good if she were acquainted with the Cumanian tongue as well as the men.

And from Tana traveling to Gittarchan[4] you should take with you twenty-five days' provisions, that is to say, flour and salt fish; as for meat, you will find enough of it at all the places along the road. And also at all the chief stations [along the way]. . . . , you should replenish yourself with flour and salt fish; other things you will find in sufficient quantities, especially meat.

The road you travel from Tana to Cathay is perfectly safe, whether by day or by night, according to what the merchants say who have used it. But if the merchant, in going or coming, should die enroute, everything belonging to him will become the property of the lord of the country in which he dies, and the officers of the lord will take possession of all. So also if he dies in Cathay. But if his brother is with him, or an intimate friend and comrade calling himself his brother, then they will surrender the property of the deceased to this person, and so it will be rescued.

And there is another danger: this is when the lord of the country dies, and before the new lord who is to have the lordship is proclaimed. During such intervals there have sometimes been irregularities perpetrated on the Franks, and other foreigners. (They call "Franks" all the Christians of these parts from Romania[5] westward.) And the roads will not be safe to travel until another lord be proclaimed who is to reign in place of him who died.

Cathay is a province that contains a multitude of cities and towns. Among others there is one in particular, that is to say the capital city, to which merchants flock, and in which there is a vast amount of trade; and this city is called Cambalec.[6] And the said city has a circuit of one hundred miles,[7] and is all full of people and houses and of dwellers in the said city. . . .

You may reckon also that from Tana to Sara[8] the road is less safe than on any other part of the journey; and yet even when this part of the road is at its worst, if there are some sixty men in your company you will go as safely as if you were in your own house.

Anyone from Genoa or from Venice, wishing to go to the places above-named, and to make the journey to Cathay, should carry linens with him, and if he visits Organci[9] he will dispose of these at a profit. In Organci he should purchase *sommi* of silver,[10] and with these he should pro-

---

[1]The present-day city of Azov on the northeast coast of the Sea of Azov, which is an extension of the Black Sea. Tana was the easternmost point to which a person could sail from the Mediterranean.

[2]An interpreter fluent in Arabic, Persian, or Turkish.

[3]A Turkic people inhabiting the Middle Volga.

[4]Present-day Astrakhan, a city in the Volga Delta, just north of the Caspian Sea.

[5]The European term for the Byzantine Empire.

[6]Khanbalik. See source 83.

[7]Compare this with Odoric of Pordenone's account (source 83).

[8]Sarai on the Volga, the capital of the il-khans of Kipchak (also known as the *Golden Horde*), who ruled Russia and Kazakhstan.

[9]Urgench on the Oxus River in Central Asia.

[10]*Sommi* were weights of silver. Each *sommo* was equivalent to five golden florins (see source 83, note 8). Pegolotti calculated that the average merchant would carry merchandise worth about 25,000 florins and that the expenses for the merchant, interpreter, and two personal servants would amount to a combined sixty to eighty *sommi*, or 300–400 florins.

ceed without making any further investment, unless for some bales of the very finest textiles of small bulk, and that cost no more for transportation than coarser textiles.

Merchants who travel this road can ride on horseback or on asses, or mounted in any way that they choose to be mounted.

Whatever silver the merchants might carry with them as far as Cathay the lord of Cathay will take from them and put into his treasury.[11] And to merchants who bring silver they give that paper money of theirs in exchange. This is

of yellow paper, stamped with the seal of the aforementioned lord. And this money is called *balishi*; and with this money you can readily buy silk and all other merchandise that you desire to buy. And all the people of the country are bound to receive it. And yet you shall not pay a higher price for your goods because your money is of paper. And there are three kinds of paper money, one being worth more than another, according to the value which has been established for each by that lord.[12]

[11]The Chinese (and Mongol) policy of demanding silver for paper money resulted in a significant flow of silver from the West to China before, during, and well after the fourteenth century.

[12]See source 83, note 7.

Long-Distance Travel Beyond the Mongol Peace

Important as the Mongol Peace was in facilitating movement and trade across Eurasia, it was not the sole factor behind the general upsurge of long-distance travel and cultural exchange after 1000. Religious motives and ties were equally important driving factors, and this was especially true for the ecumenical community that called itself *Dar al-Islam* (The House of Islam). Educated Muslims, no matter their ethnic origins or native tongues, shared a sacred language — Arabic — and could communicate with one another. They also shared the obligation of *hajj*. The pilgrimage routes that enabled African, Spanish, Turkish, Iranian, Indian, and East Asian Muslims to travel to Arabia's holy sites equally served as important avenues of cultural and material exchange. Moreover, merchants and scholars spread Islam to such faraway regions as sub-Saharan Africa and the coastal lands of Southeast Asia. Once the faith had taken root, there was even more reason to maintain contact with these societies, many of which were quite distant from Islam's Southwest Asian birthplace.

In addition to religious devotion, other factors fueled long-distance travel and commerce for both Muslims and non-Muslims before and after the breakup of the Mongol Empire. Arabs, Persians, East Africans, Indians, Southeast Asians, Chinese, and Western Europeans had taken to the seas with increasing zeal long before the rise of Chinggis Khan and continued their interests in seafaring and naval technology throughout the thirteenth and fourteenth centuries and beyond. Chinese and Western European seafarers were in the forefront of the effort to build more seaworthy craft capable of bigger payloads and safer transportation. Borrowing extensively from the Arabs and other maritime cultures, Chinese and

Western European sailors adopted and created better navigational tools, including superior coastal charts. Such efforts paid rich rewards to the merchant mariners of China and the West. By the mid thirteenth century, Chinese mariners were a major force in the seaborne commerce of Southeast Asia, and Western Europeans, especially the Italians, dominated the shipping lanes of the Mediterranean.

Early in the fifteenth century, Ming China sent seven massive naval expeditions into the Indian Ocean, and portions of several of those fleets reached the shores of East Africa and Arabia. Also in the fifteenth century, Western Europe, finding the overland roads to Cathay now mostly blocked, began to seek sea routes to the Indies. The consequences of those explorations were astounding. Before the century was over, Europeans had sailed to East Africa, India, and the Americas.

Developments in naval engineering and navigation held the key to a new stage in human history — the joining of the Eastern and Western Hemispheres — but long-distance transportation across Inner Asia also enjoyed a brief renaissance in the period following the dissolution of the Mongol Ecumene. We might think of it as the Silk Road's Indian Summer. From 1370 to 1405, the armies of *Tamerlane* swept across Eurasia, from Anatolia to the borders of China, from Russia to India. Their destructive fury became legendary and deservedly so. But they also established a new but short-lived Central Asian empire, whose capital, *Samarqand*, became the dynamic meeting place for merchants, travelers, and artisans from all over Eurasia.

The land routes of Inner Africa, particularly of West Africa, were equally vital in the thirteenth and fourteenth centuries, and remained so until new markets blossomed along Africa's west coast in the sixteenth century. Between about 1230 and 1591, the grasslands trading empires of Mali and Songhai successively flourished as a consequence of their ability to control the traffic in gold, goods, salt, and slaves that passed along the trans-Saharan caravan routes.

A Moroccan Visitor in Sub-Saharan Africa
▼▼▼

85 ▼ *Ibn Battuta,*
A GIFT TO THOSE WHO CONTEMPLATE
THE WONDERS OF CITIES

The life and world travels of Abu Abdallah Muhammad ibn Battuta (1304–1369) provide eloquent testimony to the cosmopolitanism of fourteenth-century Islam. Ibn Battuta was born into the religious upper class of Tangier, Morocco, where he received an education in Islamic law and Arabic literature. In 1325 he left home to make the first of what would be several pilgrimages to Mecca. In the course of the next twenty-six years, he visited Constantinople, Mesopotamia, Iran, India (where he resided and worked as a *qadi*, or religious judge, for seven years), Burma, Sumatra, Spain, Mali, and probably southern China. In all, his travels covered about 73,000 miles, and most of his stops along the way were within the cultural confines of *Dar al-Islam*, where Sharia (see source 48) prevailed.

In 1351 Ibn Battuta returned to Morocco, but one more journey awaited him. In February 1352 he joined a camel caravan of merchants as he embarked on his last great adventure — a trip to the West African kingdom of Mali, which lay some 1,500 miles to the south across one of the world's most inhospitable deserts. Two years later he arrived back home with marvelous tales to tell of this land of gold, whose leaders had converted to Islam in the early thirteenth century.

His days of long-distance travel now over, Ibn Battuta narrated his many travel experiences and observations to Ibn Juzayy, a professional scribe who fashioned these stories into one of the most popular forms of literature in the Islamic World: a *rihla*, or book of travels centering on the hajj to Mecca.

The following selection does not describe any of Ibn Battuta's several pilgrimages to Mecca; rather, it tells of his journey into the kingdom of Mali in West Africa's Niger River region.

QUESTIONS FOR ANALYSIS

1. What did Ibn Battuta admire most about these people? What did he find hardest to accept? Why?
2. Did Ibn Battuta understand fully all that he encountered? Can you find any evidence of tension or misunderstanding?
3. In what ways were the cultures of the people whom Ibn Battuta encountered a mixture of indigenous West African and Islamic elements?
4. How organized and controlled does the state of Mali appear to be?
5. Compare fourteenth-century Mali with eleventh-century Ghana (see source 72). What are their similarities and differences? Which seem more significant? What do you conclude from that answer?
6. Based on a careful study of sources 72 and 74, as well as of this document, what inferences do you draw about the social status of women in sub-Saharan West Africa?

Then we reached the town of Iwalatan . . . after a journey . . . of two whole months. It is the first district of the Sudan and the sultan's[1] deputy there is Farba Husayn. *Farba* means "deputy." When we arrived there the merchants[2] placed their belongings in an open space, where the Sudan[3] took over the guard of them while they went to the *farba*. He was sitting on a carpet under a *saqif*[4] with his assistants in front of him with lances and bows in their hands and the chief men of the Masufa[5] behind him. The merchants stood before him while he addressed them, in spite of their proximity to him, through an interpreter, out of contempt for them. At this I repented at having come to their country because of their ill manners and their contempt for white men.[6] I made for the house of Ibn Badda, a respectable man of Sala to whom

---

[1]The sultan, or king, of Mali, for whom this was an outlying province.
[2]Berbers and Arabs from North Africa.
[3]Here this Arabic word, which means "blacks," refers to the local people and not to the region.

[4]A colonnade.
[5]A Berber people of the western Sahara.
[6]Merchants from North Africa: Berbers and Arabs.

I had written to rent a house for me. He had done so. Then the *mushrif*[7] (of Iwalatan), who is called the *manshaju*, invited those who had come with the caravan to receive his reception-gift (*diyafa*). I declined to go but my companions entreated me urgently, so I went with those who went. Then the *diyafa* was brought. It was *anili*[8] meal mixed with a little honey and yogurt which they had placed in half a gourd made into a kind of bowl. Those present drank and went away. I said to them: "Was it to this that the black man invited us?" They said: "Yes, for them this is a great banquet." Then I knew for certain that no good was to be expected from them and I wished to depart with the pilgrims of Iwalatan. But then I thought it better to go to see the seat of their king.

My stay in Iwalatan lasted about fifty days. Its inhabitants did me honor and made me their guest. Among them was the qadi[9] of the place Muhammad b. Abd Allah b. Yanumur and his brother the faqih[10] and teacher Yahya. The town of Iwalatan is extremely hot. There are a few little palm trees there in the shade of which they sow watermelons. . . . Mutton is abundant there and the people's clothes are of Egyptian cloth of good quality. Most of the inhabitants there belong to the Masufa, whose women are of surpassing beauty and have a higher status than the men.

THE MASUFA LIVING IN IWALATAN

These people have remarkable and strange ways. As for their men, they feel no jealousy. None of them traces his descent through his father, but from his maternal uncle, and a man's heirs are the sons of his sister only, to the exclusion of his own sons. This is something that I have seen nowhere in the world except among the Indian infidels. . . . , whereas these are Muslims who observe the prayer and study fiqh[11] and memorize

the Quran. As for their women, they have no modesty in the presence of men and do not veil themselves in spite of their assiduity in prayer. If anybody wishes to marry one of them he may do so, but they do not travel with the husband, and if one of them wished to do so her family would prevent her.

The women there have friends and companions among the foreign men, just as the men have companions from among the foreign women. One of them may enter his house and find his wife with her man friend without making any objection. . . .

One day I went into the presence of Abu Muhammad Yandakan al-Masufi in whose company we had come and found him sitting on a carpet. In the courtyard of his house there was a canopied couch with a woman on it conversing with a man seated. I said to him: "Who is this woman?" He said: "She is my wife." I said: "What connection has the man with her?" He replied: "He is her friend." I said to him: "Do you acquiesce in this when you have lived in our country and become acquainted with the precepts of the Shar?"[12] He replied: "The association of women with men is agreeable to us and a part of good conduct, to which no suspicion attaches. They are not like the women of your country." I was astonished at his laxity. I left him, and did not return thereafter. He invited me several times but I did not accept.

When I resolved to travel to Mali . . . I hired a guide from the Masufa, since there is no need to travel in company because of the security of that road, and set off with three of my companions . . . [and] I arrived at the town of Mali, the seat of the king of the Sudan. . . .

THE SULTAN OF MALI

He is the sultan Mansa Sulayman.[13] *Mansa* means "sultan" and Sulayman is his name. He is

---

[7]The sultan's overseer of the town's markets.
[8]Millet.
[9]An Islamic religious judge.
[10]A teacher of religion.

[11]Religion.
[12]*Sharia*, or Islamic Sacred Law (see source 48).
[13]The brother of Mansa Musa (see source 50), Mansa Sulayman ruled Mali from 1341 to 1360.

a miserly king from whom no great donation is to be expected. It happened that I remained for this period without seeing him on account of my illness. Then he gave a memorial feast for our Lord Abul-Hasan[14] (may God be content with him) and invited the emirs and faqihs and the qadi and khatib,[15] and I went with them. They brought copies of the Quran and the Quran was recited in full. They prayed for our lord Abul-Hasan (may God have mercy on him) and prayed for Mansa Sulayman. When this was finished I advanced and greeted Mansa Sulayman and the qadi and the khatib and Ibn al-Faqih told him who I was. He answered them in their language and they said to me: "The sultan says to you: 'I thank God.'" I replied: "Praise and thanks be to God in every circumstance."

THEIR TRIVIAL RECEPTION GIFT AND THEIR RESPECT FOR IT

When I departed the reception gift was sent to me and dispatched to the qadi's house. The qadi sent it with his men to the house of Ibn al-Faqih. Ibn al-Faqih hastened out of his house barefooted and came in to me saying: "Come! The cloth and gift of the sultan have come to you!" I got up, thinking that it would be robes of honor and money, but behold! it was three loaves of bread and a piece of beef fried in *gharti*[16] and a gourd containing yogurt. When I saw it I laughed, and was long astonished at their feeble intellect and their respect for mean things.

MY SPEAKING TO THE SULTAN AFTER THIS AND HIS KINDNESS TOWARDS ME

After this reception gift I remained for two months during which nothing was sent to me by

the sultan and the month of Ramadan[17] came in. Meanwhile I frequented the *mashwar* [council-place] and used to greet him and sit with the qadi and the khatib. I spoke with Dugha the interpreter, who said: "Speak with him, and I will express what you want to say in the proper fashion." So when he held a session at the beginning of Ramadan and I stood before him and said: "I have journeyed to the countries of the world and met their kings. I have been four months in your country without your giving me a reception gift or anything else. What shall I say of you in the presence of other sultans?" He replied: "I have not seen you nor known about you." The qadi and Ibn al-Faqih rose and replied to him saying: "He greeted you and you sent to him some food." Thereupon he ordered that a house be provided for me to stay in and an allowance to be allotted to me. Then, on the night of 27 Ramadan, he distributed among the qadi and the khatib and the faqihs a sum of money which they call *zakah*[18] and gave to me with them 33⅓ mithqals.[19] When I departed he bestowed on me 100 mithqals of gold. . . .

THE SELF-DEBASEMENT OF THE SUDAN BEFORE THEIR KING AND THEIR SCATTERING OF DUST ON THEMSELVES BEFORE HIM AND OTHER PECULIARITIES

The Sudan are the humblest of people before their king and the most submissive towards him. They swear by his name, saying: "*Mansa Sulayman ki.*" When he calls to one of them at his sessions in the pavilion which we have mentioned the person called takes off his clothes and puts on ragged clothes, and removes his turban and puts on a dirty *shashiyya*[20] and goes in holding up his garments and trousers half-way up his

---

[14]The late sultan of Morocco (r. 1331–1351).
[15]A public preacher at Friday mosque services.
[16]A vegetable oil.
[17]The month during which Muslims fast from sunrise to sunset.

[18]Alms distributed at the end of Ramadan.
[19]One *mithqal* was 4.72 grams of gold.
[20]A skullcap.

leg, and advances with submissiveness and humility. He then beats the ground vigorously with his two elbows, and stands like one performing a *raka*[21] to listen to his words.

If one of them addresses the sultan and the latter replies he uncovers the clothes from his back and sprinkles dust on his head and back, like one washing himself with water. I used to marvel how their eyes did not become blinded. . . .

WHAT I APPROVED OF AND WHAT I DISAPPROVED OF AMONG THE ACTS OF THE SUDAN

One of their good features is their lack of oppression. They are the farthest removed of people from it and their sultan does not permit anyone to practice it. Another is the security embracing the whole country, so that neither traveler there nor dweller has anything to fear from thief or usurper. Another is that they do not interfere with the wealth of any white man who dies among them, even though it be *qintar* upon *qintar*.[22] They simply leave it in the hands of a trustworthy white man until the one to whom it is due takes it. Another is their assiduity in prayer and their persistence in performing it in congregation and beating their children to make them perform it. If it is a Friday and a man does not go early to the mosque he will not find anywhere to pray because of the press of the people. It is their habit that every man sends his servant with his prayer-mat to spread it for him in a place which he thereby has a right to until he goes to the mosque. Their prayer-carpets are made from the fronds of the tree resembling the palm which has no fruit. Another of their good features is their dressing in fine white clothes on Friday. If any one of them possesses nothing but a ragged shirt he washes it and cleanses it and attends the Friday prayer in it. Another is their eagerness to memorize the great Quran. They place fetters on their children if there appears on their part a failure to memorize it and they are not undone until they memorize it.

I went into the house of the qadi on the day of the festival and his children were fettered so I said to him: "Aren't you going to let them go?" He replied: "I shan't do so until they've got the Quran by heart!" One day I passed by a youth of theirs, of good appearance and dressed in fine clothes, with a heavy fetter on his leg. I said to those who were with me: "What has this boy done? Has he killed somebody?" The lad understood what I had said and laughed, and they said to me: "He's only been fettered so that he'll learn the Quran!"

One of their disapproved acts is that their female servants and slave girls and little girls appear before men naked, with their privy parts uncovered. During Ramadan I saw many of them in this state, for it is the custom of the *farariyya*[23] to break their fast[24] in the house of the sultan, and each one brings his food carried by twenty or more of his slave girls, they all being naked. Another is that their women go into the sultan's presence naked and uncovered, and that his daughters go naked. On the night of 25 Ramadan I saw about two hundred slave girls bringing out food from his palace naked, having with them two of his daughters with rounded breasts having no covering upon them. Another is their sprinkling dust and ashes on their heads out of good manners. . . . Another is that many of them eat carrion, and dogs, and donkeys.[25]

---

[21]A set sequence of utterances and gestures that form the *salah*, or obligatory ritual prayer, that Muslims must engage in five times daily.
[22]"Weight upon weight" (i.e., a large amount of wealth).
[23]Emirs, or chief men.

[24]The daily fast of the month of Ramadan ends at sunset (see note 17).
[25]Unclean meat, according to quranic law.

Samarqand in the Age of Tamerlane
▼▼▼

86 ▼ Ruy González de Clavijo,
EMBASSY TO TAMERLANE

The Byzantines retook Constantinople from its Latin overlords in 1261 but soon thereafter faced a new enemy in the *Ottoman Turks*, who appeared as a new force to be reckoned with in Anatolia around 1300. During the fourteenth century, the Ottomans established a foothold in the Balkans and squeezed Byzantium from two directions — Asiatic Anatolia and southeastern Europe. As the Byzantine Empire contracted in the face of this pressure, various popes and lords in Western Europe roused themselves to call for and wage crusades in defense of the Christian Byzantines, despite the deep religious differences and historical animosities that separated Eastern and Western Christians, especially since 1204 (see Multiple Voices VII). In 1396 a combined French and Hungarian crusade army marched into the Balkans to confront the Ottomans, but Sultan Bayazid I (The Thunderbolt) crushed it at Nicopolis in Bulgaria. It seemed as though the few remnants of the Byzantine Empire would soon be overrun, and then the full fury of the Ottomans would fall upon nearby Latin Christian states, such as Hungary.

In the midst of this crisis, Byzantium and Latin Europe were given a temporary reprieve when the armies of *Timur-i leng* (Timur, or Temür, the Lame), known in the West as *Tamerlane* (1336?–1405), destroyed Sultan Bayazid's army at Ankara in July 1402. The captive sultan was transported east and died soon after. Constantinople was given another half century of life and did not fall to the Ottomans until May 29, 1453.

Although Tamerlane was a Turkish Muslim who presented himself as the champion of Islam, he was not averse to destroying Islamic enemies in bloodbaths. Was it possible that the Christian West could ally with him against common Islamic enemies, such as the Ottomans and the Mamluks of Egypt and Syria? Tamerlane, who had conquered substantial portions of the lands of the former Mongol Empire, was more interested in China than the West. Indeed, he died in early 1405, just as he was preparing a campaign against the Ming Empire. For a few months in the period 1402–1403, however, Tamerlane conducted diplomatic exchanges with a variety of Western princes who courted an alliance with him. It was in this context that King Henry III of Castile-León dispatched several embassies to the Turkish warlord. The second of these, sent out in May 1403, included Ruy González de Clavijo, the royal chamberlain.

After a little less than fifteen months and almost 3,000 miles of travel, Clavijo and a surviving colleague (a third envoy had died in Iran) caught up with Tamerlane at his capital, Samarqand (in present-day Uzbekistan). Tamerlane, who was already preparing for his ill-fated invasion of China, received the ambassadors cordially but refused to commit to any alliance with the Christian West. In fact, the two ambassadors and their retinue were forced to depart Samarqand in November 1404 without even a final audience with the aged and ill Tamerlane (who died two months later).

What did come out of this adventure, however, is Clavijo's detailed account of the embassy and the people and places they visited. Our selection comes from the chamberlain's description of Samarqand, an ancient city of the Silk Road.

QUESTIONS FOR ANALYSIS

1. What master plan did Tamerlane seem to have for Samarqand?
2. Tamerlane has often been described as essentially a plunderer rather than a state-builder. Based on this source, what is your considered judgment of that characterization?
3. Tamerlane's campaigns, which were often accompanied by wholesale destruction and slaughter, have been pointed to as one of many factors that helped close down the Silk Road. Based on this source, what is your considered judgment of that statement?

Now therefore that I have narrated in detail all that befell us during our stay in Samarqand, I must describe that city for you, telling of all that is there to be seen in and round and about, and of all that Timur has accomplished there to embellish his capital. Samarqand stands in a plain, and is surrounded by a rampart or wall of earth, with a very deep ditch. The city itself is rather larger than Seville, but lying outside Samarqand are great numbers of houses which form extensive suburbs. These are spread out on all sides for indeed the township is surrounded by orchards and vineyards, extending in some cases to a league and a half or even two leagues[1] beyond Samarqand which stands in their center. In between these orchards pass streets with open squares; these all are densely populated, and here all kinds of goods are on sale with bread stuffs and meat. Thus it is that the population outside the city is more numerous than the population within the walls. Among these orchards outside Samarqand are found the most noble and beautiful houses, and here Timur has his many palaces and pleasure grounds. Round and about the great men of the government also here have their estates and country houses, each standing within its orchard: and so numerous are these gardens

and vineyards surrounding Samarqand that a traveler who approaches the city sees only a great mountainous height of trees and the houses embowered among them remain invisible. Through the streets of Samarqand, as through its gardens outside and inside, pass many water-conduits, and in these gardens are the melon-beds and cotton-growing lands. . . .

Further, this land of Samarqand is not only rich in food stuffs but also in manufactures, such as factories of silk. . . , also crapes, taffetas and the stuffs we call tercenals in Spain, which are all produced here in great numbers. Further, they make up special fur linings for silk garments, and manufacture stuffs in gold and blue with other colors of diverse tints dyed, and besides all these kinds of stuffs there are the spices. Thus trade has always been fostered by Timur with the view of making his capital the noblest of cities: and during all his conquests wheresoever he came he carried off the best men of the population to people Samarqand, bringing there the master-craftsmen of all nations. Thus from Damascus he carried away with him all the weavers of that city, those who worked at the silk looms.[2] Further, the bow-makers who produce those cross-bows which are so famous: likewise

---

[1] One league is about three miles.

[2] Tamerlane sacked the Syrian cities of Aleppo and Damascus in 1400–1401, wreaking great devastation and leaving the economy of Syria in shambles.

armorers: also the craftsmen in glass and porcelain, who are known to be the best in all the world. From Turkey he had brought their gunsmiths who make the arquebus,[3] and all men of other crafts wheresoever he found them, such as silversmiths and masons. These all were in very great numbers, indeed so many had been brought together of craftsmen of all sorts that of every denomination and kind you might find many master-workmen established in the capital. Again he had gathered to settle here in Samarqand artillery men, both engineers and bombardiers, besides those who make the ropes by which these engines work. Lastly hemp and flax had been sown and grown for the purpose in the Samarqand lands, where never before this crop had been cultivated.

So great therefore was the population now of all nationalities gathered together in Samarqand that of men with their families the number they said must amount to 150,000 souls. Of the nations brought here together there were to be seen Turks, Arabs and Moors[4] of diverse sects, with Christians who were Greeks and Armenians, Catholics, Jacobites[5] and Nestorians,[6] besides those [Indian] folk who baptize with fire in the forehead, who are indeed Christians but of a faith that is peculiar to their nation.[7] The population of Samarqand was so vast that lodging for them all could not be found in the city limits, nor in the streets and open spaces of the suburbs and villages outside, and hence they were to be found quartered temporarily for lodgment even in the caves and in tents under the trees of the gardens, which was a matter very wonderful to see. The markets of Samarqand further are amply stored with merchandise imported from distant and foreign countries. From Russia and Tartary[8] come leathers and linens, from Cathay silk stuffs that are the finest in the whole world, and of these the best are those that are plain without embroideries. Thence too is brought musk which is found in no other land but Cathay, with balas rubies and diamonds which are more frequently to be met with in those parts than elsewhere, also pearls, lastly rhubarb with many other spiceries. The goods that are imported to Samarqand from Cathay indeed are of the richest and most precious of all those brought thither from foreign parts, for the craftsmen of Cathay are reputed to be the most skillful by far beyond those of any other nation. . . .

From India there are brought to Samarqand the smaller spices, which indeed are the most costly of the kind, such as nutmegs and cloves and mace with cinnamon . . . all these with many other kinds that are never to be found in the markets of Alexandria.[9] Throughout the city of Samarqand there are open squares where butchers' meat ready cooked, roasted or in stews, is sold, with fowls and game suitably prepared for eating, also bread and excellent fruit both are on sale. All these viands and victuals are there set out in a decent clean manner, namely in all those squares and open spaces of the town, and their traffic goes on all day and even all through the night time. Butchers' shops are numerous, also those booths where fowls, pheasants and partridges are on sale: and these shops are kept open by night as by day. On the one part of Samarqand stands the Castle which is not built on a height, but is protected by deep ravines on all its sides: and through these water flows which makes the position of the Castle impregnable. It

---

[3]A heavy but portable matchlock gun.

[4]Normally the term means a Muslim from western North Africa. Here, however, context demands that we understand it to mean a non-Arab Muslim.

[5]Syrian Christians.

[6]See source 44.

[7]Possibly the so-called Saint Thomas Christians of the western coast of India, who claim origins from the missionary work of the Apostle Thomas (see Multiple Voices IV), but they are not Gnostics. More likely, however, he refers to

Parsis (Persians), or Indian Zoroastrians (see source 17), a small but important group in western India that traces its origins to Persian refugees who left their homeland in the eighth century fearing persecution from Muslim conquerors. Parsis engage mainly in commerce.

[8]Lands of the il-khanate of the Golden Horde north of the Caucasus Mountains.

[9]The Mediterranean's major port of entry and wholesale center for spices from the East.

is here that his Highness keeps his treasure, and none from the city without may enter save the governor of the Castle and his men. Within its walls however Timur holds in captivity upwards of a thousand workmen; these labor at making plate-armor and helmets with bows and arrows, and to this business they are kept at work throughout the whole of their time in the service of his Highness. . . .

At that time when we were his guests in Samarqand there had arrived certain ambassadors sent by the emperor of China[10] who came to Timur bearing this message, namely: that all men knew that he, Timur, was in occupation of lands formerly held in fief to China, and hence that tribute for the same yearly had been due from him to the Chinese emperor: but seeing that for seven years past no tribute had ever been paid, he, Timur, must now forthwith pay down the sum. The answer of his Highness to these ambassadors was that this was most true, and that he was about to pay what was due: but that he would not burden them, the ambassadors, to take it back to China on their return, for he himself, Timur, would bring it. This of course was all said in scorn and to spite them, for his Highness had no intention to pay that tribute. . . .

We heard presently that his Highness had issued orders that those Chinese ambassadors should forthwith all of them be hung, but whether this order was actually carried out . . . is not known to us. Now from the city of Samarqand it is six months' march to the capital of China, which is called Cambaluc,[11] and this is the largest town in that empire: and of this six months' journey two are passed going across a desert country entirely uninhabited, except by nomad herdsmen who wander over the plains feeding their flocks. During the month of June of this year, immediately before the date of our coming to Samarqand, there had arrived a caravan of eight hundred camels bringing merchandise from China. Then it was that Timur having come home from his western campaigns had received that Chinese embassy bearing the message sent him by the emperor of China: and he forthwith had ordered the whole of this caravan, men and goods, to be taken into custody and that none should return to China. . . .

Good order is maintained in Samarqand with utmost strictness and none dare fight with another or oppress his neighbor by force: indeed, as to fighting, that Timur makes them do enough but abroad.

---

[10]The Yongle Emperor, who was attempting to re-establish a Chinese-dominated Silk Road, such as had existed in the early Tang Dynasty. See also source 87.

[11]Khanbalik. See source 83. Actually, the capital was Nanjing. See source 87, note 5.

Zheng He's Western Voyages
▼▼▼

87 ▼ *Ma Huan,*
THE OVERALL SURVEY
OF THE OCEAN'S SHORES

Vigorous expansionism characterized the early Ming Dynasty (1368–1644), particularly during the reign of Chengzu, known as the *Yongle Emperor* (r. 1402–1424). Between 1405 and 1421, he sent out six great fleets under the command of China's most famous admiral, a Muslim eunuch of Mongolian ancestry named *Zheng He* (1371–1433). If we can believe the records, several fleets carried in excess of 27,000 sailors, soldiers, and officials. The first expedition of 1405–1407 reportedly consisted of 317 vessels, including 62 massive treasure ships, some of which had 9 masts and were more than 400 feet long, more than 150 feet wide (imagine a ship larger than a football field), and around 3,100 tons in weight. These armadas — as well as a seventh, which went out in 1431 and returned in 1433 — sailed through the waters of Southeast Asia and the Indian Ocean, visiting numerous ports of call in such faraway places as the Spice Islands, India, East Africa, and the Arabian Peninsula.

Following long-established Arab and Chinese sailing routes, the expeditions were not voyages of exploration. Rather, their main purpose appears to have been the reassertion of Chinese prestige to the south and west. In essence, they were commissioned to accept the submission and tribute of the foreign rulers they encountered. A secondary purpose seems to have been to stimulate China's economy and strengthen its commercial position in South Asia, particularly in light of the fact that the armies of Tamerlane had disrupted certain routes along the Silk Road.

A book that appeared in 2002, *1421: The Year China Discovered America* by Gavin Menzies, claims that the sixth expedition, which went out in 1421 and returned in 1423, divided into a number of squadrons. This was usual for the fleets, but what followed was not. One squadron supposedly circumnavigated the globe, sailing to both American continents, as well as to Australia and New Zealand, before returning to home port. Another squadron is said to have visited the east coast of North America and then to have gone north to Greenland and Iceland and across the Arctic Ocean until it reached the eastern tip of Siberia. From there it sailed south to China. A third allegedly sailed to South America, then to the top of Antarctica, back across the Atlantic and Indian oceans to Australia, and then home. Historians reject this story as a fantasy based on imagination rather than credible evidence, and they agree that the squadrons of this fleet, as was true of earlier voyages, sailed no farther west than East Africa.

Wherever they sailed, all of the fleets made an impression on those whom they visited. In one area of Thailand, for example, Zheng He was remembered as a god. Despite the awe that these shows of strength engendered, China failed to gain dominance over the Indian Ocean. After the Yongle Emperor's death, the imperial court did not follow through on what had begun so well. The reasons are not difficult to discern. The cost of mounting the expeditions was prohibitively high, and the return was disproportionately low. Moreover, the Confucian bureaucracy, with its traditional contempt for commerce and foreign cultures, was on the ascendance after the Yongle Emperor's death. Although Zheng He was allowed to lead a seventh expedition westward, it proved to be China's last moment of transoceanic greatness. The court called a halt to further overseas adventures; the fleet was allowed to decay; and China deliberately and effectively forgot much of the naval technology that had made it the world's greatest maritime power in the ages of Song and early Ming.

The following account, by Ma Huan, whom we have already seen in the Prologue's sample Multiple Voices, describes various sites visited in the course of several of Zheng He's expeditions in western waters.

QUESTIONS FOR ANALYSIS

1. What evidence is there that the emperor saw these expeditions as a way of extending Chinese influence abroad?
2. How did Zheng He use both diplomacy and military force to achieve this objective?
3. What evidence is there that these expeditions also served commercial purposes?
4. What evidence is there that a high level of international commerce existed in the Indian Ocean well before the coming of Zheng He's fleets?

THE COUNTRY OF MANLAJIA[1] (MALACCA)

Formerly this place was not designated a "country." . . . There was no king . . . and it was controlled only by a chief. This territory was subordinate to the jurisdiction of Xian Luo;[2] it paid an annual tribute of forty *liang*[3] of gold, and if it were not paid, then Xian Luo would send men to attack it.

In the seventh year of the Yongle period,[4] the Emperor ordered the principal envoy, the grand eunuch Zheng He, and others to assume command (of the treasure-ships), and to take the imperial edicts and to bestow upon this chief two silver seals, a hat, a belt and a robe. Zheng He set up a stone tablet and raised the place to [the status of a] city; and it was subsequently called the "country of Manlajia." Thereafter Xian Luo did not dare to invade it.

The chief, having received the favor of being made king, conducted his wife and son, and went to the court at the capital[5] to return thanks and to present tribute of local products. The court also granted him a sea-going ship, so that he might return to his country and protect his land. . . .

Whenever the treasure-ships of the Central Country[6] arrived there, they at once erected a line of stockading, like a city-wall, and set up towers for the watchdrums at four gates; at night they had patrols of police carrying bells; inside, again, they erected a second stockade, like a small city-wall, within which they constructed warehouses and granaries; and all the money and provisions were stored in them. The ships which had gone to various countries[7] returned to this place and assembled; they marshaled the foreign goods and loaded them in the ships; then waited till the south wind was perfectly favorable. In the middle decade of the fifth moon they put to sea and returned home.[8]

Moreover, the king of the country made a selection of local products, conducted his wife and son, brought his chiefs, boarded a ship and followed the treasure-ships; and he attended at court and presented tribute. . . .

---

[1]Malacca, a port on the west coast of the Malay Peninsula and along the north shore of the Strait of Malacca, the main route from the South China Sea to the Indian Ocean.
[2]Thailand.
[3]About forty-eight ounces.
[4]1409. This would be the third expedition of 1409–1411.
[5]Nanjing (the southern capital). The Ming court moved from the seaport capital of Nanjing to inland Beijing (the northern capital) in 1421, signaling a shift in China's focus toward the Middle Kingdom's age-old area of primary concern — the steppes and the steppe peoples who inhabited them. The Ming Dynasty also rebuilt and extended the Great Wall into the edifice we see today — massive frontier fortifications to protect China from invasions from the west and the north.
[6]China, the Middle Kingdom.
[7]Elements were detached from the main fleet and sent off on special missions.
[8]1433, the last expedition.

THE COUNTRY OF SUMENDALA[9] (SEMUDERA, LHO SEUMAWE)

. . . The king of the country of Sumendala had previously been raided by the "tattooed-face king" of Naguer; and in the fighting he received a poisoned arrow in the body and died. He had one son, who was young and unable to avenge his father's death. The king's wife made a vow before the people, saying "If there is anyone who can avenge my husband's death and recover his land, I am willing to marry him and to share with him the management of the country's affairs." When she finished speaking, a fisherman belonging to the place was fired with determination, and said "I can avenge him."

Thereupon he took command of an army and at once put the "tattooed-face king" to flight in battle; and later he avenged the former king's death when the "tattooed-face king" was killed. The people of the latter submitted and did not dare to carry on hostilities.

Whereupon the wife of the former king, failing not to carry out her previous vow, forthwith married the fisherman. He was styled "the old king," and in such things as the affairs of the royal household and the taxation of the land, everybody accepted the old king's decisions. In the seventh year of the Yongle period[10] the old king, in fulfillment of his duty, brought tribute of local products,[11] and was enriched by the kindness of Heaven;[12] and in the tenth year of the Yongle period[13] he returned to his country.

When the son of the former king had grown up, he secretly plotted with the chiefs, murdered his adoptive father the fisherman, usurped his position, and ruled the kingdom.

The fisherman had a son by his principal wife; his name was Suganla; he took command of his people, and they fled away, taking their families; and, after erecting a stockade in the neighboring mountains, from time to time he led his men in incursions to take revenge on his father's enemies. In the thirteenth year of the Yongle period[14] the principal envoy, the grand eunuch Zheng He, and others, commanding a large fleet of treasure-ships, arrived there; they dispatched soldiers who captured Suganla; and he went to the capital;[15] and was publicly executed. The king's son was grateful for the imperial kindness, and constantly presented tribute of local products to the court. . . .

At this place there are foreign[16] ships going and coming in large numbers, hence all kinds of foreign goods are sold in great quantities in the country.

In this country they use gold coins and tin coins. The foreign name for the gold coin is *dinaer*;[17] they use pale gold, seventy percent pure, for casting it. . . . The foreign name for the tin coin is *jiashi*[18] and in all their trading they regularly use tin coins. . . .

THE COUNTRY OF HULUMOSI[19] (HORMUZ)

Setting sail from the country of Guli,[20] you go towards the north-west; and you can reach this place after traveling with a fair wind for twenty-five days. The capital lies beside the sea and up against the mountains.

Foreign ships from every place and foreign merchants traveling by land all come to this

---

[9]Semudera, on the north coast of the island of Sumatra and across the Strait of Malacca from Malaysia.
[10]1409.
[11]To the Ming court at Nanjing.
[12]The emperor.
[13]1412.
[14]1415.
[15]Presumably Nanjing.

[16]Non-Chinese.
[17]From the Arabic *dinar*.
[18]The English would later transliterate this local word as "cash."
[19]Hormuz, an island off the coast of Iran and at the mouth of the Persian Gulf.
[20]Calicut. See the Prologue's sample Multiple Voices.

country to attend the market and trade; hence the people of the country are all rich. . . .

The king of this country, too, took a ship and loaded it with lions, *qilin*,[21] horses, pearls, precious stones, and other things, also a memorial to the throne written on a golden leaf; and he sent his chiefs and other men, who accompanied the treasure-ships dispatched by the Emperor, which were returning from the Western Ocean; and they went to the capital and presented tribute.[22]

---

[21]A giraffe. This animal caused a tremendous amount of excitement at the Ming court.

[22]This probably took place at the end of the seventh expedition.

The Origins of Portugal's Overseas Empire
▼▼▼

88 ▼ *Gomes Eannes de Azurara,* *THE CHRONICLE OF GUINEA*

At the same time that Zheng He's fleets were sailing majestically through the western seas and Muslim sailors dominated the coastal traffic of virtually every inhabited land washed by the Indian Ocean (except Australia), the Portuguese were tentatively inching down the west coast of Africa. From 1419 onward, Prince Henry (1394–1460), third son of King John I (r. 1385–1433), almost annually sent out a ship or two in an attempt to push farther toward the sub-Saharan land the Portuguese called *Guinea*; only in 1434, however, did one of his caravels manage to round the feared Cape Bojador, along the western Sahara coast. Once this psychological and navigational barrier had been broken, the pace of exploration quickened. By 1460 Portuguese sailors had ventured as far south as present-day Sierra Leone, an advance of about 1,500 miles in twenty-six years. Finally, Bartholomeu Dias rounded the southern tip of Africa in early 1488, and Vasco da Gama, seeking, in his words, "Christians and spices," dropped anchor off Calicut on May 20, 1498 (see the Prologue's sample Multiple Voices). Although da Gama lost two of his four ships and many of his crew, the profits from this small enterprise were astounding. Portugal was now in the Indian Ocean to stay.

Portugal's commercial empire was still more than half a century in the future when, in 1452, Gomes Eannes de Azurara (ca. 1400–after 1472) began to compose a history of the life and work of Prince Henry "the Navigator," in so many ways the father of an empire-to-be. Azurara's history details Portuguese explorations along the coast of West Africa down to 1448. He promised a sequel because Henry was still alive and actively promoting voyages to Africa when Azurara completed *The Chronicle of Guinea* in 1453. Azurara's other duties apparently intervened, and he never returned to the topic. Still, the chronicle he managed to write is a revealing picture of the spirit behind Portugal's first generation of oceanic exploration and colonialism.

In the following excerpts, Azurara explains why Prince Henry sponsored the expeditions and defends the consequent enslavement of West Africans. Trade in Guinean slaves, which became an integral part of Portugal's commercial imperialism, began in 1441 with the capture of 10 Africans, and Azurara estimated that 927 West African slaves had come into Portugal by 1448. This humane man, who was disturbed by many of the aspects of this exploitation, could not foresee that between 1450 and 1500 roughly 150,000 more Africans would enter Portugal as slaves, and over the next four centuries millions of so-called heathens would be transported out of Africa by European and Euro-American slavers.

QUESTIONS FOR ANALYSIS

1. What were Henry's motives? What seems to have been foremost in his mind — commercial, political, or religious gain or simple curiosity?
2. Some modern commentators argue that Europeans initially entered the African slave trade out of a sense of racial superiority. Based on this account, do you think Azurara would agree with that assessment? In other words, how does he justify the enslavement of Africans? Please be specific in your answer.
3. It has been said that Henry was a fifteenth-century crusader. From the evidence, does this seem to be a fair judgment? Why or why not?
4. Compare the purposes behind the Portuguese explorations with those of Zheng He's expeditions. In what ways do they differ, and to what do you ascribe those differences?

We imagine that we know a matter when we are acquainted with the doer of it and the end for which he did it. And since in former chapters we have set forth the Lord Infant[1] as the chief actor in these things, giving as clear an understanding of him as we could, it is proper that in this present chapter we should know his purpose in doing them. And you should note well that the noble spirit of this Prince, by a sort of natural constraint, was ever urging him both to begin and to carry out very great deeds. For which reason, after the taking of Ceuta[2] he always kept ships well armed against the Infidel, both for war, and because he had also a wish to know the land that lay beyond the isles of Canary and that Cape called Bojador, for that up to his time, neither by writings, nor by the memory of man, was known with any certainty the nature of the land beyond that Cape. Some said indeed that Saint Brendan[3] had passed that way; and there was an-

other tale of two galleys rounding the Cape, which never returned. But this does not appear at all likely to be true, for it is not to be presumed that if the said galleys went there, some other ships would not have endeavored to learn what voyage they had made. And because the said Lord Infant wished to know the truth of this — since it seemed to him that if he or some other lord did not endeavor to gain that knowledge, no mariners or merchants would ever dare to attempt it — (for it is clear that none of them ever trouble themselves to sail to a place where there is not a sure and certain hope of profit) — and seeing also that no other prince took any pains in this matter, he sent out his own ships against those parts, to have manifest certainty of them all. And to this he was stirred up by his zeal for the service of God and of the King Edward his Lord and brother,[4] who then reigned. And this was the first reason of his action.

---

[1]Prince Henry. An *infante* (feminine *infanta*) was any son of a Portuguese or Spanish monarch who was not an heir to the throne.
[2]A Muslim naval base in Morocco that Portugal captured in 1415. In 1580 possession passed to Spain, which still controls it.

[3]A wandering Irish monk of the sixth century; according to legend, he set sail into the Atlantic.
[4]King Duarte (r. 1433–1438).

The second reason was that if there chanced to be in those lands some population of Christians, or some havens, into which it would be possible to sail without peril, many kinds of merchandise might be brought to this realm, which would find a ready market, and reasonably so, because no other people of these parts traded with them, nor yet people of any other that were known; and also the products of this realm might be taken there, which traffic would bring great profit to our countrymen.

The third reason was that, as it was said that the power of the Moors in that land of Africa was very much greater than was commonly supposed, and that there were no Christians among them, nor any other race of men; and because every wise man is obliged by natural prudence to wish for a knowledge of the power of his enemy; therefore the said Lord Infant exerted himself to cause this to be fully discovered, and to make it known determinately how far the power of those infidels extended.

The fourth reason was because during the one and thirty years that he had warred against the Moors, he had never found a Christian king, nor a lord outside this land, who for the love of our Lord Jesus Christ would aid him in the said war. Therefore he sought to know if there were in those parts any Christian princes, in whom the charity and the love of Christ was so ingrained that they would aid him against those enemies of the faith.

The fifth reason was his great desire to make increase in the faith of our Lord Jesus Christ and to bring to him all the souls that should be saved, — understanding that all the mystery of the Incarnation, Death, and Passion of our Lord Jesus Christ was for this sole end — namely the salvation of lost souls — whom the said Lord Infant by his travail and spending would fain bring into the true path. For he perceived that no better offering could be made unto the Lord than this; for if God promised to return one hundred goods for one, we may justly believe that for such great benefits, that is to say for so many souls as were saved by the efforts of this Lord, he will have so many hundreds of rewards in the kingdom of God, by which his spirit may be glorified after this life in the celestial realm. For I who wrote this history saw so many men and women of those parts turned to the holy faith, that even if the Infant had been a heathen, their prayers would have been enough to have obtained his salvation. And not only did I see the first captives,[5] but their children and grandchildren as true Christians as if the Divine grace breathed in them and imparted to them a clear knowledge of itself.

----

[5]West African slaves who had been captured and transported to Portugal by licensed slave hunters. As the slave trade developed, the vast majority of slaves transported out of Africa by Europeans and, later, Euro-Americans would be purchased from native African slavers (see source 93).

Chapter 13

Transoceanic Encounters
1500–1700

AGGRESSIVE EXPANSION HAD BEEN a driving force in Western European civilization for more than 700 years, but its transoceanic explorations that began in the fifteenth century mark a turning point in the history not only of the West but of the entire world. Europe's push across wide expanses of ocean eventually became the single most important factor in the breakdown of regional isolation around the world and the creation of a true global community in the years after 1500.

The story is not simple. By 1700 Europeans had culturally and demographically altered forever large areas of the Americas, but they had yet to visit much of those two great continents. The major civilizations of East Asia were still successfully resisting most unwanted European influences, and European penetration of India's interior had hardly begun. At the end of the seventeenth century, Western exploration and direct exploitation of the regions of Africa beyond the coasts were even less advanced. Moreover, although it is easy from a twenty-first-century perspective to see in its early transoceanic ventures the origins of Europe's eventual dominance of the world, this would not have been apparent to most people living during these two centuries. For every area into which Europeans were expanding their influence, there was another from which they were retreating or being rebuffed. For example, sixteenth- and seventeenth-century Europeans fearfully witnessed the advancing menace of the Ottoman Turks into southeastern Europe.

Under Sultan *Suleiman I* (r. 1520–1566), the Ottoman Empire became a major force to be reckoned with as far as Europe was concerned. In 1522 Suleiman's armies established control over the eastern Mediterranean by seizing the island of Rhodes from the crusading order of the Knights Hospitaler. In 1526 the Turks destroyed a Hungarian army and within two decades controlled most of that Christian kingdom. By the autumn of 1529, Ottoman forces besieged Vienna but were forced to withdraw. The Ottoman Turks remained Europe's greatest challenger for the next two centuries, and many believed that the next time Ottoman soldiers advanced on Vienna, they would not be stopped. Indeed, the siege of 1683 failed by the slightest margin.

Equally impressive was the expansion of Chinese borders, especially during the reign of Emperor *Kangxi* (r. 1661–1722), when China took control of the island of Formosa (present-day Taiwan), incorporated Tibet into its empire, turned the nomads of Mongolia into quiescent vassals, and entered into a border treaty with imperial Russia that inaugurated a long period of Sino-Russian peace. On its part, Russia carved out the largest land empire of its day through a steady process of exploration and colonization across Eurasia's eastern forests and steppes. In 1637 Russian pioneers reached the Pacific, and colonists were not far behind. Given this state of affairs, Western Europeans did not see expansion as a one-way street, nor did they see themselves as aggressors and the rest of the world as their victims.

▼▼▼

Europeans in the Americas

In the wake of Columbus's four voyages to the Americas, Europeans discovered that the world across the Atlantic contained exploitable sources of wealth, such as silver, gold, timber, and furs, and was capable of supporting large-scale agricultural production of such crops as sugar and tobacco, for which there was an eager European market. All these things seemed theirs for the taking, not only in the thinly populated regions of North America and eastern and southern South America, but even in the densely populated regions of Mexico, Peru, and the Caribbean.

The consequences of this attitude were catastrophic for America's indigenous peoples. By 1650 Spaniards and Portuguese ruled and exploited Mexico, the Caribbean, Central and South America, and southern portions of North America; the English, French, Dutch, and other Europeans had begun to settle the northern portions of North America's Atlantic coast and the Saint Lawrence River Basin. As a consequence of these European incursions, Native American political structures disintegrated, uncounted millions of American Indians died, and traditional patterns of life and belief managed only a tenuous (but tenacious) survival.

While this sad story is true enough, it would be incorrect to say that the majority of the European colonists and the governments that supported them attempted to exterminate the Native Americans. Certainly most European colonists sought to exploit them, and even the American Indians' protectors sought to convert them to Western European forms of Christianity, thereby offering the natives a form of cultural suicide. There is also no denying the fact that the European newcomers contained within their ranks a number of ruthless thugs who did not hesitate to brutalize and kill, sometimes on a large scale. Still, there is no credible evidence of any widespread attempts at *genocide*, or the systematic, state-sponsored annihilation of an entire people. Such a notion was inconsistent with the worldview and aims of the European colonizers who sought souls to save and slaves for servitude.

Europeans might have lacked the intention of killing off millions of Native Americans, but they managed to do so unintentionally, as a consequence of the viruses, bacteria, and other parasites that they carried across the Atlantic in their bodies and ships. Moreover, when West African slaves were brought to the Caribbean to replace the native populations that were rapidly dying off, additional fatal diseases came into the Americas. Smallpox, measles, diphtheria, chickenpox, whooping cough, influenza, malaria, yellow fever — all of these and more became killers when introduced into populations that lacked genetic resistance, due to their thousands of years of isolation from the Afro-Eurasian World.

The Tainos, who greeted Columbus, numbered about 1 million in 1492; by 1530 they numbered a few thousand. In 1519, the year of Cortés's arrival, the population of Mexico was about 21.5 million people; in 1532 it had fallen to about 16 million; at midcentury, following the epidemic of 1545–1548, it was possibly as low as 2.5 million. That is a 90 percent decrease in the short space of thirty years! No part of the Americas was untouched; even areas not visited by Europeans felt the devastating effects of killer epidemics. The Mississippian Mound Culture of North America probably disappeared as an identifiable entity in the mid sixteenth century as a result of European diseases that traveled along native trade routes to its population centers, well before Europeans ever saw the mound complexes that this culture left behind as silent witnesses of its former greatness.

The first of the following two documents hints at the critical role played by the hidden ally of disease in the Spanish *conquistadors'* conquest of Mexico. It also suggests other factors that combined to give the Spaniards their victory. The second source reveals the devastating effects of simple greed on the part of Spanish entrepreneurs in Peru.

The Battle for Tenochtitlan: A Mexica Perspective

▼▼▼

89 ▼ *Bernardino de Sahagún,* GENERAL HISTORY OF THE THINGS OF NEW SPAIN

Bernardino de Sahagún (ca. 1499–1590), a member of the Franciscan Order, was one of the earliest Spanish missionaries in Mexico, arriving in 1529. He soon developed a keen interest in the culture of the natives of Mexico, for whom he had deep affection and respect. He mastered the *Nahuatl* language, spoken by the Mexica (Aztecs) and other central Mexican peoples, and in 1545 began a systematic collection of oral and pictorial information about the culture of the native Mexicans. The result was our principal source of information about Mexican culture at the time of the Spanish conquest.

The following selection comes from the twelfth and last book of his *General History of the Things of New Spain*. Based on interviews Sahagún and his American Indian assistants had with Mexica who had experienced the conquest some twenty-five years earlier, Book Twelve, which exists in both Nahuatl and Spanish versions, recounts events in Mexico from the time Cortés arrived on the coast in April 1519 until the days immediately following the Mexica capitulation in August 1521. Although scholars hotly debate the exact role of Sahagún and his assistants in composing and organizing Book Twelve, most agree that it accurately portrays Mexica views and perceptions of the events that unfolded between 1519 and 1521.

The following excerpt, translated from the Nahuatl text, picks up the story in November 1519. By then the Spaniards had gained as allies the Tlaxcalans, the Aztecs' bitter enemies, and were leaving Cholula, an ancient city that the Spaniards and their allies had subjected to slaughter and sack (see Multiple Voices VIII). They were on their way to Tenochtitlan, the Mexica capital on Lake Texcoco, for an anticipated meeting with the emperor, Moctezuma.

QUESTIONS FOR ANALYSIS

1. What does the source reveal about the motives of the Spaniards and their allies for their attack on the Mexica?
2. What was Moctezuma's strategy for dealing with the Spaniards? Why did it fail?
3. What impression did Spanish firearms and cannons have on the Mexica? What evidence is there that the Mexica adjusted their strategy to counter the Spanish weapons?
4. Aside from their firearms, what other military advantages did the Spaniards have over their opponents? How decisive do these other advantages seem to have been?

5. On occasion the Mexica routed the Spaniards. What explains these victories?
6. How did the Mexica view of war differ from that of the Spaniards?
7. What does the source reveal about Mexica religious beliefs, values, and practices?

And after the dying in Cholula,[1] the Spaniards set off on their way to Mexico,[2] coming gathered and bunched, raising dust. . . .

Thereupon Moteucçoma[3] named and sent noblemen and a great many other agents of his . . . to go meet [Cortés]. . . . They gave [the Spaniards] golden banners of precious feathers, and golden necklaces.

And when they had given the things to them, they seemed to smile, to rejoice and to be very happy. Like monkeys they grabbed the gold. It was as though their hearts were put to rest, brightened, freshened. For gold was what they greatly thirsted for; they were gluttonous for it, starved for it, piggishly wanting it. They came lifting up the golden banners, waving them from side to side, showing them to each other. They seemed to babble; what they said to each other was in a babbling tongue. . . .

Another group of messengers — rainmakers, witches, and priests — had also gone out for an encounter, but nowhere were they able to do anything or to get sight of [the Spaniards]; they did not hit their target, they did not find the people they were looking for, they were not sufficient. . . .

▷ Cortés and his entourage continue their march.

Then they set out in this direction, about to enter Mexico here. Then they all dressed and equipped themselves for war. They girded them-

selves, tying their battle gear tightly on themselves and then on their horses. Then they arranged themselves in rows, files, ranks.

Four horsemen came ahead going first, staying ahead, leading. . . .

Also the dogs, their dogs, came ahead, sniffing at things and constantly panting.[4]

By himself came marching ahead, all alone, the one who bore the standard on his shoulder. He came waving it about, making it spin, tossing it here and there. . . .

Following him came those with iron swords. Their iron swords came bare and gleaming. On their shoulders they bore their shields, of wood or leather.

The second contingent and file were horses carrying people, each with his cotton cuirass,[5] his leather shield, his iron lance, and his iron sword hanging down from the horse's neck. They came with bells on, jingling or rattling. The horses, the deer,[6] neighed, there was much neighing, and they would sweat a great deal; water seemed to fall from them. And their flecks of foam splatted on the ground, like soapsuds splatting. . . .

The third file were those with iron crossbows, the crossbowmen. Their quivers went hanging at their sides, passed under their armpits, well filled, packed with arrows, with iron bolts. . . .

The fourth file were likewise horsemen; their outfits were the same as has been said.

The fifth group were those with harquebuses,[7] the harquebusiers, shouldering their harquebuses;

---

[1]For more on Cholula, see source 76 and Multiple Voices VIII.

[2]Throughout the text, the term *Mexico* refers to Tenochtitlan, the capital of the Aztec Empire.

[3]One of several acceptable modern spellings of the emperor's name, including *Moctezuma, Motecuhzoma,* and *Montezuma.*

[4]Specially bred war dogs for use in combat.

[5]A piece of armor that covered the body from neck to waist.

[6]Having never before seen horses, some Mexica considered them to be large deer.

[7]Also spelled *arquebuses.* See source 86, note 3.

some held them [level]. And when they went into the great palace, the residence of the ruler, they repeatedly shot off their harquebuses. They exploded, sputtered, discharged, thundered, disgorged. Smoke spread, it grew dark with smoke, everyplace filled with smoke. The fetid smell made people dizzy and faint.

Then all those from the various altepetl[8] on the other side of the mountains, the Tlaxcalans, the people of Tliliuhquitepec, of Huexotzinco, came following behind. They came outfitted for war with their cotton upper armor, shields, and bows, their quivers full and packed with feathered arrows, some barbed, some blunted, some with obsidian[9] points. They went crouching, hitting their mouths with their hands yelling, singing, . . . whistling, shaking their heads. . . .

▷   Cortés and his army entered Tenochtitlan in November 1519 and were amicably received by Moctezuma, who was nonetheless taken captive by the Spaniards. Cortés's army was allowed to remain in a palace compound, but tensions grew the following spring. Pedro de Alvarado, in command while Cortés left to deal with a threat to his authority from the governor of Cuba, became increasingly concerned for the Spaniards' safety as the people of Tenochtitlan prepared to celebrate the annual festival in honor of Huitzilopochtli, the warrior god of the sun.

And when it had dawned and was already the day of his festivity, very early in the morning those who had made vows to him[10] unveiled his face. Forming a single row before him they offered him incense; each in his place laid down before him offerings of food for fasting and rolled amaranth dough.[11] And it was as though all the youthful warriors had gathered together and had hit on the idea of holding and observing the festivity in order to show the Spaniards

something, to make them marvel and instruct them.[12] . . .

When things were already going on, when the festivity was being observed and there was dancing and singing, with voices raised in song, the singing was like the noise of waves breaking against the rocks.

When it was time, when the moment had come for the Spaniards to do the killing, they came out equipped for battle. They came and closed off each of the places where people went in and out. . . . And when they had closed these exits, they stationed themselves in each, and no one could come out any more. . . . Then they surrounded those who were dancing, going among the cylindrical drums. They struck a drummer's arms; both of his hands were severed. Then they struck his neck; his head landed far away. Then they stabbed everyone with iron lances and struck them with iron swords. They struck some in the belly, and then their entrails came spilling out. They split open the heads of some, they really cut their skulls to pieces, their skulls were cut up into little bits. And if someone still tried to run it was useless; he just dragged his intestines along. There was a stench as if of sulfur. Those who tried to escape could go nowhere. When anyone tried to go out, at the entryways they struck and stabbed him.

And when it became known what was happening, everyone cried out, "Mexica warriors, come running, get outfitted with devices, shields, and arrows, hurry, come running, the warriors are dying; they have died, perished, been annihilated, O Mexica warriors!" Thereupon there were war cries, shouting, and beating of hands against lips. The warriors quickly came outfitted, bunched together, carrying arrows and shields. Then the fighting began; they shot at them with barbed darts, spears, and tridents,

---

[8]The Nahuatl term for any sovereign state, especially the local ethnic states of central Mexico.
[9]A volcanic glass that can be sharpened to a razor-sharp edge.
[10]Huitzilopochtli. As god of the sun, he needed daily sacrifices of human hearts and blood in order to rise from the east each morning.

[11]An image of the god was fashioned from amaranth seed flour and the blood of recently sacrificed victims.
[12]An integral part of the ceremony was the singing of hymns that extolled battle, blood, and honor on the field of conflict.

and they hurled darts with broad obsidian points at them. . . .

> ▷ The fighting that ensued drove the Spaniards and their allies back to the palace enclave. Without a reliable supply of food and water, in June or July 1520, Cortés, who had returned with his power intact, led his followers on a desperate nocturnal escape from the city, but they were discovered and suffered heavy losses as they fled. They retreated to the other side of the lake, and the Mexica believed that the Spanish threat had passed.

Before the Spanish appeared to us [again], first an epidemic broke out, a sickness of pustules.[13] . . . Large bumps spread on people; some were entirely covered. They spread everywhere, on the face, the head, the chest, etc. The disease brought great desolation; a great many died of it. They could no longer walk about, but lay in their dwellings and sleeping places, no longer able to move or stir. They were unable to change position, to stretch out on their sides or face down, or raise their heads. And when they made a motion, they called out loudly. The pustules that covered people caused great desolation; very many people died of them, and many just starved to death; starvation reigned, and no one took care of others any longer.

On some people, the pustules appeared only far apart, and they did not suffer greatly, nor did many of them die of it. But many people's faces were spoiled by it, their faces and noses were made rough. Some lost an eye or were blinded.

This disease of pustules lasted a full sixty days; after sixty days it abated and ended. When people were convalescing and reviving, the pustules disease began to move in the direction of Chalco.[14] And many were disabled or paralyzed

by it, but they were not disabled forever. . . . The Mexica warriors were greatly weakened by it.

And when things were in this state, the Spaniards came. . . .

> ▷ Having resupplied his army and having constructed a dozen cannon-carrying brigantines for use on the lake, Cortés resumed his offensive late in 1520. In April 1521 he reached Tenochtitlan and besieged the city.

When their twelve boats had [arrived] . . . then the Marqués[15] went about searching where the boats could enter, where the canals were straight, whether they were deep or not, so that they would not be grounded somewhere. But the canals were winding and bent back and forth, and they could not get them in. They did get two boats in. . . .

And the two boats came gradually, keeping on one side. . . . They came ahead, fighting as they came; there were deaths on both sides, and on both sides captives were taken. . . . Once they got two of their boats into the canal at Xocotitlan.[16] When they had beached them, then they went looking into the house sites of the people of Xocotitlan. But Tzilacatzin[17] and some other warriors who saw the Spaniards immediately came out to face them; they came running after them, throwing stones at them, and they scattered the Spaniards into the water. . . .

When they got to Tlilhuacan,[18] the warriors crouched far down and hid themselves, hugging the ground, waiting for the war cry, when there would be shouting and cries of encouragement. When the cry went up, "O Mexica, up and at them!" the Tlappanecatl Ecatzin,[19] a warrior of Otomi[20] rank, faced the Spaniards and threw himself at them, saying, "O Tlatelolca[21] warriors, up and at them, who are these barbarians?

[13]Smallpox.
[14]A city on the southeast corner of Lake Texcoco.
[15]Cortés.
[16]A district of Tenochtitlan.
[17]A warrior-hero who distinguished himself in this battle. He was of the Otomi order (see note 20).
[18]A district of the city.
[19]The title of a local governor.

[20]Elite Mexica warriors bound by oath never to retreat, they wore their hair in the style of the fierce Otomi warriors as a mark of their special status. See Multiple Voices VIII for more on the Otomis.
[21]Formerly an independent city located next to Tenochtitlan, it was absorbed by the latter and became its vast market district. This district remained loyal to the Mexica cause to the end.

Come running!" Then he went and threw a Spaniard down, knocking him to the ground; the one he threw down was the one who came first, who came leading them. And when he had thrown him down, he dragged the Spaniard off.

And at this point they let loose with all the warriors who had been crouching there; they came out and chased the Spaniards in the passageways, and when the Spaniards saw it they, the Mexica, seemed to be intoxicated. Then captives were taken. Many Tlaxcalans, and people of Acolhuacan, Chalco, Xochimilco, etc.,[22] were captured. A great abundance were captured and killed. . . .

Then they took the captives to Yacacolco,[23] hurrying them along, going along herding their captives together. Some went weeping, some singing, some went shouting while hitting their hands against their mouths. When they got them to Yacacolco, they lined them all up. Each one went to the altar platform where the sacrifice was performed.[24] The Spaniards went first, going in the lead; the people of the different altepetl just followed, coming last. And when the sacrifice was over, they strung the Spaniards' heads on poles on skull racks; they also strung up the horses' heads. They placed them below, and the Spaniards' heads were above them, strung up facing east.[25] . . .

▷ Despite this victory, the Mexica could not overcome the problems of shortages of food, water, and warriors. In mid July 1521, the Spaniards and their allies resumed their assault, and in early August the Mexica decided to send into battle a quetzal-owl warrior, whose success or failure, it was believed, would reveal if the gods wished them to continue the war.

And all the common people suffered greatly. There was famine; many died of hunger. They no longer drank good, pure water, but the water they drank was salty. Many people died of it, and because of it many got dysentery and died. Everything was eaten: lizards, swallows, maize straw, grass that grows on salt flats. And they chewed at . . . wood, glue flowers, plaster, leather, and deerskin, which they roasted, baked, and toasted so that they could eat them, and they ground up medicinal herbs and adobe bricks. There had never been the like of such suffering. The siege was frightening, and great numbers died of hunger. And bit by bit they came pressing us back against the wall, herding us together. . . . There was no place to go; people shoved, pressed and trampled one another; many died in the press. But one woman came to very close quarters with our enemies, throwing water at them, throwing water in their faces, making it stream down their faces.

And when the ruler Quauhtemoctzin[26] and the warriors Coyohuehuetzin, Temilotzin, Topantemoctzin, the Mixcoatlailotlac Ahuelitoctzin, Tlacotzin, and Petlauhtzin took a great warrior named Tlapaltecatl opochtzin . . . and outfitted him, dressing him in a quetzal-owl costume.[27] . . . "Let him wear it, let him die in it. Let him dazzle people with it, let him show them something; let our enemies see and admire it." When they put it on him he looked very frightening and splendid. And they ordered four [others] to come helping him, to accompany him. They gave him the darts of the devil,[28] darts of wooden rods with flint tips. And the reason they did this was that it was as though the fate of the rulers of the Mexica were being determined.

---

[22]American Indian allies of the Spaniards.
[23]A suburb of the city.
[24]Traditionally, the sacrifice consisted of cutting the heart out of the victim.
[25]The direction of the god Huitzilopochtli. See note 10. Reportedly fifty-three Spaniards and four horses were among those sacrificed.

[26]Quauhtemoctzin was now the emperor, Moctezuma having died while in Spanish captivity.
[27]This rare bird had been sacred to the Maya and was equally sacred to the Mexica. Its four iridescent blue-green tail feathers were highly prized.
[28]Battle darts sacred to Huitzilopochtli.

When our enemies saw him, it was as though a mountain had fallen. Every one of the Spaniards was frightened; he intimidated them, they seemed to respect him a great deal. Then the quetzal-owl climbed up on the roof. But when some of our enemies had taken a good look at him they rose and turned him back, pursuing him. Then the quetzal-owl turned to them again and pursued them. Then he snatched up the precious feathers and gold and dropped down off the roof. He did not die, and our enemies did not carry him off. Also three of our enemies were captured. At that the war stopped for good.

There was silence, nothing more happened. Then our enemies went away. It was silent and nothing more happened until it got dark.

And the next day nothing more happened at all, no one made a sound. The common people just lay collapsed. The Spaniards did nothing more either, but lay still, looking at the people. Nothing was going on, they just lay still. . . .

▷ Two weeks passed before the Mexica capitulated on August 13, 1521, after a siege of more than three months' duration.

The "Mountain of Silver" and the Mita System

▼▼▼

90 ▼ Antonio Vazquez de Espinosa, COMPENDIUM AND DESCRIPTION OF THE WEST INDIES

Queen Isabella of Spain was, by most accounts, disquieted by the idea of enslaving American Indians, but forced labor came to the new Spanish colonies nevertheless, largely because it proved economically advantageous for the colonizers, especially on their plantations and in their mines.

In 1545 the Spaniards discovered the world's richest silver mine at Potosí. Located two miles above sea level in a cold, desolate region of present-day Bolivia, Potosí became the site of the Western Hemisphere's first and greatest silver rush. Within four decades Potosí had a racially mixed population of 160,000 inhabitants, making it the largest, wildest, gaudiest, and richest city in the New World. With one-fifth of all the silver extracted going directly to the Spanish crown, Potosí was a major reason why the kings of Spain were able to launch a huge naval armada against England in 1588, carry on a crusade against the Ottoman Empire in the eastern Mediterranean, and send armies off to campaigns in France, the Low Countries, and central Europe. The silver of Potosí also contributed significantly to massive inflation throughout Europe and in China, as the wealth filtered out of Spanish hands.

The backbone of the Potosí operation was the *mita* system of labor, described by Antonio Vazquez de Espinosa (d. 1630), a Spanish Carmelite missionary-friar. He returned to Spain in 1622, where he wrote half a dozen books on the Americas and topics relating to priestly work. His best-known book is *Compendium and Description of the West Indies*, an extensive summary of observations made during his travels through Mexico and Spanish South America.

In the first part of the selection that follows, Espinosa describes the mine and facilities at Huancavelica for extracting mercury, a necessary element in the refining of silver. The second portion provides a wealth of details on the mining of silver at Potosí. Throughout the document, Espinosa presents insights into the functioning of the mita system of labor, which had its roots in the Inca Empire when villages had been required to provide an annual quota of laborers for public works projects. The Spaniards continued the practice of enforced labor quotas, at first for public works, and later for work in mines, factories, and fields owned by private individuals.

QUESTIONS FOR ANALYSIS

1. What was the range of annual wages for each laborer at Huancavelica? How did this amount of money compare with the annual salary of the royal hospital chaplain? How did the annual sum of their wages compare with the cost of tallow candles at Potosí? Compare the wages of the mita workers at Potosí with the wages paid those American Indians who freely hired themselves out. What do you conclude from all these figures?
2. What were the major hazards of the work connected with the extraction and production of mercury and silver?
3. What evidence does Espinosa provide of Spanish concern for the welfare of the American Indian workers? What evidence is there of unconcern? Where does the weight of the evidence seem to lie?
4. Wherever huge profits justify the risks, there will be people who function beyond the constraints of the law. What evidence does Espinosa provide of this phenomenon in Spanish South America?
5. How did the mita system work?
6. What appears to have been the impact of the mita system on native Peruvian society?

HUANCAVELICA

And so at the rumor of the rich deposits of mercury . . . in the years 1570 and 1571, they started the construction of the town of Huancavelica de Oropesa. . . . It contains 400 Spanish residents, as well as many temporary shops of dealers in merchandise and groceries, heads of trading houses, and transients, for the town has a lively commerce. It has a parish church with vicar and curate,[1] a Dominican convent, and a Royal Hospital under the Brethren of San Juan de Diós for the care of the sick, especially Indians on the range; it has a chaplain with a salary of 800 pesos[2] contributed by His Majesty; he is curate of the parish of San Sebastian de Indios, for the Indians who have come to work in the mines and who have settled down there. There is another parish on the other side of the town, known as Santa Ana, and administered by Dominican friars.

---

[1] A parish priest and his assistant priest.

[2] A standard Spanish currency weight of twenty-seven grams of 92 percent silver (see note 11).

Every two months His Majesty sends by the regular courier from Lima[3] 60,000 pesos to pay for the mita of the Indians, for the crews are changed every two months, so that merely for the Indian mita payment . . . 360,000 pesos are sent from Lima every year, not to speak of much besides, which all crosses at his risk that cold and desolate mountain country which is the puna[4] and has nothing on it but llama ranches.

Up on the range there are 3,000 or 4,000 Indians working in the mine; it is colder up there than in the town, since it is higher. The mine where the mercury is located is a large layer which they keep following downward. When I was in that town (which was in the year 1616) I went up on the range and down into the mine, which at that time was considerably more than 130 stades[5] deep. The ore was very rich black flint, and the excavation so extensive that it held more than 3,000 Indians working away hard with picks and hammers, breaking up that flint ore; and when they have filled their little sacks, the poor fellows, loaded down with ore, climb up those ladders or rigging, some like masts and others like cables, and so trying and distressing that a man empty-handed can hardly get up them. That is the way they work in this mine, with many lights and the loud noise of the pounding and great confusion. Nor is that the greatest evil and difficulty; that is due to thievish and undisciplined superintendents. As that great vein of ore keeps going down deeper and they follow its rich trail, in order to make sure that no section of that ore shall drop on top of them, they keep leaving supports or pillars of the ore itself, even if of the richest quality, and they necessarily help to sustain and insure each section with less risk. This being so, there are men so heartless that for the sake of stealing a little rich ore, they go down out of hours and de-

prive the innocent Indians of this protection by hollowing into these pillars to steal the rich ore in them, and then a great section is apt to fall in and kill all the Indians, and sometimes the unscrupulous and grasping superintendents themselves, as happened when I was in that locality; and much of this is kept quiet so that it shall not come to the notice of the manager and cause the punishment of the accomplices. . . .

This is how they extract the mercury. On the other side of the town there are structures where they grind up the mercury ore and then put it in jars with molds like sugar loaves on top of them, with many little holes, and others on top of them, flaring and plastered with mud, and a channel for it to drip into and pass into the jar or place where it is to fall. Then they roast the ore with a straw fire from the plant growing on the puna, like esparto grass, which they call ichu; that is the best sort of fire for the treatment of this ore. Under the onset of this fire it melts and the mercury goes up in vapor or exhalation until, passing through the holes in the first mold, it hits the body of the second, and there it coagulates, rests, and comes to stop where they have provided lodging for it; [but] if it does not strike any solid body while it is hot, it rises as vapor until it cools and coagulates and starts falling downward again. Those who carry out the reduction of this ore have to be very careful and test cautiously; they must wait till the jars are cold before uncovering them for otherwise they may easily get mercury poisoning and if they do, they are of no further use; their teeth fall out, and some die. . . . In the treatment of the silver [at Potosí] they use up every year more than 6,000 quintals[6] [of mercury], plus 2,000 more derived from the ore dust, i.e., the silver and mercury which was lost and escaped from the first washing of the ore, made in vats.

---

[3]Lima was the capital city of the viceroyalty of Peru, one of the two major administrative units of Spanish America.
[4]A high, cold plateau.

[5]A *stade* was approximately one-eighth of a mile.
[6]A *quintal* was measure of weight equaling anywhere from 100 to 130 pounds.

POTOSÍ

The famous Potosí range, so celebrated all over the world for the great wealth which God has created unique in its bowels and veins, lies in . . . [a] region [that] is usually colder than Germany, so much so that it was uninhabitable for the native tribes. . . .

According to His Majesty's warrant, the mine owners on this massive range have a right to the mita of 13,300 Indians in the working and exploitation of the mines, both those which have been discovered, those now discovered, and those which shall be discovered. It is the duty of the Corregidor of Potosí[7] to have them rounded up and to see that they come in from all the provinces between Cuzco over the whole of El Collao and as far as the frontiers of Tarija and Tomina;[8] this Potosí Corregidor has power and authority over all the Corregidors in those provinces mentioned; for if they do not fill the Indian mita allotment assigned each of them in accordance with the capacity of their provinces as indicated to them, he can send them, and does, salaried inspectors to report upon it, and when the remissness is great or remarkable, he can suspend them, notifying the Viceroy[9] of the fact.

These Indians are sent out every year under a captain whom they choose in each village or tribe, for him to take them and oversee them for the year each has to serve; every year they have a new election, for as some go out, others come in. This works out very badly, with great losses and gaps in the quotas of Indians, the villages being depopulated; and this gives rise to great extortions and abuses on the part of the inspectors toward the poor Indians, ruining them and thus depriving the . . . chief Indians of their property and carrying them off in chains because they do not fill out the mita assignment, which they cannot do, for the reason given and for others which I do not bring forward.

These 13,300 are divided up every 4 months into 3 mitas, each consisting of 4,433 Indians, to work in the mines on the range and in the 120 smelters in the Potosí and Tarapaya areas; it is a good league[10] between the two. These mita Indians earn each day, or there is paid each one for his labor, 4 reals.[11] Besides these there are others not under obligation, who are mingados or hire themselves out voluntarily: these each get from 12 to 16 reals, and some up to 24, according to their reputation of wielding the pick and knowing how to get the ore out. These mingados will be over 4,000 in number. They and the mita Indians go up every Monday morning to the locality of Guayna Potosí which is at the foot of the range; the Corregidor arrives with all the provincial captains or chiefs who have charge of the Indians assigned them, and he there checks off and reports to each mine and smelter owner the number of Indians assigned him for his mine or smelter; that keeps him busy till 1 P.M., by which time the Indians are already turned over to these mine and smelter owners.

After each has eaten his ration, they climb up the hill, each to his mine, and go in, staying there from that hour until Saturday evening without coming out of the mine; their wives bring them food, but they stay constantly underground, excavating and carrying out the ore from which they get the silver. They all have tallow candles, lighted day and night; that is the light they work with, for as they are underground, they have need of it all the time. The mere cost of these candles used in the mines on this range will amount every year to more than 300,000 pesos, even though tallow is cheap in that country, being abundant; but this is a very

---

[7]A district military leader.
[8]This region consisted of approximately 139 Indian villages.
[9]Literally "the royal deputy," he was appointed by the Crown to serve as chief military and civil administrator over a vast region.

[10]A league is three miles.
[11]A Spanish silver coin, eight of which equaled one peso (see note 2).

great expense, and it is almost incredible, how much is spent for candles in the operation of breaking down and getting out the ore.

These Indians have different functions in the handling of the silver ore; some break it up with bar or pick, and dig down in, following the vein in the mine; others bring it up; others up above keep separating the good and the poor in piles; others are occupied in taking it down from the range to the mills on herds of llamas; every day they bring up more than 8,000 of these native beasts of burden for this task. These teamsters who carry the metal do not belong to the mita, but are mingados — hired.

So huge is the wealth which has been taken out of this range since the year 1545, when it was discovered, up to the present year of 1628, which makes 83 years that they have been working and reducing its ores, that merely from the registered mines, as appears from an examination of most of the accounts in the royal records, 326,000,000 assay pesos have been taken out. At the beginning when the ore was richer and easier to get out, for then there were no mita Indians and no mercury process, in the 40 years between 1545 and 1585, they took out 111,000,000 of assay silver. From the year 1585 up to 1628, 43 years, although the mines are harder to work, for

they are deeper down, with the assistance of 13,300 Indians whom His Majesty has granted to the mine owners on that range, and of other hired Indians, who come there freely and voluntarily to work at day's wages, and with the great advantage of the mercury process, in which none of the ore or the silver is wasted, and with the better knowledge of the technique which the miners now have, they have taken out 215,000,000 assay pesos. That, plus the 111 extracted in the 40 years previous to 1585, makes 326,000,000 assay pesos, not counting the great amount of silver secretly taken from these mines . . . to Spain, paying no 20 percent or registry fee,[12] and to other countries outside Spain; and to the Philippines and China, which is beyond all reckoning; but I should venture to imagine and even assert that what has been taken from the Potosí range must be as much again as what paid the 20 percent royal impost.

Over and above that, such great treasure and riches have come from the Indies in gold and silver from all the other mines in New Spain and Peru, Honduras, the New Kingdom of Granada, Chile, New Galicia, New Vizcaya,[13] and other quarters since the discovery of the Indies, that they exceed 1,800 millions.

---

[12]The 20 percent registry fee was the royal tax on all New World silver.

[13]New Galicia and New Vizcaya were regions and administrative jurisdictions in New Spain located in north-central and northwestern Mexico.

▼▼▼

African Reactions to the European Presence

Due mainly to the catastrophic decline of the American Indian population, Spanish and Portuguese colonists increasingly turned to African slaves for labor in the sixteenth century. Portugal, which had begun to explore the west coast of Africa in 1418, was initially in an advantageous position to supply this human chattel. During the 1480s the Portuguese established fortified posts along West Africa's Gold Coast, where it traded with coastal kingdoms such as Benin for gold, slaves, and ivory. By 1500 some 700 kilos of gold and approximately 10,000 slaves were arriving annually in Lisbon from West Africa. While engaging in this trade, the Portuguese were also pushing down the coast. Finally, in 1487–1488 Bartholomeu Dias rounded the Cape of Good Hope, opening the east coast of Africa to direct Portuguese contact. Under the leadership of Francisco de Almeida (ca. 1450–1510), the Portuguese set up fortified trading posts along Africa's east coast, thereby successfully challenging Arab hegemony over East African trade.

The Portuguese led the way, but other European maritime powers were close behind in establishing their presence in coastal Africa. While the Spaniards concentrated on North Africa, capturing Tunis in 1535 and holding it until 1574, the English under John Hawkins instituted their own slave trade from West Africa to the New World between 1562 and 1568. After 1713, when England won the right of *asiento*, by which it was granted license to transport African slaves to the Spanish Americas, the English came to dominate the African slave trade. In 1595 the Dutch began to trade on the Guinea coast, and in 1652 they founded Cape Town on the southern tip of the continent. The first French forts in Africa appeared in 1626 on the island of Madagascar, which France annexed in 1686, and by 1637 the French were building numerous forts on West Africa's Gold Coast and exploring Senegal. Even the Prussians had a minor presence in West Africa by 1683.

Slaves and gold were the two major attractions for all these European powers on the African coasts, and many Africans were quite willing to deal in these commodities with the outside world. Arab and Berber traders had already been crossing the Sahara for centuries to purchase the goods of inner Africa, including millions of slaves. European merchants now simply opened a new door — a coastal door — to this lucrative, long-booming market.

Although Europeans were becoming a major presence along the coasts, their penetration of the interior would have to wait for a later age. The general social and political strength of most African regional kingdoms, the wide variety of debilitating and often deadly African diseases, against which Europeans had no immunities, and the absence of safe and fast inland transportation combined to block significant European thrust into the interior until the nineteenth century. The Europeans were thus forced to come largely as traders and not colonizers, and they had to negotiate with local African leaders for goods and slaves.

An African Voice of Ambivalence?

▼▼▼

91 ▼ *Nzinga Mbemba (Afonso I), LETTERS TO THE KING OF PORTUGAL*

The largest state in central West Africa in 1500 was the kingdom of Kongo, stretching along the estuary of the Congo River in territory that today lies within the nations of Angola and the Democratic Republic of the Congo. In 1483 the Portuguese navigator Diogo Cão made contact with Kongo and several years later visited its inland capital. When he sailed home, he brought with him Kongo emissaries, whom King Nzinga a Kuwu dispatched to Lisbon to learn European ways. They returned in 1491, accompanied by Portuguese priests, artisans, and soldiers, who brought with them a wide variety of European goods, including a printing press. In the same year, the king and his son, Nzinga Mbemba, were baptized into the Catholic faith.

Around 1506 Nzinga Mbemba, whose Christian name was *Afonso*, succeeded his father and ruled until about 1543. Afonso promoted the introduction of European culture into his kingdom by adopting Christianity as the state religion (although most of his subjects remained followers of the ancient ways), imitating the etiquette of the Portuguese royal court, and using Portuguese as the language of state business. His son Henrique was educated in Portugal and returned to serve as West Africa's first native-born Roman Catholic bishop. European firearms, horses, and cattle, as well as new foods from the Americas, became common in Kongo, and Afonso dreamed of achieving a powerful and prosperous state through cooperation with the Europeans. By the time of his death, however, his kingdom was on the verge of disintegration, in no small measure because of the Portuguese. As many later African rulers were to discover, the introduction of European products and customs caused dissension and instability. Worse yet, Portuguese involvement in the slave trade undermined Afonso's authority and made his subjects restive.

In 1526 King Afonso wrote the following three letters to King João III of Portugal. The three documents are part of a collection of twenty-four letters that Afonso and his Portuguese-educated native secretaries dispatched to two successive kings of Portugal on a variety of issues. This collection is our earliest extant source of African commentary on the European impact.

QUESTIONS FOR ANALYSIS

1. According to King Afonso, what have been the detrimental effects of the Portuguese presence in his kingdom?
2. What do the letters reveal about the mechanics of the slave trade in the kingdom? Who participated in it?
3. What do the letters reveal about King Afonso's attitude toward slavery? Was he opposed to the practice in its entirety or only to certain aspects of it?
4. What steps has the king taken to deal with the problems caused by the Portuguese? What do the letters suggest about the effectiveness of these steps?
5. How would you characterize Afonso's attitude toward the power and authority of the king of Portugal? Does he consider himself inferior to the Portuguese king or his equal?
6. Based on this evidence, what do you conclude was King Afonso's conception of the ideal relationship between the Portuguese and his kingdom?

JULY 6, 1526

Sir, Your Highness should know how our Kingdom is being lost in so many ways that it is convenient to provide for the necessary remedy, since this is caused by the excessive freedom given by your agents and officials to the men and merchants who are allowed to come to this Kingdom to set up shops with goods and many things which have been prohibited by us, and which they spread throughout our Kingdoms and Domains in such an abundance that many of our vassals, whom we had in obedience, do not comply because they have the things in greater abundance than we ourselves; and it was with these things that we had them content and subjected under our vassalage and jurisdiction, so it is doing a great harm not only to the service of God, but the security and peace of our Kingdoms and State as well.

And we cannot reckon how great the damage is, since the mentioned merchants are taking every day our natives, sons of the land and the sons of our noblemen and vassals and our relatives, because the thieves and men of bad conscience grab them wishing to have the things and wares of this Kingdom which they are ambitious of; they grab them and get them to be sold; and so great, Sir, is the corruption and licentiousness that our country is being completely depopulated, and Your Highness should not agree with this nor accept it as in your service. And to avoid it we need from those (your) Kingdoms no more than some priests and a few people to teach in schools, and no other goods except wine and flour for the holy sacrament. That is why we beg of Your Highness to help and assist us in this matter, commanding your

factors that they should not send here either merchants or wares, because it is *our will that in these Kingdoms there should not be any trade of slaves nor outlet for them.*[1] Concerning what is referred [to] above, again we beg of Your Highness to agree with it, since otherwise we cannot remedy such an obvious damage. Pray Our Lord in His mercy to have Your Highness under His guard and let you do forever the things of His service. I kiss your hands many times.

At our town of Kongo, written on the sixth day of July,

João Teixeira did it[2] *in 1526.*

The King. Dom[3] *Affonso.*

[On the back of this letter the following can be read: To the most powerful and excellent prince Dom João, King our Brother.]

UNDATED

Moreover, Sir, in our Kingdoms there is another great inconvenience which is of little service to God, and this is that many of our people, keenly desirous as they are of the wares and things of your Kingdoms, which are brought here by your people, and in order to satisfy their voracious appetite, seize many of our people, freed and exempt men, and very often it happens that they kidnap even noblemen and the sons of noblemen, and our relatives, and take them to be sold to the white men who are in our Kingdoms; and for this purpose they have concealed them; and others are brought during the night so that they might not be recognized.

And as soon as they are taken by the white men they are immediately ironed and branded with fire, and when they are carried to be em-

---

[1]The emphasis appears in the original letter.
[2]That is, wrote the letter. João Teixeira was probably a Kongo-born secretary who had been baptized and educated by Portuguese missionaries.

[3]Portuguese for "lord."

barked, if they are caught by our guards' men the whites allege that they have bought them but they cannot say from whom, so that it is our duty to do justice and to restore to the freemen their freedom, but it cannot be done if your subjects feel offended, as they claim to be.

And to avoid such a great evil we passed a law so that any white man living in our Kingdoms and wanting to purchase goods in any way should first inform three of our noblemen and officials of our court whom we rely upon in this matter, and these are Dom Pedro Manipanza and Dom Manuel Manissaba, our chief usher, and Gonçalo Pires our chief freighter, who should investigate if the mentioned goods are captives[4] or free men, and if cleared by them there will be no further doubt nor embargo for them to be taken and embarked. But if the white men do not comply with it they will lose the aforementioned goods. And if we do them this favor and concession it is for the part Your Highness has in it, since we know that it is in your service too that these goods are taken from our Kingdom, otherwise we should not consent to this. . . .

OCTOBER 18, 1526

Sir, Your Highness has been kind enough to write to us saying that we should ask in our letters for anything we need, and that we shall be provided with everything, and as the peace and the health of our Kingdom depend on us, and as there are among us old folks and people who have lived for many days, it happens that we

have continuously many and different diseases which put us very often in such a weakness that we reach almost the last extreme; and the same happens to our children, relatives and natives owing to the lack in this country of physicians and surgeons who might know how to cure properly such diseases. And as we have got neither dispensaries nor drugs which might help us in this forlornness, many of those who had been already confirmed and instructed in the holy faith of Our Lord Jesus Christ perish and die; and the rest of the people in their majority cure themselves with herbs and breads and other ancient methods, so that they put all their faith in the mentioned herbs and ceremonies if they live, and believe that they are saved if they die; and this is not much in the service of God.

And to avoid such a great error and inconvenience, since it is from God in the first place and then from your Kingdoms and from Your Highness that all the good and drugs and medicines have come to save us, we beg of you to be agreeable and kind enough to send us two physicians and two apothecaries and one surgeon, so that they may come with their drugstores and all the necessary things to stay in our kingdoms, because we are in extreme need of them all and each of them. We shall do them all good and shall benefit them by all means, since they are sent by Your Highness, whom we thank for your work in their coming. We beg of Your Highness as a great favor to do this for us, because besides being good in itself it is in the service of God as we have said above.

---

[4]Captives taken by King Afonso in his wars of expansion (made possible by Portuguese firearms) were sold into slavery.

Images of the Portuguese in the Art of Benin
▼▼▼
92 ▼ *A BENIN-PORTUGUESE SALTCELLAR and A BENIN WALL PLAQUE*

For many centuries sub-Saharan Africans have crafted some of the world's most impressive artworks, especially sculptures. Since at least 500 B.C.E., West African sculptors used clay, wood, ivory, and bronze to create a variety of works that were of central importance to their various cultures. These include masks, animal figures, ceremonial weapons, religious objects, and images of rulers and other important people (see source 74). In some regions bronze casting and ivory carving were royal monopolies carried on by highly trained professionals.

Such was the case in the kingdom of Benin, located on the west coast of tropical Africa in an area that today is part of Nigeria. The kingdom took shape around 1300, when a number of agricultural villages accepted the authority of an *oba*, or divine king, who ruled from the capital, Benin City. When the Portuguese arrived in 1485, Benin was a formidable military and commercial power and a center of state-sponsored artistic activity. Ivory carvers and bronze casters were organized into hereditary guilds and resided in neighborhoods set aside for them in Benin City. They produced bronze heads, animal and human figures, pendants, plaques, musical instruments, drinking vessels, and armlets, all of which were used for ceremonial and personal purposes or exchanged in trade.

The arrival of the Portuguese affected Benin's artistic development in two important ways. First, Portuguese merchants, unable to establish Benin as a major source of slaves, turned to other commodities, including artworks, as objects of trade. Benin ivory carvers received numerous commissions from Portuguese merchants to produce condiment sets, utensils, and hunting horns for sale in Europe. Second, the Portuguese also stimulated the production of bronze sculpture by providing an increased supply of copper, the major component of bronze.

The two works reproduced in this section provide an opportunity to appreciate the high quality of Benin art and to draw some inferences about the attitudes of the people of Benin toward Europeans. The first item, an ivory carving crafted in the sixteenth or early seventeenth century, is usually identified as a *salario*, or saltcellar. It depicts two Portuguese officials, flanked by two assistants. Above them is a Portuguese ship, with a man peering out of a crow's-nest.

The second work, which also dates from the sixteenth or early seventeenth century, is a copper plaque, approximately eighteen inches high and designed to be hung on a wall in the oba's palace in Benin City. (We can see the holes on the top and bottom of the plaque where it was attached.) The central figure is the oba, shown holding a spear and shield. To his right stand two attendants. The one farther away holds a C-shaped iron bar, which was used as currency in trade; the figure closer to the oba holds an *eban*, a ceremonial sword. To the oba's left stands another attendant playing a flute. The two figures in the background, on each side of the oba's head, represent the Portuguese. In one hand each figure holds a rectangular glass mirror and in the other hand a goblet. Both were items the Portuguese traded for the goods of Benin.

A Benin-Portuguese Saltcellar

A Benin Wall Plaque

QUESTIONS FOR ANALYSIS

1. In the saltcellar, notice what hangs around the standing figure's neck, what he holds in his hands, and his facial expression. What is the sculptor trying to communicate?
2. Why might this image of the Portuguese official have appealed to the European purchasers for whom the work was intended?
3. Consider the plaque. What distinguishes the oba from all the other figures? Which details illustrate the oba's power and perhaps his divinity?
4. How does the representation of the Portuguese in the plaque differ from that of the saltcellar?
5. Compare the representation of the Portuguese official in the saltcellar with that of the oba in the plaque. Which strike you as more significant, the similarities or the differences? What inferences do you draw from your answer?
6. What might we infer from these works about Portuguese-Benin relations and the attitudes of the people of Benin toward the Portuguese?

The Economics of the West African Slave Trade

▼▼▼

93 ▼ James Barbot,
A VOYAGE TO NEW CALABAR RIVER
IN THE YEAR 1699

Source 91 illustrates how an African king's attempt to control commerce between his subjects and the Portuguese was at least partially frustrated and how the slave trade had a number of tragic consequences for African society. This source offers another perspective. James Barbot, a French member of a late-seventeenth-century English slave-trading expedition to Ibani, describes trade negotiations with its king, William, in 1699. Ibani, or *Bonny*, as the English called it, was an island state in the Niger Delta. By the late eighteenth century, it was the principal slave market of the entire Guinea coast. One English captain, who sailed to Bonny between 1786 and 1800, estimated that at least 20,000 slaves were bought and sold there annually. In this document we see how the trading system worked a century earlier.

QUESTIONS FOR ANALYSIS

1. How would you characterize trade at Ibani? Was it haphazard bartering? A well-developed system with specific currency? Something else?
2. How did the English benefit from the way in which trade was conducted?
3. What benefits did the king enjoy from this arrangement?
4. What was Barbot's attitude toward Ibani society?

5. How did the Ibani seem to regard the English?
6. What do the prices of the other commodities purchased by the English say about the relative value of one slave?
7. Who was the exploiter, and who was the exploited?
8. What does this account reveal about social structure in Ibani?

June 30, 1699, being ashore, had a new conference which produced nothing. Then Pepprell [Pepple], the king's brother, delivered a message from the king:

> He was sorry we would not accept his proposals. It was not his fault, since he had a great esteem and regard for the whites, who had greatly enriched him through trade. His insistence on thirteen bars[1] for male and ten for female slaves was due to the fact that the people of the country maintained a high price for slaves at their inland markets, seeing so many large ships coming to Bonny for them. However, to moderate matters and to encourage trade with us, he would be content with thirteen bars for males and nine bars and two brass rings for females, etc.

We offered thirteen bars for men and nine for women and proportionately for boys and girls, according to their ages. Following this we parted, without concluding anything further.

On July 1, the king sent for us to come ashore. We stayed there till four in the afternoon and concluded the trade on the terms offered them the day before. The king promised to come aboard the next day to regulate it and be paid his duties. . . .

The second [of July]. . . . At two o'clock we fetched the king from shore, attended by all his *Caboceiros*[2] and officers, in three large canoes. Entering the ship, he was saluted with seven guns. The king had on an old-fashioned scarlet coat, laced with gold and silver, very rusty, and a fine hat on his head, but bare-footed. All his attendants showed great respect to him and, since our arrival, none of the natives have dared to come aboard or sell the least thing, till the king adjusted trade matters.

We had again a long talk with the king and Pepprell, his brother, concerning the rates of our goods and his customs. This Pepprell was a sharp black and a mighty talking black, perpetually making objections against something or other and teasing us for this or that *dassy*[3] or present, as well as for drinks, etc. Would that such a one as he were out of the way, to facilitate trade. . . .

Thus, with much patience, all our affairs were settled equitably, after the fashion of a people who are not very scrupulous when it comes to finding excuses or objections for not keeping to the word of any verbal contract. For they do not have the art of reading and writing, and we therefore are forced to stand to their agreement, which often is no longer than they think fit to hold it themselves. The king ordered the public crier to proclaim permission to trade with us, with the noise of his trumpets . . . , we paying sixteen brass rings to the fellow for his fee. The blacks objected against our wrought pewter and tankards, green beads, and other goods, which they would not accept. . . .

We gave the usual presents to the king. . . . To Captain Forty, the king's general, Captain Pepprell, Captain Boileau, alderman Bougsbyu, my lord Willyby, duke of Monmouth, drunken Henry, and some others[4] two firelocks, eight hats, nine narrow Guinea stuffs. We adjusted with them the reduction of our merchandise into bars of iron, as the standard coin, namely: one bunch of beads, one bar; four strings of rings, ten

---

[1]Bars of iron. See source 92.
[2]A Portuguese term. Here it means "chiefs and elders."
[3]A trade term meaning "gift."
[4]The king's chiefs and elders.

rings each, one ditto; four copper bars, one ditto. . . . And so on *pro rata* for every sort of goods. . . .

The price of provisions and wood was also regulated. Sixty king's yams, one bar; one hundred and sixty slave's yams, one bar; for fifty thousand yams to be delivered to us. A butt[5] of water, two rings. For the length of wood, seven bars, which is dear, but they were to deliver it ready cut into our boat. For one goat, one bar. A cow, ten or eight bars, according to its size. A hog, two bars. A calf, eight bars. A jar of palm oil, one bar and a quarter.

We also paid the king's duty in goods; five hundred slaves, to be purchased at two copper rings a head.

---

[5]A large cask.

▼▼▼

Chinese and Japanese Reactions to the West

China and Japan were no exception to the rule that most societies in Asia and Africa were able to successfully resist European efforts during the sixteenth and seventeenth centuries to impose trade on Western terms and Christianity. Although ultimately rebuffed by the Chinese and Japanese, European merchants and missionaries nonetheless had good reason to believe during the sixteenth century that their labors in East Asia would be richly rewarded.

Portuguese traders reached south China in 1513, opened trade at Guangzhou (Canton) in 1514, and established a permanent trading base in Macao in 1557. In 1542 the first Portuguese merchants reached Japan and soon were reaping healthy profits by carrying goods between China and Japan. Later in the century, the Dutch and English successfully entered the East Asian markets. Roman Catholic Europeans, especially the Portuguese, energetically supported missionary efforts in China and Japan, usually in cooperation with the newly founded Society of Jesus, more popularly known as the *Jesuits*. Francis Xavier and other Jesuits began preaching in Japan in 1549, and by the early 1600s they had won approximately 300,000 converts to Christianity. Catholic missionary activities in China began later, in 1579. There the Jesuits did less preaching to the common people and instead sought the support of Chinese intellectuals, government officials, and members of the imperial court. The Jesuits were moderately successful because they impressed Confucian scholars with their erudition, especially in mathematics and science, and the Chinese appreciated the missionaries' willingness to understand and respect China's culture.

For all their efforts, Europeans' economic and religious gains in China were meager. The Chinese tolerated learned Jesuit missionaries, but they viewed Europe's merchants as boorish, overly aggressive, and purveyors of shoddy goods. Preferring to deal with Arabs and other non-Westerners, they limited trade with Europeans to Guangzhou and Macao and placed it under numerous restrictions. Missionary activity resulted in some converts, but feuding among Catholic religious orders, staunch opposition from many Chinese officials, and the unwillingness of most

Chinese, even converts, to abandon ancient rites, especially veneration of the ancestors, caused the enterprise to wither and die.

Although European efforts to win souls and trade had a more promising start in Japan, by the mid seventeenth century the Japanese had suppressed Christianity and restricted European trade to only one Dutch ship a year. This turn of events resulted from attempts by Japanese leaders to bring stability to Japan after a century of civil war and rebellion. Convinced that European merchants and Catholic missionaries had contributed to Japan's disorder, the government outlawed Christianity and essentially closed Japan to the outside world.

The Jesuits in China
▼▼▼
94 ▼ *Matteo Ricci, JOURNALS*

The most celebrated Jesuit scholar-missionary to work in China was the Italian Matteo Ricci (1552–1610), who arrived in 1582. A trained mathematician and scientist, Father Ricci dazzled the Chinese literarchy and court with clocks, a world map, and various pieces of scientific equipment, many of which he constructed himself. A gifted linguist, he composed more than twenty-five essays in Chinese on mathematics, literature, ethics, geography, astronomy, and, above all else, religion. He so impressed Confucian scholars that they accorded him the title *Doctor from the Great Western Ocean.* In 1601 Emperor Wanli summoned Ricci to his court at Beijing and provided him with a subsidy to carry on his study of mathematics and astronomy. When Ricci died, the emperor donated a burial site outside the gates of the imperial city as a token of special honor.

During his twenty-seven years in China, Ricci kept a journal. Shortly after Ricci's death, a Jesuit colleague edited and published the journal. It became one of Europe's major sources of information about China until the late eighteenth century, when accounts by European travelers to the Middle Kingdom became more common.

When Father Ricci became the superior of the tiny Chinese mission in 1597, there were probably no more than 100 Chinese Catholics throughout the entire empire, excluding the Portuguese trading station at Macao. Thanks in large part to his and his colleagues' policy of trying to accommodate as many Chinese traditions as they could to Catholic Christianity and their genuine admiration for Confucian moral philosophy, the Jesuits were able to add to these numbers in a significant way. In 1603 Ricci instructed his Jesuits that traditional ceremonies honoring Confucius and essential ancestral services were "civil rites," and therefore acceptable practices for Chinese Catholics. At Ricci's death in 1610, an estimated 2,500 converts lived in the vicinity of the Jesuits' five resident churches. By 1650 as many as 150,000 Chinese professed Catholic Christianity, out of a total population of about 150 million. Fifty years later the Christian population had risen to almost 300,000, but it was still around 1 percent of the overall population.

Many Catholic missionaries who followed Ricci, especially from other religious orders, such as the Franciscans, were not willing to accept a syncretic Chinese

Catholicism that retained some vestiges of traditional Chinese worship. A heated controversy erupted regarding the so-called "rites question" and the Jesuits' missionary tactics. In the end, Catholic traditionalists won out, and the Jesuits' efforts to fuse some Chinese customs with Christianity lost out. In 1742 Pope Benedict XIV decreed that Chinese Catholics must abandon all vestiges of Confucianism. In response, the Qianlong Emperor (r. 1736–1795), a friend of the Jesuits and an admirer of Western technology and architecture, expelled the Catholic missionaries, and Chinese Catholicism was doomed. But even had the Jesuit vision prevailed, one wonders if Christianity could ever have become a major force in China. As Protestant missionaries to China later learned, too many differences separated European Christianity from a culture that was already well over 3,000 years old.

In the following selection from Ricci's *Journals*, we can glimpse some of the barriers and attitudes that defeated the Jesuits' efforts to transform China into a Christian civilization, despite their willingness to make limited accommodations.

QUESTIONS FOR ANALYSIS

1. What most offended the Confucians who brought charges against the Jesuits and their religion?
2. How do you think the Jesuits' Confucian opponents viewed this confrontation and its resolution?
3. Why did Ricci view the outcome as a Christian victory?
4. Imagine that you are the Chief Justice and are preparing a report to the imperial court concerning the incident, your decision, the reasoning behind it, and what you believe will be its consequences. Compose that report.
5. Compare the charges brought against the Jesuits with Han Yu's *Memorial on Buddhism* (Multiple Voices VI). Which are more significant, the differences or the similarities? What do you conclude from your answer?
6. Compare the failure of Christianity to permeate Chinese culture with the relative success of Buddhism 1,000 years earlier (see Multiple Voices VI), despite opposition to it. Why did one succeed and the other fail?

During 1606 and the year following, the progress of Christianity in Nancian[1] was in no wise retarded. . . . The number of neophytes[2] increased by more than two hundred, all of whom manifested an extraordinary piety in their religious devotions. As a result, the reputation of the Christian religion became known throughout the length and breadth of this metropolitan city. . . .

Through the efforts of Father Emanuele Dias another and a larger house was purchased, in August of 1607, at a price of a thousand gold pieces. This change was necessary, because the house he had was too small for his needs and was situated in a flood area. Just as the community was about to change from one house to the other, a sudden uprising broke out against them. . . .

---

[1]Nanchang, in the southern province of Kiangsi.

[2]New converts.

At the beginning of each month, the Magistrates hold a public assembly . . . in the temple of their great Philosopher.[3] When the rites of the new-moon were completed in the temple, and these are civil rather than religious rites, one of those present took advantage of the occasion to speak on behalf of the others, and to address the highest Magistrate present. . . . "We wish to warn you," he said, "that there are certain foreign priests in this royal city, who are preaching a law, hitherto unheard of in this kingdom, and who are holding large gatherings of people in their house." Having said this, he referred them to their local Magistrate, . . . and he in turn ordered the plaintiffs to present their case in writing, assuring them that he would support it with all his authority, in an effort to have the foreign priests expelled. The complaint was written out that same day and signed with twenty-seven signatures. . . . The content of the document was somewhat as follows.

> Matthew Ricci, Giovanni Soerio, Emanuele Dias, and certain other foreigners from western kingdoms, men who are guilty of high treason against the throne, are scattered amongst us, in five different provinces. They are continually communicating with each other and are here and there practicing brigandage on the rivers, collecting money, and then distributing it to the people, in order to curry favor with the multitudes. They are frequently visited by the Magistrates, by the high nobility and by the Military Prefects, with whom they have entered into a secret pact, binding unto death.
>
> These men teach that we should pay no respect to the images of our ancestors, a doctrine which is destined to extinguish the love of future generations for their forebears. Some of them break up the idols, leaving the temples empty and the gods to be pitied, without any patronage. In the beginning they lived in small houses, but by this time they have bought up large and magnificent residences.

> The doctrine they teach is something infernal. It attracts the ignorant into its fraudulent meshes, and great crowds of this class are continually assembled at their houses. Their doctrine gets beyond the city walls and spreads itself through the neighboring towns and villages and into the open country, and the people become so wrapt up in its falsity, that students are not following their course, laborers are neglecting their work, farmers are not cultivating their acres, and even the women have no interest in their housework. The whole city has become disturbed, and, whereas in the beginning there were only a hundred or so professing their faith, now there are more than twenty thousand. These priests distribute pictures of some Tartar or Saracen, who they say is God, who came down from Heaven to redeem and to instruct all of humanity, and who alone, according to their doctrine, can give wealth and happiness; a doctrine by which the simple people are very easily deceived. These men are an abomination on the face of the Earth, and there is just ground for fear that once they have erected their own temples, they will start a rebellion. . . . Wherefore, moved by their interest in the maintenance of the public good, in the conservation of the realm, and in the preservation, whole and entire, of their ancient laws, the petitioners are presenting this complaint and demanding, in the name of the entire province, that a rescript of it be forwarded to the King, asking that these foreigners be sentenced to death, or banished from the realm, to some deserted island in the sea. . . .

Each of the Magistrates to whom the indictment was presented asserted that the spread of Christianity should be prohibited, and that the foreign priests should be expelled from the city, if the Mayor saw fit, after hearing the case, and notifying the foreigners. . . . But the Fathers,[4] themselves, were not too greatly disturbed, placing their confidence in Divine Providence,

---

[3]Confucius.

[4]The Jesuit fathers, or priests.

which had always been present to assist them on other such dangerous occasions.

▷   Father Emanuele is summoned before the Chief Justice.

Father Emanuele, in his own defense, . . . gave a brief outline of the Christian doctrine. Then he showed that according to the divine law, the first to be honored, after God, were a man's parents. But the judge had no mind to hear or to accept any of this and he made it known that he thought it was all false. After that repulse, with things going from bad to worse, it looked as if they were on the verge of desperation, so much so, indeed, that they increased their prayers, their sacrifices, and their bodily penances, in petition for a favorable solution of their difficulty. Their adversaries appeared to be triumphantly victorious. They were already wrangling about the division of the furniture of the Mission residences, and to make results doubly certain, they stirred up the flames anew with added accusations and indictments. . . .

The Mayor, who was somewhat friendly with the Fathers, realizing that there was much in the accusation that was patently false, asked the Magistrate Director of the Schools,[5] if he knew whether or not this man Emanuele was a companion of Matthew Ricci, who was so highly respected at the royal court, and who was granted a subsidy from the royal treasury, because of the gifts he had presented to the King. Did he realize that the Fathers had lived in Nankin[6] for twelve years, and that no true complaint had ever been entered against them for having violated the laws. Then he asked him if he had re-

ally given full consideration as to what was to be proven in the present indictment. To this the Director of the Schools replied that he wished the Mayor to make a detailed investigation of the case and then to confer with him. The Chief Justice then ordered the same thing to be done. Fortunately, it was this same Justice who was in charge of city affairs when Father Ricci first arrived in Nancian. It was he who first gave the Fathers permission, with the authority of the Viceroy, to open a house there. . . .

After the Mayor had examined the charges of the plaintiffs and the reply of the defendants, he subjected the quasi-literati[7] to an examination in open court, and taking the Fathers under his patronage, he took it upon himself to refute the calumnies of their accusers. He said he was fully convinced that these strangers were honest men, and that he knew that there were only two of them in their local residence and not twenty, as had been asserted. To this they replied that the Chinese were becoming their disciples. To which the Justice in turn replied: "What of it? Why should we be afraid of our own people? Perhaps you are unaware of the fact that Matthew Ricci's company is cultivated by everyone in Pekin,[8] and that he is being subsidized by the royal treasury. How dare the Magistrates who are living outside of the royal city expel men who have permission to live at the royal court? These men here have lived peacefully in Nankin for twelve years. I command," he added, "that they buy no more large houses, and that the people are not to follow their law." . . .

A few days later, the court decision was pronounced and written out . . . and was then posted at the city gates as a public edict. The

---

[5]The director of the local Confucian academy was one of the Jesuits' chief opponents.

[6]Nanjing, the southern auxiliary capital.

[7]Those who are almost learned or learned to a limited degree. This is Ricci's term for the chief tormenters of the Jesuits in Nanchang. They were Confucian scholars who had passed the first and most basic of the three Confucian civil-service examinations (offered respectively at the local, provincial, and capital levels) and thereby earned the title *Cultivated Talents*. By passing the first examination level,

they earned recognition simply as competent students. Hence, Ricci dismisses them as *quasi-literati*. Cultivated Talents were subject to periodic re-examination at that level and could lose their status and privileges. Only scholars who passed the provincial-level examination and became *Elevated Men* attained a permanent rank and were eligible for appointment to one of the lower civil posts. Apparently the Cultivated Talents felt threatened by the Jesuits.

[8]Beijing, the Ming capital.

following is a summary of their declaration. Having examined the cause of Father Emanuele and his companions, it was found that these men had come here from the West because they had heard so much about the fame of the great Chinese Empire, and that they had already been living in the realm for some years, without any display of ill-will. Father Emanuele should be permitted to practice his own religion, but it was not considered to be the right thing for the common people, who are attracted by novelties, to adore the God of Heaven. For them to go over to the religion of foreigners would indeed be most unbecoming. . . . It would therefore seem to be . . . [in] . . . the best interests of the Kingdom, to . . . [warn] . . . everyone in a public edict not to abandon the sacrifices of their ancient religion by accepting the cult of foreigners. Such a movement might, indeed, result in calling together certain gatherings, detrimental to the public welfare, and harmful also to the foreigner, himself. Wherefore, the Governor of this district, by order of the high Magistrates, admonishes the said Father Emanuele to refrain from perverting the people, by inducing them to accept a foreign religion. The man who sold him the larger house is to restore his money and Emanuele is to buy a smaller place, sufficient for his needs, and to live there peaceably, as he has done, up to the present. Emanuele, himself, has agreed to these terms and the Military Prefects of the district have been ordered to make a

search of the houses there and to confiscate the pictures of the God they speak of, wherever they find them. It is not permitted for any of the native people to go over to the religion of the foreigners, nor is it permitted to gather together for prayer meetings. Whoever does contrary to these prescriptions will be severely punished, and if the Military Prefects are remiss in enforcing them, they will be held to be guilty of the same crimes. To his part of the edict, the Director of the Schools added, that the common people were forbidden to accept the law of the foreigners, and that a sign should be posted above the door of the Father's residence, notifying the public that these men were forbidden to have frequent contact with the people.

The Fathers were not too disturbed by this pronouncement, because they were afraid that it was going to be much worse. In fact, everyone thought it was rather favorable, and that the injunction launched against the spread of the faith was a perfunctory order to make it appear that the literati were not wholly overlooked, since the Fathers were not banished from the city, as the literati had demanded. Moreover it was not considered a grave misdemeanor for the Chinese to change their religion, and it was not customary to inflict a serious punishment on those violating such an order. The neophytes, themselves, proved this when they continued, as formerly, to attend Mass.

The Seclusion of Japan
▼▼▼

95 ▼ *Tokugawa Iemitsu,* *CLOSED COUNTRY EDICT OF 1635 and EXCLUSION OF THE PORTUGUESE, 1639*

When the first Europeans reached Japan, they encountered a land plagued by civil war and rebellion. The authority of the *shoguns*, military commanders who had ruled Japan on behalf of the emperor since the twelfth century, was in eclipse, as the *daimyo* (great lords) fought for power. Turbulence ended toward the close of the sixteenth century, when three military heroes — Oda Nobunaga (1534–1582), Toyotomi Hideyoshi (1536–1598), and Tokugawa Ieyasu (1543–1616) — forced the daimyo to accept central authority. In 1603 the emperor recognized Tokugawa Ieyasu as shogun; the era of the Tokugawa Shogunate, which lasted to 1868, had begun.

Between 1624 and 1641, Iemitsu, grandson of Ieyasu and shogun from 1623 to 1651, issued edicts that closed Japan to almost all foreigners. This was the culmination of policies begun under Toyotomi Hideyoshi, who had sought to limit contacts between Japanese and foreigners, especially Catholic missionaries. He and his successors viewed the missionaries' aggressive proselytizing as a potential source of social unrest and rebellion. The first document that follows, the most celebrated of Tokugawa Iemitsu's edicts, is directed to the two *bugyo*, or commissioners, of Nagasaki, a port city in southwest Japan and a center of Japanese Christianity; the second more specifically deals with the missionary activities of the Portuguese.

QUESTIONS FOR ANALYSIS

1. To what extent was the edict of 1635 directed against the activities of foreigners? To what extent was it directed against certain presumed antisocial activities by Japanese?
2. Much of the 1635 edict dealt with trade issues. What do the various trade provisions suggest about the shogun's attitude toward commerce?
3. What was the major purpose behind the 1635 edict?
4. What can you infer about the reasons for promulgating the 1639 edict?

CLOSED COUNTRY EDICT OF 1635

1. Japanese ships are strictly forbidden to leave for foreign countries.
2. No Japanese is permitted to go abroad. If there is anyone who attempts to do so secretly, he must be executed. The ship so involved must be impounded and its owner arrested, and the matter must be reported to the higher authority.
3. If any Japanese returns from overseas after residing there, he must be put to death.[1]
4. If there is any place where the teachings of padres[2] is practiced, the two of you must order a thorough investigation.
5. Any informer revealing the whereabouts of the followers of padres must be rewarded accordingly. If anyone reveals the whereabouts

of a high ranking padre, he must be given one hundred pieces of silver. For those of lower ranks, depending on the deed, the reward must be set accordingly.
6. If a foreign ship has an objection [to the measures adopted] and it becomes necessary to report the matter to Edo,[3] you may ask the Omura domain[4] to provide ships to guard the foreign ship. . . .
7. If there are any Southern Barbarians[5] who propagate the teachings of padres, or otherwise commit crimes, they may be incarcerated in the prison. . . .
8. All incoming ships must be carefully searched for the followers of padres.
9. No single trading city shall be permitted to purchase all the merchandise brought by foreign ships.

[1]Since 1597 well over 1,000 Japanese and European Christians had already been executed.
[2]Fathers (Catholic priests).
[3]Present-day Tokyo, the seat of Tokugawa government.
[4]The area around Nagasaki.
[5]Westerners.

10. Samurai are not permitted to purchase any goods originating from foreign ships directly from Chinese merchants in Nagasaki.
11. After a list of merchandise brought by foreign ships is sent to Edo, as before you may order that commercial dealings may take place without waiting for a reply from Edo.
12. After settling the price, all white yarns[6] brought by foreign ships shall be allocated to the five trading cities[7] and other quarters as stipulated.
13. After settling the price of white yarns, other merchandise [brought by foreign ships] may be traded freely between the [licensed] dealers. However, in view of the fact that Chinese ships are small and cannot bring large consignments, you may issue orders of sale at your discretion. Additionally, payment for goods purchased must be made within twenty days after the price is set.
14. The date of departure homeward of foreign ships shall not be later than the twentieth day of the ninth month. Any ships arriving in Japan later than usual shall depart within fifty days of their arrival. As to the departure of Chinese ships, you may use your discretion to order their departure after the departure of the Portuguese *galeota*.[8]
15. The goods brought by foreign ships which remained unsold may not be deposited or accepted for deposit.
16. The arrival in Nagasaki of representatives of the five trading cities shall not be later than the fifth day of the seventh month. Anyone arriving later than that date shall lose the quota assigned to his city.
17. Ships arriving in Hirado[9] must sell their raw silk at the price set in Nagasaki, and are not permitted to engage in business transactions until after the price is established in Nagasaki.

You are hereby required to act in accordance with the provisions set above. It is so ordered.

EXCLUSION OF THE PORTUGUESE, 1639

1. The matter relating to the proscription of Christianity is known [to the Portuguese]. However, heretofore they have secretly transported those who are going to propagate that religion.
2. If those who believe in that religion band together in an attempt to do evil things, they must be subjected to punishment.
3. While those who believe in the preaching of padres are in hiding, there are incidents in which that country [Portugal] has sent gifts to them for their sustenance.

In view of the above, hereafter entry by the Portuguese *galeota* is forbidden. If they insist on coming [to Japan], the ships must be destroyed and anyone aboard those ships must be beheaded. We have received the above order and are thus transmitting it to you accordingly.

The above concerns our disposition with regard to the *galeota*.

Memorandum
With regard to those who believe in Christianity, you are aware that there is a proscription, and thus knowing, you are not permitted to let padres and those who believe in their preaching to come aboard your ships. If there is any violation, all of you who are aboard will be considered culpable. If there is anyone who hides the fact that he is a Christian and boards your ship, you may report it to us. A substantial reward will be given to you for this information.

This memorandum is to be given to those who come on Chinese ships. [A similar note to the Dutch ships.]

---

[6]Raw silk.
[7]The cities of Kyoto, Edo, Osaka, Sakai, and Nagasaki.

[8]A *galleon*, an oceangoing Portuguese ship.
[9]A small island in the southwest, not far from Nagasaki.

The Great Mughals and the West

Between 1526 and his death in 1530, the Turkish lord of Afghanistan, Babur, subdued north-central India with a small, well-equipped army that enjoyed the advantage of firearms received from the Ottoman Turks. This new Muslim lord of Hindustan, a direct descendant of the Mongol Chinggis Khan and the Turk Tamerlane, initiated India's *Mughal* (the Persian word for *Mongol*) Age and laid the base for the reign of his grandson Jalal ad-Din Akbar (r. 1556–1605), known to history as simply *Akbar* (the Great).

Akbar's empire encompassed only the northern half of the Indian subcontinent. His great-grandson Aurangzeb (r. 1658–1707), the last effective Mughal emperor, reigned over twice that amount of land, holding all the subcontinent except its southern tip and the island of Ceylon (present-day Sri Lanka). Nevertheless, Akbar fully deserved to be known as the *Great Mughal*, a title that awed European visitors to his court at Fatehpur-Sikri (the City of Victory) bestowed on him. From this court Akbar forged a centralized empire, which during his reign of almost half a century enjoyed prosperity and a fair level of peace between Hindus and Muslims. Although the Portuguese had established three major bases along the west Indian coast by 1535, Akbar was secure enough in his power to keep them and other Europeans at arm's length throughout the last half of the sixteenth century.

The European presence, however, increased in the seventeenth century. In 1603 the English East India Company — chartered on December 31, 1600, the last day of the sixteenth century — sent its first envoy to Akbar's court. After defeating a Portuguese squadron in 1639, the English established their first trading station at Madras (present-day Chennai) on India's east coast and in 1661 acquired Bombay (today called Mumbai) on the west coast. As Portuguese influence in India declined, other European maritime powers secured trading privileges in the Mughal Empire. The Dutch acquired several important sites on both coasts between 1640 and 1663; in 1664 France founded an East India Company, and several French trading bases followed. In time, the Dutch shifted their focus away from India to the islands of Southeast Asia, leaving the French and English to fight for control of the Indian markets.

Despite all these late-seventeenth-century incursions along India's coasts, Emperor Aurangzeb was able to hold the West and its merchants at bay for the most part, even dealing the English a military setback in the 1680s. In 1700 the directors of the English East India Company rejected as unrealistic the notion of acquiring additional territory or establishing colonies in India. The decline of Mughal authority in the eighteenth century, however, changed the situation substantially, and toward midcentury the French and British were engaged in armed struggle for control of Indian territory.

Dealing with the Faringis
▼▼▼
96 ▼ *Abul Fazl, AKBARNAMA*

Assisting Akbar in formulating and carrying out his largely successful policies of state was Abul Fazl (1551–1602), the emperor's chief advisor and confidant from 1579 until Abul Fazl's assassination at the instigation of Prince Salim, the future Emperor Jahangir (r. 1605–1627). Abul Fazl's death cut short his composition of the *Akbarnama*, a gigantic, laudatory history of Akbar's distinguished ancestors and the emperor's own reign. Before he was murdered, Abul Fazl carried his history to Akbar's forty-sixth year, creating a work universally regarded as one of the masterpieces of Mughal literature.

These thousands of pages of elegant Persian prose and poetry provide surprisingly few references to Akbar's or even India's relations with Europeans, or *Faringis* (Franks), as they were called at the Mughal court. This silence speaks eloquently of the level of early Mughal concern with these foreigners. The following excerpts constitute the work's major references to Europeans in India.

QUESTIONS FOR ANALYSIS

1. What aspects of European culture most fascinated Akbar?
2. What did he and Abul Fazl believe they could gain from the Faringis?
3. What did they believe they could offer the Europeans?
4. How did Akbar and Abul Fazl regard the Portuguese coastal bases?
5. What does the discussion with Padre Radif (Father Rodolfo) suggest about Akbar and Abul Fazl's attitudes toward the teachings of Europe's Christian missionaries?
6. Jesuit missionaries to Akbar's court often believed they were on the verge of converting him to Roman Catholicism. Why do you suppose they believed this? What evidence strongly indicates there was never any chance Akbar would become a Christian?

THE SIEGE OF SURAT

One of the occurrences of the siege[1] was that a large number of Christians came from the port of Goa[2] and its neighborhood to the foot of the sublime throne, and were rewarded by the bliss of an interview. Apparently they had come at the request of the besieged in order that the latter might make the fort over to them, and so convey themselves to the shore of safety. But when that crew saw the majesty of the imperial power, and had become cognizant of the largeness of the army, and of the extent of the siege-train they represented themselves as ambassadors and performed the *kornish*.[3] They produced many of the rarities of their country, and the appreciative

---

[1]The siege of the west-coast port of Surat in 1573 during Akbar's campaign in Gujarat (see note 6). This successful expedition gave Akbar access to the sea. Through his conquests Akbar more than tripled the empire he had inherited.

[2]The chief Portuguese stronghold in India since 1510.
[3]The act of obeisance.

Khedive[4] received each one of them with special favor and made inquiries about the wonders of Portugal and the manners and customs of Europe. It seemed as if he did this from a desire of knowledge, for his sacred heart is a storehouse of spiritual and physical sciences. But his . . . soul wished that these inquiries might be the means of civilizing this savage race.[5]

THE COMMODITIES OF GOA

One of the occurrences was the dispatch of Haji Habibu-llah Kashi to Goa. At the time when the country of Gujarat became included among the imperial dominions, and when many of the ports of the country came into possession, and the governors of the European ports became submissive,[6] many of the curiosities and rarities of the skilled craftsmen of that country became known to His Majesty. Accordingly the Haji,[7] who for his skill, right thinking and powers of observation was one of the good servants of the court, was appointed to take with him a large sum of money, and the choice articles of India to Goa, and to bring for His Majesty's delectation the wonderful things of that country. There were sent with him clever craftsmen, who to ability and skill added industry, in order that just as the wonderful productions of that country [Goa and Europe] were being brought away, so also might rare crafts be imported [into Akbar's dominions].

THE MUSICIANS OF GOA

One of the occurrences was the arrival [at court] of Haji Habibu-llah. It has already been mentioned that he had been sent to the port of Goa with a large sum of money and skillful craftsmen in order that he might bring to his country the excellent arts and rarities of that place. On the 9th he came to do homage, attended by a large number of persons dressed up as Christians and playing European drums and clarions. He produced before His Majesty the choice articles of that territory. Craftsmen who had gone to acquire skill displayed the arts which they had learned and received praises in the critical place of testing. The musicians of that territory breathed fascination with the instruments of their country, especially with the organ. Ear and eye were delighted and so was the mind.

THURSDAY NIGHT AT THE HOUSE OF WORSHIP

One night, the assembly in the Ibadatkhana[8] was increasing the light of truth. Padre Radif,[9] one of the Nazarene[10] sages, who was singular for his understanding and ability, was making points in that feast of intelligence. Some of the untruthful bigots[11] came forward in a blundering way to answer him. Owing to the calmness of the august assembly, and the increasing light of justice, it became clear that each of these was weaving a circle of old acquisitions, and was not following the highway of proof, and that the explanation of the riddle of truth was not present to their thoughts. The veil was nearly being stripped, once for all, from their procedure. They were ashamed, and abandoned such discourse, and applied themselves to perverting the words of the Gospels. But they could not silence their antagonist by such arguments. The Padre quietly and with an air of conviction said, "Alas, that such things should be thought to be true! In fact, if

---

[4]Akbar.

[5]The Portuguese.

[6]In 1573 Akbar conquered the northwest coastal region of Gujarat, where the Portuguese held the ports of Diu and Bassein. In theory, but not fact, these Portuguese bases were now under Akbar's control.

[7]Haji Habibu-llah. He bore the title *Haji* because he had completed the hajj, or pilgrimage, to Mecca.

[8]*The House of Worship*, where Akbar held weekly Thursday-night discussions on theological issues with Muslim, Hindu, Parsi (Zoroastrian), and Christian religious teachers.

[9]Father Rodolfo Acquaviva, a Jesuit missionary.

[10]Christian (a follower of Jesus of Nazareth).

[11]Here he refers to the *ulama*, Muslim religious teachers. Abul Fazl, who pursued a vigorous policy of religious and cultural toleration, considered the ulama to be narrow-minded hypocrites.

this faction have such an opinion of our Book, and regard the *Furqan* [the Quran] as the pure word of God, it is proper that a heaped fire be lighted. We shall take the Gospel in our hands, and the Ulama[12] of that faith shall take their book, and then let us enter that testing-place of truth. The escape of any one will be a sign of his truthfulness." The liverless and black-hearted fellows wavered, and in reply to the challenge had recourse to bigotry and wrangling. This cowardice and effrontery displeased Akbar's equitable soul, and the banquet of enlightenment was made resplendent by acute observations. Continually, in those day-like nights, glorious subtleties and profound words dropped from his pearl-filled mouth.

Among them was this: "Most persons, from intimacy with those who adorn their outside but are inwardly bad, think that outward semblance, and the letter of Islam, profit without internal conviction. Hence we by fear and force compelled many believers in the Brahman [i.e., Hindu] religion to adopt the faith of our ancestors. Now that the light of truth has taken possession of our soul, it has become clear that in this distressful place of contrarities [the world], where darkness of comprehension and conceit

are heaped up, fold upon fold, a single step cannot be taken without the torch of proof, and that creed is profitable which is adopted with the approval of wisdom. To repeat the creed, to remove a piece of skin [i.e., to become circumcised] and to place the end of one's bones on the ground [i.e., the head in adoration] from dread of the Sultan,[13] is not seeking after God.

EUROPEAN-HELD PORTS

One of the occurrences was the appointing of an army to capture the European ports.[14] Inasmuch as conquest is the great rule of princes, and by the observance of this glory-increasing practice, the distraction of plurality[15] places its foot in the peacefulness of unity, and the harassed world composes her countenance, the officers of the provinces of Gujarat and Malwa were appointed to this service under the leadership of Qutbu-d-din Khan on 18 Bahman, Divine month (February 1580). The rulers of the Deccan were also informed that the troops had been sent in that direction in order to remove the Faringis who were a stumbling-block in the way of the pilgrims to the Hijaz.[16]

---

[12]See note 11.

[13]Akbar.

[14]The ports of Diu and Bassein (see note 6). This expedition was unsuccessful, and Abul Fazl tells us nothing more about it.

[15]The distraction of multiple rulers.

[16]Pilgrims to Mecca (Mecca is located in the Hijaz, Arabia's west coast). Many Muslim pilgrims complained that, when embarking at Portuguese ports, they were forced to purchase letters of passage imprinted with images of Jesus and Mary. Orthodox Muslims consider such images blasphemous, and some Muslim ulama (see note 11) went so far as to argue that it was better to forgo the pilgrimage than to submit to such sacrilege.

Seventeenth-Century Commerce in India

▼▼▼

97 ▼ *Jean-Baptiste Tavernier, TRAVELS IN INDIA*

The increasing volume of French trade with seventeenth-century Mughal India attracted Jean-Baptiste Tavernier (1605–after 1689), a Parisian gem merchant who arrived in India in 1640 on the first of five trips to the empire of the Great Mughal. Following his last voyage to India, which ended in 1668, Tavernier was able to live in wealthy semiretirement thanks to his profitable Eastern ventures. In 1670 he settled down to write his memoirs, probably from notes he had made during his career in the East.

His *Travels in India* covers a pivotal period in Mughal-European relations. French and English merchants were becoming increasingly important in India, just as cracks were beginning to appear in the Mughal Empire under Shah Jahan (r. 1627–1658) and Aurangzeb (r. 1658–1707), whose respective building programs (Shah Jahan constructed the Taj Mahal) and military campaigns placed severe strains on the economy and general well-being of Indian society. In the following selection, Tavernier details the manner in which the Mughal government attempted to control and profit from the Western merchants and the tactics some Europeans employed to circumvent these controls and raise their profit margins.

QUESTIONS FOR ANALYSIS

1. Why do you think the English and Dutch East India companies paid a lower tariff on their imported goods and gold? What added to their costs of doing business in India, and why do you think they paid these extra expenses?
2. Did the European merchants take advantage of the Indian officials with whom they dealt? Did the Indian officials seem to resent or not want this business with the Europeans? What do your answers suggest?
3. Why do you think the officers of the Dutch and English East India companies were treated as described? Why did they refuse to engage in smuggling? What do your answers suggest about relations between the Mughal government and these trading companies?
4. What does the story of the roast pig suggest?
5. Do you perceive any significant differences in Indian-European relations between the era of Akbar and the period described by Tavernier? If so, what are they? What do these changes suggest to you?

As soon as merchandise is landed at Surat[1] it has to be taken to the custom-house, which adjoins the fort. The officers are very strict and search persons with great care. Private individuals pay as much as four and five percent duty on all their goods; but as for the English and Dutch Companies, they pay less. But, on the other hand, I believe that, taking into account what it costs them in . . . presents, which they are obliged to make every year at court, the goods cost them nearly the same as they do private persons.

Gold and silver are charged two percent,[2] and as soon as they have been counted at the custom-

house the Mintmaster removes them, and coins them into money of the country, which he hands over to the owner, in proportion to the amount and standard of the bullion. You settle with him, according to the nature of the amount, a day when he is to deliver the new coins, and for as many days as he delays to do so beyond the term agreed upon, he pays interest in proportion to the sum which he has received. The Indians are cunning and exacting in reference to coin and payments; for when money has been coined for three or four years it has to lose one-half percent, and it continues in the same proportion according to

---

[1] A city on the west coast that served as India's main port of entry for Dutch, English, and French merchants and their goods at this time.

[2] The exchange commission charged the Dutch and English East India companies.

age, not being able, as they say, to pass through many hands without some diminution.[3] . . .

As regards gold, the merchants who import it use so much cunning in order to conceal it, that but little of it comes to the knowledge of the customs' officers. The former do all they can to evade paying the customs, especially as they do not run so much risk as in the custom-houses of Europe. For in those of India, when anyone is detected in fraud, he is let off by paying double, ten percent instead of five, the Emperor comparing the venture of the merchant to a game of hazard, where one plays double or quits.[4] . . . The Emperor has conceded to the English Captains that they shall not be searched when they leave their vessels to go on shore; but one day an English Captain, when going to Tatta,[5] one of the largest towns of India, . . . which is at the mouth of the river Indus, as he was about to pass, was arrested by the customs' guards, from whom he could not defend himself, and they searched him in spite of anything he could say. They found gold upon him; he had in fact already conveyed some in sundry journeys which he had made between his vessel and the town; he was, however, let off on payment of the ordinary duty. The Englishman, vexed by this affront, resolved to have his revenge for it, and he took it in a funny manner. He ordered a suckling-pig to be roasted, and to be placed with the grease in a china plate, covered with a napkin, and gave it to a slave to carry with him to the town, anticipating exactly what would happen. As he passed in front of the custom-house, where the Governor of the town, the Shah-bandar,[6] and the Master of the Mint were seated in a divan, they did not fail to stop him, but the slave still advancing with his covered plate, they told his master that he must

needs go to the custom-house, and that they must see what he carried. The more the Englishman protested that the slave carried nothing liable to duty, the less was he believed; and after a long discussion he himself took the plate from the hands of the slave, and proceeded to carry it to the custom-house. The Governor and the Shah-bandar thereupon asked him, in a sharp tone, why he refused to obey orders, and the Englishman, on his part, replied in a rage that what he carried was not liable to duty, and rudely threw the plate in front of them, so that the suckling-pig and the grease soiled the whole place, and splashed up on their garments. As the pig is an abomination to the Muslims, and by their Law they regard as defiled whatever is touched by it, they were compelled to change their garments, to remove the carpet from the divan, and to have the structure rebuilt, without daring to say anything to the Englishman, because the Shah-bandar and the Master of the Mint have to be careful with the Company,[7] from which the country derives so much profit. As for the Chiefs of the Companies, both English and Dutch, and their deputies, they are treated with so much respect that they are never searched when they come from their vessels; but they, on their part, do not attempt to convey gold in secret as the private merchants do, considering it beneath their dignity to do so.

The English, seeing that the custom of searching them had been adopted, had recourse to little stratagems in order to pass the gold, and the fashion of wearing wigs having reached them from Europe, they bethought themselves of concealing . . . [gold coins] . . . in the nets of their wigs every time they left their vessels to go on shore.

---

[3]Because of the metal that had been rubbed off.
[4]Tavernier writes elsewhere that another reason the Mughals had such a lenient policy in regard to smuggling was because quranic law forbids charging interest and tariffs, and they were troubled by the practice.

[5]A city in present-day Pakistan.
[6]The Mughal commissioner in charge of merchants.
[7]The English East India Company.

Multiple Voices VIII ▼▼▼
The Spaniards and the Tlaxcalans

BACKGROUND

When Hernán Cortés began his march into the interior of Mexico in June 1519, his army included roughly 350 Spanish soldiers. Although he received subsequent reinforcements, an army of this size was inadequate to topple the mighty Aztec Empire of the Mexica and capture its capital city, Tenochtitlan, which probably had a population of between 150,000 and 200,000. The fact is that Cortés enjoyed the help of tens of thousands of indispensable Indian allies, chief of whom were the people of Tlaxcala (or Tlaxcalteca), bitter enemies of the Mexica. With the coming of the Spaniards, the Tlaxcalans converted to Catholic Christianity, and following the conquest, their land became a privileged, largely self-governing province that was showered with honors and exemptions during colonial times.

Cortés's initial attempt to win over the Tlaxcalans through diplomacy failed, and they and the Spaniards clashed in a series of bloody skirmishes and battles between August 31 and September 20, 1519. The Spaniards prevailed, but only barely. Following his victory, Cortés entered into an alliance with the Tlaxcalans, who then joined the Spaniards' march on Tenochtitlan. Around October 15, this combined force perpetrated a massacre at Cholula (see source 76, note 3), a city located only twenty miles from the Mexica capital. Thereafter, the Tlaxcalans were ever at the side of the Spaniards as they toppled the Aztec Empire.

THE SOURCES

Accounts of early Spanish-Tlaxcalan relations differ, and those differences present students of the conquest of Mexico with an interesting case study of source veracity and perspective. Our first two sources are Spanish — the accounts of Hernán Cortés and Bernal Díaz del Castillo. Our next two sources are Indian: The first is Mexica; the second is Tlaxcalan. The last source is a Spanish-colonial image of a Catholic saint.

Cortés sent back to the Holy Roman Emperor Charles V (who was also King Charles I of Spain) as many as six lengthy *cartas de relación*, or reports, four of which are extant. In the report excerpted here, possibly the second one sent to the royal court (but the first to survive), which he dated October 30, 1520, Cortés describes his war with the Tlaxcalans and the subsequent victory and peace accord.

Cortés's account was written a little more than a year after he encountered the Tlaxcalans. Almost half a century later, during the 1560s, one of the soldiers who marched with him, Bernal Díaz del Castillo (1492 or 1496–1584), composed his own detailed history of the entire campaign. Despite the passage of time, Díaz is the most reliable Spanish eyewitness of the conquest. Entitled *True History of the Conquest of New Spain*, Díaz's account was written, at least on one level, to

counter the inaccuracies in a history of the conquest by Francisco López de Gó-
mara, who had never set foot in the Americas but who served as Cortés's secretary
upon the captain-general's return to Spain.

In the first of the two excerpts from his history, Bernal Díaz tells how the Tlax-
calans and Cortés sealed their alliance. The second excerpt takes place after the
Spaniards and their allies were driven out of Tenochtitlan on either June 30 or
July 10, 1520 (there are conflicting accounts as to the date), on the *Noche Triste*
(Night of Sorrow). Badly mauled in a disastrous retreat that cost the lives of a re-
ported 150 Spaniards and numerous Indian allies, the combined army returned to
Tlaxcala to recuperate and refit.

The third source is a Mexica account in the Nahuatl language preserved in Friar
Bernardino de Sahagún's *General History of the Things of New Spain*, which we
have already seen (see source 89). This excerpt details the Tlaxcalans' alliance with
the Spaniards and their combined attack on Cholula.

The fourth source is pictorial: five scenes from the *Lienzo de Tlaxcala*. A *lienzo* is
a picture or series of pictures on fabric that tells a story. Around 1550, Tlaxcalan
artists crafted three identical renderings of a lienzo that told, in a series of more
than eighty scenes that follow one another in chronological sequence, the story of
their people's critical role in Cortés's conquest of Mexico. At least one of the three
lienzos was a gift for the viceroy of New Spain, Luis de Velasco. All three originals
were later lost, but faithful nineteenth-century copies survive.

The five images shown here, which appear sequentially in the lienzo, are (1) the
Tlaxcalans' initial greeting of Cortés, in which their rulers offer the Spanish leader
tokens of peace; (2) Tlaxcalan chiefs helping Cortés to erect a cross in their territory; (3) the Tlaxcalans' further offering of gifts; (4) the baptism of the Tlaxcalan
caciques (chiefs); and (5) the assault on Cholula. A few further words of explanation will help you understand these images. In the first scene, two chiefs, a Tlaxcalan and an Otomi, greet the bearded Cortés with flowers and food at the
Waterfall (*Atliuetzyan*). The woman acting as interpreter is Cortés's native guide
and mistress, Doña Marina. Marina was the name given her at baptism; her original name was probably Malinal or Malinalli. As Cortés's trusted advisor, she was
more instrumental than any other single person for his success in Mexico. In the
next scene, in which Tlaxcalan chiefs help Cortés erect a cross, the inscription
translates as "Received in Tlaxcala with open arms." The inscription in the third
scene translates as "They offered gifts," and the gifts proffered here are gold and
jade artifacts, textiles, and women. In the fourth scene, a Nahuatl caption in the
upper left corner states, "When they baptized the leaders." Beneath the image of
the Virgin Mary and Jesus, four male leaders kneel and receive the Eucharistic
host of holy communion from a priest. Three noble Tlaxcalans, probably women,
stand behind the priest. Cortés dominates the upper register on our right. He sits
on a Spanish *jarmuga*, a chair that the Moors had introduced into Spain, and holds
a crucifix and a book, presumably a Bible or a book of prayer. To his left stands
Doña Marina.

The final scene shows the assault on Cholula. Cholulan warriors, who are identified by their topknots, are shown in various states of capture, dismemberment,
dying, death, and defensive retreat. A Tlaxcalan warrior and Spanish soldier fight

side by side as they victoriously advance up the stairs of Cholula's great temple dedicated to Quetzalcoatl, the divine archenemy of Tezcatlipoca, the chief god and defender of Tlaxcala. The two figures in dark robes who stand between the captive Cholulans are Tlaxcalan nobles, one of whom turns toward Doña Marina to warn her of putative Cholulan treachery, thereby precipitating an attack on the city that turned into a massacre. Doña Marina, who plays a prominent role throughout the lienzo, here is pointing toward the temple. Below her is a warrior on horseback. The rearing horse and thrust lance bring to mind sixteenth-century Spanish (and later Spanish-colonial) depictions of *Santiago Matamoros* — Saint James the Moor-Slayer — patron saint of the Spanish Reconquest. Our fifth source (and sixth illustration) is a Latin American statuette of a mounted Santiago (the lance is lost). Cortés and a number of his subordinate commanders were associated with the Order of Santiago, a Spanish crusading order founded in 1170. Other sources tell us that the conquistadors regularly shouted out the traditional Spanish battle cry "Santiago" as they went into battle in the Americas.

QUESTIONS FOR ANALYSIS

1. How does Cortés present the Tlaxcalans?
2. How does Díaz's account deal with the manner in which the Tlaxcalans showed their support of the Spaniards and their willingness to convert to Christianity?
3. How does the Mexica account differ from those of Díaz and Cortés?
4. Provide a verbal narrative for the five images in the *Lienzo de Tlaxcala*. In other words, what is the story, and what is its message?
5. "It is wrong to speak of an Indian or a Spanish perspective on these events. It was not that simple. Perspectives differed due to a variety of factors." What does this anonymous commentator mean? Do you agree? Why or why not?

I ▾ Hernán Cortés, REPORT

I left before dawn . . . without being observed, with the horsemen, a hundred foot soldiers and my Indian allies. I burnt more than ten villages, in one of which there were more than three thousand houses, where the inhabitants fought with us, although there was no one there to help them. As we were carrying the banner of the Cross and were fighting for our Faith and in the service of Your Sacred Majesty in this Your Royal enterprise, God gave us such a victory that we killed many of them without ourselves receiving any hurt. Having gained our victory, we returned to camp a little after midday, for the enemy was gathering from all directions.

The following day messengers arrived from the chieftains saying that they wished to be vassals of Your Highness and my friends; and they begged me to forgive them for what they had done. I replied that they had done wrong, but that I was content to be their friend and to forgive what they had done. The next day some fifty Indians who, it seemed, were people of importance among them, came to the camp saying they were bringing food, and began to inspect the entrances and exits and some huts where we were living. The men from Cempoal[1] came to me and said I should take notice of the fact that the newcomers were bad men and had come to spy and see how we could be harmed, and I could be certain that that was their only purpose in coming. I ordered one of them to be captured discreetly so that the others did not see, and I took him aside and through the interpreters threatened him so that he should tell me the truth. He confessed that Sintengal,[2] who is captain general of this province, was waiting with many men behind some hills opposite the camp to fall on us that night, because, they said, they had fought with us by day and gained nothing and now wished to try by night, so that their people should fear neither the horses nor the guns nor the swords. They had been sent to spy out our camp and to see where it could be entered, and how they might burn the straw huts. Then I had another Indian seized and questioned him likewise, and he repeated what the other had said and in the same words. Then I took five or six and they all confirmed what I had heard, so I took all fifty and cut off their hands and sent them to tell their chief that by day or by night, or whenever they chose to come, they would see who we were. I had the camp fortified as best I could, and deployed my men where I thought most advantageous, and so remained on the alert until the sun set. . . .

When we had rested somewhat, I went out one night, after inspecting the first watch, with a hundred foot soldiers, our Indian allies and the horsemen. . . . Before it was dawn I attacked two towns, where I killed many people, but I did not burn the houses lest the fires should alert the other towns nearby. At dawn I came upon another large town containing, according to an inspection I had made, more than twenty thousand houses. As I took them by surprise, they rushed out unarmed, and the women and children ran naked through the streets, and I began to do them some harm. When they saw that they could not resist, several men of rank of the town came to me and begged me to do them no more harm, for they wished to be Your Highness's vassals and my allies. They now saw that they were wrong in not having been willing to assist me; from thenceforth I would see how they would do all that I, in Your Majesty's name, commanded them to do, and they would be Your faithful vassals. Then, later, more than four thousand came to me in peace and led me outside to a spring and fed me very well. . . .

On the following day at ten o'clock, Sintengal, the captain general of this province, came to see me, together with some fifty men of rank, and he begged me on his own behalf, and on behalf of Magiscasin,[3] who is the most important person in the entire province, and on behalf of many other lords, to admit them to Your Highness's Royal service and to my friendship, and to forgive them their past errors, for they did not know who we were. They had tried with all their forces both by day and by night to avoid being subject to anyone, for this province never had been, nor had they ever had an over-all ruler. For they had lived in freedom and independence from time immemorial and had always defended themselves against the great power of Mutezuma and against his ancestors, who had subjugated all those lands but had never been able to reduce them to servitude, although they were surrounded on all sides and had no place by which to leave their land. They ate no salt because there was none in their land; neither could they go and buy it elsewhere, nor did they wear cotton because it did not grow there on account of the cold; and they were lacking in many other things through being so enclosed.

---

[1]Cempoala, a Totonac town near Veracruz on the coast of the Gulf of Mexico. Realizing that he needed to win over allies through diplomacy, Cortés had convinced the Totonacs to rebel against the Mexica and join in the march to Tenochtitlan.

[2]Xicotencatl, the leading war chieftain of the Tlaxcalans.
[3]Maxixcatzin, one of the major caciques, or chiefs, of Tlaxcala.

All of which they suffered willingly in return for being free and subject to no one, and with me they had wished to do the same; to which end, as they said, they had used all their strength but saw clearly that neither it nor their cunning had been of any use. They would rather be Your Hightness's vassals than see their houses destroyed and their women and children killed. I replied that they should recognize they were to blame for the harm they had received, for I had come to their land thinking that I came to a land of friends. . . . I had sent my messengers on ahead to tell them that I was coming and that I wished to be their friend. But without reply they had attacked me on the road while I was unprepared and had killed two horses and wounded others. And after they had fought me, they sent messengers to tell me that it had been done without their consent by certain communities who were responsible; but they were not involved and had now rebuked those others for it and desired my friendship. I had believed them and had told them that I was pleased and would come on the following day and go among them as I would among friends. And again they had attacked me on the road and had fought all day until nightfall. And I reminded them of everything else that they had done against me and many other things which in order not to tire Your Highness I will omit. Finally, they offered themselves as vassals in the Royal service of Your Majesty and offered their persons and fortunes and so they have remained until today and will, I think, always remain so for what reason Your Majesty will see hereafter.

---

2 ▼ Bernal Díaz del Castillo, TRUE HISTORY OF THE CONQUEST OF NEW SPAIN

Early the following day, Cortés ordered an altar erected and that Mass be said, for we now had wine and [eucharistic] wafer bread. The cleric Juan Díaz said the Mass because Padre de la Merced[1] was sick with fever and quite feeble. Present were Mase-Escaci[2] and the elder Xicotenga,[3] and other *caciques*. At the conclusion of Mass, Cortés entered his dwelling, accompanied by some of us soldiers who were accustomed to accompany him, and also by elderly *caciques* and our translators. Xicotenga said to him that they wished to bring him a gift, and Cortés showed them great affection, saying to them that they should bring it whenever they wished. And so some mats were immediately spread out, covered by a cloth, and they brought in six or seven small pieces of gold and stones of little value and some quantity of henequen rope.[4] It was all very poor and not even worth twenty *pesos*.[5] And when they had presented it, those *caciques* said, as they laughed, "*Malinche*[6] we know well that, inasmuch as what we have given you is so paltry, you will not accept it with good grace. We have already sent word on to tell you that we are poor and possess neither gold nor fantastic riches, and the cause of this is that those traitorous and evil Mexica and Montezuma, who is now their lord, took all that we once possessed in return for peace and a truce, when we requested that they not make war on us. So, do not consider its poor

---

[1]Cortés's chief chaplain.
[2]Maxixcatzin. See note 3 of the previous source.
[3]Xicotencatl, father of the warrior chieftain of the same name. See note 2 of the previous source.
[4]A fiber made from a native plant.
[5]The Spanish *peso* was the silver eight-*real* coin, popularly known as "pieces of eight." See source 90, note 2.

[6]A term of respect used for both Cortés and Doña Marina. It is a Spanish corruption of *Malinaltzim*, a reverential form of Marina's Nahuatl name. According to Díaz del Castillo, when applied to Cortés, it meant "Malinal's Captain."

value, but accept it with good grace as the gift of friends and servants, which we will be to you." Then they brought, apart from this, bounteous food. Cortés accepted it cheerfully, and he told them that he valued it more for coming from their hands with the good will with which it was offered than he would a house filled with gold dust brought by others, and it was in this spirit that he accepted it, and he showed them great affection.

It seems that it had been agreed upon by all the *caciques* to give us those daughters and nieces of theirs who were the most beautiful, marriage-ready maidens, and the elderly Xicotenga said: "*Malinche*, in order that you might know more clearly our good will toward you and our wish to satisfy you in every way, we want to give you our daughters as your wives, so that you might have children by them. For we wish to consider you as our brothers, given that you are so good and courageous. I have a very lovely daughter who has not been married, and I want to present her to you." Likewise Mase-Escaci and all of the other *caciques* said that they would bring their daughters and that we should accept them as wives, and they offered many other things. Throughout the day, both Mase-Escaci and Xicotenga never left Cortés's side. Inasmuch as Xicotenga was blind from old age, he felt Cortés with his hand all over his head, face, beard, and entire body.

In regard to the women, Cortés replied to them that he and all of us were most grateful and, as time passed, we would repay them with good deeds. Padre de la Merced was present, and Cortés said to him: "Señor Padre, it seems to me to be a propitious time to attempt to induce these *caciques* to abandon their idols and sacrifices, for they will do anything we require of them because of their great fear of the Mexica." The friar replied: "Señor, true enough, but let the matter be until they bring their daughters, and then there will be material to work on, and Your Honor can say that you do not wish to accept them until

they abandon sacrifices. If that succeeds, excellent! If not, we have done our duty." . . .

The next day the same elderly *caciques* arrived with five beautiful Indian maidens. . . . and all were daughters of *caciques*. Xicotenga said to Cortés: "*Malinche*, this is my daughter . . . take her as your own. . . . and let the others be given to the captains." Cortés expressed his gratitude and . . . said that he accepted them and received them as our own, but for the present they should remain under the care of their fathers. The *caciques* asked why he would not take them now, and Cortés replied: "First, I desire to obey the mandate of Our Lord God . . . and that for which our lord the king has sent me: to induce you to abandon your idols and no longer sacrifice or butcher any humans . . . and that you believe what we believe, namely faith in one true God." And he told them much more regarding our holy faith. . . .

They replied to it all as follows: "*Malinche*, we firmly believe that this God of yours and this great Lady[7] are very good, but consider that you have only recently arrived in our land and at our homes. As time goes on we will understand your points much more clearly, and seeing what they are, we will do what is right. But how can you ask that we abandon our *teules*,[8] which now for so many years our ancestors have held to be gods and have worshiped and sacrificed to? Even if we, the old men, might wish to do so to please you, what about our priests, and all our neighbors, and the youth and children throughout the province, who would rise up against us? This is especially true of the priests who have already consulted our *teules*, who answered that they not forget the human sacrifices and all the rites that we formerly practiced. Otherwise, they would devastate the entire province with famine, pestilence, and war." And so they replied, saying that we should not trouble ourselves to talk to them on that subject again because they were not about to stop the sacrifices, even if they were killed for it.

---

[7]The Virgin Mary. See the fourth scene in the *lienzo*.

[8]Nahua deities.

When we had heard this response, which they gave forthrightly and fearlessly, Padre de la Merced, a wise man who was learned in theology, said: "Señor, take care not to press them further on the subject, for it is not right that we use force to make them Christians, and . . . we should not destroy their idols until they have some knowledge of our holy faith." Furthermore, three gentlemen . . . told Cortés: "The padre has spoken well. You have fulfilled your duty with what you have done. Do not raise the matter again when talking with these *caciques*." And so the matter was dropped. What we managed to entreat the *caciques* to do was to clear out at once one of their nearby and recently built temples, and, after removing the idols, to clean and whitewash it so that we could place therein a cross and the image of Our Lady. This they did promptly. Then Mass was said there, and the *cacicas*[9] were baptized. The daughter of Xi-

cotenga was given the name Doña Luisa, and Cortés took her by the hand and gave her to Pedro de Alvarado,[10] saying to Xicotenga that he to whom he gave her was his brother and captain, and he should be pleased, for she would be well cared for by him. And Xicotenga was pleased. . . .

▾▾▾

When we arrived at Tlaxcala,[11] . . . Xicotenga "the Elder" . . . and almost all the other *caciques* of Tlaxcala offered Cortés their service . . . for the war against the Mexica. Cortés embraced them with great affection. . . . and soon persuaded them to choose to become Christian. And the good old Xicotenga with great willingness said he desired to be a Christian. With the greatest possible ceremony that one could arrange at that time, he was baptized in Tlaxcala by Padre de la Merced and given the name Lorenzo de Vargas.

---

[9]The daughters and nieces of the chieftains.
[10]Cortés's chief lieutenant.

[11]Following the retreat from Tenochtitlan on the Night of Sorrow.

---

3 ▾ Bernardino de Sahagún, *GENERAL HISTORY OF THE THINGS OF NEW SPAIN*

And when they[1] reached Tecoac, which is in the land of the Tlaxcalans, where their Otomis lived, the Otomis met them with hostilities and war.[2] But they annihilated the Otomis of Tecoac, who were destroyed completely. They lanced and stabbed them, they shot them with guns, iron bolts, crossbows. Not just a few but a huge number of them were destroyed.

After the great defeat at Tecoac, when the Tlaxcalans heard it and found out about it and it was reported to them, they became limp with

fear, they were made faint; fear took hold of them. Then they assembled, and all of them, including the lords and rulers, took counsel among themselves, considering the reports.

They said, "How is it to be with us? Should we face them? For the Otomis are great and valiant warriors, yet they thought nothing of them, they regarded them as nothing; in a very short time, in the blink of an eyelid, they destroyed the people. Now let us just submit to them, let us make friends with them, let us be

---

[1]The Spaniards.
[2]The Otomis were a non-Nahua people of central Mexico who resided along the frontier of Tlaxcala and served both the Mexica and Tlaxcalans as warriors. They were so noted for their fierceness in combat that the Mexica designated

their own warrior-elites as "Otomi rank" (see source 89, note 20). The Spaniards and their Indian allies skirmished with a mixed force of Otomis and Tlaxcalans when they crossed into Tlaxcalan territory on August 31.

friends, for something must be done about the common people."

Thereupon the Tlaxcalan rulers went to meet them, taking along food: turkey hens, eggs, white tortillas, fine tortillas. They said to them, "Welcome, our lords."

[The Spaniards] answered them back, "Where is your homeland? Where have you come from?"

They said, "We are Tlaxcalans. Welcome, you have arrived, you have reached the land of Tlaxcala, which is your home." . . .

[The Tlaxcalans] guided, accompanied, and led them until they brought them to their palace[s] and placed them there. They showed them great honors, they gave them what they needed and attended to them, and then they gave them their daughters.

Then [the Spaniards] asked them, "Where is Mexico? What kind of a place is it? Is it still far?"

They answered them, "It's not far now. Perhaps one can get there in three days. It is a very favored place, and [the Mexica] are very strong, great warriors, conquerors, who go about conquering everywhere."

Now before this there had been friction between the Tlaxcalans and the Cholulans. They viewed each other with anger, fury, hate, and disgust; they could come together on nothing. Because of this they put [the Spaniards] up to killing them treacherously.

They said to them, "The Cholulans are very evil; they are our enemies. They are as strong as the Mexica, and they are the Mexica's friends."

When the Spaniards heard this, they went to Cholula. The Tlaxcalans and Cempoalans went with them, outfitted for war. When they arrived, there was a general summons and cry that all the noblemen, rulers, subordinate leaders, warriors, and commoners should come, and everyone assembled in the temple courtyard. When they had all come together, [the Spaniards and their friends] blocked the entrances, all of the places where one entered. Thereupon people were stabbed, struck, and killed. No such thing was in the minds of the Cholulans; they did not meet the Spaniards with weapons of war. It just seemed that they were stealthily and treacherously killed, because the Tlaxcalans persuaded [the Spaniards] to do it.

4 ▾ LIENZO DE TLAXCALA

Tlaxcalans Greet Cortés at Atlihuetzyan

Erecting a Cross

Offering Gifts

Baptism

The Battle of Cholula

5 ▾ SANTIAGO MATAMOROS

Statue of Santiago Matamoros

▲▲▲

Sources

Prologue

(1) From E. G. Ravenstein, ed. and trans., *A Journal of the First Voyage of Vasco da Gama, 1497–1499* (Hakluyt Society, 1898), First Series, No. 99. Reproduced by Burt Franklin, 1963, pp. 77–78. Modernized by A. J. Andrea. (2) *Travels in Asia and Africa, 1325–1354*, H. A. R. Gibb, trans. (New York: Robert M. McBride & Co., 1929), pp. 234–237, passim. Modernized by A. J. Andrea. (3) From Ma Huan, Ying-Yai Sheng-Lan, *The Overall Survey of the Ocean's Shores* [1433], J. V. G. Mills, trans. The Hakluyt Society at the University Press, 1970, pp. 138–143, passim. Romanization to Pinyin style from Wade Giles by A. J. Andrea. (4) *The Catalan World Atlas*, © British Library, London, UK / The Bridgeman Art Library.

Part One ▾ The Ancient World

Chapter 1

Source 1: From *The Epic of Gilgamesh*, translated by Nancy K. Sandars, Penguin Classics, Third Edition, 1972, pp. 81–83, 102, 106–110, 111–114, 118. Copyright © N. K. Sandars, 1960, 1964, 1972. **Source 2:** Chilperic Edwards, *The Hammurabi Code* (1904), pp. 23–80, passim. Reprinted without copyright by Kennikut Press, 1971. **Source 3:** William Kelly Simpson, ed., *The Literature of Egypt: An Anthology of Stories, Instructions, Stelae, Autobiographies, and Poetry*, 3rd ed. Yale University Press, 2003, pp. 183–187, passim. Reprinted with permission of Yale University Press. **Source 4:** From William Kelly Simpson, ed., *The Literature of Egypt: An Anthology of Stories, Instructions, Stelae, Autobiographies, and Poetry*, 3rd ed., Yale University Press, 2003, pp. 41–42, passim. Reprinted with permission of Yale University Press. **Source 5:** James Legge, trans., *The Sacred Books of China: The Texts of Confucianism*, in F. Max Mueller, ed., *The Sacred Books of the East*, 50 vols. (Oxford: Clarendon Press, 1879–1910), vol. 3, pp. 92–95. **Source 6:** From *The Book of Songs*, translated by Arthur Waley, edited with additional translations by Joseph R. Allen, 1996, pp. 23–26, 65, 78, 318, and 283–285. Copyright © 1996 by Grove Press, Inc. Reprinted with permission of Grove/Atlantic, Inc. **Source 7:** (1–6) Walter A. Fairservis Jr. *The Roots of Ancient India: The Archeology of Early Indian Civilization*, illustrated with drawings by Jan Fairservis (New York: Macmillan, 1971), pp. 276, 276, 279, 278, 274, 276. Copyright © by Walter A. Fairservis. Reprinted with the permission of Macmillan Publishing Company. (7–8) Courtesy of the Trustees of the British Museum. (9) Courtesy of the Ashmolean Museum, Oxford University, Oxford. **Source 8:** (1) Courtesy of Hamlyn Publishing, London. (2) Sudan Archeological Museum, Khartoum. Courtesy of Werner Forman/Art Resource, NY.

Multiple Voices I

(1, 2, and 3) Miriam Lichtheim, *Ancient Egyptian Literature: A Book of Readings, Vol. II: The New Kingdom* (University of California Press, 1976), pp. 124–126. Reprinted with permission of University of California Press via Rightslink.

Chapter 2

Source 9: Excerpts from *The Rig Veda: An Anthology of One Hundred and Eight Hymns*, selected, annotated, and translated by Wendy Doniger O'Flaherty, Penguin Classics, 1981, pp. 160–162. Copyright © Wendy Doniger O'Flaherty. Reproduced by permission of Penguin Books. **Source 10:** A. J. Andrea, trans. *The Odyssey of Homer*. Copyright © 2008 by A. J. Andrea. **Sources 11 and 12:** From the New Revised Standard Version of the Bible. Copyright © 1989 by the National Council of Churches of Christ in the USA. Used by permission. All rights reserved.

Chapter 3

Source 13: F. Max Mueller, trans., *The Upanishads*, in Mueller, ed., *The Sacred Books of the East*, 50 vols. (Oxford: Clarendon Press, 1879–1910), vol. 1, pp. 92, 104–105; vol. 15, pp. 168–169, 173, 175–177, passim. **Source 14:** Tashinath Trmibak Telang, trans., *The Bhagavad Gita*, in F. Max Mueller, ed., *The Sacred Books of the East*, 50 vols. (Oxford: Clarendon Press, 1879–1910), vol. 8, pp. 43–46, 48–49, 51–52, 126–128, passim. **Source 15:** T. W. Rhys Davids and Hermann Oldenberg, trans., *Vinaya Texts*, in F. Max Mueller, ed., *The Sacred Books of the East*, 50 vols. (Oxford: Clarendon Press, 1879–1910), vol. 13, pp. 94–97, 100–102, passim. **Source 16:** The Buddha, "Questions That Tend Not to Edification," in Henry C. Warrant, ed. and trans., *Buddhism in Translations* (Cambridge: Harvard University Press, 1896), pp. 117–122, passim (modernized). **Source 17:** James Hope Moulton, Yasnas 43, 44, 45, in *Early Zoroastrianism* (London: Williams and Norgate, 1913), pp. 367–370, passim. **Source 18:** From the New Revised Standard Version of the Bible. Copyright © 1989 by the National Council of Churches of Christ in the USA. Used by permission. All rights reserved.

Chapter 4

Source 19: F. Max Mueller, ed., *The Sacred Books of the East*, 50 vols. (Oxford: Clarendon Press, 1879–1910), vol. 39, passim. **Source 20:** From *The Analects of Confucius (Lun Yu)*, a Literal Translation with an Introduction and Notes by Chichung Huang, 1997, pp. 47–49, 52–53, 56, 58, 77–80, 84–85, 87, 90, 94, 106, 125, 129, 131–132, 136, 144, 155–157, 162, 168, 172, passim. Reprinted with permission of Oxford University Press. **Source 21:** Reprinted with the permission of the Free Press, a Division of Simon & Schuster Adult Publishing Group, from *Chinese Civilization: A Sourcebook*, 2nd ed., by Patricia Buckley Ebrey, pp. 51–53, passim. Copyright © 1993 by Patricia Buckley Ebrey. All rights reserved. **Source 22:** Thucydides, *The Peloponnesian War*, trans. by A. J. Andrea. Copyright © 2008 by A. J. Andrea. **Source 23:** From *Euripides: The Complete Greek Tragedies*, volume 3, 1959, pp. 184–187. Excerpts from *The Bacchae*, translated by William Arrowsmith. Reprinted with permission of University of Chicago Press. **Source 24:** Plato, *Phaedo*, Benjamin Jowett, trans., *The Dialogues of Plato*, 3rd ed. (London: Humphrey Milford, 1892), pp. 205–207, passim. **Source 25:** (1) Staatliche Antikensammlungen und Glyptothek Munchen. Photograph by Kuppermann. (2) Hellenic Republic Ministry of Culture/Athens, Greece. (3) Metropolitan Museum of Art, Fletcher Fund, 1927 (27.45).

Multiple Voices II

(1) Ilza Veith, trans., *Huang Nei Ching Su Wen: The Yellow Emperor's Classic of Internal Medicine*, pp. 102–105. Copyright © 1996 by The Regents of the University of California. (2) From Emma Jeanette Edelstein and Ludwig Edelstein, *Asclepius: A Collection and Interpretation of the Testimonies*, Vol. I & II, pp. 230–235, 237. Copyright © 1945 The Johns Hopkins University Press. Reprinted with permission of The Johns Hopkins University Press. (3) *Hippocrates*, A. J. Andrea, trans. Copyright © 2008 by A. J. Andrea.

Chapter 5

Source 26: (1) German Archeological Institute, Rome (neg. #33.23). (2) Alinari/Art Resource, NY. (3) The Metropolitan Museum of Art, Rogers Fund, 1909 (09.39). (4) Alinari/Art Resource, NY. **Source 27:** Publius Vergilius Maro, *Aeneid*, Book 6. Selections translated by A. J. Andrea. Copyright © 2008 by A. J. Andrea. **Source 28:** From Esson M. Gale, trans., *Discourses on Salt and Iron: A Debate on State Control of Commerce and Industry in Ancient China*, 1967, pp. 1–7, 3–16; modified by A. J. Andrea. Original publishers E. J. Brill, Ltd. of Leiden, 1931. Reprinted with permission of Brill Academic Publishers/The Netherlands. **Source 29:** Nancy Lee Swann, trans., *Pan Chao: Foremost Woman Scholar of China* (New York: Century Co., 1932), pp. 111–114. Reprinted with the permission of Gest Oriental Library, Princeton. **Source 30:** Excerpts from *The Edicts of Asoka*, trans. and ed. by N. A. Nikam and Richard McKeon, 1958. Reprinted with permission of the University of Chicago Press. **Source 31:** James Legge, trans., *A Record of Buddhistic Kingdoms* (Oxford: Clarendon Press, 1886), 42–45, 77–79.

Multiple Voices III

(1) Translated from the Latin by A. J. Andrea. Copyright © 2008 by A. J. Andrea. (2) James Legge, trans., *A Record of Buddhistic Kingdoms* (Oxford: Clarendon Press, 1886). (3) (1) Classical Exchange Fund, 1979.5576 Photograph © 2003 Museum of Fine Arts, Boston. (2) Courtesy of Iraq Museum.

(3) University of Pennsylvania Museum neg. #29-68-1. (4) The Metropolitan Museum of Art, John Stewart Kennedy Fund, 1926 (26.123).

Part Two ▾ Faith, Devotion, and Salvation: Great World Religions to 1500

Chapter 6

Source 32: From Donald S. Lopez Jr. (ed.), *Religions of China in Practice*. Copyright © 1996 Princeton University Press. Reprinted by permission of Princeton University Press. **Source 33:** (1) Freer Gallery of Art, Smithsonian Institution, Washington, DC: Purchase F1979.51. (2) Courtesy of the National Museum of Phnom Penh, Cambodia. (3) Bildarchiv Preussischer Kulturbesitz/Art Resource, NY. **Source 34:** From William Theodore de Bary, et al., *Sources of Indian Tradition*, 1958, pp. 332–335. Copyright © 1958 Columbia University Press. Reprinted with permission of the publisher. **Source 35:** National Museum Madura, Tamil Nadu India; Courtesy Giraudon Art Resource, NY. **Source 36:** Reprinted by permission of the publishers and the Trustees of the Loeb Classical Library from *Josephus: Life Against Apion — Volume 1*, LCL 196, translated by H. J. St. Thackeray, Cambridge, Mass.: Harvard University Press. Copyright 1926 by the President and Fellows of Harvard College. The Loeb Classical Library® is a registered trademark of the President and Fellows of Harvard College. **Source 37:** From *The Talmud*, translated by Ben Zion Bokser, Copyright © 1989 Baruch M. Bokser. Used with permission of Paulist Press, Inc., New York/Mahwah, NJ, www.paulistpress.com.

Chapter 7

Sources 38 and 39: From the New Revised Standard Version of the Bible. Copyright © 1989 by the National Council of Churches of Christ in the USA. Used by permission. All rights reserved. **Source 40:** Arthur C. McGiffert, trans., in *A Select Library of Nicene and Post-Nicene Fathers*, 14 vols., 2nd series (Christian Literature, 1890), vol. 1, pp. 349–350, 369–370, 386–387, passim (modified). **Source 41:** From *The Theodosian Code* from P. R. Coleman-Norton, trans. and ed., *Roman State and Christian Church*, 1966, Vol. 1, pp. 74, 76, 216, 254, 342, 354; vol. 2, pp. 387–388, 392–393, 436–437, 438, 452, 459, 510, 559–560, passim. Reprinted with permission of the Society for Promoting Christian Knowledge. **Source 42:** Scala/Art Resource, NY/Museo Arcivescovile/Ravenna, Italy. **Source 43:** From R. Philip and S. J. Amidon, *The Church History of Rufinus of Aquileia: Books 10 and 11*, 1997, pp. 20–23. Reprinted with permission of Oxford University Press. **Source 44:** Bishop Adam, "The Christian Monument," in P. Y. Saeki, *The Nestorian Documents and Relics in China* (Tokyo: Maruzen, 1951), pp. 56–61 (modified).

Multiple Voices IV

(1) From *The Secret Teachings of Jesus* by Marvin W. Meyer, pp. 19–20, 23–24, 26–29, 32–33, 38, passim. Copyright © 1984 by Marvin W. Meyer. Used by permission of Random House, Inc. (2) From Joseph Cullen Ayers, *A Source Book for Ancient Church History*, Charles Scribner's Sons, 1939, p. 103. (3) The Homilies of Clement from *New Testament Apocrypha*, Vol. 2, ed. William Schneemelcher, 2nd ed. Cambridge/Louisville: Lutterworth Press and Westminster John Knox Press. Reprinted with permission of Westminster John Knox Press. (4) Reprinted by permission of the publishers and the Trustees of the Loeb Classical Library from *Eusebius: Volume 1*, Loeb Classical Library Volume 153, translated by Kirsopp Lake, pp. 191, 193, 257, 259, Cambridge, Mass.: Harvard University Press, Copyright 1926 by the President and Fellows of Harvard College. The Loeb Classical Library® is a registered trademark of the President and Fellows of Harvard College. (5) *The Ecclesiastical History of Socrates* (London: Henry G. Bohn, 1853), 21.

Chapter 8

Source 45: From *The Koran Interpreted*, trans. by Arthur J. Arberry, 2 Vols., 1955, George Allen & Unwin, HarperCollins Publishers, Inc. Reprinted with permission of Anna Evans. Source 46: M. Aftab-ud-din Ahmad, trans., English Translation of *Sahih-al-Bukhari* (Lahore: Ahmadiyya Anjuman Ishaat-i-Islam, [n.d.]), pp. 2–4, 53, 56–57, 59–60, 112, 128, 194, 241, 243–244. Source 47: A. Guillaume, trans., *The Life of Muhammad: A Translation of Ishaq's Sirat Rasul Allah* (Oxford University Press, 1955), 181–187, passim. Reprinted by permission of Oxford University Press, Pakistan. Source 48: Jihad in Medieval and Modern Islam: The Chapter on Jihad from *Averroes' Legal Handbook*, translated and annotated by Rudolph Peters, Brill Academic, 1977, pp. 9–18. Reprinted with permission of the author. Source 49: Hasan ibn Yusuf, "Creed Concerning the Imams," in A. A. A. Fyzec, ed. and trans., *A Shi'ite Creed* (New Delhi: Oxford, 1942). Copyright © 1942. Used by permission of Oxford University Press, New Delhi. Source 50: Bernard Lewis, ed. and trans., *Islam from the Prophet Muhammad to the Capture of Constantinople*, Volume I, Politics and War, Translation copyright © 1987 by Bernard Lewis, Oxford University Press. Reprinted with permission of Oxford University Press, Inc. Source 51: From *The Mathnawi of Jalalu'addin Rumi*, trans. by Reynold A. Nocholson, Volume 2, Cambridge University Press, 1926, p. 76. Reprinted with permission of Cambridge University Press.

Multiple Voices V

(1) Al-Baladhuri, *Kitab Futah al-Buldan* (The Origins of the Islamic State), P. K. Hitti, trans. (New York, 1916), pp. 316–317. (2) T. W. Arnold, trans., *The Preaching of Islam*, 2nd ed. (London, 1913), pp. 57–59 (modified). (3) Benjamin Ben Jonah, *The Itinerary of Benjamin of Tudela*, trans. Marcus N. Adler (London: H. Frowde, 1907), pp. 35–42, passim. (4) H. M. Elliott and John Dowson, eds. and trans., *The History of India as Told by Its Own Historians*, 8 vols. (London: Truebner, 1867–1877), vol. 3, pp. 374–388, passim.

Part Three ▾ Continuity, Change, and Interchange: 500–1500

Chapter 9

Source 52: "Chronicles of Japan," in W. G. Aston, trans., *Nihongi: Chronicles of Japan from the Earliest Times to A.D. 697*, 2 vols. (London: Kegan, Paul, Trench, Truebner, 1896), vol. 2, pp. 128–133, passim. Source 53: From *The Pillow Book of Sei Sh'onagan*, trans. and ed. by Ivan I. Morris, pp. 21–23, 39–40, 45–50, 117, passim. Copyright © 1991 Columbia University Press. Reprinted with the permission of the publisher. Source 54: From *The Taiheki: A Chronicle of Medieval Japan*, trans. by Helen Craig McCullough. Copyright © 1959 Columbia University Press. Reprinted with the permission of the publisher. Source 55: From *The Selected Poems of Du Fu*, trans. Burton Watson, pp. 2, 8–9, 26–27, 52. Copyright © 2002 Columbia University Press. Reprinted with the permission of the publisher. Source 56: From Colin Mackerras, ed and trans., *The Uighur Empire According to the T'ang Dynasty Histories: A Study in Sino-Uighur Relations, 744–840*, 1972, 62–68. Reprinted with permission of University of South Carolina Press. Source 57: Reprinted with the permission of The Free Press, a Division of Simon & Schuster Adult Publishing Group, from *Chinese Civilization and Society: A Sourcebook* by Patricia Buckley Ebrey. Copyright © 1981 by The Free Press. All rights reserved. Source 58: Charles Pellat, *The Life and Works of Jahiz*, trans. D. M. Hawkes (Berkeley, CA: University of California Press, 1969), pp. 251, 257–258, 265–267, passim. Source 59: From *The Travels of Ibn Jubayr* translated by R. J. C. Broadhurst, published by Jonathan Cape. Reprinted by permission of The Random House Group Ltd. Source 60: *The Arabian Nights' Entertainments* (London: George Routledge, 1890), pp. 113–116. Source 61: Edward C. Sachau, trans., *Alberuni's India* (Delhi, 1910), pp. 17–25, passim. Source 62: Franklin Edgerton, ed. and trans., *Vikrama's Adventures*, 2 vols. (Cambridge, Mass.: Harvard University Press, 1926), vol. 1, pp. 228–230. Copyright © 1926 by Harvard University Press. Reprinted by permission.

Multiple Voices VI

(1) From *Lives of the Nuns: Biographies of Chinese Nuns from the Fourth to Sixth Centuries*, pp. 20–21. A translation of *Pi-ch'iu-ni chuan*, compiled by Shih Pao-ch'ang. Translated by Kathryn Ann Tai, 1994. Romanization from Wade-Giles to Pinyin by A. J. Andrea. (2) From *Ennin's Travels in T'ang China*, Edwin O. Reischauer, pp. 221–224. Copyright © 1955. Reprinted with permission of John Wiley & Sons, Inc. (3) From *Ennin's Travels in Tang China*, Edwin O.

Reischauer, pp. 225–227. Copyright © 1955. Reprinted by permission of John Wiley & Sons, Inc. (4) Excerpts from Daniel K. Gardner, ed. and trans., *Learning to Be a Sage: Selections from the Conversations of Master Chu*, 1990, University of California Press, pp. 128–134. Reprinted with permission of University of California Press via Rightslink.

Chapter 10

Source 63: (1 and 2): Alinari/Art Resource, NY. **Source 64:** From *Fourteen Byzantine Rulers: The Chronographia of Michael Psellus* by Marcus Psellus, translated with an introduction by E. R. A. Sewter (Penguin Classics, 1966), pp. 237–241. Copyright © the Estate of E. R. A. Sewter, 1966. Reprinted with permission of Penguin Group UK. **Source 65:** Alinari/Art Resource, NY. **Source 66:** Oliver J. Thatcher and Edgar H. McNeal, trans., *A Source Book for Medieval History* (New York: Charles Scribner's Sons, 1905), p. 107; D. C. Munro, trans., University of Pennsylvania Translations and Reprints (Philadelphia: University of Pennsylvania, 1900), vol. 6, no. 5, pp. 16–27, passim. **Source 67:** From *The Works of Liudprand of Cremona*, translated by F. A. Wright. Copyright © 1930 E. P. Dutton & Company. Reproduced by permission of Taylor & Francis Books UK. **Source 68:** (1) Courtesy Bayerische Staatsbibliothek, München. (2) Herzog August Bibliothek Wolfenbüttel. **Source 69:** *Dictatus Papae* translated by A. J. Andrea. Copyright © 2008 Alfred J. Andrea; Oliver J. Thatcher and Edgar H. McNeal, trans., *A Source Book for Medieval History* (New York: Charles Scribner's Sons, 1905), 151–152; Brian Tierney, trans., *The Crisis of Church and State, 1050–1300* (Englewood Cliffs, NJ: Prentice-Hall, Inc., 1964), pp. 208–209, passim. **Source 70:** From *The Alexiad of the Princess Anna Comnena*, translated by Elizabeth A. S. Dawes. Copyright © 1967. Reproduced by permission of Taylor & Francis Books UK.

Multiple Voices VII

(1) Baldric of Dol, "The Jerusalem History," in A. C. Krey, trans., *The First Crusade: The Accounts of Eye-Witnesses and Participants* (Princeton, NJ: Princeton University Press, 1921), pp. 33–36. (2) From *The Alexiad of the Princess Anna Comnena*, translated by Elizabeth A. S. Dawes. Copyright © 1967. Reproduced by permission of Taylor & Francis Books UK. (3) Robert of Clari, *La Conquête de Constantinople*. Translated from the Old French by A. J. Andrea. Copyright © 2008 by A. J. Andrea. (4) Reprinted material from Harry J. Magoulias, trans., *O City of Byzantium: Annals of Niketas Choniates*, 1984, pp. 314–317, with the permission of Wayne State University Press. (5) *Register Innocentii III*. Translated from the Latin by A. J. Andrea. Copyright © 2008 A. J. Andrea.

Chapter 11

Source 71: G. S. P. Freeman-Greenville, ed. and trans., *The East African Coast: Select Documents* (Oxford: Clarendon Press, 1962), pp. 14–17, passim. Reprinted by permission of Mr. Freeman-Greenville. **Source 72:** From N. Levtzion

and J. F. P. Hopkins, eds., *Corpus of Early Arabic Sources for West African History*, Cambridge University Press, 1981, pp. 79–83, passim. Reprinted with permission of Cambridge University Press. **Source 73:** From G. W. B. Huntingford, *The Glorious Victories of Amda Seyon, King of Ethiopia*, 1965, pp. 53–65, passim. Reprinted with permission of Oxford University Press. **Source 74:** *Yoruba Woman of Authority* from 1978 Ibadan University Press and the Nigerian Federal Department of Antiquities. Photograph courtesy of the Library of Congress. **Source 75:** (1) Maya People, "Ball Player as a War Captive," terra-cotta with traces of pigment, Late Classic period, circa 600–900, New Orleans Museum of Art: Museum purchase, Women's Volunteer Committee Fund, 74.211. (2) Denver Art Museum Collection: Gift of William I. Lee, 1986.617. Photo by Denver Art Museum © 2003. All rights reserved. (3) The Detroit Institute of Arts, acc #77.49. Founders Society Purchase, Katherine Margaret Kay Bequest Fund and New Endowment Fund. Photograph © 1993 The Detroit Institute of Arts. **Source 76:** From Fray Diego Durán, *Book of the Gods and Rites and the Ancient Calendar*, trans. by Fernando Horcasitas and Doris Heyden, 1971, pp. 137–139, 273–280, 284–286, passim., and illustration 29, page 351. Reprinted with permission of University of Oklahoma Press. **Source 77:** From *The Incas of Pedro de Cieza de Leon*, Translated by Harriet de Onis; edited, with an introduction by Victor Wolfgang von Hagen, 1959, pp. 165–167, 169–174, 177–179, passim. Reprinted with permission of University of Oklahoma Press.

Part Four ▼ Travel, Encounter, and Exchange: 1000–1700

Chapter 12

Source 78: Friederich Hirth and W. W. Rockhill, *Chau Ju-Kau: His Work on the Chinese and Arab Trade in the Twelfth and Thirteenth Centuries*, entitled *Chu-fan-chï* (Saint Petersburg: Imperial Academy of Sciences, 1911), pp. 111–116, 124–125, 142–143, revised by A. J. Andrea. **Source 79:** The "Cotton Manuscript" of the British Museum, printed 1625, ch. 20, 30; adapted into modern English by A. J. Andrea. Copyright © 2008 by A. J. Andrea. **Source 80:** Courtesy Omiya Library at Ryukoku University. **Source 81:** Christopher Dawson, ed., *The Mongol Mission* (New York: Sheed and Ward, 1955), pp. 93–98, 103–104, passim. Reprinted with permission of Sheed & Ward, Rowman & Littlefield Publishing. **Source 82:** From *The Travels of Marco Polo*, translated by Ronald Latham, Penguin Classics 1958, pp. 82–85, 87–88. Copyright © Ronald Latham, 1958. Reprinted by permission of Penguin Books Ltd. **Source 83:** Translated from the Latin by A. J. Andrea. Copyright © 2008 by A. J. Andrea. **Source 84:** Henry Yule, ed. and trans., *Cathay and the Way Thither*, 2nd ed. (rev. by H. Cordier), 4 vols. (London: Hakluyt Society, 1913–1916), vol. 3, pp. 151–155. Modernized by A. J.

Andrea. **Source 85:** From N. Levtzion and J. F. P. Hopkins, eds., *Corpus of Early Arabic Sources for West African History*, Cambridge University Press, 1981, pp. 284–286, 288–291, 296–297. Reprinted with permission of Cambridge University Press. **Source 86:** From *Ruy Gonzalez de Clavijo, Embassy to Tamerlane, 1403–1406*, trans. by Guy Le Strange, Harper & Bros., 1928, pp. 285–292 and 294–295, passim. **Source 87:** Ma Huan, *The Overall Survey of the Ocean's Shores* (London: Hakluyt Society, 1970), pp. 108–109, 113–117, 120, 137–140, 165, 172. Copyright © 1970. Used by permission of the publisher. **Source 88:** Gomes Eannes de Azurara, *The Chronicle of the Discovery and Conquest of Guinea*, trans. Charles Raymond Beazely and Edgar Prestage, 2 vols. (London: Hakluyt Society, 1896), vol. 1, pp. 27–29, 83–85.

Chapter 13

Source 89: James Lockhart, ed. and trans., *We People Here: Nahuatl Accounts of the Conquest of Mexico* (Berkeley: University of California Press, 1993), pp. 96, 98, 100, 106, 110, 112, 132, 134, 136, 180, 182, 186, 188, 210, 216, 218, 238, 240, 242. **Source 90:** From Antonio Vasquez de Espinosa, *Compendium and Description of the West Indies* (Washington, DC: Smithsonian Institution, 1942), pp. 621–625, 629, 631–634, passim. **Source 91:** Extracts from Letters of King Afonso to King of Portugal, 1526. Translated and published in *The African Past* by Basil Davidson. Copyright © 1964 by Basil Davidson. Reprinted by permission of Curtis Brown, Ltd. **Source 92:** (1) A Benin-Portuguese Saltcellar, courtesy of the Trustees of The British Museum. (2) A Benin Wall Plaque, Multiple Figures, Edo Peoples, Benin Kingdom, Nigeria, Photograph by Franko Khoury, mid 16th–17th century, copper alloy, H × W × D: 45.6 × 35 × 8.9 cm. Purchased with funds provided by the Smithsonian Collection Acquisition Program, National Museum of African Art, 82-5-3, Smithsonian Institution. **Source 93:** Awnsham Churchill and John Churchill, eds., *Collections of Voyages and Travels*, 3rd ed., 8 vols. (London: H. Lintor, 1744–1747), vol. 5, p. 459; modernized by A. J. Andrea. **Source 94:** From *China in the Sixteenth Century* by Matteo Ricci, translated by Louis J. Gallagher, S.J., Copyright 1942, 1953 and renewed 1970 by Louis J. Gallagher, S.J. Used by permission of Random House, Inc. **Source 95:** From *Japan: A Documentary History*, ed. and trans. David J. Lu (Armonk, NY: M. E. Sharpe, 1997), pp. 221–222, 223. Translation copyright © 1997 by David J. Lu. Reprinted with permission of M. E. Sharpe, Inc. **Source 96:** Henry Beveridge, trans., *The Akbar Nama of Abu-l-Fazl*, 3 vols. (New Delhi: Ess Ess Publications, 1902–1939), vol. 1, pp. 37, 207, 322–323, 368-370, 410–411. **Source 97:** Jean-Baptiste Tavernier, *Travels in India*, 2nd ed., ed. William Ball, trans. V. Ball (Oxford: Oxford University Press, 1925), pp. 7–11. Used by permission of the publisher.

Multiple Voices VIII

(1) From Hernán Cortés, *Letters from Mexico*, translated and edited by Anthony Pagen, 1986, pp. 60–63, 66, passim. Reprinted with permission of Yale University Press. (2) Bernal Díaz del Castillo, *Historia verdadera de la conquista de la Nueva España*, Edición de Miguel León-Portilla, 2 vols., 5th edition (Madrid: 1992), 1: 267–271 and 510, translated by A. J. Andrea. Copyright © 2008 by A. J. Andrea. (3) James Lockhart, ed. and trans., *We People Here: Nahuatl Accounts of the Conquest of Mexico* (Berkeley: University of California Press, 1993), pp. 90, 92, and 94 (4) (1) Washington State University / Special Collections Library. (2) The Art Archive / Antochiw Collection Mexico / Mireille Vautier. (3–4) © Private Collection / Archives Charmet / The Bridgeman Art Library. (5) The Bancroft Library / University of California. (5) Private collection of A. J. Andrea.